WOMEN RETURNE

RETURNING TO WORK

1996/7

A DIRECTORY
OF EDUCATION & TRAINING
FOR WOMEN

8TH EDITION

Paul Chapman Publishing in association with
The Women Returners' Network

P·C·P
Paul Chapman
Publishing Ltd

ШRN
The Women Returners' Network

First published in Great Britain in 1987 by
Longman Group UK Limited
Second edition 1988
Third edition 1989
Fourth edition 1990, published by
Kogan Page Limited
Fifth edition 1991
Sixth edition 1992, published by MJ Publishing
Seventh edition 1993
Eighth edition 1996, published by Paul Chapman Publishing
144 Liverpool Rd, London N1 1LA

British Library Cataloguing in Publication Data
Returning to work : a directory of education and training
for women. – 8th ed.
  1. Women – Employment   2. Adult education of women
  I. Women Returners Network
  331.4'12

  ISBN 1 85396 337 2

Typeset by Dorwyn Ltd, Rowlands Castle
Printed and bound in Great Britain

A B C D E F G H   9 8 7 6

Contents

ENGLAND

NORTHERN IRELAND

SCOTLAND

WALES

This Book Can Help You

- if you are a woman wishing to return to work after a break or to improve your career prospects by following a course of training.

- if you are an adviser to whom women returners may come for educational guidance or you have an interest in the opportunities available to women.

The aim of this Directory is to help women returners and does this by providing information on education and training initiatives which offer opportunities and facilities that enable women returners to take them up, for example:

- shortened-day timetables to fit in with school hours

- hands-on experience with computers and other information technology equipment

- job-sampling experience

- the opportunity to assess abilities, discover new interests, widen horizons and develop confidence

- guidance and counselling sessions

About This Book

This Directory is unique in focusing attention on the needs of women hoping to return to the labour market after a break. For every copy sold, hundreds of women seeking guidance have benefitted. It contains vital information on courses that have been designed for them.

Women returners need help in managing their return to work. Our aim is that the Directory should help them do this by providing them with both specific and general information. If they are able to discover: whether training and job opportunities exist in their own locality and the extent to which these initiatives are designed to suit women returners, then it may be possible for them to take full advantage of the education and training opportunities available to them. If these do not exist, then the general information provided may help them find out why not.

Women returners should make their needs known to everyone who provides training in their area. They can ask at colleges and Training and Enterprise Councils (TECs) about shortened-day timetables, about childcare facilities and about educational advisory services. Professional women should urge their professional associations to set up career-break services, for example, updating courses. Employers, especially large ones, should be approached by female staff about keeping-in-touch schemes. Most women will have a far longer period in employment after their return to work than they had before taking a break and it is essential that they are made fully aware of all the opportunities to update, retrain, change careers, obtain grants or sponsorship and make an informed choice based on sound information and advice.

Were you aware that:

- Nearly half the workforce is female
- Over 11 million women are in employment
- Two-thirds of them are married/co-habiting
- Over 8 million married/co-habiting women are working, which means that around one in three of all workers is a married/cohabiting woman
- Eight out of ten women who take a career break return to employment within five years

It is clear that women are vitally important in meeting current and future skills shortages. If employers are to remain productive, they must take full advantage of the potential and existing skills and experience of women. Opportunities for employment will alter with changes in the economy, but the indications are that, long term, the existing shortage of skilled people will remain and it is advisable for women to take every available opportunity to train and update their qualifications.

The Directory makes it immediately possible to read about the many initiatives directed at recruiting and retaining women. We hope that it will help you, if you are a woman returner, or your clients, if you are an educational adviser, to make a happy return.

Women Returners' Network
8 John Adam Street
London WC2N 6EZ
Phone: 0171 839 8188
Fax: 0171 930 8620

The eighth edition has been updated by Gill Heath, WRN's Information Officer, and has received support from a WRN project under the European Union New Opportunities for Women Initiative.

Sources of Information: National Schemes and Organisations

1. Who can inform you?

Finding out what is available by way of training and education remains a problem for women. This section lists the organisations to approach for information. The Directory includes, at the end of every county or regional section, details of local advisers who can direct you to specific providers of courses or to adult guidance services.

In the UK, women returning to work are not a marginal group. Over 11 million women are in the workforce; of those, more than two-thirds (i.e. over 8 million) are either married or cohabiting.

Women returners are women who stop work because of family commitments, usually to have children but sometimes to care for a dependent adult, and who later wish to return to work, either in the same field or one that requires them to retrain.

Why do women returners need help to manage their return to work? The problems facing women returners are: lack of flexible entry to jobs and education; loss of confidence; the costs of retraining and how to offset them (see Section 3); lack of childcare facilities (see Section 4); and the difficulties of keeping in touch (see Section 4). Women should ask for information on whichever of these issues affects them.

Once you have found these organisations, it is essential to ask the right questions in order to be able to take advantage of what they offer.

Many women who return to work continue to perform a dual role at work and at home, maintaining their domestic and family commitments and juggling to do so as well as perform well in their job. If this is generally recognised, return to work or training can be eased. However, many women looking for work take whatever job is available in order to solve short term needs. All too often, this means a drop in pay and status, or loss of employment protection, job security and opportunities to retrain. The Directory lists below sources of information on flexible working and jobshare registers.

- Flexible training programmes and flexible work patterns will help overcome returning to work problems for women. Do they exist in your area and in your field?

- For many women living in rural areas or beyond the reach of a suitable college and with no means of transport, Distance Learning may be the only option. It combines a correspondence course with tutorial help and possibly audio-visual aids. Is Distance Learning an option or perhaps the only option for you?

Frequently, many women find the domestic break is characterised by lowered self-esteem and ambition, making the return more difficult. This can be the case for an under-achiever at school, or someone who made little career progress while at work, or a professional woman. Too few employers help their employees to plan a career break.

In education and training, lack of self-confidence can be overcome if 'gateway' women-only courses are provided. The essential need to express their aspirations and explore opportunities is best done in an atmosphere of mutual understanding which women-only courses can provide. One requirement is well-recognised, namely that training be provided during school hours.

- Do women-only courses, timetabled within school hours, take place in your locality?

The opportunity to progress from starter courses to more vocational and focused courses is not always available. Some education and training providers have made major efforts to provide progression routes.

- Do women-only courses, shortened-day timetables, planned progression from one course to another exist in your locality?

- Is Credit Accumulation and Transfer available in your area? (CATS allows students to move from one college to another without having to start another course from scratch. This can be very helpful to women who have to move because of their own or their partner's work, or who need, for a variety of reasons, to interrupt their study.)

Information and Guidance Services

Careers Services

Careers Services, traditionally provided by Local Education Authorities, can now be provided under contract by a variety of organisations. Their primary responsibility is to meet the needs of young people for careers information and guidance. They are not obliged to make provision for the needs of adult returners to education/training/employment, although some do. In some cases, those Careers Services which do offer guidance and counselling may charge for their services.

Check County Contacts for careers advisory services in your area (contact the Adult Guidance Officer). In addition the National Association of Educational Guidance Advisers (see below) has a network of branches which you may contact.

Opportunity Shops

Run by many Training and Enterprise Councils (TECs), Opportunity or Guidance Shops offer 'one stop' information and guidance concerning local training and employment initiatives. See County Contacts for local details.

Other sources of information and advice:

Association of Graduate Careers Advisory Services, c/o Careers Service, University of Warwick, Coventry CV4 7AL 01203 523498   *Contact:* Margaret Wallis

Career Assessment and Guidance Counselling, Northland Farmhouse, Ketches Lane, Sheffield Park, Uckfield, East Sussex TN22 3RX 01825 791337   *Contact:* Pat Frank
CAGS specialises in helping women returning to work and offers talks, one day workshops and courses for women returners at bases in Sussex and London. Also co-ordinates a list of independent professional Career Guidance Counsellors in different parts of the country. In-depth consultations for individuals cost from £50 to £100. Some offer concessionary rates for the unemployed. All listed counsellors are members of the British Association for Counselling, the Institute of Careers Guidance or similar recognised organisations.

Career Development Centre for Women, 97 Mallard Place, Strawberry Vale, Twickenham, Middlesex TW1 4SW 0181 892 3806   *Contact:* Linda Greenbury
Personalised career/life planning programmes for women only, specialising in partner relocation, older adults and returners. A charge is payable for this service.

Careerwise, 127 Lansdowne Road, London N17 0NN 0181 808 4584   *Contact:* Penny Redwood. Careerwise is a supportive career counselling service, based in North London, for people making career decisions, specialising in women returners. A charge is payable for this service.

ECCTIS 2000, Oriel House, Oriel Road, Cheltenham, Gloucestershire GL50 1XP 01242 252627
ECCTIS (Educational Counselling and Credit Transfer Information Service) 2000 is a national computerised service providing information about courses in further and higher education and their entry requirements. It holds information on over 80,000 courses, from postgraduate and first degree courses to further education opportunities throughout the UK. Courses of more than 6 weeks' full-time (or equivalent part-time) duration leading to recognised

qualifications (except GCSE and SCE) are covered. Course information includes subject, duration, method of study, education institution, normal entry requirements, course structure and content, and credit transfer opportunities. The database is available on CD-ROM by annual subscription.

Individuals seeking information should contact a local careers or guidance officer for information about their nearest ECCTIS database access point.

Higher Education Careers Service Unit, Armstrong House, Oxford Road, Manchester M1 7ED 0161 236 8677   *Contact:* Pat Raderecht

Infinite Reach, 4 Holmes Cottages, Pebble Hill Road, Betchworth, Surrey RH3 7BP 01737 842713. Runs workshops for women considering job/career change or returning to work after a break. One-to-one advice also available. Fees are charged for these services.

Instant Muscle, Springside House, 84 Northend Road, London W14 9ES 0171 603 2604 *Contact:* Sue Ellis, Information Officer
National charity which seeks to help unemployed people who face disadvantage in the labour market to take up the challenge of self-employment or return to a satisfying job. Free training is available for both sexes. Instant Muscle offers a high level of individual counselling in all its employment and enterprise training programmes.

Kelly Services, UK Headquarters, Rodwell House, 100 Middlesex Street, London E1 7HD 0171 247 4494. Runs specially targetted programmes throughout its network of branches aimed at helping women who have had a break return to the workplace. Every participating branch has a Working Mother Adviser who is able to assist mothers return to employment. Branches are able to provide testing and free computer technology as well as basic keyboard skills, backed up by a range of factsheets covering topics such as CVs, job interviews, stress at work, etc.

Learning from Experience Trust (LET), Anglia Polytechnic University, Victoria ÆRoad South, Chelmsford, Essex CM1 1LL 01245 348779
LET is an educational charity established to develop ways in which people can make maximum use of their knowledge and skills, however they acquired them, through the assessment of experiential learning. It seeks to develop procedures for identifying and evaluating informal learning, and to encourage their use in assessing people who hope to progress through further or higher education or employment. LET offers a useful service for trainers and advisers.

Low Pay Unit, 27-29 Amwell Street, London EC1R 1UN 0171 713 7616
The Low Pay Unit is an independent charity set up in 1974 to investigate and highlight the problems of low pay, poverty and inequality, to advise low paid individuals and train advisers on wages and employment law. It is now the main organisation representing the interests of the 'working poor', ensuring that the issues remain high on the political agenda and can respond to individual enquiries.

NIACE (National Institute of Adult Continuing Education), 21 De Montfort Street, Leicester LE1 7GE 0116 255 1451
NIACE is the national organisation for adult learning; promoting the study and general advancement of adult continuing education. It seeks to enable consultation and co-operation between all those concerned in the provision of education and training for adults. It also provides an information and advice service for organisations and individuals, undertakes research, organises conferences and produces a range of publications. NIACE also co-ordinates the annual Adult Learners' Week, a nationwide event promoting adult education and training opportunities. Publications include an annual 'Adult Continuing Education Yearbook' which lists organisations concerned with adult education across the UK and overseas.

For details of NIACE in Wales, contact: Wales Committee NIACE/NIACE Cymru, Welsh Joint Education Committee, Education Department, 245 Western Avenue, Cardiff CF5 2YX; 01222 265000.

National Association for Educational Guidance for Adults (NAEGA), 10b Leny Road, Callander, Scotland FK17 8BA 01877 330996   *Contact:* Anne Docherty, Secretary
This is the national body representing the view and aims for local Education Guidance Services for Adults. It plays an active role in national discussions aimed at promoting educational guidance and the requirements of adult learners. NAEGA has regional branches, newsletters and an annual conference for members and others interested in provision of guidance for adults. A 'UK Directory of Educational Guidance Services for Adults' is available from the Secretary, as well as other publications covering educational guidance matters. See County Contacts for details of regional representatives.

For details of NAEGA in Northern Ireland, contact: Eileen Kelly, Director, Educational Guidance Service for Adults, 2nd Floor, Glendinning House, Murray Street, Belfast BT1 6DN; 01232 244274

New Ways to Work, 309 Upper Street, London N1 2TY 0171 226 4026
New Ways to Work is the leading organisation in the UK advising on more flexible ways of working. It runs a national information and advice service dealing with enquiries about flexible working from individuals, employers, trade unions and others. It publishes booklets, leaflets and a quarterly newsletter and also runs seminars and training sessions for employers and personnel officers.

Opportunities for People with Disabilities, 1 Bank Buildings, Princes Street, London EC2R 8EU 0171 726 4961 or 0171 726 4963 Minicom
Contact: Information Officer
Aim, through training, preparation and guidance, to help people with disabilities to secure and maintain worthwhile employment matched to their talents and aspirations, by persuading employers to recognise positively ability and potential, not disability. Services are offered free of charge from a network of 12 regional centres and 4 Special Need job clubs around the country.

Ownbase, 68 First Avenue, Bush Hill Park, Enfield Middlesex EN1 1BN   *Contact:* Enquiries Secretary. Founded in 1986, Ownbase is a national organisation focusing on the social and psychological problems of working from home. Contact is maintained with members through regular newsletters, project teams, exhibitions and the AGM. Many members are in full time employment, but would like to know more about working from home, while others are freelancers running small businesses. SAE for further details.

Small Business Bureau, Curzon House, Church Road, Windlesham, Surrey GU20 6BH 01276 452010. Lobbyists for small businesses.

The Basic Skills Agency, 1-19 New Oxford Street, London WC1A 1NU 0171 405 4017
This is the national development agency for literacy, numeracy and related basic skills in England and Wales. If you want to join a programme anywhere in England or Wales to improve your reading, writing, spelling or basic maths, ring the Basic Skills Agency Helpline 0800 700987.

The Industrial Society, Robert Hyde House, 48 Bryanston Square London W1H 7LN 0171 262 2401   *Contact: Jo Gardiner*
Women's development is, and has long been, one of the Industrial Society's key campaign areas. This is reflected in the Pepperell Network as well as in an exciting range of up-to-date courses. Because many women find it easier to learn in a non-threatening, single gender environment, their women-only courses enable them to take stock of the challenges they face. They are then able more effectively to plan the actions they will implement on their return to work; which makes good business sense.

Access to further/higher education

Access Courses

Access to higher education courses are designed for adults as an alternative to A levels or Scottish Highers. They normally take one year full-time or two years part-time.

Access courses need no formal entry requirements, other than a willingness to study and ability to benefit from the course. Some are linked to specific degree programmes, so that success on the Access Course leads directly to entry to the degree course. Not all Access courses lead automatically to further study, so it is important to check where the course leads.

Accreditation of Prior Learning (APL)

Accreditation of Prior Learning is a process which enables people to gain certification for their past achievement, often outside the formal education system, for example in work, leisure or community activities. Identified learning can be matched against nationally recognised qualifications at various levels. Contact your local university or College of Higher Education for more information.

In Scotland, the Scottish Vocational Council is the major awarding body for Further Education. For information on APL, contact: SCOTVEC, Hanover House, 24 Douglas Street, Glasgow G2 7NQ; 0141 248 7900.

For information on APL in childcare and education, contact: Council for Early Years Awards, 8 Chequer Street, St Albans, Hertfordshire AL1 3XZ; 01727 847636

Associate Student Schemes

Many universities and CHEs, including the Open University, offer associate student schemes. Generally these allow adult students to choose single units from any current programme of study on offer without having to enrol for the whole programme, whether this is a degree, diploma or other type of provision. It is a useful opportunity for women to gain specialist expertise to further their careers, update knowledge in their field and pace their return to study. Credits gained from passing single units can be accumulated towards a degree whether in that college or by credit transfer to another. Contact your local university, College of Higher Education or Open University regional office for more details.

Credit Accumulation and Transfer (CATS)

Credit Accumulation and Transfer (CATS). The Scheme seeks to break down the many barriers that prevent people from taking advantage of higher education, enabling them to accumulate academic credit towards awards (undergraduate or postgraduate degrees). These credits can be achieved through learning at work, unpaid or voluntary work, professional courses, as well as formal study at college.

Further information on the higher education opportunities available and the credit enquirers may already have accumulated is available from your local university or College of Higher Education.

Scottish Wider Access Programme (SWAP)

Scottish Wider Access Programme (SWAP) works to create new ways into higher education through the design of access courses and of individual programmes guaranteeing entry to higher education, and through credit transfer and flexible study plans. Contact the regional offices below for further information.

North of Scotland Consortium, Summerhill Education Centre, Stronsay Drive, Aberdeen AB2 6JA 01224 313142

South East of Scotland Consortium, Stevenson College, Bankhead Avenue, Edinburgh EH11 4DF 0131 458 5468

West of Scotland Consortium, Allan Glen's Building, 190 Cathedral Street, Glasgow G4 0AD
0141 553 2471

Awards

BTEC Continuing Education Qualifications

The Customer Enquiries Unit, Central House, Upper Woburn Place, London WC1H 0HH 0171 413 8400
Certificate and Diploma programmes designed specifically for people with either previous qualifications or experience in a responsible job (usually at least three years) to extend and develop their previous education and experience. Students are eligible for certain BTEC Continuing Education Certificates on completion of specified combinations of modules.

BTEC Certificates of Achievement

Certificates of Achievement are awarded to students who successfully complete: – Continuing Education modules, ie short programmes of study designed to meet particular employers' or students' needs, including updating, refresher training or preparing to return to work; – modules drawn from BTEC initial programmes which may equally meet the needs of adults, especially for technological updating; – groups of modules studied together, which have been designed to meet specific needs.

BTEC Initial Qualifications

Full programmes – a mature person may wish to follow the full programme of studies leading to a BTEC National or Higher National Certificate or Diploma. There is no maximum age limit to these programmes.

Shorter courses – Adults who have developed or acquired skills and knowledge through their work may be able to follow a shortened course leading to a BTEC National or Higher National qualification because their experience may give them exemption from up to 50% of the total requirements of a full course.

City and Guilds of London Institute

76 Portland Place, London W1N 4AA
City and Guilds of London Institute offers a wide range of occupational qualifications, including NVQs.

National Vocational Qualifications (NVQs)

National Council for Voluntary Qualifications, 222 Euston Road, London NW1 2BZ 0171 387 9898
NVQs are available across the range of occupational areas and can be awarded at up to 5 different levels, starting with level 1 (routine and straightforward tasks) through to level 5 (complex managerial and professional activities). For example, students in a management post or with management responsibilities and experience may gain an NVQ level 4 or 5 in Management.

General National Vocational Qualifications (GNVQs) are available in a range of occupational areas and can be awarded at Foundation, Intermediate and Advanced levels. The Advanced GNVQ is comparable to A levels and is known as the Vocational A Level.

RSA Examinations Board

Westwood Way, Coventry CV4 8HS 01203 470033
The Royal Society of Arts (RSA) offers over 200 qualifications, including NVQs in a range of administrative and management subjects.

Scottish Vocational Education Council (SCOTVEC)

Hanover House, 24 Douglas Street, Glasgow G2 7NQ 0141 242 2052
SCOTVEC is the national body with responsibility for accrediting, awarding and developing vocational qualifications in Scotland. Within its qualifications framework, SCOTVEC offers unit-based provision at non-advanced (National Certificate Modules) and advanced (Higher National Units) levels. Modules and units can be taken individually or in groups and can lead to nationally recognised qualifications such as HNC, HND, Scottish Vocational Qualifications (SVQs) or General Scottish Vocational Qualifications (GSVQs). In addition, programmes can be designed to meet the needs of particular organisations or companies. National Certificate Modules, Higher National Units and courses are designed by SCOTVEC in collaboration with educationalists, employers, industry lead bodies and professional/technical bodies, and are recognised routes to careers and to further study at degree level and beyond.

Distance Learning

Chartered Insurance Institute, Distance Learning Division, Churchill Court, Kippington Road, Sevenoaks, Kent TN13 2LL 01732 450888
Range of distance learning provision, leading to Certificates in Proficiency, Financial Planning, Advanced Financial Planning, Insurance Practice, also Associateship

Holborn College, 200 Greyhound Road, London W14 9RY 0171 385 3377
Offers distance learning degrees and diplomas in Law and related subjects such as Public Relations in conjunction with the University of Wolverhampton.

National College of Technology, NCT Ltd, PO Box 11, High Street, Wendover, Buckinghamshire HP22 6XA 01296 624270
Offers a range of technological training/education courses leading to BTEC and other awards.

National Extension College, 18 Brooklands Avenue, Cambridge CB2 2HN 01223 316644
The College, founded in 1963, is a non-profit making educational trust. NEC enrols over 15000 students annually on over 150 distance learning courses, ranging from basic skills to GCSE, A level, NVQ, degree and professional qualifications. Other courses of particular interest to women include Return to Work and Return to the Office. Also available are courses covering business, accounting and management skills, counselling, childcare, computing, engineering, languages, writing skills and University of London degrees.

Open College of the Arts, Houndhill, Worsborough, Barnsley, South Yorkshire S70 6TU 0891 168902 (Information)/ 01226 730495
The College was founded in 1987 and is an educational charitable trust with no government funding support. Over 10,000 students have taken OCA courses. They include unemployed people and women who have to work mainly or entirely at home for reasons of family or of disability. Courses are available throughout Great Britain in art and design, drawing, painting, sculpture, textiles, photography, writing, garden design, music and history of art. In addition to home study, tutorial back-up is provided by tutors in various colleges of art, universities, schools, art centres, studios or, in some cases, by post. A Record of Satisfactory Completion is offered to all students and a graded Award scheme is available for students who need written evidence of their level of achievement

Open University, Central Enquiry Service, The Open University, PO Box 2000, Milton Keynes MK7 6YZ 01908 653231
The Open University offers home-based, part-time study using distance learning texts and kits, television, radio, audio and video cassettes and local tuition. Students can study for a degree in a wide range of Arts, Social Sciences, Education or Science and Technology subject areas and usually take about six years to complete. Diplomas or Masters degrees are also available, as well as a wide range of short courses for those wishing to develop a personal interest or further a career. These include various Women's Studies options, Women into Management and a Women Returners' Scheme. The Open Business School caters for managers at all levels in industry and commerce and offers a Certificate, a Diploma and an MBA degree.

There are no entry requirements for most OU programmes. A good first degree or OU diploma is usually needed for higher degrees. Courses run from February to October and some also have week-long residential summer schools.

The College of Law, Distance Learning Department, Braboeuf Manor, St Catherines, Guildford, Surrey GU3 1HA 01483 460385
Runs 'Fresh Start': a distance learning course for people seeking to return to legal practice after a career break and for those wishing to change specialisation.

Unison Education, 20 Grand Depot Road, London SE18 6SF 0181 854 2244   *Contact:* Jim Sutherland, Director of Education
The amalgamated NALGO, NUPE and COHSE union offers distance learning provision in various subjects

Residential Colleges for Adults

There are eight publicly funded residential colleges for adults in England and Wales. Most offer one- or two-year full-time courses but in some cases it is possible for local students to attend on a full-time or part-time basis. In many cases, there are no formal entry qualifications for these colleges and Department for Education and Employment grants are available for most full-time students. Contact individual colleges for details of their courses (some courses are listed in the appropriate County pages). Two of the colleges, Hillcroft College and Lucy Cavendish College, are for women.

Co-operative College, Stanford Hall, Loughborough, Leicestershire LE12 5QR 01509 852333

Coleg Harlech, Harlech, Gwynedd LL46 2PU 01766 780363

Fircroft College, 1018 Bristol Road, Selly Oak, Birmingham B29 6LH 0121 472 0116

Hillcroft College, South Bank, Surbiton, Surrey KT6 6DF 0181 399 2688

Lucy Cavendish College, Cambridge CB3 0BU 01223 332190

Northern College, Wentworth Castle, Stainborough, Barnsley, South Yorkshire S75 3ET 01226 285426

Plater College, Pullens Lane, Oxford OX3 0DT 01865 741676

Ruskin College, Oxford OX1 2HE 01865 54331

2.   Who can train you?

The essential question to ask about any course, programme or job on offer is whether it has been designed for women returners. Does it have the features that will attract women returners – flexible entry, flexible training, an accessible creche or assistance with childcare, a clear progression route onwards from the course or job, an adviser for women returners on the campus or at the workplace, a clear equal opportunities policy?

Often you will find workshops or training centres for women which offer training for non-traditional occupations, while others concentrate on hands-on sampling of computing and associated technology. Updating courses, and conversion courses which allow women to build on their training and experience, retrain and reassess their abilities, may be available. Educational guidance services and careers services can help you find the right training, at the right level and with progression routes. (See listings for your county.)

For those women returning to work without taking time to retrain, update or prepare for a career change, it is important to enquire about training provided on the job and available to both full and part time workers. Personnel managers or personnel directors should be aware of these. Despite unemployment, employers frequently find it difficult to recruit skilled staff. If you indicate your willingness to be trained, it should fall on receptive ground. If it does not, look elsewhere.

If training provision is not available locally, contact your education authority or Training and Enterprise Council. Try to exert pressure to obtain the education or training that you want. Currently, many organisations are working to help women find the appropriate means. This includes training funded by the European Union under a number of initiatives for women.

Training providers

Training and Enterprise Councils

82 Training and Enterprise Councils, covering England and Wales, have been established regionally. Their role is to plan and deliver employment training and enterprise support which will meet local labour market and business needs throughout each area.

TECs are independent companies under contract to the Department for Education and Employment and currently administer the Training for Work programme as well as a range of local and national employment training and support initiatives. The role of TECs in relation to women returners: TECs have a fundamental role to play in 1. planning for a wide-ranging programme of training and education initiatives for women workers and women returners; 2. budgeting for the support and funding of such programmes; 3. encouraging employers to offer employment and career development for women workers and women returners. TECs can be the continuing resource for providing career and educational guidance for women in their areas. See County Contacts for individual TECs

Local Enterprise Councils

Local Enterprise Councils cover the various Scottish Regions, operating within a policy framework set by their co-ordinating body Scottish Enterprise. Each LEC has its own contract with Scottish Enterprise and each provides the local focus and knowledge to develop employment and training initiatives within its own area and to innovate and adapt national programmes.

Local Enterprise Councils are listed in the County Contacts pages. Scottish Enterprise is based at: 120 Bothwell Street, Glasgow G2 7JP; 0141 248 2700.

Training for Work

Training for Work is funded by the Department for Education and Employment and delivered through local Training and Enterprise Councils (England and Wales) and Local Enterprise Councils (Scotland).

Citizens Advice Bureaux: CAB Training

National Association of Citizens Advice Bureaux, 115-123 Pentonville Road, London N1 9LZ 0171 833 2181
Every adviser working in CAB's 724 main bureaux receives professional training both in interviewing and in finding the information the client needs. All advisers attend CAB Basic Training which takes place in-bureau as well as through a series of training courses provided locally. Regular update courses are held to brief advisers on new legislation and helping particular clients. CAB training equips new workers to make full use of the CAB Information System which contains over 1200 subject headings and thousands of pages of guidance. Subjects covered range from welfare benefits to consumer rights and housing problems to legal matters. Anyone interested in becoming a volunteer should contact their CAB direct.

Women's Training Network

Aizelwood's Mill, Nursery Street, Sheffield S3 8GG 0114 282 3172/3/5   Contact: Kalpana Joshi
WTN is a national, non-profit-making membership organisation and a Sector Co-ordinator of Objectve 3 of the European Social Fund. WTN promotes targeted vocational training to

disadvantaged women in areas where women are substantially under-represented such as electronics, information technology and construction. See County Contacts pages for details of local Centres.

Workers' Educational Association

Temple House, 17 Victoria Park Square, London E2 9PB 0181 983 1515
The WEA is a voluntary, democratic and nationwide organisation which aims to stimulate and satisfy the demand for education and to further its advancement. Women's education is among the key areas promoted by WEA branches. It offers a variety of courses including Return to Learn/Access/Return to Work/Confidence Building and Assertiveness/IT and vocational training/Women's Studies and other tailored courses. There are no entrance requirements or exams. Costs are kept to a minimum and, where possible, childcare facilities are provided. For more details, contact the Women's Co-ordinator in the various English and Scottish Districts, listed in County Contacts.

WEA Women's National Co-ordinator: 88 Nether Ridge Road, Sheffield S7 1RX 0114 258 4530
Contact: Chris Scarlett

Working for a Charity

44-46 Caversham Road, London NW5 2DS 0171 911 0353   *Contact:* Catherine Mortier
Runs a programme aimed at those wishing to return to work, or seeking a new career, in a charity, including those considering part-time and flexible employment options. The Foundation Course combines seven days of seminars with a twenty-day voluntary placement in a host charity. Courses are usually run three times a year, starting in January, May and September. Send an A4 SAE for more information.

Young Women's Christian Association

Youth and Community Department, 52 Cornmarket Street, Oxford OX1 3EJ 01865 726110
Contact: Caroline McCleary
The YWCA has run adult education courses for women for over 30 years. These are focused on personal, social and vocational education and are person centred in their approach, particularly in regard to accessibility, offering a range of options to women. Courses for women who wish to gain access to the employment market are offered within YWCA centres throughout the UK.

Industry Lead Bodies for Training and Development

Advice, Guidance, Counselling and Psychotherapy Lead Body, 40a High Street, Welwyn, Hertfordshire AL6 9EQ 01438 840511

Arts and Entertainment Training Council, 3 St Peters Building, York Street. Leeds LS9 8AJ 0113 244 8845

Banking Industry Training Council, 10 Lombard Street, London EC3V 9AT 0171 398 4246

British Polymer Training Association, Coppice House, Halesfield 7, Telford, Shropshire TF7 4NA 01952 587020

Construction Industry Training Board, Bircham Newton, King's Lynn, Norfolk PE31 6RH 01553 776677

Engineering Training Authority (ENTRA), Vector House, 41 Clarendon Road, Watford, Hertfordshire WD1 1HS 01923 238441

Food and Drink Qualifications Council, 6 Catherine Street, London WC2B 5JJ 0171 836 2460

HBTTB (Health and Beauty), PO Box 21, Bognor Regis, West Sussex PO21 2PF 01243 860339

Hairdressing Training Board, 3 Chequer Road, Doncaster, South Yorkshire DN1 2AA 01302 342837

Hotel and Catering Training Company, International House, High Street, Ealing, London W5 5DB 0181 579 2400

Industry Lead Body for Design, 29 Bedford Square, London WC1B 3EG 0171 486 1510

Kingscourt PLC (Clothing and allied products industry), 80 Richardshaw Lane, Pudsey, Leeds LS28 6BN 0113 239 3355

Languages Lead Body, c/o Centre for Information on Language Teaching, 20 Bedfordbury, London WC2N 4LB 0171 379 5134

Management Charter Initiative, Russell Square House, 10-12 Russell Square, London WC1B 5BZ 0171 872 9000

National Retail Training Council, 4th Floor, Bedford House, 66-79 Fulham High Street, London SW6 3JW 0171 371 5021

Road Transport Industry Training Services, Capitol House, Empire Way, Wembley, Middlesex HA9 0NG 0181 902 8880

Science, Technology and Mathematics Council, St Bartholomews Court, 18 Christmas Street, Bristol BS1 5BT 0117 929 8578

Sport and Recreation Lead Body, c/o The Sports Council, 16 Upper Woburn Place, London WC1H 0QP 0171 388 1277

European Initiatives

European Social Fund

Department for Education and Employment, European Social Fund Unit, Level 1, 236 Grays Inn Road, London WC1X 8HL 0171 211 4741
The ESF provides financial support for various vocational training schemes and job creation initiatives. It has five priority areas: 1) Encouraging the development of under-developed regions 2) Regenerating areas of industrial decline 3) Addressing long-term unemployment and encouraging employment for young people, those traditionally unable to find work, and encouraging equal opportunities 4) Helping employees adapt to change at work (not implemented in the UK) 5) Promoting rural development. Schemes concentrating upon training, retraining or job creation fall within the European Social Fund remit.

IRIS

19-21 Rue Capouillet, bte 21, B-1060, Brussels Belgium
The European Network on Women's Training was set up in 1988 to facilitate access for women across Europe to employment-related training.

New Opportunities for Women

Department for Education and Employment, European Social Fund Unit, Level 1, 236 Grays Inn Road, London WC1X 8HL 0171 211 3000
Aims to promote equal opportunities for women in the field of employment and training. NOW targets women who are long-term unemployed or wishing to return to work after a break of several years, as well as unemployed women under 25.

New Opportunities for Women (Northern Ireland), EC Unit, Training and Employment Agency, Clarendon House, Adelaide Street, Belfast Northern Ireland BT2 01232 239944

3.   Who can fund you: fees and subsistence

Fees for higher education

Finding adequate funding to take up higher education is a major problem for many women. If you have a firm place on a full-time degree course then you can apply for a mandatory (Local Education Authority) award. LEAs will grant you a mandatory award if you have not previously had experience of higher education. Most people who have already undertaken previous higher education are thereby ineligible for further mandatory grants. While LEAs may make discretionary awards, these are in practice increasingly infrequent as authorities continue to cope with funding cuts. However, it is always worth making an application for a discretionary grant. If you are intending to study part-time, you can apply only for a discretionary grant and, if unsuccessful, you may have to find the funding for the course yourself.

For training or updating

Enquire of the college, local TEC (Training and Enterprise Council) or local advisory service whether the particular course is funded. Many are funded by the European Social Fund (ESF).

Grants

Subsistence grants for higher education courses depend upon whether previous higher education has been undertaken. If this is the case, mandatory awards will not be available. You may apply to your Local Education Authority for a discretionary award, but these are increasingly uncommon.

Sources of private funding

Various trusts and other agencies may offer awards to women seeking to study in certain fields, for example, scientific, technical or postgraduate courses. These are detailed below and the *Useful Publications* section includes directories of grant-making bodies.

Grants for travel and childcare

Some training courses, particularly those with ESF funding, have travel and childcare grants available; these are listed under the relevant courses.

Grants and loans

Mandatory awards

You are entitled to a mandatory award from your Local Education Authority if you are attending a full-time course (or sandwich course) at a UK university or other publicly funded college, leading to a first degree (BA, BSc, BEd), Diploma of Higher Education, Higher National Diploma, Postgraduate Certificate of Education, a specified equivalent qualification, or NVQ at level 4 where this is awarded along with a first degree, DipHE or HND. You will also need to have been ordinarily resident in the British Isles for three years prior to the start of the academic year in which your course begins. If you have been away because you or your family were temporarily employed abroad, you may still qualify (contact your LEA for advice). In most cases, people who have already received a grant for previous higher education are not then eligible for mandatory grants (contact your LEA for more information).

Discretionary awards

Your LEA may still give you an award if you fail to satisfy the mandatory regulations. To help them make their decision, you will need to explain all your circumstances. It is now very difficult to obtain discretionary grants as local authorities are under severe financial restraint, but it is always worth making an application.

Additional maintenance grants

In addition to the basic maintenance grant there are allowances which provide extra financial support to mature students, those with dependants, those required to maintain a second home and single parents with dependants.

Maintaining a home

£650 (1996/7 rate) is payable if you have to maintain a home for yourself and a dependant, other than the home you live in when you attend the course. Contact your LEA for more details.

Dependants

If your partner is financially dependent on you, or you have dependent children or other adults, you may be eligible for an extra allowance. All income of dependants is assessed. The allowance is available for 52 weeks of the year and is as follows: £1,865 (1996/7 rate) for your partner or other adult dependants, or for your eldest or only dependent child if you have no adult dependants. Allowances for dependent children vary according to their ages. Contact your LEA for further information.

Student loans

Loans may be available to students who meet the residence requirements, are studying for eligible full-time courses and are aged under 50 when the course begins. Certain bank or building society conditions must also be met. You may apply for a loan only once in each academic year of the course and for only one course at a time. Unlike grants, loans are not means-tested. They are however index-linked, normally in line with the rate of inflation (currently 2.3%). Repayments are normally made monthly.

Student loans are administered by the Student Loans Company, 100 Bothwell Street, Glasgow, G2 7JD. 0141 306 2000

Entitlement to Social Security Benefits

These are not normally available to students who attend full-time courses (21 hours/week or more). From October 1996, benefits may not be claimed by people undertaking 'guided learning' for more than 16 hours/week. Social security benefits may still be claimed by students in certain vulnerable groups such as lone parents or students with disabilities. Contact your local benefits agency office or Freeline Social Security 0800 666555 for more information.

The Unemployment Unit has produced a briefing 'Studying while unemployed: the Jobseekers' Allowance and the 16 Hour Rule' available from the Unemployment Unit, 322 St John Street, London EC1V 4NT, 0171 833 1222

Scotland:

In Scotland, applications for grants for full-time HNC, HND, degree, diploma or equivalent course should be made to the Students Awards Agency for Scotland, Gyleview House, 3 Redheughs Rigg, South Gyle, Edinburgh EH12 9HH, 0131 244 5868. Apply to the Bursaries Department of the local authority education department for awards for school-level courses, National Certificate or Diploma, Open University or part-time courses.

Northern Ireland:

In Northern Ireland, applications for undergraduate level courses should be made to the local Education Library Board; for most postgraduate courses to the DES. For more information, contact the Department of Education, Northern Ireland, Rathgael House, Balloo Road, Bangor BT19 7PR, 01247 279100.

Other sources of funding:

Daphne Jackson Memorial Fellowships Trust, Department of Physics, University of Guildford, Guildford, Surrey GU2 5XH 01483 259166
Fellowships for women or men who have had a career break for family reasons, to enable them to resume careers in science or engineering, in industry or academia. Aimed at people over the age of 27 who have attained at least a first degree.

Successful candidates will be given research facilities and the opportunity of training in recent developments and new techniques under the supervision of a university tutor. They will be supported by fixed-term, part-time Fellowships (usually for two years) in the fields of science and engineering.

EPSRC Fellowships and Research Grants, EPSRC Swindon Office, Polaris House, North Star Avenue, Swindon, Wiltshire SN2 1ET 01793 444000 (Fellowships)/ 01793 444010 (Grants)
The Engineering and Physical Sciences Research Council (EPSRC) recognises that many women returning to academic life after a period away prefer to do their post graduate study part-time. It offers a limited number of Fellowships and Research Grants, all of which can be taken up on a full-time or part-time basis and are open to 'mature' applicants, although precise employment terms rest with the grantmaking institution. Full details are set out in the handbooks 'EPSRC Research Grants' and 'EPSRC Fellowships', both available from the address above.

The EPSRC has also selected 16 pilot courses ranging from innovative manufacturing to chemistry for support for the new Masters of Research degree.

Laura Ashley Foundation, 33 King Street, London WC2E 8JD 0171 497 2503   *Contact:* Annabel Thompson, Administrator
The Foundation helps individuals between the ages of 18 and 50 years who did not succeed in gaining GCSE, O or A Levels at school. Financial help is given to individuals for course fees and some travel costs.

The Foundation helps only students on the following types of courses at further education colleges: GCSE and A Level, Access, NNEB, BTEC Foundation and City & Guilds. The Foundation also funds projects for: the development of ability; opportunities for low achievers; gaining skills for employment; FE group courses; adult education for advancement to further and higher education; other educational skills for employment or training.

Lucy Cavendish College, Cambridge: Bursaries and other Awards, Lucy Cavendish College, Cambridge CB3 0BU 01223 332190   *Contact:* The Secretary (Awards)
Lucy Cavendish College, which specialises in offering mature women students (21 or over) the opportunity to work for a first degree, is normally able to offer bursaries to undergraduates to augment other funding. Some awards give preference to women from certain geographical areas, such as Merseyside, some give preference to particular subjects. Awards are also available to graduate students, and from time to time the College advertises Research Fellowships. The Ruth Tomlinson Award of £1000 is offered by the Federation of Business and Professional Women to a graduate or undergraduate who is disabled. Awards available to graduate students include the Lord Frederick Cavendish Studentships, the Becker for lawyers and the Masterman/Braithwaite for research in linguistics, computer science or philosophy and for clinical medicine or veterinary surgery. All awards must be held at the College which is part of the University of Cambridge. All enquiries should be addressed to The Secretary (Awards)

The Royal Society Research Fellowships, Research Appointments Department, 6 Carlton House Terrace, London SW1Y 5AG 0171 451 2547
Dorothy Hodgkin Fellowships offer a high level of support and flexibility which should be particularly useful and encouraging to women. They offer four years guaranteed tenure on Research Staff IA/II Scale, up to £5000 annual research grant, the option to take part in mentor and networking schemes, the option of part-time working, career advice and support and flexibility with maternity cover.

University of Warwick Bursaries for Women, Warwick Business School, University of Warwick, Coventry CV4 7AL 01203 524306

In order to encourage more women to join postgraduate programmes, the University of Warwick Business School offers a number of special bursaries. These bursaries, worth between £1,000 and £4,500, are awarded to women applying to enter the MBA and MA courses. Women accepted on the courses are eligible to apply. For further information, contact the Academic Director of the Programme you are interested in, at the address above.

4. Who can provide other forms of support?

While the path back to education, training or employment is not always easy, there are many types of organisations which can offer you support along the way.

Women's support groups

A wide range of national statutory and independent organisations exists to support and inform women. Only those directly pertinent to women in education, training and employment are listed here, as other directories cover the whole range of women's organisations in greater depth. Foremost among these, of course, is The Women Returners' Network.

Employers

A growing number of employers have set up career-break policies enabling their staff to take time off for domestic responsibilities and to return to work at the same level in due course. Banks, Building Societies and various branches of the Civil Service lead the way in this field, but many key industrial and commercial companies have also adopted 'family-friendly' career-break policies.

Professional associations

Women who belong to professional associations may also find that their association offers 'keeping-in-touch' facilities enabling updating of skills and a smoother return to work. If you are a member of a professional association, enquire whether it has any facilities to assist members on a career break, and if not, why not?

Childcare organisations

After-school clubs and other childcare facilities are not necessarily available across the country, and where they do exist, often have long waiting lists. Childcare can also be expensive for parents on low incomes. National sources of information on childcare provision are listed here, but also check the County Contacts pages for your area as local facilities are also sometimes listed.

Employers' career break schemes

Abbey National PLC, 215-221 Baker Street, London NW1 6XL 0171 612 4000

Offers a career break scheme for up to five years which allows staff to return to the same level of work. Reduced grade and part-time schemes are also offered, which allow staff to step down a grade for a period and then return to the original grade. A range of flexible working options is available.

Barclays Bank PLC, Fleetway House, 25 Farringdon Street, London EC4A 4LP 0171 489 1995

Runs a Career Break Scheme which provides a complete break or part-time work (at least 14 hours per week) for up to two years for eligible staff. The scheme starts at the expiry of the Maternity Break. Also available is an extended Maternity Break of up to 52 weeks for staff with at least 2 years' service. For staff with more than six months but less than two years' service a Maternity Break of up to 26 weeks is available. The Bank also offers a Responsibility Break of up to six months which could be a complete break from work or a period of reduced working hours. This scheme is available to staff with caring responsibilities for sick, elderly or disabled people.

Boots the Chemist, Head Office, Nottingham NG2 3AA
Operates a career-break scheme for both Store and Head Office staff, as well as flexible working hours, term-time working and job share.

British Council, Employment Relations Service, 10 Spring Gardens, London SW1A 2BN 0171 930 8466   *Contact:* Felicity Harris (recruitment information)
For all staff on indefinite contract unpaid leave schemes are available after a qualifying period of two years' service for: 1. employees with family responsibiliites; 2. employees who need to accompany a partner overseas; 3. compassionate or domestic reasons. The Council allows a break in service of up to seven years. Information, including job vacancies, is regularly sent to staff taking up these options and staff in category 1 undertake to return to the workplace for a period of two to four weeks each year for updating and to aid the keeping-in-touch process. Return to work at the end of unpaid leave is at the same grade/seniority. Flexible working patterns are available to staff (flexible working hours, part time working, job-sharing including a job-sharers' network, and parents' contracts). Nursery places, a childcare voucher scheme and a Women's Development Programme are available.

British Gas PLC, Corporate Human Resources, Rivermill House, 152 Grosvenor Road, London SW1V 3JL 0171 821 1444
Operates a career support scheme which includes the following provisions: at the end of maternity leave an employee is eligible to return to work on their existing contract or an alternative contract which may include arrangements such as jobsharing, flexible hours, or shorter contractual hours, subject to operational requirements. Employees who have completed at least 12 months service at the beginning to the 11th week before their, or their partner's, expected week of confinement, are eligible to take a career break (3 months-2 years). On return to work the Company will offer an appropriate post to the employee. Alternatively, an employee may opt to join the Reservist Scheme for up to five years, during which time they are kept in touch with the company, offered temporary work and are given preference over external applicants if they wish to return at the end of the period. A childcare allowance for pre-school children is available for employees returning from maternity leave or a career break.

Civil Service, Equal Opportunities Division, Office of Public Service, Horse Guards Road, London SW1P 3AL
A variety of flexible working arrangements has been introduced to help staff who wish to combine work with domestic responsibilities. These include part-time working, job-sharing, term-time working and home working. 19% of women now work part-time at senior as well as junior grades. In departments and agencies, 43 keeping-in-touch schemes have now been established, while long-term special leave arrangements provide an opportunity to take a career break and maintain employment rights. Former members of staff are welcome to apply for reinstatement. There are about 120 holiday playschemes around the country for children aged 5 to 12 years and 52 Civil Service nurseries. Some women-only development training courses have been set up, and there is increasing provision of alternatives to traditional residential training. Contact the personnel officer of individual departments and agencies.

Esso UK PLC, Esso House, Victoria Street, London SW1E 5JW 0171 834 6677
Has introduced a career break scheme for male and female staff who can take up to five years off for domestic reasons. A keeping-in-touch scheme is in operation and staff are encouraged to return to work for short periods to keep their skills up to date.

Grand Metropolitan PLC, 20 St James's Square, London SW1Y 4RR 0171 321 6000   *Contact:* Catherine Parsons, Human Resources Officer
Employees at all levels, with more than 2 years service, can take up to 3 years maternity leave, with an option of returning on a part-time basis (20 hours per week) for a period of two years. There are adoptive leave arrangements of one week's paid leave within the month of the

adoption, or where the child is under the age of 6 months the provisions of the maternity policy will apply. There is also a Family Responsibility Leave policy which allows employees to take between 6 months and 3 years unpaid leave to undertake responsibilities such as caring for an elderly relative or seriously ill member of the family.

ICI, 9 Millbank, London SW1P 3JF 0171 834 4444
Has introduced a career-break scheme of up to five years with a guaranteed return to own or equivalent job, with formal keeping-in-touch arrangements during the break, and flexible re-introduction to work.

J Sainsbury PLC, Stamford Street, London SE1 9LL 0171 921 6000
Offers a career-bridge scheme of up to five years' full-time leave, with protection of contractual employment benefits on return to work, or the opportunity to return to work part-time for a defined period. Homeworking, term-time contracts and day nurseries are other options available to men and women.

Lloyds Bank, PO Box 112, Canons House, Canons Way, Bristol BS99 7LB 0117 943 3433
Contact: Sally Evans, Manager, Equal Opportunities
Employees at all levels with at least five years continuous service and good performance are eligible for a five-year career break with guaranteed employment on return at the same grade as when they left. Several breaks are possible as long as total absence is not more that five years. Regular contact will be maintained to keep staff abreast of developments whilst on career break. On return to work any request for flexible working patterns will be carefully considered.

Rank Xerox Ltd, Bridge House, Oxford Road, Uxbridge, Middlesex UB8 1HS 01895 51133
Runs a career break scheme which allows staff to take a maximum of two career breaks totalling up to five years. Emergency Parental Leave, to take account of emergency childcare leave, and flexible working patterns are also available.

The BP Group, Britannic House, 1 Finsbury Circus, London EC2M 7BA 0171 496 4000
Uses its parental break policy as a guideline for career-break practices (ie schemes open to both sexes; two years per child; full-time absence or alternative working; life-assurance coverage and retention of car while absent). Childcare Networks provide support groups for working parents and maintain contact with staff on maternity absence or career breaks. Range of nursery provision. Contact Department Manager or Personnel Officer.

The Littlewoods Organisation, 100 Old Hall Street, Liverpool L70 1AB 0151 235 2222
The Littlewoods Organisation PLC offers a career break scheme to male and female staff who have a minimum of one year's service. The scheme includes keeping in touch, updating of skills and knowledge and a phased return. The scheme allows for a maximum break of 5 years. Every endeavour is made to provide an opportunity to return. Service will be deemed to be continuous only excluding the career break period.

Unilever PLC, Unilever House, PO Box 68, Blackfriars, London EC4P 4BQ 0171 822 5252
Operates a career break scheme lasting up to five years open to staff with at least three years' service. A keeping-in-touch scheme is available for managerial staff during their break.

Other organisations operating career break schemes include:

Avon Cosmetics Ltd; Bank of England; Bank of Scotland; British Airways PLC; Clydesdale Bank; Contributions Agency; Co-operative Bank; Glaxo Wellcome PLC; Halifax Building Society; Hampshire County Council; Inland Revenue; London Boroughs of Greenwich and Hillingdon; London Electricity; Lucas Industries PLC; Mast International Organisation PLC; Metropolitan Police; Midland Bank PLC; Midland Electricity PLC; National Westminster Bank; Nationwide Building Society; NHS Management Executive; Northern Electric PLC; Northern Arts; Northern Ireland Housing Association; Nuclear Electric PLC; Oxfordshire County Council; Queen Mary's University of Belfast; Royal Bank of Scotland; Royal Mail; Sheffield Hallam University; Staffordshire County Council; Surrey County Council; Texaco

PLC; TSB Group PLC; Ulster Bank Ltd; Universities of Southampton and Ulster; Wales Tourist Board; West Midlands Police; Woolwich Building Society; Yorkshire Bank

Professional and vocational organisations

Association for Women in Science and Engineering, 1 Park Square West, London NW1 4LJ 0171 935 5202   Contact: Dr Joan Mason, 12 Hills Avenue, Cambridge, CB1 4XA
Aims to advance the participation of women in the various sciences and engineering, at all levels, in industry, research institutes, education, administration and the media, by acting as a forum, a resource centre, support network and collective voice, linking with sister organisations at home and abroad. Organises national and regional meetings and other branch activities, collecting and providing information, networking and mentoring.

Association of Women Solicitors, c/o Judith McDermott, The Law Society, Law Society House, 50 Chancery Lane, London WC2A 1SX 0171 320 5793
Promotes the professional, business and social interests of women solicitors

British Association for Dental Nurses, 110 London Street, Fleetwood, Lancashire FY7 6EU 01253 778631. Professional association for dental nurses.

British Association of Women Entrepreneurs, 114 Gloucester Place, London W1H 3DB 0171 935 0085   Contact: Arline Woutersz, National President
Affiliates in 32 different countries

British Telecom Women's Network, BT Centre, 81 Newgate Street, London EC1A 7AJ 0171 356 6554   Contact: Allison Davies

Chartered Institute of Public Finance and Accountancy, 3 Robert Street, London WC2N 6BH 0171 895 8823 x258/ Women in CIPFA x262
As part of its remit, the Institute's Recruitment and Retention Board works to ensure that the interests of women members are represented and attended to. A career break membership category is offered. CIPFA is represented on the Women in Accountancy Board

City Women's Network, PO Box 353, Uxbridge, Middlesex UB10 0UN 01895 272178 Contact: Alison Thorne, Chairman
A network for senior executive women. Offers peer support for women in London and holds five events a year from wine tastings to serious career development. Minimum criteria for membership: five years at senior level. Members may join the CWN Register for non-executive directorships and public appointments.

Medical Women's Federation, Tavistock House North, Tavistock Square, London WC1H 9HX 0171 387 7765   Contact: Mrs L Perry
Independent nationwide network of women doctors and medical students. Membership by subscription.

National Association of Women Pharmacists, c/o Office Manager, Royal Pharmaceutical Society, 1 Lambeth High Street, London SE1 7JN 0171 735 9141   Contact: Janet Davis, Secretary
Founded in 1905, publishes a newsletter, has local branches in England and Wales, produces a Women in Pharmacy information pack, organises an annual weekend school and study days. Provides a link with the profession by contacting those who have temporarily left the Register of the Royal Pharmaceutical Society

North West Women into Management, 26 Windsor Avenue, Flixton, Manchester M41 5GP 0161 748 6081   Contact: Pam Crompton

Royal College of Nursing, 20 Cavendish Square, London W1M 0AB 0171 409 3333
Operates a Career Break category of membership which enables professional nurses to take a break of up to five years to care for children or other dependants or to undertake further education. Members are kept in touch with professional developments and receive free careers advice when they wish to return to work.

Royal Pharmaceutical Society of Great Britain, 1 Lambeth High Street, London SE1 7JN 0171 735 9141

Registered pharmacists in England may attend residential or day Return to Practice courses run by the Centre for Pharmacy Postgraduate Education (CPPE). Courses update knowledge and skills in community pharmacy practice and are intended for pharmacists wishing to return after a break and those changing from one branch of pharmacy to another. Further information from: Jennifer Archer, Assistant Director (Direct Learning), CPPE, University of Manchester, Oxford Road, Manchester, M13 9PL. 0161 275 2324

Pharmacists in Wales and Scotland should contact the following for details of return to practice courses: Dr DJ Temple, Director of Postgraduate Pharmaceutical Studies for Wales, Welsh School of Pharmacy, UWCC, PO Box 13, Cardiff, CF1 3XF. 01222 874784; Miss R Parr, Director of Postgraduate Education for Scotland, Department of Pharmacy, Royal College, 204 George Street, Glasgow, G1 1XW. 0141 552 4400 x4273/4274.

WAVES (Women's Audio Visual Education Scheme), London Women's Centre, 4 Wild Court, London WC2B 5AU 0171 430 1076   *Contact:* Margeret Trotter

Provides a structured framework of intermodular training courses in audio vidual media skills to enable women to make their own work, take further education and training or enter and advance within the audio visual industry

Women Architects' Committee, RIBA, 66 Portland Place, London W1N 4AD 0171 580 5533

Women in Banking and Finance, 55 Bourne Vale, Bromley, Kent BR2 7NW 0181 462 3276 *Contact:* Ann Leverett, Administrator

Develops and promotes the role of women throughout the financial community

Women in CIPFA (Chartered Institute of Public Finance & Accountancy), 3 Robert Street, London WC2N 6BH 0171 895 8823 x262

Women in Dentistry, Motcombe, Manchester Road, Thornton Heath, Surrey CR7 8NH *Contact:* Ms S Tuck

Women in Film and Television (UK) Ltd, Garden Studios, 11-15 Betterton Street, London WC2H 9BP 0171 379 0344   *Contact:* Kate Wallbank

A networking/membership organisation for women with a minimum three years experience in the film/television industries. Aims to provide information and promote the position of women in the industry. Publishes: monthly calendar, quarterly magazine, annual Directory of members. Programme of events includes: networking, workshops, seminars, screenings and Annual Awards.

Women in Management, 64 Marryat Road, Wimbledon, London SW19 5BN 0181 944 6332 *Contact:* Liz Marryat

Women in Manual Trades, 52-54 Featherstone Street, London EC1Y 8RT 0171 251 9192

Offers information, advice and resources for tradeswomen, including training and careers advice, courses for women setting up in business, meetings, newsletter, conferences and a resource library for tradeswomen.

Women in Medicine, 21 Wallingford Avenue, London W10 6QA

Provides support and a political voice for women doctors and medical students

Women in Physics Professional Group, Institute of Physics, 47 Belgrave Square, London SW1X 8QX 0171 235 6111

Works to advise on matters of interest to professional women with careers in physics. Current activities include a regular newsletter for women members, professional briefs on various topics, holding meetings and workshops and encouraging the formation of local networks. Publications of particular interest are 'A Career Break Kit for Physicists' and 'Professional Training for Women'.

Women in Property, c/o McLean Aylwin Communications, 39 King Street, London WC2E 8JS 0171 497 9707   *Contact:* Melissa Kojan

Business network for professional women employed in property and related industries. Members include architects, lawyers, surveyors, planners, etc. Promotes the advancement of women in the industry through educational seminars, visits to developments, forums, networking and social events. There are 900 members in 10 branches nationwide.

Women in Publishing, c/o The Bookseller, 12 Dyott Street, London WC1A 1DF   *Contact:* Information Officer

Women in Technology (WITEC), Sheffield Hallam University, Room 317, Heriot House, City Campus, Sheffield S1 1WB 0114 253 2041   *Contact:* Claire Molyneux, National Co-ordinator
Aims to promote equality of opportunity in science and technology.

Women into Business, Small Business Bureau Ltd, 46 Westminster Palace Gardens, Artillery Row, London SW1P 1RR 0171 976 7262/3
Network for women running their own business.

Women into Information Technology Campaign, Concept 2000, 250 Farnborough Road, Farnborough, Hampshire GU14 7LU 01252 528329
WIT offers advice/information for education, professional development and women returners to the IT workforce. It looks generally at the gender imbalance and equal opportunities of girls and women in IT with the aim of increasing the overall national skills base.

Women into Science and Engineering (WISE), The Engineering Council, 10 Maltravers Street, London WC2R 3ER 0171 240 7891   *Contact:* Marie Noelle Barton
Encourages women and girls to consider careers in science and engineering. Advice on career breaks for engineers and technicians, also publication of a directory of special initiatives to encourage women to enter engineering. The directory 'Awards, courses, visits' includes details of awards and scholarships available solely for women

Women's Computer Centre, Third Floor, Wesley House, 4 Wild Court, London WC2B 5AU 0171 430 0112
WCC runs courses in general computing and is also a City & Guilds certified centre

Women's Education in Building, 12-14 Malton Road, London W10 5UP 0181 968 9139
Construction skills training centre offering taster courses, single trade courses, one day and evening courses for women.

Women's Engineering Society, Imperial College of Science and Technology, Department of Civil Engineering, Imperial College Road, London SW7 2BU 0171 594 6025   *Contact:* C J MacGillivray
Promotes the education, training and practice of engineering among women. Ensures the voice of women engineers is heard. Annual Conference, quarterly journal.

Women's Farm and Garden Association, 175 Gloucester Street, Cirencester, Gloucestershire GL7 2DP 01285 658339   *Contact:* Patricia McHugh, Organiser
Voluntary organisation for women working in, or connected with agriculture, horticulture or allied industries. Promoting the interests of members at national and international levels. Organising training scheme for women returners offering practical training under supervision

Childcare organisations

BAND, 81 St Nicholas Road, St Pauls, Bristol BS2 9JJ 0117 954 2128
BAND is an umbrella organisation, set up in 1978 to link up out-of-school schemes, which are run independently by an elected management of parent users. All schemes particularly acknowledge the needs of single parent families and those on low incomes. Full membership is open to Schemes that are providing out-of-school facilities for children of working parents, and are managed by parent users; and to individuals who share BAND's aims. Affiliate membership is open to both organisations and individuals.

Childcare Links, 0171 405 5617
Run by the Daycare Trust, this is a telephone helpline based on a computerised database of

childcare services, offering information and leaflets to parents and carers as well as providers of childcare services.

Choices in Childcare, Holly Building, Holly Street, Sheffield S1 2GT 0114 276 6881
Choices in Childcare can put parents in touch with their nearest children's information service – who hold detailed local information on childcare – childminders, nurseries and out of school clubs. Supports and links to local children's information services in the UK, promoting their development and quality through the provision of specialist advice, publications and training events.

Kids Club Network, Bellerive House, 3 Muirfield Crescent, London E14 9SZ 0171 512 2112
Provides information about out-of-school clubs which provide care for school-age children outside school hours and during school holidays.

National Childminding Association, 8 Masons Hill, Bromley, Kent BR2 9EY 0181 464 6164
Information and advice on choosing and using child-minders.

Parents at Work, 45 Beech Street, London EC2Y 8AD 0171 628 3565
Provides information on all aspects of child care; members are put in touch with a network of local support groups; promotes 'family friendly' work practices.

Pre-School Learning Alliance, National Centre, 69 Kings Cross Road, London WC1X 9LL 0171 833 0991
The Pre-School Learning Alliance (formerly Pre-School Playgroups Association) is a national educational charity with over 30 years of experience in pre-school care and education. Through its 19,500 playgroups, it involves an enormous number of people, the large majority of whom are women returning to work. The PLA offers nationally developed and validated courses for work with pre-school age children. These courses provide underpinning knowledge and understanding for NVQs in Childcare and Education.

Support organisations

British Federation of Women Graduates, 4 Mandeville Courtyard, 142 Battersea Park Road, London SW11 4NB 0171 498 8037
A national organisation which brings women graduates together. It provides stimulation, encouragement and friendship through local, national and international networks for all women graduates.

Business and Professional Women UK Ltd (BPW), 23 Ansdell Street, London W8 5BN 0171 938 1729   *Contact:* Rita Bangle
Networking, training and personal development

Equal Opportunities Commission, England: Overseas House, Quay Street, Manchester M3 3HN 0161 833 9244
The EOC is the national body which was set up to work towards the elimination of discrimination and to promote equality of opportunity between men and women. It keeps under review the working of the Sex Discrimination Act and the Equal Pay Act. It is active in pursuit of these responsibilities and publishes excellent pamphlets on contemporary issues. It is the body in the UK to whom both individuals and organisations may turn for advice in this area.

EOC Press Office: 36 Broadway, London SW1H 0XH 0171 222 1110

EOC Scotland: Stock Exchange House, 7 Nelson Mandela Place, Glasgow G2 1QW 0141 248 5833

EOC Wales: Caerwys House, Windsor Lane, Cardiff CF1 1LB 01222 43552

Fawcett Society, Fifth Floor, 45 Beech Street, London EC2Y 8AD 0171 628 4441
Membership organisation, campaigning for women's equality

Federation of Army Wives, Central Office, HQ Land, Old Sarum, Salisbury, Wiltshire SP4 6BN 01722 438231

Gingerbread, 35 Wellington Street, London WC2E 7BN 0171 240 0953
Information and support for single parents provided through a network of local groups around the country.

Maternity Alliance, 45 Beech Street, London EC2P 2LX 0171 588 8582   *Contact:* Jenny McLeish, Information Officer
The Maternity Alliance is an independent national organisation which campaigns for improvements in rights and services for mothers, families and babies. It works for better provision before conception and during pregnancy, childbirth and the first year of life. The Telephone Advice Line is open 10-1 on Mon, Tues, Thurs, Fri and 2-5pm on Wed. Leaflets on benefits and employment rights are available.

National Alliance of Women's Organisations, PO Box 257, Twickenham, Middlesex TW1 4XG 0181 891 1419
NAWO campaigns for equal opportunities in the fields of education and training for women. The Resource Centre holds information on education and training developments as they affect women.

National Childbirth Trust, Alexandra House, Oldham Terrace, Acton London W3 6NH 0181 992 8637
Offers information and support in pregnancy, childbirth and early parenthood and aims to enable all parents to make informed choices. 400 branches running specialist help for women returners, on breastfeeding and for parents with disabilities.

National Council for One Parent Families, 225 Kentish Town Road, London NW5 7EE 0171 267 1361
Offers a range of information and services for one parent families, including an information pack covering returning to work.

National Council of Women, 36 Danbury Street, Islington, London N1 8JU 0171 354 2395

National Federation of Women's Institutes, 104 New King's Road, London SW6 4LY 0171 371 9300
The Women's Institute provides a democratic, non-sectarian, non-party political, educational and social organisation for women, enabling the development of skills and talents to improve quality of life in the community. All women and girls in England, Wales, Channel Islands and Isle of Man are welcome to join. The WI publishes a monthly magazine 'Home and Country' and also has its own publishing company WI Books. It also runs its own short stay adult education establishment near Oxford which provides an increasing range of courses, some of which can lead to accreditation.

National Women's Register, National Office, 3a Vulcan House, Vulcan Road North, Norwich NR6 5LX 01603 406767
The NWR enables women to meet informally in one another's homes, to hold discussions on topics unconnected with their everyday surroundings, thus promoting friendship and communication skills, and building confidence. It runs educational workshops and day conferences affiliated to its activities, publishes a newsletter and national correspondence magazines and runs a research bank for members. Contact NWR for a local group in your area.

Soroptimist International of Great Britain and Ireland, 127 Wellington Road South, Stockport SK1 3TS 0161 480 7686
Women's international service organisation.

Townswomen's Guilds, Chamber of Commerce House, 75 Harborne Road, Edgbaston, Birmingham B15 3DA 0121 456 3435

Women's National Commission, Department for Education & Employment, Caxton House, Tothill Street, London SW1H 9NF 0171 273 5486
Publishes 'Women Returners' Employment Potential: an Agenda for Action' (supplied free on request).

About the Women Returners' Network

The Women Returners' Network (a registered charity) was set up in 1984 to facilitate women's re-entry into the labour force by:

a. Promoting education, training and employment opportunities.

b. Providing information to employers in all sectors about the schemes available to facilitate the retention and re-entry of women employees, with particular emphasis on flexibility and training provision.

c. Encouraging providers of education and training to develop flexible programmes to meet the needs of women with families, whether they are young children or elderly dependants.

d. Developing links with appropriate national, international and local voluntary organisations.

e. Producing publications on issues concerning women returners.

f. Disseminating information and experience of successful strategies, techniques and methods in meeting the needs of women returners.

WRN Activities

So far, we have been involved in conferences for employers on career breaks, on professional updating for women, on ageism, on recruitment and retention of women returners, on skills shortages and recruitment potential, on promoting jobs for women in rural areas.

WRN is active in Europe; in 1993, it held a conference covering Quality, Equality and the European Community. In 1994, WRN played a prime role in establishing the European Women Returners' Network, based at Erasmus University in Rotterdam, and which seeks to co-ordinate and promote the cause of women returners throughout the European Union. During 1995, WRN was funded by the European Commission to undertake a major research project, focusing on the professional updating available to women returners and examining employment and training implications for the UK and other selected EU states.

WRN provides a national information service from its London office, dealing with over 2,500 enquiries annually. A series of free Resource Sheets is available, covering topics most frequently requested by enquirers. This Directory, *Returning to Work*, forms the flagship of WRN's information work and has been used as a model by European partners.

Women returners and those concerned with their education, training or employment are welcome to become members of WRN. Members receive WRN's quarterly newsletter *ReTurn* which covers a wide variety of issues covering women's employment and training, and are also invited to regular network meetings, seminars and conferences and other events.

For further information, contact: WRN, 8 John Adam Street, London WC2N 6EZ; 0171 839 8188; Fax: 0171 930 8620.

Useful Publications

Childcare

Shaw, Clare *The 5-minute mum: time management for busy parents* Headway 1995 £4.99
The working parents' handbook Parents at Work, 45 Beech Street, London EC2Y 8AD, 0171 628 3565

Education/training

Adult continuing education yearbook, 1995/6 NIACE (National Institute of Adult Continuing Education) 1995 £12.99
British qualifications: a comprehensive guide to educational, technical, professional and academic qualifications in Britain, 25th ed Kogan Page 1994
Colleges and institutes of higher education annual guide Standing Conference of Principals, Edge Hill College, Ormskirk, L39 4QP Free
Compendium of higher education, 1996/7 LASER Advisory Council, 0171 637 3073 1995 £20
Degree course guide, 1995/6 Hobsons/CRAC 1995
Directory of further education, 1995/6 Hobsons/CRAC
Directory of higher education, 1995/6 Hobsons/CRAC
Entrance guide to higher education in Scotland, 1996 The Herald/Committee of Scottish Higher Education Principals 1995
Graduate studies, 1995/6 Hobsons/CRAC 1995
How to choose your Higher National Diploma course Trotman 1993 £14.95
Bourner, Tom & Race, Phil *How to win as a part-time student, 2nd ed* Kogan Page 1995 £7.99
Maynard, Liz & Pearsall, Simon *Mature students' guide: getting into higher education for 21+* Trotman 1994
Open learning directory, 1995 Pergamon Open Learning 1995
Second chances: a national guide to adult education and training opportunities COIC/NIACE
Stepping up: mature students' guide Universities and Colleges Admissions Service (01242 227788)
Taggart, Caroline *The essential handbook for mature students* Kyle Cathie 1994 £9.99
The training and enterprise directory, 7th ed Kogan Page 1995
UCAS handbook: how to apply for admission to a university, 1996 Universities and Colleges Admissions Service (01242 227788)
University and college entrance: the official guide, 1996 UCAS (Universities and Colleges Admissions Service) 1995 £12
Which degree? 1996 Hobsons/CRAC 1995

Flexible working

Change at the top: working flexibly in senior and managerial jobs New Ways to Work £12.50
Bibby, Andrew *Home is where the heart is: a practical handbook for teleworking from home* Headway 1991 £6.99
Walton, Pam *Job sharing: a practical guide* New Ways to Work £7.99
Read, Sue *The complete guide to working from home* Headline 1992 £6.99

Grants/funding

A guide to grants for individuals in need Directory of Social Change 1994
Directory of grant-making trusts, 1995 Charities Aid Foundation 1995
Educational grants directory Directory of Social Change
Guide to students' allowances (Scotland) Scottish Office Education Dept, Awards Branch, Gyleview, 3 Redheughs Riggs, Edinburgh EH12 9AH 1995 Free
Student grants and loans (England and Wales) Department for Education & Employment,

Publications Centre, PO Box 2193, London E15 2EU 1995 Free
Student grants and loans to students: a brief guide (Northern Ireland) Department of Education, Scholarships Branch, Rathgael House, Balloo Road, Bangor, Co. Down BT19 2PR 1995 Free
The grants register, 1995-1997 Macmillan 1995

Returning to work

Back to work: a resource guide for women returners Industrial Society 1995 £4.95
Flanders, Margaret L *Breakthrough: the career woman's guide to shattering the glass ceiling* Paul Chapman 1994 £10.95
Dyson, Sue & Hoare, Stephen *Changing course: how to take charge of your career* Sheldon 1990
Wallis, Margaret *Getting there: job hunting for women, 2nd ed* Kogan Page 1990
Dobson, Ann *How to return to work* How To Books 1995 £8.99
Hutt, Jane *Making opportunities: a guide for women and employers* NCVO 1992
Making the most: women in science, engineering and technology building a workforce for sustained competitiveness Department of Trade and Industry/Opportunity 2000 1995
Returning to work: a guide for lone parents National Council for One Parent Families 1995 £4.75
Returning without fears: a support package for women returning to work Domino Consultancy Ltd, 01509 650505 1995 £19.95
Secretaries: onwards and upwards Industrial Society, 48 Bryanston Square, London W1H 7LN 1995 £20
Sampson, Eleri *The image factor: a guide to effective self-presentation for career enhancement* Kogan Page 1994 £9.99
Sitterly, Connie *The woman manager: how to develop essential skills for success* Kogan Page 1993 £6.99
Bird, Polly *The working woman's handbook: the essential reference guide for every working woman* Piatkus 1995 £9.99
McGowan, Frankie *Women going back to work* NTP Publishing 1993 £7.99
Women mean business: a practical guide for women returners BBC Books 1991 £5.99
Stoker, Linda *Women returners' guide* Bloomsbury 1991 £7.99
Sadek, Jackie & Egan, Sheila *Working out: a woman's guide to career success* Arrow 1995 £6.99

List of Abbreviations

General

APL Accreditation of Prior Learning is a process which enables people to gain certificates for their past achievement, often outside the formal education system in work, leisure or community activities.

CATS Credit Accumulation and Transfer

DfEE Department for Education and Employment

EOC Equal Opportunities Commission

ESF European Social Fund

ESOL English as a Second Language

IT Information Technology

LEA Local Education Authority

LEC Local Enterprise Council (Scotland)

NOW New Opportunities for Women

SED Scottish Education Department

TAP Training Access Point

TEC Training and Enterprise Council (England and Wales)

WP Word-processing

Education Providers

AEC Adult Education Centre

College of FE/HE, CFE, CHE College of Further Education/Higher Education

LOCN London Open College Network

MOCF Manchester Open College Federation

OCFNW Open College Federation of the North West

OCN Open College Network

OU Open University

SWAF South West Access Federation

SWAP Scottish Wider Access Programme

SWWOCAC South West Wales Open College Access Consortium

SYOC/SYOLF South Yorkshire Open College/South Yorkshire Open Learning Federation

WEA Workers' Educational Association. Has district offices throughout the country

WNYAN West and North Yorkshire Access Network

Examining Bodies and Qualifications

BA/BSc/BEd Bachelor of Arts/Science/Education. Most common 'first' degrees, usually taking three years full-time, four to six years part-time.

BTEC Business and Technology Education Council

CACHE   Council for Awards in Children's Care and Education

C&G   City and Guilds

CLAIT   Computer Literacy and Information Technology (an award offered by the Royal Society of Arts)

CNAA   Council for National Academic Awards

CSE   Certificate of Secondary Education. Replaced by the GCSE in 1988.

DipHE   Diploma in Higher Education. Usually awarded after two years of full-time study or its part-time equivalent; can lead on to a degree or teaching qualification.

DipSW   Diploma in Social Work

GCE O and A level   General Certificate of Education Ordinary and Advanced level. The conventional route to higher education. GCE O Level has been replaced by the GCSE.

GCSE   General Certificate of Secondary Education. Qualification which combined and replaced CSE and O level in 1988.

GNVQ   General National Vocational Qualification

HNC/D   Higher National Certificate/Diploma

HEQC   Higher Education Quality Council

LCCI   London Chamber of Commerce and Industry

MA/MSc/MEd   Master of Arts/Science/Education. Postgraduate qualifications, usually taking one year of full-time study. Part-time study over a longer period of time may also be available.

NC/D   National Certificate/Diploma

NEBSM   National Examining Board for Supervisory Management

NNEB   National Nursery Examination Board

NVQ   National Vocational Qualification

PGCE   Postgraduate Certificate in Education

QTS   Qualified Teacher Status

RSA   Royal Society of Arts. Some business studies courses lead to RSA certificates.

SCE   Scottish Certificate of Education. Standard Ordinary Grade is generally considered equivalent to GCSE. The Higher Grade examination serves as an entry to higher education in Scotland.

SCOTVEC   Scottish Vocational Education Council

TEFLA   Teaching English as a Foreign Language

Description of courses

Subject headings
Within each county the courses are listed alphabetically under subject headings (e.g. Access or Management or Practical or Preparatory). Many courses could fit under several headings and so they are placed under what seems the most appropriate, given what is known about the content and intention of the course.

The following subject headings may require clarification:

Access
These are courses designed to give students access by a recognised route into a university or college of higher education. They have been validated by an institution which recognises the course as an acceptable access route, but other places may also accept them. There is no GUARANTEE that successful completion of the course will AUTOMATICALLY lead to acceptance, but it provides a recognised alternative qualification. In most cases such courses replace the need for A levels. In some areas, several colleges have grouped together with higher education institutions and formed an Open College system. Details of these are given under the county where appropriate.

Preparatory
These courses are seen essentially as a starting-point for those wanting to return to education or training. Under this heading are included return to study courses, return to work provision and Open University preparatory courses. GCSE courses are not listed since these are provided by almost all further education colleges.

NOW (New Opportunities for Women)
These are courses designed specifically for women who have been out of paid employment for some time and want to prepare for a return to education, training or paid employment. Many of these courses contain a component which includes advice and guidance, as well as different subjects or skills. NOW courses are run by colleges as well as by organisations like the Workers' Educational Association, and some fee may be payable.

Professional Updating
These courses are for women wishing to return to a profession. They are available in various parts of the country and are usually short courses (e.g. 12 to 15 weeks) which include practical advice on returning, such as interview techniques, plus academic study to allow updating in the student's subject area and work experience in a professional capacity.

Women's studies
These are included in a separate category because most are not specifically provided for women returners and do not necessarily provide a recognised route back into education or training. However, many such courses have given women the opportunity to reassess their lives in a wider context and to find out what is available and what they might wish to do. There are two types of women's studies courses; those, usually short ones, which are open to anyone; and those, often one- or two-year courses, which lead to a postgraduate diploma or degree. The first type tends to change the topic and the title each year. Where these are listed the current course title is given; the contact person will provide more information if it has changed.

All other courses are listed by subject or main content. This includes courses leading to traditional academic or vocational qualifications. Also listed are courses designed to provide skills training which will enable women to look for work on completing the course. However, many such courses also enable their students to go on to further education and training. Skills training includes refresher courses for those who previously had some experience (e.g. updating office skills), new skills training which requires no previous experience, and non-traditional skill centres for women.

Course information
Each course lists as many details as possible. In every case the same format is used.

Title
This gives the title of the course.

Place

This indicates the college or place where the course is held. For the postal address see the index of colleges at the end of the Directory. Where a college occupies several sites, the contact name and telephone number may be at a different address from that where the course is held.

Length

This gives the duration of the course in weeks, terms or years. For some part-time courses the length of time needed to complete the course varies, depending on how many sessions are taken each week.

Start

Most courses start in the Autumn term, in September or October. Other start dates are noted. It is a good idea to phone and enquire well in advance but, even if a course has started, late applicants are sometimes accepted.

Day(s) and time(s)

In most cases, the day of the week is given; otherwise it states 'one day/week' or whatever is appropriate. The actual times of the class are given whenever possible or the number of hours/week.

Cost

The figure given is for the latest full fee known. If concessions are available this is stated. It is ALWAYS worth asking if a concessionary rate is available; local regulations vary.

Entry requirements (Entry Reqs)

This indicates for whom the course is designed and whether any entry qualifications are needed. ALL the courses listed are open to women and we have indicated if the provision is for women only. The title of the course usually makes this clear. Some courses operate within age limits and these are stated if known.

Award

This indicates if any certificate or other qualification is obtained at the end of the course, Often the course may lead to an examination, but this may be optional.

Creche

Always ASK about childcare provision and about classes coinciding with school hours. The actual creche provision varies both in the number of hours covered and the age range of children accepted. Ask the contact person for details. Charges for childcare are included where known.

Contact

The name of the person is provided whenever possible. If no name is given, ask for the person responsible for the course. The college or centre phone number is given, with extension number if known.

County contacts

The county contact section at the end of each county lists local people, places and organisations to approach for information and advice.

DIRECTORY OF COURSES
AND
COUNTY CONTACTS

COURSES

- **SUBJECT** Access/Art & Design   1
- **TITLE** Access to Higher Education: Pathway for Art & Design
- **PLACE** South Bristol College

Length 1 year   **Start** September   **Cost** Contact College   **Entry Reqs** Selection by interview
Award Open College Network accredited   **Creche** Yes
- **CONTACT** Student Services 0117 963 9033

- **SUBJECT** Access/Built Environment   2
- **TITLE** Access to the Built Environment
- **PLACE** Soundwell College

Length 1 year   **Start** September   **Days** Full time 9.30-3.30   **Cost** Enrolment £21, otherwise free   **Entry Reqs** None. Entry by interview   **Award** Entry to degree/diploma courses at Univ of West of England in Housing, Planning, Building   **Creche** Yes
- **CONTACT** Jenny Newley or Student Services 0117 947 9270/80/90

- **SUBJECT** Access/Business   3
- **TITLE** Access to Higher Education: Pathway for Business
- **PLACE** South Bristol College

Length 1 year   **Start** September   **Cost** Contact College   **Entry Reqs** Selection by interview
Award Open College Network accredited   **Creche** Yes
- **CONTACT** Student Services 0117 963 9033

- **SUBJECT** Access/Business Studies   4
- **TITLE** Access to Bookkeeping and Accountancy for Mature Students
- **PLACE** Weston-super-Mare College

Length 1 year (1 day/week)   **Start** September   **Days** Wed 9.30-3.00   **Cost** Approx £162 Concessions may apply   **Entry Reqs** Open, assumes basic arithmetic   **Award** Preparation for further study   **Creche** No
- **CONTACT** Fiona L Waters 01934 411411 x481

- **SUBJECT** Access/Business Studies   5
- **TITLE** Access to Business Studies
- **PLACE** Soundwell College

Length 1 year   **Start** September   **Days** Full time 9.30-3.30   **Cost** Enrolment £21, otherwise free   **Entry Reqs** None. Entry by interview   **Award** Entry to degree/diploma courses at Univ of West of England in Housing, Planning, Building   **Creche** Yes
- **CONTACT** Annie Angell or Student Services 0117 947 9270/80/90

- **SUBJECT** Access/Business Studies/Humanities/Science/Social Science/Teaching   6
- **TITLE** Access to Higher Education
- **PLACE** Brunel College of Arts and Technology

Length 1 year full time, 2 years part time   **Start** September   **Days** 4 days/week 9.15-3.30 Full time £618, part time £301 (100% concessions)   **Entry Reqs** Interview   **Award** Access to Higher Education Certificate (OCN)   **Creche** Nursery
- **CONTACT** Jane Wills 0117 924 1241 x2354

- **SUBJECT** Access/Computing/Information Technology   7
- **TITLE** Access to Computing and Information Technology
- **PLACE** Soundwell College

Length 1 year   **Start** September   **Days** Full time 9.30-3.30   **Cost** Enrolment £21, otherwise free   **Entry Reqs** None. Entry by interview   **Award** Entry to degree/diploma courses at Univ of West of England in Housing, Planning, Building   **Creche** Yes
- **CONTACT** Rhona Trueman or Student Services 0117 947 9270/80/90

- **SUBJECT** Access/Environmental Studies 8
- **TITLE** Access to Higher Education: Pathway for Environmental Studies
- **PLACE** South Bristol College

Length 1 year **Start** September **Cost** Contact College **Entry Reqs** Selection by interview **Award** Open College Network accredited **Creche** Yes
- **CONTACT** Student Services 0117 963 9033

- **SUBJECT** Access/Health Studies 9
- **TITLE** Access to Health Studies (including Physiotherapy)
- **PLACE** Soundwell College

Length 1 year **Start** September **Days** Full time 9.30-3.30 **Cost** Enrolment £21, otherwise free **Entry Reqs** None. Entry by interview **Award** Entry to Dip HE & Reg Nurse Training/ degrees in Nursing, Radiography, Physiotherapy **Creche** Yes
- **CONTACT** Martyn Pape or Student Services 0117 947 9270/80/90

- **SUBJECT** Access/Health Studies 10
- **TITLE** Access to Higher Education: Pathway for Health
- **PLACE** South Bristol College

Length 1 year **Start** September **Cost** Contact College **Entry Reqs** Selection by interview **Award** Open College Network accredited **Creche** Yes
- **CONTACT** Student Services 0117 963 9033

- **SUBJECT** Access/Humanities 11
- **TITLE** Access to Higher Education: Pathway for Humanities
- **PLACE** South Bristol College

Length 1 year **Start** September **Cost** Contact College **Entry Reqs** Selection by interview **Award** Open College Network accredited **Creche** Yes
- **CONTACT** Student Services 0117 963 9033

- **SUBJECT** Access/Languages 12
- **TITLE** Access to Modern Languages: French
- **PLACE** Soundwell College

Length 1 year **Start** September **Days** Full time 9.30-3.30 **Cost** Enrolment £21, otherwise free **Entry Reqs** Some knowledge of French. Entry by interview **Award** Reserved place on Modern Language degree course at Univ of West of England **Creche** Yes
- **CONTACT** Tricia Thorpe or Student Services 0117 947 9270/80/90

- **SUBJECT** Access/Law 13
- **TITLE** Access to Higher Education: Pathway for Law
- **PLACE** South Bristol College

Length 1 year **Start** September **Cost** Contact College **Entry Reqs** Selection by interview **Award** Open College Network accredited **Creche** Yes
- **CONTACT** Student Services 0117 963 9033

- **SUBJECT** Access/Science/Engineering 14
- **TITLE** Access to Science and Engineering
- **PLACE** Brunel College of Arts and Technology

Length 1 year **Start** September **Entry Reqs** By interview **Award** Guaranteed place at University of the West of England **Creche** Nursery
- **CONTACT** Peter Gulliver 0117 924 1241

- **SUBJECT** Access/Social Science 15
- **TITLE** Access to Higher Education: Pathway for Social Science
- **PLACE** South Bristol College

Length 1 year **Start** September **Cost** Contact College **Entry Reqs** Selection by interview **Award** Open College Network accredited **Creche** Yes
- **CONTACT** Student Services 0117 963 9033

Avon

- **SUBJECT** Access/Social Science 16
- **TITLE** Access to Social Science
- **PLACE** Soundwell College

Length 1 year **Start** September **Days** Full time 9.30-3.30 **Cost** Enrolment £21, otherwise free **Entry Reqs** None. Entry by interview **Award** Reserved place on Social Science degree course at Univ of West of England, Bath or Bristol Univ **Creche** Yes
- **CONTACT** Irene Mcgrath or Student Services 0117 947 9270/80/90

- **SUBJECT** Access/Social Work/Community Studies 17
- **TITLE** Access to Social Work, Access to Community and Youth Work
- **PLACE** Soundwell College

Length 1 year **Start** September **Days** Full time 9.30-3.30 **Cost** Enrolment £21, otherwise free **Entry Reqs** None. Entry by interview **Award** Entry to Diploma in Social Work or Youth & Community Work at Univ of the West of England **Creche** Yes
- **CONTACT** Judie Jancovich or Student Services 0117 947 9270/80/90

- **SUBJECT** Access/Systems Engineering 18
- **TITLE** Access to Systems Engineering
- **PLACE** Soundwell College

Length 1 year **Start** September **Days** Full time 9.30-3.30 **Cost** Enrolment £21, otherwise free **Entry Reqs** None. Entry by interview **Award** Entry to Foundation Course or related dip/degree courses at Univ of the West of England **Creche** Yes
- **CONTACT** John Turton or Student Services 0117 947 9270/80/90

- **SUBJECT** Access/Teaching 19
- **TITLE** Access to Higher Education: Pathway for Teacher Training
- **PLACE** South Bristol College

Length 1 year **Start** September **Cost** Contact College **Entry Reqs** Selection by interview **Award** Open College Network accredited **Creche** Yes
- **CONTACT** Student Services 0117 963 9033

- **SUBJECT** Access/Travel & Tourism/Secretarial/Law 20
- **TITLE** Access to 1. Travel and Tourism 2. Secretarial Studies 3. Law
- **PLACE** Weston-super-Mare College

Length 1 year (1 day/week) **Start** September **Days** 1. Fri 10.00-3.00 2. Thurs 9.30-3.00 3. 9.30-3.00 **Cost** £162 Concessions may apply **Entry Reqs** None 1. Background in general business desirable, not essential 2. All topics from basics **Award** 1. ABTA Travel Agents Certificate Primary & Advanced including air. 2. RSA exams 3. ILEX pt 1/yr 1 **Creche** No
- **CONTACT** Fiona L Waters 01934 411411 x481

- **SUBJECT** Access/Women's Studies 21
- **TITLE** Access Units in Women's Studies: Women in Society
- **PLACE** South Bristol College

Cost £499 (free if in receipt of benefit) **Entry Reqs** 21+, few formal qualifications **Award** Open College Network Credits
- **CONTACT** Kath Tudor 0117 963 9033

- **SUBJECT** Art & Design 22
- **TITLE** Foundation Studies in Art & Design
- **PLACE** Weston-super-Mare College

Length 2 years (2 days/week) **Start** September **Days** Mon & Tues 9.00-4.30 **Cost** £463+£35 studio fee+cost of external visits. Concessions may apply. **Entry Reqs** Interview **Award** Access to higher education **Creche** No
- **CONTACT** Fiona L Waters 01934 411411 x481

- **SUBJECT**   Business   23
- **TITLE**   Record Keeping for Small Businesses
- **PLACE**   Weston-super-Mare College

Length 6 weeks   **Start** November, February   **Days** Tues 6.30-9.00   **Cost** £45 No concession
Entry Reqs None   **Award** Progress to Payroll for Small Businesses course   **Creche** No
- **CONTACT**   Fiona L Waters 01934 411411 x481

- **SUBJECT**   Business   24
- **TITLE**   Setting Up Your Own Small Business
- **PLACE**   Weston-super-Mare College

Length 6 weeks   **Start** September, January   **Days** Tues 6.30-9.00   **Cost** £45 No concession
Entry Reqs None   **Award** Leads to Record Keeping for Small Businesses course   **Creche** No
- **CONTACT**   Fiona L Waters 01934 411411 x481

- **SUBJECT**   Business Administration   25
- **TITLE**   Business Start Up Skills
- **PLACE**   Soundwell College, Management & Professional Studies Centre

Length 12 weeks   **Start** Various   **Days** Flexible   **Cost** Free tuition, £25 enrolment, £60 exam
fee   **Award** NVQ III   **Creche** Yes
- **CONTACT**   Jenny Tucker 0117 956 2406

- **SUBJECT**   Childcare   26
- **TITLE**   NVQ Childcare and Education Levels II & III
- **PLACE**   College of Care and Early Education, Lawrence Weston Site

Length Contact College   **Start** Flexible   **Days** Flexible according to need   **Entry Reqs** By
interview and assessment   **Award** NVQ Level II & III   **Creche** Yes
- **CONTACT**   Sue Kingswood 0117 923 5706

- **SUBJECT**   Childcare   27
- **TITLE**   Part Time NNEB Diploma
- **PLACE**   Various sites in Bristol

Length 5 years maximum   **Start** Various   **Days** Flexible   **Entry Reqs** Interview and
assessment   **Award** NNEB Diploma   **Creche** Contact College
- **CONTACT**   Sue Kingswood 0117 923 5706

- **SUBJECT**   Childcare   28
- **TITLE**   Pre-School Playgroups Association
- **PLACE**   Weston-super-Mare College

Length 1 year (1 day/week)   **Start** September   **Days** Tues 9.45-2.30, Thurs 7.15-9.45   **Cost**
£180 Concessions may apply   **Entry Reqs** None. Contact with playgroups useful but not
essential   **Award** NVQ   **Creche** Yes, daytime only. Contact College
- **CONTACT**   Fiona L Waters 01934 411411 x481

- **SUBJECT**   Community Studies/Social Work   29
- **TITLE**   DipHE in 1. Community and Youth Work 2. Social Work
- **PLACE**   University of the West of England, St Matthias Campus

Length 2 years full time or 3 years part time   **Start** September, October   **Days** Full time Mon-
Fri   **Cost** Contact University   **Entry Reqs** 1. Minimum 1 yr relevant experience 2. Equivalent
to 5 GCSEs/2 at A Level (Mature students welcome)   **Award** Diploma in Higher Education 1.
Community & Youth Work 2. Social Work   **Creche** Yes 0117 965 6100
- **CONTACT**   1. & 2. Cathy Benjamin 3. Maria Michael 0117 965 5384

- **SUBJECT**   Construction   30
- **TITLE**   Construction Crafts for Women
- **PLACE**   South Bristol College

Length Variable   **Entry Reqs** None   **Award** College Certificate
- **CONTACT**   Kath Tudor 0117 963 9033

- **SUBJECT**   English   31
- **TITLE**   Workshop for Developing Reading & Writing Skills in English
- **PLACE**   Soundwell College
Length 30 weeks   **Start** September   **Days** 1 eve/week (Mon, Tues, Wed or Thurs) 7.00-9.00
Cost Free   **Entry Reqs** None   **Creche** Yes
- **CONTACT**   Sandie Watkins or Student Services 0117 947 9270/80/90

- **SUBJECT**   Geography/Social Science   32
- **TITLE**   MSc in Society and Space (Geography & Planning)
- **PLACE**   University of Bristol, School of Policy Studies & Geography Dept
Length 1 year full time or 2 years (extended study)   **Start** October   **Entry Reqs** First degree in
Geography or other relevant Social Science   **Award** MSc   **Creche** No
- **CONTACT**   Kit Kelly, Dept of Geography 0117 928 7875

- **SUBJECT**   Housing   33
- **TITLE**   MA/Diploma in Housing Studies
- **PLACE**   University of Bristol & University of the West of England, Bristol
Length Diploma 2 years, MA 3 years   **Start** October   **Days** Contact Admissions Office, UWE
0117 9656261   **Entry Reqs** First degree or equivalent qualification/experience   **Award**
Diploma and/or MA in Housing Studies   **Creche** No
- **CONTACT**   Professor Peter Malpass, Course Director 0117 9656261

- **SUBJECT**   Information Technology   34
- **TITLE**   Fast Track IT Skills
- **PLACE**   Soundwell College, Downend Campus
Length 10 weeks   **Start** September, January, April   **Days** Wed, Thur, Fri 11.00-3.30   **Cost**
Free   **Entry Reqs** None   **Creche** Nursery
- **CONTACT**   Brenda Higson 0117 967 5101/Student Services 0117 947 9270/80/90

- **SUBJECT**   Information Technology   35
- **TITLE**   MSc Information Technology
- **PLACE**   University of the West of England, Frenchay Campus
Length 1 year full time, 2 years part time   **Start** September   **Days** 1 day/week   **Cost** £2760
Award MSc   **Creche** Playgroup
- **CONTACT**   Sue Follows 0117 965 6261 x3354

- **SUBJECT**   Languages   36
- **TITLE**   Intermediate ESOL (English for Speakers of Other Languages) for Women
- **PLACE**   South Bristol College
Length Variable   **Entry Reqs** None   **Award** College Certificate
- **CONTACT**   Kath Tudor 0117 963 9033

- **SUBJECT**   Management   37
- **TITLE**   Women into Management
- **PLACE**   Soundwell College, Management & Professional Studies Centre
Length 15 weeks   **Start** September, January, April   **Days** 15 hours/week   **Cost** Free   **Entry
Reqs** Experience of, or intending to work within supervisory management   **Award** NEBSN
Certificate in Supervisory Management Skills   **Creche** Yes
- **CONTACT**   Jenny Tucker 0117867 5101/0117 956 7406

- **SUBJECT**   Management Development   38
- **TITLE**   MSc in Management Development & Social Responsibility
- **PLACE**   University of Bristol, School for Policy Studies
Length 2 years   **Start** October   **Days** Mon-Wed 2.5 days a month in 1st year, Wed-Fri once a
month in 2nd year   **Cost** Tuition fees £3300. Residential charges additional   **Entry Reqs**
Graduate, or non-graduate able to demonstrate ability to benefit. Some work experience
Award MSc
- **CONTACT**   Sarah Harding 0117 9741117

- **SUBJECT** Manufacturing 39
- **TITLE** MSc in Manufacturing and Management Information Systems
- **PLACE** University of the West of England, Faculty of Engineering

Length 1 year full time **Start** September **Days** Wed-Fri + 3-month industrial placement **Cost** ESF funded **Entry Reqs** Hons Degree (2:2+) in any discipline **Award** MSc in Manufacturing and Management Information Systems **Creche** Yes

- **CONTACT** James Scanlon 0117 976 2545

- **SUBJECT** Mathematics/Computing 40
- **TITLE** BA/HND Business Decison Analysis & other BSc/HND Maths/Stats/ Computing Courses
- **PLACE** University of the West of England, Frenchay Campus

Length BA, BSc 3/4 years full time, HND 2 years **Start** September **Days** Arranged to suit needs **Cost** Contact University **Entry Reqs** Mature students considered individually **Award** BA(Hons), BSc(Hons), HND **Creche** Playgroup

- **CONTACT** Sue Follows 0117 965 6261 x3354

- **SUBJECT** Office Skills 41
- **TITLE** Typing, Database Training, Pascal, WP, Spreadsheet Training
- **PLACE** Brunel College of Arts & Technology

Length Flexible open learning **Start** Flexible **Days** Mon-Fri 9.00-8.00 **Cost** £40/course (concessions available) **Entry Reqs** None **Award** College Certificate **Creche** Nursery

- **CONTACT** Alison Rugg 0117 924 1241

- **SUBJECT** Office Skills 42
- **TITLE** Secretarial Subjects
- **PLACE** Soundwell College, Open Learning Centre in Office Skills

Length 10 weeks **Start** September, January, April **Days** 3 days/week **Cost** Free **Entry Reqs** None **Award** RSA single subject exams **Creche** Yes

- **CONTACT** Brenda Higson or Student Services 0117 947 9270/80/90

- **SUBJECT** Office Skills/Computing/Community Studies/Construction/Catering 43
- **TITLE** Start Programme/Open Access
- **PLACE** Weston-super-Mare College

Length Flexible, 9-week modules **Start** September, January, April **Days** Weekday 3-hour sessions or Open Access by booking system. **Cost** £3/hour No concessions **Entry Reqs** None **Award** RSA Levels 1, 2, 3, NVQ Levels II, III **Creche** No

- **CONTACT** Fiona L Waters 01934 411411 x481

- **SUBJECT** Office Technology 44
- **TITLE** New Office Technology
- **PLACE** College of Care and Early Education, Lawrence Weston Site

Length 12 weeks **Start** September, January, April **Days** 3-5 days/week 9.30-3.00 **Cost** Contact College **Entry Reqs** Basic skills in IT **Award** RSA WP - various stages, CLAIT, CIT **Creche** Yes fee varies

- **CONTACT** Admissions and Guidance Officer 0117 923 5706

- **SUBJECT** Photography 45
- **TITLE** What Can a Woman Do With a Camera?
- **PLACE** South Bristol College

Length 10 weeks **Start** Contact College **Cost** Contact College **Entry Reqs** None **Award** College Certificate

- **CONTACT** Kath Tudor 0117 963 9033

- **SUBJECT**   Policy Studies   46
- **TITLE**   MSc in Policy Studies
- **PLACE**   University of Bristol, School for Policy Studies

Length 2 years   **Start** October   **Days** Mon-Wed 2.5 days a month in 1st year, Wed-Fri once a month in 2nd year   **Cost** Tuition fees approx £1400. Residential charges additional   **Entry Reqs** Graduate or non-graduate able to benefit. Some work experience   **Award** MSc
- **CONTACT**   Dinah Foweraker 0117 974 1117

- **SUBJECT**   Practical   47
- **TITLE**   Practical Skills for Women (Foundation, Woodwork, Finishing, Marketable Skills)
- **PLACE**   Bristol Women's Workshop

Length Various   **Start** Various   **Days** Day, eve, weekend, intensive courses   **Cost** Contact Workshop   **Entry Reqs** Contact Workshop
- **CONTACT**   0117 971 1672

- **SUBJECT**   Practical   48
- **TITLE**   Woodwork for Women
- **PLACE**   South Bristol College

Length 6 months   **Days** Tues, Wed, Thurs   **Cost** Free to women in receipt of benefit   **Entry Reqs** None   **Award** City & Guilds
- **CONTACT**   Kath Tudor 0117 963 9033

- **SUBJECT**   Preparatory   49
- **TITLE**   New Directions for Women
- **PLACE**   South Bristol College

Length 10 weeks   **Start** Contact College   **Days** 10.00-3.00   **Entry Reqs** None   **Award** College Certificate
- **CONTACT**   Kath Tudor 0117 963 9033

- **SUBJECT**   Preparatory   50
- **TITLE**   Return to Study
- **PLACE**   Brunel College of Arts & Technology

Length 1.5 weeks 2.10 weeks 3.1 year   **Start** 2. October 3. September   **Days** 1.1 day/week 2. & 3.4 days/week   **Cost** 1. £37 2. £118 3. £618 (100% concessions in all cases)   **Entry Reqs** 1. None 2. &3. Informal interview   **Award** 1. , 2. &3. OCN Credits Levels 1 & 2 3. Also GCSEs   **Creche** Nursery
- **CONTACT**   Judy Weeks/Sandra Beckett 0117 924 1241 x2477

- **SUBJECT**   Preparatory   51
- **TITLE**   Return to Study
- **PLACE**   Weston-super-Mare College

Length 6 weeks   **Start** September   **Days** Tues 9.30-12.30 or Wed 7.15-9.15   **Cost** £26.50 day course, £20 evening course   **Entry Reqs** None   **Award** Preparation for return to study   **Creche** No
- **CONTACT**   Fiona L Waters 01934 411411 x481

- **SUBJECT**   Preparatory   52
- **TITLE**   Women into Work
- **PLACE**   Filton College, Shield House

Length 30 weeks   **Start** September   **Days** Tues or Thurs 10.00-3.00   **Cost** £129 (Concessions available)   **Award** Optional RSA Word Processing exams or Open College Network accreditation
- **CONTACT**   0117 931 2121

- **SUBJECT** Preparatory/Mathematics 53
- **TITLE** Developing Maths Skills
- **PLACE** Soundwell College

Length 30 weeks **Start** September **Cost** Free **Entry Reqs** None **Award** C&G Foundation or Level 1 Certificate **Creche** Yes
- **CONTACT** Sandie Watkins or Student Services 0117 947 9270/80/90

- **SUBJECT** Professional Updating/Teaching 54
- **TITLE** Returning to Teaching
- **PLACE** University of the West of England, Faculty of Education

Length 6 weeks **Start** Contact University **Cost** Free (ESF funded) **Entry Reqs** Qualified women primary & secondary teachers returning to teaching
- **CONTACT** Partnership Office 0117 974 1251 x4126/7

- **SUBJECT** Social Science 55
- **TITLE** BA(Hons) Social Science
- **PLACE** University of the West of England, Frenchay Campus

Length 3 years full time or 6 years part time **Start** September, October **Cost** Contact University **Entry Reqs** Mature students considered individually **Award** BA(Hons) Social Science, Politics, Economics or Sociology **Creche** Yes 0117 965 6261 x2434 May be concessions
- **CONTACT** John Brookes, Admissions Tutor 0117 965 6261

- **SUBJECT** Social Science 56
- **TITLE** Certificate in Social Science
- **PLACE** University of Bristol, Dept of Continuing Education

Length 2 years **Start** January **Days** Mon+Wed 6.00-9.30 **Cost** Approx £400/year **Entry Reqs** None **Award** Certificate in Social Science **Creche** No
- **CONTACT** Liz Bird 0117 928 7172

- **SUBJECT** Social Science 57
- **TITLE** MSc Gender and Social Policy
- **PLACE** University of Bristol

Length 1 year full time, 2 years part time **Start** October **Days** 1 day/week (part time) **Cost** Contact University **Entry Reqs** Normally upper second class hons degree. Exceptions made. Option to study for diploma **Award** MSc or Diploma **Creche** No
- **CONTACT** Jackie West 0117 928 7172

- **SUBJECT** Women's Studies 58
- **TITLE** BA/MA/Postgraduate Diploma in Women's Studies (Part time or full time)
- **PLACE** University of the West of England, St Matthias Campus

Length BA 3 yrs ft; MA 1yr ft, 7 terms pt; PgD 1 yr ft; 5 terms pt **Start** October **Cost** Contact University **Entry Reqs** Applications taken on their own merits **Award** BA/MA/Postgraduate Diploma **Creche** No
- **CONTACT** D Baldwin 0117 965 5384

COUNTY CONTACTS

Information and advice:

Careers Service West, 4 Colston Avenue, Bristol BS1 4ST 0117 987 3700
Careers Service West, 45 Boulevard, Weston-super-Mare BS23 9PG 01934 644443
Careers Service West, 5 The Kingsway, Kingswood, Bristol BS15 1BE 0117 9612760

Careers Service West, Northgate House, Upper Borough Walls, Bath BA1 2JD 01225 461501
Careers Service West, St Stephens House, Station Road, Filton, Bristol BS12 7JG 0117 969 8101
Guidance Service, City of Bath College, Avon Street, Bath BA1 1UP 01225 312191   *Contact:* Louise Davidson, Alison Maynard, Linda Mayford. Free service for students and all people in receipt of certain benefits, otherwise £75 for an interview and £25 for a group guidance session to all non-college students currently in employment
TAP West, 6 Iddesleigh Road, Bristol BS6 6YJ 0117 973 2585   *Contact:* Amanda Bennison Comprehensive information on local education/training opportunities in the South West. Free public-access terminals at various locations in Bristol/Bath/Weston-super-Mare.

Open University:

The Open University, South West Region, 4 Portwall Lane, Bristol BS1 6ND 0117 925 6523

Training and Enterprise Council:

WESTEC, PO Box 164, St Lawrence House, 29-31 Broad Street, Bristol BS99 7HR 0117 927 7116 Funding from the Childcare Initiative to develop, support and deliver out of school childcare in Avon; Targetted support for women entrepreneurs; vocational training grant scheme for women returners in South Bristol, including childcare grants

WEA office:

WEA Western District, 40 Morse Road, Redfield, Bristol BS5 9LB 0117 935 1764   *Contact:* Mavis Zutchi, Kath Ryder

---

BEDFORDSHIRE

COURSES

- **SUBJECT**   Access/Art & Design/Business Studies/Health Studies/Law/Science/Social **59** Studies/Teaching
- **TITLE**   Access Courses
- **PLACE**   Bedford College
Length 1 year   **Start** September   **Days** Day and evening   **Cost** Contact College   **Entry Reqs** 21+, interview   **Award** Progression to further/higher education   **Creche** Nursery places available Small charge
- **CONTACT**   Access Group 01234 271492

- **SUBJECT**   Access/Health Studies   **60**
- **TITLE**   Access to Nursing/Midwifery
- **PLACE**   Barnfield College, Faculty of Secretarial and Community Studies
Length 1 year   **Start** September   **Days** Full time 10.00-3.00 Mon-Fri   **Cost** Contact College
Entry Reqs Interview   **Award** Access Certificate   **Creche** Yes £4/day
- **CONTACT**   Maggie Clark 01582 507531 x420

- **SUBJECT**   Administration   **61**
- **TITLE**   Administration NVQ Levels I, II, III
- **PLACE**   Barnfield College, Office Technology and Retail
Length Flexible Learning Programme   **Cost** Contact College   **Entry Reqs** Open Entry   **Award** RSA NVQ Levels I, II, III and single subjects   **Creche** Yes
- **CONTACT**   Jean Scott-Brown 01582 507531 x420

- **SUBJECT**   Beauty/Hairdressing/Catering   62
- **TITLE**   1. Beauty Therapy 2. Hairdressing 3. Foundation Catering NVQ
- **PLACE**   Barnfield College, Faculty of Service Industries

Length 1 or 2 years   **Start** September   **Cost** Contact College   **Entry Reqs** Interview   **Award** 1. HBC (Beauty Therapy) 2. C&G LI Hairdressing/NVQ LII 3. C&GLI/NVQ Catering   **Creche** Yes £4/day

- **CONTACT**   1. Loraine Winslade 01582 507531/2. Jan Lear x258/3. Neil Pulling x302

- **SUBJECT**   Care Studies   63
- **TITLE**   BTEC National Caring Services (Nursery Nursing)
- **PLACE**   Barnfield College, Faculty of Secretarial and Community Studies

Length 2 years   **Start** September   **Days** Part time or full time   **Cost** Contact College   **Entry Reqs** Interview   **Award** BTEC National Certificate (part time), BTEC National Diploma (full time)   **Creche** Yes £4/day

- **CONTACT**   Helen Evans 01582 507531 x429

- **SUBJECT**   Care Studies   64
- **TITLE**   BTEC National Caring Services (Social Care)
- **PLACE**   Barnfield College, Faculty of Secretarial and Community Studies

Length 2 years   **Start** September   **Days** Part time or full time   **Cost** Contact College   **Entry Reqs** Interview   **Award** BTEC National Certificate (part time), BTEC National Diploma (full time)   **Creche** Yes £4/day

- **CONTACT**   Helen Evans 01582 507531 x429

- **SUBJECT**   Catering   65
- **TITLE**   C&G Cookery Certificate
- **PLACE**   Dunstable College

Length 2 years part time   **Start** September   **Cost** Contact College   **Award** C&G Cookery Certificate   **Creche** No

- **CONTACT**   Joanna Merrils 01582 696451

- **SUBJECT**   Computing/Office Skills   66
- **TITLE**   Women into Office Technology
- **PLACE**   Barnfield College, Office Technology and Retail

Length 17 weeks   **Start** September, February   **Days** Tues, Wed, Thurs 10.00-3.00   **Cost** £15 inclusive   **Entry Reqs** Interview   **Award** RSA single subject exams   **Creche** Yes

- **CONTACT**   Sue Hingston 01582 507531 x429

- **SUBJECT**   Engineering/Manufacturing   67
- **TITLE**   MSC in Engineering and Management of Manufacturing Systems
- **PLACE**   Cranfield University

Length 1 year   **Start** October   **Days** Full time and part time   **Cost** Funding possible. Some industrial sponsorships   **Entry Reqs** Degree or equivalent in Engineering, Science or Technology   **Award** MSc in Engineering and Management of Manufacturing Systems   **Creche** Contact University

- **CONTACT**   Linda Nichols 01234 750111 x2403

- **SUBJECT**   Health Studies   68
- **TITLE**   BTEC GNVQ Health and Social Care
- **PLACE**   Dunstable College

Length 2 years   **Start** September   **Cost** Contact College   **Award** BTEC GNVQ Intermediate Health and Social Care   **Creche** No

- **CONTACT**   Jane Rouse 01582 696451

● **SUBJECT**	Manufacturing	69
● **TITLE**	Innovative Manufacturing: Pilot Research Masters Course	
● **PLACE**	Cranfield University	

Length 2 years **Start** October **Cost** Engineering & Physical Sciences Research Council award available **Entry Reqs** Graduates with first or upper second honours degree in an appropriate subject **Award** Master of Research
● **CONTACT** Dr DJ Stephenson 01234 754041

● **SUBJECT**	Multi-Subject	70
● **TITLE**	BA, BSc, HND (Various subjects)	
● **PLACE**	University of Luton	

Start September **Days** Full time, part time **Award** BA/BSc/HND
● **CONTACT** Marketing Unit 01582 489012

● **SUBJECT**	Preparatory	71
● **TITLE**	New Horizons for Women	
● **PLACE**	University of Luton	

Length 10 weeks **Start** October, January, April **Days** 1 day/week 10.00-3.00, usually Wed or Thurs **Cost** Free **Entry Reqs** None **Award** Attendance Certificate
● **CONTACT** Jane Knowles 10582 486318

● **SUBJECT**	Teaching	72
● **TITLE**	Introduction to Teaching English as a Foreign Language	
● **PLACE**	Bedford College	

Length 11 weeks **Start** September, January, April **Days** Eves 2 hours/week **Cost** Approx £90 **Entry Reqs** Contact College **Creche** Not evenings
● **CONTACT** 01234 271492

● **SUBJECT**	Teaching	73
● **TITLE**	Teaching English as a Foreign Language to Adults	
● **PLACE**	Bedford College	

Length 1 year **Start** September **Days** Mon & Thurs 6.45-9.00 + 2 hours daytime (variable) **Cost** Approx £695 **Entry Reqs** Graduates, non-graduates considered **Award** RSA/Cambridge Certificate TEFLA **Creche** No
● **CONTACT** Ken Wilford 01234 271492

COUNTY CONTACTS

Information and advice:

Bedford College, Cauldwell Street, Bedford MK42 9AH 01234 345151   *Contact:* Norma Squibb, Jacquie Fillmore. Information and guidance, also Access and New Horizons courses
Dunstable Guidance Centre, 21 West Street, Dunstable LU6 1SL 01582 662949   *Contact:* Anne Barber
SALP (Bedfordshire North Special Adult Learning Programmes), Westbourne Centre, Bedford 10234 364454   *Contact:* Meryl Harris. Community languages spoken
SALP (Bedfordshire South Special Adult Learning Programmes), Charles Street, Luton LU2 0EB 01582 22566   *Contact:* Meryl Harris. Community languages spoken
University of Luton Careers Service, Park Square, Luton LU1 3JU 01582 34111   *Contact:* Claire Rees
Women's Network, Bedford College, Cauldwell Street, Bedford MK42 9AH 01234 345151

Open University:

The Open University, East Anglia Region, 12 Hills Road, Cambridge CB2 1PF 01223 61650

Training and Enterprise Council:

Bedfordshire TEC, 2 Railton Road, Woburn Road Industrial Estate, Kempston MK42 7PN
01234 843100
Ethnic minority grant; Enterprise for African, Caribbean and Asian women; Out of school
initiative, Employment Department Scheme; Information and support service; NVQ in Playwork
Level 2, TEC/ESF funded; 'Who's Who in Bedfordshire for Women'.

WEA office:

WEA Eastern District, Botolph House, 17 Botolph Lane, Cambridge CB2 3RE 01223 350978
Contact: Sue Young

BERKSHIRE

COURSES

- **SUBJECT**   Access/Humanities/Social Science   74
- **TITLE**   Access Course in Humanities and Social Sciences
- **PLACE**   Newbury College

Length 1 year part time   **Start** September   **Days** 2 eves/week   **Cost** Contact College   **Entry Reqs** 21+. No formal entry requirements   **Award** Access to higher education
- **CONTACT**   Science & Humanities 01635 37000 x212

- **SUBJECT**   Administration   75
- **TITLE**   NVQ Administration
- **PLACE**   Bracknell College

Length 18 weeks   **Start** September, January   **Days** Mon-Fri times vary   **Cost** Contact College, free if unemployed   **Entry Reqs** None   **Award** NVQ II and/or III   **Creche** Yes
- **CONTACT**   Jean Robbins 01344 420411

- **SUBJECT**   Administration   76
- **TITLE**   NVQ Administration
- **PLACE**   Newbury College

Length 1 year   **Start** September   **Days** Part time   **Cost** Contact College   **Entry Reqs** Contact College   **Award** NVQ I/II/III   **Creche** Yes
- **CONTACT**   Student Services 01635 550066

- **SUBJECT**   Business   77
- **TITLE**   Business 1. GNVQ Intermediate 2. GNVQ Advanced
- **PLACE**   Newbury College

Length 1.1 year 2.2 years   **Start** September   **Days** Part time   **Cost** Contact College   **Entry Reqs** Contact College   **Award** 1. GNVQ Intermediate 2. GNVQ Advanced   **Creche** Yes
- **CONTACT**   Student Services 01635 550066

- **SUBJECT**   Business Studies   78
- **TITLE**   Business Skills Workshop
- **PLACE**   Newbury College

Length Flexible   **Start** Roll-on, roll-off   **Days** Flexible   **Cost** £2/hour. Tax relief possible   **Entry Reqs** None
- **CONTACT**   Student Services 01635 550066

Berkshire

79

- **SUBJECT**　Catering
- **TITLE**　Cooks' Professional Certificate
- **PLACE**　Windsor College

Length 2 years　**Start** September　**Cost** Contact College　**Entry Reqs** None　**Award** C&G 332/1 & 2 Certificate　**Creche** No
- **CONTACT**　Sue Bridger 01753 862111

80

- **SUBJECT**　Environmental Sciences
- **TITLE**　Earth and Atmospheric Sciences: Research Masters Training Programme
- **PLACE**　University of Reading

Length 1 year　**Start** October　**Cost** Natural Environment Research Council award available **Entry Reqs** Graduates with first or upper second honours degree in an appropriate subject **Award** Master of Research
- **CONTACT**　Dr Stephen Northcliff 01734 316559/316557

81

- **SUBJECT**　Management
- **TITLE**　Certificate in Supervisory Management Studies
- **PLACE**　Newbury College

Length 1 year　**Start** September　**Days** Part time　**Cost** Contact College　**Entry Reqs** Contact College　**Award** NEBSM Certificate　**Creche** Yes
- **CONTACT**　Student Services 01635 550066

82

- **SUBJECT**　Office Skills
- **TITLE**　Office Procedures
- **PLACE**　Newbury College, at Denefield School, Ticehurst

Length 25 weeks　**Start** September　**Days** Wednesday 3.30-5.50　**Cost** £50　**Entry Reqs** None　**Award** Various qualifications
- **CONTACT**　Student Services 01734 835035/01491 873745

83

- **SUBJECT**　Preparatory
- **TITLE**　Back to Work and Office Skills
- **PLACE**　Reading Adult College

Length 10-20 weeks　**Start** September, January, April　**Days** Various, 10 hours/week maximum　**Cost** No fees. £10 registration covers all course units　**Entry Reqs** Unwaged, actively seeking employment or intending to return to job market
- **CONTACT**　Maggie Walker 01734 575575

84

- **SUBJECT**　Preparatory
- **TITLE**　New Horizons
- **PLACE**　Newbury College, various community venues

Length Various　**Start** Various　**Cost** Free　**Entry Reqs** None
- **CONTACT**　Adult Studies 01635 37000 x215/01635 35353

85

- **SUBJECT**　Preparatory
- **TITLE**　Return to Learn
- **PLACE**　Newbury College

Length 10 weeks　**Days** Daytime　**Cost** Free　**Entry Reqs** None　**Creche** Yes
- **CONTACT**　Adult Studies 01635 37000 x215/01635 35353

86

- **SUBJECT**　Preparatory
- **TITLE**　Stepping Stones
- **PLACE**　Newbury College

Length Various　**Start** Various　**Cost** Contact College　**Entry Reqs** Unemployed　**Creche** Yes
- **CONTACT**　Adult Studies 01635 37000 x215/01635 35353

- **SUBJECT**   Preparatory   87
- **TITLE**   Women Returners' Courses
- **PLACE**   Bracknell College, various sites

Length Varies   **Start** Varies   **Cost** Some courses are subsidised/industry sponsored   **Entry Reqs** None   **Award** None   **Creche** Yes £1.50/morning or afternoon session

- **CONTACT**   Ros Scarth/Terry Kenyon 01344 420411

COUNTY CONTACTS

Information and advice:

Know How (TAP Point), Thames Valley Enterprise, 5th Floor, King's Point, 120 King's Road, Reading RG1 3BZ 0800 775566
REGSA (Reading Educational Guidance Service for Adults), Reading Adult College, Wilson Centre, Wilson Road, Reading RG30 2RW 01734 581754. Non-biased education guidance service for adults, giving information on local and national education and training opportunities across the board.

Open University:

The Open University, South Region, Foxcombe Hall, Boars Hill, Oxford, OX1 5HR 01865 328038

Training and Enterprise Council:

Thames Valley TEC, 6th Floor, Kings Point, 120 Kings Road, Reading RG1 3BZ 01734 568156   *Contact:* Joanna Stapeley

WEA office:

WEA Thames and Solent, 6 Brewer Street, Oxford OX1 1QN 01865 246270   *Contact:* Annie Winner

BUCKINGHAMSHIRE

COURSES

- **SUBJECT**   Access/Humanities/Social Science/Teaching   88
- **TITLE**   Access to Higher Education/Humanities/Social Science/Teaching
- **PLACE**   Milton Keynes College, Chaffron Way Centre

Length 30 weeks   **Start** September   **Days** Mon-Fri 10.00-3.00   **Cost** £65   **Entry Reqs** Interview and diagnostic test   **Award** Access to degree courses   **Creche** Yes Contact College

- **CONTACT**   Wendy Ashcroft 01908 684444

- **SUBJECT**   Multi-Subject   89
- **TITLE**   Open Learning (vocational courses, GCSE, A Levels)
- **PLACE**   Home/Workshop study through Milton Keynes College, Bletchley

Length Varies, 10 weeks-2 years depending on subject   **Start** Anytime between September and June   **Entry Reqs** None   **Award** Varies   **Creche** No

- **CONTACT**   Amanda McBride 01908 684444

Buckinghamshire

- **SUBJECT**   Office Skills   **90**
- **TITLE**   Essential Office Training
- **PLACE**   Milton Keynes College, Chaffron Way Centre

Length 15 weeks   **Start** September, February   **Days** Mon-Thurs 9.00-1.00   **Cost** £45   **Creche** Yes

- **CONTACT**   Mary Cartwright 01908 684444

- **SUBJECT**   Preparatory   **91**
- **TITLE**   Fresh Start: Guidance Course for Women Returners
- **PLACE**   Milton Keynes College, Bletchley Centre

Length 10 weeks   **Start** September, January, April   **Days** Tues+Wed 10.00-3.00   **Cost** £5
Entry Reqs Must be aged 25+ and unemployed for at least 1 year   **Award** None   **Creche** Yes
Contact College

- **CONTACT**   Jane Morgan 01908 684444

- **SUBJECT**   Preparatory   **92**
- **TITLE**   Return to Work: General and Pre-Vocational
- **PLACE**   Milton Keynes Women and Work Group

Length 1-8 weeks   **Start** February, May, September   **Days** 2 days/week 9.30-2.30   **Cost** Free
Entry Reqs None   **Award** None   **Creche** Yes free

- **CONTACT**   Jenny Charlwood 01908 310372

COUNTY CONTACTS

Information and advice:

Amersham and Wycombe College, Stanley Hill, Amersham HP7 9HN 01494 536654
Contact Customer Services Unit about information and guidance services run in centres at Amersham and High Wycombe
Milton Keynes College, Leadenhall Street, Milton Keynes MK6 5LP 01908 684444   *Contact:* Jane Morgan. 'Fresh Start' course for women returners.
Milton Keynes Women and Work Group, Acorn House, 365 Midsummer Boulevard, Milton Keynes MK9 3HP 01908 200186   *Contact:* Lori Hope. Free short courses, advice service and resource club for unemployed women in Milton Keynes. Also specialist Asian Women's Project.

Open University:

The Open University, Walton Hall, Milton Keynes MK7 6AA 01908 653861

Training and Enterprise Council:

Milton Keynes & North Buckinghamshire Chamber of Commerce Training & Enterprise, Old Market Halls, Creed Street, Wolverton, Milton Keynes MK12 5LY 01908 222555

WEA office:

WEA Thames and Solent, 6 Brewer Street, Oxford OX1 1QN 01865 246270   *Contact:* Annie Winner

Publication:

Jobs and Training Guide: a guide for women in Milton Keynes. Milton Keynes Women and Work Group

COURSES

- **SUBJECT** Access/Health Studies/Nursing 93
- **TITLE** Access to Nursing & Health Studies
- **PLACE** Huntingdonshire Regional College

Length 1 year **Start** September **Days** Mon-Fri 9.15-3.30 **Cost** Free for full-time students **Entry Reqs** Interview **Award** Entry to nurse training **Creche** Yes £1 per hour

- **CONTACT** Adrian Howells 01480 52346

- **SUBJECT** Access/Humanities/Social Science 94
- **TITLE** Adult Access to Humanities, Social Science
- **PLACE** Huntingdonshire Regional College

Length 1 year **Start** September **Days** Flexible **Cost** Full time no charge, part time max £55 per term (concessions available) **Entry Reqs** Interview **Award** Access Certificate for Higher Education **Creche** Yes £1 per hour

- **CONTACT** Sue Edgington 01480 52346

- **SUBJECT** Access/Science/Mathematics 95
- **TITLE** Adult Access to Science, Mathematics
- **PLACE** Huntingdonshire Regional College

Length 1 year **Start** September **Days** Flexible **Cost** Full time no charge, part time max £55 per term (concessions available) **Entry Reqs** Interview **Award** Access Certificate for Higher Education **Creche** Yes £1 per hour

- **CONTACT** Stephen Draper 01480 52346

- **SUBJECT** Law 96
- **TITLE** Residential Returner Course for Solicitors
- **PLACE** Lucy Cavendish College, Cambridge

Length Contact College **Days** Residential **Cost** £300 **Entry Reqs** Solicitors wishing to return to private practice after an absence of a few years

- **CONTACT** Association of Women Solicitors 0171 242 1222

- **SUBJECT** Management Studies 97
- **TITLE** Diploma
- **PLACE** Judge Institute of Management Studies, Cambridge

Length 9 months **Start** October **Days** Full time, residential during term **Cost** Contact Admissions Office **Entry Reqs** Good first degree in any discipline **Award** Diploma in Management Studies **Creche** No

- **CONTACT** Admissions Office 01223 339640

- **SUBJECT** Management Studies 98
- **TITLE** M Phil
- **PLACE** Judge Institute of Management Studies, Cambridge

Length 9 months **Start** October **Days** Full time, residential during term **Cost** Contact Admissions Office **Entry Reqs** Good first degree in a relevant discipline **Award** M Phil in Management Studies **Creche** No

- **CONTACT** Admissions Office 01223 339640

- **SUBJECT** Management Studies 99
- **TITLE** MBA
- **PLACE** Judge Institute of Management Studies, Cambridge

Length 21 mths: 1 term residence, 1 yr placement, 2 terms residence **Start** October **Cost** 1st year £8000, 2nd year £14, 500 **Entry Reqs** Good first degree, GMAT and company sponsorship **Award** MBA **Creche** No

- **CONTACT** John Hendry 01223 339700

- **SUBJECT** Multi-Subject   100
- **TITLE** BA, MBA, Postgraduate Degrees, Certificates, Diplomas of University of Cambridge
- **PLACE** Lucy Cavendish College, Cambridge

Length Varies **Start** October **Days** Full time **Entry Reqs** Women 21+. Contact College **Award** Degree/Certificate/Diploma **Creche** No (childcare bursaries available)

- **CONTACT** Margaret Pullen, Admissions Secretary, 01223 330280

- **SUBJECT** Office Skills   101
- **TITLE** Office Opportunities
- **PLACE** Huntingdonshire Regional College

Length 36 weeks **Start** September **Days** 5 days/week 9.30-1.30 **Cost** £50 **Entry Reqs** None **Award** RSA single subject certificate **Creche** Yes £1 per hour

- **CONTACT** Michelle Snell 01480 52346

- **SUBJECT** Office Skills   102
- **TITLE** Workshop
- **PLACE** Huntingdonshire Regional College, Huntingdon & St Neots

Length Flexible **Start** Flexible **Days** Mon-Fri 9.30-12.30/7.00-9.00 **Cost** £25 for 20 hours **Entry Reqs** None **Award** RSA Single Subjects **Creche** Yes at Huntingdon £2.50/2 hour session

- **CONTACT** Michelle Snell 01480 52346

- **SUBJECT** Preparatory   103
- **TITLE** Open University Preparatory Course
- **PLACE** Anglia Polytechnic University

Length 5 weeks **Start** November **Days** Mon 6.00-8.00 **Cost** £35 **Entry Reqs** None **Award** Preparation for OU courses **Creche** No

- **CONTACT** G Wisker/C Rigglesford 01223 363271 x2062/2055

- **SUBJECT** Preparatory   104
- **TITLE** Preparatory Training
- **PLACE** Peterborough College of Adult Education

Length 4-6 weeks **Start** On-going throughout year **Days** Mon-Fri 21 hours/week **Cost** None **Entry Reqs** Unemployed, even if not getting benefits **Award** College Certificate or Accreditation **Creche** Yes 74p/hour

- **CONTACT** Vivienne Galvin 01733 61830

- **SUBJECT** Preparatory   105
- **TITLE** SCOPE (Second Chance Opportunities & Education)
- **PLACE** OU Regional Office, Cintra House, Hills Road, Cambridge CB2 1PF

Length 11 weekly sessions **Start** January, September **Days** Tues 9.45-2.45 **Cost** £55 (£10 concessions) **Entry Reqs** None **Award** NRA & Certificate of completion **Creche** No Some help with childcare costs possible

- **CONTACT** Kate Grillet 01223 364185/Clare Gilmour 01223 262808

- **SUBJECT** Preparatory   106
- **TITLE** Training for Work
- **PLACE** Peterborough College of Adult Education

Length According to NVQ Level; minimum 21 hours/week **Start** Continuous throughout the year **Days** Full time **Cost** None **Entry Reqs** Employment-ready **Award** Occupationally-related NVQ **Creche** Yes Contact College

- **CONTACT** Vivienne Galvin 01733 61830

COUNTY CONTACTS

Information and advice:

Cambridge Careers Centre, 62 Burleigh Street, Cambridge CB1 1DN 01223 62345   *Contact* Gill Aslett

Cambridgeshire Careers Guidance Ltd, 7 The Meadow, Huntingdon PE17 4LG 01480 463463. Non-profit company offering information and advice on education, training and careers. Drop-in desks are held at various venues throughout Cambridgeshire. Contact local office for details.

Cambridge Guidance Shop, Central Library, Lion Yard, Cambridge 01223 311189   *Contact* Hilary Cundale

Ely Guidance Shop, 59 Market Street, Ely CB7 4LP 01353 669099   *Contact* Tricia Brassington

Huntingdon Careers Centre, Walden House, Market Hill, Huntingdon PE18 6NR 01480 425827   *Contact* Chris Parsons

Huntingdon Guidance Shop, 2/3 George Street, Huntingdon 01480 450810   *Contact* Julia Jones

March Careers Centre, Town Hall, Market Square, March PE15 9JF 01354 51703   *Contact* Julie Cooper

Peterborough Careers Centre, 9-11 Cavell Court, Peterborough PE1 2RQ 01733 311094   *Contact* Jake Sanders

Wisbech Careers Centre, 2 Stermyn Street, Wisbech PE13 1EQ 01945 585128   *Contact* Julie Cooper

National Association for Educational Guidance for Adults, Regional representative, Cambridgeshire Careers Guidance Ltd, 7 The Meadow, Meadow Lane, St Ives, Huntingdon PE17 4LG 01480 463463   *Contact* Sue Claydon. Covers East Anglia region

Open University:

The Open University. East Anglia Region, 12 Hills Road, Cambridge CB2 1PF 01223 61650

Other agencies:

Cambridge Women's Resources Centre, Hooper Street, Cambridge CB1 2NZ 01223 321148   *Contact* Jean Anker. Training, education and support centre. All women are welcomed regardless of race, age, sexuality or disability. Free creche

Training and Enterprise Councils:

CAMBSTEC (Central and South Cambridgeshire), Trust Court, The Vision Park, Histon, Cambridge CB4 4PW 01223 235635/3. Women Returners workshops

Greater Peterborough TEC, Unit 4, Blenheim Court. Peppercorn Close, off the Lincoln Road, Peterborough PE1 2DU 01733 890808. Women into Technology course; IT for Ethnic Minorities course

WEA office:

WEA Eastern District Office, Botolph House, 17 Botolph Lane, Cambridge CB2 3RE 01223 350978 *Contact* Sue Young

COURSES

- **SUBJECT** Access   107
- **TITLE** Access to Higher Education
- **PLACE** Macclesfield College

Length 9 months   **Start** September, January, March   **Days** 3.5 days/week 10.00-3.00   **Cost** £596   **Entry Reqs** Interview and letter   **Award** Kitemarked Certificate of Access Studies, accredited by Manchester Open College Federation   **Creche** No

- **CONTACT** Mary Brown/Bill Humphreys 01625 427744

- **SUBJECT** Access   108
- **TITLE** Access to Higher Education
- **PLACE** Mid-Cheshire College, Verdin Centre, Winsford

Length 36 weeks   **Start** September   **Days** 3.5 days/week 10.00-3.00   **Cost** Contact College   **Entry Reqs** None. Interview   **Award** CNAA Access Certificate   **Creche** Yes

- **CONTACT** John Feather 01606 558278

- **SUBJECT** Access   109
- **TITLE** Access to Higher Education
- **PLACE** South Cheshire College

Length 1 year   **Start** September   **Days** Wed, Thurs 9.30-3.00 or Mon, Tues 9.30-3.00   **Cost** Contact College   **Entry Reqs** Interview   **Award** UCAN   **Creche** Yes Contact College

- **CONTACT** Sue Bonner 01270 69133

- **SUBJECT** Access   110
- **TITLE** Access to HE/Opportunities for Women: Media, Leisure, Social Science, Maths, Science, Arts
- **PLACE** Warrington Collegiate Institute, Padgate Campus

Length 15 weeks (short courses)   **Start** September, January   **Days** Various 9.00-4.00   **Cost** Contact College   **Entry Reqs** By letter   **Award** MOCF Level 3 and some Level 2   **Creche** No

- **CONTACT** Kay Owen 01925 814343

- **SUBJECT** Accounting   111
- **TITLE** Adult Updates in Accounting
- **PLACE** Macclesfield College

Length 30 weeks   **Start** October   **Days** 4 days/week 9.30-3.00   **Cost** Free   **Entry Reqs** By interview   **Award** Association of Accounting Technicians Foundation Award (NVQ II) **Creche** No

- **CONTACT** Peter Matthews 01625 427744

- **SUBJECT** Business/Travel & Tourism   112
- **TITLE** Adult Updates in Business with Travel Studies
- **PLACE** Macclesfield College

Length 30 weeks   **Start** October   **Days** 4 days/week 9.30-3.00   **Cost** Free   **Entry Reqs** By interview   **Award** BTEC National Certificate in Business   **Creche** No

- **CONTACT** Dennis Smith/Julie Robinson 01625 427744

- **SUBJECT**   Business Administration
- **TITLE**   Adult Updates in Business Administration
- **PLACE**   Macclesfield College

113

Length 32 weeks   **Start** September/October or by arrangement   **Days** 16 hours/week (9.15-3.00 flexible access 4 days/week)   **Cost** Free   **Entry Reqs** By interview   **Award** NVQ II/III in Administration   **Creche** No

- **CONTACT**   Sadie Munro 01625 427744

- **SUBJECT**   Business Studies
- **TITLE**   1. BA (Hons) Business Studies 2. BTEC HNC in Business Studies
- **PLACE**   Manchester Metropolitan University, Crewe Campus

114

Length 1.2. 5 years part time 2.2 years part time   **Entry Reqs** Contact University   **Award** 1. BA(Hons) Business Studies 2. BTEC HNC in Business Studies

- **CONTACT**   Crewe Site 0161 247 5053

- **SUBJECT**   Catering/Hospitality Management
- **TITLE**   Adult Updates in Catering and Hospitality
- **PLACE**   Macclesfield College

115

Length 30 weeks   **Start** September/October   **Days** 4 days/week 9.30-3.00   **Cost** Free   **Entry Reqs** By interview   **Award** NVQ II in Catering and Hospitality   **Creche** No

- **CONTACT**   Georgina Wright 01625 427744

- **SUBJECT**   Childcare
- **TITLE**   1. Nursery Management 2. Childcare Management
- **PLACE**   Macclesfield College

116

Length 1.20 weeks 2.30 weeks   **Start** 1. May 2. Contact College   **Days** 1. Mon, Tues, Wed 9.30-1.00 2.21 hours/week   **Cost** 1. Free 2. Free (fees paid by South & East Cheshire TEC)   **Entry Reqs** Age 25+, unemployed for 12 months, some childcare experience   **Award** 1. College Certificate   **Creche** No (Help with childcare & travel costs)

- **CONTACT**   1. Marian Burns 01625 427744/2. Advice & Admissions 01625 501633

- **SUBJECT**   Computing
- **TITLE**   Adult Updates in Computer Studies (Programming)
- **PLACE**   Macclesfield College

117

Length 32 weeks   **Start** September/October   **Days** 4 days/week 9.15-3.00   **Cost** Free   **Entry Reqs** By interview   **Award** BTEC National Certificate in Computer Studies   **Creche** No

- **CONTACT**   Lynn Parchment 01625 427744

- **SUBJECT**   Computing
- **TITLE**   Adult Updates in Computer Studies (Small Business Systems)
- **PLACE**   Macclesfield College

118

Length 32 weeks   **Start** September/October   **Days** 4 days/week 9.15-3.00   **Cost** Free   **Entry Reqs** By interview   **Award** BTEC National Certificate in Computer Studies/RSA LAIT Certificate/RSA Typing qualifications   **Creche** No

- **CONTACT**   Lynn Parchment 01625 427744

- **SUBJECT**   Desk Top Publishing
- **TITLE**   Adult Updates in Desk Top Publishing
- **PLACE**   Macclesfield College

119

Length 30 weeks   **Start** September/October   **Days** 4 days/week 9.30-3.00   **Cost** Free   **Entry Reqs** By interview   **Award** BTEC Continuing Education Certificate   **Creche** No

- **CONTACT**   John Edwards 01625 427744

Cheshire

- **SUBJECT**   Management   **120**
- **TITLE**   Management: BTEC Advanced GNVQ
- **PLACE**   Macclesfield College

Length 30 weeks **Start** October **Days** 3 days/week 9.30-3.00 **Cost** Free **Entry Reqs** By interview **Award** BTEC GNVQ Advanced Management **Creche** No

- **CONTACT** Doreen Graham 01625 427744

- **SUBJECT**   NOW   **121**
- **TITLE**   New Opportunities for Women
- **PLACE**   Macclesfield College

Length 25 weeks **Start** September **Days** 2 hours/week, Thurs 1.00-3.00 **Cost** £32 **Entry Reqs** None **Award** 2 Credits at Level 2 or 3 accredited by Manchester Open College Federation **Creche** No

- **CONTACT** Mary Brown/Bill Humphreys 01625 427744

- **SUBJECT**   Office Skills   **122**
- **TITLE**   Fresh Start
- **PLACE**   Warrington Collegiate Institute, Winwick Road Campus

Length 1 year **Start** September **Days** 4 days/week 10.00-12.00 + 1.00-3.00 **Entry Reqs** None **Award** RSA NVQ Level 2 Business Admin/RSA Typing/RSA WP, Audio, CLAIT, IT Level 2 **Creche** No

- **CONTACT** Audrey Caulderwood 01925 814343 x3445

- **SUBJECT**   Preparatory   **123**
- **TITLE**   City Course for Returners
- **PLACE**   West Cheshire College, Business IT Dept

Length 12 weeks **Start** September, January **Days** Mon-Thurs 15 hours/week **Cost** Free. Travel expenses paid **Entry Reqs** None **Award** Various **Creche** Yes Free

- **CONTACT** Lesley Roberts 01244 677677 x234

- **SUBJECT**   Preparatory   **124**
- **TITLE**   Fresh Start Course
- **PLACE**   Mid-Cheshire College, Verdin Centre, Winsford

Length 5 weeks **Start** Throughout the year **Days** Thurs+Fri 10.15-12.15 **Cost** Free **Entry Reqs** None **Award** College Certificate **Creche** Yes Free to claimants

- **CONTACT** Chris Cody 01606 558278

- **SUBJECT**   Preparatory   **125**
- **TITLE**   Learning Skills
- **PLACE**   Macclesfield College

Length 10 weeks **Start** September, April **Days** 2 hours/week, Fri **Cost** £14.40 **Entry Reqs** None **Award** 1 Credit at Level 2 accredited by Manchester Open College Federation **Creche** No

- **CONTACT** Mary Brown/Bill Humphreys 01625 427744

- **SUBJECT**   Preparatory   **126**
- **TITLE**   Access Foundation Course
- **PLACE**   South Cheshire College, various Adult Centres in Cheshire

Length 30 weeks **Start** September **Days** Interview **Entry Reqs** Interview **Award** UCAN **Creche** Possibly Contact College

- **CONTACT** Chris Brookes 01270 69133 x250

- **SUBJECT**   Preparatory
- **TITLE**   Pick and Mix for Adults
- **PLACE**   West Cheshire College, Human Sciences Division

127

Length Modular, usually 10 weeks/module hours/week in school hours   **Start** September, January, April   **Days** Up to 15 hours/week: times to accommodate school hours   **Cost** Depends on courses taken, free if in receipt of benefit   **Entry Reqs** None   **Award** Varies to suit individuals   **Creche** Yes

- **CONTACT**   Pauline Gibbons 01244 677677 x252

- **SUBJECT**   Social Studies
- **TITLE**   BA (Hons) Applied Social Studies (by Independent Study)
- **PLACE**   Manchester Metropolitan University, Alsager Campus

128

Length 3 years   **Start** September   **Days** Full time   **Entry Reqs** Contact University. Traditionally recruits a high proportion of mature students   **Award** BA (Hons) Applied Social Studies

- **CONTACT**   Dept of Humanities & Applied Social Studies 0161 247 5056/5118/5055

COUNTY CONTACTS

Information and advice:

Warrington Education and Training Advice Centre, The Horsa Building, Warrington Collegiate Institute, Museum Street, Warrington WA1 1HU 01925 633260Open Mon-Fri 10am-4pm. Personal guidance interviews to help with education/training/career choices.

Open University:

The Open University. North West Region, Chorlton House, 70 Manchester Road, Chorlton cum Hardy, Manchester M21 9UN 0161 862 6824

Other agencies:

Beechcroft Training, Beechcroft House, Dee Hills Park, Boughton, Chester CH3 5AR 01244 323495. Range of training programmes, including Women Returning to Work courses

Training and Enterprise Councils:

NORMIDTEC, Spencer House, Dewhurst Road, Birchwood, Warrington WA3 7PP 01925 826515. Covers north and mid Cheshire
South and East Cheshire TEC, PO Box 37, Middlewich Industrial and Business Park, Dalton Way, Middlewich CW10 0HU 01606 737009

WEA offices:

WEA North Western District, 4th Floor, Crawford House, Oxford Road, Manchester M13 9GH 0161 273 7652   *Contact:* Linda Pepper. Covers east Cheshire
WEA West Mercia District, 78/80 Sherlock Street, Birmingham B5 6LT 0121 666 6101   *Contact:* Jill Bedford. Covers south Cheshire

COURSES

- **SUBJECT** Access   129
- **TITLE** Access to Higher Education 1. Full time 2. Part time evening
- **PLACE** Hartlepool College of Further Education

Length 1.30 weeks 2.2 years **Start** September **Days** 1.15 hours/week between 10.00-3.00, term time only 2.2eves/week 6.30-9.00 **Cost** Free if in receipt of benefit, otherwise £11 **Entry Reqs** 1. None 2. By interview with course tutor **Award** Access Certificate validated by Tees-Wear Access Federation **Creche** Nursery Some places available at student rates

- **CONTACT** Student Services 01429 863466

- **SUBJECT** Access   130
- **TITLE** Gateway to Higher Education
- **PLACE** University of Teeside

Length 1 year or 2 years **Start** September **Days** 3 days/week or 2 eves/week **Cost** £76 daytime, £52 eve **Entry Reqs** Interview **Award** Kitemarked Access Certificate from Tees-Wear Access Federation **Creche** Yes

- **CONTACT** Information & Guidance 01642 360205

- **SUBJECT** Access/Business Studies   131
- **TITLE** Access to Higher Education: Business Studies
- **PLACE** Hartlepool College of Further Education

Length 30 weeks **Start** September **Days** 10½ hours/week **Cost** £11 **Entry Reqs** None, over 21 years **Award** Access Certificate validated by Tees-Wear Access Federation **Creche** Nursery Some places available at student rates

- **CONTACT** Student Services 01429 863466

- **SUBJECT** Access/Care Studies   132
- **TITLE** Access to Vocational Caring Professions
- **PLACE** Teeside Tertiary College, Longlands Campus

Length 1 year **Start** September **Days** Full time or part time (less than 21 hours/week) **Cost** Free if in receipt of benefit **Entry Reqs** By interview. Need to show commitment, enthusiasm, interest **Award** CNAA award **Creche** Yes free

- **CONTACT** Margaret Walters 01642 300100 x233

- **SUBJECT** Access/Nursing/Health Studies   133
- **TITLE** Access to Health Studies & Nurse Training
- **PLACE** Stockton & Billingham College of Further Education

Length 1 year or 2 years **Start** September **Days** 3 days/week or 2 eves/week **Cost** £76 daytime, £52 eve **Entry Reqs** Interview **Award** Kitemarked Access Certificate from Tees-Wear Access Federation **Creche** Yes

- **CONTACT** Information & Guidance 01642 360205

- **SUBJECT** Access/Science   134
- **TITLE** Access to Science
- **PLACE** Hartlepool College of Further Education

Length 1 year **Start** September **Days** Mon-Thurs 10.00-3.00 (16 hours/week) **Cost** £11 **Entry Reqs** None, over 21 years **Award** Access to Science Certificate validated by Tees-Wear Access Federation **Creche** Nursery Some places available at student rates

- **CONTACT** Student Services 01429 863466

- **SUBJECT** Access/Science/Technology **135**
- **TITLE** Access to Higher Education: Science and Technology
- **PLACE** Stockton & Billingham College of Further Education

Length 4 terms **Start** September **Days** Daytime or evening **Cost** £76 daytime, £52 eve
Entry Reqs Interview **Award** Kitemarked Access Certificate from Tees-Wear Access
Federation **Creche** Yes
- **CONTACT** Information & Guidance 01642 360205

- **SUBJECT** Access/Science/Technology **136**
- **TITLE** Access to Science and Technology
- **PLACE** Teeside Tertiary College

Length Up to 15 months **Start** Contact College **Days** Up to 16 hrs/week part time **Cost**
Free if in receipt of benefit **Entry Reqs** Enthusiasm, commitment, interest **Award** HEQC
Access Certificate, A levels, BTEC modules **Creche** Yes free
- **CONTACT** Alan Massey 01642 300100 x295

- **SUBJECT** Accounting **137**
- **TITLE** Newstart: Modern Electronic Office Skills - Accounts
- **PLACE** Hartlepool College of Further Education

Length 30 weeks **Start** September **Days** Mon-Thurs 10.00-3.00 (16 hours/week) **Cost** £11
Entry Reqs None, over 21 years **Award** RSA/NCFE qualifications **Creche** Nursery Some
places available at student rates
- **CONTACT** Student Services 01429 863466

- **SUBJECT** Catering **138**
- **TITLE** Food Preparation and Cooking
- **PLACE** Middlesbrough College, Kirby site

Length 1 year **Start** September **Days** Various, day or evening depending on course **Cost**
Contact College **Entry Reqs** Contact College **Award** NVQ Levels I/II Food Preparation and
Cooking **Creche** Yes
- **CONTACT** Chris Mann 01642 333260/Alison Cocking 01642 333232

- **SUBJECT** Childcare **139**
- **TITLE** Childhood Studies (BTEC National Certificate)
- **PLACE** Middlesbrough College

Length 2 years **Start** September **Days** 1 day + 1 eve/week **Cost** £190/year plus BTEC
registration fee **Entry Reqs** By interview **Award** BTEC National Certificate **Creche** Yes
£3/4 hour session
- **CONTACT** Hilary Lee 01642 333246

- **SUBJECT** Computing **140**
- **TITLE** Computing in Business
- **PLACE** Hartlepool College of Further Education

Length 30 weeks **Days** 4 days/week Mon-Thurs (16 hours/week) **Cost** Free if in receipt of
benefit, otherwise £11 **Entry Reqs** None **Award** RSA exams, BTEC CE Units, business
employment, higher education **Creche** Nursery Some places available at student rates
- **CONTACT** Student Services 01429 863466

- **SUBJECT** Computing/Business Administration **141**
- **TITLE** Adult Business Computing
- **PLACE** Middlesbrough College

Length Up to 3 terms **Start** September, January, April **Days** Mon-Fri 10.00-3.00 **Cost**
Remission of fees for Cleveland residents, otherwise £209 **Entry Reqs** None **Award** RSA
Computing/NCFE Micro Accounts/BTEC Certificate IT & Business Studies **Creche** Yes £3
hour
- **CONTACT** Mrs Nicola Errington 01642 333341

- **SUBJECT** Counselling   **142**
- **TITLE** Basic Counselling Skills
- **PLACE** Teeside Tertiary College

Length 2 study blocks of 13 weeks   **Start** September, January, April   **Days** 2 hours/week **Cost** Contact College   **Entry Reqs** None   **Award** NCFE Certificate in Counselling Skills **Creche** Yes free

- **CONTACT** Geraldine Oliver 01642 300100 x540

- **SUBJECT** Engineering/Information Technology   **143**
- **TITLE** Software & Hardware Engineering Programme (SHEP)
- **PLACE** Hartlepool College of Further Education

Length Modular   **Start** Flexible   **Days** Modular   **Cost** Free if in receipt of benefit, otherwise £11   **Entry Reqs** None   **Award** Employment, higher education   **Creche** Nursery Some places available at student rates

- **CONTACT** Student Services 01429 863466

- **SUBJECT** Hospitality Management   **144**
- **TITLE** Hotel Reception
- **PLACE** Middlesbrough College

Length 1 year   **Start** Anytime   **Days** Wed 9.00-3.00   **Cost** £150   **Entry Reqs** Good spoken and written English   **Award** NVQ Level II Hotel Reception   **Creche** Yes

- **CONTACT** Mrs D Grant 01642 333218

- **SUBJECT** Information Technology   **145**
- **TITLE** Application of Computers and IT in Medicine
- **PLACE** Teeside Tertiary College

Length 1 term   **Start** September, January, April   **Days** 3 hours/week   **Cost** Contact College **Entry Reqs** Interest in computers and IT   **Award** College Certificate, BTEC Certificate   **Creche** Yes free

- **CONTACT** Margaret Hawkins 01642 300100

- **SUBJECT** Information Technology   **146**
- **TITLE** BTEC Continuing Education Information Technology
- **PLACE** Teeside Tertiary College

Length 1 term/unit, maximum 5 units   **Start** September   **Days** 3 hours/week   **Cost** Contact College   **Entry Reqs** Basic computing   **Award** BTEC CE Certificate   **Creche** Yes free

- **CONTACT** Margaret Hawkins 01642 300100

- **SUBJECT** Information Technology   **147**
- **TITLE** Computer Literacy
- **PLACE** Teeside Tertiary College

Length 1 year   **Start** September, January, April   **Days** 2 hours/week   **Cost** Contact College **Entry Reqs** None   **Award** RSA IT Computer Literacy Certificate   **Creche** Yes free

- **CONTACT** Sally Craven 01642 300100 x579

- **SUBJECT** Information Technology   **148**
- **TITLE** IT Workshops
- **PLACE** Middlesbrough College

Length Variable   **Start** Roll-on roll-off   **Days** Flexible   **Cost** £1/hour for 20 hours   **Entry Reqs** None   **Award** Progress to other IT/Wordprocessing courses   **Creche** Yes

- **CONTACT** Shelagh Clarke 01642 333333 x3213

- **SUBJECT** Information Technology   149
- **TITLE** IT Workshops and Distance Learning
- **PLACE** Learning Resources Centre, Kirby

Length 20 hours   **Start** Any time   **Days** Flexible   **Cost** £20 for 20 hours   **Entry Reqs** None
Award RSA WP I/II/III/CLAIT

- **CONTACT** Elaine Heard/Sheelagh Clarke 01642 333200

- **SUBJECT** Management   150
- **TITLE** Women into Management
- **PLACE** Hartlepool College of Further Education

Length 6 weeks   **Start** Termly   **Days** Thurs 6.30-8.30   **Cost** £15, £3 if in receipt of state
benefit   **Entry Reqs** None   **Award** College Certificate   **Creche** No

- **CONTACT** Student Services 01429 863466

- **SUBJECT** Media Studies   151
- **TITLE** Media Techniques: Radio and Journalism
- **PLACE** Teeside Tertiary College

Length September   **Start** 20 hours/week   **Days** Contact College   **Cost** Contact College
Entry Reqs Competence in writing skills   **Award** C&G 779   **Creche** Yes free

- **CONTACT** Alastair Smith 01642 248351 x233

- **SUBJECT** Multi-Subject   152
- **TITLE** Women Returners' Course
- **PLACE** Teeside Tertiary College Outreach, EastWest Women's Centre

Length 3 terms   **Start** Contact College   **Days** Up to 12 hours/week   **Cost** Free to Task Force
residents   **Entry Reqs** Contact College   **Award** College Certificate and GCSEs   **Creche** Yes
free

- **CONTACT** Kate Brown 01642 248351 x246

- **SUBJECT** NOW   153
- **TITLE** New Start: New Opportunities for Women
- **PLACE** Various locations in Hartlepool

Length Two 12 week terms, 1 day/week   **Start** September   **Days** Tues, Wed 9.15-3.15   **Cost**
Free   **Entry Reqs** Enthusiasm, interest and time. All ages welcome   **Award** Open College
Network Certificate   **Creche** Yes £1.50/day

- **CONTACT** Maggie Heaps 01642 563285

- **SUBJECT** NOW   154
- **TITLE** New Start: New Opportunities for Women
- **PLACE** Various locations in Langbaurgh

Length Two 12 week terms, 1 day/week   **Start** September   **Days** Mon   **Cost** Free   **Entry
Reqs** Enthusiasm, interest and time. All ages welcome   **Award** Open College Network
Certificate   **Creche** Yes £1.50/day

- **CONTACT** Julie Kenrick 01642 490409

- **SUBJECT** NOW   155
- **TITLE** New Start: New Opportunities for Women with Introduction to Computing
- **PLACE** Various locations in Stockton district

Length Two 12 week terms, 1 day/week   **Start** September   **Days** Mon, Tues, Wed, Thurs
Cost Free   **Entry Reqs** Enthusiasm, interest and time. All ages welcome   **Award** Open College
Network Certificate   **Creche** Yes £1.50/day

- **CONTACT** Maggie Heaps 01642 563285/554001

Cleveland

- **SUBJECT** Office Skills 156
- **TITLE** Newstart: Modern Electronic Office Skills - Secretarial
- **PLACE** Hartlepool College of Further Education

Length 30 weeks **Start** September **Days** Mon-Thurs 10.00-3.00 (16 hours/week) **Cost** £11 **Entry Reqs** None, over 21 years **Award** RSA/NCFE qualifications **Creche** Nursery Some places available at student rates

- **CONTACT** Student Services 01429 863466

- **SUBJECT** Preparatory 157
- **TITLE** Adult Basic Education: English for Women Speaking Other Languages
- **PLACE** Teeside Tertiary College

Length Open/flexible learning **Start** Continuous **Days** Daily between 8.30 and 5.00 **Cost** Usually free **Entry Reqs** Interest **Award** Can lead to Pitmans examination (various levels) **Creche** Yes free

- **CONTACT** Lynn Sampson 01642 300100 x315

- **SUBJECT** Preparatory 158
- **TITLE** Confidence Building
- **PLACE** Stockton & Billingham College of Further Education

Length 1 term **Start** September **Days** Tues 6.00-8.00 **Cost** Contact College **Creche** Yes

- **CONTACT** Information & Guidance 01642 360205

- **SUBJECT** Preparatory 159
- **TITLE** Women into Work
- **PLACE** Stockton & Billingham College of Further Education

Length 1 term **Days** Thurs 10.00-12.00 **Cost** Contact College **Entry Reqs** None **Award** None **Creche** Yes

- **CONTACT** Information & Guidance 01642 360205

- **SUBJECT** Science/Technology 160
- **TITLE** Women into Science and Technology
- **PLACE** Hartlepool College of Further Education

Length 20 weeks **Start** September **Days** Wed 10.00-3.00 **Cost** £9 **Entry Reqs** None **Award** College Certificate **Creche** Nursery Some places available at student rates

- **CONTACT** Student Services 01429 863466

COUNTY CONTACTS

Information and advice:

Hartlepool College of Further Education, Stockton Street, Hartlepool TS24 7NT 01429 863466 Mon-Thurs 9.00-8.00, Fri 9.00-4.00 and during college holidays
National Association for Educational Guidance for Adults, Regional representative, 53 High Street, Ormseby Road, Middlesbrough TS7 9BP 01642 454601 *Contact:* Dennis Burns. Covers northern region
Prospects, TAD Centre Ltd, Ormesby Road, Middlesbrough 01642 203050. Provide adult guidance services

Open University:

Open University Resource Centre, 37 Harrow Road, Middlesbrough TS5 5NT 01642 816227
The Open University. North Region, Eldon House, Regent Centre, Gosforth, Newcastle upon Tyne NE3 3PW 0191 284 1611

WEA office:

WEA Northern District, 51 Grainger Street, Newcastle upon Tyne NE1 5JE 0191 232 3957
Contact: Clare Brown, Ann Staines

CORNWALL

COURSES

- **SUBJECT**   Access   161
- **TITLE**   Access to Higher Education
- **PLACE**   Cornwall College, Helston & Falmouth Open Learning Centres

Length 30 weeks   **Start** September   **Days** 3 days/week 10.00-3.00   **Cost** Contact College
Entry Reqs None, but evidence of recent study an advantage. Age 21+   **Award** South West
Access Federation Certificate   **Creche** Yes £60/week

- **CONTACT**   Andrea Smith 01209 712911 x2253

- **SUBJECT**   Access/Art & Design   162
- **TITLE**   Access Foundation Course in Art & Design
- **PLACE**   Saltash College & Falmouth College of Art

Length 2 years, 25 weeks/year   **Start** September   **Days** 1 day+1 eve (10 hours week)+8 hours
self study   **Cost** Approx £450/year   **Entry Reqs** Under 21, 5 GCSEs or 3 GCSEs A Level or
similar. Over 21, portfolio of work+interview   **Award** BTEC Diploma in Foundation Studies.
Prepares students for HE courses   **Creche** No

- **CONTACT**   Foundation Secretary Falmouth 01326 211077/Gill Hayles Saltash 01752 848147
                 x222

- **SUBJECT**   Access/Business Studies   163
- **TITLE**   Access to Higher Education in Business Studies
- **PLACE**   Saltash College

Length 35 weeks   **Start** September   **Days** Mon+Wed 9.30-3.00   **Cost** Contact College   **Entry
Reqs** Interview   **Award** South West Access Federation Certificate   **Creche** No

- **CONTACT**   Steve Warnes 01752 848147

- **SUBJECT**   Access/Health Studies/Technology   164
- **TITLE**   Access to 1. Health & Social Care 2. Technology
- **PLACE**   Saltash College

Length 35 weeks   **Start** September   **Days** Mon+Wed 9.30-3.00   **Cost** Contact College   **Entry
Reqs** Interview   **Award** South West Access Federation Certificate   **Creche** No

- **CONTACT**   Steve Warnes 01752 848147

- **SUBJECT**   Access/Science   165
- **TITLE**   Access to Foundation Science
- **PLACE**   Cornwall College

Length 1 year   **Start** September   **Days** 2 days/week 9.30-3.30   **Cost** £350   **Entry Reqs**
None   **Award** South West Access Federation Certificate   **Creche** Yes £1.80/hour Subsidy
possible

- **CONTACT**   Claire Wilson 01209 712911 x2226

- **SUBJECT** Beauty/Hairdressing   **166**
- **TITLE** 1. Beauty Therapy CIBTAC Diploma 2. Hairdressing C&G
- **PLACE** Saltash College

Length 1.1 year 2. Approx 2 years (maximum)   **Start** September   **Days** Mon-Fri 9.00-4.00 **Cost** £590 College support for fees. Possible loans towards equipment   **Entry Reqs** 1. & 2. Interview and practical test   **Award** 1. CIBTAC Diploma NVQ 2. City & Guilds NVQ Level II **Creche** No

- **CONTACT** 1. Lesley Cheetham 01752 848147/ 2. Christine Thomas 01752 844777

- **SUBJECT** Catering   **167**
- **TITLE** Bakery and Cake Decoration
- **PLACE** Cornwall College

Length 2 years   **Start** September   **Cost** Contact College   **Entry Reqs** College interview and work experience   **Award** NVQ Level II

- **CONTACT** 01209 712911

- **SUBJECT** Catering   **168**
- **TITLE** Food Production and Cooking (with Food and Drink Service)
- **PLACE** Cornwall College

Length 2 years   **Start** September (flexible)   **Cost** Contact College   **Entry Reqs** College interview and work experience   **Award** NVQ Level II

- **CONTACT** 01209 712911

- **SUBJECT** Childcare   **169**
- **TITLE** 1. BTEC National Certificate in Childhood Studies 2. BTEC Higher National Certificate in Early Childhood Studies
- **PLACE** Cornwall College, Centre for Community & Health Studies

Length 2 years   **Start** 1. September 2. January   **Days** College study + 2 days/week in a childcare setting   **Cost** £289   **Entry Reqs** 1. Discretional entry 2. BTEC National, NNEB, A Levels or equivalent   **Award** 1. BTEC National Certificate 2. BTEC Higher National Certificate

- **CONTACT** Sian Brown 01209 712911

- **SUBJECT** Childcare   **170**
- **TITLE** Nursery Nursing/Childcare
- **PLACE** Saltash College

Length 2 years   **Start** September   **Days** Mon-Fri 9.00-4.00   **Cost** £538/year College grant towards fees possible   **Entry Reqs** Observation work, interview and references   **Award** NNEB Diploma in Nursery Nursing   **Creche** No

- **CONTACT** Pat Gregory 01752 848147 x234

- **SUBJECT** Craft   **171**
- **TITLE** Furniture Crafts for Women Returners to Work
- **PLACE** Cornwall College

Length 1 year   **Start** September   **Days** Mon, Tues 9.00-4.30, Wed 9.00-12.15   **Cost** Contact College. Free if in receipt of benefit   **Entry Reqs** None   **Award** NVQ Level I   **Creche** Yes

- **CONTACT** Derek Roach 01209 712911 x2235

- **SUBJECT** Health Studies   **172**
- **TITLE** BTEC Certificate in Health Studies
- **PLACE** Cornwall College, Centre for Community & Health Studies

Length 1 or 2 years   **Start** September   **Days** 1 or 2 days/week 9.30-3.00   **Cost** £488   **Entry Reqs** Each candidate considered on individual merits   **Award** BTEC Certificate in Health Studies   **Creche** Yes

- **CONTACT** Sally Pitcher 01209 712911 x2176

- **SUBJECT** Hospitality Management 173
- **TITLE** Hotel Reception and Front Office Administration
- **PLACE** Cornwall College

Length 1 year **Start** September **Cost** Contact College **Entry Reqs** Contact College **Award** NVQ Level II

- **CONTACT** 01209 712911

- **SUBJECT** Hospitality Management 174
- **TITLE** Hotel Reception with Catering and Hospitality Studies
- **PLACE** Cornwall College

Length 1/2 years **Start** September **Cost** Contact College **Entry Reqs** Contact College **Award** NVQ Level II (NVQ option for 2nd year in Hotel Reception and House Keeping)

- **CONTACT** 01209 712911

- **SUBJECT** Information Technology 175
- **TITLE** Women into Computing
- **PLACE** Cornwall College, Computing Centre

Length 10 weeks **Start** September, January, April **Days** Tues 9.15-12.30 **Cost** Contact College **Entry Reqs** None **Award** None **Creche** Yes £60/week Subsidy possible

- **CONTACT** Christine Jenkins 01209 712911 x2086

- **SUBJECT** Information Technology/Computing 176
- **TITLE** 1. Access to Higher Education in IT 2. Flexible Modules IT Workshop
- **PLACE** Saltash College

Length 1.36 weeks 2. Flexible **Start** 1. September 2. Flexible **Days** 1. Mon+Wed 9.30-3.00 2. Flexible **Cost** 1. and 2. Contact College **Entry Reqs** 1. Interview 2. Open entry **Award** 1. South West Access Federation Certificate 2. C&G 726/NVQ **Creche** No

- **CONTACT** Steve Warnes 01752 848147

- **SUBJECT** Multi-Subject 177
- **TITLE** Modular Degree, HND, Dip HE, Certificate, Postgraduate Courses
- **PLACE** University of Plymouth (at various centres in Cornwall)

Length Flexible **Start** Flexible **Cost** Contact University **Entry Reqs** Mature students positively encouraged to apply with appropriate life/work experience **Award** Degree, HND, Dip HE, University Certificate, Postgraduate qualifications

- **CONTACT** Mature Student Enquiry Service 01752 232382

- **SUBJECT** Preparatory 178
- **TITLE** Access to Further Education
- **PLACE** Cornwall College

Length 30 weeks **Start** September **Days** 2 days/week **Cost** Contact College **Award** Pre Access Certificate **Creche** Yes £60/week

- **CONTACT** Briege Caldwell 01209 712911 x2253

- **SUBJECT** Preparatory 179
- **TITLE** Make Your Experience Count
- **PLACE** Cornwall College

Length 2-day workshops **Start** September, January, April **Days** 10.15-3.00 **Cost** £10 **Creche** Yes £60/week Subsidy possible

- **CONTACT** Briege Caldwell 01209 712911 x2253

Cornwall

- **SUBJECT** Preparatory   **180**
- **TITLE** Return to Study
- **PLACE** Saltash College

Length 10 weeks   **Start** September, January, April   **Days** 1 day/week 9.30-3.00   **Cost** Contact College   **Entry Reqs** Everyone welcome   **Award** OC Federation Accreditation   **Creche** No

- **CONTACT** Chris Wiseman 01752 847994

- **SUBJECT** Preparatory   **181**
- **TITLE** Return to Work: Clerical/Secretarial Course
- **PLACE** Saltash College

Length 3 terms, 10 weeks/term   **Start** September   **Days** 1 day College+1 day work experience (optional)/week and assignment/self study   **Cost** £36/term Concessions £10   **Entry Reqs** By interview   **Award** RSA Certificates   **Creche** No

- **CONTACT** Chris Wiseman 01752 847994

- **SUBJECT** Science   **182**
- **TITLE** BTEC National Certificate in Science
- **PLACE** Cornwall College

Length 2 years   **Start** September   **Days** Thurs (year 1), Tues (year 2) 9.00-7.00   **Cost** £350/year approx   **Entry Reqs** 4 GCSEs or equivalent + experience   **Award** BTEC National Certificate in Science   **Creche** Yes £1.80/hour Subsidy possible

- **CONTACT** John Baldock 01209 712911 x2108

- **SUBJECT** Science   **183**
- **TITLE** Extended Science Foundation Programme
- **PLACE** Cornwall College

Length 1 year (1st year of 4 year course)   **Start** Cornwall College   **Days** 5 days/week   **Cost** Contact College (attracts mandatory grant)   **Entry Reqs** Flexible. Contact College   **Award** Leads to various degree courses at University of Plymouth   **Creche** Yes £1.80/hour Subsidy possible

- **CONTACT** Roger Harding 01209 712911 x2108

- **SUBJECT** Secretarial/Business Administration   **184**
- **TITLE** Intensive Secretary
- **PLACE** Saltash College

Length 36 weeks   **Start** September   **Days** Mon-Fri 9.30-3.00   **Cost** Contact College   **Entry Reqs** By interview   **Award** RSA NVQ Business Admin Level II & III   **Creche** No

- **CONTACT** Chris Burns 01752 848147

- **SUBJECT** Social Science   **185**
- **TITLE** Combined Honours Degree (Year 1)
- **PLACE** Cornwall College

Length 33 weeks   **Start** September   **Days** Days vary depending on whether student is full time or part time   **Cost** Depends on whether full time or part time   **Entry Reqs** Access Certificate/A Level/BTEC National Diploma   **Award** Certificate in Higher Education, entry to 2nd year of degree course   **Creche** Yes £60/week

- **CONTACT** Briege Caldwell 01209 712911 x2253

- **SUBJECT**   Social Studies/Care Studies   186
- **TITLE**   BTEC National Certificate in Social Care
- **PLACE**   Cornwall College

Length 1 or 2 years   **Start** September   **Days** 1 or 2 days/week 9.30-4.30   **Cost** £206/year
Entry Reqs Interview, maturity and experience taken into account   **Award** BTEC National Certificate   **Creche** Yes

- **CONTACT**   J Mann, P Rendall 01209 712911 x2267/2176

COUNTY CONTACTS

Information and advice:

Cornwall College, Pool, Redruth TR15 3RD 01209 712911 x2253   *Contact:* Briege Caldwell
Cornwall Education Guidance Service for Adults, 61 Lemon Street, Truro TR1 2HG 01872 40555   *Contact:* Rita Watkins. Free, impartial advice, information and counselling on the full range of opportunities available for returning to education, training and employment. Training & Education Shop open daily in Truro and appointments at venues around the county
Pool Careers Centre, Carnon Building, Wilson Way, Pool, Redruth TR15 3RS 01209 315171   *Contact:* Carol Bloomfield
Truro Careers Centre, Helford Building, The Daniell Road Centre, Daniell Road, Truro TR1 2DA 01872 77993   *Contact:* John Case
National Association for Educational Guidance for Adults, Regional representative, Education Guidance Service, 61 Lemon Street, Truro TR1 2PE 01872 40555   *Contact:* Joyce Tabbner. Covers south west region

Open University:

The Open University. South West Region, 4 Portwall Lane, Bristol BS1 6ND 0117 925 6523

Other agencies:

Cornwall Women in Engineering Science & Technology, c/o Camborne School of Mines, University of Exeter, Pool, Redruth TR15 3SE 01209 714866   *Contact:* Lesley Atkinson. Runs Women into Technology courses
Fair Play South West, Roses Barn, Caradon Tain, Upton Cross, Liskeard PL14 5AR 01579 363767   *Contact:* Pat McCarthy. Directory of women's groups in the South West.
Women's Enterprise Centre, Enterprise Tamar, St Thomas Road, Launceston PL15 8BU 01566 775632   *Contact:* Mary Gleeson. Launceston Telecentre: training for computer literacy and running a small business.

Training and Enterprise Council:

Devon and Cornwall TEC, see Devon County Contacts

WEA office:

WEA South Western District, Martin's Gate, Bretonside, Plymouth PL4 0AT 01752 664989   *Contact:* Gail Brooks

CUMBRIA

COURSES

- **SUBJECT** Access   187
- **TITLE**   Access Initiative for Mature Students
- **PLACE**   Carlisle College

Length 1 year (variable) **Start** September **Days** Full or part time modular **Cost** Contact College **Entry Reqs** Age 21+. No formal requirements **Award** Kitemarked Higher Education Foundation Certificate, validated by University of Northumbria

- **CONTACT** Information Unit 01228 24464

- **SUBJECT** Business   188
- **TITLE**   1. HND Business 2. HND Business (Tourism) 3. HND Business (Information Technology)
- **PLACE**   Carlisle College

Length 2 years **Start** September **Cost** Contact College **Entry Reqs** Mature students accepted with relevant experience + interview **Award** HND 1. Business 2. Business (Tourism) 3. Business (Information Technology)

- **CONTACT** Information Unit 01228 24464

- **SUBJECT** Business Administration   189
- **TITLE**   Bookkeeping for Small Businesses
- **PLACE**   Carlisle College

Length 10 weeks **Start** September **Days** Tues 6.00-8.00 **Cost** £35 **Entry Reqs** None

- **CONTACT** Information Unit 01228 24464

- **SUBJECT** Combined Studies   190
- **TITLE**   BA Combined Honours
- **PLACE**   Carlisle College

Length 3 years full time, part time variable **Start** September **Cost** £750 full time, £250 per part-route **Entry Reqs** Contact College **Award** BA (Hons) Combined Honours

- **CONTACT** Dr J Luffrum CHP Co-ordinator 01228 24464

- **SUBJECT** Catering   191
- **TITLE**   BTEC HNC Food and Consumer Studies
- **PLACE**   Carlisle College

Length 2 years **Start** September **Days** Part time **Cost** Contact College **Entry Reqs** Mature students accepted with relevant vocational experience **Award** BTEC Higher National Certificate

- **CONTACT** Information Unit 01228 24464

- **SUBJECT** Childcare   192
- **TITLE**   CACHE (NNEB) Diploma in Nursery Nursing
- **PLACE**   Carlisle College

Length 2 years full time, up to 5 years part time **Start** September **Days** Modular **Cost** Contact College **Entry Reqs** Entrance test and interview **Award** CACHE (NNEB) Diploma

- **CONTACT** Information Unit 01228 24464

- **SUBJECT** Community Studies   193
- **TITLE**   Consumer Studies Programme
- **PLACE**   Carlisle College

Length 1-2 years   **Start** September   **Cost** Contact College   **Entry Reqs** Discretionary entrance for students 21+   **Award** BTEC National Diploma in Home Economics

- **CONTACT** Information Unit 01228 24464

- **SUBJECT** Computing   194
- **TITLE**   Computer Applications
- **PLACE**   Carlisle College

Length 18 weeks   **Start** September, January   **Days** Tues 10.00-1.00   **Cost** £59   **Entry Reqs** None   **Award** RSA CLAIT

- **CONTACT** Information Unit 01228 24464

- **SUBJECT** Computing   195
- **TITLE**   HNC in Computer Aided Technology
- **PLACE**   Carlisle College

Length 1 year   **Start** September   **Days** Part time   **Cost** Contact College   **Entry Reqs** Mature students accepted with relevant experience + interview   **Award** BTEC Higher National Certificate

- **CONTACT** Information Unit 01228 24464

- **SUBJECT** Engineering   196
- **TITLE**   1. Preparation Engineering Programme 2. Advanced Engineering Programme
- **PLACE**   Carlisle College

Length 1.1 year 2.2 years   **Start** September   **Cost** Contact College   **Entry Reqs** Mature students welcome   **Award** 1. BTEC Intermediate GNVQ, C&G 2. BTEC Advanced GNVQ, NVQ Level II

- **CONTACT** Information Unit 01228 24464

- **SUBJECT** Engineering/Science   197
- **TITLE**   Foundation Year: Extended Degree Programme for Engineering and Science
- **PLACE**   Carlisle College

Length 1 year   **Start** September   **Days** Full time   **Cost** Contact College   **Entry Reqs** Mature students welcome   **Award** Progression to degree or HND courses

- **CONTACT** Information Unit 01228 24464

- **SUBJECT** Hairdressing   198
- **TITLE**   Hairdressing Refresher
- **PLACE**   Carlisle College

Length 6 weeks   **Start** September   **Days** Tues 6.00-9.00   **Cost** £33   **Entry Reqs** People who are or who have been employed in hairdressing

- **CONTACT** Information Unit 01228 24464

- **SUBJECT** Horticulture   199
- **TITLE**   Horticulture
- **PLACE**   Newton Rigg College, Penrith

Length Various, including Open Learning   **Start** Various   **Cost** Contact College   **Entry Reqs** None   **Creche** Local provision, free or subsidised

- **CONTACT** Information Unit/Student Services 01768 63791

- **SUBJECT**   Information Technology   200
- **TITLE**   Information Technology
- **PLACE**   Newton Rigg College, Penrith

Length Various, including Open Learning   **Start** Various   **Cost** Various   **Award** BTEC/RSA/ NVQ awards   **Creche** Local provision, free or subsidised

- **CONTACT**   Information Unit/Student Services 01768 63791

- **SUBJECT**   Management   201
- **TITLE**   Certificate in Management
- **PLACE**   Carlisle College

Length 1 year   **Start** September   **Days** Tues eves + 2 Saturday workshops   **Cost** Contact College   **Entry Reqs** 21+ with relevant experience   **Award** Certificate in Management awarded by Institute of Management

- **CONTACT**   Information Unit 01228 24464

- **SUBJECT**   Office Skills   202
- **TITLE**   PA/Administrator Course
- **PLACE**   Carlisle College

Length 18-36 weeks, depending on requirements   **Days** Full or part time   **Cost** Contact College   **Entry Reqs** Contact College   **Award** RSA exams

- **CONTACT**   Information Unit 01228 24464

- **SUBJECT**   Office Skills   203
- **TITLE**   Typewriting, Audio, Word Processing, Desk Top Publishing, Shorthand
- **PLACE**   Carlisle College

Length 10-18 weeks   **Start** September, January   **Days** Part time day or evening   **Cost** Contact College   **Entry Reqs** None   **Award** RSA I/II/III or NVQ Level II Administration Units

- **CONTACT**   Information Unit 01228 24464

- **SUBJECT**   Secretarial   204
- **TITLE**   Advanced Secretarial Skills
- **PLACE**   Carlisle College

Length 1 year   **Start** September   **Cost** Contact College   **Entry Reqs** Mature students accepted with relevant experience   **Award** RSA Advanced Certificates + NVQ Units

- **CONTACT**   Information Unit 01228 24464

- **SUBJECT**   Secretarial   205
- **TITLE**   STEP: Secretarial Training in Electronic Procedures
- **PLACE**   Carlisle College

Length 1 year   **Start** September   **Days** Mon-Fri 10.00-3.00   **Cost** Contact College   **Entry Reqs** Mature students seeking employment in modern office environment. Interview   **Award** NVQ Level II Administration/RSA qualifications

- **CONTACT**   Information Unit 01228 24464

- **SUBJECT**   Technology   206
- **TITLE**   HNC in Advanced Manufacturing Technology
- **PLACE**   Carlisle College

Length 2 years   **Start** September   **Days** Part time   **Cost** Contact College   **Entry Reqs** Mature students accepted with relevant experience + interview   **Award** BTEC Higher National Certificate

- **CONTACT**   Information Unit 01228 24464

- **SUBJECT**   Tourism & Leisure   207
- **TITLE**   Leisure and Tourism 1. GNVQ Intermediate 2. GNVQ Advanced
- **PLACE**   Carlisle College

Length 1.1 year 2.2 years   **Start** September   **Cost** Contact College   **Entry Reqs** Discretionary entrance for students 21+   **Award** 1. GNVQ Intermediate 2. GNVQ Advanced

- **CONTACT**   Information Unit 01228 24464

- **SUBJECT**   Tourism & Leisure   208
- **TITLE**   Leisure and Tourism 1. GNVQ Intermediate 2. GNVQ Advanced
- **PLACE**   West Cumbria College

Length 1.1 year 2.2 years   **Start** September   **Cost** Contact College   **Award** 1. GNVQ Intermediate 2. GNVQ Advanced

- **CONTACT**   01900 64331

COUNTY CONTACTS

Information and advice:

Carlisle College, Victoria Place, Carlisle CA1 1HS 01228 24464
West Cumbria College, Park Lane, Workington CA14 2RW 01900 64331

Open University:

Resource Centre, Newton Rigg College, Penrith CA11 0AH 01768 63791
The Open University. North Region, Eldon House, Regent Centre, Gosforth, Newcastle upon Tyne NE3 3PW 0191 284 1611

Training and Enterprise Council:

Cumbria TEC, Venture House, Regents Court, Guard Street, Workington CA14 4EW 01900 66991

WEA offices:

WEA Cheshire, Merseyside & West Lancashire District, 7/8 Bluecoat Chambers, School Lane, Liverpool L1 3BX 0151 709 8023   *Contact:* Christine Pugh. Covers south west Cumbria
WEA Northern District, 51 Grainger Street, Newcastle upon Tyne NE1 5JE 0191 232 3957   *Contact:* Clare Brown, Ann Staines. Covers north and east Cumbria
Workers' Educational Association, Trades Hall Centre, Brow Top, Workington 01900 822253   *Contact:* Clare Brown

COURSES

- **SUBJECT** Access   209
- **TITLE** Access 2000
- **PLACE** Mackworth College, Derby

Length 4x9-week modules to obtain full Access Certificate   **Start** Ongoing   **Days** Up to 15 hours/week as appropriate   **Cost** 69p/hour   **Entry Reqs** None   **Award** Kitemarked Access Certificate validated by NEMAP, CNAA approved   **Creche** Nursery

- **CONTACT** Director of Student Services 01332 519951

- **SUBJECT** Access   210
- **TITLE** Access Pathways: Modular Access Course
- **PLACE** North Derbyshire Tertiary College, Clowne

Length 1 year   **Start** September   **Days** Full or part time. Full time 9.30-3.30, 5 days/week   **Cost** Usually eligible for minor award or under 21 hour rule   **Entry Reqs** No formal requirements   **Award** Access Certificate NEMAP   **Creche** Yes & playgroup Free

- **CONTACT** Geoff Bright 01246 810332

- **SUBJECT** Access/Art & Design   211
- **TITLE** Access to Higher Education: Art & Design
- **PLACE** Chesterfield College

Length Flexible   **Start** September   **Days** Various days 9.00-4.30   **Cost** Free if in receipt of benefits   **Entry Reqs** Contact College   **Award** SYOC credits   **Creche** Nursery Contact College

- **CONTACT** Sandra Heap 01246 500500 x648

- **SUBJECT** Access/English   212
- **TITLE** Access to Higher Education: English Studies
- **PLACE** Chesterfield College

Length Flexible   **Start** September   **Days** Various days 9.00-4.30   **Cost** Free if in receipt of benefits   **Entry Reqs** Contact College   **Award** SYOC credits   **Creche** Nursery Contact College

- **CONTACT** Sandra Heap 01246 500500 x648

- **SUBJECT** Access/Health Studies   213
- **TITLE** Access to Higher Education: Health and Nursing
- **PLACE** Chesterfield College

Length Flexible   **Start** September   **Days** Various days 9.00-4.30   **Cost** Free if in receipt of benefits   **Entry Reqs** Contact College   **Award** SYOC credits   **Creche** Nursery Contact College

- **CONTACT** Sandra Heap 01246 500500 x648

- **SUBJECT** Access/Mathematics   214
- **TITLE** Access Maths (GCSE Equivalent)
- **PLACE** Chesterfield College

Length Flexible   **Start** Negotiable   **Days** Various days 9.00-4.30   **Cost** Free if in receipt of benefits   **Entry Reqs** Contact College   **Award** SYOC credits   **Creche** Nursery Contact College

- **CONTACT** Sandra Heap 01246 500500 x648

- **SUBJECT** Access/Science/Technology/Environmental Studies   215
- **TITLE** Access to Higher Education: Science, Technology, Environmental Studies
- **PLACE** Chesterfield College

Length Flexible   **Start** September   **Days** Various days 9.00-4.30   **Cost** Free if in receipt of benefits   **Entry Reqs** Contact College   **Award** SYOC credits   **Creche** Nursery Contact College
- **CONTACT** Sandra Heap 01246 500500 x648

- **SUBJECT** Access/Social Studies   216
- **TITLE** Access to Higher Education: Social Studies
- **PLACE** Chesterfield College

Length Flexible   **Start** September   **Days** Various days 9.00-4.30   **Cost** Free if in receipt of benefits   **Entry Reqs** Contact College   **Award** SYOC credits   **Creche** Nursery Contact College
- **CONTACT** Sandra Heap 01246 500500 x648

- **SUBJECT** Access/Social Studies   217
- **TITLE** Living in a Changing Society
- **PLACE** Mackworth College, Derby

Length 1 year, possibility of extending to 2 years   **Start** September   **Days** Tues 6.00-8.00 or Thurs 7.00-9.00   **Cost** Contact College   **Entry Reqs** No formal requirements. Competency in written English essential   **Award** Open College Network Credits leading to kitemarked Access Certificate
- **CONTACT** Student Services 01332 519951

- **SUBJECT** Access/Tourism & Leisure/Information Technology   218
- **TITLE** Access to Higher Education: Travel & Tourism and Business Information Technology
- **PLACE** Chesterfield College

Length Flexible   **Start** September   **Days** Various days 9.00-4.30   **Cost** Free if in receipt of benefits   **Entry Reqs** Contact College   **Award** SYOC credits   **Creche** Nursery Contact College
- **CONTACT** Sandra Heap 01246 500500 x648

- **SUBJECT** Information Technology   219
- **TITLE** Women into Information Technology
- **PLACE** Chesterfield College

Length 34 weeks   **Start** September   **Days** 1-4 mornings/week 9.30-12.15   **Cost** Contact College   **Entry Reqs** Contact College   **Award** C&G 726   **Creche** Yes
- **CONTACT** Nev Parkes 01246 500746

- **SUBJECT** Information Technology   220
- **TITLE** Women into New Technology
- **PLACE** Derby Tertiary College, Wilmorton

Length 36 weeks   **Start** September   **Days** 9.30-3.00 4 days/week during College term times (not Thurs)   **Cost** Free (ESF funded)   **Entry Reqs** None   **Award** Certificates of Achievement in BTEC, National Diploma in Computer Studies, RSA CLAIT & WP   **Creche** Yes
- **CONTACT** Jane McKenna 01332 757570

- **SUBJECT** Management   221
- **TITLE** Women into Management
- **PLACE** Chesterfield College

Length 48 weeks   **Start** September   **Days** Tues 6.00-9.00+open learning element   **Cost** Contact College (£65 NEBSM registration+£40 book hire)   **Entry Reqs** Age 21+   **Award** NEBSM Certificate in Supervisory Management   **Creche** Yes free
- **CONTACT** Rosie Gilligan 01246 500621

Derbyshire

- **SUBJECT** Office Skills   222
- **TITLE** Typewriting, Wordprocessing, Information Processing
- **PLACE** Chesterfield College, Office Skills Workshop

Length Flexible   **Start** Various, September-June   **Days** Mon-Thurs 10.30-12.30+1.00-3.00 **Cost** £80/subject   **Entry Reqs** No entry qualifications for Stage 1, other levels according to existing qualifications   **Award** RSA exams   **Creche** Yes

- **CONTACT** Eileen Limb/Susan Bannister 01246 500626

- **SUBJECT** Preparatory   223
- **TITLE** Confidence Building/Assertion Training
- **PLACE** Chesterfield College

Length 12 week modules   **Start** September, January, April   **Days** Tues 5.30-8.30   **Cost** Contact College   **Creche** Not in evenings

- **CONTACT** Gail Freeman 01246 500500 x648

- **SUBJECT** Preparatory   224
- **TITLE** Fresh Start
- **PLACE** Mackworth College, Derby

Length 5 weeks   **Cost** Free (ESF funded)   **Entry Reqs** None   **Award** OCN Credits at Level I/II   **Creche** Yes

- **CONTACT** Student Services 01332 519951

- **SUBJECT** Preparatory   225
- **TITLE** Learning Opportunities:English, Maths, Computers, Core Skills, Job Search Skills
- **PLACE** North Derbyshire Tertiary College & Community Learning Centres

Length Various. Halfday, 1 day sessions, Open Learning, etc   **Start** Flexible   **Days** Various **Cost** Free   **Entry Reqs** All welcome   **Award** Learning/updating skills. Open Learning accreditation. Entry to AEB/GCSE Maths, CLAIT, C&G   **Creche** Contact College

- **CONTACT** Student Services 01246 810332

- **SUBJECT** Preparatory   226
- **TITLE** New Directions
- **PLACE** Mackworth College, Derby, Normanton Road Site

Length 12 weeks   **Start** September, January, April   **Days** Fri 9.45-2.30   **Cost** Free (ESF funded)   **Entry Reqs** None   **Award** OCN Credits at Level I/II   **Creche** Yes Free

- **CONTACT** Sue Poxon 01332 519951

- **SUBJECT** Preparatory   227
- **TITLE** Return to Learning
- **PLACE** WEA, St Helen's House Adult Education Centre, King Street, Derby

Length 8 or 10 weeks   **Start** September   **Days** 1 weekday/1 evening/week   **Cost** Contact Centre   **Entry Reqs** None   **Creche** No

- **CONTACT** Jill Duncan 01332 346013/01332 205305

- **SUBJECT** Preparatory   228
- **TITLE** Return to Learning: Study Skills
- **PLACE** Mackworth College, Derby

Length 8 weeks   **Days** 2 hours/week   **Cost** Contact College   **Entry Reqs** None   **Award** OCN Credits at Level I/II   **Creche** Yes

- **CONTACT** Student Services 01332 519951

- **SUBJECT** Preparatory
- **TITLE** Time for a Change
- **PLACE** WEA, St Helen's House Adult Education Centre, King Street, Derby

229

Length 10 weeks **Start** September **Days** 1 day/week **Cost** Contact Centre **Entry Reqs** None **Creche** No

- **CONTACT** Jill Duncan 01332 346013

COUNTY CONTACTS

Open University:

The Open University. East Midlands Region, The Octagon, 143 Derby Road, Nottingham NG7 1PH 0115 924 0121

Other agencies:

Derwent Childcare Centre, St Mark's Road, Derby DE21 6AH 01332 372245. Women's centre

Training and Enterprise Councils:

North Derbyshire TEC, Block C, St Mary's Court, St Mary's Gate, Chesterfield S41 7TD 01246 551158
Southern Derbyshire Chamber of Commerce Training & Enterprise Ltd, St Helen's Court, St Helen's Street, Derby DE1 3GY 01332 200550

WEA offices:

WEA East Midland District, Alfreton Hall, Church Street, Alfreton DE55 7AH 01773 832185 *Contact:* Chris Scarlett. Covers south Derbyshire
WEA North Western District, 4th Floor, Crawford House, Oxford Road, Manchester M13 9GH 0161 273 7652 *Contact:* Linda Pepper. Covers north west Derbyshire
WEA Yorkshire South District, Chantry Buildings, Corporation Street, Rotherham S60 1NG 01709 837001 *Contact:* Trish Lands. Covers north east Derbyshire

---

DEVON

COURSES

- **SUBJECT** Access
- **TITLE** Access to Higher Education
- **PLACE** University of Plymouth, Plymouth Campus

230

Length 1 year **Start** September **Cost** Contact University **Entry Reqs** No formal requirements **Award** South West Access Federation Access to Higher Education Kitemarked Certificate **Creche** Yes

- **CONTACT** Mature Student Enquiry Service 01752 232382

- **SUBJECT** Access/Arts/Music   **231**
- **TITLE** Access to the Arts, Music, Theatre, Visual Arts
- **PLACE** Dartington College of Arts

Length 1 year   **Start** October   **Days** 2 days/week   **Cost** Contact College. Concessions available   **Entry Reqs** 21+, no formal requirements   **Award** Nationally recognised Access Certificate validated by SW Access Federation   **Creche** No

- **CONTACT** Access Co-ordinator 01803 862224

- **SUBJECT** Access/Humanities/Social Studies/Science/Health Studies/Business   **232** Studies/Electronics/Construction
- **TITLE** Access to HE: 1. Humanities/Social Studies 2. Science/Health Studies 3. Business Studies/Social Science 4. Electronics 5. Construction
- **PLACE** South Devon College

Length 1 year   **Start** September   **Days** 16 hours/week 9.30-3.00   **Cost** Tuition £395 (concessions possible); accreditation £45   **Entry Reqs** Evidence of recent study   **Award** Access to HE Certificate   **Creche** Pre-school 3+, £3.50/session

- **CONTACT** Mike Herbert 01803 386489

- **SUBJECT** Access/Mathematics   **233**
- **TITLE** Access to Higher Education: Advancing in Maths
- **PLACE** University of Plymouth, Plymouth Campus

Length 1 year part time   **Start** September   **Days** 2 eves/week   **Cost** Contact University **Entry Reqs** Recent study in Maths an advantage   **Award** Access to HE Kitemarked Certificate, University Certificate   **Creche** No

- **CONTACT** Ted Graham 01752 232773

- **SUBJECT** Access/Preparatory   **234**
- **TITLE** 1. Access to Humanities, Fine Art 2. Return to Study
- **PLACE** North Devon College

Length 1.1 year 2.6 weeks   **Start** 1. September 2. Termly   **Days** Contact College

- **CONTACT** Steve Edwards 01271 888103

- **SUBJECT** Access/Science/Humanities/Social Science   **235**
- **TITLE** Access to Science, Humanities and Social Science
- **PLACE** Plymouth College of Further Education

Length 1 or 2 years   **Start** September   **Cost** Contact College   **Entry Reqs** Interview   **Award** Access Certificate   **Creche** Yes

- **CONTACT** Information Unit 01752 385300

- **SUBJECT** Beauty   **236**
- **TITLE** 1. Beauty Specialist Certificate 2. Manicure and Make-up
- **PLACE** Exeter College

Length 35 weeks   **Start** September   **Days** 1.1 day/week 2.1 eve/week or 1 afternoon/week **Cost** Contact College   **Entry Reqs** None   **Award** College Certificate   **Creche** Yes

- **CONTACT** Customer Services 01392 384001/2/3

- **SUBJECT** Business Information Technology   **237**
- **TITLE** HND Business Information Technology
- **PLACE** Exeter College

Length 2 years   **Start** September   **Cost** Contact College   **Entry Reqs** Contact College **Award** HND   **Creche** Yes

- **CONTACT** Marge Clarke 01392 384157

- **SUBJECT** Business Studies 238
- **TITLE** Computer Skills, WP, Book-keeping, Typing, Shorthand
- **PLACE** Plymouth College of Further Education

Length Flexible   **Start** Flexible   **Cost** From £20 Concessions available   **Entry Reqs** None
Award Various   **Creche** Yes

- **CONTACT** Hilary Kilborn 01752 383827

- **SUBJECT** Care Studies 239
- **TITLE** Social Care
- **PLACE** Exeter College

Length 2 years   **Start** September   **Days** Modular, 1 day/week   **Cost** Contact College   **Entry
Reqs** Interview   **Award** BTEC National Certificate   **Creche** Yes

- **CONTACT** Customer Services 01392 384001/2/3

- **SUBJECT** Computing 240
- **TITLE** Computer Studies
- **PLACE** Exeter College

Length 2 years   **Start** September   **Days** 1 day/week   **Cost** Contact College   **Entry Reqs**
Contact College   **Award** BTEC National Certificate   **Creche** Yes

- **CONTACT** Customer Services 01392 384001/2/3

- **SUBJECT** Information Technology 241
- **TITLE** HNC Information Technology
- **PLACE** University of Plymouth, Plymouth Campus

Length 2 years part time   **Start** February   **Days** Tues, Wed, Thurs 10.00-2.30   **Cost** Contact
University   **Award** HNC Information Technology   **Creche** Playgroup 01752 2322338

- **CONTACT** Mary Squire 01752 232541/2

- **SUBJECT** Information Technology 242
- **TITLE** Open Learning: Information Technology
- **PLACE** South Devon College, Open Learning Centre

Length Flexible, open learning   **Days** Flexible   **Cost** Contact College   **Entry Reqs** Contact
College   **Award** RSA CLAIT, RSA Integrated Business Technology, Modular Text Processing,
Spreadsheets, etc   **Creche** Yes

- **CONTACT** Open Learning Reception 01803 386459

- **SUBJECT** Multi-Subject 243
- **TITLE** Credit Accumulation & Transfer Scheme (CATS)
- **PLACE** University of Plymouth, Plymouth, Exeter, Newton Abbott

Length Flexible   **Start** September   **Cost** Contact University   **Entry Reqs** Mature students
welcome   **Award** Leads to University Certificate in HE, Dip HE, leading to degree   **Creche**
Playgroup

- **CONTACT** Roger Adams 01752 232370

- **SUBJECT** Multi-Subject 244
- **TITLE** Modular Degree, HND, Dip HE, Certificate, Postgraduate Courses
- **PLACE** University of Plymouth at 4 campus sites and other centres in Devon

Length Flexible, full time or part time   **Start** Flexible   **Cost** Contact University   **Entry Reqs**
Mature students positively encouraged to apply with appropriate life/work experience   **Award**
Degree, HND, Dip HE, University Certificate, Postgraduate qualifications   **Creche** Playgroup

- **CONTACT** Mature Student Enquiry Service 01752 232382

- **SUBJECT** NOW   245
- **TITLE** Making Change Happen/New Opportunity Workshops
- **PLACE** South Devon College

Length 1 day workshop **Start** May, June (workshop 4 times) **Days** Fri 10.00-3.00 **Cost** £5
Creche Pre-school 3+, £3.50/session

- **CONTACT** Eve Spencer 01803 386314

- **SUBJECT** Office Skills   246
- **TITLE** Office Skills Workshop
- **PLACE** Exeter College

Length Flexible **Days** Various **Cost** Contact College **Entry Reqs** None **Award** RSA
CLAIT & single subjects **Creche** Yes

- **CONTACT** Customer Services 01392 384001/2/3

- **SUBJECT** Office Skills/Information Technology   247
- **TITLE** Refreshers - Updating Office Skills and Information Technology
- **PLACE** South Devon College

Days Thurs 9.30-3.00 **Cost** Contact College **Entry Reqs** Contact College **Creche** Yes

- **CONTACT** Admissions Office 01803 291212

- **SUBJECT** Preparatory   248
- **TITLE** Confidence Building, Personal Effectiveness, Career/Training/Job Seeking
  Guidance
- **PLACE** Plymouth Returners' Ltd

Length 2 weeks+Open/Distance Learning+Open Access **Start** Monthly (9 courses/year)
Days Full time 9.30-3.00 **Cost** Free (ESF & Plymouth City Council funding) **Entry Reqs**
Women only **Award** Fact finding on progressions routes/self development/enhancement of
work possibilities **Creche** No (limited help with childcare costs)

- **CONTACT** Tina Massey/Gill Thomas 01752 673466

- **SUBJECT** Preparatory   249
- **TITLE** Fresh Start
- **PLACE** South Devon College

Length 10 weeks **Start** September, January, April **Days** 1 day/week 9.30-11.30 **Cost** £10
waged, free if unwaged **Entry Reqs** None **Creche** Yes

- **CONTACT** Eve Spencer 01803 386317

- **SUBJECT** Preparatory   250
- **TITLE** Make Your Experience Count
- **PLACE** East Devon College

Length 10 weeks **Start** October, January **Cost** £6 (free if on benefit) **Entry Reqs** None
Award SWAF Accreditation **Creche** No

- **CONTACT** Jude Painter 01884 235245

- **SUBJECT** Preparatory   251
- **TITLE** Pre Access: Into Science, Maths and Technology
- **PLACE** South Devon College

Length 10 weeks **Start** October, March **Days** Oct: Wed 7.00-9.00, March: Fri 10.00-12.00
Cost Free to unwaged, £32 waged **Entry Reqs** None **Award** South West Access Federation
Creche Pre-school 3+, £3.50/session daytime only

- **CONTACT** Eve Spencer 01803 386314

- **SUBJECT** Preparatory
- **TITLE** Pre Access: Preparation for Study
- **PLACE** South Devon College

252

Length 10 weeks   **Start** January, April, September   **Days** Mon 1.00-3.00 or 7.00-9.00   **Cost** Free to unwaged, £32 waged   **Entry Reqs** None   **Award** South West Access Federation   **Creche** Pre-school 3+, £3.50/session
- **CONTACT** Eve Spencer 01803 386314

- **SUBJECT** Preparatory
- **TITLE** Pre Access: Preparation for Study Through the Living Arts
- **PLACE** South Devon College

253

Length 10 weeks   **Start** January, April   **Days** Mon 9.30-11.30   **Cost** Free to unwaged, £32 waged   **Entry Reqs** None   **Award** South West Access Federation   **Creche** Pre-school 3+, £3.50/session
- **CONTACT** Eve Spencer 01803 386314

- **SUBJECT** Preparatory
- **TITLE** Return to Learn
- **PLACE** South Devon College

254

Length 10 weeks   **Start** January, April, September   **Days** Tues & Wed 10.00-3.00   **Cost** Free to unwaged, £10 waged   **Entry Reqs** None   **Award** South West Access Federation accreditation available   **Creche** Pre-school 3+, £3.50/session
- **CONTACT** Eve Spencer 01803 386314

- **SUBJECT** Preparatory
- **TITLE** Return to Learn: Getting Back to Study
- **PLACE** South Devon College

255

Length 10 weeks   **Start** January, April, September   **Days** Wed 7.00-9.00   **Cost** Free to unwaged, £10 waged   **Entry Reqs** None   **Award** South West Access Federation   **Creche** Pre-school 3+, £3.50/session
- **CONTACT** Eve Spencer 01803 386314

- **SUBJECT** Preparatory
- **TITLE** Return to Learn: Fresh Start
- **PLACE** South Devon College

256

Length 10 weeks   **Start** January, April, September   **Days** Wed 10.00-12.00   **Cost** Free to unwaged, £10 waged   **Entry Reqs** None   **Award** South West Access Federation accreditation available   **Creche** Pre-school 3+, £3.50/session
- **CONTACT** Eve Spencer 01803 386314

- **SUBJECT** Preparatory
- **TITLE** Springboard
- **PLACE** East Devon College

257

Length 10 weeks   **Start** September, January, April/May   **Days** Mon-Thurs 9.30-3.00   **Cost** £55 or free if in receipt of benefit   **Entry Reqs** Women only aged 25+   **Award** SWAF Certificate   **Creche** Yes 2-5 years subsidised
- **CONTACT** Gill Unstead 01884 254247

- **SUBJECT** Preparatory
- **TITLE** Time for Change
- **PLACE** East Devon College with Community Agencies: location varies

258

Length 6 weeks   **Start** November, January, May   **Days** 2 hours/week usually 1.00-3.00   **Cost** None   **Entry Reqs** Open Access to women   **Creche** Yes minimal charges
- **CONTACT** Gill Unstead 01884 235245

- **SUBJECT** Science   259
- **TITLE** Biological Research Methods
- **PLACE** University of Exeter

Length 1 year   **Start** October   **Cost** Biotechnology & Biological Sciences Research Council award available   **Entry Reqs** Graduates with first or upper second honours degree in an appropriate subject   **Award** MSc

- **CONTACT** Dr V Essex, BBSRC, 01793 413200

- **SUBJECT** Social Science   260
- **TITLE** Joint Social Science Modular Scheme
- **PLACE** University of Plymouth, Plymouth Campus

Length 3 years full time, 5 years part time   **Start** September   **Cost** Contact University   **Entry Reqs** Mature students welcome, evidence of recent appropriate academic study required   **Award** Various. Contact University   **Creche** Playgroup Contact University 01752 232338

- **CONTACT** Mai Lowe 01752 233191

- **SUBJECT** Social Work   261
- **TITLE** Devon and Somerset Diploma in Social Work Programme
- **PLACE** University of Plymouth

Length 2 years   **Start** September   **Cost** Contact University   **Entry Reqs** Age 20+. Interview   **Award** DipHE, DipSW   **Creche** Yes

- **CONTACT** Course Administrator 01752 233192

- **SUBJECT** Social Work   262
- **TITLE** Diploma in Social Work
- **PLACE** East Devon College

Length 2 years   **Start** September   **Days** Full time   **Cost** Contact College   **Entry Reqs** Age 21+. Access and mature students welcomed   **Award** Diploma in Social Work   **Creche** Yes 2-5 years

- **CONTACT** Admissions Officer 01884 254247

- **SUBJECT** Women's Studies   263
- **TITLE** Short Courses: Assertiveness Training, Access Courses, Wider Opportunities
- **PLACE** WEA, Martin's Gate, Bretonside, Plymouth & other sites

Length 5-25 hours   **Start** Continuous   **Days** Varies   **Cost** £1.00-£1.50/hour (concessions available)   **Entry Reqs** None   **Award** Open College Federation Accredited or Non-Accredited   **Creche** At some locations

- **CONTACT** WEA District Secretary 01752 664989

- **SUBJECT** Women's Studies   264
- **TITLE** Women's Studies 1. Certificate 2. Postgraduate Diploma 3. MA
- **PLACE** University of Plymouth, Faculty of Human Science, Plymouth

Length 1 year full time, 2 years part time   **Start** September   **Days** Mon 10.00-4.00   **Cost** Contact University   **Entry Reqs** Degree/relevant professional qualification with experience   **Award** 1. Certificate (after 1 year part time) 2. Postgraduate Diploma 3. MA   **Creche** Playgroup Contact University 01752 232338

- **CONTACT** Course Administrator 01752 233243

COUNTY CONTACTS

Information and advice:

East Devon Careers Centre, 1st Floor, Queen's House, Little Queen Street, Exeter EX4 3LJ 01392 384272
North Devon Careers Centre, The Red House, Castle Street, Barnstaple
01271 388630
South Devon Careers Centre, First Floor, Union House, 89 Union Street, Torquay TQ1 3YA 01803 386000
West Devon Careers Centre, 10 Derry's Cross, Plymouth PL1 2SH 01752 385000
Mature Student Enquiry Service, University of Plymouth, Drake Circus, Plymouth 01752 232382. *Contact:* Beth Scott, Nicola Opie Scott. Information, advice and guidance on opportunities in, and routes to, higher education. Mature Students Guide available, also one-to-one guidance and counselling.
Plymouth Returners Ltd, 40 Tavistock Place, Plymouth PL4 8AX 01752 673466   *Contact:* Gill Thomas. Guidance, information, support and advice

Open University:

The Open University. South West Region, 4 Portwall Lane, Bristol BS1 6ND 0117 925 6523

Other agencies:

The Devon Centre, Lord Halden Hotel, Dunchideock
01803 862267   *Contact:* Sylvia Eglington. The Centre is Devon Education Committee's residential centre for teaching and social services courses; also available to anyone wishing to run courses or have them put on.

Training and Enterprise Council:

Devon and Cornwall TEC, Foilot House, Brooklands, Budshead Road, Crownhill, Plymouth PL6 5XR 01752 767929. Options for Learning.

WEA office:

WEA South Western District, Martin's Gate Annexe, Bretonside, Plymouth PL4 0AT 01752 664989   *Contact:* Gail Brooks

---

DORSET

COURSES

- **SUBJECT**   Access   265
- **TITLE**   Access to Higher Education
- **PLACE**   Bournemouth and Poole College of Further Education

Length 1 year   **Start** September   **Days** Full time   **Cost** Contact College   **Entry Reqs** Age 21+. Interview   **Award** Access to higher education   **Creche** Yes

- **CONTACT**   Student Services 01202 205660

- **SUBJECT** Access/Business Studies/Computing   **266**
- **TITLE** Access to Higher Education in Business Studies and Computing
- **PLACE** Bournemouth and Poole College of Further Education, Bournemouth

Length 1 year   **Start** September   **Days** Full time   **Cost** Contact College   **Entry Reqs** 21+, no formal qualifications but competent in English Language. Interview   **Award** Access to higher education   **Creche** Yes

- **CONTACT** Student Services 01202 205660

- **SUBJECT** Access/Engineering/Science   **267**
- **TITLE** Foundation Years to BEng/BSc Degree Programmes
- **PLACE** Bournemouth University

Length 1 year+degree programme (varies)   **Start** September   **Days** Full time   **Cost** Contact University. Financial support may be available   **Entry Reqs** Contact University   **Award** Entry to BEng/BSc degree programmes   **Creche** Yes Contact University

- **CONTACT** N Richardson 01202 524111

- **SUBJECT** Access/Humanities/Social Science   **268**
- **TITLE** Access to Higher Education (Humanities and Social Science)
- **PLACE** Weymouth College

Length 1 year   **Start** September   **Days** 2 days/week Mon+Tues 10.00-3.00   **Cost** £618 Fee concessions possible   **Entry Reqs** 21+, motivation to study   **Award** Access Certificate from Weymouth College validated by Wessex Access Federation   **Creche** Yes £2/hour

- **CONTACT** Pamela Bradford 01305 208837

- **SUBJECT** Access/Science/Technology   **269**
- **TITLE** Access to Higher Education (Science and Technology)
- **PLACE** Weymouth College

Length 1 year   **Start** September   **Days** 3 days/week 9.30-3.30   **Cost** Contact College   **Entry Reqs** 21+, motivation to study, career path   **Award** Access Certificate from Weymouth College validated by Wessex Access Federation   **Creche** Yes £2/hour

- **CONTACT** Irene Robinson 01305 208868

- **SUBJECT** Accounting   **270**
- **TITLE** Practical Book-keeping Stages I & II
- **PLACE** Weymouth College Flexible Learning Centre

Length 50 hours over 1 year   **Days** Open learning   **Cost** £67, concessions available   **Entry Reqs** Contact College   **Award** RSA Practical Book-keeping Levels I & II

- **CONTACT** Flexible Learning Centre 01305 208989

- **SUBJECT** Beauty Therapy   **271**
- **TITLE** Adult Students' Certificate in Massage and Exercise
- **PLACE** Bournemouth and Poole College of Further Education, Bournemouth

Length 1 year   **Start** September   **Days** Full time   **Cost** Contact College   **Entry Reqs** Age 25+, commitment. Interview   **Award** College Certificate, NVQ verification awaited   **Creche** Yes

- **CONTACT** Student Services 01202 205660

- **SUBJECT** Business/Languages 272
- **TITLE** Euroqualifications (European Business Administration)
- **PLACE** Bournemouth and Poole College of Further Education, Bournemouth

Length 1 year **Start** September **Days** Full time **Cost** Contact College **Entry Reqs** HND, degree or equivalent or relevant commercial experience **Award** Diploma in European Business Administration **Creche** Yes

- **CONTACT** Student Services 01202 205660

- **SUBJECT** Business Studies/Information Technology 273
- **TITLE** Business Studies and Information Technology: Foundation
- **PLACE** Bournemouth and Poole College of Further Education

Length 1 year **Start** September **Days** Full time **Cost** Contact College **Entry Reqs** Interview. No formal entry requirements **Award** Progress to employment, NVQ 2 Business Admin or GNVQ Intermediate Business/IT **Creche** Yes

- **CONTACT** Student Services 01202 205660

- **SUBJECT** Electronics 274
- **TITLE** 1. BEng (Hons) Microelectronics & Computing Foundation 2. BEng (Hons) Electronic Systems Design Foundation
- **PLACE** Bournemouth and Poole College of Further Education, Poole

Length 1 year **Start** September **Days** Full time **Cost** Contact College **Entry Reqs** No formal entry requirements for mature students **Award** Entry to honours degree studies at Bournemouth University **Creche** Yes

- **CONTACT** Student Services 01202 205660

- **SUBJECT** Engineering 275
- **TITLE** BSc (Hons) Engineering Business Development Foundation
- **PLACE** Bournemouth and Poole College of Further Education, Poole

Length 1 year **Start** September **Days** Full time **Cost** Contact College **Entry Reqs** No formal entry requirements for mature students **Award** Entry to honours degree studies at Bournemouth University **Creche** Yes

- **CONTACT** Student Services 01202 205660

- **SUBJECT** Floristry 276
- **TITLE** Adult Students' Certificate in Floristry
- **PLACE** Bournemouth and Poole College of Further Education, Bournemouth

Length 1 year **Start** September **Days** Full time **Cost** Contact College **Entry Reqs** Age 25+, commitment. Interview **Award** NVQ Level II **Creche** Yes

- **CONTACT** Student Services 01202 205660

- **SUBJECT** Hairdressing 277
- **TITLE** Adult Students' Certificate in Hairdressing
- **PLACE** Bournemouth and Poole College of Further Education, Bournemouth

Length 1 year **Start** September **Days** Full time **Cost** Contact College **Entry Reqs** 25+ with an interest in hairdressing. Interview **Award** NVQ Level II **Creche** Yes

- **CONTACT** Student Services 01202 205660

- **SUBJECT** Information Technology 278
- **TITLE** BTEC GNVQ Intermediate in Information Technology
- **PLACE** Bournemouth and Poole College of Further Education, Poole

Length 1 year **Start** September **Days** Full time **Cost** Contact College **Entry Reqs** Contact College **Award** BTEC GNVQ Intermediate **Creche** Yes

- **CONTACT** Student Services 01202 205660

Dorset

- **SUBJECT**   Multi-Subject   279
- **TITLE**   Degree/Diploma/Certificate Courses
- **PLACE**   Bournemouth University

Length Varies   **Start** September, usually   **Days** Full time, part time, sandwich courses
Entry Reqs Contact University   **Award** BA/BSc/LLB/BEng/DipHE/HND/HNC   **Creche**
Yes Contact University

- **CONTACT**   N Richardson 01202 524111

- **SUBJECT**   Multi-Subject   280
- **TITLE**   MBA/MA/MSc/Postgraduate Diploma
- **PLACE**   Bournemouth University

Length Varies   **Start** Varies   **Days** Full time, part time   **Cost** Contact University. Financial
support may be available   **Entry Reqs** Normally first degree   **Award** MBA/MA/MSc/PG
Dip   **Creche** Yes Contact University

- **CONTACT**   N Richardson 01202 524111

- **SUBJECT**   Preparatory   281
- **TITLE**   Gateway I: Introduction to Study
- **PLACE**   Bournemouth & Poole College of FE

Length 10 weeks   **Start** April   **Days** 4 hours/week, day to be arranged   **Cost** Contact
College   **Award** College Letter of Certification   **Creche** No

- **CONTACT**   Secretary 01202 205849

- **SUBJECT**   Preparatory   282
- **TITLE**   Women Returners' Programme
- **PLACE**   Weymouth College Flexible Learning Centre

Length 9 months   **Days** Open learning   **Cost** Approx £25   **Entry Reqs** None, reasonable level
of verbal/written communication & enthusiasm   **Award** RSA Diploma in IT/ISM Certificate in
Supervisory Management

- **CONTACT**   Flexible Learning Centre 01305 208989

- **SUBJECT**   Psychology/Computing   283
- **TITLE**   BSc (Hons) Applied Psychology and Computing Foundation Year
- **PLACE**   Bournemouth and Poole College of Further Education, Bournemouth

Length 1 year   **Start** September   **Days** Full time   **Cost** Contact College   **Entry Reqs** No
formal entry requirements for mature students   **Award** Entry to honours degree study at
Bournemouth University   **Creche** Yes

- **CONTACT**   Student Services 01202 205660

- **SUBJECT**   Science   284
- **TITLE**   BTEC National Diploma in Science
- **PLACE**   Weymouth College

Length At least 2 years   **Start** September   **Days** Negotiable   **Cost** Contact College
Award BTEC National Diploma in Science, or if not completed, Certificate of Performance for
units covered   **Creche** Yes £2/hour

- **CONTACT**   Irene Robinson 01305 208868

COUNTY CONTACTS

Information and advice:

Adult Access Unit, Bournemouth & Poole College of Further Education, Lansdowne Centre, Bournemouth BH1 3JJ 01202 205660/205896   *Contact:* Shaun Kelly, Felicity Bond

Guidance Service for Adults, Access and Guidance Unit, Weymouth College, Cranford Avenue, Weymouth DT4 7LQ 01305 208837   *Contact:* Pam Bradford

Dorset Careers Guidance Services, Station Approach, Weymouth Avenue, Dorchester DT1 1GA 01305 225284

Blandford Careers Centre, The Tabernacle, Blandford Forum DT11 7DW 01258 454454

Bournemouth Careers Centre, 5th Floor, Dorset House, 20-22 Christchurch Road, Bournemouth BH1 3NL 01202 221172

Poole Careers Centre, Jademanor Court, West Quay Road, Poole BH15 1JG 01202 221450

Weymouth Careers Centre, 29 St Thomas Street, Weymouth DT4 8EJ 01305 782180

Open University:

The Open University. South Region, Foxcombe Hall, Boars Hill, Oxford OX1 5HR 01865 328038

Training and Enterprise Council:

Dorset TEC, 25 Oxford Road, Bournemouth BH8 8EY 01202 299284. Training & Enterprise Shop provides information on learning opportunities together with help and advice on job searching, CV production and appropriate training. Details of local and national courses.

WEA office:

WEA Western District, 40 Morse Road, Redfield, Bristol BS5 9LB 0117 935 1764   *Contact:* Mavis Zutchi, Kath Ryder

DURHAM

COURSES

- **SUBJECT**   Access   285
- **TITLE**   Higher Education Foundation Course
- **PLACE**   Derwentside College

Length Flexible   **Start** September   **Days** Day and/or eve   **Cost** Contact College   **Entry Reqs** None   **Award** University of Northumbria at Newcastle HE Foundation Certificate   **Creche** Yes

- **CONTACT**   Information Centre 01207 502906

- **SUBJECT**   Access   286
- **TITLE**   Higher Education Foundation Course
- **PLACE**   East Durham Community College, Howletch Centre & Burnhope Way Centre

Length 1 year   **Start** September   **Cost** Contact College   **Award** Higher Education Foundation Certificate   **Creche** Yes Contact College

- **CONTACT**   Student Services 0191 518 8222

Durham

- **SUBJECT**   Access/Business Studies   287
- **TITLE**   Access to Higher Education: Business Studies
- **PLACE**   Darlington College of Technology

Length 30 weeks   **Start** September   **Days** 4 days/week   **Cost** £432   **Entry Reqs** Subject to interview, age 21+   **Award** Kitemarked Access Certificate   **Creche** Yes

- **CONTACT**   Clarie Strickland 01325 503266

- **SUBJECT**   Access/Humanities/Social Science   288
- **TITLE**   Access to Higher Education: Humanities and Social Science
- **PLACE**   Darlington College of Technology

Length 1 year   **Start** September   **Days** 3 days/week 9.30-4.30   **Cost** £423   **Entry Reqs** None   **Award** Kitemarked Course leads to degrees in Humanities, Social Science, BEd & Diploma in Social Work   **Creche** Yes daytime hours

- **CONTACT**   J Tindall 01325 467651 x255

- **SUBJECT**   Access/Mathematics/Science   289
- **TITLE**   Access to Higher Education: Maths and Sciences
- **PLACE**   Darlington College of Technology

Length 36 weeks   **Start** September   **Days** 6 halfdays/week   **Cost** Contact College   **Entry Reqs** None. Interview and counselling   **Award** Access Certificate kitemarked by Tees-Wear Access Federation and TROCN   **Creche** Yes daytime hours

- **CONTACT**   Vic Brown 01325 503170

- **SUBJECT**   Access/Science   290
- **TITLE**   Access to Higher Education: Science
- **PLACE**   Darlington College of Technology

Length 40 weeks   **Start** September   **Days** 2 eves/week   **Cost** Contact College   **Entry Reqs** None. Interview and counselling   **Award** Access Certificate kitemarked by Tees-Wear Access Federation and TROCN

- **CONTACT**   Vic Brown 01325 503170

- **SUBJECT**   Administration   291
- **TITLE**   NVQ II Administration
- **PLACE**   East Durham Community College, Town Centre

Length 1 year   **Start** September   **Days** 2 days College+3 days work placement/week   **Cost** Contact College   **Award** LCC/NVQ Level II   **Creche** Yes Contact College

- **CONTACT**   Student Services 0191 518 8222

- **SUBJECT**   Care Studies/Community Studies   292
- **TITLE**   Community Care Practice NVQ Level 2 Care
- **PLACE**   East Durham Community College, Howletch Centre

Length 1 year   **Start** September   **Days** Tues+Wed 9.15-12.15   **Cost** Approx £135   **Entry Reqs** Contact College   **Award** NVQ Level 2   **Creche** Yes Contact College

- **CONTACT**   Student Services 0191 518 8222

- **SUBJECT**   Childcare   293
- **TITLE**   BTEC Certificate Caring Services (Nursery Nursing)
- **PLACE**   Derwentside College

Length 2 years part time   **Start** September   **Days** Contact College   **Cost** Contact College   **Entry Reqs** Adults in paid or voluntary employment with children under 8 years   **Award** BTEC Certificate   **Creche** Yes

- **CONTACT**   Mick Horgan 01207 502906

- **SUBJECT** Childcare
- **TITLE** Childcare for Adults
- **PLACE** East Durham Community College, Howletch Centre

294

Length 1 year **Start** September **Days** Tues 9.30-3.00 **Cost** Contact College **Entry Reqs** Contact College **Award** NVQ Level 2 **Creche** Yes Contact College
- **CONTACT** Student Services 0191 518 8222

- **SUBJECT** Childcare
- **TITLE** Creche Workers Course: Pre School Care
- **PLACE** Derwentside College

295

Length Flexible **Start** September **Days** Contact College **Cost** Contact College **Entry Reqs** Age 20+ **Award** NCFE Certificate **Creche** Yes
- **CONTACT** Joan Beveridge 01207 502906

- **SUBJECT** Childcare
- **TITLE** Playgroup Leaders
- **PLACE** East Durham Community College, Howletch Centre

296

Length 1 year **Start** September **Days** Thurs 7.00-9.00 **Cost** Approx £48 **Entry Reqs** Contact College **Award** College Certificate **Creche** Yes Contact College
- **CONTACT** Student Services 0191 518 8222

- **SUBJECT** Counselling
- **TITLE** Basic Counselling Skills
- **PLACE** East Durham Community College or by negotiation

297

Length 20 hours **Start** Negotiable **Days** By negotiation **Cost** Contact College **Award** C&G 3701/2 **Creche** Yes Contact College
- **CONTACT** Student Services 0191 518 8222

- **SUBJECT** Hairdressing
- **TITLE** Adult Opportunities in Hairdressing
- **PLACE** East Durham Community College, Howletch Centre

298

Length 2 years **Start** September **Days** 15 hours/week **Cost** Contact College **Award** C&G (NVQ Level 2) **Creche** Yes Contact College
- **CONTACT** Student Services 0191 518 8222

- **SUBJECT** Office Skills
- **TITLE** Office Skills for Adults
- **PLACE** Derwentside College

299

Length Flexible **Start** September, January, April **Days** Part time **Cost** Contact College **Entry Reqs** None **Award** Recognised certificates **Creche** Yes
- **CONTACT** J Gallagher 01207 502906

- **SUBJECT** Preparatory
- **TITLE** Assertiveness Training for Women
- **PLACE** East Durham Community College, Burnhope Way Centre

300

Length 10 weeks **Start** September **Days** Sat 9.30-11.30 **Cost** £16 approx **Entry Reqs** None **Award** College Certificate **Creche** Yes Contact College
- **CONTACT** Student Services 0191 518 8222

- **SUBJECT** Preparatory
- **TITLE** Focus on Opportunity
- **PLACE** Centres in Derwentside

301

Length 10 weeks **Start** Ongoing **Days** 2 days/week 9.45-2.45 **Cost** Free **Entry Reqs** None **Award** Tyneside Open College Federation Certificate **Creche** Depends on venue
- **CONTACT** Beveley Hill, Newcastle Women's Training Centre, 0191 232 6159

Durham

- **SUBJECT**   Preparatory   302
- **TITLE**   Introduction to Maths and Sciences
- **PLACE**   Darlington College of Technology

Length 8 weeks   **Start** Contact College   **Days** 4 halfdays/week   **Cost** Contact College
Entry Reqs None   **Creche** Yes, daytime hours

- **CONTACT**   Vic Brown 01325 503173

- **SUBJECT**   Preparatory   303
- **TITLE**   Return to Work
- **PLACE**   Derwentside College

Length 12 weeks   **Start** October   **Cost** Free   **Entry Reqs** None   **Award** Could lead to NVQs
via APL   **Creche** No Help with childminding costs

- **CONTACT**   Mina Eaves 01207 502906

- **SUBJECT**   Teaching   304
- **TITLE**   Adult and Further Education Teaching
- **PLACE**   Darlington College of Technology

Length 31 weeks   **Start** September, January   **Days** Mon or Wed 9.00-4.00 or Mon+Wed
6.00-9.00, or Thurs 2.30-9.00   **Cost** Approx £180 (subject to revision)   **Entry Reqs** Vocational
qualification   **Award** Further Education Teaching Certificate (C&G 7307)   **Creche** Yes

- **CONTACT**   Margaret Reay 01325 467651

COUNTY CONTACTS

Information and advice:

Peterlee College, Lee House, Peterlee SR8 1NU 0191 518 0690

Open University:

The Open University. North Region, Eldon House, Regent Centre, Gosforth, Newcastle upon
Tyne NE3 3PW 0191 284 1611

Training and Enterprise Council:

County Durham TEC, Valley Street North, Darlington DL1 1TJ 01325 351166. 'Taster Days' in
various community centre locations; Range of Access programmes; ESF joint funded Wider
Opportunities for Women; after school childcare & holiday care initiative; Working for Women
Advisory Group produces annual plan of activities responding to identified needs

WEA office:

WEA Northern District, 51 Grainger Street, Newcastle upon Tyne NE1 5JE 0191 232
3957   *Contact* Clare Brown, Ann Staines

COURSES

- **SUBJECT** Access   305
- **TITLE** Access to Higher Education
- **PLACE** Lewes Tertiary College

Length 1 year   **Start** September   **Days** Full time or part time   **Cost** Contact College   **Entry Reqs** Age 21+, interview, attendance at June Pre-Access Course   **Award** Access Certificate, entry to higher education   **Creche** Yes

- **CONTACT** College Information Officer 01273 483188

- **SUBJECT** Access/Humanities/Science   306
- **TITLE** Access to Higher Education, Science Pathway/Humanities Pathway
- **PLACE** Eastbourne College of Arts & Technology

Length 34 weeks   **Start** September, April   **Days** 2 part time days/week or 2 part time eves/week   **Cost** £170 Humanities, £220 Science (both free if in receipt of benefit)   **Entry Reqs** None   **Award** Access Certificate   **Creche** Yes

- **CONTACT** Mick Scruton/Hilary Pusyer 01323 644711 x209

- **SUBJECT** Access/Humanities/Science   307
- **TITLE** Access to Higher Education
- **PLACE** Hastings College of Arts & Technology

Length 1 year   **Start** September, May   **Cost** £190   **Entry Reqs** None   **Award** Access to higher education

- **CONTACT** Juliet Millican 01424 442222x241 (Humanities)/Chris Morrell x269 (Science)

- **SUBJECT** Access/Humanities/Science/Social Science/Mathematics/Physics/   308
  Business Studies
- **TITLE** Access to Higher Education
- **PLACE** Brighton College of Technology

Length 1 year   **Start** September   **Cost** Contact College   **Entry Reqs** None, 21+   **Award** Access to higher education

- **CONTACT** Mandy Foyster/Carolyn Knott 01273 667759

- **SUBJECT** Administration   309
- **TITLE** Administration: NVQ
- **PLACE** Brighton College of Technology

Days 1 day or eve/week   **Cost** Contact College   **Entry Reqs** Contact College   **Award** NVQ Level II/III Business Administration

- **CONTACT** Mandy Foyster/Carolyn Knott 01273 667759

- **SUBJECT** Art & Design   310
- **TITLE** Foundation Studies in Art and Design
- **PLACE** Hastings College of Arts & Technology

Length 2 years   **Days** Part time   **Cost** £190 + BTEC registration fee   **Award** BTEC Diploma

- **CONTACT** Tony Anderson 01424 442222 x231

- **SUBJECT** Health Studies   311
- **TITLE** Introduction to Health and Social Care
- **PLACE** Hastings College of Arts & Technology

Length 10 weeks   **Start** September, January, April   **Days** Mon-Thur 10.00-1.00   **Cost** Contact College   **Award** RSA Initial Award in Care

- **CONTACT** Vivienne Bannister 01424 442222 x348/241

- **SUBJECT**   Horticulture   312
- **TITLE**   Garden Services
- **PLACE**   Brighton College of Technology

Length 1 year   **Start** September   **Days** Full time or part time   **Cost** Contact College   **Entry Reqs** None   **Award** NVQ Levels I/II, C& G Horticultural Skills/Garden Design

- **CONTACT**   Mandy Foyster/Carolyn Knott 01273 667759

- **SUBJECT**   Information Technology   313
- **TITLE**   Information Technology: City & Guilds
- **PLACE**   Hastings College of Arts & Technology

Length 20 weeks   **Start** Roll on roll off   **Days** Flexible, maximum 20 hours/week   **Cost** £199 + C&G fees   **Award** City & Guilds Diploma

- **CONTACT**   Judith Cubison 01424 442222 x226/228

- **SUBJECT**   Office Skills   314
- **TITLE**   Fresh Return to Office Work
- **PLACE**   Hastings College of Arts & Technology

Length 18 weeks   **Start** September, February   **Days** Mon-Fri 9.30-3.00   **Cost** Contact College   **Entry Reqs** None   **Award** NVQ Levels/single subject exams

- **CONTACT**   Pat Collings 01424 442222 x244/241

- **SUBJECT**   Preparatory   315
- **TITLE**   New Horizons
- **PLACE**   Hastings College of Arts & Technology

Length 10 weeks   **Start** April   **Days** Mon 1.00-3.00   **Cost** Contact College   **Entry Reqs** None   **Creche** Yes

- **CONTACT**   Gina Standen 01797 222318

- **SUBJECT**   Preparatory   316
- **TITLE**   Way in for Women
- **PLACE**   Hastings College of Arts & Technology

Length 6 weeks   **Start** June   **Days** Wed-Thurs 10.00-12.00, 1.00-3.00   **Cost** Contact College   **Entry Reqs** None   **Award** Progress to further courses such as GNVQ Intermediate   **Creche** Yes

- **CONTACT**   Alison Hay 01424 442222 x310

- **SUBJECT**   Retail   317
- **TITLE**   Retailing and Distribution: BTEC Intermediate GNVQ
- **PLACE**   Hastings College of Arts & Technology

Length 1 year   **Start** September   **Days** Mon-Tues 9.20-1.00   **Cost** £148 + BTEC registration fee   **Entry Reqs** Interview   **Award** BTEC Intermediate GNVQ

- **CONTACT**   Hilary Armfield 01424 442222 x242/241

- **SUBJECT**   Secretarial   318
- **TITLE**   Secretarial Skills
- **PLACE**   Brighton College of Technology

Start Flexible   **Days** 2 hours/week   **Cost** Contact College   **Entry Reqs** None   **Award** RSA Single Subject/Pitman

- **CONTACT**   Mandy Foyster/Carolyn Knott 01273 667759

COUNTY CONTACTS

Information and advice:

Guidance Centre, Hastings College of Arts and Technology, Archery Road, St Leonards on Sea TN38 0HX 01424 44222   *Contact:* Susan McGrath, Gina Sanderson. Guidance on courses and options. (Course fee waivers for women on a range of benefits)

Open University:

The Open University. South East Region, St James's House, 150 London Road, East Grinstead RH19 1ES 01342 410545

Other agencies:

Brighton College of Technology, Pelham Street, Brighton BN1 4FA 01273 667788   *Contact:* Alison Hastings. Range of vocational/access courses available full or part time
Friends' Centre, Ship Street, Brighton BN1 1AF 01273 327835. Independent adult education centre providing range of general adult education courses

Training and Enterprise Council:

Sussex TEC, see West Sussex County Contacts

WEA office:

WEA South Eastern District, 4 Castle Hill, Rochester ME1 1QQ 01634 842140   *Contact:* Wilma Fraser, Joy Pascoe

---

ESSEX

COURSES

- **SUBJECT**   Access   319
- **TITLE**   Access Main Course Programme
- **PLACE**   Braintree Tertiary College

Length 36 weeks   **Start** September   **Days** 5 days/week   **Cost** Contact College   **Entry Reqs** Completion of planning period and personal statement   **Award** Access to higher education/ further education/employment   **Creche** Playgroup £2.25/9.00-12.00, £1.50/1.00-3.00

- **CONTACT**   Elizabeth Hawton, Access Co-ordinator 01376 321711

- **SUBJECT**   Access   320
- **TITLE**   Access Planning Period
- **PLACE**   Braintree Tertiary College

Length 70 hours over 10 weeks, day or evening   **Start** April, June   **Days** Wed 9.15-3.15+Fri 9.15-12.15 or Tues+Thurs eves 6.30-9.30   **Cost** Daytime £47.50, evening £46.80   **Entry Reqs** Age 21+   **Award** CNAA validated Access Certificate after completion of Access Main Course **Creche** Playgroup £2.25/9.00-12.00, £1.50/1.00-3.00

- **CONTACT**   Elizabeth Hawton, Access Co-ordinator 01376 321711

- **SUBJECT**   Access   321
- **TITLE**   Access to Higher Education
- **PLACE**   Basildon College

Length 4 terms   **Start** October, January, April   **Days** Various   **Entry Req** By interview
Award Access Certificate   **Creche** Playgroup 3-5 years
- **CONTACT**   Gillian Beeston 01268 532015

- **SUBJECT**   Access   322
- **TITLE**   Access to Higher Education
- **PLACE**   Chelmsford College

Length 1 year   **Start** September   **Days** Full time   **Cost** Contact College   **Entry Reqs** Age
21+   **Award** Essex Access Certificate   **Creche** Yes
- **CONTACT**   Sector of Professional & Management Studies 01245 265611

- **SUBJECT**   Access   323
- **TITLE**   Access to Higher Education
- **PLACE**   South East Essex College

Length 1 year full time, 2 years part time   **Start** September   **Days** Full time day, part time
eves   **Cost** Contact College   **Entry Reqs** Age 19+   **Award** Access Certificate   **Creche** Yes
- **CONTACT**   01702 220400

- **SUBJECT**   Access   324
- **TITLE**   Essex Access Scheme
- **PLACE**   Colchester Institute, Sheepen Road Site

Length 4 terms, including Access Planning   **Start** January, April   **Days** Full or part time
Cost Varies, concessions available   **Entry Reqs** None   **Award** EOCF Credits for Planning
Period; Access Certificate validated by Essex Access Consortium   **Creche** Yes Contact Institute
- **CONTACT**   Cathy Cook 01206 718614 / Clare Hawkins 01206 718000

- **SUBJECT**   Access / Arts / Business Studies / Psychology / Social Science / Science /   325
  Teaching / Women's Studies
- **TITLE**   Access Specialist Modules
- **PLACE**   Harlow College

Length 1 year   **Start** September   **Cost** £35 / module   **Entry Reqs** None   **Award** Access to
higher education
- **CONTACT**   Client Adviser Team 01279 868000

- **SUBJECT**   Accounting   326
- **TITLE**   Accountancy
- **PLACE**   Chelmsford College

Length 2 years   **Start** September   **Days** Full time   **Cost** Contact College   **Entry Reqs**
Contact College. Mature students welcome   **Award** NVQ Levels II / III / IV   **Creche** Yes
- **CONTACT**   Sector of Professional & Management Studies 01245 265611

- **SUBJECT**   Administration   327
- **TITLE**   Administration
- **PLACE**   Chelmsford College

Length 1-2 years   **Start** September   **Days** Full time   **Cost** Contact College   **Entry Reqs**
Contact College. Mature students may not need formal qualifications   **Award** NVQ Level II
Adminstration, RSA Text Processing Modules, RSA Higher Diploma   **Creche** Yes
- **CONTACT**   Sector of Computing, Office & IT 01245 265611

- **SUBJECT**   Administration   328
- **TITLE**   Administration: 1. NVQ Level II 2. NVQ Level III
- **PLACE**   South East Essex College

Length 1.1 year 2.2 years   **Start** September   **Days** Full time   **Cost** Contact College   **Entry**
Reqs Contact College   **Award** 1. NVQ Level II 2. NVQ Level III   **Creche** Yes
- **CONTACT**   01702 220400

- **SUBJECT** Administration
- **TITLE** Administration: Adult Modular Programme
- **PLACE** Thurrock College

329

Length Modular **Days** 10.00-12.00, 1.00-3.00 **Cost** Financial help with fees usually available **Entry Reqs** No formal qualifications. **Award** RSA NVQ 1-4 **Creche** Yes
- **CONTACT** Admissions Unit 01375 391199

- **SUBJECT** Beauty Therapy
- **TITLE** Beauty Therapy
- **PLACE** Thurrock College

330

Length 2 years **Start** September **Days** Full time **Cost** Contact College **Entry Reqs** Contact College. Mature students wishing to start a new career as beauty therapists welcome **Award** C&G NVQ II/III **Creche** Yes
- **CONTACT** Admissions Unit 01375 391199

- **SUBJECT** Business
- **TITLE** Business GNVQ: 1. Foundation 2. Intermediate 3. Advanced
- **PLACE** Chelmsford College

331

Length 1. &2.1 year 3.2 years **Start** September **Days** Full time **Cost** Contact College **Entry Reqs** Contact College. Mature students welcome **Award** 1. GNVQ Foundation 2. GNVQ Intermediate 3. GNVQ Advanced **Creche** Yes
- **CONTACT** Sector of Business Studies 01245 265611

- **SUBJECT** Business
- **TITLE** Business BTEC GNVQ: 1. Intermediate 2. Advanced
- **PLACE** South East Essex College

332

Length 1.1 year 2.2 years **Start** September **Days** Full time **Cost** Contact College **Entry Reqs** Contact College **Award** 1. BTEC GNVQ Intermediate 2. BTEC GNVQ Advanced **Creche** Yes
- **CONTACT** 01702 220400

- **SUBJECT** Business
- **TITLE** BTEC National Certificate Business and Finance
- **PLACE** South East Essex College

333

Length 2 years **Start** September **Days** 1 day/week or 2 eves/week 6.30-9.30 **Cost** Contact College **Entry Reqs** Contact College **Award** BTEC National Certificate **Creche** Yes
- **CONTACT** 01702 220400

- **SUBJECT** Business Administration
- **TITLE** Diploma in Business Administration: NVQ Levels 1, 2, 3, 4 (Legal, Medical, Languages, DTP, Shorthand, Audio)
- **PLACE** Thurrock College

334

Length Flexible **Start** September **Days** Mon-Fri 10.00-3.00 **Cost** Contact College **Entry Reqs** None **Award** NVQ Level 1 equiv/RSA Cert, 2 equiv/RSA Dip, 3 equiv/RSA Advanced Dip/Business Admin **Creche** Playgroup
- **CONTACT** June Laushway 01375 391199 x609

- **SUBJECT** Business Information Technology
- **TITLE** IT for Business
- **PLACE** Harlow College

335

Length 1 year **Start** September **Days** Mon-Fri 9.15-2.45 **Cost** £221 **Entry Reqs** Interest in IT and a working knowledge of 1 or more applications **Award** RSA NVQ Level II Using Information Technology
- **CONTACT** Client Adviser Team 01279 868000

● **SUBJECT**   Business Studies   336
● **TITLE**   Administration: RSA/NVQ
● **PLACE**   Harlow College

Length 1 year   **Start** September   **Days** Open/distance learning or Mon-Fri 9.15-2.45   **Cost** Contact College   **Award** RSA NVQ Administration Levels I/II/III
● **CONTACT**   Client Adviser Team 01279 868000

● **SUBJECT**   Care Studies   337
● **TITLE**   Care in the Community
● **PLACE**   Thurrock College

Length 1 year   **Start** September   **Days** Wed 9.00-4.00 + 1 day/week placement   **Cost** Contact College   **Entry Reqs** 19+, aptitude test and interview   **Award** Essex Open College Federation Accreditation
● **CONTACT**   Charlotte Suttle 01375 391199 x2616

● **SUBJECT**   Care Studies   338
● **TITLE**   HNC in Caring Services (Community Care)
● **PLACE**   Thurrock College

Length 2 years   **Start** January   **Days** Thurs 5.30-9.30   **Cost** Contact College   **Entry Reqs** Contact College   **Award** HNC in Caring Services (Community Care)
● **CONTACT**   Charlotte Suttle 01375 391199 x2616

● **SUBJECT**   Care Studies   339
● **TITLE**   Management for Care 1. C&G Foundation 2. C&G Advanced
● **PLACE**   Thurrock College

Length 36 weeks   **Start** September   **Days** 1. Wed 9.00-5.00 2. Tues 9.00-5.00   **Cost** Contact College   **Entry Reqs** Contact College   **Award** 1. C&G 3250/2 Foundation Management for Care 2. C&G 3250/3 Advanced Management for Care
● **CONTACT**   Charlotte Suttle 01375 391199 x2616

● **SUBJECT**   Childcare   340
● **TITLE**   1. Certificate in Children's Care and Education 2. BTEC National Diploma Childhood Studies 3. NNEB Diploma in Nursery Nursing
● **PLACE**   South East Essex College

Length 1.1 year 2. &3.2 years   **Start** September   **Days** Full time   **Cost** Contact College   **Entry Reqs** Contact College   **Award** 1. Certificate 2. BTEC National Diploma 3. NNEB Diploma   **Creche** Yes
● **CONTACT**   01702 220400

● **SUBJECT**   Computing   341
● **TITLE**   Computer Studies
● **PLACE**   Chelmsford College

Length 2 years   **Start** September   **Days** Full time   **Cost** Contact College   **Entry Reqs** No formal requirements for mature students   **Award** BTEC National Diploma in Computer Studies   **Creche** Yes
● **CONTACT**   Sector of Computing, Office & IT 01245 265611

● **SUBJECT**   Computing   342
● **TITLE**   Computer Studies
● **PLACE**   South East Essex College

Length 2 years   **Start** September   **Days** 2 eves/week   **Cost** Contact College   **Entry Reqs** GCSEs or equivalent, or existing computing skills and experience   **Award** BTEC National Certificate in Computer Studies
● **CONTACT**   01702 220400

- **SUBJECT** Engineering 343
- **TITLE** Engineering: 1. BTEC GNVQ Intermediate 2. BTEC GNVQ Advanced
- **PLACE** South East Essex College

Length 1.1 year 2.2 years **Start** September **Days** Full time **Cost** Contact College **Entry Reqs** Contact College. Female applicants welcome **Award** 1. BTEC GNVQ Intermediate 2. BTEC GNVQ Advanced **Creche** Yes
- **CONTACT** 01702 220400

- **SUBJECT** Hairdressing 344
- **TITLE** Hairdressing for Mature Students
- **PLACE** Thurrock College

Length 36 weeks **Start** September **Days** 4 days/week between 9.00-3.00 **Cost** Assistance available. Contact College **Entry Reqs** Age 20+, interview, reference **Award** C&G NVQ Level 2 Hairdressing **Creche** Playgroup 3-5 years
- **CONTACT** Secretariat 01375 362704

- **SUBJECT** Health Studies 345
- **TITLE** Health and Social Care: 1. BTEC GNVQ Intermediate 2. BTEC GNVQ Advanced
- **PLACE** South East Essex College

Length 1.1 year 2.2 years **Start** September **Days** Full time **Cost** Contact College **Entry Reqs** Contact College **Award** 1. BTEC GNVQ Intermediate 2. BTEC GNVQ Advanced **Creche** Yes
- **CONTACT** 01702 220400

- **SUBJECT** Health Studies 346
- **TITLE** Training for the Health and Social Care Professions
- **PLACE** South East Essex College

Length 1 year **Start** September **Days** 18 hours/week **Cost** Contact College **Entry Reqs** Adults seeking employment-related qualifications or seeking a career change **Award** BTEC GNVQ Intermediate Health and Social Care **Creche** Yes
- **CONTACT** 01702 220400

- **SUBJECT** Information Technology 347
- **TITLE** BTEC GNVQ Intermediate Information Technology
- **PLACE** South East Essex College

Length 1 year **Start** September **Days** Full time **Cost** Contact College **Entry Reqs** 2 GCSEs, reasonable standard of literacy and numeracy **Award** BTEC GNVQ Intermediate **Creche** Yes
- **CONTACT** 01702 220400

- **SUBJECT** Information Technology 348
- **TITLE** IT: Introduction to Programming, Communications, Small Business Systems, WP, DTP, Spreadsheets, Databases
- **PLACE** Thurrock College

Length Flexible **Start** September **Entry Req** None **Award** RSA Computer Literacy, C&G Communications, RSA Database, RSA Word Processing **Creche** Playgroup
- **CONTACT** John Blick 01375 391199

- **SUBJECT** Information Technology 349
- **TITLE** Information Technology: Adult Modular Programme
- **PLACE** Thurrock College

Length Modular **Days** 10.00-12.00, 1.00-3.00 **Cost** Financial help with fees usually available **Entry Reqs** No formal qualifications **Award** NVQ 1-3 **Creche** Yes
- **CONTACT** Admissions Unit 01375 391199

- **SUBJECT** Information Technology/Multi-Subject **350**
- **TITLE** Modular Programmes: Keyboarding/IT/WP/DTP/Computer Applications/ Business Admin/Law/Medical/Languages/Audio
- **PLACE** Thurrock College

Length Flexible **Start** September **Cost** Contact College **Entry Reqs** None for beginners, some wp training/shorthand/typing for intermediate/advanced **Award** RSA, Pitmans examinations **Creche** Playgroup
- **CONTACT** June Laushway 01375 391199 x609

- **SUBJECT** Management **351**
- **TITLE** Institute of Supervisory Management Cert/NVQ L3 or Management Cert/NVQ L4
- **PLACE** Braintree Tertiary College

Length 10 months (1 day/week) **Start** September **Days** Tues 1.15-8.00 **Cost** CSM £310, CM £325 **Entry Reqs** For CM preferably a management qualification/Level 3 or supervisory management experience **Award** ISM Certificate in Supervisory Mgt (CSM) or Certificate in Management (CM) **Creche** Daytime only, not eves
- **CONTACT** Linda Bywater 01376 312711

- **SUBJECT** Management **352**
- **TITLE** Modern Manager
- **PLACE** Harlow College

Length 25 weeks **Start** January **Days** Tues, Wed, Thurs 9.30-4.00 **Cost** Free, ESF funded **Entry Reqs** Unemployed for six months or more **Award** NVQ Level IV Information Systems & Applications; Human, Financial & Resource Management
- **CONTACT** Client Adviser Team 01279 868000

- **SUBJECT** Media Studies **353**
- **TITLE** Entry into Media Occupations
- **PLACE** South East Essex College

Length 1 year **Start** September **Cost** Contact College **Entry Reqs** 2 GCSEs, reasonable standard of literacy and numeracy **Award** Progress to full or part time BSc Media degree courses or employment **Creche** Yes
- **CONTACT** 01702 220400

- **SUBJECT** Multi-Subject **354**
- **TITLE** BA/BSc Foundation Programme (Part Time)
- **PLACE** Harlow College

Length 11 weeks/module **Start** September, January, March **Days** Mon, Tues, Wed 6.30-9.30 **Cost** £92/module Reductions possible **Entry Reqs** Interview **Award** Middlesex University Certificate in Higher Education
- **CONTACT** Client Adviser Team 01279 868000

- **SUBJECT** Office Skills/Secretarial **355**
- **TITLE** Flexi-Sec: Secretarial Skill Modules
- **PLACE** Harlow College

Length 22 hours/module **Start** Flexible **Cost** £20/module
- **CONTACT** Client Adviser Team 01279 868000

- **SUBJECT** Preparatory **356**
- **TITLE** Access Planning Period
- **PLACE** Colchester Institute

Length 10 weeks **Start** January, April or at other times **Days** Part time, various days or evenings **Cost** Approx £65 (remission for those on qualifying benefits) **Entry Reqs** Age 21+ **Award** Credits from EOCF plus entry to Access Main Course **Creche** Playgroup
- **CONTACT** Cathy Cook 01206 718614/Clare Hawkins 01206 718000

- **SUBJECT** Preparatory 357
- **TITLE** Choices: a Programme for Adult Returners
- **PLACE** Harlow College

Length 10 weeks   **Start** September, January, April   **Days** Wed 9.15-12.30   **Cost** Free   **Entry Reqs** None   **Award** Progress to further/higher education   **Creche** Possible help with childcare
- **CONTACT** Client Adviser Team 01279 868000

- **SUBJECT** Preparatory 358
- **TITLE** New Directions
- **PLACE** Harlow College

Length 8 weeks   **Start** September, January, April   **Days** Wed 9.30-12.45   **Cost** £20   **Entry Reqs** None
- **CONTACT** Client Adviser Team 01279 868000

- **SUBJECT** Preparatory 359
- **TITLE** Wider Opportunities for Women
- **PLACE** Adult Community College, Colchester

Length 10 weeks   **Start** September, January   **Days** Wed-Thurs   **Cost** £42/half term   **Entry Reqs** None   **Creche** Yes £2.80 session
- **CONTACT** Administration Office 01206 42242

- **SUBJECT** Preparatory 360
- **TITLE** Work Preparation
- **PLACE** Adult Community College, Colchester

Length 10 weeks   **Start** October   **Days** Mon & Fri   **Cost** £4   **Entry Reqs** None   **Creche** Yes £2.80 session
- **CONTACT** Administration Office 01206 42242

- **SUBJECT** Travel & Tourism 361
- **TITLE** Gateway to a Career in Travel & Tourism
- **PLACE** Thurrock College

Length 36 weeks   **Start** September   **Days** Mon-Fri 9.30-4.45 or part time   **Cost** Contact College   **Entry Reqs** 19+, by interview   **Award** ABTA/Travel Training Co.   **Creche** Playgroup £5/day
- **CONTACT** Kathy Regan 01708 863011

COUNTY CONTACTS

Information and advice:

Braintree College, Church Lane, Bocking, Braintree CM7 5SN 01376 321711   *Contact:* Sally Breen. Education advice and guidance
Castle Point and Rochford Adult Community College, Rochford Centre, Rocheway, Rochford SS4 1DQ 01702 544900. Adult education provision at Benfleet, Canvey, Hadleigh, Hockley, Rayleigh and Rochford
Client Adviser Team, Harlow College, West Site, The High, Harlow CM20 1LT 01279 868000   *Contact:* Dee Clarke
Educational and Careers Guidance Service, Anglia Polytechnic University, Victoria Road South, Chelmsford CM1 1LL 01245 493131 x3298 or Brentwood 01277 264504   *Contact:* Joan Boyton/ Barry Buckton. Pre-entry advice and guidance to mature applicants to Higher Education

National Association for Educational Guidance for Adults, Regional representative, Anglia University Student Services, Victoria Road, Chelmsford CM1 1LL 01245 493131 x3298/9 *Contact:* Joan Boyton. Covers London region
South East Essex College, Carnarvon Road, Southend on Sea SS2 6LS 01702 220400   *Contact:* Student Services

Open University :

The Open University East Anglia Region, 12 Hills Road, Cambridge CB2 1PF 01223 61650

Other agencies:

Returners' Unit, Chelmsford College of Further Education, Moulsham Street, Chelmsford CM2 0JQ 01245 494472   *Contact:* Joy Macmillan

Training and Enterprise Council:

Essex TEC, Redwing House, Hedgerows Business Park, Colchester Road, Chelmsford CM2 5PB 01245 450123. After School Care Project, setting up 15 schemes, joint funded; Essex Returners' Unit - a decision and policy making unit, co-ordinating and advising employers and returners throughout Essex

WEA offices:

WEA Eastern District, Botolph House, 17 Botolph Lane, Cambridge CB2 3RE 01223 350978 *Contact:* Sue Young. Covers north Essex
WEA London District, 44 Crowndale Road, London NW1 1TR 0171 388 7261   *Contact:* Ann Deutch. Covers south Essex

GLOUCESTERSHIRE

COURSES

● **SUBJECT**	Access/Arts/Humanities/Management/Social Work/Teaching	**362**
● **TITLE**	Access to Art, Education, Humanities, Management and Social Work	
● **PLACE**	Stroud College	

Length 1 year   **Start** September   **Days** Full time   **Cost** Contact College   **Entry Reqs** Age 21+   **Award** Access to higher education   **Creche** Yes
- ● **CONTACT**   1. Art Colin Gerard 01453 762524/2. Other subjects Rosemary Coop 01453 763424

● **SUBJECT**	Access/Science/Social Science/Arts/Business	**363**
● **TITLE**	Access to Higher Education	
● **PLACE**	Cirencester College, Fossway Campus, Stroud Road, Cirencester	

Length 1 or 2 years   **Start** September   **Cost** Contact College   **Entry Reqs** None   **Award** Entry to higher education   **Creche** Yes £7/session (Concessions available)
- ● **CONTACT**   Christine Peacock 01285 640994

- **SUBJECT** Care Studies 364
- **TITLE** BTEC Higher & National Certificate in Caring Services
- **PLACE** Cheltenham & Gloucester College of Higher Education, Park Campus

Length 2-5 years, day release basis **Start** September **Days** Thurs (1996 registration) **Cost** £120/module, £1175 full programme, £72 BTEC registration **Entry Reqs** In paid or voluntary caring work 2 days/week. Over 21 no formal qualifications **Award** BTEC HNC Caring Services **Creche** Yes & playgroup
- **CONTACT** Gwen Chaney 01242 543242/Penny Taylor 01242 532995

- **SUBJECT** Information Technology 365
- **TITLE** Women into Technology
- **PLACE** Royal Forest of Dean College, Five Acres Campus

Length 12 weeks **Start** September, January, April **Days** Tues, Wed, Thurs 9.00-4.30 **Cost** Free plus assistance with travel costs **Entry Reqs** Age 25+, unemployed and unwaged 12 months+. Interview **Award** RSA CLAIT **Creche** Yes Free
- **CONTACT** Mary Jones 01594 833416

- **SUBJECT** Management 366
- **TITLE** Professional Qualifications in Management
- **PLACE** Cheltenham & Gloucester College of Higher Education

Length Various, part time **Start** September/October **Days** Various **Cost** Contact College **Award** Professional awards in Personnel Management, Marketing, Accounting, Purchasing **Creche** No
- **CONTACT** Course Administrator 01242 543205

- **SUBJECT** Management 367
- **TITLE** Women into Management
- **PLACE** Royal Forest of Dean College, Five Acres Campus

Length 1 year **Start** September **Days** Tues, Wed, Thurs 9.00-4.30 **Cost** Free **Entry Reqs** Age 25+, unemployed and unwaged 12 months+. Interview **Award** BTEC Continuing Education Units **Creche** Yes Free
- **CONTACT** Mrs K Mills 01594 833416

- **SUBJECT** Marketing 368
- **TITLE** CIM Certificate, Advanced Certificate, Diploma
- **PLACE** Cheltenham & Gloucester College of Higher Education, Park Campus

Length 3 terms at each level **Start** September **Days** Tues & Wed 6.15-9.15 **Cost** Certificate £80/module, Diploma £120-£240/module **Entry Reqs** Contact College **Award** Chartered Institute of Management Certificate, Advanced Certificate, Diploma **Creche** No
- **CONTACT** Derek Pitts 01242 543254

- **SUBJECT** Multi-Subject 369
- **TITLE** BA, BSc, BEd (Hons) Degree, Diploma, Certificate: Undergraduate Modular Scheme
- **PLACE** Cheltenham & Gloucester College of Higher Education

Length Full time 3/2/1 year, part time available **Start** September (ft), September/Feb (pt) **Days** Mon-Fri 9.15-5.15 **Cost** £2500/full honours degree. Payments can be made monthly **Award** Degree/diploma/certificate **Creche** Possibly, contact creche 01242 532856
- **CONTACT** Schools Liaison Officer 01242 532825

- **SUBJECT** NOW 370
- **TITLE** New Opportunities for Women
- **PLACE** Cirencester College & community locations

Length 12 sessions **Start** September, January, April **Days** Daytime or evening depending on venue **Cost** Contact College **Entry Reqs** None **Creche** Yes, cost varies according to venue
- **CONTACT** Lois Thorn 01285 640994

- **SUBJECT** Office Skills 371
- **TITLE** Personal Assistants' Course
- **PLACE** Stroud College

Length 1 year+ **Start** September **Cost** Contact College **Entry Reqs** Mature students with previous experience **Award** RSA Higher Diploma in Administrative Procedures **Creche** Yes
- **CONTACT** Christine Hart/Christine Mauler 01453 763424

- **SUBJECT** Preparatory 372
- **TITLE** Preparing for Higher Education
- **PLACE** Cheltenham & Gloucester College of Higher Education

Length 20 hours **Start** April **Days** Thurs 7.15-9.15 for 10 weeks or 1 week block (daytime) in July **Cost** £48 (£24 concessionary rate) **Entry Reqs** None **Award** None **Creche** No
- **CONTACT** Ann Bullers 01242 532958

- **SUBJECT** Preparatory 373
- **TITLE** Women Returners: Preparatory/Exploratory Course
- **PLACE** Stroud College, Dursley & Highwood Education Centres

Length 10 weeks **Start** September, January, April **Days** 1 day/week, hours to fit in with school hours **Cost** £33.80, free if on benefit or low income (funding from Stroud District Council) **Entry Reqs** Women 21+ **Creche** Yes £2.50/session (approx)
- **CONTACT** Mary Moore 01453 763424

- **SUBJECT** Preparatory 374
- **TITLE** Work Link (targets women, includes men)
- **PLACE** Stroud College, Dursley Education Centre

Length 12/24/36 weeks **Start** September, January, April **Days** Mon-Fri (pick and mix subjects), flexible hours to fit in with school hours **Cost** £17.33/2-hour module + registration. Free if on benefit **Entry Reqs** Adults only **Award** Exams where appropriate **Creche** Yes £2.50/session (approx)
- **CONTACT** Rosemary Coop 01453 761175

- **SUBJECT** Secretarial 375
- **TITLE** Intensive Secretarial Course
- **PLACE** Stroud College

Length 1 term **Start** September, January, April **Cost** Contact College **Entry Reqs** Contact College. Suitable for adult returners **Award** RSA exams, Teeline Shorthand exams **Creche** Yes
- **CONTACT** Jeannette Glastonbury 01453 763424

- **SUBJECT** Teaching 376
- **TITLE** MEd, MPhil, Certificate, Advanced Diploma, Short Courses for Returners to Teaching
- **PLACE** Cheltenham & Gloucester College of Higher Education

Length Part time, varies, 2-5 years, or short courses **Start** September **Days** Varies **Entry Req** QTS or teaching experience **Award** Masters, Degree, Certificate, Advanced Diploma in Education **Creche** Yes Contact College
- **CONTACT** Angela Hodgkinson 01242 532898

COUNTY CONTACTS

Information and advice:

Adult Guidance Service, Cirencester College, Fosseway Campus, Stroud Road, Cirencester GL7 1XA 01285 640994 *Contact:* Liza Howes, Penny Smith

Gloscat Guidance Service (Gloucester College of Arts & Technology), Brunswick Campus, Brunswick Road, Gloucester GL1 1HU 01452 426529 *Contact:* Glyn Holloway. Free educational guidance service

Gloscat Guidance Service (Gloucester College of Arts & Technology), Park Campus, The Park, Cheltenham GL50 2RR 01242 532415 *Contact:* Anne Clement. Free educational guidance service

Guidelines, Royal Forest of Dean College, Five Acres Campus, Berry Hill, Coleford GL16 7JT 01594 822191. Adult guidance service

Stroud College, The British School, Slad Road, Stroud GL5 1QW 01453 751408. Adult guidance service

Pathfinder Trust Ltd: Careers and Guidance Service HQ, 92-96 Westgate Street, Gloucester GL1 2PE 01452 425421

Pathfinder Trust Ltd: Cheltenham and North Gloucestershire, County Offices, St George's Road, Cheltenham GL50 3EW 01242 532350

Pathfinder Trust Ltd: Gloucester and Forest of Dean, 92 Westgate Street, Gloucester GL1 2PE 01452 426900

Pathfinder Trust Ltd: Stroud and South Gloucestershire, 9 John Street, Stroud GL5 2HA 01453 757133/758588

Open University:

The Open University South West Region, 4 Portwall Lane, Bristol BS1 6ND 0117 925 6523

Training and Enterprise Council:

Gloucestershire TEC, Conway House, Worcester Street, Gloucester GL1 3AJ 01452 524488 *Contact:* Freephone Guidance Helpline 0800 220262 ask for Angie. Individual training grants for unemployed people; Training for Work; Springboard Initiative

WEA office:

WEA Western District, 40 Morse Road, Redfield, Bristol BS5 9LB 0117 935 1764 *Contact:* Mavis Zutchi, Kath Ryder

GREATER MANCHESTER

COURSES

- **SUBJECT** Access   377
- **TITLE** Access to Higher Education
- **PLACE** Tameside College of Technology

Length Usually 1 year   **Start** September   **Days** Mon-Fri during school hours   **Cost** Contact College   **Entry Reqs** Contact College   **Award** Access to higher education   **Creche** Yes

- **CONTACT** Course Enquiry Service 0161 330 6911

- **SUBJECT**   Access   **378**
- **TITLE**   Access to Higher Education
- **PLACE**   Manchester College of Arts & Technology, Moston & City Centre Campuses

Length 1 or 2 years   **Start** September   **Days** 5 days/week or 2 eves/week   **Cost** Costs vary. Fees may be remitted or grants available   **Entry Reqs** No formal requirements   **Award** Exams at MOCF Level 4, GCSE English & Maths, Computing & Statistics   **Creche** Yes Limited Places

- **CONTACT**   Mel Smith/Margaret Sherwood 0161 953 4290

- **SUBJECT**   Access   **379**
- **TITLE**   Pathway (Level 1/2 Access Course)
- **PLACE**   City College, Manchester, Arden Centre

Length 1 year or 2 years part time   **Start** September   **Days** 3 halfdays/week 10.00-3.00   **Cost** Varies, many concessions   **Entry Reqs** None   **Award** MOCF Levels 1 & 2   **Creche** Yes (6 mnths-5 yrs) Limited spaces £1/session

- **CONTACT**   Eddie Little 0161 957 1767/Dorothy Shelston 0161 957 1546

- **SUBJECT**   Access/Community Studies/Science/Humanities/Tourism & Leisure/   **380** Performing Arts
- **TITLE**   Access: Community Studies, Science & Humanities, Tourism & Leisure, Performing Arts
- **PLACE**   Bolton College

Length 1 year   **Start** September   **Days** Varies   **Cost** Contact College   **Entry Reqs** Open access   **Award** Manchester Open College Federation   **Creche** Yes

- **CONTACT**   Course Enquiries 01204 31411

- **SUBJECT**   Access/Information Technology/Engineering/Cultural Studies/Marketing   **381**
- **TITLE**   Access to IT, Engineering & Technology, Cultural Studies, Marketing
- **PLACE**   Bolton College

Length 1 year   **Start** September   **Days** Varies   **Cost** Contact College   **Entry Reqs** Open access   **Award** Manchester Open College Federation   **Creche** Yes

- **CONTACT**   Course Enquiries 01204 31411

- **SUBJECT**   Access/Science   **382**
- **TITLE**   Access into Science
- **PLACE**   Tameside College of Technology

Length 1 year   **Start** September, but can be joined anytime   **Days** Wed 6.30-8.30   **Cost** Contact College   **Entry Reqs** Contact College   **Award** Access to higher education

- **CONTACT**   Course Enquiry Service 0161 330 6911

- **SUBJECT**   Access/Social Science/Humanities   **383**
- **TITLE**   Gateway
- **PLACE**   City College, Manchester

Length 1 year   **Start** September   **Days** 5 days/week 9.15-3.00   **Entry Req** None   **Award** MOCF Level 2, MOCF Validation   **Creche** Yes (6 mnths-5 yrs) Limited spaces £1/session

- **CONTACT**   Mike Taylor 0161 957 1764

- **SUBJECT**   Accounting   **384**
- **TITLE**   Accountancy (Association of Accounting Technicians)
- **PLACE**   Hopwood Hall College

Length Flexible   **Days** Flexible learning   **Cost** Contact College   **Entry Reqs** None, interview and guidance report   **Award** AAT Foundation/Intermediate/Technician

- **CONTACT**   Jeffrey Horner 0161 643 7650 x266

- **SUBJECT**   Accounting   385
- **TITLE**   Accounting
- **PLACE**   Stockport College of Further and Higher Education

Length 1 year   **Start** Flexible   **Cost** Contact College   **Entry Reqs** None   **Award** RSA Stage II, progress to further accounting courses
- **CONTACT**   Flexible Learning Centre 0161 958 3366

- **SUBJECT**   Biological Sciences   386
- **TITLE**   Biological Sciences: Masters Degree by Research
- **PLACE**   University of Manchester

Length 1 year   **Start** October   **Cost** Biotechnology & Biological Sciences Research Council award available   **Entry Reqs** Graduates with first or upper second honours degree in an appropriate subject   **Award** MSc
- **CONTACT**   Dr V Essex, BBSRC, 01793 413200

- **SUBJECT**   Biological Sciences/Medicine   387
- **TITLE**   Biological Sciences and Medicine: Research Masters Pilot Course
- **PLACE**   University of Manchester

Length 1 year   **Start** October   **Cost** Medical Research Council award available   **Entry Reqs** Graduates with first or upper second honours degree in an appropriate subject   **Award** MSc
- **CONTACT**   Professor R Balment 0161 275 5608

- **SUBJECT**   Business   388
- **TITLE**   Business and Finance
- **PLACE**   Tameside College of Technology

Length 1 year   **Start** September   **Cost** Contact College   **Entry Reqs** Contact College   **Award** BTEC GNVQ Intermediate Business and Finance   **Creche** Yes
- **CONTACT**   Course Enquiry Service 0161 330 6911

- **SUBJECT**   Business Administration   389
- **TITLE**   Marketing, Export, Bookkeeping, Customer Service, Supervisory Management
- **PLACE**   Stockport College of F&HE, Flexible Learning Centre

Length Flexible   **Start** Various   **Cost** Variable Contact College   **Entry Reqs** Various. All students must have an advice session before enrolment   **Award** Various
- **CONTACT**   Chris Marsden 0161 958 3366

- **SUBJECT**   Computing   390
- **TITLE**   Women and Computing
- **PLACE**   Tameside College of Technology

Length 1 year   **Start** September   **Days** Daytime, within school hours   **Cost** Contact College   **Entry Reqs** Contact College   **Creche** Yes
- **CONTACT**   Course Enquiry Service 0161 330 6911

- **SUBJECT**   Design   391
- **TITLE**   Women and Computer Aided Draughting
- **PLACE**   Tameside College of Technology

Length 1 year   **Start** September   **Days** Thurs 9.30-12.30 or 6.30-9.00   **Cost** Contact College   **Entry Reqs** Contact College   **Creche** Yes
- **CONTACT**   Course Enquiry Service 0161 330 6911

- **SUBJECT**   Economics   392
- **TITLE**   BA(Hons) Economics
- **PLACE**   Manchester Metropolitan University, Mabel Tylecote Building, All Saints

Length 5 years   **Start** September   **Days** Daytime attendance, days dependent on units selected. Average 10 hours/week   **Cost** Approx £450/year   **Entry Reqs** Standard or non-standard entry   **Award** BA(Hons) Economics   **Creche** Very limited places, approx £10/day
- **CONTACT**   Helen Dawson 0161 247 3888

- **SUBJECT** Education 393
- **TITLE** BA (Hons) Professional Studies (Learning Difficulties)
- **PLACE** Stockport College of Further and Higher Education

Length 3 years, full time **Start** September **Days** 3 days/week 9.30-4.30; 5 day full time placements in first 2 years **Cost** Mandatory award **Entry Reqs** College entrance test for mature applicants **Award** BA Honours Classified Degree of the University of Manchester **Creche** Yes

- **CONTACT** Course Secretary 0161 958 3484/Course Team 0161 958 3487

- **SUBJECT** Engineering 394
- **TITLE** Computational and Experimental Fluids Engineering: Research Masters Pilot Course
- **PLACE** University of Manchester Institute of Science and Technology

Length 2 years **Start** October **Cost** Engineering & Physical Sciences Research Council award available **Entry Reqs** Graduates with first or upper second honours degree in an appropriate subject **Award** Master of Research Degree

- **CONTACT** Professor M Leschziner 0161 200 3704

- **SUBJECT** Engineering/Science 395
- **TITLE** Surface and Interface Science and Engineering: Pilot Masters Research Course
- **PLACE** University of Manchester

Length 2 years **Start** October **Cost** Engineering & Physical Sciences Research Council award available **Entry Reqs** Graduates with first or upper second honours degree in an appropriate subject **Award** Master of Research Degree

- **CONTACT** Professor R Grice 0161 275 4653

- **SUBJECT** English 396
- **TITLE** MA Critical Theory
- **PLACE** Manchester Metropolitan University, All Saints Campus

Length 2 years **Start** September **Days** 1 eve/week 6.00-9.00 **Cost** Approx £130/year **Entry Reqs** Appropriate Honours Degree **Award** MA Critical Theory **Creche** Yes

- **CONTACT** Linda Irish 0161 247 1728

- **SUBJECT** Health Studies 397
- **TITLE** Health and Social Care
- **PLACE** Manchester College of Arts & Technology, Moston Campus

Length 2 year part time **Start** February **Days** Variable **Cost** Costs vary. Fees may be remitted **Entry Reqs** No formal requirements **Award** GNVQ Intermediate or Advanced **Creche** Yes Limited places

- **CONTACT** Leone Dunk 0161 953 4290

- **SUBJECT** History 398
- **TITLE** MA History of the Manchester Region
- **PLACE** Manchester Metropolitan University, Mabel Tylecote Building, All Saints

Length 3 years **Start** September **Days** Tues eves (normally) 6.00-9.00 **Cost** Approx £130/year **Entry Reqs** Background in historical studies, degree or non-standard entry **Award** MA/Postgrad Diploma History of the Manchester Region **Creche** No

- **CONTACT** Helen Dawson 0161 247 3888

- **SUBJECT** Information Technology 399
- **TITLE** Information Technology Workshops
- **PLACE** Stockport College of F&HE, Flexible Learning Centre

Length Flexible **Start** Every month except August **Days** Students can choose how quickly/slowly they use up their sessions **Cost** £36/12x2-hr sessions, £24/subsequent 12 sessions. Free for students on benefits. **Entry Reqs** None **Award** Cambridge Certificate in IT, RSA CLAIT, NVQ

- **CONTACT** Chris Marsden 0161 958 3366

- **SUBJECT** Law   **400**
- **TITLE** Women's Refresher Course
- **PLACE** Manchester Metropolitan University, School of Law

Length Contact College   **Start** Contact College   **Cost** Contact College   **Entry Reqs** None **Award** None   **Creche** No

- **CONTACT** Ms D Hughes 0161 247 3062/3076

- **SUBJECT** Library & Information Management   **401**
- **TITLE** BA/BSc (Hons) Information and Library Management
- **PLACE** Manchester Metropolitan University

Length 6 years   **Start** September   **Days** 1 day/week   **Cost** Contact University   **Entry Reqs** Contact University   **Award** BA/BSc (Hons) Information and Library Management   **Creche** Yes

- **CONTACT** Dept of Library & Information Studies 0161 247 6146

- **SUBJECT** Library & Information Management   **402**
- **TITLE** 1. MA Information and Library Studies 2. MSc Information Management
- **PLACE** Manchester Metropolitan University

Length 1.3 years 2.7 terms   **Start** September   **Days** 1 day/week   **Cost** 1. Approx £400/year 2. Approx £450/year   **Entry Reqs** 1. Degree in any subject & at least 6 months experience in library/information work 2. Degree or equiv   **Award** 1. MA/PgDip Information and Library Studies 2. MSc/PgDip Information Management   **Creche** Yes

- **CONTACT** Dept of Library & Information Studies 0161 247 6146

- **SUBJECT** Management   **403**
- **TITLE** Supervisory Skills
- **PLACE** Hopwood Hall College

Length Flexible   **Days** Flexible learning   **Cost** Contact College   **Entry Reqs** None   **Award** NEBSM Introductory Award/NEBSM Certificate

- **CONTACT** Jeffrey Horner 0161 643 7650 x266

- **SUBJECT** Multi-Subject   **404**
- **TITLE** BA(Hons) Humanities/Social Studies
- **PLACE** Manchester Metropolitan University, All Saints Campus

Length 5 years   **Start** September   **Days** 2 eves/week or day/eve attendance averaging 6 hours/week   **Cost** Approx £270/year   **Entry Reqs** None, though most students will have some GCSEs or A Levels   **Award** BA(Hons) Humanities/Social Studies   **Creche** Limited places Approx £10/day (daytime only)

- **CONTACT** Linda Irish 0161 247 1728

- **SUBJECT** Multi-Subject   **405**
- **TITLE** BA(Hons) Independent Study
- **PLACE** Manchester Metropolitan University

Length 5-6 years   **Days** Variable   **Entry Req** Contact University   **Award** BA(Hons) Independent Study

- **CONTACT** Dept of Sociology & Interdisciplinary Studies 0161 247 3026

- **SUBJECT** Multi-Subject   **406**
- **TITLE** BA(Hons) Modern Studies
- **PLACE** Manchester Metropolitan University, All Saints Campus

Length 2 years   **Start** September   **Days** Day or day/eve attendance averaging 6 hours/week   **Cost** Approx £270/year   **Entry Reqs** Diploma of Higher Education, or OU Credits, etc   **Award** BA(Hons) Modern Studies   **Creche** Limited places Approx £10/day (daytime only)

- **CONTACT** Linda Irish 0161 247 1728

- **SUBJECT** Multi-Subject   407
- **TITLE** Diploma of Higher Education
- **PLACE** Manchester Metropolitan University

Length 5 years maximum to complete 2 stages of 120 credits each   **Start** September   **Days** Variable, daytime attendance   **Cost** Variable, approx £90/unit 2 hours/week study   **Entry Reqs** Contact University. Mature applicants welcome   **Award** Diploma of HE, access to final year of a first degree course   **Creche** Limited places Approx £10/day (daytime only)

- **CONTACT** Dept of Sociology & Interdisciplinary Studies 0161 247 3026

- **SUBJECT** Multi-Subject   408
- **TITLE** Open Learning Courses
- **PLACE** Stockport College of F&HE, Flexible Learning Centre

Length Negotiable, minimum 12 weeks   **Start** Every month except August   **Days** Supported self-study courses, tutorials once a month by arrangement   **Cost** Variable   **Entry Reqs** None **Award** A Level, RSA, NVQ etc   **Creche** Yes

- **CONTACT** J Robinson 0161 958 3366

- **SUBJECT** Office Skills   409
- **TITLE** Office Skills Workshop
- **PLACE** Stockport College of F&HE, Flexible Learning Centre

Length Flexible   **Start** Every month except August   **Days** Students can choose how quickly/slowly they use up their sessions   **Cost** £36/12x2-hr sessions, £24/subsequent 12 sessions. Free for students on benefits.   **Entry Reqs** Basic typing skills required for wordprocessing   **Award** RSA exams (all levels)

- **CONTACT** Chris Marsden 0161 958 3366

- **SUBJECT** Preparatory   410
- **TITLE** Adult Basic Education: Maths, English, Basic Computer Skills
- **PLACE** Stockport College of F&HE, Open Learning Workshop

Length Flexible   **Start** Every month except August   **Days** Mon-Thurs 9.30-3.00, Mon+Wed 5.00-8.00, closed Friday   **Cost** None   **Entry Reqs** None   **Award** Entry to other pre GCSE, RSA etc courses   **Creche** Yes

- **CONTACT** Liz Money 0161 958 3122/3133

- **SUBJECT** Preparatory   411
- **TITLE** Adult Returners' Workshop
- **PLACE** Tameside College of Technology

Start Join anytime   **Days** Flexible   **Cost** Free   **Entry Reqs** None   **Creche** Yes

- **CONTACT** Course Enquiry Service 0161 330 6911

- **SUBJECT** Preparatory   412
- **TITLE** Flying Start
- **PLACE** Manchester College of Arts & Technology, Moston & City Centre Campuses

Length 1 term or less   **Start** January, May   **Days** Variable   **Cost** Costs vary. Fees may be remitted   **Entry Reqs** No formal requirements   **Award** Open University Credits, GMOCF qualifications   **Creche** Yes Limited places

- **CONTACT** Shirley Hindley 0161 953 4290

- **SUBJECT** Preparatory   413
- **TITLE** Make Your Experience Count
- **PLACE** Birtles Adult Education Centre, Wythenshawe

Days Tues 10.00-12.00   **Award** Manchester Open College Federation Certificate

- **CONTACT** Birtles Centre 0161 499 1455

- **SUBJECT** Preparatory   **414**
- **TITLE** Make Your Experience Count
- **PLACE** Tameside College of Technology

Length 10 weeks   **Days** Mon 1.00-3.00   **Cost** Free   **Entry Reqs** None   **Creche** Yes

- **CONTACT** Course Enquiry Service 0161 330 6911

- **SUBJECT** Preparatory   **415**
- **TITLE** New Training Opportunities for Women
- **PLACE** Tameside College of Technology

Length 24 weeks   **Days** Wed 9.30-2.30 or Thurs 9.30-3.00   **Cost** £5   **Entry Reqs** None **Creche** Yes

- **CONTACT** Course Enquiry Service 0161 330 6911

- **SUBJECT** Preparatory   **416**
- **TITLE** PACE: Progress and Access to College and Education
- **PLACE** Birtles Adult Education Centre, Wythenshawe

Start September   **Days** 15 hours/week   **Award** RSA Maths, English, CLAIT

- **CONTACT** Martin/Estelle 0161 499 1455

- **SUBJECT** Preparatory   **417**
- **TITLE** Pathfinder: Optional Subjects, Counselling and Careers Guidance
- **PLACE** Manchester College of Arts & Technology, Moston & City Centre Campuses

Length 1 or 2 years   **Start** September   **Days** 5 days/week 9.30-3.00 for all units (fewer can be studied)   **Cost** Costs vary. Fees may be remitted or grants available   **Entry Reqs** No formal qualifications   **Award** GCSE, MOCF Level 2 or 3, or College Certificate   **Creche** Yes Limited places

- **CONTACT** Ms Shirley Hindley 0161 953 4290

- **SUBJECT** Preparatory   **418**
- **TITLE** Return to Learning for Women
- **PLACE** City College, Manchester, Arden Centre

Length 10 weeks   **Start** January, April   **Days** 1 day/week 10.00-3.00   **Cost** Free to those on Income Support & other benefits, £28 otherwise   **Entry Reqs** None   **Award** MOCF Level I **Creche** Yes (6 mnths-5 yrs) Limited spaces £1/session

- **CONTACT** Dorothy Shelston 0161 957 1546

- **SUBJECT** Preparatory   **419**
- **TITLE** Return to Work: Learn New Technology or Update Existing Skills
- **PLACE** Tameside College of Technology

Length 30 weeks   **Start** September   **Days** Mon-Thurs 9.00-2.00   **Cost** Contact College **Entry Reqs** Contact College   **Creche** Yes

- **CONTACT** Course Enquiry Service 0161 330 6911

- **SUBJECT** Professional Updating   **420**
- **TITLE** Professional Updating for Women
- **PLACE** Manchester Metropolitan University

Length 15 weeks   **Start** September, Spring   **Days** Mon-Fri 10.00-12.00 & 1.00-3.00   **Cost** No fees (ESF funded) Travel expenses & some childcare paid   **Entry Reqs** Degree or equivalent professional qualification. Unemployed for at least 12 months   **Creche** No

- **CONTACT** Mary Taylor 0161 247 3857

- **SUBJECT** Public Administration 421
- **TITLE** BA(Hons) Public Administration
- **PLACE** Manchester Metropolitan University, All Saints Campus

Length 3 to 5 years **Start** September **Days** 1 day/eve week **Cost** Approx £270/year **Entry Reqs** Varies: standard entry or appropriate work experience **Award** BA(Hons) Public Administration **Creche** Limited places Approx £10/day (daytime only)

- **CONTACT** Carole Burns 0161 247 3436

- **SUBJECT** Science 422
- **TITLE** Molecular Engineering: Research Masters Pilot Course
- **PLACE** University of Manchester

Length 2 years **Start** October **Cost** Engineering & Physical Sciences Research Council award available **Entry Reqs** Graduates with first or upper second honours degree in an appropriate subject **Award** Master of Research Degree

- **CONTACT** Dr PM Budd 0161 275 4706

- **SUBJECT** Science 423
- **TITLE** Informatics: Research Masters Pilot Course
- **PLACE** University of Manchester

Length 2 years **Start** October **Cost** Engineering & Physical Sciences Research Council award available **Entry Reqs** Graduates with first or upper second honours degree in an appropriate subject **Award** Master of Research Degree

- **CONTACT** Professor DS Bree 0161 275 6180

- **SUBJECT** Social Science 424
- **TITLE** BA (Hons) Social Science
- **PLACE** Manchester Metropolitan University

Length 6 years **Start** September **Days** 2 days/week or negotiable **Cost** Approx £270/year **Entry Reqs** Contact University **Award** BA (Hons) Social Science **Creche** Limited places Approx £10/day (daytime only)

- **CONTACT** Dept of Sociology & Interdisciplinary Studies 0161 247 3026

- **SUBJECT** Social Science 425
- **TITLE** Living in a Changing Society (Introduction to Social Sciences)
- **PLACE** Tameside College of Technology

Length 10 weeks/module **Days** Thurs 9.30-12.30 and/or 6.30-9.00 **Cost** Contact College **Entry Reqs** Contact College **Creche** Yes

- **CONTACT** Course Enquiry Service 0161 330 6911

- **SUBJECT** Teaching 426
- **TITLE** Certificate in TEFL (Teaching English as a Foreign Language)
- **PLACE** Manchester College of Arts & Technology, City Centre Campus

Length 25 weeks **Start** September/October **Days** Part time day or evening, 3 hours/week **Cost** Varies **Entry Reqs** Usually graduate entry but interest in TEFL more important than experience **Award** College Certificate **Creche** Yes Limited places

- **CONTACT** Judith Porter 0161 953 5995

- **SUBJECT** Technology 427
- **TITLE** Women into Technology
- **PLACE** Manchester Adult Education Service, various centres

Length 1 year **Start** September **Days** 6 hours/week, Wed **Cost** Free to women who are unemployed or in receipt of benefit **Award** Progression to Women's Access to Science & Technology course at University College Salford **Creche** Yes

- **CONTACT** Karmit Sidhu 0161 736 6541/Jane Ward 0161 226 0428

- **SUBJECT**   Women's Studies   **428**
- **TITLE**   Women's Studies
- **PLACE**   Manchester Metropolitan University, Mabel Tylecote Building, All Saints

Length Up to 4 years   **Start** September   **Days** Evenings (number dependent on how many units studied at any one time)   **Cost** Approx £450 for MA   **Entry Reqs** Hons Degree/Postgrad Dip or equiv professional qualification or approp prior experience   **Award** MA/Postgraduate Diploma Women's Studies   **Creche** No (for weekend day schools only)

- **CONTACT**   Linda Irish 0161 247 1728

COUNTY CONTACTS

Information and advice:

Adult Guidance Service, Oldham Careers Service, Brunswick House, Brunswick Square, Union Street, Oldham OL1 1DE 0161 911 4296   *Contact:* Elizabeth Ainley, Carol Dack

Adult Guidance Service, Rochdale Careers Service, c/o Rochdale TEC, St James Place, Yorkshire Street, Rochdale 01706 44909

Bolton Careers Service, PO Box 53, Paderborn House, Civic Centre, Bolton BL1 1JW 01204 22311 x2155

Bury Careers Service, Link House, 35 Walmersley Road, Bury BL9 5AE 0161 764 9904

Guidance Centre, Bolton College, Manchester Road, Bolton BL2 1ER 01204 365980   *Contact:* Margaret Boardman, Beverley Baker, Peter Sugden

Manchester Adult Education Service, Crown Square, Manchester M60 3BB 0161 234 7107   *Contact:* Dick Corbridge, Head of Services. Runs adult education facilities at 10 neighbourhood centres across Manchester

National Association for Educational Guidance for Adults, Regional representative, EPB (Wigan) Ltd, The Careers Service, Wigan Development Centre, Waterside Drive, Wigan WN3 5BA 01942 705705   *Contact:* Steve Burbage. Covers Lancashire, Merseyside, Manchester and Tameside regions

Outreach Guidance Service, Platt Bridge Community Enterprise Centre, John Tiernan House, 92-102 Ribble Road, Platt Bridge, Wigan WN2 5EL 01942 702121   *Contact:* Pam Potts

SETAS (Salford Education and Training Advice Service), Salford Opportunities Centre, 2 Paddington Close, Salford M6 5PL 0161 745 7233   *Contact:* Jane Barrett

Stepping Stones, Stockport 0161 958 3359   *Contact:* Sue Hasty. Return to learn/work advice and guidance

Stockport College Guidance and Assessment Services, Stockport 0161 958 3144

Stockport and High Peak Careers Guidance Services, Strathblane House, Ashfield Road, Cheadle SK8 1BB 0161 282 2220   *Contact:* Tony Brunner

Trafford Careers Service, Town Hall, Tatton Road, Sale M33 1YR 0161 872 2101 x3177

Women's Opportunities Centre, 101 Wellington Road North, Stockport SK1 2LP 0161 477 0824   *Contact:* Liz Cole. Career counselling for women

Open University:

The Open University, North West Region, Chorlton House, 70 Manchester Road, Chorlton cum Hardy, Manchester M21 9UN 0161 862 6824

Other agencies:

Bolton Institute, Deane Road, Bolton BL3 5AB 01204 528851 x3811   *Contact:* Pauline Ward, Linda Clayson (Access Officers). Taster courses for women returners, advice & guidance for entry to higher education, information about Access courses.

City College Manchester, Barlow Moor, West Didsbury, Manchester M20 8PQ 0161 957 1721

Greater Manchester Open College Federation, Sixth Floor, Manchester Metropolitan University, All Saints Building, Manchester M15 6BH 0161 228 0510   *Contact:* John Sanders

RVA-Opportunities for Women Ltd, Block B, Brunswick Square, Union Street, Oldham OL1 1DE 0161 628 9294. Delivers women returner training in conjunction with a variety of TECs. Also offers Women into Management and Springboard programmes for women returners and a range of personal development programmes for women.

Rochdale Asian Women's Training Project, 104-106 Drake Street, Rochdale OL16 1PQ 01706 40761. Asian women's training centre

Training and Enterprise Councils:

Bolton/Bury TEC, Clive House, Clive Street, Bolton BL1 1ET 01204 397350. Women Returners Project at Bury College; Two eight-week part time New Opportunities for Adults courses (majority being women); Ethnic Minorities Women into Management Project at Bolton Institute - 15 week course to achieve units in Management NVQs

METROTEC (Wigan) Ltd, Buckingham Row, Northway, Wigan WN1 1XX 01942 36312

Manchester TEC, Boulton House, 17-21 Chorlton Street, Manchester M1 3HY 0161 236 7222

Oldham TEC, Block D, 3rd Floor, Brunswick Square, Union Street, Oldham OL1 1DE 0161 628 9294   *Contact:* Janette Melia. Initiatives funded by Oldham TEC and ESF, delivered by RVA-Opportunities for Women Ltd: Opportunities for Women Centre offering guidance and information, Women into Work, Business Skills Update, Telework and Business Enterprise programmes; Mobile Resource Unit for women from the Asian communities of Oldham, offering information and guidance, a range of Work Awareness programmes, an Introduction to Childcare programme and a creche.

Rochdale TEC, St James Place, 160-162 Yorkshire Street, Rochdale OL16 2DL 01706 44909

Stockport and High Peak TEC, 1 St Peter's Square, Stockport SK1 1NN 0161 477 8830

WEA office:

WEA North Western District, 4th Floor, Crawford House, University Precinct Centre, Oxford Road, Manchester M13 9GH 0161 273 7652   *Contact:* Linda Pepper

---

HAMPSHIRE

COURSES

- **SUBJECT**   Access   **429**
- **TITLE**   Access:Adults' Pre-Degree Course
- **PLACE**   Farnborough College of Technology, Aldershot

Length 1 year full time, 2 years part time   **Start** September   **Days** Part time students infill full time timetable, Mon-Fri daytime   **Cost** £612, free if on benefits   **Entry Reqs** Age 21+   **Award** Access Certificate, entry to higher education   **Creche** Crche 6 mos-5 yrs £25 4dys/wk, Kindergarten £85/wk

- **CONTACT**   Information Centre 01252 391391

- **SUBJECT** Access   430
- **TITLE** Access to Higher Education
- **PLACE** Brockenhurst College

Length 1 year   **Start** September   **Days** Mon-Fri 9.30-3.00   **Cost** Contact College   **Entry Reqs** Age 21+   **Award** Access Certificate, entry to higher education   **Creche** Yes

- **CONTACT** Student Admissions 01590 623565

- **SUBJECT** Access   431
- **TITLE** Access to Higher Education
- **PLACE** Fareham College

Length 1 year   **Start** September   **Days** Mon-Fri   **Cost** Contact College   **Award** Wessex Access Federation Certificate   **Creche** Yes & playgroup

- **CONTACT** Angus Reid 01329 815357

- **SUBJECT** Access   432
- **TITLE** Access to Higher Education
- **PLACE** Highbury College

Length 1 year full time, 2-3 years part time   **Start** Autumn   **Days** 5 days/week 10.00-3.00 full time   **Cost** Discretionary grants available   **Entry Reqs** Interview   **Award** Access Certificate **Creche** Yes

- **CONTACT** Information Unit 01705 383131

- **SUBJECT** Access   433
- **TITLE** Access to Higher Education
- **PLACE** South Downs College

Length 1 year   **Start** September   **Days** Day or eve study possible   **Cost** Contact College **Entry Reqs** None   **Award** Kitemarked Access Certificate   **Creche** Yes and playgroup, daytime only

- **CONTACT** Access Co-ordinator 01705 257011

- **SUBJECT** Access/Business Studies   434
- **TITLE** Access to Higher Education: Business Studies
- **PLACE** Fareham College

Length 30 weeks   **Start** September   **Days** Tues, Wed, Thurs 9.15-3.15   **Cost** Free   **Award** College Certificate   **Creche** Yes

- **CONTACT** Tony Tetchner 01329 815235

- **SUBJECT** Access/Humanities/Health Studies/Social Studies   435
- **TITLE** Access to Higher Education 1. Humanities 2. Health and Social Studies
- **PLACE** Fareham College

Length 1 year   **Start** September   **Days** 1. Tues 6.30-9.30 2. Thurs 6.30-9.30   **Cost** Contact College   **Award** Wessex Access Federation Certificate

- **CONTACT** Angus Reid 01329 815357

- **SUBJECT** Access/Humanities/Social Science/Science   436
- **TITLE** Acess to Humanities, Social Science, Science
- **PLACE** Alton College

Length 1 year full time, 2 years part time   **Start** September   **Days** Modular course, day or evening study   **Cost** Contact College   **Entry Reqs** No formal entry qualifications   **Award** Kitemarked Access Certificate   **Creche** Yes Approx £1.50/hour

- **CONTACT** Access Co-ordinator 01420 88118

- **SUBJECT** Access/Humanities/Social Science/Science 437
- **TITLE** Acess to Humanities, Social Science, Science (Pre-Degree Course)
- **PLACE** Basingstoke College of Technology

Length 1 year full time, 2 years part time **Start** September **Days** Varies according to individual timetables **Cost** Full time free; part time fees waived if student is in receipt of benefit. **Entry Reqs** Interview **Award** Access Certificate from the University of Portsmouth **Creche** No

- **CONTACT** Christine Smart 01256 54141

- **SUBJECT** Administration 438
- **TITLE** Administration
- **PLACE** Basingstoke College of Technology

Length Flexible **Start** Anytime **Days** Mon-Fri between 9.00-5.00 **Cost** Free **Entry Reqs** Dependent on level studied **Award** NVQ Levels I, II, III or IV **Creche** No

- **CONTACT** Levels I-III Pamela Matthews/Level IV Gill Dunn 01256 54141

- **SUBJECT** Administration/Information Technology 439
- **TITLE** IT and Administration Short Course
- **PLACE** Basingstoke College of Technology

Length 10 weeks **Start** January, May, September **Days** 4 days/week 9.15-3.15 **Cost** Free **Entry Reqs** None **Award** RSA CLAIT Certificate **Creche** No

- **CONTACT** Carol Wilshaw 01256 54141 x249

- **SUBJECT** Administration/Secretarial 440
- **TITLE** Secretarial Day Study
- **PLACE** Fareham College

Length 30 weeks **Start** September **Days** Wed 9.00-5.30 **Cost** £80 **Entry Reqs** Discussion on course content and workload **Award** NVQ 2/3 Administration and RSA Certificates **Creche** Yes & playgroup

- **CONTACT** Vivian Stewart 01329 815277

- **SUBJECT** Antiques 441
- **TITLE** HND Antiques and Collections Management
- **PLACE** Farnborough College of Technology

Length 2 years full time (part time elements possible) **Start** September **Days** 19 hours/week daytime **Cost** Approx £1600/year full time (grants available) **Entry Reqs** 4 GCSEs + 1 or more A Levels; or commercial or craft practice **Award** BTEC Higher National Diploma **Creche** Kindergarten 2-5 years Approx £85/week

- **CONTACT** Information Centre 01252 391391

- **SUBJECT** Art & Design 442
- **TITLE** BTEC GNVQ Intermediate Art and Design
- **PLACE** Brockenhurst College

Length 1 year full time **Start** September **Cost** Contact College **Entry Reqs** Mature students considered individually (with portfolio) **Award** BTEC GNVQ Intermediate **Creche** Yes

- **CONTACT** Student Admissions 01590 623565

- **SUBJECT** Business 443
- **TITLE** Business for Adults
- **PLACE** Brockenhurst College

Length 1 year full time **Start** September **Days** 9.30-3.30 **Cost** LEA grants available **Entry Reqs** 21+, wishing to update or improve business skills **Award** BTEC GNVQ Advanced **Creche** Yes

- **CONTACT** Student Admissions 01590 623565

- **SUBJECT** Chemistry   444
- **TITLE** Chemistry: Research Masters Pilot Course
- **PLACE** University of Southampton

Length 2 years **Start** October **Cost** Engineering and Physical Sciences Research Council award available **Entry Reqs** Graduates with first or upper second class honours degree in an appropriate subject **Award** Master of Research Degree
- **CONTACT** Professor D Fletcher 01703 593519

- **SUBJECT** Childcare   445
- **TITLE** 1. NNEB Nursery Nursing 2. Childcare and Education
- **PLACE** Brockenhurst College

Length 1.2 years 2.1 year **Start** September **Days** Full time + placements **Cost** Contact College **Entry Reqs** Mature students considered individually **Award** 1. NNEB Diploma NVQ level III 2. NNEB Certificate NVQ level II **Creche** Yes
- **CONTACT** Student Admissions 01590 623565

- **SUBJECT** Construction   446
- **TITLE** Building Studies (Mature Entry)
- **PLACE** Southampton City College

Length 1 year **Start** September **Days** Tues+Wed 9.00-3.00, Thurs 9.00-4.00 **Cost** £440 **Entry Reqs** Contact College **Award** BTEC National Certificate **Creche** Yes
- **CONTACT** Information Officer 01703 635222 x253

- **SUBJECT** Counselling   447
- **TITLE** Counselling Skills and Theory
- **PLACE** Brockenhurst College

Length 1 year **Start** September **Days** Mon 1.00-3.00 **Cost** £57 **Entry Reqs** Contact College **Award** Open College Certificate **Creche** Yes
- **CONTACT** Student Admissions 01590 623565

- **SUBJECT** Design   448
- **TITLE** BTEC National Certificate/Higher National Certificate in Design (Graphics)
- **PLACE** Farnborough College of Technology

Length 2 years part time **Start** September **Days** 1 day + same evening **Cost** Contact College **Entry Reqs** Contact College. Includes interview & portfolio of work **Award** BTEC National Certificate or Higher National Certificate
- **CONTACT** Information Centre 01252 391391

- **SUBJECT** Desk Top Publishing   449
- **TITLE** RSA Desk Top Publishing
- **PLACE** Brockenhurst College

Length 15 or 16 weeks **Start** September, January, February **Days** Tues 10.00-1.00 (Jan) or Wed 9.30-12.00 (Sept/Feb) **Cost** Contact College **Entry Reqs** Contact College **Award** RSA NVQ Level II **Creche** Yes
- **CONTACT** Student Admissions 01590 623565

- **SUBJECT** Hairdressing   450
- **TITLE** Hairdressing for Mature Students
- **PLACE** Farnborough College of Technology, Farnborough

Length 1 year **Start** September **Days** Approx 20 hours/week daytime **Cost** Approx £618, free if on benefits **Entry Reqs** Age 20+ **Award** NVQ Level II Hairdressing (C&G 3010) **Creche** Kindergarten 2-5 years Approx £85/week
- **CONTACT** Information Centre 01252 391391

- **SUBJECT** Health Studies 451
- **TITLE** Preparation for Training for Health Service Careers
- **PLACE** Basingstoke College of Technology

Length 1 year **Start** September **Days** 6 hours/week Wed 12.15-3.15, Fri 9.30-11.00+11.30-1.00
Cost Approx £180 **Entry Reqs** Interview **Award** College Certificate **Creche** No

- **CONTACT** Pam Lonsdale 01256 54141 x342

- **SUBJECT** Information Technology 452
- **TITLE** Information Technology: a Practical Foundation Approach for Women
- **PLACE** Fareham College

Length 30 weeks **Start** September **Days** Mon+Thurs 1.15-3.15, 4 hours/week **Cost** Contact
College **Entry Reqs** None **Award** RSA Information Technology Certificates **Creche** Yes &
playgroup

- **CONTACT** Sue Gainford 01329 815226

- **SUBJECT** Information Technology 453
- **TITLE** Women into IT
- **PLACE** Fareham College

Length 30 weeks **Start** September **Days** Mon, Tues, Thurs 10.00-3.00, Fri 1.00-1.00 **Cost**
Contact College **Entry Reqs** Interview **Award** Various RSA Certificates & Access
Accreditation **Creche** Yes

- **CONTACT** Sue Gainford 01329 815226

- **SUBJECT** Information Technology 454
- **TITLE** Women into Information Technology
- **PLACE** Southampton City College & community venues

Length 18 weeks **Start** September, February **Days** Mon-Fri 10.00-3.00 **Cost** Free **Entry
Reqs** Contact College **Award** C&G 7261 NVQ Levels I/II **Creche** Yes

- **CONTACT** Information Officer 01703 635222 x253

- **SUBJECT** Interior Design 455
- **TITLE** Interior Design
- **PLACE** Southampton City College

Length 1 year **Start** September **Days** Tues 9.00-12.00 + 1.00-3.00 **Cost** £185 **Entry Reqs**
Contact College **Award** C&G 7900 **Creche** Yes

- **CONTACT** Information Officer 01703 635222 x253

- **SUBJECT** Management 456
- **TITLE** 1. Women into Management 2. Women into Management: Advanced Course
- **PLACE** Fareham College

Length 1.20 weeks 2.10 weeks **Start** 1. September 2. March **Days** 1. +2. Wed 6.00-8.00 **Cost**
1. £60 2. £30 **Entry Reqs** 1. Managers or those aspiring to be managers 2. Managers, those
completing first course **Award** College Certificate **Creche** No

- **CONTACT** 01329 815200

- **SUBJECT** NOW 457
- **TITLE** New Opportunities for Women
- **PLACE** Farnborough College of Technology, Aldershot

Length 10 weeks **Start** September, January, April **Days** 1 day (3 hours/week) **Cost** £12, free
if on benefit **Entry Reqs** None **Award** College Certificate, C&G Wordpower **Creche** Creche
6 mos-5 yrs £3/halfday

- **CONTACT** Chris Gilfoyle 01252 336090

- **SUBJECT** Office Skills   **458**
- **TITLE** Flexible Learning Centre for Office Skills
- **PLACE** Brockenhurst College, Adult Education Centre, New Milton

Length Flexible   **Start** Flexible   **Cost** Contact College   **Entry Reqs** None   **Award** RSA Wordprocessing, Spreadsheets, Databases or NVQ 2/3 Business Administration
- **CONTACT** Student Admissions 01590 623565

- **SUBJECT** Office Skills   **459**
- **TITLE** Flexible Office Skills including Software Applications
- **PLACE** Basingstoke College of Technology

Length Flexible   **Start** Flexible   **Days** Day or evening   **Cost** Contact College   **Entry Reqs** None   **Award** NVQ Levels I, II, III or IV   **Creche** No
- **CONTACT** Levels I-III Deirdre O'Rourke/Level IV Gill Dunn 01256 54141

- **SUBJECT** Office Skills   **460**
- **TITLE** Office and Word Processing Skills for Ethnic Minority Women
- **PLACE** Southampton City College

Length 12 weeks   **Days** Mon 1.00-3.00   **Cost** Free   **Entry Reqs** None   **Creche** Yes
- **CONTACT** Information Officer 01703 635222 x253

- **SUBJECT** Office Skills   **461**
- **TITLE** Word Processing, Shorthand & Options in DTP, Spreadsheets or Book-keeping
- **PLACE** Brockenhurst College

Length 20 weeks   **Start** September   **Days** Mon 1.00-3.00, Tues & Fri 9.30-12.30   **Cost** £152 **Entry Reqs** Contact College   **Creche** Yes
- **CONTACT** Student Admissions 01590 623565

- **SUBJECT** Preparatory   **462**
- **TITLE** Courses for Women Returners: Preparation for Work or Further Study (Part-Sponsored by Local Employers, Agencies & ESF)
- **PLACE** Cricklade College, Cricklade House

Length 10 weeks   **Start** September, January, April or May   **Days** 3 hours/week, Wed   **Cost** £2.50 session (concessions available)   **Entry Reqs** None   **Award** All elements accredited through Hampshire Open College Network   **Creche** Yes Tel: 01264 336310
- **CONTACT** Val Ryland/Jean Lannie 01264 334523

- **SUBJECT** Preparatory   **463**
- **TITLE** Get Qualified (Part-Sponsored by European Social Fund)
- **PLACE** Cricklade College, Cricklade House

Length 36 weeks   **Start** September   **Days** Flexible, negotiatied with tutor to suit individual needs   **Cost** Free if unemployed 12 mnths + some help with travel/childcare costs   **Entry Reqs** None. By interview   **Award** GCSE/A level/NVQ/C&G Diploma of Vocational Education **Creche** Yes Tel: 01264 336310
- **CONTACT** Isobel Johnston/Jean Lannie 01264 334523

- **SUBJECT** Preparatory   **464**
- **TITLE** Make Your Experience Count: a Course for Women
- **PLACE** Southampton City College

Length 10 weeks   **Start** September   **Days** Wed 7.00-9.00   **Cost** Free   **Entry Reqs** None
- **CONTACT** Information Officer 01703 635222 x253

- **SUBJECT** Preparatory   **465**
- **TITLE** Opening Doors: Second Chance for Women
- **PLACE** Southampton City College

Length 10 weeks   **Start** September, January   **Days** Wed 1.00-3.00   **Cost** Free   **Entry Reqs** None   **Creche** Yes
- **CONTACT** Information Officer 01703 635222 x253

Hampshire

- **SUBJECT** Preparatory — 466
- **TITLE** Return to Study
- **PLACE** Brockenhurst College
Length Various   **Days** Various   **Cost** Contact College   **Entry Reqs** None   **Award** Progress to further education   **Creche** Yes
- **CONTACT** Student Admissions 01590 623565

- **SUBJECT** Preparatory — 467
- **TITLE** Return to Study
- **PLACE** University of Southampton
Length 30 weeks   **Start** Various   **Days** 1 eve/week   **Cost** Contact University   **Entry Reqs** Contact University   **Award** None   **Creche** No
- **CONTACT** Dept of Adult & Continuing Education 01703 593649

- **SUBJECT** Preparatory — 468
- **TITLE** SuperWOW (Wider Opportunities for Women)
- **PLACE** Farnborough College of Technology, Aldershot
Length 1 year   **Start** September   **Days** 3 days/week (15 hours/week)   **Cost** £25/term, free if on benefits   **Entry Reqs** None   **Award** College Certificate, CLAIT, C&G Wordpower   **Creche** Yes approx £18 for 3 days/week
- **CONTACT** Chris Gilfoyle 01252 336090

- **SUBJECT** Preparatory — 469
- **TITLE** Wider Opportunities for Women
- **PLACE** Farnborough College of Technology, Aldershot
Length 1 year   **Start** September   **Days** 1 day (4 hours/week)   **Cost** £10/term, free if on benefit   **Entry Reqs** None   **Award** College Certificate, C&G Wordpower   **Creche** Crche 6 mos-5 yrs £6/day, Kindergarten £18/day
- **CONTACT** Chris Gilfoyle 01252 336090

- **SUBJECT** Preparatory — 470
- **TITLE** Wider Opportunities for Women
- **PLACE** Highbury College
Length 5 weeks   **Start** Various   **Days** 3 days/week 9.30-3.00   **Cost** Contact College, concessions possible   **Entry Reqs** Interview   **Creche** Yes
- **CONTACT** Information Unit 01705 383131

- **SUBJECT** Preparatory — 471
- **TITLE** Wider Opportunities for Women
- **PLACE** South Downs College
Length 12 weeks   **Start** September, January, April   **Days** 1 day/week   **Cost** Contact College   **Entry Reqs** None   **Award** Course Certificate   **Creche** Yes & playgroup
- **CONTACT** Course Information Unit 01705 257011

- **SUBJECT** Professional Updating — 472
- **TITLE** Professional Updating for Women
- **PLACE** Southampton City College
Length 3 months   **Start** January/April   **Days** 15 hours/week   **Cost** £115   **Entry Reqs** Contact College   **Award** Hampshire Open College Network Accreditation   **Creche** Yes
- **CONTACT** Information Officer 01703 635222 x253

- **SUBJECT** Secretarial — 473
- **TITLE** Intensive Secretarial
- **PLACE** Fareham College
Length 15 weeks   **Start** September   **Days** Mon, Tues, Wed, Thurs 9.15-3.15, Fri 9.15-2.15   **Cost** £303   **Entry Reqs** Discussion on course content and workload   **Award** RSA Certificates   **Creche** Yes & playgroup
- **CONTACT** Judith Oakes 01329 815275

- **SUBJECT**   Preparatory   684
- **TITLE**   Look Forward and Look Further
- **PLACE**   Cricklade College, Cricklade House

Length 10 weeks   **Start** September, January, April   **Days** Flexible, 15 hours/week   **Cost** Free   **Entry Reqs** None   **Award** Hampshire Open College Network Accreditation of all modules   **Creche** Yes Tel: 01264 336310

- **CONTACT**   Jean Lannie 01264 334523

COUNTY CONTACTS

Information and advice:

Eastleigh College, Chestnut Avenue, Eastleigh SO5 5HT 01703 326326   *Contact:* Sue Rogers. Guidance interviews to current full and part time students.
Guidelines Shop, 6 Hanover Buildings, Southampton SO14 1JW 01703 212141. Run by Hampshire TEC. Open days for women returners seeking advice on training and employment options
Hampshire Childcare Links, 27 Guildhall Walk, Portsmouth PO1 2RP 01705 669066. Helpline for parents on childcare options. 01345 581636 (local rates)
Hampshire Guidance and Careers Service, Aldershot Office. 01252 331107
Alton Office. 01420 83966
Andover Office. 01264 323271
Basingstoke Office. 01256 467666
Eastleigh Office. 01703 641655
Fareham Office. 01329 232918
Gosport Office. 01705 583115
Havant Office. 01705 484719
Portsmouth Office. 01705 756756
Southampton Office. 01703 235523
Totton Office. 01703 871344
Waterlooville Office. 01705 254271
Winchester Office. 01962 868411
Southampton City College, St Mary Street, Southampton SO14 1AR 01703 635222. Community based vocational training, advice and guidance. 'Learning in the home' and community based courses available.

Open University:

The Open University, South Region, Foxcombe Hall, Boars Hill, Oxford OX1 5HR 01865 328038

Training and Enterprise Council:

Hampshire TEC, 25 Thackeray Mall, Fareham PO16 0PQ 01329 230099. Expansion of out of school initiative with 37 projects in Hampshire; Survey of part time work and training needs of employees; Recruitment and Training Grants of £1000 for Hampshire companies recruiting and training women returning to work; Business Training Vouchers available toward the cost of a Springboard self development programme for women employed by small businesses

WEA office:

WEA Thames and Solent, 6 Brewer Street, Oxford OX1 1QN 01865 246270   *Contact:* Annie Winner

COURSES

- **SUBJECT** Access 474
- **TITLE** Access Foundation: Study Skills, Basic Maths & Computing, English, Sociology
- **PLACE** Evesham College

Length 1 year **Start** September **Days** Mon, Thurs, Fri 9.15-1.15+negotiated tutorial time **Cost** Normally none **Entry Reqs** 21+ **Award** Access Foundation Certificate, optional GCSEs **Creche** Yes £6/day

- **CONTACT** Lindsay Parfitt 01386 41091 x156

- **SUBJECT** Access 475
- **TITLE** Access to Higher Education
- **PLACE** North East Worcestershire College, Bromsgrove

Length 1 academic year **Start** September **Days** 3 days/week 9.15-3.00 **Cost** No fee (full time course) **Entry Reqs** 21+, no formal requirements **Award** Nationally recognised Access qualification **Creche** Playgroup £7.50/day

- **CONTACT** Phil Logan 01527 570020

- **SUBJECT** Access 476
- **TITLE** Access to Higher Education
- **PLACE** Worcester College of Technology

Length 1 year **Start** September **Days** Mon-Fri 9.00-4.00 **Cost** Tuition free **Award** Accredited Access Certificate **Creche** Yes

- **CONTACT** D Bragg 01905 723383

- **SUBJECT** Access/Health Studies/Tourism & Leisure 477
- **TITLE** Access to 1. Health and Social Care 2. Hospitality, Tourism and Leisure
- **PLACE** Herefordshire College of Technology

Length 1.3 weeks 2.6 weeks **Days** 1. 9.00-1.00 2 mornings/week 2. Mon 9.30-12.30 **Cost** Free **Entry Reqs** None **Award** Progession to other courses, including GNVQ Foundation courses **Creche** Yes Tel: 01432 352235 x460

- **CONTACT** Adult Vocational Training & Guidance Centre 01432 352235

- **SUBJECT** Access/Humanities/Teaching 478
- **TITLE** Access to Higher Education
- **PLACE** Evesham College

Length Daytime 1 year, evening 2 years **Start** September **Days** Tues, Wed, Thurs 9.15-1.15+negotiated tutorial time, evenings Tues+Thurs 6.00-9.00 **Cost** None **Entry Reqs** 21+, O Level English Language or equivalent, interview **Award** CNAA Validated Certificate **Creche** Yes £6/day

- **CONTACT** Wendy Logan 01386 41091

- **SUBJECT** Access/Nursing 479
- **TITLE** Access to Nursing & Health Care Professions: Preparation for Nurse Training
- **PLACE** North East Worcestershire College, Bromsgrove

Length 36 weeks full time, 72 weeks part time **Start** September **Days** 5 days/week 9.30-3.00 full time, 2.5 days/week part time **Cost** £15 **Entry Reqs** Minimum age 21 **Award** Access Certificate adapted for entry to nurse training **Creche** Playgroup £7.50/day

- **CONTACT** Lisa Read 01527 572714

- **SUBJECT**   Accounting   480
- **TITLE**   Association of Accounting Technicians Foundation Stage NVQ 2
- **PLACE**   North East Worcestershire College, Bromsgrove & Redditch

Length 1 year part time   **Start** September   **Days** Mon-Fri 9.00-4.30 or Mon+Tues eves 6.00-9.00   **Cost** Contact College   **Entry Reqs** No fixed entry requirements   **Award** AAT(NVQ2). Completion of 3 stages gives entry to Association of Accounting Technicians **Creche** Playgroup £7.50/day

- **CONTACT**   Martin Bate 01527 572634

- **SUBJECT**   Business   481
- **TITLE**   Women into Business (IT/Business Administration, Finance, Communications & Law)
- **PLACE**   Evesham College

Length 1 year   **Start** September   **Days** Mon-Thurs 9.15-2.15 (term time only)   **Cost** None **Entry Reqs** None   **Award** RSA Single Subjects (optional), College Certificate   **Creche** Yes £3.85/halfday session

- **CONTACT**   Lynn Phillips 01386 41091 x162

- **SUBJECT**   Business Administration   482
- **TITLE**   Business Administration Foundation Level
- **PLACE**   Herefordshire College of Technology

Length 6 weeks   **Days** 10 hours/week over 3 days   **Cost** Free, College fee of £10 (£5 if on benefit) payable on enrolment   **Entry Reqs** None   **Creche** Yes Tel: 01432 352235 x460

- **CONTACT**   Adult Vocational Training & Guidance Centre 01432 352235

- **SUBJECT**   Business Administration   483
- **TITLE**   Business Administration: Return to Work
- **PLACE**   Worcester College of Technology

Length 1 year   **Start** September   **Days** Mon-Fri 10.00-3.00   **Cost** Tuition free   **Award** NVQ Level 3   **Creche** Yes

- **CONTACT**   A Hardwick 01905 723383

- **SUBJECT**   Business Studies/Secretarial   484
- **TITLE**   Intensive Secretarial, Beginners
- **PLACE**   Evesham College

Length 12 weeks   **Start** September, December, March   **Days** Mon-Fri 9.00-3.15   **Cost** Contact College   **Entry Reqs** Age 18+   **Award** RSA Single Subjects, College Certificate   **Creche** Yes £3.85/halfday session

- **CONTACT**   Jean Davis 01386 41091 x150

- **SUBJECT**   Childcare   485
- **TITLE**   Diploma in Playgroup Practice
- **PLACE**   North East Worcestershire College, Bromsgrove & Redditch

Length 36 weeks   **Start** September   **Days** Fri (Redditch) 9.30-3.00 or Thurs (Bromsgrove) 9.15-2.45   **Cost** £139   **Award** Diploma in Playgroup Practice   **Creche** Playgroup £7.50/day

- **CONTACT**   Dept Secretary, Redditch 01527 572702/Bromsgrove 01527 572701

- **SUBJECT**   Childcare   486
- **TITLE**   National Association for Maternal and Child Welfare (NAMCW) Child Care
- **PLACE**   North East Worcestershire College, Bromsgrove & Redditch

Length 34 weeks   **Start** September   **Days** Tues or Wed eves 7.00-9.00   **Cost** £74   **Award** NAMCW Stage 3   **Creche** Daytime only

- **CONTACT**   Julie Bagley 01527 572713

- **SUBJECT** Childcare/Care Studies   **487**
- **TITLE** 1. Dip in Nursery Nursing 2. Caring for Children C&G 324 3. Caring for Elderly C&G
- **PLACE** North East Worcestershire College 1. Bromsgrove 2. &3. Redditch

Length 1.3 years part time 2.33 weeks 3.34 weeks   **Start** 1. Sept 2. &3. Sept, Oct, Dec, Jan, March   **Days** 1. Mon-Fri 9.30-2.30 2. &3. Mon or Thurs 9.30-3.30   **Cost** 1. £15 2. £115+exam fees 3. £155+exam fees   **Entry Reqs** 1. Good general education 2. &3. Minimum age 17   **Award** 1. Dip in Nursery Nursing 2. C&G 324 3. C&G325   **Creche** Playgroup £7.50/day

- **CONTACT** 1. Diane White 01527 572713/2. &3. Janet Turberville 01527 572716

- **SUBJECT** Craft   **488**
- **TITLE** Furniture Studies: The Design and Manufacture of Furniture
- **PLACE** Herefordshire College of Technology

Length 2 years   **Start** September   **Days** 36 weeks at 23 hours/week   **Cost** Variable, related to circumstances   **Entry Reqs** Discretionary   **Award** CGLI 555/Furniture Craft subjects **Creche** Yes & nursery 6 mnths-5yrs £3.25/session

- **CONTACT** P Denton 01432 352235 x252/253

- **SUBJECT** Information Technology   **489**
- **TITLE** IT for Business
- **PLACE** North East Worcestershire College, Bromsgrove

Length 12 weeks   **Start** September, January, April   **Days** 3 days/week 9.00-3.00   **Cost** £15 **Entry Reqs** Over 25, unwaged   **Award** Award in Computer Literacy & Information Technology (CLAIT)   **Creche** Playgroup £7.50/day

- **CONTACT** Frank Page 01527 572613

- **SUBJECT** Information Technology   **490**
- **TITLE** Modern Office Technology
- **PLACE** Evesham College

Length 12 weeks   **Start** September, December, March   **Days** 9.00-3.15 4 days/week   **Cost** Contact College   **Entry Reqs** Age 18+, keyboard skills   **Award** RSA CLAIT, Single Subjects, College Certificate   **Creche** Yes £3.85/halfday session

- **CONTACT** Jean Davis 01386 41091 x150

- **SUBJECT** Management   **491**
- **TITLE** Women Returners Management Course
- **PLACE** Worcester College of Technology

Length 25 weeks   **Start** January   **Days** 2 days/week 9.15-3.00   **Cost** Free (funded by ESF & HAWTEC)   **Entry Reqs** Women, 23+, paid, voluntary or home-based management experience   **Award** NEBS Management Certificate/NVQ 3   **Creche** Yes Free

- **CONTACT** Ann Turner 01905 619031

- **SUBJECT** Office Skills   **492**
- **TITLE** Office Skills (Beginner)
- **PLACE** North East Worcestershire College, Redditch

Length Up to 3 terms   **Start** September   **Days** 5 days/week 18 hours total   **Cost** £15   **Entry Reqs** Desire to benefit from subjects covered. Good standard of written English helpful   **Award** Opportunity to take exam for RSA I&II Typing & WP; RSA Audio Transcription: Speedwriting **Creche** Playgroup £7.50/day

- **CONTACT** Jenny Jones 01527 57634

- **SUBJECT** Office Skills 493
- **TITLE** Office Skills Refresher Course
- **PLACE** North East Worcestershire College, Redditch

Length 17 weeks **Start** September, February **Days** 5 days/week, up to 20 hours total. Hours usually 9.30-2.30 **Cost** £15 **Entry Reqs** Some office experience and preferably some keyboarding skills **Award** Opportunity to take various Office/Secretarial and CLAIT exams **Creche** Playgroup £7.50/day

- **CONTACT** Jenny Jones 01527 57634

- **SUBJECT** Personnel Management 494
- **TITLE** Certificate in Personnel Practice
- **PLACE** North East Worcestershire College, Bromsgrove

Length 30 weeks **Start** October **Days** Thurs 2.30-8.30 **Cost** £300 **Entry Reqs** Minimum age 20 **Award** Certificate in Personnel Practice (IPM) **Creche** Playgroup £7.50/day

- **CONTACT** Denzil Lewis 01527 572615

- **SUBJECT** Practical/Craft 495
- **TITLE** Furniture Studies: The Design and Manufacture of Furniture
- **PLACE** Herefordshire College of Technology

Length 2 years **Start** September **Days** 23 hours/week **Cost** Variable, related to circumstances **Entry Reqs** Discretionary **Award** CGLI 555/Furniture Craft Subjects **Creche** Yes & nursery 6 months-5 yrs £3.25/session

- **CONTACT** Phil Thomas 01432 352235 x252/253

- **SUBJECT** Preparatory 496
- **TITLE** Breakthrough
- **PLACE** Worcester College of Technology

Length 1 year, study of individual modules possible **Start** September **Days** Mon-Thurs 10.00-3.00 **Cost** Free if unwaged, £10 full time registration fee **Entry Reqs** None **Award** WMAP Credit Record and/or GCSEs English, Maths, Sociology **Creche** Yes £1.40/hour

- **CONTACT** Jane Tope 01905 723383 x223

- **SUBJECT** Preparatory 497
- **TITLE** Choices for Women
- **PLACE** Herefordshire College of Technology

Length 4 weeks **Start** Contact College **Days** Tues, Wed, Thurs 10.00-1.00 **Cost** Free to unwaged **Entry Reqs** None **Creche** Yes Tel: 01432 352235 x460

- **CONTACT** Ashlyn Dunlop/Liz Norman 01432 352235 x429

- **SUBJECT** Preparatory 498
- **TITLE** Choices for Women: Examination of Options in Education, Training & Development
- **PLACE** Herefordshire College of Technology

Length 36 hours over 4 weeks **Start** Variable (not July or August) **Days** 4 weeks, Tues-Thurs 10.00-1.00 **Cost** None **Entry Reqs** None **Award** None **Creche** Yes £3.25/halfday

- **CONTACT** Liz Norman 01432 352235

- **SUBJECT** Preparatory 499
- **TITLE** Flexistudy and Open Learning
- **PLACE** Herefordshire College of Technology

Length Flexible **Start** At any time or Sept, Jan, April **Days** Flexible **Cost** Varies, some free **Entry Reqs** None **Award** College or external qualifications **Creche** Yes £3.25/session

- **CONTACT** S Morgan 01432 353336. I Macklin 01432 278344

Hereford and Worcester

- **SUBJECT** Preparatory   **500**
- **TITLE** Foundation Education: Basic English/Mathematics/IT/Social Studies
- **PLACE** North East Worcestershire College, Bromsgrove & Redditch

Length 1 academic year   **Start** Sept or anytime, roll on roll off   **Days** Mon-Fri 9.30-2.45   **Cost** Free   **Entry Reqs** None   **Award** GCSE English, RSA Maths & English, Wordpower, Numberpower   **Creche** Playgroup £7.50/day

- **CONTACT** Sara Nugent 01527 570020

- **SUBJECT** Preparatory/Nursing   **501**
- **TITLE** 1. Preparation Course for Nurse Training Entry Test 2. Health Care:Study Skills
- **PLACE** North East Worcestershire College 1. Redditch 2. Bromsgrove

Length 1.8 weeks (eves) or 12 weeks (mornings) 2.10 weeks   **Start** September, January, April/May   **Days** 1. Wed 6.30-9.00 2. Mon7.00-9.00   **Cost** 1. &2. £20   **Entry Reqs** None   **Award** 1. Preparation for Nurse Training Entry Test 2. No formal award   **Creche** Playgroup daytime only, £3.50/morning

- **CONTACT** Mrs O'Gorman 01527 572714

- **SUBJECT** Science/Engineering   **502**
- **TITLE** BSc or BEng Degree
- **PLACE** North East Worcestershire College, Year 1/Coventry Univ, Years 2-4

Length 4 years   **Start** September   **Days** 5 days/week 10.00-3.00   **Cost** Full time course, no fee (course attracts mandatory grant)   **Entry Reqs** GCSE Maths or equivalent   **Award** BSc or BEng   **Creche** Playgroup £7.50/day

- **CONTACT** Graham Bishop 01527 570020

COUNTY CONTACTS

Information and advice:

Adult Vocational Training & Guidance Service, Herefordshire College of Technology, Folly Lane, Hereford HR1 1LS 01432 352235   *Contact:* Chris Bucknall

Open University:

The Open University. West Midlands Region, 66-68 High Street, Harborne, Birmingham B17 9NB 0121 428 1550

Training and Enterprise Councils:

Central England TEC, The Oaks, Clewes Road, Redditch B98 7ST 01527 545415
HAWTEC (Hereford and Worcester), Hazwell House, St Nicholas Street, Worcester WR1 1UW 01905 723200

WEA office:

WEA West Mercia District, 78-80 Sherlock Street, Birmingham B5 6LT 0121 666 6101   *Contact:* Jill Bedford

COURSES

- **SUBJECT** Access   503
- **TITLE** Access to Higher Education
- **PLACE** Hertford Regional College, Broxbourne and Ware Centres

Length Flexible modular programme   **Start** September   **Days** Flexible including day (9.30-3.00) and/or evening   **Cost** No tuition fees   **Entry Reqs** None   **Award** Access to Higher Education Certificate (HEQC validated), GCSEs also available   **Creche** No

- **CONTACT** Christine Vial 01992 466451 x4423

- **SUBJECT** Access   504
- **TITLE** Access to Higher Education
- **PLACE** Oaklands College, Borehamwood

Length 1 year   **Start** September   **Days** Contact College   **Cost** Free   **Entry Reqs** Interview and assessment   **Award** Access to Degree or HND course   **Creche** No

- **CONTACT** Wanda Verity 0181 953 6024

- **SUBJECT** Access   505
- **TITLE** Access to Higher Education: Multi-Subject
- **PLACE** Hertford Regional College 1. Ware Centre 2. Broxbourne

Length 1 year full time, 2 years part time day or evening   **Start** April 1 day or eve/wk; main course Sept   **Days** Mon-Fri 9.30-3.30 (flexible) or 2 eves/week   **Cost** Free (LEA funded) **Entry Reqs** 21+   **Award** Hertfordshire Access Certificate (CNAA/CVCP validated), entry to higher education   **Creche** Yes Ware Centre only

- **CONTACT** 1. Nick Spenceley 01920 46544x2223/2. Chris Vial 01992 466451 x4423

- **SUBJECT** Access   506
- **TITLE** Access to Higher Education: Multi-Subject
- **PLACE** Oaklands College, Welwyn Garden City

Length 36 weeks   **Start** September   **Days** Mon-Fri 10.00-3.00   **Cost** Contact College   **Entry Reqs** Interview   **Award** Hertfordshire Access Certificate (CNAA validated), entry to higher education   **Creche** Yes Contact College

- **CONTACT** Eira Beddall 01707 362318

- **SUBJECT** Access   507
- **TITLE** Access Planning Period (Pre-Access)
- **PLACE** Hertford Regional College, Broxbourne and Ware Centres

Length 8-10 weeks   **Days** Part time day & evening options   **Cost** No tuition fees   **Entry Reqs** None   **Award** OCN accreditation in progress   **Creche** No

- **CONTACT** Christine Vial 01992 466451 x4423

- **SUBJECT** Access/Business/Computing   508
- **TITLE** Access to Business and Computing
- **PLACE** Oaklands College, Welwyn Garden City

Length 1 year   **Start** September   **Days** Mon-Fri 10.00-3.00   **Cost** Registration fee   **Entry Reqs** None. Interview for suitability   **Award** Hertfordshire Access Scheme Award   **Creche** Yes

- **CONTACT** Sue Pearce 01707 362318 x4425

- **SUBJECT** Access/Business Studies/Life Sciences/Information Technology   **509**
- **TITLE** Access to Business Studies, Life Sciences, IT & Mathematics
- **PLACE** Oaklands College, St Albans City Campus

Length 9 months, full time day or 1-2 years part time evening   **Start** September   **Days** 5 days/week 9.30-3.00, variable eves   **Cost** Tuition free to Herts residents. Enrolment & materials charge   **Entry Reqs** Interview and letter of application. No formal qualifications   **Award** Hertfordshire Access Certificate. Entry to higher education   **Creche** Yes

- **CONTACT** Paul Fielding 01727 847070 x4802/Jim Bailey x4322

- **SUBJECT** Access/Preparatory   **510**
- **TITLE** Preparing for Training/Education/Work 1. Access to Higher Education 2. Return to Learn
- **PLACE** North Herts College, Monkswood Way Campus

Length 1.1 year 2. Contact College   **Start** 1. September 2. Anytime   **Days** 1. Full time 9.00-3.00 2. Tues 9.15-11.15   **Cost** Free   **Entry Reqs** Interview to assess suitability   **Award** 1. Access Certificate, entry to HE 2. Entry to English/Communications qualifications   **Creche** Playgroup Approx £3/session

- **CONTACT** 1. Judith Richell/2. Sue Hartga 01438 312822

- **SUBJECT** Access/Social Science/Humanities   **511**
- **TITLE** Access to Social Science, Humanities
- **PLACE** Oaklands College, St Albans City Campus

Length 9 months, full time day or 1-2 years part time evening   **Start** September   **Days** 5 days/week 9.30-3.00, variable eves   **Cost** Tuition free to Herts residents. Enrolment & materials charge   **Entry Reqs** Interview and letter of application. No formal qualifications   **Award** Hertfordshire Access Certificate. Entry to higher education   **Creche** Yes Contact College

- **CONTACT** Paul Fielding 01727 847070 x4802/Jim Bailey x4322

- **SUBJECT** Access/Social Work   **512**
- **TITLE** Access to Higher Education (Social Work option)
- **PLACE** Oaklands College, Welwyn Garden City

Length 1 year full time, 2 years part time   **Start** September   **Days** Mon-Fri 10.00-12.00, 1.00-3.00   **Cost** Registration fee   **Entry Reqs** Some voluntary experience in social work   **Award** Diploma in Social Work   **Creche** Yes Contact College

- **CONTACT** Tony West 01707 326318 x4263

- **SUBJECT** Administration   **513**
- **TITLE** NVQ Administration
- **PLACE** Oaklands College, School of Business and Computing, Welwyn & Hatfield

Length Varies   **Start** September, January   **Days** Varies daytime/eves   **Cost** Contact College   **Entry Reqs** None   **Award** NVQ, LCCI   **Creche** Yes Contact College

- **CONTACT** Pauline Gormley 01707 326318 x4413

- **SUBJECT** Administration/Teaching   **514**
- **TITLE** RSA Teacher/Trainer Certificate in Administration Skills
- **PLACE** West Herts College, Dacorum Campus, Cassio Campus Watford

Length Varies but theoretical tuition 30 weeks   **Start** September, January   **Days** Mon & Wed 6.00-9.99   **Cost** £450 approx less 25% tax relief   **Entry Reqs** Background in administration/secretarial work   **Award** RSA Teacher/Trainers Certificate in Administration Skills   **Creche** No

- **CONTACT** Glenda Tizard/Beatrice Birch 01442 221605/01923 812477

- **SUBJECT** Administration   **515**
- **TITLE** NVQ Administration Levels II and III (Text & Information Processing/Business Admin)
- **PLACE** West Herts College, Dacorum Campus

Length Modular courses   **Start** Continuous enrolment   **Days** Mon-Fri 2 hr blocks 9.00-3.00, eves 6-9   **Cost** Contact College   **Entry Reqs** Varies   **Award** NVQ Administration Levels II & III   **Creche** Yes

- **CONTACT** Glenda Tizard/G Braine 01442 221610/221605

- **SUBJECT** Business Administration/Information Technology   **516**
- **TITLE** Business Administration, Information Technology
- **PLACE** Oaklands College, Borehamwood

Length 18 weeks   **Start** September   **Days** 5 days/week + work placement   **Cost** Contact College   **Entry Reqs** None   **Award** NVQ Levels I & II   **Creche** No

- **CONTACT** Margaret Ward 0181 953 6024

- **SUBJECT** Care Studies   **517**
- **TITLE** BTEC First Certificate in Caring
- **PLACE** North Herts College, Shephalbury Campus

Length 35 weeks+2-day residential block   **Start** September   **Days** 1 day/week in College, 1 day/week on placement   **Cost** Approx £253+exam fees. Concessions apply   **Entry Reqs** 21+, desire to work as care assistant or similar   **Award** BTEC 1st Cetificate   **Creche** Yes

- **CONTACT** Lin Martin-Haugh 01462 424242 x1149

- **SUBJECT** Catering   **518**
- **TITLE** Food Preparation & Cooking (Level 2)
- **PLACE** Hertford Regional College, Ware Centre

Length 26 weeks; 13 weeks/College & 13 weeks/placement   **Start** September, January   **Days** Mon, Tues, Thurs   **Cost** Free course for mature applicants   **Entry Reqs** None   **Award** C&G NVQ Level 2 Food Preparation & Cooking   **Creche** No

- **CONTACT** Mrs D Squire 01920 465441 x2350

- **SUBJECT** Childcare   **519**
- **TITLE** Advanced Certificate in Childcare and Education
- **PLACE** North Herts College, Shephalbury Campus

Length 1 year   **Start** September   **Days** Thurs 9.00-3.30 + 1 day/week placement   **Cost** Approx £253 Reduced fees if on benefit or low income   **Entry Reqs** 18+. Provision for learning-impaired/physically disabled students   **Award** NAMCH   **Creche** Yes

- **CONTACT** Louella Hodgson 01462 424242

- **SUBJECT** Childcare   **520**
- **TITLE** Advanced Diploma in Childcare and Education
- **PLACE** Oaklands College, St Albans City Campus

Length 2 years   **Start** September, January, April   **Days** Thurs 9.30-4.00   **Cost** £105 per termly module   **Entry Reqs** NNEB or similar childcare qualification   **Award** Advanced Diploma in Childcare Education   **Creche** Yes £5.50 halfday session

- **CONTACT** Ann Lexton 01727 847070

- **SUBJECT** Childcare   **521**
- **TITLE** Playgroup Introductory Course
- **PLACE** Oaklands College, Lemsford Lane Campus

Length 10 weeks   **Start** January   **Days** Mon 12.30-2.30   **Cost** £40   **Award** College Certificate in conjunction with Herts Social Services   **Creche** Yes £5.50 halfday session

- **CONTACT** Wendy Taylor 01727 847070

- **SUBJECT** Childcare 522
- **TITLE** Diploma Course: Child Development/Pre-School Play
- **PLACE** Oaklands College, St Albans City Campus & Welwyn GC Campus

Length 1 year **Start** September **Days** 1 day/week 9.30-2.30 **Cost** £110 **Award** Diploma awarded by College and Herts Social Services **Creche** Yes £5.50 halfday session

- **CONTACT** Gill Forrest 01438 717673

- **SUBJECT** Childcare 523
- **TITLE** NNEB Diploma Nursery Nursing
- **PLACE** Hertford Regional College, Ware Centre

Length 2 years full time **Start** September **Days** 3 days/week 9.00-3.15 + days/week practical placement **Cost** Course fee £615 Course registration etc approx £120 **Entry Reqs** Good standard of English plus experience of working with children **Award** NNEB Diploma awarded by CACHE **Creche** No

- **CONTACT** Rosemary Chandler 01920 465441 x2400

- **SUBJECT** Childcare 524
- **TITLE** NNEB Nursery Nursing for Mature Students
- **PLACE** Oaklands College, St Albans City Campus

Length 2 years **Start** September **Days** Mon-Fri 60% College attendance 10.00-3.00, 40% work placements 8.30-4.00 **Cost** Discretionary grant may be available **Award** NNEB Nursery Nursing **Creche** Yes £5.50 halfday session

- **CONTACT** Angela Underdown 01727 847070 x2431

- **SUBJECT** Childcare 525
- **TITLE** NVQ Level 2 & 3 Childcare and Education
- **PLACE** Oaklands College, St Albans City Campus

Length 1-2 years **Start** September, January, April **Days** 1 evening + 1 day **Cost** Level 2 £300, Level 3 £350 **Entry Reqs** Desire to work with children **Award** NVQ Levels 2 or 3 **Creche** Yes £5.50 halfday session

- **CONTACT** Lorna Fitzjohn 01727 847070

- **SUBJECT** Computing 526
- **TITLE** Business Computing
- **PLACE** Oaklands College, Dept of Information Systems

Length 18 weeks **Start** September **Cost** Free **Entry Reqs** None **Award** NVQ Level II **Creche** No

- **CONTACT** John Parry 0181 953 6024

- **SUBJECT** Design 527
- **TITLE** Auto CAD Training Programme
- **PLACE** Oaklands College, Welwyn Garden City

Length 1.12 weeks 2.7 weeks **Start** 1. Sept, Jan, April 2. Roll on **Days** 1. Fri 2. Tues, Wed, Thurs **Cost** Free (Government funded) **Entry Reqs** Registered unemployed 6 months **Award** 1. &2. C&G 4351 **Creche** Yes

- **CONTACT** I Gibbs 01707 326318 x4303

- **SUBJECT** Design 528
- **TITLE** Computer Aided Draughting (Auto CAD+CAD)
- **PLACE** Oaklands College, Welwyn Garden City

Length 34 weeks **Start** September **Days** Tues 4.30-6.30 **Cost** £80 (Concessions available) **Entry Reqs** Competence as a draughtswoman or tracer **Award** C&G 230 **Creche** Yes Contact College

- **CONTACT** Tricia Kane 01707 326318 x4302

- **SUBJECT**   Electrical Engineering   **529**
- **TITLE**   Electrical Installations C&G 236/1
- **PLACE**   Oaklands College, Welwyn Garden City

Length 1.36 weeks 2.4 terms   **Start** 1. September 2. September, January   **Days** 1. Wed 9.00-6.30 2. Mon & Wed 6.45-8.45   **Cost** 1. £181.25 (includes tax exemption) 2. £185/year   **Entry Reqs** None   **Award** C&G Certificate 236 Part 1   **Creche** Yes Contact College
- **CONTACT**   Peter Thompson 01707 326318 x4312/Peter Holgate 01707 326318 x4316

- **SUBJECT**   Hairdressing   **530**
- **TITLE**   NVQ Hairdressing (C&G NVQ)
- **PLACE**   Hertford Regional College, Ware Centre

Length 1 year approx   **Start** September onwards by arrangement   **Days** 3 days/week 9.00-3.15   **Cost** £1.55/hour   **Entry Reqs** None   **Award** C&G Hairdressing Training Board, Foundation Certificate in Hairdressing NVQ Level II   **Creche** No
- **CONTACT**   Julie Curr 01920 465441 x2350

- **SUBJECT**   Health Studies   **531**
- **TITLE**   Diploma in Osteopathy
- **PLACE**   The College of Osteopaths: Regents College, London & Hertfordshire

Length 5 years part time   **Start** September   **Days** 12 weekends/year+exams 3 weekends/year   **Cost** £2000/year   **Entry Reqs** 3 A Levels. Mature student entry possible. Interview   **Award** Diploma in Osteopathy   **Creche** No
- **CONTACT**   Christine Slade 0181 905 1937

- **SUBJECT**   Health Studies/Social Studies   **532**
- **TITLE**   GNVQ/NVQ/BTEC Early Learning Studies
- **PLACE**   Oaklands College, Welwyn Garden City & St Albans Campus

Length Various   **Start** Various modules   **Days** Various   **Cost** Contact College   **Entry Reqs** Various   **Award** Further study/employment in social work or nursing   **Creche** Yes Contact College
- **CONTACT**   Tony West 01707 326318 x4263/Lorna Fitzjohn, Beverley Seaborn 01727 847070

- **SUBJECT**   Humanities/Social Science/Social Work   **533**
- **TITLE**   1. +2. BA (Hons)/BA/DipHE 3. BA (Hons) with DipSW
- **PLACE**   University of Hertfordshire, Hatfield or Watford Campus

Length 1. +2.3 years, 4/5 years part time 3.3 years full time   **Start** September   **Days** Part time 2-3 days/week; 2 days/week for BA Social Science   **Cost** Part time approx £400/year   **Entry Reqs** A Level, Access or essay   **Award** BA(Hons)/BA/DipHE/DipSW   **Creche** Yes, at Hatfield and Watford
- **CONTACT**   1. S Southgate 01707 284416 2. A Nicholas 284492 3. R Goatley 284432

- **SUBJECT**   Management   **534**
- **TITLE**   Returners Link
- **PLACE**   University of Hertfordshire, Hatfield and St Albans

Length 20-30 weeks   **Start** September/October   **Days** 3 days/week plus home study   **Cost** Free (TEC funded)   **Entry Reqs** Degree or equivalent plus employment experience   **Award** CATS points to Postgraduate Certificate level   **Creche** Yes
- **CONTACT**   Hilary Fyson, Course Co-ordinator 01727 813622

- **SUBJECT**   Multi-Subject   **535**
- **TITLE**   CATS: Credit Accumulation and Transfer Scheme
- **PLACE**   University of Hertfordshire, Hatfield, Watford or St Albans

Length Half year or 1 year or more   **Start** September   **Days** 2-4 hours/week (+ home study) per unit of study   **Cost** £90-£100/unit of study. Concessions for those in receipt of benefit   **Entry Reqs** None   **Award** Choice of none, Certificate or Diploma of HE, Degree, Masters Degree   **Creche** Yes
- **CONTACT**   Sam Swift 01707 285224

- **SUBJECT**   NOW   **536**
- **TITLE**   New Opportunities for Women
- **PLACE**   University of Hertfordshire, Hatfield and St Albans

Length 10 weeks   **Start** 2/3 times/year   **Days** 1 day/week   **Cost** Contact College   **Entry Reqs** None   **Award** Contact College for details   **Creche** Yes

- **CONTACT**   Maggie Goodchild 01707 285222

- **SUBJECT**   Office Skills   **537**
- **TITLE**   Office Skills (Admin, Spreadsheet, Typing, WP, Dbase, Office Management)
- **PLACE**   Oaklands College, Welwyn Garden City

Length Roll on roll off   **Start** September onwards every 12 weeks   **Days** Choice of days available   **Cost** £1.15/hour   **Entry Reqs** None   **Award** RSA/LCCI exams available   **Creche** Yes

- **CONTACT**   Lynn Burling 01707 362318

- **SUBJECT**   Preparatory   **538**
- **TITLE**   Assertion Training
- **PLACE**   Oaklands College, Borehamwood

Length 12 weeks   **Start** September, January   **Days** Tues 10.00-12.00, Wed 7.00-9.00   **Cost** Contact College   **Entry Reqs** None   **Award** None   **Creche** No

- **CONTACT**   School of Arts, Humanities and Sciences 0181 953 6024

- **SUBJECT**   Preparatory   **539**
- **TITLE**   Fresh Start: Confidence Building, Learning to Study
- **PLACE**   Oaklands College, Borehamwood

Length 34 weeks   **Start** September   **Days** Wed 9.30-11.30   **Cost** Approx £50   **Entry Reqs** None   **Award** None   **Creche** No

- **CONTACT**   School of Arts, Humanities and Sciences 0181 953 6024

- **SUBJECT**   Preparatory   **540**
- **TITLE**   Return to Learning
- **PLACE**   Oaklands College, St Albans City Campus

Length 1.8 weeks evenings 2.6 weeks daytime   **Start** May   **Days** 1.7. 00-9.30 2.10. 00-3.00   **Cost** £6 enrolment charge   **Entry Reqs** None   **Creche** Yes contact College for charges

- **CONTACT**   Mari Sved 01727 847070 x4830

- **SUBJECT**   Preparatory   **541**
- **TITLE**   Return to Learning: Fresh Start (Study Skills, English/Written & Spoken)
- **PLACE**   Oaklands College, Borehamwood

Length 1 year   **Start** September   **Days** Wed 9.30-11.30   **Cost** Contact College   **Entry Reqs** None   **Award** Optional exams eg LCCI English for Commerce (3 levels)   **Creche** No

- **CONTACT**   School of Arts, Humanities and Sciences 0181 953 6024

- **SUBJECT**   Preparatory   **542**
- **TITLE**   Return to Study: Study Skills, Personal Development, Education & Careers Guidance
- **PLACE**   Hertford Regional College 1. Broxbourne 2. Ware

Length 1 year part time   **Start** Usually Sept, but anytime possible   **Days** 1. Broxbourne Mon am or Tues eve 2. Ware Wed am or Thurs eve   **Cost** Halfday core free. Other subjects vary   **Entry Reqs** None   **Award** OCN accreditation in progress   **Creche** No

- **CONTACT**   1. C Vial/N Williams 01992 466451 x4423/2. N Spenceley 01920 465441 x2223

- **SUBJECT** Preparatory   543
- **TITLE** Returners' Courses
- **PLACE** Dow Stoker & Women Returners Ltd at various venues in Herts

Length 6 weeks   **Start** Various   **Days** Varies   **Cost** Free (funded by Herts TEC & ESF)
Entry Reqs Not in employment for 2 years   **Creche** No

- **CONTACT** Sally Payne 01279 466660

- **SUBJECT** Preparatory   544
- **TITLE** UNIPREP
- **PLACE** University of Hertfordshire, Hatfield

Length 12 weeks (term time only)   **Start** Courses throughout the year   **Days** 4 hours/week +
home study   **Cost** £90 Concessions for those in receipt of benefit   **Entry Reqs** Interest in
returning to study   **Award** 12 credit points Level 1   **Creche** Yes

- **CONTACT** Maggie Goodchild 01707 285222

- **SUBJECT** Professional Updating   545
- **TITLE** Professional Updating for Women
- **PLACE** University of Hertfordshire, Hatfield and St Albans

Length 12 weeks   **Start** 1/2 times/year   **Days** 4 days/week   **Cost** Free or small charge
Entry Reqs Professional qualifications and experience   **Award** CATS points at Postgraduate
level   **Creche** Yes

- **CONTACT** Hilary Fyson, Course Co-ordinator 01727 813622

- **SUBJECT** Retail   546
- **TITLE** Intermediate GNVQ in Retail and Distributive Services
- **PLACE** Hertford Regional College, Ware Centre

Length 36 weeks   **Start** September   **Days** 4 days/week 9.00-4.30   **Cost** Tuition free, up to
£150 registration, certification and on-course costs   **Entry Reqs** By interview   **Award** BTEC
Intermediate GNVQ in Retail and Distributive Services   **Creche** No

- **CONTACT** Jill White 01920 465441 x2219

- **SUBJECT** Secretarial   547
- **TITLE** Secretarial Administration
- **PLACE** Hertford Regional College, Ware & Broxbourne Centres

Length 36 weeks   **Start** September   **Days** Mon, Tues, Thurs, Fri 9.15-3.15   **Cost** Tuition free,
up to £150 registration, certification and on-course costs   **Entry Reqs** By interview   **Award**
RSA NVQ Administration Level 2, + wordprocessing & other secretarial/office skills
qualifications   **Creche** No

- **CONTACT** Audrey Skitt 01920 465441 x2232/Maxine Levy 01920 465441 x2222

COUNTY CONTACTS

Information and advice:

Adult Guidance Service, Hertford Regional College, Broxbourne Centre, Turnford, Broxbourne
EN10 6AF 01992 470648   *Contact:* Information Helpline. Offers Guidance Service on
appointment basis.
Ware Centre, Scotts Road, Ware SG12 9JF 01920 463730   *Contact:* Information Officer. Drop-in
sessions Mon 10.00-12.30, 1.30-4.00; Tues 10.00-12.30. Higher Education Workshops Wed 1.30-4.00.
Free provision.

Hertfordshire

Hertfordshire Careers Service, Bishops Stortford Office 01279 654898
Cheshunt Office 01992 621426 Also covers Hoddesdon
Hatfield Office 01707 263048
Hemel Hempstead Office 01442 61511 Also covers Tring and Berkhamstead
Letchworth Office 01462 685123 Also covers Royston, Buntingford, Hitchin and surrounding areas
St Albans Office 01992 556944
Stevenage Office 01438 351582
Ware Office 01920 466314
Watford Office 01923 231132
Oaklands College, Oaklands Campus, St Albans AL4 0JA 0727 850651   *Contact:* Helen Mason. Helpline 01727 868888
Rural Adult Guidance Service, Broadway House, 43 The Broadway, Letchworth SG6 3PA 01462 685123   *Contact:* Susan Whittaker, Mary Walsh. Also covers Royston, Hitchin and surrounding areas. Individual careers counselling to women in Herts.
Watford Adult Guidance Centre, 12 Market Street, Watford WD1 7AD 01923 816970   *Contact:* Pete Coleman. Free drop-in open access sessions Mon-Thurs 10.00-2.00, individual guidance appointments where appropriate. TEC funded Back to Work courses.
West Herts College, Dacorum Campus, Marlowes, Hemel Hempstead HP1 1HD 01442 63771   *Contact:* Sue Page. Information on courses and training appropriate for returners and how to access careers guidance.
Watford Campus, Hempstead Road, Watford WD1 3EZ 01923 257500   *Contact:* Julie Griffin

Open University:

The Open University, East Anglia Region, 12 Hills Road, Cambridge CB2 1PF 01223 61650

Other agencies:

Watford Women's Centre, 18b Clarendon Road, Watford 01923 816229   *Contact:* Sylvia Harvey. Offers WEA-run Planning for Employment courses

Training and Enterprise Council:

Hertfordshire TEC, New Barnes Mill, Cotton Mill Lane, St Albans AL1 2HA 01727 813600
Women's Inititatives Group; Back to Work Foundation course; Business Administration Skills Training; Adult Guidance Shop, Watford, joint funded; Guidance Vouchers for Returners.

WEA offices:

WEA Eastern District, Botolph House, 17 Botolph Lane, Cambridge CB2 3RE 01223 350978
Contact: Sue Young. Covers most of Hertfordshire
WEA London District, 44 Crowndale Road, London NW1 1TR 0171 388 7261   *Contact:* Ann Deutch. Covers south Herts

COURSES

- **SUBJECT** Access
- **TITLE** Access to Higher Education
- **PLACE** East Yorkshire College

548

Length 1 year   **Start** September   **Days** 11 hours/week (various)   **Cost** £275/year   **Entry Reqs** None   **Award** Access Certificate   **Creche** Available for part time students
- **CONTACT** Access Co-ordinator 01262 672676

- **SUBJECT** Access
- **TITLE** Action Programme
- **PLACE** Hull College of Further Education

549

Length 1 year part time   **Start** Rolling programme   **Days** Dependent upon individual programme   **Cost** Contact College   **Entry Reqs** Open Access. Entry by interview. Commitment and motivation   **Award** College Certificate   **Creche** Nurseries
- **CONTACT** Byron Edwards 01482 329988 x2816

- **SUBJECT** Access/Preparatory
- **TITLE** Pathway for Women
- **PLACE** Hull College of Further Education, Park Street Centre

550

Length Termly, 3 different options available over year   **Start** Fits in with school terms   **Days** Varies   **Cost** Contact College   **Entry Reqs** None. Interview   **Award** SYOLF accreditation on unit   **Creche** Yes
- **CONTACT** Gwyneth Yates 01482 329988 x2811

- **SUBJECT** Business
- **TITLE** GNVQ Intermediate Business
- **PLACE** Priory Lane Adult Education Centre, Scunthorpe

551

Length 12 weeks/unit   **Start** September, April   **Cost** £28, free if in receipt of benefit   **Entry Reqs** Knowledge of word processing an advantage   **Award** NVQ/RSA Certificate
- **CONTACT** Priory Lane Centre 01724 862217/281376

- **SUBJECT** Computing
- **TITLE** Word Processing Update
- **PLACE** Boothferry Adult Education Service, Howden Centre

552

Length 10 weeks   **Start** September   **Days** Thurs 9.30-11.30   **Cost** £26.40
- **CONTACT** Howden Centre 01430 430131

- **SUBJECT** Preparatory
- **TITLE** Working Towards Work
- **PLACE** Boothferry Adult Education Service, South Axholme Centre

553

Length 12 weeks   **Start** September   **Days** Wed 9.30-3.30   **Cost** Free
- **CONTACT** Parkside Centre 01405 762714

- **SUBJECT** Professional Updating
- **TITLE** Professional Updating for Women
- **PLACE** Humberside University

554

Length 15 weeks   **Start** September, February   **Days** Mon, Wed, Thurs, Fri 10.00-3.00, Tues work placement   **Cost** Free (funded by European Social Fund)   **Entry Reqs** Primarily graduates with professional experience   **Award** University Certificate   **Creche** No (childcare allowance available)
- **CONTACT** Jenny Wells 01482 440550 x4210

- **SUBJECT**   Sociology/Psychology   **555**
- **TITLE**   Social & Behavioural Studies 1. Certificate 2. Diploma 3. BA
- **PLACE**   University of Hull and Franklin College, Grimsby

Length 6 years part time   **Start** September   **Cost** 1. Certificate £260/year 2. &3. £360/year
Entry Reqs 1. Open access to Certificate stage. 2. & 3. Via credit transfer to Diploma & Degree stages   **Award** 1. Certificate 2. Diploma 3. BA in Social & Behavioural Studies   **Creche** No

- **CONTACT**   Mike Somerton 01482 465974

COUNTY CONTACTS

Information and advice:

Educational Guidance Service for Adults, Adult Education Area Office, Lincoln Gardens, Scunthorpe DN16 2ED 01724 849996   *Contact:* Kim Ellis
Adult Education Area Office, Parkside, Western Road, Goole DN14 6RQ 01405 762714   *Contact:* Denise Wilson
Adult Education Centre, Hull Road, Withernsea HU19 2EQ 01964 612750   *Contact:* Dave Walker
Riby Square Resource Centre, 10-12 Riby Square, Grimsby DN31 3HA 01472 245041   *Contact:* Angela Shipway
The Avenues Centre, Park Avenue, Hull HU5 4DA 01482 346489   *Contact:* Nieca MacKinder

Open University:

The Open University, East Midlands Region, The Octagon, 143 Derby Road, Nottingham NG7 1PH 0115 924 0121Covers South Humberside
The Open University, Yorkshire Region, 2 Trevelyan Square, Boar Lane, Leeds LS1 6ED 0113 245 1466Covers North Humberside

Training and Enterprise Council:

Humberside TEC, The Maltings, Silvester Square, Silvester Street, Hull HU1 3HL 01482 226491Accreditation of prior learning, case studies produced on/for women returners; expansion of out of school childcare facilities to provide support to women returners to enable them to take up training/education/work opportunities; wide range of training programmes supported at a local Women's Centre to prepare women for further training or employment

WEA office:

WEA Yorkshire South District, Chantry Buildings, Corporation Street, Rotherham S60 1NG 01709 837001   *Contact:* Trish Lands

COURSES

- **SUBJECT**   Accounting   556
- **TITLE**   Accounting: NVQ Modules
- **PLACE**   Isle of Wight College

Length Flexible   **Start** Anytime   **Cost** Contact College   **Entry Reqs** Contact College **Award** NVQ II/III   **Creche** Day Nursery

- **CONTACT**   Marketing Centre 01983 526631

- **SUBJECT**   Administration   557
- **TITLE**   Administration: NVQ Modules
- **PLACE**   Isle of Wight College

Length Flexible   **Start** Anytime   **Cost** Contact College   **Entry Reqs** Contact College **Award** NVQ II/III   **Creche** Day Nursery

- **CONTACT**   Marketing Centre 01983 526631

- **SUBJECT**   Animal Care   558
- **TITLE**   Animal Care: NVQ
- **PLACE**   Isle of Wight College

Length 36 weeks part time   **Start** September   **Days** Tues 9.00-4.00   **Cost** £158.50+£70.60 exam fees Concessions possible   **Entry Reqs** None, keen & experience of small animals an advantage   **Award** NVQ Level II, progression to BTEC/HNC   **Creche** Day Nursery

- **CONTACT**   Marketing Centre 01983 526631

- **SUBJECT**   Art   559
- **TITLE**   GNVQ Art: 1. Intermediate 2. Advanced
- **PLACE**   Isle of Wight College

Length 1. 1 year 2. 2 years   **Start** September   **Cost** Free if in receipt of benefit   **Entry Reqs** Art portfolio   **Award** GNVQ Intermediate or Advanced, GCSE, A Level   **Creche** Day Nursery

- **CONTACT**   Judith Salmon 01983 826631 x212

- **SUBJECT**   Business   560
- **TITLE**   BTEC HNC Business
- **PLACE**   Isle of Wight College

Length 36 weeks part time   **Start** September   **Days** Wed 9.00-6.00   **Cost** £311+£74.00 exam fees Concessions possible   **Entry Reqs** Contact College   **Award** BTEC HNC, access to Business Studies   **Creche** Day nursery

- **CONTACT**   Marketing Centre 01983 526631

- **SUBJECT**   Care Studies   561
- **TITLE**   1. Essential Skills for Caring 2. Further Skills for Caring 3. BTEC HNC Caring Services
- **PLACE**   Isle of Wight College

Length 1. 1 year 2. 18 weeks 3. 2 years All part time   **Start** Contact College   **Cost** 1. £55 2. £158.50 3. £245 Concessions possible   **Entry Reqs** Contact College   **Award** 1. NVQ Level II 2. NVQ Level III 3. BTEC HNC Caring Services (Social Care)   **Creche** Day nursery

- **CONTACT**   Marketing Centre 01983 526631

- **SUBJECT**   Care Studies/Social Studies   562
- **TITLE**   Certificate in Welfare Studies
- **PLACE**   Isle of Wight College

Length 32 weeks part time   **Start** September   **Days** Tues & Thurs 6.00-9.00 or Mon 1.00-8.00   **Cost** £158.50 Concessions possible   **Entry Reqs** Contact College   **Award** Certificate in Welfare Studies, progression to nursing or social work training   **Creche** Day nursery

- **CONTACT**   Marketing Centre 01983 526631

- **SUBJECT**   Computing   563
- **TITLE**   Computing Workshops
- **PLACE**   Isle of Wight College

Length 10 weeks   **Start** Roll on, roll of   **Days** Flexible   **Cost** £40 Concessions possible   **Entry Reqs** None   **Award** RSA Text Processing/NVQ Administration & IT   **Creche** Day nursery

- **CONTACT**   Marketing Centre 01983 526631

- **SUBJECT**   Electronics   564
- **TITLE**   BTEC Electronics
- **PLACE**   Isle of Wight College

Length 1 year part time   **Start** September   **Days** Tues 9.00-5.30, Wed 6.00-7.45   **Cost** £314+£72 exam fee Concessions possible   **Entry Reqs** Contact College   **Award** BTEC National Certificate Electronics   **Creche** Day nursery

- **CONTACT**   Marketing Centre 01983 526631

- **SUBJECT**   Horticulture   565
- **TITLE**   Horticulture Phase II:City & Guilds
- **PLACE**   Isle of Wight College

Length 30 weeks part time   **Start** September   **Days** Thurs 9.00-4.00   **Cost** £158.50 Concessions possible   **Entry Reqs** None, keen interest essential   **Award** C&G 022, progression to RHS Diploma   **Creche** Day nursery

- **CONTACT**   Marketing Centre 01983 526631

- **SUBJECT**   Information Technology   566
- **TITLE**   Information Technology
- **PLACE**   Isle of Wight College

Length 1 year part time   **Start** September   **Days** Wed 9.00-4.00   **Cost** £158.50 Concessions possible   **Entry Reqs** Contact College   **Creche** Day nursery

- **CONTACT**   Marketing Centre 01983 526631

- **SUBJECT**   Management   567
- **TITLE**   Women into Management
- **PLACE**   Isle of Wight College

Length 6 weeks   **Start** September   **Days** Tues 6.00-9.00   **Cost** £95 Concessions possible   **Entry Reqs** Contact College   **Creche** Day nursery

- **CONTACT**   Marketing Centre 01983 526631

- **SUBJECT**   Preparatory   568
- **TITLE**   Basic Skills: Wordpower & Numberpower
- **PLACE**   Isle of Wight College

Length 18 weeks-1 year   **Start** September, January or at any time   **Days** 12½ hours/week minimum   **Cost** Free   **Entry Reqs** Enthusiasm and commitment   **Award** Wordpower/Numberpower Levels Foundation to 2   **Creche** Day nursery

- **CONTACT**   Bob Atkins 01983 526631 x212

- **SUBJECT** Preparatory   **569**
- **TITLE** Skills for Work
- **PLACE** Isle of Wight College

Length Contact College   **Days**   **Cost** Contact College   **Entry Reqs** None   **Creche** Day nursery

- **CONTACT** Marketing Centre 01983 526631

COUNTY CONTACTS

Information and advice

ASET, Isle of Wight College, Medina Way, Newport PO30 5TA 01983 526631. Adult guidance services
New Directions Adult Guidance Service, Wight Training and Enterprise 01983 822818

Open University

The Open University, South Region, Foxcombe Hall, Boars Hill, Oxford OX1 5HR 01865 328038

Training and Enterprise Council

Isle of Wight TEC, Mill Court, Furlongs, Newport PO30 2AA 01983 822818

WEA office

WEA Thames and Solent, 6 Brewer Street, Oxford OX1 1QN 01865 246270   *Contact:* Annie Winner

KENT

COURSES

- **SUBJECT** Access   **570**
- **TITLE** Access to Higher Education
- **PLACE** West Kent College, Tonbridge

Length 1 year   **Start** September   **Days** 3 days/week 9.00-3.00   **Cost** £500   **Entry Reqs** A commitment to study and benefit from the course   **Award** Access Certificate (HEQC kitemarked)   **Creche** Nursery

- **CONTACT** Isabel Gill/Jean Hayes 01732 358101 x4414

- **SUBJECT** Access/Art   **571**
- **TITLE** Access to Fine Art
- **PLACE** Kent Institute of Art & Design

Length 1 year   **Start** September   **Days** 1 day+1 eve/week   **Cost** Contact College   **Entry Reqs** Some prior experience of art or design + folder of visual work   **Award** Access Certificate   **Creche** No

- **CONTACT** Janice Thompson 01622 757286 (after 1pm)

- **SUBJECT** Access/Art & Design   572
- **TITLE** Access to Art & Design
- **PLACE** Thanet College

Length 1 year   **Start** September   **Days** Up to 18 hours over 3 days/week   **Cost** £325   **Entry Reqs** Age 21+ by end of course   **Award** Entry to higher education institutions   **Creche** No

- **CONTACT** Central Admissions 01843 865111

- **SUBJECT** Access/Business Studies   573
- **TITLE** Access to Business Studies
- **PLACE** South Kent College, Ashford and Dover

Length 1 year (16 hours/week)   **Start** September   **Days** 4 days/week 9.30-2.30   **Cost** Contact College. Grants available   **Entry Reqs** Interview   **Award** Access Certificate, entry to degree programmes   **Creche** No

- **CONTACT** Access Co-ordinator 01304 204573

- **SUBJECT** Access/Business Studies   574
- **TITLE** Access to Business Studies
- **PLACE** Thanet College

Length 1 year   **Start** September   **Days** 12 hours over up to 4 days/week   **Cost** Contact College   **Entry Reqs** Age 21+ by end of course   **Award** Entry to higher education institutions   **Creche** No

- **CONTACT** Central Admissions 01843 865111

- **SUBJECT** Access/Business Studies/Computing/Humanities/Media Studies/   575
  Science/Social Science/Teaching/Law/Art & Design/Technology
- **TITLE** Modular Access Programme
- **PLACE** North West Kent College of Technology

Length 1 year   **Start** September   **Days** Modular, Mon-Fri 10.00-3.00   **Cost** Contact College   **Entry Reqs** By interview   **Award** Access to Higher Education   **Creche** Playgroup

- **CONTACT** Mr M Webber 01322 225471 x2461

- **SUBJECT** Access/Community Studies/Health Studies   576
- **TITLE** Access to Social and Health Care
- **PLACE** Thanet College

Length 1 year   **Start** September   **Days** 15 hours/week spread over 5 days   **Cost** Approx £300   **Entry Reqs** Age 21+ by end of course   **Award** Entry to higher education institutions   **Creche** No

- **CONTACT** Central Admissions 01843 865111

- **SUBJECT** Access/Computing   577
- **TITLE** Access to Computing
- **PLACE** Canterbury College

Length 1 year   **Start** September   **Cost** Contact College   **Entry Reqs** None   **Award** Entry to higher level courses in computing/employment   **Creche** Yes, contact College for fees

- **CONTACT** Course Information 01227 766081

- **SUBJECT** Access/Computing/Accounting/Business Studies   578
- **TITLE** Access to Computing, Accounts and Business Studies
- **PLACE** Mid-Kent College of H & FE, Horsted, Chatham

Length 1 year   **Start** September   **Days** Mon-Fri 9.30-2.30   **Cost** Free   **Entry Reqs** None   **Award** Entry to higher education   **Creche** No

- **CONTACT** Helpline 01634 402020

- **SUBJECT** Access/Engineering   579
- **TITLE** Access to Engineering
- **PLACE** Canterbury College

Length 1 year   **Start** October   **Cost** Contact College   **Entry Reqs** Interview   **Award** Entry to higher level courses in engineering/employment   **Creche** Yes, contact College for fees

- **CONTACT** Course Information 01227 766081

- **SUBJECT** Access/English/History/Social Studies   580
- **TITLE** Access to English Literature, History and Social Studies
- **PLACE** Mid-Kent College of H & FE, Horsted, Chatham

Length 2 years   **Start** September   **Days** Year 1: Mon+Tues 6.00-9.00, year 2: Tues 6.00-9.00   **Cost** Year 1: £130, year 2: £90   **Entry Reqs** No formal requirements   **Award** Entry to higher education   **Creche** No

- **CONTACT** Helpline 01634 402020

- **SUBJECT** Access/Environmental Studies   581
- **TITLE** Access to Geography and Environmental Studies
- **PLACE** South Kent College, Ashford

Length 1 year   **Start** September   **Days** 3 days/week 9.30-2.30   **Cost** Contact College. Grants available   **Entry Reqs** Interview   **Award** HEQC validated award leading to entry to degree programmes   **Creche** No

- **CONTACT** Course Information 01233 624513

- **SUBJECT** Access/Health Studies   582
- **TITLE** Access to Health Care
- **PLACE** Mid-Kent College of H & FE, Horsted, Chatham

Length 1 year   **Start** September   **Days** Mon-Fri 9.30-2.30   **Cost** Free   **Entry Reqs** None   **Award** Entry to higher education   **Creche** No

- **CONTACT** Helpline 01634 402020

- **SUBJECT** Access/Health Studies   583
- **TITLE** Access to Health and Caring Professions
- **PLACE** South Kent College, Ashford

Length 1 year   **Start** September   **Days** 3 days/week 9.30-2.30   **Cost** Contact College. Grants available   **Entry Reqs** Interview   **Award** HEQC validated award leading to entry to diploma and degree programmes   **Creche** No

- **CONTACT** Course Information 01233 624513

- **SUBJECT** Access/Humanities/Social Science   584
- **TITLE** Access to Humanities/Social Science
- **PLACE** Canterbury College

Length 1 year   **Start** September   **Days** 1 day/week or 2 eves/week   **Cost** Contact College. Concessions available   **Entry Reqs** Interview   **Award** Entry to higher education   **Creche** Yes, contact College for fees

- **CONTACT** Course Information 01227 766081

- **SUBJECT** Access/Humanities/Social Science   585
- **TITLE** Access to Humanities/Social Science
- **PLACE** Mid-Kent College of H & FE, Horsted, Chatham

Length 1 year   **Start** September, January   **Days** Mon-Fri 9.30-2.30   **Cost** Free   **Entry Reqs** None   **Award** Entry to higher education   **Creche** No

- **CONTACT** Helpline 01634 402020

- **SUBJECT**   Access/Humanities/Social Science   586
- **TITLE**   Access to Humanities/Social Science
- **PLACE**   Thanet College

Length 1 year or 2 year Evening Access   **Start** September   **Days** 1 year: up to 16 hours over 3-4 days/week   **Cost** Contact College   **Entry Reqs** Age 21+ by end of course   **Award** Entry to higher education institutions   **Creche** No

- **CONTACT**   Central Admissions 01843 865111

- **SUBJECT**   Access/Humanities/Social Studies   587
- **TITLE**   Access to Humanities and Social Studies
- **PLACE**   University of Kent, Canterbury

Length 1 or 2 years   **Start** September   **Days** 1-2 eves/week or 1 day/week   **Cost** Contact University. Concessions available   **Entry Reqs** None   **Award** Preparation for degree and diploma courses   **Creche** Creche and playgroup may be available

- **CONTACT**   Course Information 01227 764000

- **SUBJECT**   Access/Languages   588
- **TITLE**   Access to Languages and European Studies
- **PLACE**   Mid-Kent College of H & FE, Horsted, Chatham

Length 1 year   **Start** September   **Days** Mon-Fri 9.30-2.30   **Cost** Free   **Entry Reqs** Some knowledge of French, preferably to GCSE standard or equivalent   **Award** Entry to higher education   **Creche** No

- **CONTACT**   Helpline 01634 402020

- **SUBJECT**   Access/Law   589
- **TITLE**   Access to Law
- **PLACE**   Mid-Kent College of H & FE, Horsted, Chatham

Length 1 year   **Start** September   **Days** Mon-Fri 9.30-2.30   **Cost** Free   **Entry Reqs** No formal requirements   **Award** Entry to higher education   **Creche** No

- **CONTACT**   Helpline 01634 402020

- **SUBJECT**   Access/Law   590
- **TITLE**   Access to Law Studies
- **PLACE**   South Kent College, Ashford

Length 1 year   **Start** September   **Days** 1 day+same eve+1 eve/week   **Cost** Contact College. Concessions available   **Entry Reqs** None   **Award** Entry to degree courses in Law and Law-related subjects   **Creche** No

- **CONTACT**   Course Information 01233 624513

- **SUBJECT**   Access/Mathematics   591
- **TITLE**   Access to Mathematics/Statistics
- **PLACE**   Thanet College

Length 1 year   **Start** September   **Days** Approx 18 hours over 3-4 days/week   **Cost** £300   **Entry Reqs** Age 21+ by end of course   **Award** Entry to higher education institutions   **Creche** No

- **CONTACT**   Central Admissions 01843 865111

- **SUBJECT**   Access/Mathematics/Computing/Economics   592
- **TITLE**   Access to 1. Mathematics & Computing 2. Mathematics & Economics
- **PLACE**   South Kent College, Ashford

Length 1 year   **Start** September   **Days** Mon-Fri 9.30-2.30   **Cost** Contact College. Grants available   **Entry Reqs** Interview   **Award** HEQC validated award leading to entry to degree programmes   **Creche** No

- **CONTACT**   Course Information 01233 624513

- **SUBJECT** Access/Mathematics/Information Technology 593
- **TITLE** Access to Mathematics & Information Technology
- **PLACE** Thanet College

Length 1 year **Start** September **Days** Approx 18 hours over 3-4 days/week **Cost** Approx £300 **Entry Reqs** Age 21+ by end of course **Award** Entry to higher education institutions **Creche** No
- **CONTACT** Central Admissions 01843 865111

- **SUBJECT** Access/Science 594
- **TITLE** Access to Science
- **PLACE** Canterbury College

Length 1 year **Start** September **Days** 15 hours/week over 3 days between 9.30-3.30 **Cost** Contact College **Entry Reqs** Interview **Award** Entry to higher level courses **Creche** Yes, contact College for fees
- **CONTACT** Course Information 01227 766081

- **SUBJECT** Access/Science 595
- **TITLE** Access to Science
- **PLACE** Mid-Kent College of H & FE, Horsted, Chatham

Length 1.1 year 2.2 years 3.2 years **Start** September **Days** 1. &2. Mon-Fri 9.30-2.30, 3. Mon+Tues 6.00-9.00 **Cost** 1. Free 2. £95/year 3. £150/year **Entry Reqs** No formal requirements **Award** Entry to higher education **Creche** No
- **CONTACT** Helpline 01634 402020

- **SUBJECT** Access/Science 596
- **TITLE** Access to Science
- **PLACE** Thanet College

Length 1 year **Start** September **Days** 16 hours over 4 days/week **Cost** Contact College **Entry Reqs** Age 21+ by end of course **Award** Entry to higher education institutions **Creche** No
- **CONTACT** Central Admissions 01843 865111

- **SUBJECT** Access/Science/Information Technology/Humanities 597
- **TITLE** Access to Science, IT, Humanities
- **PLACE** West Kent College, Tonbridge

Length 1 year **Start** September **Days** 3 days/week 10.00-3.00 **Cost** Contact College **Entry Reqs** Commitment to study and benefit from course **Award** Access Certificate **Creche** Nursery
- **CONTACT** Course Information 01732 358101

- **SUBJECT** Access/Social Science/Humanities 598
- **TITLE** Access to 1. Social Science 2. Humanities
- **PLACE** South Kent College, Ashford

Length 1 year **Start** September **Cost** Contact College. Grants available **Entry Reqs** Interview **Award** HEQC validated award leading to entry to degree programmes **Creche** No
- **CONTACT** Course Information 01233 624513

- **SUBJECT** Access/Teaching 599
- **TITLE** Access to Teaching
- **PLACE** South Kent College, Dover

Length 1 year (12 hours/week) **Start** September **Days** 3 days/week 9.30-2.30 **Cost** Contact College. Grants available **Entry Reqs** Interview **Award** HEQC validated award leading to entry to degree programmes **Creche** No
- **CONTACT** Course Information 01303 850061

- **SUBJECT**   Access/Tourism & Leisure   600
- **TITLE**   Access to Tourism and Leisure Studies
- **PLACE**   South Kent College, Dover

Length 1 year (16 hours/week)   **Start** September   **Days** 4 days/week 9.30-2.30   **Cost** Contact College. Grants available   **Entry Reqs** Interview   **Award** HEQC validated award leading to entry to degree programmes   **Creche** No

- **CONTACT**   Course Information 01303 850061

- **SUBJECT**   Art   601
- **TITLE**   BA(Hons) Fine Art
- **PLACE**   Kent Institute of Art & Design, Canterbury

Length 5 years part time   **Days** 1 day+2 eves/week   **Cost** Contact College   **Entry Reqs** Folder of art work & completion of Access Course or equivalent   **Award** BA(Hons), interim awards of Certificate & Diploma HE   **Creche** No

- **CONTACT**   Anthony Heywood 01227 769371

- **SUBJECT**   Beauty   602
- **TITLE**   1. Beauty 2. Make Up & Manicure
- **PLACE**   Mid-Kent College of H & FE, City Way, Rochester

Length 1.1 year 2.2 years   **Start** September   **Days** 1. Mon 9.30-4.30 2. Tues 6.00-9.00   **Cost** 1. £230 2. £150   **Entry Reqs** Mature/retraining students by interview and assessment **Award** 1. NVQ Level 2 (Vocational Training Charitable Trust) 2. NVQ 2 Records of Achievement (VTCT)   **Creche** No

- **CONTACT**   Jillian Edwards 01634 830644

- **SUBJECT**   Business/Finance   603
- **TITLE**   HNC in Business & Finance
- **PLACE**   Mid-Kent College of H & FE, Horsted, Chatham

Length 2 years   **Start** September   **Days** Day option Thurs 9.15-6.15 or Mon-Thurs eves 5.45-9.15   **Cost** £560/year including residential weekend   **Entry Reqs** Mature students with suitable experience   **Award** HNC in Business & Finance   **Creche** No

- **CONTACT**   Helpline 01634 402020

- **SUBJECT**   Business Administration   604
- **TITLE**   National Certificate for Farm Secretaries/College Diploma: Business Administration
- **PLACE**   Hadlow College of Agriculture & Horticulture

Length 1 year (32 weeks)   **Start** September   **Days** Full time 5 days/week (part time options available)   **Cost** £594   **Entry Reqs** 3 GCSE passes A-C (Maths/Arithmetic subject & English)   **Award** National Certificate for Farm Secretaries/College Diploma in Business Admin   **Creche**

- **CONTACT**   Heather Coppock 01732 850551

- **SUBJECT**   Care Studies   605
- **TITLE**   Community Care
- **PLACE**   Dartford Adult Education Centre

Length 1 year   **Start** October   **Days** Fri 9.15-4.00   **Cost** Contact Centre   **Award** C&G Certificate in Community Care   **Creche** Yes & playgroup, small charge

- **CONTACT**   Maureen Green 01322 221897

- **SUBJECT** Careers Guidance 606
- **TITLE** Diploma in Careers Guidance
- **PLACE** 1. The College of Careers Guidance 2. Distance Learning

Length 1.1 year full time 2.2 years part time/distance learning **Start** 1. Jan/April/Sept 2. Jan/April/June/Sept **Days** 1.5 days/week 9.30-5.00 2. Distance Learning **Cost** 1. £1800 2. £3600 **Entry Reqs** Age 25+, competent communications skills, interest in people **Award** Diploma in Careers Guidance (LGMB) **Creche** No

- **CONTACT** Administrative Assistants, Careers Guidance Programmes (UK) 01322 664407

- **SUBJECT** Community Studies 607
- **TITLE** Advanced Diploma in Community Organisations
- **PLACE** Dartford Adult Education Centre

Length 1 year **Start** October **Days** Fri 1.00-3.30 **Cost** Contact Centre **Entry Reqs** Some experience in a community group **Award** RSA Diploma in the Organisation of Community Groups **Creche** Yes & playgroup, small charge

- **CONTACT** Kath France 01322 221897

- **SUBJECT** Counselling 608
- **TITLE** Introductory, Certificate and Diploma Courses
- **PLACE** Adult Education Service, centres in Maidstone area

Length Various **Start** Various **Cost** Contact College **Entry Reqs** None

- **RI1** Ian Forward 01622 752165

- **SUBJECT** Design 609
- **TITLE** Graphic Design BTEC Higher National Diploma
- **PLACE** Kent Institute of Art & Design, Maidstone

Length 2 years part time **Start** September/October **Days** 1 day/week **Cost** Contact College **Entry Reqs** 3 GCSEs or equiv+Foundation or BTEC Nat Dip. Mature entry with prior graphic experience **Award** BTEC HND **Creche** No

- **CONTACT** Mike Tappenden 01622 757286

- **SUBJECT** Floristry 610
- **TITLE** Floristry
- **PLACE** Mid-Kent College of H & FE, City Way, Rochester

Length 2 years **Start** September, January **Days** Mon-Thurs 9.00-4.00 **Cost** £230/year **Entry Reqs** Mature/retraining students **Award** C&G NVQ 2 Floristry **Creche** No

- **CONTACT** Linda Parr 01634 830644 x271

- **SUBJECT** Hairdressing 611
- **TITLE** Hairdressing City & Guilds 3010
- **PLACE** Mid-Kent College of H & FE, City Way, Rochester

Length 2 years **Start** September **Days** Wed 9.00-4.00 **Cost** £230 **Entry Reqs** Mature/retraining students by interview and assessment **Award** Hairdressing Training Board/C&G 3010 Certificate NVQ Level 2 status **Creche** No

- **CONTACT** June Strouts 01634 830644

- **SUBJECT** Health Studies 612
- **TITLE** Complementary Therapies
- **PLACE** Holmesdale Evening Centre, Snodland

Length Various **Start** September, January **Days** Eves **Cost** Contact Centre **Entry Reqs** Contact Centre **Award** CIBTAC, ITEC Certificates and Diplomas **Creche** No

- **CONTACT** Malcolm Mitchell 01674 245855/01622 752165

Kent

- **SUBJECT** Information Technology   613
- **TITLE**   Keyboarding Skills and Computing
- **PLACE**   Hadlow College of Agriculture & Horticulture
Length 32 weeks   **Start** September   **Days** Tues+Fri afternoons   **Cost** £135   **Entry Reqs** None   **Award** RSA qualifications in Wordprocessing and Computer Literacy   **Creche** No
- **CONTACT** Heather Coppock 01732 850551

- **SUBJECT** Management   614
- **TITLE**   MA Employment Strategy
- **PLACE**   University of Greenwich, Kings Hill, West Kent
Length 1 year   **Start** October   **Days** Block release (3 days/week)   **Cost** £1950   **Entry Reqs** Managers with CM, DMS or members of IPD Stage II   **Award** MA Employment Strategy   **Creche** No
- **CONTACT** Janet Winter 0181 331 8590

- **SUBJECT** Marketing   615
- **TITLE**   MA Marketing
- **PLACE**   University of Greenwich, Kings Hill, West Kent
Length 1 year   **Start** October   **Days** Block release   **Cost** £1950   **Entry Reqs** Chartered Institute of Marketing Diploma or equivalent   **Award** MA Marketing   **Creche** No
- **CONTACT** Keith Lewis 0181 331 8590

- **SUBJECT** Multi-Subject   616
- **TITLE**   Combined Studies Programme
- **PLACE**   University of Kent at Canterbury
Length Various   **Start** Contact University   **Cost** Contact University   **Award** Courses are accredited
- **CONTACT** School of Continuing Education 01732 352316

- **SUBJECT** Multi-Subject   617
- **TITLE**   Part Time Diplomas and Degrees
- **PLACE**   University of Kent, various venues
Length Various (2-6 years)   **Start** October   **Cost** Various   **Entry Reqs** A Levels, Access or evidence of mature study   **Award** University of Kent Diploma or BA(Hons)   **Creche** Creche and playgroup may be available
- **CONTACT** School of Continuing Education 01732 352316

- **SUBJECT** NOW   618
- **TITLE**   Assertiveness for Women
- **PLACE**   Dartford Adult Education Centre
Length 10 weeks   **Start** October, January, April   **Days** Contact Centre   **Cost** Contact Centre   **Entry Reqs** None   **Award** None   **Creche** Yes & playgroup daytime, small charge
- **CONTACT** Doreen Parris 01322 221897

- **SUBJECT** Office Skills   619
- **TITLE**   Business Skills Update
- **PLACE**   Mid-Kent College of H & FE 1. Maidstone 2. Rochester
Length 1.10 weeks 2.15 weeks   **Start** 1. Sept, Jan, April 2. Sept, February   **Days** 1. Mon-Fri 9.15-2.45 2. Mon-Fri 9.00-2.00   **Cost** Free   **Entry Reqs** None   **Award** NVQ I/II/III Administration   **Creche** No
- **CONTACT** Helpline 01634 402020

- **SUBJECT** Office Skills/Information Technology   620
- **TITLE**   Office Skills, Information Technology
- **PLACE**   St Luke's Adult Education Centre, Sittingbourne Road, Maidstone
Length Contact College   **Start** Contact College   **Cost** Contact College
- **CONTACT** Joy Ackroyd 01622 755808

- **SUBJECT** Preparatory — 621
- **TITLE** Fresh Start
- **PLACE** North West Kent College of Technology, Dartford and Gravesend

Length 1 term **Start** September, January, April **Days** Various **Cost** Contact College **Entry Reqs** None **Award** NVQ Modules **Creche** Playgroup
- **CONTACT** Mrs E Croker 01474 352049

- **SUBJECT** Preparatory — 622
- **TITLE** Fresh Start
- **PLACE** West Kent College, Tonbridge

Length 1 year **Start** September **Days** Flexible **Cost** £500 (free to Kent residents) **Entry Reqs** None **Award** GCSEs or other qualifications **Creche** No
- **CONTACT** 01732 358101

- **SUBJECT** Preparatory — 623
- **TITLE** Job Seeking Skills/Basic Education
- **PLACE** St Luke's Adult Education Centre, Sittingbourne Road, Maidstone

Length 3 terms or as appropriate **Start** Roll on roll off **Cost** Contact College **Entry Reqs** None **Award** Various **Creche** No
- **CONTACT** Joy Ackroyd 01622 755808

- **SUBJECT** Preparatory — 624
- **TITLE** Return to Study
- **PLACE** University of Kent, various venues

Length Various **Start** September **Days** Various days/eves **Cost** Contact University **Entry Reqs** Open entry **Award** None **Creche** Ask for details
- **CONTACT** chool of Continuing Education 01732 352316
School of Continuing Education 01732 352316

- **SUBJECT** Preparatory — 625
- **TITLE** Skills Shop for Women
- **PLACE** Dartford Adult Education Centre

Length 5 weeks **Start** Continuous October to April **Days** Tues morning **Cost** Contact Centre **Entry Reqs** None **Award** None **Creche** Yes & playgroup, small charge
- **CONTACT** Doreen Parris 01322 221897

- **SUBJECT** Preparatory — 626
- **TITLE** Study Skills Workshops
- **PLACE** University of Kent at Canterbury

Length 2 Saturdays **Start** Various **Days** Sat 10.00-4.00 **Cost** £24 Concessions available **Entry Reqs** None
- **CONTACT** Jean Field 01227 827647

- **SUBJECT** Preparatory/Computing — 627
- **TITLE** Return to Study: Computing
- **PLACE** Mid-Kent College of H & FE, Horsted, Chatham

Length 4 weeks **Start** June, August **Days** Mon-Wed 9.30-2.30 **Cost** £50 **Entry Reqs** None **Creche** No
- **CONTACT** Helpline 01634 402020

- **SUBJECT** Science — 628
- **TITLE** Biotechnology: Masters Degree by Research
- **PLACE** University of Kent at Canterbury

Length 1 year **Start** October **Cost** Biotechnology & Biological Sciences Research Council award available **Entry Reqs** Graduates with first or upper second honours degree in an appropriate subject **Award** MSc
- **CONTACT** Dr V Essex, BBSRC, 01793 413200

Kent

- **SUBJECT**   Social Science   629
- **TITLE**   Social Science 1. Diploma 2. Degree
- **PLACE**   Mid-Kent College of H & FE, Horsted, Chatham

Length 1. 2 years 2. 3 years   **Start** September   **Days** 1. Tues 2. Mon+Wed 8.00-9.00   **Cost** 1. £110/year 2. £180/year   **Entry Reqs** 1.5 GCE/GCSE passes, 2 at A Level or equivalent. Mature students may bypass these   **Award** Social Science Diploma or Degree   **Creche** No

- **CONTACT**   Helpline 01634 402020

COUNTY CONTACTS

Information and advice:

Kent Adult Careers Guidance, Head Office 01634 841400
A specialist free careers advisory service for adults is run by Kent County Council, available to all adults including those seeking to return to work or learning. Information is available on opportunities for employment, training and education, skills assessment and practical help with CV preparation, interview skills and modern selection methods. The three main Bureaux are equipped with interactive computer programmes and comprehensive library facilities. Careers Advisers are also available at various libraries and Jobcentres.
Canterbury Office, 3rd Floor, Lombard House, 12-17 Upper Bridge Street, Canterbury 01227 456808. Open Mon-Thurs 9.30-5.00 and 3rd Saturday of the month 9.30-12.30
Chatham Office, 85 High Street, Chatham. 01634 819137. Open Tues-Fri 9.30-5.00 and 1st Saturday of the month 9.30-12.30
Tunbridge Wells Office, 10 Lonsdale Gardens, Tunbridge Wells 01892 538430. Open Mon, Tues, Thurs & Fri 9.30-5.00 and 2nd Saturday of the month 9.30-12.30

Open University:

The Open University. South East Region, St James's House, 150 London Road, East Grinstead RH19 1ES 01342 410545

Other agencies:

Libertum, Ash House, Ash Road, New Ash Green DA3 8JD 01474 879494   *Contact:* Sharon Brine. Career guidance consultancy, psychometric analysis. Career change/development specialists.

Training and Enterprise Council:

Kent TEC, 5th Floor, Mountbatten House, 28 Military Road, Chatham ME4 4JE 01634 844411. Runs Training Access Points (01634 818188) for information and details of nearest TAP

WEA office:

WEA South Eastern Office, 4 Castle Hill, Rochester ME1 1QQ 01634 842140   *Contact:* Wilma Fraser, Joy Pascoe

110

COURSES

- **SUBJECT** Access   **630**
- **TITLE** Access to Health & Social Studies, Business, IT
- **PLACE** Morecambe Community Education Centre

Length 1 year   **Start** September   **Days** Mon-Fri 9.45-3.00   **Cost** Variable. Remitted fees for full time students   **Entry Reqs** None   **Award** Open College Full Certificate   **Creche** Nursery Contact College

- **CONTACT** Janet Jones 01524 831374 (answerphone available)

- **SUBJECT** Access   **631**
- **TITLE** Open College A & B Units
- **PLACE** Blackburn College

Length A units 16 weeks, B units 32 weeks   **Start** September, February   **Days** 3 hours/week per unit   **Cost** Contact College   **Entry Reqs** None   **Award** Access to higher education with B units   **Creche** Yes Contact College for fees

- **CONTACT** Course Enquiries 01254 55144

- **SUBJECT** Access   **632**
- **TITLE** Open College A & B Units/Foundation Programme/Multi-Subject
- **PLACE** Preston College, Main Campus, St Vincent's Road

Length 1 year or 2 years, full or part time   **Start** September, February (B Units)   **Days** Mon-Fri 9.30-4.30, ft 16 hours/week, pt 7.5 hours/week   **Cost** Full time free, concessions for part time students available   **Entry Reqs** None   **Award** Open College Full Certificate, GCSE Maths & English   **Creche** Yes

- **CONTACT** Adult Team 01772 772200

- **SUBJECT** Access   **633**
- **TITLE** Open College A & B Units
- **PLACE** Preston College, Main Campus, St Vincent's Road

Length 1-2 years   **Start** September   **Days** Mon-Fri 9.30-4.30 (16 hours/week)   **Cost** Free. Grant aided for those with disrupted educational background   **Entry Reqs** None   **Award** Open College Full Certificate   **Creche** Yes

- **CONTACT** Adult Team 01772 772250/1

- **SUBJECT** Access   **634**
- **TITLE** Open College of the North West
- **PLACE** Lancaster & Morecambe College or Morecambe CE Centre

Length Modular units approx 50-100 hours+ Open Learning   **Start** September, January   **Days** Varies   **Cost** Contact College. Concessions available   **Entry Reqs** None   **Award** Open College of the North West kitemarked accreditation   **Creche** Nursery Contact College

- **CONTACT** Janet Jones 01524 831374 (answerphone available)

- **SUBJECT** Access   **635**
- **TITLE** What Next for Women
- **PLACE** Morecambe CE Centre and Lancaster & Morecambe College

Length Modular 16032 weeks   **Start** September/October   **Days** Flexible to suit individual needs   **Cost** £25-£50 Concessions available, free for full time students   **Entry Reqs** None   **Award** Open College of the North West kitemarked accreditation   **Creche** Nursery Contact College

- **CONTACT** Janet Jones 01524 831374 (answerphone available)

- **SUBJECT**   Access/Teaching 636
- **TITLE**   Access to Teacher Training
- **PLACE**   Morecambe Community Education Centre

Length 1 year   **Start** September   **Days** Mon-Fri full or part time   **Cost** Contact College. Concessions available   **Entry Reqs** Contact College   **Award** Open College of the North West kitemarked accreditation   **Creche** Nursery Contact College
- **CONTACT**   Janet Jones 01524 831374 (answerphone available)

- **SUBJECT**   Computing 637
- **TITLE**   Introduction to Computing
- **PLACE**   Myerscough College

Length Various   **Start** Contact College   **Cost** Contact College
- **CONTACT**   Academic Registry 01995 640611

- **SUBJECT**   Electronics/Mathematics/Technology 638
- **TITLE**   Foundation Year in Technology for Women
- **PLACE**   University of Central Lancashire

Length 1 year   **Start** October   **Days** Full time 10.00-3.00   **Cost** Grant from LEA   **Entry Reqs** None   **Creche** Yes Approx £5/day
- **CONTACT**   Liz Bennett 01772 893242

- **SUBJECT**   Engineering 639
- **TITLE**   Women into Engineering
- **PLACE**   Burnley College

Length 20 weeks   **Start** Varies   **Days** Varies   **Cost** Free   **Entry Reqs** None   **Award** College Certificate   **Creche** Yes Contact College
- **CONTACT**   Annette Williams 01282 36111 x213

- **SUBJECT**   Engineering 640
- **TITLE**   Women into Technology
- **PLACE**   Burnley College

Length 1 year full time   **Start** September   **Days** 5 days/week 10.00-3.00   **Cost** Mandatory grant, no fee   **Entry Reqs** Interview   **Award** University Certificate in Technology, Year 1 of BEng   **Creche** Yes Contact College
- **CONTACT**   Annette Williams 01282 36111 x213

- **SUBJECT**   Environmental Sciences 641
- **TITLE**   Science of the Environment: Research Masters Training Programme
- **PLACE**   University of Lancaster

Length 1 year   **Start** October   **Cost** Natural Environment Research Council award available   **Entry Reqs** Graduates with first or upper second honours degree in an appropriate subject   **Award** MSc
- **CONTACT**   Professor Nick Hewitt 01524 65201

- **SUBJECT**   Multi-Subject 642
- **TITLE**   Multi-Subject Short Courses
- **PLACE**   Myerscough College

Length Various   **Cost** Contact College
- **CONTACT**   Academic Registry 01995 640611

- **SUBJECT**   NOW 643
- **TITLE**   Competence in IT/Communications/Maths/Personal & Career Development/ Other Vocational Modules
- **PLACE**   Preston College

Length 1 year   **Start** September   **Days** Wed + Fri 9.30-2.30; 10 hours/week part time, 15 hours/week full time   **Cost** Free if full time   **Entry Reqs** None   **Award** University Certificate   **Creche** Yes
- **CONTACT**   Linda Barton/Phyllis Williams 01772 772250/1

Lancashire

- **SUBJECT** NOW
- **TITLE** New Opportunities for Women
- **PLACE** Morecambe Community Education Centre

644

Length 1 year **Days** Mon-Fri full or part time **Cost** Contact College. Concessions available **Entry Reqs** None **Award** Open College of the North West kitemarked accreditation **Creche** Nursery Contact College
- **CONTACT** Janet Jones 01524 831374 (answerphone available)

- **SUBJECT** Preparatory
- **TITLE** Access for Women
- **PLACE** Burnley College

645

Length 5 weeks **Start** March **Days** 2 hours/week day and evening **Cost** Free **Entry Reqs** None **Award** College Certificate **Creche** Yes Contact College
- **CONTACT** Annette Williams 01282 36111 x213

- **SUBJECT** Preparatory
- **TITLE** Assertiveness
- **PLACE** Preston College, Trinity Centre

646

Length 10 weeks **Start** September, January **Days** Tues+Wed 7.00-9.00 **Cost** £22 **Entry Reqs** None **Award** Leads to further study: New Opportunities for Women Course, Open College Units, Foundation & Access **Creche** No
- **CONTACT** Vera Conway 01772 253558

- **SUBJECT** Preparatory
- **TITLE** Open College of the North West Stage A & B Units
- **PLACE** The Adult College, Lancaster

647

Length Stage A: 13 weeks, Stage B: 34 weeks **Start** September, January **Days** Day and eve **Cost** Stage A: £30, Stage B: £60 **Entry Reqs** Age 21+ **Award** OCNW Certificate **Creche** Nursery for 23 2-5 year olds
- **CONTACT** Jean Latimer 01524 60141

- **SUBJECT** Preparatory
- **TITLE** Courses for Women Returners: Starting Points
- **PLACE** The Adult College, Lancaster

648

Length 6-7 weeks **Start** Every 2 months **Days** Various hours between 10.00-3.00 **Cost** Free Course funded by Lancashire Enterprise/ESF. Allowance for travel/childcare **Entry Reqs** None **Award** RSA Practical Skills Certificate **Creche** Nursery for 23 2-5 year olds
- **CONTACT** Heather Armer/Murial Lobley 01524 60141

- **SUBJECT** Women's Studies
- **TITLE** Women in Society 1. Stage A 2. Stage B
- **PLACE** Burnley College

649

Length 1.16 weeks 2.32 weeks **Start** 1. September, February 2. September **Days** Varies, daytime **Cost** 1. £25 2. £74 (approximately) **Entry Reqs** None **Award** 1. OCFNW Stage A 2. OCFNW Stage B **Creche** Yes Contact College
- **CONTACT** Annette Williams 01282 36111 x213

- **SUBJECT** Women's Studies
- **TITLE** Women's Studies
- **PLACE** Morecambe Community Education Centre

650

Length 1 year **Start** September **Days** Mon-Fri full or part time **Cost** Contact College. Concessions available **Entry Reqs** None **Award** Open College of the North West kitemarked accreditation **Creche** Nursery Contact College
- **CONTACT** Janet Jones 01524 831374 (answerphone available)

COUNTY CONTACTS

Information and advice

Educational Guidance for Adults Service, Student Recruitment Office, University of Central Lancashire, Preston PR1 2HE 01772 892400   *Contact:* Shelagh Murphy

Myerscough College, Myerscough Hall, Bilsborrow, Preston PR3 0RY 01995 640611. Women's information and guidance centre

Opportunities for Women, MBW Training, Rigby Road, Blackpool 01253 291110. Information, guidance and training for women

Opportunities for Women, Northbrook Training, Northbrook Road, Leyland 01772 451921

Opportunities for Women, TP Training Ltd, The Centre, Railway Road, Skelmersdale 01695 24477. Drop-in centre providing advice and guidance to women, also short courses

The Adult College Lancaster, PO Box 603, White Cross Education Centre, Quarry Road, Lancaster LA1 3SE 01524 60141. Information, advice and guidance to women on education and training opportunities. College also runs specialist courses for women returners funded by Lancashire Enterprises PLC and Lancashire County Council

Open University

The Open University, North West Region, Chorlton House, 70 Manchester Road, Chorlton cum Hardy, Manchester M21 9UN 0161 862 6824

Other agencies

Blackpool & The Fylde College, Ashfield Road, Bispham, Blackpool 01253 52352   *Contact:* Pat Stevens

Training and Enterprise Councils

ELTEC Ltd (East Lancashire), Red Rose Court, Petre Road, Clayton Business Park, Clayton Le Moor BB5 5JR 10254 301333. ESOL and job search training; NVQ training for textile industry; clerical and IT for Asian women; 'Into Engineering' for women; women's training centres; women's management; out of school childcare (contact Elizabeth Guha)

LAWTEC (Lancashire Area West), Caxton Road, Fulwood, Preston PR2 9ZB 01772 792111. Opportunities for Women Centres, Women into Work courses, resource centre for guidance and information, ESF joint funded

WEA offices

WEA Cheshire, Merseyside & West Lancashire District, 7/8 Bluecoat Chambers, School Lane, Liverpool L1 3BX 0151 709 8023   *Contact:* Christine Pugh. Covers west Lancs

WEA North Western District, 4th Floor, Crawford House, Oxford Road, Manchester M13 9GH 0161 273 7562   *Contact:* Linda Pepper. Covers east Lancs

COURSES

- **SUBJECT**   Access   651
- **TITLE**   Access: Foundation Skills
- **PLACE**   RNIB Vocational College

Length Various   **Start** Various   **Days** 5 days/week   **Cost** Contact College   **Entry Reqs** Assessment   **Creche** No
- **CONTACT**   Geoff Jackman 01509 611077

- **SUBJECT**   Access/Business Studies   652
- **TITLE**   Open Access to Business Studies
- **PLACE**   Charles Keene College

Length 1 year   **Start** September   **Days** Mon-Fri   **Cost** Contact College   **Entry Reqs** Interview   **Award** Access to higher education   **Creche** Playgroup
- **CONTACT**   Business & Management Faculty 0116 251 6037

- **SUBJECT**   Access/Health Studies/Social Science/Business Studies/Sports Studies/   653
  Chemistry/English Literature/History
- **TITLE**   Modular Access Programme
- **PLACE**   Hinckley College

Length 1 year   **Start** September   **Cost** Contact College   **Entry Reqs** None   **Award** Access to higher education
- **CONTACT**   Information Centre 01455 251222

- **SUBJECT**   Access/Humanities/Science/Social Science/Art & Design   654
- **TITLE**   Access to Humanities, Science, Social Science, Art & Design
- **PLACE**   Coalville Technical College

Length 36 weeks   **Start** January, September   **Days** Flexible   **Cost** Free to women in receipt of benefit, otherwise small cost   **Entry Reqs** Ability to achieve at least GCSE level   **Award** Access to higher education. Course validated by Leicestershire Open College Network **Creche** Yes Small charge
- **CONTACT**   Jill Dransfield 01530 836136

- **SUBJECT**   Access/Humanities/Social Science/Sports Studies   655
- **TITLE**   Open Access Humanities, Social Science, Sports Studies
- **PLACE**   Charles Keene College

Length 1 year   **Start** September   **Days** Mon-Fri, part time eves possible   **Cost** Contact College   **Entry Reqs** Interview   **Award** Access to higher education   **Creche** Playgroup
- **CONTACT**   Adult Access Co-ordinator 0116 251 6037

- **SUBJECT**   Access/Multi-Subject   656
- **TITLE**   Fully Supported Access to Mainstream Courses
- **PLACE**   Run by RNIB at Loughborough College

Length Various   **Start** September   **Days** 5 days/week, usual College terms   **Cost** Usually paid under Training for Work scheme or FE Funding Council   **Entry Reqs** Various   **Award** Various including BTEC/City & Guilds/GCSEs/GNVQ/A Levels   **Creche** No
- **CONTACT**   Geoff Jackman 01509 611077

- **SUBJECT**   Access/Nursing/Teaching   657
- **TITLE**   Access to Higher Education
- **PLACE**   Wigston College of Further Education

Length 1 year   **Start** September   **Days** Varies   **Cost** Full time free   **Entry Reqs** None   **Award** LOCN Access Certificate   **Creche** Yes
- **CONTACT**   Bob Holt 0116 288 5051

Leicestershire

- **SUBJECT** Access/Science/Engineering **658**
- **TITLE** Access to Higher Education: Science and Engineering
- **PLACE** Charles Keene College

Length 1 year full time or 4 terms part time   **Start** September, April (part time)   **Cost** Contact College   **Entry Reqs** Age 21+, interview   **Award** Access to higher education   **Creche** Playgroup

- **CONTACT** Adult Access Co-ordinator 0116 251 6037

- **SUBJECT** Biological Sciences/Medicine **659**
- **TITLE** Biological Sciences and Medicine: Research Masters Pilot Course
- **PLACE** University of Leicester

Length 1 year   **Start** October   **Cost** Medical Research Council award available   **Entry Reqs** Graduates with first or upper second honours degree in an appropriate subject   **Award** MSc

- **CONTACT** Professor R Camp 0116 252 3061

- **SUBJECT** Business Administration **660**
- **TITLE** Certificate in Business Administration
- **PLACE** Charles Keene College

Length 1 year   **Start** September   **Cost** Contact College   **Entry Reqs** Contact College   **Award** BTEC Certificate in Business Administration   **Creche** Playgroup

- **CONTACT** Business & Management Faculty 0116 251 6037

- **SUBJECT** Business Administration **661**
- **TITLE** Certificate in Business Administration
- **PLACE** Coalville Technical College

Length 1 year   **Start** January, September   **Days** Mon, Thurs 6.00-9.00, Wed occasional tutorials   **Cost** £385   **Entry Reqs** Age 21 years+ or 3 years' experience in responsible position in industry or commerce   **Award** BTEC Certificate in Business Administration

- **CONTACT** Frances Frandon 01530 836136

- **SUBJECT** Childcare **662**
- **TITLE** Childcare and Education: 1. NVQ Level II 2. Level III
- **PLACE** Coalville Technical College

Length 1.1 year 2.2 years   **Start** Flexible, roll on, roll off   **Days** Tues eves   **Cost** Contact College   **Entry Reqs** Either paid or voluntary work in a childcare setting   **Award** 1. NVQ Level II 2. NVQ Level III

- **CONTACT** Mrs S Hughes 01530 836136 x153

- **SUBJECT** Finance/Business/Law/Marketing/Communications **663**
- **TITLE** Business Enterprise Training (with Personal Presentation Option)
- **PLACE** RNIB Vocational College

Length 1-day modules   **Start** Various   **Days** 9.00-5.00   **Cost** Contact College   **Creche** No

- **CONTACT** Mark Braithwaite 01509 611077

- **SUBJECT** Hairdressing **664**
- **TITLE** Hairdressing for Women Returners
- **PLACE** Coalville Technical College

Length Flexible roll-on roll-off or 36 weeks full time or part time   **Start** September onwards   **Days** Flexible   **Cost** Free to unemployed women; free to unwaged women doing less than 9 hours tuition   **Entry Reqs** None   **Award** C&G National Preferred Scheme Levels 1 & 2   **Creche** Yes Small charge

- **CONTACT** Lorraine Gammon 01530 836136

- **SUBJECT**   Information Technology   665
- **TITLE**   BTEC Certificate in Information Technology
- **PLACE**   Charles Keene College

Length 1 year   **Start** September   **Days** Mon-Fri   **Cost** Contact College   **Entry Reqs**
Interview   **Award** BTEC Certificate   **Creche** Playgroup
- **CONTACT**   Course Enquiries 0116 251 6037

- **SUBJECT**   Information Technology   666
- **TITLE**   Information Technology
- **PLACE**   RNIB Vocational College

Length 52 weeks   **Start** Various   **Days** Full time 9.00-5.00, 5 days/week   **Cost** Contact
College   **Entry Reqs** Good keyboard and study skills, assessment   **Award** NVQ Information
Technology Level I/II   **Creche** No
- **CONTACT**   Geoff Jackman 01509 611077

- **SUBJECT**   Multi-Subject   667
- **TITLE**   Stepping Stones
- **PLACE**   Linwood Centre, Leicester

Length Flexible, according to requirements   **Start** September onwards, roll on, roll off   **Days**
Mon-Fri pick & mix, according to subject   **Cost** None   **Entry Reqs** None   **Award** Centre
Certificate   **Creche** Yes Contact College
- **CONTACT**   Deb Shackleton 0116 283 2335

- **SUBJECT**   Multi-Subject   668
- **TITLE**   Stepping Stones
- **PLACE**   Wigston College of Further Education

Length Flexible, according to requirements   **Start** September onwards, roll on, roll off   **Days**
Mon-Fri pick & mix, according to subject   **Cost** Tuition free, small administration fee   **Entry**
Reqs None   **Award** Single Subject Certificates, RSA, EMFEC, GCSE, LCCI, NVQ   **Creche**
Yes Contact College
- **CONTACT**   Sheila Chamberlain 0116 288 5051

- **SUBJECT**   Multi-Subject   669
- **TITLE**   Various Short Courses: Technical, Vocational and Academic
- **PLACE**   Charles Keene College

Length Varies   **Cost** Varies   **Award** BTEC, GCSE, A Level, C&G, Open Access Course,
RSA   **Creche** Playgroup
- **CONTACT**   Short Course Unit 0116 251 6037

- **SUBJECT**   Preparatory   670
- **TITLE**   Exploring Opportunities: Building on Your Skills: Starting to Build a Portfolio
- **PLACE**   Leicester Adult Education Service

Start September   **Days** 3 hours/week   **Entry Req** By interview   **Award** Open College
Network Accreditation
- **CONTACT**   Gill Green 0116 233 4344

- **SUBJECT**   Preparatory   671
- **TITLE**   Planning Your Future
- **PLACE**   Wigston College of Further Education

Length 20 hours   **Start** Varies   **Days** Varies on demand   **Cost** £5   **Entry Reqs**
None   **Award** OCN Credits   **Creche** Yes
- **CONTACT**   Bob Holt 0116 288 5051

Leicestershire

- **SUBJECT** Preparatory   672
- **TITLE** Vocational Skills Updating: Main and Alternative College Programmes
- **PLACE** Hinckley College

Length 1 year   **Start** September   **Days** Full time 9.00-4.00   **Cost** Benefit recipients £1.50 registration fee, no course fee. Full time courses free   **Entry Reqs** Unemployed/ unwaged   **Award** Access route/BTEC/C&G/RSA/GCSE/NVQs/GNVQs   **Creche** Off-site. Contact College for fees
- **CONTACT** Mike Strong 01455 251222

- **SUBJECT** Secretarial   673
- **TITLE** Business Administration Secretarial or Telephone Reception
- **PLACE** RNIB Vocational College

Length 52 weeks   **Start** Various   **Days** 5 days/week   **Cost** Contact College   **Entry Reqs** Assessment   **Award** NVQ Business Administration Level I/II, RSA single subject examinations   **Creche** No
- **CONTACT** Geoff Jackman 01509 611077

- **SUBJECT** Technology/Computing   674
- **TITLE** Short and Refresher Courses: Access Technology & Computer Software
- **PLACE** RNIB Vocational College

Length 3 days   **Start** Various   **Days** 9.00-5.00   **Cost** Contact College   **Creche** No
- **CONTACT** Mark Braithwaite 01509 611077

COUNTY CONTACTS

Information and advice

Leicester Adult Education College, Wellington Street, Leicester LE1 6HL 0116 233 4343   *Contact:* Meg Green, Head of Student Services
Leicestershire Careers Service, 1 Pocklington's Walk, Leicester LE1 6BT 0116 262 7254

Open University

The Open University, East Midlands Region, The Octagon, 143 Derby Road, Nottingham NG7 1PH 0115 924 0121

Training and Enterprise Council

Leicestershire TEC, Meridian East, Meridian Business Park, Leicester LE3 2WZ 0116 265 1515. Childcare Provision for Rural Women project: voucher system for access to employment and training systems for women returners and lone parents

WEA offices

Leicester Office, 101 Hinckley Road, Leicester LE3 0TD 0116 255 6614   *Contact:* Frances Pollard,
Quest House Adult Education Centre, Loughborough College Buildings, Loughborough LE11 3BS 01509 268636   *Contact:* Christine Cubberley, Development Officer. 'Make Your Experience Count' courses for women.
Tutor Organiser Leicestershire, Melton Mowbray College, Asfordby Road, Melton Mowbray LE13 0HJ 01664 66816   *Contact:* Douglas Clinton
Vaughan College, St Nicolas Circle, Leicester LE1 4LB 0116 251 9740   *Contact:* Cherry Heinrich, Tutor Organiser
WEA East Midland District, Alfreton Hall, Church Street, Alfreton DE55 7AH 01773 832185 *Contact:* Chris Scarlett

COURSES

- **SUBJECT** Access   675
- **TITLE** Access to Higher Education
- **PLACE** Boston College

Length 1 year **Start** September or by negotiation **Days** Mon-Fri (up to 14 hours/week) **Cost** Free **Entry Reqs** Interview **Award** Access to Higher Education Certificate **Creche** Playgroup
- **CONTACT** 01205 365701

- **SUBJECT** Access   676
- **TITLE** Access to Higher Education
- **PLACE** Grantham College

Length 1 year **Start** September **Days** Various **Cost** Contact College **Entry Reqs** 21 years + **Award** NEMAP Certificate of Access **Creche** Yes Contact College
- **CONTACT** Maggie O'Donoghue 01476 63141

- **SUBJECT** Access/Art & Design/Multi-Subject   677
- **TITLE** Access: Post-Experience/Re-Training/New Opportunities in Art & Design
- **PLACE** Lincolnshire College of Art & Design

Length Varies **Start** Varies **Days** Part time **Cost** Contact College **Award** BTEC **Creche** Playgroup
- **CONTACT** Colin Measures 01522 512912

- **SUBJECT** Access/Humanities/Social Science   678
- **TITLE** Access to Humanities, Social Science
- **PLACE** Stamford College

Length 1 year **Start** September **Days** 12-15 hours/week between 9.30-3.30 Mon-Fri **Cost** Varies, concessions available **Entry Reqs** Evidence of ability and motivation, no exams necessary **Award** College Certificate of Readiness for HE **Creche** Yes
- **CONTACT** Jim Beard 01780 64141

- **SUBJECT** Catering   679
- **TITLE** Food and Drink Supervision Skills
- **PLACE** Boston College

Length Approx 2 years **Start** Anytime **Days** 3 or 4 days/week 10.00-3.00 **Cost** Contact College. Purchase of equipment required **Entry Reqs** None **Award** NVQ III **Creche** Playgroup £3/session
- **CONTACT** C Jackson 01205 357007

- **SUBJECT** Catering   680
- **TITLE** Food Preparation/Food and Drink Service
- **PLACE** Boston College

Length 1 year **Start** Throughout year **Days** 3 days/week 8.30 (if poss)-2.00 or 10.00-3.00 **Cost** Contact College. Purchase of equipment required **Entry Reqs** Contact College **Award** NVQ II **Creche** Playgroup £3/session
- **CONTACT** 01205 365701 x243

- **SUBJECT** Childcare   681
- **TITLE** Diploma in Nursery Nursing
- **PLACE** Grantham College

Length 3 years **Start** September **Days** 3 days/week **Cost** Free **Entry Reqs** Interview **Award** Diploma in Nursery Nursing **Creche** Yes
- **CONTACT** Eileen Bonner 01476 63141

Lincolnshire

- **SUBJECT** Hairdressing/Beauty 682
- **TITLE** 1. Hairdressing 2. Beauty Therapy Certificate NVQ Levels 1, 2, 3
- **PLACE** Lincolnshire College of Art & Design

Length Variable **Start** Varies **Days** Flexible programmes **Cost** Contact College **Entry Reqs** None **Award** Accreditation of Prior Learning is available, NVQ Levels 1, 2 & 3 **Creche** Playgroup

- **CONTACT** 1. Carol McFarlande/2. Maxine/Anna 01522 512912

- **SUBJECT** Information Technology 683
- **TITLE** Information for End Users
- **PLACE** Boston College

Start January **Days** 1 day/week 10.00-3.00 + 5 day summer school **Cost** Contact College **Entry Reqs** None **Award** BTEC NVQ Level II

- **CONTACT** 01205 365701

- **SUBJECT** Management 685
- **TITLE** Women into Management
- **PLACE** Boston College

Length 20 weeks **Start** October **Days** Mon-Thurs **Cost** Free. Fully funded **Entry Reqs** Unemployed **Award** NEBSM Certificate in Supervisory Management **Creche** Playgroup £3/session

- **CONTACT** A G Burton 01205 365701

- **SUBJECT** Management 686
- **TITLE** Women into Management
- **PLACE** Grantham College

Length 19 weeks **Start** Various **Days** 21 hours/week **Cost** Free **Entry Reqs** Must be unemployed and have considerable work experience or A Levels **Award** Certificate in Marketing, BTEC **Creche** Yes

- **CONTACT** Phil Goodliffe 01476 63141

- **SUBJECT** New Technology 687
- **TITLE** Training for Women in New Technology Skills
- **PLACE** Grantham College

Length 15 weeks **Start** Various **Days** Flexible **Cost** Free (European Social Fund provision) **Award** RSA, Pitmans, C&G, NVQ **Creche** Yes Contact College

- **CONTACT** Barbara Watt 01476 63131

- **SUBJECT** Office Skills/Office Technology 688
- **TITLE** Secretarial/Office Technology
- **PLACE** Stamford College

Length 10-17 weeks **Start** Flexible **Days** Mon-Fri 9.00-3.00 **Cost** According to hours attended **Entry Reqs** None **Award** RSA/Pitmans/LCC Office Skills Certificates **Creche** Yes

- **CONTACT** Lesley Julian 01780 64141

- **SUBJECT** Office Technology 689
- **TITLE** Office Technology/Intensive Technology Skills
- **PLACE** Grantham College

Length Various **Start** Continuous **Cost** Contact College **Entry Reqs** None **Award** RSA, LCC, Pitmans **Creche** Yes Contact College

- **CONTACT** Nicola Parry 01476 63141

- **SUBJECT** Preparatory   690
- **TITLE** Open Door
- **PLACE** North Lincolnshire College and locations in North Lincolnshire

Length 12 weeks   **Days** 2 hours/week   **Cost** Free   **Entry Reqs** Contact College   **Award** NEMAP Credits Levels 1&2 (Open College Network)   **Creche** Yes Free
- **CONTACT** Jane Summers 01652 610530

- **SUBJECT** Preparatory   691
- **TITLE** Return to Learning
- **PLACE** WEA Lincoln

Length 12 weeks   **Start** October   **Days** 10.00-11.30am   **Cost** £28.50 + £7.50 registration Concessions   **Entry Reqs** None
- **CONTACT** Beaumont Fee Education Centre 01522 528414

- **SUBJECT** Science/Technology   692
- **TITLE** Women into Science and Technology
- **PLACE** Grantham College

Length 19 weeks   **Start** Various   **Days** Tues + Wed 9.45-3.00   **Cost** Free   **Entry Reqs** Must be unemployed   **Award** Open College Network Into Science Course   **Creche** Yes
- **CONTACT** Alan Hudson 01476 63141

- **SUBJECT** Secretarial   693
- **TITLE** Secretarial Workshop (Typewriting, Word Processing, Computer Applications)
- **PLACE** Boston College

Length Flexible   **Start** September and as required   **Days** Mon-Fri various times   **Cost** Contact College   **Entry Reqs** None   **Award** RSA examinations   **Creche** Playgroup £3/session
- **CONTACT** Sue Brackenbury 01205 365701

- **SUBJECT** Travel & Tourism   694
- **TITLE** Training in Travel and Tourism Skills
- **PLACE** Grantham College

Length 13 weeks   **Start** Various   **Days** Various   **Cost** Free   **Entry Reqs** Must be unemployed   **Award** ABTAC, RSA, AVis Car Hire, Units towards NVQ Level II   **Creche** Yes
- **CONTACT** Nicola Parry 01476 63141

COUNTY CONTACTS

Information and advice

Guidance and Counselling Service, Boston College, Skirbeck Road, Boston PE21 6JF 01205 313218   *Contact:* Mike Peck, Val Price. Information centres at Boston, Sleaford (Moneys Mill Tel: 01529 415195), Spalding and Skegness.

Lincolnshire Careers and Education Services, Head Office, Brayford House, Brayford Wharf, Lincoln LN1 1XN 01522 553510

Boston Office 01205 310010
Gainsborough Office 01427 612096
Grantham Office 01476 66379
Lincoln Office 01522 528412
Louth Office 01507 600800
Skegness Office 01754 762595
Sleaford Office 01529 414144
Spalding Office 01775 766151
Stamford Office 01708 622328

Open University

The Open University, East Midlands Region, The Octagon, 143 Derby Road, Nottingham NG7 1PH 0115 924 0121

Training and Enterprise Council

Lincolnshire TEC, Beech House, Waterside South, Witham Park, Lincoln LN5 7JH 01522 567765 *Contact:* Sylvia Wardley. Lift-Off Project offers access to training, education and employment to women returners through events, confidence building and personal development courses. It supports working women and raises awareness of career opportunities. Produces 'Steps to Success: a Guide for Women Returners' and 3 other local directories. Out of School childcare project

WEA offices

WEA East Midland District, Alfreton Hall, Church Street, Alfreton DE55 7AH 01773 832185   *Contact:* Chris Scarlett. Covers south Lincolnshire
WEA North Lincolnshire and Lincoln, Beaumont Fee Education Centre, Beaumont Fee, Lincoln LN1 1UU 01522 528414   *Contact:* Pam Burton, Centre Secretary
WEA Spalding, 56 Woolram Wygate, Spalding PE11 1PB 01775 725319   *Contact:* Rodney Lines, Tutor Organiser
WEA Yorkshire North District, 6 Woodhouse Square, Leeds LS3 1AD 0113 245 3304   *Contact:* Wendy Formby. Covers north Lincolnshire

---

LONDON

COURSES

- **SUBJECT** Access   695
- **TITLE** Access Preparation
- **PLACE** Carshalton College

Length 10 weeks   **Days** 1. Wed 7.00-9.00 2.2 days/week   **Cost** Contact College   **Entry Reqs** 21+. No formal entry requirements   **Award** College Certificate 1. Entry to Access Intensive 2. Entry to Access to Degree Programme (Modular)
- **CONTACT** Advice and Guidance Centre 0181 770 6800

- **SUBJECT** Access   696
- **TITLE** Access to Degree Programmes (Modular)
- **PLACE** Carshalton College

Length 1 year   **Start** September   **Days** 4 days/week 9.30-3.00   **Cost** Contact College **Entry Reqs** 21+. No formal entry requirements   **Award** Access Certificate, entry to higher education
- **CONTACT** Advice and Guidance Centre 0181 770 6800

- **SUBJECT** Access   697
- **TITLE** Access to Higher Education
- **PLACE** Richmond Adult & Community College

Length Contact College   **Award** Access Diploma validated by Surrey & SW London Access Agency   **Creche** Yes
- **CONTACT** 0181 891 5907

- **SUBJECT** Access 698
- **TITLE** Access to Higher Education
- **PLACE** City & Islington College, Islington Campus

Length 1 year **Start** September **Days** 2½ days/week (16 hours) or 2 eves (6 hours) **Cost** Contact College **Entry Reqs** By interview **Award** LOCF Access Certificate **Creche** Nursery, sliding scale for charges
- **CONTACT** Course Information Centres 0171 607 1132/0171 614 0200

- **SUBJECT** Access 699
- **TITLE** Access to Higher Education
- **PLACE** Morley College

Length 1 year **Start** September **Cost** Contact College **Entry Reqs** Contact College **Award** Access to higher education **Creche** Creche, playgroup
- **CONTACT** 0171 928 8501

- **SUBJECT** Access 700
- **TITLE** Access to Higher Education
- **PLACE** West Thames College

Length 1 year **Start** Flexible **Days** Usually evenings, flexible **Cost** £90 **Entry Reqs** None **Award** Access Certificate **Creche** No
- **CONTACT** Brenda Sharman 0181 568 0244

- **SUBJECT** Access 701
- **TITLE** Fresh Horizons Access Programme 1. Full time 2. Part time 3. Evening
- **PLACE** The City Lit

Length 29 weeks **Start** September (apply early) **Days** 1.4 days/week 2.2 days/week 3. eves **Cost** 1. £500/year 2. £280/year 3. £200/year (Concessions no fee in each case) **Entry Reqs** None **Award** Access Certificate **Creche** Daytime only. £1/day
- **CONTACT** 3

- **SUBJECT** Access/Accounting/Arts/Business/Computing/Health Studies/ 702 Hospitality Management/Languages/Music/Social Science/Science
- **TITLE** Access to Higher Education
- **PLACE** Merton College

Length Flexible **Start** September **Days** Mon-Fri 9.30-1.00 **Cost** Contact College **Entry Reqs** By interview **Award** Access Certificate, entry to higher education
- **CONTACT** Guidance and Entry Unit 0181 640 8001

- **SUBJECT** Access/Art & Design 703
- **TITLE** Access to Art and Design
- **PLACE** West Thames College

Length 1 year **Start** September **Days** Full time 16-20 hours/week, part time 10 hours minimum by arrangement **Cost** £200+£50 studio charge, £45 TRAC qualification + £8 registration **Entry Reqs** Some evidence of potential to progress and succeed in Art & Design **Award** TRAC Certificate, opportunity to enter higher education **Creche** Yes
- **CONTACT** Ken Newlan/Jenny Lagnado 0181 568 0244

- **SUBJECT** Access/Art & Design/Business/Law/Cultural Studies/Electronics/ 704 Health Studies/Computing/Science/Social Science/Teaching
- **TITLE** Access Programmes
- **PLACE** Barnet College

Length 1 year **Start** September **Days** Full time **Cost** Contact College **Entry Reqs** Age 20+. Interview **Award** Access to higher education **Creche** Yes
- **CONTACT** 0181 440 6321/0181 361 5101

London

- **SUBJECT** Access/Arts/Business/Computing/Languages/ **705**
  Science/Social Science/Teaching
- **TITLE** Access to Higher Education Modular Programme
- **PLACE** Ealing Tertiary College, Acton Site

Length 1 year **Start** September **Days** 20 hours/week **Cost** Contact College **Entry Reqs** By interview **Award** Access to higher education **Creche** No (financial help with childcare)
- **CONTACT** Information Centre 0181 231 6008

- **SUBJECT** Access/Arts/Business/Computing/Nursing/Social Science/Teaching **706**
- **TITLE** Access to Higher Education Modular Programme
- **PLACE** Ealing Tertiary College, Southall Centre

Length 1 year **Start** September **Days** 20 hours/week **Cost** Contact College **Entry Reqs** By interview **Award** Access to higher education **Creche** No (financial help with childcare)
- **CONTACT** Information Centre 0181 231 6008

- **SUBJECT** Access/Black Studies **707**
- **TITLE** Access to Higher Education in African and Caribbean Studies
- **PLACE** Kensington and Chelsea College, Wornington Centre

Length 1 year **Start** September **Days** Fri 10.00-12.00+1.00-3.30 or Mon 6.30-9.00 **Cost** Contact College **Entry Reqs** No formal qualifications. GCSE standard of written & spoken English **Award** Access to higher education **Creche** Yes, limited
- **CONTACT** 0181 964 1311

- **SUBJECT** Access/Black Studies **708**
- **TITLE** Return to Study in Caribbean Studies: History and Literature
- **PLACE** Hammersmith & Fulham Community Learning and Leisure, Macbeth Centre

Length 30 weeks **Start** September, possible up to February **Days** Thurs 6.30-8.30 **Cost** LEA fees. Concessions available **Entry Reqs** Good command of written & spoken English and commitment **Award** LOCF Credits (Levels 2&3) **Creche** No
- **CONTACT** Nigel Leyland 0181 563 2185

- **SUBJECT** Access/Business **709**
- **TITLE** Access to Business
- **PLACE** Lewisham College

Length 1 year **Start** September **Days** 16 hours/week **Cost** £648 **Entry Reqs** Reasonable English and maths **Award** LOCF Credits for entry to higher education
- **CONTACT** Roger Fitzgibbon 0181 692 0353

- **SUBJECT** Access/Business **710**
- **TITLE** Access Course in Business Studies
- **PLACE** Orpington College

Length 1 year **Start** September **Days** 1½ days/week **Cost** Contact College **Entry Reqs** Age 21+. No formal entry requirements **Award** Access to higher education
- **CONTACT** Pauline Budden 01689 839336

- **SUBJECT** Access/Business **711**
- **TITLE** Access Diploma in Business Studies
- **PLACE** Richmond Adult & Community College, Clifden Centre

Length 1 year **Start** September **Days** Tues + eve **Cost** £305/option (£254 concessions) **Entry Reqs** O level/GCSE English or ability to cope. Diagnostic test and interview **Award** Access Diploma Surrey & SW London Access Agency **Creche** Yes
- **CONTACT** David Green 0181 891 5907

- **SUBJECT**   Access/Business   712
- **TITLE**   Access to Business Studies
- **PLACE**   College of North East London, Tottenham Centre

Length 1 year   **Start** September   **Days** 4 days/week (16 hours/week)   **Cost** Contact College   **Entry Reqs** 21+, interview   **Award** Access to Middlesex University degree courses in business related subjects   **Creche** Yes Limited places

- **CONTACT**   Admissions Officer 0181 802 3111

- **SUBJECT**   Access/Business/Media Studies/Nursing/Art/Design/Law   713
- **TITLE**   Modular Access for Mature Students: Business Studies, Media, Nursing, Art & Design, Law
- **PLACE**   Hendon College, Grahame Park Site

Length Modular 36 weeks (1 year)   **Start** September   **Days** Various   **Entry Req** 21+, by interview   **Award** LOCF Access Certificate   **Creche** Yes nursery

- **CONTACT**   Central Admissions 0181 200 8300

- **SUBJECT**   Access/Business Studies/Computing/Engineering/Science   714
- **TITLE**   Access to Computing, Life Sciences, Engineering, Business Studies
- **PLACE**   City of Westminster, Maida Vale Centre

Length 1 year   **Start** September   **Cost** Contact College   **Entry Reqs** Contact College   **Award** Access to higher education

- **CONTACT**   Mike Read 0171 723 8826 x2834

- **SUBJECT**   Access/Business Studies/Management   715
- **TITLE**   Access to HE in Business Studies and Management
- **PLACE**   Kensington & Chelsea College, Wornington Centre

Length 1 or 2 years   **Start** September   **Days** 15 hours/week (1 year); 8 hours/week (2 years)   **Cost** Contact College   **Entry Reqs** Age 20+. Numeracy and literacy assessment   **Award** LOCF Credits, access to higher education   **Creche** Yes, limited

- **CONTACT**   0181 964 1311

- **SUBJECT**   Access/Business Studies/Social Studies   716
- **TITLE**   Access Course in Social, Cultural and Business Studies
- **PLACE**   Orpington College

Length 1 year   **Start** September   **Days** Full time   **Cost** Contact College   **Entry Reqs** Age 21+. No formal entry requirements   **Award** Access to higher education

- **CONTACT**   Ken Pharoah 01689 839336

- **SUBJECT**   Access/Business Studies/Social Studies/Fashion/Media Studies/ Design/Photography/Computing/Performing Arts   717
- **TITLE**   Access Courses (Various subjects)
- **PLACE**   City and Islington College, various sites

Length 1 year   **Start** September, April   **Cost** Contact College   **Entry Reqs** Contact College   **Award** Access to higher education   **Creche** Yes

- **CONTACT**   Course Information Unit 0171 607 1132

- **SUBJECT**   Access/Community Studies   718
- **TITLE**   Access to Youth and Community Work
- **PLACE**   Lewisham College

Length 1 year   **Start** September   **Days** 16 hours/week   **Cost** £648   **Award** LOCF Credits

- **CONTACT**   Conchita Henry 0181 692 0353

- **SUBJECT** Access/Computing   719
- **TITLE** Access to Computing
- **PLACE** Lewisham College

Length 1 year **Start** September **Days** 16-20 hours/week **Cost** £648 **Entry Reqs** Maths, logic, literacy test and interview with Course Tutor **Award** LOCF Credits
- **CONTACT** Terry Creek 0181 692 0353

- **SUBJECT** Access/Computing   720
- **TITLE** Access Course in Computing
- **PLACE** Orpington College

Length 1 year **Start** September **Days** 2 days/week 9.30-3.30 **Cost** Contact College **Entry Reqs** Age 21+. No formal entry requirements **Award** LOCF Access Certificate
- **CONTACT** Kevin Armstrong 01689 839336

- **SUBJECT** Access/Cultural Studies/Information Technology/Social Science/Health 721
  Studies/Environmental Sciences
- **TITLE** Modular Access for Mature Students: Cultural Studies, Information
  Technology, Social Science, Health Education, Environmental Science
- **PLACE** Hendon College, Grahame Park Site

Length Modular 36 weeks (1 year) **Start** September **Days** Various **Entry Req** 21+, by interview **Award** LOCF Access Certificate **Creche** Yes nursery
- **CONTACT** Central Admissions 0181 200 8300

- **SUBJECT** Access/Cultural Studies/Media Studies   722
- **TITLE** Access to Modular Communications Degrees (including Journalism)
- **PLACE** Hackney Community College, Keltan House

Length 36 weeks **Start** September **Days** Full time 18 hours/week+home study **Cost** Contact College **Entry Reqs** 21+, especially women & ethnic minority applicants **Award** Access to a variety of degrees in Media Studies, Journalism and Cultural Studies **Creche** Yes
- **CONTACT** Central Admissions Unit 0181 533 5922

- **SUBJECT** Access/Engineering   723
- **TITLE** Access to Engineering Product Design (South Bank University)
- **PLACE** Lewisham College

Length 1 year **Start** September **Days** 16 hours/week **Cost** £648 **Entry Reqs** Reasonable maths and written skills **Award** Access accreditation for entry into university
- **CONTACT** Mr Suresh Jacob 0181 692 0353

- **SUBJECT** Access/Health Studies   724
- **TITLE** Access to Health Studies
- **PLACE** Waltham Forest College

Length Modular, usually 1 year **Start** September **Days** Mon-Wed 10.00-3.00, Thurs 10.00-12.00 **Cost** £464, free if in receipt of benefit **Entry Reqs** Age 21+, basic numeracy & literacy test **Award** Access Cert(NELAF validated); Degrees in Health Studies, Nursing, Psychology, Occupational Therapy, etc **Creche** Nursery (3 years+) Free
- **CONTACT** Jill Wilkens 0181 527 2311 x4286

- **SUBJECT** Access/Humanities/Social Science   725
- **TITLE** Access to Degrees in Social Sciences and Humanities (Intensive)
- **PLACE** Carshalton College

Length 1 year **Start** September **Days** 2 eves/week **Cost** Contact College **Entry Reqs** Age 21+. No formal entry requirements **Award** Access Certificate and entry to higher education
- **CONTACT** Advice and Guidance Centre 0181 770 6800

- **SUBJECT**   Access/Humanities/Social Science   726
- **TITLE**   Access to Humanities/Social Sciences
- **PLACE**   City of Westminster, Maida Vale Centre

Length 1 year   **Start** September   **Days** Evenings   **Cost** Contact College   **Entry Reqs** Contact College   **Award** Access to higher education

- **CONTACT**   Course Information 0171 723 8826

- **SUBJECT**   Access/Humanities/Social Science   727
- **TITLE**   Open Studies: Social Science, Humanities
- **PLACE**   City University, Dept of Continuing Education

Length 1 year   **Start** September   **Days** Mon 10.00-5.00   **Cost** £75/term   **Entry Reqs** By interview   **Award** University Certificate and National Accreditation   **Creche** No

- **CONTACT**   Sylvia Tyler 0171 477 8000 x3268

- **SUBJECT**   Access/Humanities/Social Science/Cultural Studies   728
- **TITLE**   Access Diploma in Arts & Social Science Study Plan Level III
- **PLACE**   Richmond Adult & Community College, Clifden & Parkshot Centres

Length 1 or 2 years   **Start** September   **Days** Daytime Tues or Wed 9.30-2.30, eves Tues+Thurs 7.00-9.00   **Cost** £305 course   **Entry Reqs** By interview and assessment   **Award** Access Diploma Surrey & SW London Access Agency   **Creche** Yes £3/session

- **CONTACT**   Myra Townsend 0181 940 0170/0181 940 5907

- **SUBJECT**   Access/Humanities/Social Science/Science   729
- **TITLE**   Access to Higher Education: Humanities, Science, Social Science
- **PLACE**   Queen's Park Community School, Brent

Length 36 weeks   **Start** September   **Days** Mon-Thurs 10.00-3.30   **Cost** £825 or £10 concessionary rate   **Entry Reqs** By interview   **Award** Access to higher education   **Creche** Yes Contact Centre

- **CONTACT**   Access Course Co-ordinator 0181 459 3418

- **SUBJECT**   Access/Humanities/Social Science/Teaching   730
- **TITLE**   Access to Humanities/Social Sciences/Teaching
- **PLACE**   City of Westminster, Maida Vale Centre

Length Modular   **Start** September   **Days** Daytime   **Cost** Contact College   **Entry Reqs** Contact College   **Award** Access to higher education

- **CONTACT**   Course Information 0171 723 8826

- **SUBJECT**   Access/Humanities/Social Science/Teaching   731
- **TITLE**   Access to Social Science, Humanities and Access to Teaching
- **PLACE**   Kensington & Chelsea College, Hortensia Road & Wornington Road

Length 33 weeks   **Start** September   **Days** Day or evening, full or part time   **Cost** Full time £350 approx, or £20 concessions   **Entry Reqs** Age 21+, assessment of written English   **Award** Access Certificate, LOCF validated   **Creche** Yes Limited places

- **CONTACT**   Lesley Croome 0171 573 5326/Course Information 0181 964 1311

- **SUBJECT**   Access/Information Technology   732
- **TITLE**   Access to Information Technology for Women
- **PLACE**   College of North East London, Tottenham Centre

Length 1 year   **Start** September   **Days** 4 days/week   **Cost** Contact College   **Entry Reqs** 21+, college test and interview   **Award** Entry to HND, HNC, BSc Computer Studies/IT at North London/Middlesex University   **Creche** Yes Limited places

- **CONTACT**   Admissions Office 0181 802 3111

- **SUBJECT**   Access/Information Technology   733
- **TITLE**   REMIT: Returners to English, Mathematics and IT
- **PLACE**   West Thames College

Length 1 year   **Start** September   **Days** Daily 10.00-3.15 during school terms   **Cost** Concessionary fees for Hounslow residents   **Entry Reqs** By interview   **Award** Access Certificate, C&G, Computer Applications, BTEC Industry & Society, GCSE Maths & English **Creche** Yes Cost varies

- **CONTACT**   Aileen Beretta 0181 568 0244 x377

- **SUBJECT**   Access/Languages   734
- **TITLE**   Access Diploma in Modern Languages with Arts or Business Studies
- **PLACE**   Richmond Adult & Community College, Clifden Centre

Length 1 year   **Start** September   **Days** Varies, 4 days/week   **Cost** £572 (£469 concessions)   **Entry Reqs** O level/GCSE English or equivalent and ability to cope. Interview and guidance   **Award** Access Diploma Surrey & SW London Access Agency   **Creche** Yes

- **CONTACT**   Amy Evans 0181 891 5907

- **SUBJECT**   Access/Law/Social Science   735
- **TITLE**   Access to Law and Social Science
- **PLACE**   Hammersmith & Fulham Community Learning & Leisure, Macbeth Centre

Length 30 weeks   **Start** September   **Days** Mon+Tues daytime   **Cost** LEA fees. Concessions available   **Entry Reqs** Good command of written & spoken English and commitment   **Award** Access Certificate, LOCF credits (levels 2&3)   **Creche** Yes, 60p/2-hour sessions

- **CONTACT**   Nigel Leyland 0181 563 2185

- **SUBJECT**   Access/Leisure Studies/Health Studies/Sports Studies   736
- **TITLE**   Access Diploma in Sports, Health, Leisure
- **PLACE**   Richmond Adult & Community College, Clifden Centre

Length 1 year   **Start** September   **Days** Mon, Thurs and as required   **Cost** part time £305 (£254 concessions); full time £572 (£469 concessions)   **Entry Reqs** GCSE English Grade C or ability; diagnostic test and advice given   **Award** Access Diploma Surrey & SW London Access Agency   **Creche** Yes

- **CONTACT**   Gill Peters 0181 891 5907

- **SUBJECT**   Access/Media Studies/Performing Arts   737
- **TITLE**   Access to 1. Media Studies for Women 2. Drama
- **PLACE**   City & Islington College, Islington Campus

Length 1 year   **Start** September   **Days** 4-5 days/week (16 hours)   **Cost** Contact College   **Entry Reqs** 1. Women, 21+; disadvantaged groups encouraged to apply 2. None. Good standard of English   **Award** LOCF Credits towards entry to BA courses   **Creche** Nursery, sliding scale for charges

- **CONTACT**   Course Information Centres 0171 607 1132/0171 614 0200

- **SUBJECT**   Access/Nursing   738
- **TITLE**   Access to Nursing
- **PLACE**   Lewisham College

Length 1 year   **Start** September   **Days** 16 hours/week   **Cost** £648   **Award** LOCF Credits for entry to Nurse Training

- **CONTACT**   Conchita Henry 0181 692 0353

- **SUBJECT** Access/Nursing/Health Studies   739
- **TITLE** Access to Nursing, Health and Allied Science
- **PLACE** Lambeth College, Norwood Centre

Length 1 year   **Start** September   **Cost** Contact College   **Award** Access to higher education
Creche Yes

- **CONTACT** Admissions Unit 0171 501 5000

- **SUBJECT** Access/Nursing/Health Studies   740
- **TITLE** Access to Nursing and Paramedical
- **PLACE** West Thames College

Length 1 year   **Start** September   **Days** Daily 9.15-3.15   **Cost** £200   Concessions available   **Entry Reqs** By interview   **Award** Access Certificate   **Creche** Yes Cost varies

- **CONTACT** Suky Binning/Margaret Edwards 0181 568 0244

- **SUBJECT** Access/Nursing/Health Studies   741
- **TITLE** Access to Nursing, Speech Therapy, Radiography
- **PLACE** City and Islington College, Bunhill Row

Length 1 year full time, Nursing 4 terms part time   **Start** September   **Days** 3 days/week or part time   **Cost** LEA fees   **Entry Reqs** 21+, courses can include students whose first language is not English   **Award** London Open College Accreditation, access to RGN training and degree courses   **Creche** No

- **CONTACT** Alison Egan 0171 638 4171 x256

- **SUBJECT** Access/Nursing/Paramedical Studies   742
- **TITLE** Access to Nursing and Paramedical Sciences
- **PLACE** West Thames College

Length 1 year   **Start** September   **Cost** Contact College   **Entry Reqs** 21+, interview
Award Access Certificate

- **CONTACT** Margaret Edwards 0181 568 0244 x264

- **SUBJECT** Access/Nursing/Social Work/Teaching   743
- **TITLE** Access to Social Work, Education, Nursing
- **PLACE** Bromley College of Further & Higher Education

Length Modular   **Start** September   **Days** Part time   **Cost** Contact College   **Entry Reqs** No formal requirements   **Award** Access to higher education

- **CONTACT** Student Enquiries 0181 295 7001

- **SUBJECT** Access/Performing Arts   744
- **TITLE** Dance Access Programme
- **PLACE** Lewisham College

Length 1 - 3 years   **Start** September   **Days** 16-24 hours/week   **Cost** £648   **Award** Access Certificate

- **CONTACT** Nick Edwards 0181 692 0353

- **SUBJECT** Access/Psychology   745
- **TITLE** Access to Psychology
- **PLACE** Hammersmith & Fulham Community Learning & Leisure, Beaufort House

Length 30 weeks   **Start** September   **Days** Thurs+Fri 1.00-3.00   **Cost** Contact College   **Entry Reqs** Good command of written & spoken English and commitment   **Award** LOCF credits (Levels 2&3)   **Creche** Yes

- **CONTACT** Nigel Leyland 0181 563 2185

- **SUBJECT**   Access/Science   746
- **TITLE**   Access to Applied Science Group A
- **PLACE**   Lambeth College, Tower Bridge Centre

Length 1 year full time, 2 years part time   **Start** September   **Days** 4 days/week 9.00-5.00 or 2 days/week 9.00-5.00 part time   **Cost** Contact College   **Entry Reqs** Entry test on numeracy and English   **Award** LOCF Access Certificate, access to university courses   **Creche** Yes

- **CONTACT**   Admissions Unit 0171 501 5000

- **SUBJECT**   Access/Social Science   747
- **TITLE**   Access to Social Science (Evening)
- **PLACE**   Barnet College

Length 1 year   **Start** September   **Days** 2 eves/week   **Cost** Contact College. Concessions available   **Entry Reqs** Aspiration to do a degree course & competence in communications   **Award** Entry to modular degree at Middlesex University, accepted by other universities   **Creche** No

- **CONTACT**   Continuing Education Unit 0181 440 6321

- **SUBJECT**   Access/Social Science   748
- **TITLE**   Modular Access to Social Sciences
- **PLACE**   Lambeth College, Vauxhall Centre

Length 36 weeks   **Start** September   **Days** 4 days/week   **Cost** Contact College   **Entry Reqs** None; experience in either voluntary or paid care work necessary   **Award** LOCF Accreditation, access to university courses   **Creche** Yes

- **CONTACT**   Admissions Unit 0171 501 5000

- **SUBJECT**   Access/Social Work   749
- **TITLE**   Access to Social Work
- **PLACE**   City and Islington College, Bunhill Row

Length 1 year full time or part time   **Start** September   **Days** 3 days/week   **Entry Req** 24+, especially African Caribbean & Asian students, relevant voluntary/paid work   **Award** London Open College Accreditation   **Creche** No

- **CONTACT**   Stephanie Boyle 0171 638 4171 x254

- **SUBJECT**   Access/Social Work   750
- **TITLE**   Access to Social Work
- **PLACE**   College of North East London, Tottenham Green Centre

Length 36 weeks   **Start** September   **Days** 18 hours or full time 5 days/week   **Cost** Contact College   **Entry Reqs** 21+, experience of working in social care setting   **Award** College Certificate, access to Diploma in Social Work or degree course   **Creche** Yes Limited Places

- **CONTACT**   Admissions Officer 0181 802 3111

- **SUBJECT**   Access/Social Work   751
- **TITLE**   Access to Social Work
- **PLACE**   Hammersmith & Fulham Community Learning & Leisure, Bryony Centre

Length 30 weeks   **Start** September   **Days** Mon+Wed 1.00-3.00   **Cost** Contact College   **Entry Reqs** Good command of written & spoken English and commitment   **Award** LOCF credits (Levels 2&3)   **Creche** Yes

- **CONTACT**   Mary Church 0181 749 1000

- **SUBJECT** Access/Social Work 752
- **TITLE** Access to Social Work
- **PLACE** Lambeth College, Clapham Centre

Length 1 year **Start** September **Days** 3/4 days/week (19 hours/week) **Cost** Contact College **Entry Reqs** None. English assessment. Some practical caring experience required **Award** Access Certificate **Creche** Yes

- **CONTACT** Admissions Unit 0171 501 5000

- **SUBJECT** Access/Social Work 753
- **TITLE** Access to Social Work
- **PLACE** Waltham Forest College

Length 1-2 years depending on route taken **Start** September **Days** 1 year course: Mon+Wed eves. 2 year course: Mon afternoons **Cost** £210 Concessions for unemployed people **Entry Reqs** 3 years caring experience in a health or social care setting **Award** Certificate of Access to Social Work **Creche** Nursery 3-5 years Free

- **CONTACT** Jaki Crossman 0181 527 2311 x4262

- **SUBJECT** Access/Teaching 754
- **TITLE** Access to Bachelor of Education (Goldsmiths University)
- **PLACE** Lewisham College

Length 1 year **Start** September **Days** 16 hours **Cost** £648 **Entry Reqs** Over 22 years. Interview and assessment tests **Award** LOCF Credits

- **CONTACT** Tudor Davies 0181 692 0353

- **SUBJECT** Access/Teaching 755
- **TITLE** Access to Teaching
- **PLACE** Bromley College of Further & Higher Education, Open Learning Centre

Length 1 year **Start** September **Cost** Contact College **Entry Reqs** Contact College **Award** Access to teacher training

- **CONTACT** Student Enquiries 0181 295 7001

- **SUBJECT** Access/Teaching 756
- **TITLE** Access to Teaching (BEd Primary) for ESOL Students
- **PLACE** College of North East London, Tottenham Green Centre

Length 1 year **Start** September **Days** Mon-Fri 10.00-3.00 **Cost** Contact College **Entry Reqs** Students whose first language is not English. Interview and assessment **Award** Access to BEd (Primary) **Creche** Yes Limited Places

- **CONTACT** Admissions Officer 0181 802 3111

- **SUBJECT** Access/Teaching/Law/Humanities 757
- **TITLE** Access to Teaching, Law, Humanities
- **PLACE** West Thames College

Length 1 year **Start** September **Days** Daily 9.15-3.15 **Cost** £200 Concessions available **Entry Reqs** By interview **Award** Access Certificate **Creche** Yes Cost varies

- **CONTACT** Suky Binning/Brenda Sharman 0181 568 0244

- **SUBJECT** Accounting 758
- **TITLE** Accounting Skills for Adults
- **PLACE** City and Islington College, Islington Campus

Length 36 weeks **Start** September **Days** Mon-Fri 10.00-3.00 **Cost** Contact College **Entry Reqs** None. Assessment and interview **Award** NVQ Level I/II **Creche** Yes

- **CONTACT** Course Information Unit 0171 607 1132

- **SUBJECT** Art & Design 759
- **TITLE** Art & Design
- **PLACE** Kensington and Chelsea College

Length 2 years **Start** September **Days** 3 days/week, extra optional **Cost** Contact College **Entry Reqs** Some evidence of drawing and visual projects **Award** BTEC National Diploma General Art & Design **Creche** Yes
- **CONTACT** Maria Donato 0181 960 1565

- **SUBJECT** Art & Design 760
- **TITLE** Art & Design GNVQ Intermediate
- **PLACE** City of Westminster College, Beethoven Street

Length 1 year full time, 2 years part time **Start** September **Cost** Contact College **Entry Reqs** Contact College **Award** GNVQ Intermediate
- **CONTACT** Course Information 0171 723 8826

- **SUBJECT** Art & Design 761
- **TITLE** Art & Design 1. GNVQ Intermediate 2. BTEC Diploma Foundation Studies
- **PLACE** Lewisham College, West Greenwich Centre

Length 1 year **Start** September **Days** 16 hours/week **Cost** £648 **Award** 1. GNVQ Intermediate 2. BTEC Diploma
- **CONTACT** Nick Edwards 0181 692 0353

- **SUBJECT** Art & Design 762
- **TITLE** Art & Design Foundation Course
- **PLACE** Kensington and Chelsea College, Wornington Road

Length 1 year **Start** September **Days** Mon, Tues, Thurs 10.00-5.00 **Cost** £45 unwaged, £475 waged **Entry Reqs** Portfolio showing maturity of work in a wide variety of media **Award** BTEC Foundation (subject to validation), entry to degree level **Creche** Yes
- **CONTACT** Charles Marriott/Simon Betts 0181 960 1565

- **SUBJECT** Art & Design 763
- **TITLE** Art & Design GNVQ Intermediate
- **PLACE** Kensington and Chelsea College, Wornington Road

Length 1 year **Start** September **Days** Wed-Fri 10.00-5.00 **Cost** £45 unwaged, £475 waged **Entry Reqs** Interview and portfolio, no formal qualifications **Award** BTEC GNVQ Intermediate, progress to BTEC Foundation Course or GNVQ Advanced **Creche** Yes
- **CONTACT** Simon Betts 0181 960 1565

- **SUBJECT** Art & Design 764
- **TITLE** Multimedia Authoring for Women
- **PLACE** Lambeth College, Vauxhall Centre

Length 1 year **Start** September **Days** Tues + Wed 9.30-5.00 **Cost** Contact College **Entry Reqs** Evidence of creative ability+portfolio **Award** LOCF Certificate **Creche** Yes Contact College. ESF supported
- **CONTACT** Admissions Unit 0171 501 5000

- **SUBJECT** Arts 765
- **TITLE** Certificate/Diploma in Arts Managment and Training (choose 3 out of 7 courses)
- **PLACE** Various locations in London area, including placements

Length 48 hours for each course, 3 courses for Certificate **Start** September, January, April **Days** 3 or 6 hours/week, day or evening **Cost** £1.77/hour. Concessionary 1/3 of full fees **Entry Reqs** No formal qualifications, must be involved in at least one arts sector **Award** Certificate/Diploma Arts Management and Training **Creche** For daytime courses. Nominal charge
- **CONTACT** Birkbeck College Social Studies Desk 0171 631 6653

- **SUBJECT** Beauty   766
- **TITLE** Beauty and Fitness
- **PLACE** Lewisham College

Length 1 year   **Start** September   **Days** 16 hours/week   **Cost** £648   **Award** NVQ Level II

- **CONTACT** Isobel Craddock 0181 692 0353

- **SUBJECT** Black Studies   767
- **TITLE** Certificate/Diploma in African Caribbean Studies
- **PLACE** Centres in North East London

Length 48-hour courses, 16 weeks, 3 courses for Certificate   **Start** September   **Days** 3 hours/week, Thurs 6.00-9.00   **Cost** £85/course £28 concessions   **Entry Reqs** None   **Award** Certificate/Diploma CATS Accredited

- **CONTACT** Birkbeck College Social Studies Desk 0171 631 6653

- **SUBJECT** Business   768
- **TITLE** Business and Finance: Fast Track
- **PLACE** Bromley College of Further & Higher Education

Length 1 year   **Start** September   **Days** 2 days/week in school hours   **Cost** Contact College   **Entry Reqs** Suitable for returners and those looking for a fresh start   **Award** BTEC National Certificate

- **CONTACT** Student Enquiries 0181 295 7001

- **SUBJECT** Business   769
- **TITLE** Business Skills for Adults 1. Level 1 2. Level 2
- **PLACE** City and Islington College, Islington Campus

Length 36 weeks   **Start** September, January   **Days** Mon-Fri 10.00-3.00   **Cost** Contact College   **Entry Reqs** 1. None 2. Contact College 1. & 2. Assessment and interview   **Award** 1. NVQ Level I/II 2. NVQ Level II/III, Pitmans, RSA Intermediate   **Creche** Yes

- **CONTACT** Course Information Unit 0171 607 1132

- **SUBJECT** Business   770
- **TITLE** GNVQ Business Foundation, Intermediate, Advanced
- **PLACE** Barnet College

Length Foundation & Intermediate 1 year, Advanced 2 years   **Start** September   **Cost** Contact College   **Entry Reqs** Contact College   **Award** GNVQ Foundation, Intermediate or Advanced   **Creche** Yes

- **CONTACT** 0181 440 6321/0181 361 5101

- **SUBJECT** Business   771
- **TITLE** GNVQ Business Foundation, Intermediate, Advanced
- **PLACE** City of Westminster College, various sites

Length Foundation & Intermediate 1 year, Advanced 2 years   **Start** September   **Days** Daytime   **Cost** Contact College   **Entry Reqs** Contact College   **Award** GNVQ Foundation, Intermediate or Advanced

- **CONTACT** Course Information 0171 723 8826

- **SUBJECT** Business   772
- **TITLE** GNVQ Business Foundation, Intermediate, Advanced
- **PLACE** Lewisham College

Length 1 or 2 years   **Start** September   **Days** 16-20 hours/week   **Cost** £648   **Entry Reqs** Contact College   **Award** BTEC GNVQ all levels

- **CONTACT** Ann Okabhai 0181 692 0353

- **SUBJECT** Business   773
- **TITLE** GNVQ Business Intermediate
- **PLACE** Brent Adult College

Length 1 year   **Start** September   **Days** 14 hours/week 10.00-12.00 & 1.00-3.00   **Cost** Free **Entry Reqs** English Language Higher Intermediate   **Award** GNVQ Level II (RSA) **Creche** Yes £2/child/term

- **CONTACT** Mariam Jazayeri 0181 838 2882

- **SUBJECT** Business   774
- **TITLE** HNC in Business
- **PLACE** Barnet College in conjunction with the University of Hertfordshire

Length 2 years   **Start** September   **Days** Part time   **Cost** Contact College   **Entry Reqs** Mature students with appropriate work experience welcome   **Award** HNC Business

- **CONTACT** Guiseppe De Cicco 0181 362 8027

- **SUBJECT** Business   775
- **TITLE** MBA
- **PLACE** University of Greenwich, Riverside House, Woolwich

Length 2.5 years   **Start** October   **Days** Mon+Wed 6.30-9.30   **Cost** £5, 500   **Entry Reqs** 3-5 years senior management experience + good 1st degree or equivalent   **Award** MBA   **Creche** No

- **CONTACT** Lynn Winter 0181 331 8590

- **SUBJECT** Business/Secretarial   776
- **TITLE** Intensive Business/Secretarial Skills
- **PLACE** Lewisham College

Length 18 weeks   **Start** September   **Days** 16-20 hours/week   **Cost** £324   **Entry Reqs** None   **Award** Various Pitman/RSA qualifications

- **CONTACT** Linda Woods 0181 692 0353

- **SUBJECT** Business Administration   777
- **TITLE** Administration
- **PLACE** City and Islington College, City Campus

Length 1 year   **Start** September   **Days** 10.00-3.30   **Cost** Contact College   **Entry Reqs** None   **Award** RSA NVQ Level I/II   **Creche** Yes

- **CONTACT** Course Information Unit 0171 607 1132

- **SUBJECT** Business Administration   778
- **TITLE** Administration
- **PLACE** City and Islington College, Willen House

Length 6 months   **Start** September, January   **Days** 16 hours/week   **Cost** Concessions available   **Entry Reqs** Some IT Knowledge   **Award** RSA Administration NVQ 2+3

- **CONTACT** Val Wilson/Eileen Farrell 0171 614 0300

- **SUBJECT** Business Administration   779
- **TITLE** Administration
- **PLACE** College of NW London, Wembley Park Centre

Length 1 year or Fast Track 18 weeks   **Start** September, February   **Days** Mon-Fri 10.00-4.00   **Cost** Contact College   **Entry Reqs** Good standard of everyday English and office work experience for Fast Track students   **Award** RSA NVQ Level II Administration   **Creche** Yes

- **CONTACT** Maria Ferguson 0181 208 5000

- **SUBJECT** Business Administration 780
- **TITLE** Administration 1. NVQ Levels 1&2 2. Level 1
- **PLACE** Lewisham College

Length 1 year **Start** 1. September 2. Flexible **Days** 1.16-20 hours 2.5 hours **Cost** 1. £648 2. £142 **Award** LCC1 NVQ Levels 1 or 2

- **CONTACT** Ann Okabhai 0181 692 0353

- **SUBJECT** Business Administration 781
- **TITLE** Administration
- **PLACE** Merton College

Length 1 year **Start** September **Cost** Contact College **Entry Reqs** Contact College **Award** RSA Diploma/NVQ Levels II & III

- **CONTACT** Guidance and Entry Unit 0181 640 8001

- **SUBJECT** Business Administration 782
- **TITLE** Administrative Procedures
- **PLACE** Bromley College of Further & Higher Education

Start September **Cost** Contact College **Entry Reqs** Postgraduates, mature students or good A Level results. **Award** RSA Higher Diploma in Administrative Procedures

- **CONTACT** Student Enquiries 0181 295 7001

- **SUBJECT** Business Administration 783
- **TITLE** Modular Training for Secretaries and Administrators
- **PLACE** Carshalton College

Length 36 weeks **Start** September **Days** 3 days/week (18 hours/week) **Cost** Contact College **Entry Reqs** Contact College. Mature students welcome **Award** NVQ Administration Levels I/II/III, RSA single subjects

- **CONTACT** Advice and Guidance Centre 0181 770 6800

- **SUBJECT** Business Administration 784
- **TITLE** Business Administration NVQ Levels 1, 2
- **PLACE** College of North East London, Tottenham Centre

Length 1 year **Start** September **Days** 4+ days/week (19 hours/week) **Cost** Contact College **Entry Reqs** None **Award** NVQ Units in Business Administration 1, 2 **Creche** No

- **CONTACT** Admissions Officer 0181 802 3111

- **SUBJECT** Business Administration 785
- **TITLE** Business Administration
- **PLACE** Lambeth College, Norwood Centre

Length 1 year **Start** September **Days** 4 days/week **Cost** Contact College **Entry Reqs** Satisfactory levels of communication & numeracy skills. Previous qualifications not necessary **Award** RSA NVQ Level II Administration **Creche** No

- **CONTACT** Admissions Unit 0171 501 5000

- **SUBJECT** Business Studies 786
- **TITLE** BTEC Business Intermediate
- **PLACE** Kensington and Chelsea College, Hortensia Road

Length 34 weeks **Start** September **Days** Mon-Thurs (15 hours/week) **Cost** 72p/hour (£15 concessions) **Entry Reqs** Reasonable command of English and numeracy **Award** BTEC Intermediate GNVQ **Creche** Yes Limited places

- **CONTACT** Kerry James 0171 573 3600

London

- **SUBJECT** Business Studies/Secretarial   787
- **TITLE** 1. Modular Business Programme 2. Secretarial Skills
- **PLACE** Kensington and Chelsea College, Hortensia Road & Wornington Road

Length Modular   **Start** September, January, April   **Days** 1. Day or eve classes 2. Mon-Thurs 10.00-4.00, 18 hours/week   **Cost** 72p/hour (£15 concessions)   **Entry Reqs** None   **Award** 1. RSA single subject exams/elementary+intermediate 2. Pitman Group Certificates/3 choices **Creche** Yes Limited places

- **CONTACT** 1. Marilyn Naden/Kerry James 2. Cordelia Gerard Sharpe 0171 573 3600

- **SUBJECT** Care Studies   788
- **TITLE** Certificate, Diploma or Foundation Course in Welfare Studies
- **PLACE** City and Islington College, Bunhill Row

Length 1 year   **Start** September   **Days** 1 day/week, Foundation 1-2 days/week   **Entry Req** 18+, some experience of relevant paid or voluntary social work   **Award** Certificate or Diploma in Welfare Studies, Institute of Welfare Officers   **Creche** No

- **CONTACT** J O'Neill 0171 638 4171 x265

- **SUBJECT** Care Studies/Childcare   789
- **TITLE** 1. Caring 2. Social Care 3. Nursery Nursing 4. Foundation Managment
            for Care 5. Advanced Management for Care
- **PLACE** Hendon College

Length 1.1 year 2.2 years 3.2 years 4. & 5.1 year part time   **Start** September   **Days** Full or part time, flexible (1 & 2 include work experience)   **Cost** Concessions available   **Entry Reqs** None for mature students, interview + references   **Award** 1. BTEC 1st Diploma/Caring 2. BTEC Nat Dip/Social Care 3. BTEC Nat Dip/Nursery 4. C&G 3052 5. C&G   **Creche** Nursery

- **CONTACT** Central Admissions 0181 200 8300

- **SUBJECT** Catering   790
- **TITLE** Cake Decoration
- **PLACE** Lewisham College

Length 1 year   **Start** September   **Days** 3 hours/week   **Cost** £79   **Award** LOCF Credits
- **CONTACT** Isobel Craddock 0181 692 0353

- **SUBJECT** Catering   791
- **TITLE** 1. Cookery Certificate 2. Cooks Professional Certificate
- **PLACE** Lewisham College

Length 1 year   **Start** September   **Days** 6 hours/week   **Cost** £234   **Award** 1. C&G 332 2. C&G 333
- **CONTACT** Isobel Craddock 0181 692 0353

- **SUBJECT** Catering   792
- **TITLE** 1. Food Preparation 2. Food and Beverage Service
- **PLACE** Carshalton College

Length 30 weeks   **Start** September   **Days** 4 days/week 10.00-3.00 (18 hours/week)   **Cost** Free (ESF funded)   **Entry Reqs** No formal entry requirements   **Award** C&G NVQ II **Creche** Help with childcare available

- **CONTACT** Advice and Guidance Centre 0181 770 6800

- **SUBJECT** Catering   793
- **TITLE** NVQ 1. General 2. Craft Catering
- **PLACE** Lewisham College

Length 1 year   **Start** September   **Days** 1.16-21 hours/week 2.8 hours/week   **Cost** 1. £648 2. £234   **Award** 1. NVQ Level I 2. NVQ Level II

- **CONTACT** Isobel Craddock 0181 692 0353

- **SUBJECT**   Chemistry   794
- **TITLE**   Analytical Chemistry
- **PLACE**   University of Greenwich/Open Learning

Length 3 months   **Start** October, April (apply early)   **Days** Flexible, 50 hours study over 10 weeks+3-day practical workshop   **Cost** £500+accommodation for workshop if needed   **Entry Reqs** Contact University. Places limited   **Award** BTEC Certificate of Achievement: 5 courses amount to BTEC Diploma in Continuing Education

- **CONTACT**   Dr Norma Chadwick 0181 3331 8483

- **SUBJECT**   Childcare   795
- **TITLE**   Childcare 1. BTEC 1st Steps 2. BTEC National Certificate
- **PLACE**   Kensington and Chelsea College 1. Hortensia/Wornington 2. Wornington

Length 1.1 term 2.2 years   **Start** 1. September, April 2. January   **Days** 1.3 days/week 10.00-3.00 2.4 days/week 10.00-3.00   **Cost** Contact College   **Entry Reqs** 1. None 2. BTEC First Certificate, 3 GCSEs   **Award** BTEC awards   **Creche** Yes

- **CONTACT**   Maureen Parris 0171 573 5240

- **SUBJECT**   Childcare   796
- **TITLE**   Childcare and Early Education
- **PLACE**   Lewisham College

Length 2 years   **Start** September   **Days** 6 hours/week   **Cost** £234   **Award** NVQ Levels II & III

- **CONTACT**   Conchita Henry 0181 692 0353

- **SUBJECT**   Childcare   797
- **TITLE**   Childcare and Education for Bilingual Learners
- **PLACE**   Lambeth College, Clapham Centre

Length 1 year   **Start** September   **Days** Tues+Fri 9.00-4.00 college, Mon+Wed work placement   **Cost** Contact College   **Entry Reqs** Bilingual. English assessment to meet course needs. Experience with children preferred including own   **Award** NVQ Level II Childcare & Education

- **CONTACT**   Admissions Unit 0171 501 5000

- **SUBJECT**   Childcare   798
- **TITLE**   1. Childcare and Education 2. Nursery Nursing
- **PLACE**   Barnet College

Length 1.1 year 2.2 years   **Start** September   **Cost** Contact College   **Entry Reqs** Contact College   **Award** 1. NNEB/CACHE Certificate 2. NNEB/CACHE Diploma   **Creche** Yes

- **CONTACT**   0181 440 6321/0181 361 5101

- **SUBJECT**   Childcare   799
- **TITLE**   1. Childcare and Education 2. Nursery Nursing
- **PLACE**   Merton College

Length 1.1 year 2.2 years   **Start** September   **Cost** Contact College   **Entry Reqs** Test, interview and practical assessment   **Award** 1. NNEB/CACHE Certificate 2. NNEB/CACHE Diploma

- **CONTACT**   Guidance and Entry Unit 0181 640 8001

- **SUBJECT**   Childcare   800
- **TITLE**   Childhood Studies 1. BTEC National Certificate 2. National Diploma
- **PLACE**   Lambeth College, Clapham Centre

Length 1.1 year part time (19 hours/week) 2.1 year full time   **Start** September   **Days** 1. Mon 9.00-5.00+Wed 6.30-9.00, Wed 9.00-3.00 placement 2. Mon-Fri inc placement   **Cost** Contact College   **Entry Reqs** 4 GCSEs + childcare experience. Other qualifications can be taken into account   **Award** 1. BTEC National Certificate 2. BTEC National Diploma   **Creche** Yes

- **CONTACT**   Admissions Unit 0171 501 5000

- **SUBJECT** Childcare 801
- **TITLE** Diploma in Nursery Nursing
- **PLACE** Kensington and Chelsea College, Hortensia Road Centre

Length 3 years **Start** January **Days** Mon-Fri 10.00-3.00 **Cost** £452 (£15 concessionary) **Entry Reqs** None **Award** NNEB Diploma **Creche** Yes

- **CONTACT** Joan Gledson 0171 573 5240

- **SUBJECT** Childcare 802
- **TITLE** Diploma in Nursery Nursing
- **PLACE** Lambeth College, Clapham Centre

Length 2 years full time **Start** September **Days** Mon-Fri **Cost** Contact College **Entry Reqs** 3 GCSEs A-C inc. English or equivalent qualification or college test + interview **Award** NNEB Diploma in Nursery Nursing **Creche** Yes

- **CONTACT** Admissions Unit 0171 501 5000

- **SUBJECT** Childcare 803
- **TITLE** Diploma in Nursery Nursing
- **PLACE** Lewisham College

Length 2 years **Start** September **Days** 16-20 hours/week **Cost** £648 **Award** BTEC National Diploma

- **CONTACT** Conchita Henry 0181 692 0353

- **SUBJECT** Childcare 804
- **TITLE** 1. Diploma in Nursery Nursing 2. Certificate in Childcare and Education
- **PLACE** City and Islington College, Finsbury Park

Length 1 year **Start** September **Cost** Contact College **Entry Reqs** College entry test, interview and references **Award** 1. NNEB Diploma, 2. Certificate in Childcare & Education **Creche** Yes

- **CONTACT** Course Information Unit 0171 607 1132

- **SUBJECT** Community Studies 805
- **TITLE** Certificate/Diploma in Development Studies
- **PLACE** Birkbeck College, Central London

Length 48-hour courses, each 16 weeks: 3 courses for Certificate **Start** September **Days** Thurs eve **Cost** £85/course £28 concessions **Entry Reqs** None **Award** Certificate CATS accredited **Creche** No

- **CONTACT** Birkbeck College Social Studies Desk 0171 631 6653

- **SUBJECT** Community Studies 806
- **TITLE** MSc in Life Course Development
- **PLACE** Birkbeck College, Central London

Length 2 years part time **Start** October **Days** 1 day/week 10.00-5.00 **Cost** Contact College **Entry Reqs** Relevant work experience, degree or professional qualification **Award** MSc

- **CONTACT** Anne Jamieson 0171 631 6649

- **SUBJECT** Community Studies/Black Studies 807
- **TITLE** Certificate and Diploma in Race and Ethnicity
- **PLACE** Birkbeck College, Central London

Length 48-hour courses, each 16 weeks: 3 courses for Certificate **Start** September **Days** Tues eve **Cost** £85/course £28 concessions **Entry Reqs** None **Award** Certificate CATS accredited **Creche** No

- **CONTACT** Birkbeck College Social Studies Desk 0171 631 6653

- **SUBJECT** Computing 808
- **TITLE** Business Computing Applications
- **PLACE** NEWTEC (Newham Women's Training & Education Centre)

Length 13 weeks **Start** September, January, April **Days** 4 days/week 10.00-3.00 **Cost** Free if unemployed/unwaged **Entry Reqs** Some office experience or basic computer skills **Award** C&G Certificates **Creche** Yes

- **CONTACT** 0181 519 5843

- **SUBJECT** Computing 809
- **TITLE** Computing and Office Technology for Graduates
- **PLACE** Carshalton College

Length 18 weeks **Start** September **Days** 3 days/week (20 hours/week) **Cost** Contact College **Entry Reqs** Graduate or equivalent **Award** Certificate in Computer Literacy Level 2, Keyboarding Level 2

- **CONTACT** Advice and Guidance Centre 0181 770 6800

- **SUBJECT** Computing 810
- **TITLE** Computer Studies for Women
- **PLACE** Lewisham College

Length 2 years **Start** September **Cost** £269 **Entry Reqs** Computerised test and interview with Course Tutor **Award** BTEC National Certificate

- **CONTACT** Sorie Rezakhani 0181 692 0353

- **SUBJECT** Computing 811
- **TITLE** Computing and Information Technology
- **PLACE** Merton College

Length 1 or 2 years **Start** September **Cost** Contact College **Entry Reqs** GSCE or equivalent **Award** C&G Certificate or Diploma

- **CONTACT** Guidance and Entry Unit 0181 640 8001

- **SUBJECT** Computing 812
- **TITLE** Computer Studies: 1. BTEC National Certificate 2. BTEC National Diploma
- **PLACE** Lewisham College

Length 1.1 year 2.2 years **Start** September **Days** 16-20 hours/week **Cost** Contact College **Entry Reqs** Computerised test and interview with Course Tutor **Award** 1. BTEC National Certificate 2. BTEC National Diploma

- **CONTACT** 1. Janet Posner 2. Andy Wick 0181 692 0353

- **SUBJECT** Computing 813
- **TITLE** Computer Systems Maintenance and Management
- **PLACE** NEWTEC (Newham Women's Training & Education Centre)

Length 6 months **Start** January **Days** Full time 10.00-3.00 **Cost** Free if unemployed/unwaged **Entry Reqs** Experience of using a computer, knowledge of computer systems **Award** C&G/NVQ Level III **Creche** Yes

- **CONTACT** 0181 519 5843

- **SUBJECT** Computing 814
- **TITLE** IT & Computing for Women
- **PLACE** Ealing Tertiary College, Acton Site

Length Termly **Start** September, January, April **Cost** Contact College **Entry Reqs** By interview, no formal qualifications **Creche** No

- **CONTACT** Information Centre 0181 231 6008

- **SUBJECT**   Computing   815
- **TITLE**   Introduction to Computing
- **PLACE**   NEWTEC (Newham Women's Training & Education Centre)

Length 12 weeks   **Start** September, January, April   **Days** 4 days/week 10.00-3.00   **Cost** Free if unemployed/unwaged   **Entry Reqs** None   **Award** RSA CLAIT Stage I, progress to further courses   **Creche** Yes

- **CONTACT**   0181 519 5843

- **SUBJECT**   Computing   816
- **TITLE**   Introduction to Computing for Women
- **PLACE**   Lewisham College

Length 1 year   **Start** September   **Days** 16-20 hours/week   **Cost** £648   **Entry Reqs** Paragraph of written work and interview with Course Tutor   **Award** LOCF Credits

- **CONTACT**   Gill Archer 0181 692 0353

- **SUBJECT**   Computing   817
- **TITLE**   Introduction to Keyboard Skills and Word Processing (Women Only)
- **PLACE**   City and Islington College, Finsbury Park

Start September, April   **Days** Fri 10.00-12.00   **Cost** Contact College   **Entry Reqs** None   **Award** London Open College Federation Accreditation   **Creche** Yes

- **CONTACT**   Course Information Unit 0171 607 1132

- **SUBJECT**   Computing   818
- **TITLE**   Using Computers at Work
- **PLACE**   Lewisham College

Length 1 year   **Start** September   **Days** 16-20 hours/week   **Cost** £648   **Entry Reqs** Aptitude test and interview with Course Tutor   **Award** LOCF Credits

- **CONTACT**   Lindy Newton 0181 692 0353

- **SUBJECT**   Computing/Electronics   819
- **TITLE**   Women into Electronics and Computing Systems
- **PLACE**   Lambeth College, Norwood Centre

Length 36 weeks   **Start** September   **Days** Mon-Fri   **Cost** ESF funded, help with childcare and travel costs   **Entry Reqs** No formal qualifications, Maths & English skills needed. Women only 18+, unemployed   **Award** City & Guilds 7261 Diploma in Electronics & Computing Systems   **Creche** Yes, help with childcare costs

- **CONTACT**   Admissions Unit 0171 501 5000

- **SUBJECT**   Construction   820
- **TITLE**   BTEC First Diploma in Construction
- **PLACE**   NEWTEC (Newham Women's Training & Education Centre)

Length 1 year   **Start** September   **Days** Full time 10.00-3.00   **Cost** Free if unemployed/ unwaged   **Entry Reqs** None   **Award** BTEC First Diploma in Construction   **Creche** Yes

- **CONTACT**   0181 519 5843

- **SUBJECT**   Construction   821
- **TITLE**   Building Maintenance and Management
- **PLACE**   NEWTEC (Newham Women's Training & Education Centre)

Length 1 year   **Start** September   **Days** Full time 10.00-3.00   **Cost** Free if unemployed/ unwaged   **Entry Reqs** None   **Award** City & Guilds Certificate in Construction   **Creche** Yes

- **CONTACT**   0181 519 5843

- **SUBJECT** Contemporary Studies   822
- **TITLE** Certificate and Diploma in Contemporary Studies
- **PLACE** Birkbeck College, Central London

Length 48-hour courses, each 12 weeks: 3 courses for Certificate   **Start** September, January, April   **Days** 6 hours or 3 hours/week, day or evening   **Cost** £1.77/hour. Concessions if unwaged   **Entry Reqs** None, but must be able to undertake written work   **Award** Certificate or Diploma   **Creche** At local day centres, free/nominal cost

- **CONTACT** Jane Hoy 0171 631 6653

- **SUBJECT** Counselling   823
- **TITLE** Certificate in Counselling and Guidance Skills in the Community
- **PLACE** Birkbeck College, Central London and North East London

Length 48-hour courses, each 16 weeks: 3 courses for Certificate   **Start** September   **Days** 3 hours/week, Friday daytime + Mon eves   **Cost** £85/course £28 concessions   **Entry Reqs** Introduction to Counselling Course completion   **Award** Certificate CATS Accredited

- **CONTACT** Birkbeck College Social Studies Desk 0171 631 6653

- **SUBJECT** Counselling   824
- **TITLE** Counselling Skills in the Development of Learning
- **PLACE** Lewisham College

Length 2 terms   **Start** September, January   **Days** 5 hours/week   **Cost** £234   **Entry Reqs** Introduction to Counselling Certificate   **Award** RSA Certificate

- **CONTACT** Val Simanowitz 0181 692 0353

- **SUBJECT** Counselling   825
- **TITLE** Diploma in Humanistic Counselling
- **PLACE** Lewisham College

Length 2 years   **Start** September   **Days** 1 day/week   **Cost** £850   **Entry Reqs** Experience+qualifications in counselling or closely related field   **Award** College Certificate

- **CONTACT** Val Simanowitz 0181 692 0353

- **SUBJECT** Counselling   826
- **TITLE** Introduction to Basic Counselling Skills
- **PLACE** Lambeth College, Clapham Centre

Length 18 weeks   **Start** September   **Days** Thurs 2.15-4.15 or Wed 5.30-9.00   **Cost** Contact College   **Entry Reqs** Interview   **Award** LOCF Certificate

- **CONTACT** Admissions Unit 0171 501 5000

- **SUBJECT** Counselling   827
- **TITLE** Introduction to Counselling
- **PLACE** Lewisham College

Length 1 term   **Start** September, January, April   **Days** 3 hours/week   **Cost** £27   **Entry Reqs** None   **Award** College Certificate

- **CONTACT** Val Simanowitz 0181 692 0353

- **SUBJECT** Counselling   828
- **TITLE** RSA Counselling Skills
- **PLACE** Lambeth College, Clapham Centre

Length 2 years   **Start** September   **Days** Thurs 11.00-5.30   **Cost** Contact College   **Entry Reqs** Interview, preferably completion of introductory course   **Award** RSA Counselling Studies

- **CONTACT** Admissions Unit 0171 501 5000

London

● **SUBJECT** Dentistry   829
● **TITLE** BTEC National Diploma in Science (Dental Technology)
● **PLACE** Lambeth College, Tower Bridge Centre

Length 3 years full time including work experience **Start** September **Days** 4 days/week 9.00-5.00 **Cost** Contact College **Entry Reqs** 4 GCSEs A-C in 2 Sciences (inc Maths), English & 1 other. Special conditions for mature students **Award** BTEC National Diploma in Dental Technology **Creche** No. Childcare allowance

● **CONTACT** Admissions Unit 0171 501 5000

● **SUBJECT** Design/Desk Top Publishing   830
● **TITLE** Computer Graphics and DTP for Women
● **PLACE** Lambeth College, Vauxhall Centre

Length 1 year **Start** September **Days** Mon-Thurs 9.30-5.00 **Cost** Contact College **Entry Reqs** Relevant experience, evidence of creative ability **Award** C&G 7261 **Creche** Yes ESF funding

● **CONTACT** Admissions Unit 0171 501 5000

● **SUBJECT** Desk Top Publishing   831
● **TITLE** Cambridge IT: Desk Top Publishing and Graphics
● **PLACE** Lewisham College

Length 18 weeks **Start** September, February **Days** 2-3 hours/week **Cost** £79 **Entry Reqs** Short WP skills test and interview **Award** UCLES Information Technology Certificate

● **CONTACT** Jack Morris 0181 692 0353

● **SUBJECT** Desk Top Publishing   832
● **TITLE** Desk Top Publishing
● **PLACE** Lewisham College

Length 1 term **Start** September, January, April **Days** 2-3 hours/week **Cost** £37 **Entry Reqs** Short WP skills test and interview **Award** Pitman DTP Certificate

● **CONTACT** Jack Morris 0181 692 0353

● **SUBJECT** Desk Top Publishing   833
● **TITLE** Desk Top Publishing & Computer Aided Graphics
● **PLACE** NEWTEC (Newham Women's Training & Education Centre)

Length 6 months **Start** September **Days** 4 days/week 10.00-3.00 **Cost** Free if unemployed/unwaged **Entry Reqs** Interest in design, some keyboard skills useful **Award** C&G 726 Desktop Publishing **Creche** Yes

● **CONTACT** 0181 519 5843

● **SUBJECT** Education   834
● **TITLE** Certificate/Diploma in Early Years Care and Education
● **PLACE** Various Centres in North East London and East London

Length 48-hour courses, each 16 weeks: 3 courses for Certificate **Start** September **Days** Fri am and Mon eve **Cost** £85/course £28 concessions **Entry Reqs** None **Award** Certificate CATS accredited

● **CONTACT** Birkbeck College Social Studies Desk 0171 631 6653

● **SUBJECT** Electrical Engineering   835
● **TITLE** Electrical Installation
● **PLACE** Bromley College of Further & Higher Education

Length 2 years **Start** September **Days** Full time **Cost** Contact College **Entry Reqs** Open to men and women seeking a career change **Award** C&G 2360 Electrical Installation Parts I/II

● **CONTACT** Student Enquiries 0181 295 7001

- **SUBJECT** Electronics 836
- **TITLE** Electronic Servicing Part 1
- **PLACE** Lewisham College

Length 1 year **Start** September **Days** 16 hours/week **Cost** £648 **Entry Reqs** Reasonable numeracy skills **Award** City & Guilds 224 part 1 Certificate

- **CONTACT** Anthony Rodgers 0181 692 0353

- **SUBJECT** Engineering 837
- **TITLE** Domestic Appliance Servicing
- **PLACE** NEWTEC (Newham Women's Training & Education Centre)

Length 1 year **Start** September **Days** Full time 10.00-3.00 **Cost** Free if unemployed/ unwaged **Entry Reqs** None **Award** BTEC Foundation GNVQ in Engineering **Creche** Yes

- **CONTACT** 0181 519 5843

- **SUBJECT** Engineering 838
- **TITLE** Engineering in Association with University of Greenwich
- **PLACE** Lewisham College

Length 1 year (+3 at University) **Start** September **Days** 24 hours/week **Cost** £648 (grant may be available) **Entry Reqs** Reasonable maths and written skills **Award** BSc (Hons) Engineering after 4 years

- **CONTACT** Dr Humphrey Jartue Giplin 0181 692 0353

- **SUBJECT** Engineering 839
- **TITLE** Engineering: 1. BTEC GNVQ Foundation 2. BTEC GNVQ Intermediate
- **PLACE** City and Islington College, Islington Campus

Length 1 year **Start** September **Days** 19 hours/week **Cost** Contact College **Entry Reqs** None. Interview and assessment **Award** 1. BTEC GNVQ Foundation 2. BTEC GNVQ Intermediate **Creche** Yes

- **CONTACT** Course Information Unit 0171 607 1132

- **SUBJECT** Engineering 840
- **TITLE** Engineering: 1. BTEC GNVQ Foundation 2. First Diploma 2. National Diploma
- **PLACE** Lewisham College

Length 1. &2.1 year 3.2 years **Start** September **Days** 16-20 hours/week **Cost** £648 **Entry Reqs** Contact College **Award** 1. BTEC GNVQ Foundation 2. BTEC First Diploma 3. BTEC National Diploma

- **CONTACT** 1. Robin Gilbert 2. Mr Kulwant Selhi 2. Anthony Nicolaides 0181 692 0353

- **SUBJECT** Engineering/Information Technology 841
- **TITLE** Engineering and Computer Aided Systems
- **PLACE** Lewisham College

Length 1 year **Start** September **Days** 16 hours/week **Cost** £648 **Entry Reqs** Interview and short test **Award** BTEC National Certificate in Engineering and C&G Certificate in IT subjects

- **CONTACT** Eddie Coode 0181 692 0353

- **SUBJECT** English/Office Skills 842
- **TITLE** 1. English as a Second Language 2. Office Skills
- **PLACE** College of NW London, Kilburn Centre

Length 1 year **Start** September **Days** 1. Maximum 5 days/week 2. Maximum 20 hours/ week 10.00-3.00 **Cost** Contact College **Entry Reqs** None **Award** 1. College Profile of Attainment 2. RSA Certificates **Creche** Playgroup

- **CONTACT** Claire Jaff 0181 208 5000

- **SUBJECT** Environmental Sciences   843
- **TITLE** Environmental Sciences: Research Masters Training Programme
- **PLACE** University College, London

Length 2 years   **Start** October   **Cost** Natural Environment Research Council award available   **Entry Reqs** Graduates with first or upper second class honours degree   **Award** MSc

- **CONTACT** Dr Kevin Pickering 0171 387 7050 x2369

- **SUBJECT** Fashion   844
- **TITLE** Fashion 1. Stage 1 2. Stage 2 3. Stage 3 4. BTEC National Diploma
- **PLACE** Lewisham College, West Greenwich Centre

Length 1. -3. 1 year 4.2 years   **Start** September   **Days** Contact College   **Cost** Contact College   **Award** 1. C&G 4569 Dressmaking 2. C&G 790 Part 1 2. C&G 790 Part 2 4. BTEC National Diploma

- **CONTACT** Kate Gibson 0181 692 0353

- **SUBJECT** Finance   845
- **TITLE** MSc 1. Finance & Financial Information Systems 2. Accounting & Finance 3. Financial Management
- **PLACE** University of Greenwich (Roehampton location)

Length 1 year full time, 2 years part time   **Start** October   **Days** Day/evening, flexible   **Cost** £3,500/year full time, £2000/year part time   **Entry Reqs** Good Honours degree/work experience in finance or IT. Numerate   **Award** MSc   **Creche** Yes

- **CONTACT** Shish Malde 0181 331 8690/9892

- **SUBJECT** Hairdressing   846
- **TITLE** Hairdressing
- **PLACE** Kensington & Chelsea College, Wornington Centre

Length 2 years   **Start** September   **Days** Tues, Wed, Fri   **Cost** £600   **Entry Reqs** 3 GCSEs or similar   **Award** NVQ Level II   **Creche** Yes

- **CONTACT** Petronella Ip 0181 960 4135

- **SUBJECT** Health Studies   847
- **TITLE** Health and Social Care
- **PLACE** Barnet College

Length 1 year   **Start** September   **Cost** Contact College   **Entry Reqs** Contact College   **Award** GNVQ Foundation or Intermediate   **Creche** Yes

- **CONTACT** 0181 440 6321/0181 361 5101

- **SUBJECT** Health Studies   848
- **TITLE** Health and Social Care
- **PLACE** City and Islington College, City Campus

Length 1 year   **Start** September   **Days** Full time   **Cost** Contact College   **Entry Reqs** Contact College   **Award** GNVQ Intermediate, College Certificate   **Creche** Yes

- **CONTACT** Departmental Secretary, Applied Social Studies Dept 0171 614 0235

- **SUBJECT** Health Studies   849
- **TITLE** Health and Social Care
- **PLACE** Kensington & Chelsea College, Hortensia Road Centre

Length 1 year   **Start** September   **Days** 2 days/week 9.30-3.30   **Cost** £267 (£15 concessions)   **Entry Reqs** None   **Award** GNVQ Intermediate Level II   **Creche** Yes

- **CONTACT** Joan Gledson 0171 573 5240

- **SUBJECT**   Health Studies   850
- **TITLE**   Health and Social Care: 1. GNVQ Foundation 2. Intermediate 3. Advanced
- **PLACE**   City of Westminster College, various sites

Length 1. &2. 1 year 3.2 years   **Start** September   **Days** Daytime   **Cost** Contact College   **Entry Reqs** Contact College   **Award** 1. GNVQ Foundation 2. GNVQ Intermediate 3. GNVQ Advanced Health and Social Care

- **CONTACT**   Course Information 0171 723 8826

- **SUBJECT**   Health Studies   851
- **TITLE**   Health and Social Care: 1. GNVQ Foundation 2. Intermediate 3. Advanced
- **PLACE**   Lambeth College, Clapham Centre

Length 1. &2.1 year 3.2 years   **Start** September   **Days** 3/4 days/week (19 hours/week)   **Cost** Contact College   **Entry Reqs** Contact College   **Award** 1. GNVQ Foundation 2. GNVQ Intermediate 3. GNVQ Advanced Health and Social Care   **Creche** Yes

- **CONTACT**   Admissions Unit 0171 501 5000

- **SUBJECT**   Health Studies   852
- **TITLE**   Health and Social Care: 1. GNVQ Foundation 2. Intermediate 3. Advanced
- **PLACE**   Lewisham College

Length 1. &2.1 year 3.2 years   **Start** September   **Days** 16-20 hours   **Cost** £648   **Entry Reqs** Contact College   **Award** 1. GNVQ Foundation 2. GNVQ Intermediate 3. GNVQ Advanced Health and Social Care

- **CONTACT**   Conchita Henry 0181 692 0353

- **SUBJECT**   Health Studies   853
- **TITLE**   NVQ Health Care
- **PLACE**   Lambeth College, Clapham Centre

Length 1 term   **Start** September, January, April   **Days** Tues, Thurs 9.00-4.00 college, Mon+Wed placement   **Cost** Contact College   **Entry Reqs** Interview   **Award** NVQ Level II Health Care

- **CONTACT**   Admissions Unit 0171 501 5000

- **SUBJECT**   Horticulture/Floristry/Landscape Design   854
- **TITLE**   Horticulture, Floristry, Landscape Design and Construction
- **PLACE**   Capel Manor Horticultural and Environmental Centre

Length Part time   **Start** Varies   **Days** Varies   **Award** C&G, BTEC   **Creche** No

- **CONTACT**   Courses Officer 0181 366 4442

- **SUBJECT**   Humanities   855
- **TITLE**   BA(Hons) Humanities Modular Scheme
- **PLACE**   University of North London, Kentish Town

Length 3 years full time, 4-6 years part time   **Start** September   **Days** Fits in with school hours if possible   **Cost** Contact University   **Entry Reqs** Subject to interview   **Award** BA(Hons)/ Diploma/Certificate   **Creche** Yes limited places.

- **CONTACT**   Course Enquiries Office 0171 753 5066/7

- **SUBJECT**   Information Technology   856
- **TITLE**   Adult Foundation into Information Technology
- **PLACE**   Lambeth College, Norwood Centre

Length 1 year   **Start** September   **Days** 3 days/week   **Cost** Contact College   **Entry Reqs** Satisfactory levels of communication & numeracy skills. Prior experience not necessary   **Award** City & Guilds 7261 IT   **Creche** No

- **CONTACT**   Admissions Unit 0171 501 5000

London

- **SUBJECT** Information Technology   857
- **TITLE** Basic Keyboarding Skills
- **PLACE** Lewisham College

Length 1 term   **Start** September, January, April   **Days** 2-3 hours/week   **Cost** £37   **Entry Reqs** Interview   **Award** LOCF Credits
- **CONTACT** Jack Morris 0181 692 0353

- **SUBJECT** Information Technology   858
- **TITLE** BTEC First Diploma in IT Applications
- **PLACE** Lewisham College

Length 1 year   **Start** September   **Days** 16-20 hours/week   **Cost** £648   **Entry Reqs** Computerised test and interview with Course Tutor   **Award** BTEC First Diploma
- **CONTACT** Paul Herbert 0181 692 0353

- **SUBJECT** Information Technology   859
- **TITLE** Business Information Systems 1. BTEC NHC 2. BTEC HND
- **PLACE** Lewisham College

Length 2 years   **Start** September   **Days** 16-20 hours/week   **Cost** 1. £284 2. Mandatory award   **Entry Reqs** Aptitude tests and interview   **Award** 1. BTEC HNC 2. BTEC HND
- **CONTACT** Richard Jones 0181 692 0353

- **SUBJECT** Information Technology   860
- **TITLE** Information Technology/Computers (Various Courses)
- **PLACE** Kensington and Chelsea College, various sites

Length Various   **Start** September   **Days** Various   **Cost** Contact College   **Entry Reqs** Contact College   **Award** NICAS/RSA/NVQ 1, 2&3/BTEC GNVQ
- **CONTACT** Course Information 0181 964 1311

- **SUBJECT** Information Technology   861
- **TITLE** Information Technology and Computing for Women
- **PLACE** College of NW London, South Kilburn, Kilburn & Wembley Centres

Length 1, 2 or 3 terms   **Days** Part time 1 day/week   **Cost** Contact College   **Entry Reqs** None. Suitable for beginners or those wishing to update skills   **Award** RSA exams   **Creche** Yes
- **CONTACT** 0181 208 5000

- **SUBJECT** Information Technology   862
- **TITLE** Information Technology for Women
- **PLACE** Lambeth College, Norwood Centre

Length Contact College   **Start** Contact College   **Cost** Contact College   **Entry Reqs** Women wishing to retrain or enhance existing skills
- **CONTACT** Suzanne D'Abo 0171 501 5721

- **SUBJECT** Information Technology   863
- **TITLE** Information Technology (Option of women-only group)
- **PLACE** City & Islington College, Islington Campus

Length 1 or 2 years   **Start** September   **Days** Under 21 hours/week 10.00-3.00   **Cost** ESF funded   **Entry Reqs** Mixed or women-only groups   **Award** City & Guilds Level 1 Wordprocessing, Spreadsheets, Pascal, Cobol, Database, Communications, Numeracy   **Creche** Nursery, sliding scale for charges
- **CONTACT** Course Information Centre 0171 607 1132

- **SUBJECT** Information Technology   864
- **TITLE** Information Technology Training
- **PLACE** Carshalton College

Length 1 year   **Start** September   **Days** 18 hours week, usually 10.00-3.00   **Cost** Free if unemployed   **Entry Reqs** None   **Award** RSA CLAIT Level 1/2
- **CONTACT** Advice and Guidance Centre 0181 770 6800

- **SUBJECT** Information Technology 865
- **TITLE** IT Skills for the Workplace
- **PLACE** Lewisham College

Length 1 year **Start** September **Days** 16-20 hours/week **Cost** £234 **Entry Reqs** Aptitude test and interview with Course Tutor **Award** LOCF Credits
- **CONTACT** Robert Evans 0181 692 0353

- **SUBJECT** Information Technology 866
- **TITLE** Introduction to Databases
- **PLACE** Lewisham College

Length 1 term **Start** September, January, April **Days** 2-3 hours/week **Cost** £37 **Entry Reqs** Interview **Award** LOCF Credits
- **CONTACT** Jack Morris 0181 692 0353

- **SUBJECT** Information Technology 867
- **TITLE** Intensive IT Skills
- **PLACE** Lewisham College

Length 18 weeks **Start** September, February **Days** 16-20 hours/week **Cost** £338 **Entry Reqs** Aptitude test and interview with Course Tutor **Award** LOCF Credits
- **CONTACT** Deirdre Alsey 0181 692 0353

- **SUBJECT** Information Technology 868
- **TITLE** MSc Information Technology
- **PLACE** City University, School of Informatics

Length 2 years **Start** October **Days** 3 days/week in school hours **Cost** Contact University **Entry Reqs** Preparatory Certificate in Information Systems & Technology or contact University **Award** MSc
- **CONTACT** Karen Leport 0171 477 8382

- **SUBJECT** Information Technology 869
- **TITLE** RSA Diploma in Information Technology
- **PLACE** City & Islington College, Willen House

Length 12 weeks **Start** September, January, April **Days** 11 hours/week **Cost** Concessions available **Entry Reqs** Some IT knowledge **Award** RSA Diploma
- **CONTACT** Val Wilson/Alison Fowles 0171 614 0300

- **SUBJECT** Information Technology 870
- **TITLE** Short Course Provision Computing and Information Technology
- **PLACE** Orpington College

Length Various **Start** Varies **Cost** Contact College **Entry Reqs** Varies. Contact College
- **CONTACT** Nicole Barber 01689 839336

- **SUBJECT** Information Technology 871
- **TITLE** Windows and Wordprocessing
- **PLACE** Lewisham College

Length 1 term **Start** September, January, April **Days** 2-3 hours/week **Cost** £37 **Entry Reqs** Interview **Award** LOCF Credits
- **CONTACT** Jack Morris 0181 692 0353

- **SUBJECT** Information Technology 872
- **TITLE** Women into Information Technology
- **PLACE** Lambeth College, Brixton Centre

Length 1 year **Start** September **Days** Mon-Fri 9.30-4.00 **Cost** Contact College **Entry Reqs** GCEs/GCSEs. College entrance test **Award** BTEC GNVQ Intermediate IT Applications **Creche** Childcare allowance
- **CONTACT** Admissions Unit 0171 501 5000

- **SUBJECT**   Information Technology   873
- **TITLE**   Women into Information Technology
- **PLACE**   Lambeth College, Norwood Centre

Length 1 year   **Start** September   **Days** 4 days/week   **Cost** Contact College   **Entry Reqs** Satisfactory levels of communication & numeracy skills. Prior experience not necessary   **Award** City & Guilds 7261 IT   **Creche** No
- **CONTACT**   Admissions Unit 0171 501 5000

- **SUBJECT**   Information Technology/Management   874
- **TITLE**   Women into Information Technology and Management
- **PLACE**   Carshalton College

Length 1 year   **Start** September   **Days** 18 hours/week   **Cost** Free (ESF funded)   **Entry Reqs** Good basic education + interview   **Award** BTEC National Certificate in Information Technology Applications   **Creche** Help with childcare available
- **CONTACT**   Advice and Guidance Centre 0181 770 6800

- **SUBJECT**   Information Technology/Secretarial   875
- **TITLE**   Intermediate Secretarial/IT RSA Diploma
- **PLACE**   Lambeth College, Norwood Centre

Length 1 year   **Start** September   **Days** 4 days/week   **Cost** Contact College   **Entry Reqs** Prior office skills & experience in use of IT applications. Good communication & numeracy skills   **Award** RSA Vocational Diploma in IT and Pitmans Book-keeping   **Creche** No
- **CONTACT**   Admissions Unit 0171 501 5000

- **SUBJECT**   Information Technology/Secretarial   876
- **TITLE**   Information Technology and Secretarial Skills
- **PLACE**   Carshalton College

Length Modular   **Days** Open learning (2 hours/module)   **Cost** Contact College   **Entry Reqs** None   **Award** RSA Single Subjects
- **CONTACT**   Advice and Guidance Centre 0181 770 6800

- **SUBJECT**   Law   877
- **TITLE**   Certificate in Legal Method
- **PLACE**   Birkbeck College, various locations in London, also Croydon

Length 48-hour courses, each 12 weeks: 3 courses for Certificate   **Start** September   **Days** Varied, evening and day   **Cost** £2.50/hour. Concessions 1/3 of full fees   **Entry Reqs** Good spoken and written English   **Award** Certificate in Legal Method   **Creche** At some Centres
- **CONTACT**   Lesley Hannigan 0171 631 6627

- **SUBJECT**   Management   878
- **TITLE**   Back to Business for Women in Management
- **PLACE**   Richmond Adult & Community College, Clifden Centre

Length 12 weeks   **Start** September, January, April   **Days** Full time Mon-Fri   **Cost** Free   **Entry Reqs** Previous experience in business   **Award** RSA Computer Literacy   **Creche** Yes
- **CONTACT**   T Saunders-Davies 0181 891 5907 x425

- **SUBJECT**   Management   879
- **TITLE**   BTEC Certificate in Management NVQ Level IV
- **PLACE**   Bromley College of Further & Higher Education

Length 1 year   **Start** September   **Days** Part time, day or evening   **Cost** Contact College   **Entry Reqs** Contact College   **Award** BTEC Certificate in Management NVQ Level IV
- **CONTACT**   Student Enquiries 0181 295 7001

- **SUBJECT**   Management   880
- **TITLE**   1. Certificate in Management 2. Diploma in Management
- **PLACE**   University of Greenwich, Riverside House, Woolwich

Length 1 year   **Start** October   **Days** Mon+Wed 6.30-9.30   **Cost** £1300   **Entry Reqs** 1. Mgt experience/aspiring managers/graduate or equivalent 2. Completion of Certificate or 3 yrs mgt   **Award** 1. Certificate 2. Diploma   **Creche** No

- **CONTACT**   Polly Carter 0181 331 8590

- **SUBJECT**   Management   881
- **TITLE**   Certificate/Diploma in Women and Management
- **PLACE**   Birkbeck College, Central London and North East London

Length 48-hour courses, each 16 weeks: 3 courses for Certificate   **Start** September   **Days** Tues & Thurs eves   **Cost** £85/course £28 concessions   **Entry Reqs** None   **Award** Certificate CATS accredited

- **CONTACT**   Birkbeck College Social Studies Desk 0171 631 6653

- **SUBJECT**   Management   882
- **TITLE**   Human Resources Management (Institute of Personnel Development)
- **PLACE**   University of Greenwich, Riverside House, Woolwich

Length 2 years   **Start** October   **Days** Mon+Wed 6.30-9.30   **Cost** £1650   **Entry Reqs** Certificate in Personnel Studies or equivalent   **Award** IPD qualifications   **Creche** No

- **CONTACT**   Barry Hutchinson 0181 331 8590

- **SUBJECT**   Management   883
- **TITLE**   Introduction to Management for Women
- **PLACE**   City University, Dept of Continuing Education

Length 10 weeks   **Start** October   **Days** Wed 6.30-8.30   **Cost** £69   **Entry Reqs** None   **Award** 1 credit

- **CONTACT**   Course for Adults 0171 477 8268

- **SUBJECT**   Management   884
- **TITLE**   MA Management
- **PLACE**   University of Greenwich, Riverside House, Woolwich

Length 1.5-3 years   **Start** October   **Days** Mon+Wed 6.30-9.30   **Cost** Depends on units taken   **Entry Reqs** Management experience, good 1st degree or equivalent   **Award** MA Management   **Creche** No

- **CONTACT**   Lynn Winter 0181 331 8590

- **SUBJECT**   Management   885
- **TITLE**   Management Development for Women
- **PLACE**   City University, Dept of Continuing Education

Length 10 weeks   **Start** January   **Days** Wed 6.30-8.30   **Cost** £69   **Entry Reqs** Some supervisory experience or attendance on introductory course   **Award** 1 credit

- **CONTACT**   Course for Adults 0171 477 8268

- **SUBJECT**   Management   886
- **TITLE**   Women into Management
- **PLACE**   University of Westminster, Marylebone Road

Length 33 weeks   **Start** October   **Days** 1 afternoon+same evening/week (Tues 1.30-8.00)   **Cost** £835   **Entry Reqs** Women only, no formal requirements   **Award** University Certificate in Management Development   **Creche** Daytime playgroup 2 yrs+

- **CONTACT**   Tricia Price 0171 911 5000 x3045

- **SUBJECT** Management/Media Studies/Craft   **887**
- **TITLE** Various Management, Media, Craft Skills Courses
- **PLACE** London College of Fashion, Oxford Circus

Length Up to 9 weeks   **Start** October, January, April   **Days** 1 eve/week or Sat morning **Cost** Approx £150-£200   **Entry Reqs** None   **Award** Certificate of Attendance **Creche** No
- **CONTACT** Antoinette Oluwafisoye 0171 514 7400 x7444

- **SUBJECT** Media Studies   **888**
- **TITLE** BTEC National Diploma Media Studies
- **PLACE** Lewisham College

Length 2 years   **Start** September   **Days** 16 hours/week   **Cost** £648   **Entry Reqs** Contact College   **Award** BTEC National Diploma
- **CONTACT** Nick Edwards 0181 692 0353

- **SUBJECT** Multi-Subject   **889**
- **TITLE** Continuing Education Scheme
- **PLACE** University of Westminster, various sites

Length 2-8 years (depending upon award)   **Start** September, February   **Days** Multi-mode, part time and full time   **Cost** Contact College. Depends on mode of study   **Entry Reqs** 21+, commitment, ability to benefit   **Award** Various: Certificate in Continuing Education, Undergraduate/PG Awards in Combined Studies   **Creche** Yes Contact Creche Supervisor
- **CONTACT** Davina Saliba 0171 911 5000 x3206

- **SUBJECT** Multi-Subject   **890**
- **TITLE** Open Learning
- **PLACE** Hammersmith & Fulham Community Learning & Leisure, Macbeth Centre

Length Open   **Start** Anytime   **Days** Mon+Wed 4.30-6.30, Tues 1.00-9.00, Thurs 4.30-9.00   **Cost** Contact College   **Entry Reqs** None   **Award** Certificates available but mainly course support   **Creche** Tues 1.00-3.00 only
- **CONTACT** Alan Carter 0171 736 0864/0181 846 9090

- **SUBJECT** Multi-Subject   **891**
- **TITLE** Various: Teaching, Psychology, Economics, Sociology, Community & Social Work, Business Studies, Study Skills
- **PLACE** Greenwich Community College, various locations

Length Varies   **Start** Varies   **Award** London Open College Federation Credits   **Creche** Yes nominal charge
- **CONTACT** Denise Hyland/Caroline James 0181 319 8088

- **SUBJECT** Music   **892**
- **TITLE** Music 1. Foundation 2. BTEC National Diploma Popular Music
- **PLACE** Lewisham College

Length 1.1 year 2.2 years   **Start** September   **Days** 16 hours/week   **Cost** £648   **Award** 1. College Certificate 2. BTEC National Diploma
- **CONTACT** Dave Moses 0181 692 0353

- **SUBJECT** NOW   **893**
- **TITLE** New Opportunities for Women
- **PLACE** Waltham Forest Adult Education Service, 3 locations

Length 11 weeks   **Start** September, January, April   **Days** 10 hours/week within school hours   **Cost** £6 (Concessions to unwaged & people with disabilities)   **Entry Reqs** Priority to local women unwaged over 6 months   **Award** Portfolio and Certificate, entry to other courses/ training   **Creche** Yes free
- **CONTACT** Jill Ross/Sue Chrimes 0181 524 4542

- **SUBJECT** NOW/Design 894
- **TITLE** New Opportunities for Women: 3D Design
- **PLACE** Kingsway College, EC1

Length 2 years **Start** September **Days** 4 days/week 9.30-12.00, 1.00-3.30 (20 hours/week)
Cost None **Entry Reqs** Women, unemployed **Award** BTEC National Diploma
Creche Yes Free

- **CONTACT** Carmel Walsh 0171 306 5700

- **SUBJECT** Office Skills 895
- **TITLE** Intensive Course: WP, Typing, Audio, Teeline, Shorthand
- **PLACE** College of NW London, Kilburn Centre

Length 18 weeks **Start** September, February **Days** 19 hours/week, afternoons **Cost**
Contact College **Entry Reqs** Minimum A Levels or similar **Creche** Yes

- **CONTACT** Pat Walters 0181 208 5000

- **SUBJECT** Office Skills 896
- **TITLE** Intensive Office Skills
- **PLACE** City and Islington College, Willen House

Length 12 weeks **Start** September, January, April **Days** 16 hours/week **Cost**
Concessions available **Entry Reqs** None **Award** RSA single subjects: Typing, WP, CLAIT

- **CONTACT** Val Wilson/Alison Fowles 0171 614 0300

- **SUBJECT** Office Skills 897
- **TITLE** New Opportunities: Office Skills
- **PLACE** Merton College

Length 12 weeks **Days** 15 hours/week over 3 days **Cost** Contact College **Entry Reqs** No
prior skills knowledge required **Award** RSA/Pitmans/College competence statements

- **CONTACT** Guidance and Entry Unit 0181 640 8001

- **SUBJECT** Office Skills 898
- **TITLE** Office Skills
- **PLACE** City and Islington College, City Campus

Length 1 term minimum **Days** Flexible **Cost** Contact College **Award** Pitman/RSA
Certificates **Creche** Yes

- **CONTACT** Departmental Secretary, Business Studies Dept 0171 614 0308

- **SUBJECT** Office Skills 899
- **TITLE** Training for Work in Offices
- **PLACE** Carshalton College

Days 3 days/week + work experience **Cost** Free (SOLOTEC funded) **Entry Reqs** Men &
women unemployed for 6 months+, or returning to work after a period of childcare **Award**
NVQ Level II Administration, RSA Single Subjects

- **CONTACT** Advice and Guidance Centre 0181 770 6800

- **SUBJECT** Office Skills 900
- **TITLE** Typing, Shorthand, Word Processing
- **PLACE** Lewisham College

Length 1 term **Start** Flexible **Days** 2.5-3 hours/week **Cost** £27-£79 **Entry Reqs** None
Award Various Pitman/RSA qualifications

- **CONTACT** Brenda Amin 0181 692 0353

- **SUBJECT**   Office Skills/Tourism & Leisure   **901**
- **TITLE**   1. Various Office Skills 2. Travel & Tourism
- **PLACE**   Hendon College

Length 1.1-12 weeks 1.1 year (includes work experience)   **Start** Varies   **Days** 5 days/week (some between 10.00-3.00)   **Cost** Contact College   **Entry Reqs** 1. None 2. Priority to unemployed men & women 18+, test & interview)   **Award** College Certificate, RSA, NVQ I or II   **Creche** Nursery
- **CONTACT**   P Clayton 0181 200 8300

- **SUBJECT**   Performing Arts   **902**
- **TITLE**   Drama Foundation
- **PLACE**   Lewisham College

Length 2 years   **Start** September   **Days** 16 hours/week   **Cost** £648   **Award** College Certificate
- **CONTACT**   Nick Edwards 0181 692 0353

- **SUBJECT**   Performing Arts   **903**
- **TITLE**   1. Performing Arts/Drama 2. Stagecraft
- **PLACE**   Lewisham College

Length 1.1 year 2.2 years   **Start** September   **Days** 16 hours/week   **Cost** £648   **Award** 1. BTEC First Diploma 2. BTEC National Diploma
- **CONTACT**   Nick Edwards 0181 692 0353

- **SUBJECT**   Photography   **904**
- **TITLE**   Photography Foundation
- **PLACE**   Lewisham College, West Greenwich Centre

Length 1 year   **Start** September   **Days** 16 hours/week   **Cost** £648   **Award** C&G 9231
- **CONTACT**   Nick Edwards 0181 692 0353

- **SUBJECT**   Photography   **905**
- **TITLE**   Photovideo Portfolio Course
- **PLACE**   Tower Hamlets College, Jubilee Street

Length 36 weeks   **Start** September   **Days** 2-3 days/week   **Cost** Contact College   **Entry Reqs** Interview and portfolio   **Award** Access Accreditation London Open College Federation (if required by student)   **Creche** Yes, sliding scale charge
- **CONTACT**   John Digance 0171 538 5888 x219

- **SUBJECT**   Practical   **906**
- **TITLE**   Furniture Crafts: Multiskills/Woodwork/Metalwork (City & Guilds Part I&II)
- **PLACE**   City and Islington College, Rochelle Street Site

Length 1 year (Part 1)+1 year (Part II)   **Start** September   **Days** 3 days/week   **Award** C&G 555 Furniture Crafts   **Creche** No
- **CONTACT**   K Payne 0171 739 7123

- **SUBJECT**   Preparatory   **907**
- **TITLE**   Access Foundation Course
- **PLACE**   City of Westminster College, Maida Vale Centre

Length 8 weeks   **Days** Daytime   **Cost** Contact College   **Entry Reqs** None   **Award** Progress to Access Courses
- **CONTACT**   Course Information 0171 723 8826

- **SUBJECT**   Preparatory   **908**
- **TITLE**   Access to Training (Basic Skills)
- **PLACE**   Carshalton College

Length 18 weeks   **Days** 18 hours/week   **Cost** Free   **Entry Reqs** None   **Award** RSA CLAIT, English/Communication, Maths
- **CONTACT**   Advice and Guidance Centre 0181 770 6800

- **SUBJECT**   Preparatory   909
- **TITLE**   1. Adult Foundation 2. Adult Foundation for Speakers of Other Languages
- **PLACE**   City and Islington College, Islington Campus

Length 1. Up to 1 year 2.1 year   **Start** September   **Days** 1. Flexible 2.16 hours/week   **Entry Reqs** 1. By interview 2. Bilingual, age 19+   **Award** 1. C&G and College Certificate, leads to further study 2. Cambridge Preliminary   **Creche** Nursery, sliding scale of charges

- **CONTACT**   Course Information Centres 0171 607 1132/0171 614 0200

- **SUBJECT**   Preparatory   910
- **TITLE**   1. Adult Foundation 2. Return to Study
- **PLACE**   Barnet College

Length Modular, part time study possible   **Cost** Contact College   **Entry Reqs** Interview   **Creche** Yes

- **CONTACT**   0181 440 6321/0181 361 5101

- **SUBJECT**   Preparatory   911
- **TITLE**   Adult Returners Course
- **PLACE**   Lewisham College

Length 1 year   **Start** Flexible   **Days** 12 hours/week   **Cost** £338   **Entry Reqs** None   **Award** C&G Numeracy & Communications Skills Levels I, II or III; LOCF Credits for IT

- **CONTACT**   Elaine Miller 0181 692 0353

- **SUBJECT**   Preparatory   912
- **TITLE**   Assertiveness for Women
- **PLACE**   Queen's Park Community School, Brent

Length 10 weeks   **Start** September   **Days** Tues 7.00-9.00   **Cost** £32 or £11 concessions   **Entry Reqs** None   **Creche** Yes

- **CONTACT**   0181 459 3418

- **SUBJECT**   Preparatory   913
- **TITLE**   Assertiveness for Women: Intensive Course
- **PLACE**   The City Lit

Length 3 days   **Start** March, June/July   **Days** Wed, Thurs, Fri 10.30-4.30   **Cost** £43.25, concessions £14.70   **Entry Reqs** None   **Award** None   **Creche** Yes £1/day or 50p/2½-hour session

- **CONTACT**   Leighton Cole 0171 430 0542

- **SUBJECT**   Preparatory   914
- **TITLE**   Breakthrough: Return to Study
- **PLACE**   The City Lit

Length 24 weeks   **Start** September   **Days** Thurs 10.00-1.00 or 6.30-9.00   **Cost** Daytime £80, evening £70 (Concessions no fee in each case)   **Entry Reqs** None   **Award** None   **Creche** Daytime only. 50p/session

- **CONTACT**   Anne Hartree/Linda Taylor 0171 430 0541

- **SUBJECT**   Preparatory   915
- **TITLE**   Career Options
- **PLACE**   Richmond Adult Guidance & Training Centre

Length 8 weeks   **Start** November onwards   **Days** Tues+Wed 9.30-1.00   **Cost** £72 if employed, otherwise free   **Entry Reqs** Good basic education to GCSE/A Level or equivalent, and a commitment to the programme   **Award** Open College Network Units   **Creche** No

- **CONTACT**   0181 891 1899

- **SUBJECT** Preparatory 916
- **TITLE** Changing Direction: Career Development
- **PLACE** The City Lit

Length 3 days **Start** November, February **Cost** £38 Concessions £13 **Entry Reqs** None
Award None **Creche** Yes £1/day or 50p/2½-hour session
- **CONTACT** Leighton Cole 0171 430 0542

- **SUBJECT** Preparatory 917
- **TITLE** Core Skills for Work
- **PLACE** Kensington and Chelsea College

Length Approx 1 year **Start** Flexible **Days** Mon-Fri 10.00-12.00, Mon-Fri 1.00-3.00
optional **Cost** None **Entry Reqs** 18+, unemployed for 6 months **Award** RSA CLAIT
Computing, Pitman Typing I & II, C&G Word/Number Power **Creche** Yes 50p/2 hour
session
- **CONTACT** Akosna Hercules 0171 573 3600

- **SUBJECT** Preparatory 918
- **TITLE** Fresh Start
- **PLACE** Carshalton College

Length 1 year **Days** 3 days/week **Cost** Free **Entry Reqs** None **Award** RSA CLAIT,
English/Communication, Maths
- **CONTACT** Advice and Guidance Centre 0181 770 6800

- **SUBJECT** Preparatory 919
- **TITLE** Fresh Start for Women
- **PLACE** City and Islington College, Finsbury Park

Length 1 year Modular **Start** September **Cost** Contact College **Award** London Open
College Federation Accreditation **Creche** Yes
- **CONTACT** Course Information Unit 0171 607 1132

- **SUBJECT** Preparatory 920
- **TITLE** Fresh Start for Women
- **PLACE** Hackney Community College, Lauriston Centre

Length 1 year **Start** September **Days** Mon, Tues, Wed 10.00-12.00 + 1.00-3.00 **Cost**
Contact College **Entry Reqs** None, basic literacy skills **Award** Access/BTEC/access to
further courses **Creche** Yes
- **CONTACT** Central Admissions Unit 0181 533 5922

- **SUBJECT** Preparatory 921
- **TITLE** Fresh Start Providing IT Services
- **PLACE** Ealing Tertiary College, Southall Centre

Length 1 year **Start** September **Days** Mon-Fri 9.00-3.00, 19 hours/week (may vary) **Cost**
Contact College. Free if registered unemployed **Entry Reqs** Men & women wishing to build
up English & IT skills **Award** C&G Record of Achievement/C&G Numeracy/AEB Literacy
Skills/Pitmans exams **Creche** No
- **CONTACT** Information Centre 0181 231 6008

- **SUBJECT** Preparatory 922
- **TITLE** Making Experience Count: Portfolio Preparation
- **PLACE** Greenwich Community College, various locations

Length Varies **Start** Varies **Entry Req** For those with no or few qualifications seeking to
return to work or education **Award** Credit for learning gained through life experience
(APEL) **Creche** Yes nominal charge
- **CONTACT** Caroline James 0181 319 8088

- **SUBJECT** Preparatory 923
- **TITLE** New Directions for Women
- **PLACE** City University

Length October **Start** 1 term **Days** 3 days/week **Cost** Free (ESF funded) **Entry Reqs**
Preference given to those unemployed for 21 months or who are returning to work
- **CONTACT** Maggie Bankart 0171 477 8252

- **SUBJECT** Preparatory 924
- **TITLE** New Directions for Women Returners
- **PLACE** University of East London

Length 5 weeks **Days** 2 hours/week **Cost** Free **Entry Reqs** Women wishing to enter
higher education **Award** LOCF credits **Creche** Yes
- **CONTACT** Continuing Education Helpline 0181 849 3433

- **SUBJECT** Preparatory 925
- **TITLE** New Horizons for Women
- **PLACE** John Ruskin College, South Croydon

Length 21 weeks **Start** September **Cost** Contact College **Entry Reqs** Interview
- **CONTACT** 0181 651 1131

- **SUBJECT** Preparatory 926
- **TITLE** Open Learning
- **PLACE** College of North East London, Bounds Green & Tottenham Green Centres

Length Flexible **Start** Flexible **Days** Flexible: drop in **Cost** £20 College registration
charge **Entry Reqs** None **Award** Various if required **Creche** Yes Limited places
- **CONTACT** Admissions Officer 0181 802 3111

- **SUBJECT** Preparatory 927
- **TITLE** Opportunities for Women
- **PLACE** Waltham Forest College

Length 16 weeks part time **Cost** £10 **Entry Reqs** Unemployed women. Guidance interview
necessary **Award** CATS Credit points
- **CONTACT** 0181 523 5449

- **SUBJECT** Preparatory 928
- **TITLE** Pre-Access Humanities
- **PLACE** Lambeth College, Vauxhall Centre

Length 36 weeks **Start** September **Days** 4 days/week 9.30-4.00 **Cost** Contact
College **Entry Reqs** None **Award** LOCF Accrediation, access to NVQ III courses **Creche**
Yes
- **CONTACT** Admissions Unit 0171 501 5000

- **SUBJECT** Preparatory 929
- **TITLE** Pre-Access Science and Health
- **PLACE** Lambeth College, Norwood Centre

Length 1 year **Start** September **Cost** Contact College **Entry Reqs** None **Creche** Yes
- **CONTACT** Admissions Unit 0171 501 5000

- **SUBJECT** Preparatory 930
- **TITLE** Pre-Access Study Skills Course
- **PLACE** Kensington and Chelsea College, Wornington Centre

Length Flexible **Start** Anytime **Days** Mon & Fri 10.00-12.00 **Cost** £15 registration
fee **Entry Reqs** Interview **Award** C&G Wordpower Level 3 Certificate, progress to further
study
- **CONTACT** Course Information 0181 964 1311

- **SUBJECT** Preparatory   931
- **TITLE** Return to Learning: English, Maths, Study Skills, Computing, Typing
- **PLACE** College of North East London, Tottenham Green Centre

Length 36 weeks, roll on roll off **Start** Anytime **Days** 5 days/week **Cost** Contact College **Entry Reqs** Interview, no formal qualifications required **Award** No **Creche** Yes Limited places
- **CONTACT** Diana Blofeld/Admissions Officer 0181 802 3111

- **SUBJECT** Preparatory   932
- **TITLE** Return to Study
- **PLACE** Lambeth College, Brixton, Norwood and Vauxhall Centres

Length 1 year **Start** September **Days** Mon-Thurs 9.30-3.00 **Cost** Contact College **Entry Reqs** None **Award** London Open College Federation Accreditation **Creche** Yes
- **CONTACT** Admissions Unit 0171 501 5000

- **SUBJECT** Preparatory   933
- **TITLE** Return to Study
- **PLACE** West Thames College

Length 1 term **Start** January, May **Days** Tues-Thurs 9.30-2.30 **Cost** Registration fee only **Entry Reqs** None **Award** OCN Credits **Creche** yes
- **CONTACT** Alison Leake 0181 568 0244 x363

- **SUBJECT** Preparatory   934
- **TITLE** Return to Work
- **PLACE** Greenwich Community College, King's Park Centre

Length 30 weeks **Start** September **Days** Wed+Thurs 10.00-12.00 + 1.00-3.00 **Cost** Free to unemployed people **Entry Reqs** RSA CLAIT 1, Pitmans Wordprocessing **Award** Yes
- **CONTACT** Karen Buttrick 0181 850 3632

- **SUBJECT** Preparatory   935
- **TITLE** 1. Return to Work 2. Management
- **PLACE** Merton College

Length Open Learning **Start** Flexible **Cost** Contact College
- **CONTACT** Rae Brimblecombe, Training Initiative Co-ordinator 0181 640 3001

- **SUBJECT** Preparatory   936
- **TITLE** Women: Assertion, Counselling Skills
- **PLACE** Greenwich Community College, various locations

Length Varies **Start** Varies **Creche** Yes nominal charge
- **CONTACT** Lesley Daniell 0181 850 3632

- **SUBJECT** Preparatory   937
- **TITLE** Women into Employment
- **PLACE** Lambeth College, Clapham Centre

Length 9 weeks (45 hours) **Start** January **Days** 2 ½-day sessions/week **Cost** Contact College **Entry Reqs** None but an interview with the tutor to assess prior experience is necessary **Award** Introductory Certificate leading to Certificate in Supervisory Management **Creche** Yes
- **CONTACT** Admissions Unit 0171 501 5000

- **SUBJECT** Preparatory   938
- **TITLE** Women Returners: New Directions
- **PLACE** Harlington Adult & Continuing Education Centre

Length 30 weeks **Start** September **Days** Mon-Fri part time **Cost** £237.50 or £22.50 concessionary **Entry Reqs** None **Award** RSA Certificates in Wordprocessing, CLAIT, Bookkeeping **Creche** Playgroup £1/session (25p concessionary)
- **CONTACT** Ros Lacey 0181 569 1613

- **SUBJECT** Preparatory 939
- **TITLE** Work Preparation Programme
- **PLACE** Croydon Continuing Education & Training Service, Addington Centre

Length Flexible **Cost** Free if unemployed **Entry Reqs** None **Award** RSA and other certificates
- **CONTACT** Addington Centre 01689 841461

- **SUBJECT** Preparatory/Access 940
- **TITLE** Adult Foundation/First Foundation
- **PLACE** City and Islington College, Bunhill Row

Length 1 year/1 term depending on need **Start** September **Days** 9.30-4.00 **Entry Req** Those requiring study skills, language support, return to study courses **Award** London Open College Accreditation **Creche** No
- **CONTACT** Irene Schwab 0171 638 4171 x254

- **SUBJECT** Preparatory/Practical/Office Skills 941
- **TITLE** Harlesden City Challenge Course for Bilingual Women
- **PLACE** Brent Adult College

Length 1 year **Start** September **Days** 9.45-2.45 **Cost** Free for residents in Harlesden City Challenge area **Entry Reqs** Students must reside in Harlesden City Challenge area **Award** External accreditation in ESOL, IT, Sewing and other options **Creche** Yes £2/child/term
- **CONTACT** Mariam Jazayeri 0181 838 2882

- **SUBJECT** Preparatory/Social Work 942
- **TITLE** Pre Access: Introduction to Community Work
- **PLACE** Lambeth College, Clapham Centre

Length 1 year **Start** September **Days** 3 days/week (13 hours/week) **Cost** Contact College **Entry Reqs** None. English assessment **Award** London Open College Federation Certificate **Creche** Yes
- **CONTACT** Admissions Unit 0171 501 5000

- **SUBJECT** Professional Updating 943
- **TITLE** Professional Updating for Women
- **PLACE** University of Westminster, Management Centre

Length 14 weeks **Start** Usually April or October **Days** 5 days/week 10.00-3.00 + 2 week work placement **Cost** None **Entry Reqs** Degree or equivalent professional work pre-career break, at least 1 year since full time work **Award** Accredited at 30 level M (Postgraduate) CATS points **Creche** Places limited Help with childcare costs
- **CONTACT** Jill Jones 0171 911 5000 x3061

- **SUBJECT** Professional Updating/Information Technology 944
- **TITLE** Return to IT: a Professional Updating Course in Information Technology
- **PLACE** City University, School of Informatics

Length 10 weeks **Start** April **Days** 3 days/week 10.00-2.00 **Cost** Contact University **Entry Reqs** Professionals with a good first degree in a non-IT subject **Award** Preparatory Certificate in Information Systems and Technology, entry to MSc course in IT
- **CONTACT** Penny Yates-Mercer 0171 477 8385

- **SUBJECT** Science 945
- **TITLE** BSc(Hons) Science Modular Degree Scheme
- **PLACE** University of North London, Holloway Road

Length 3-4 years full time, 4-6 years part time **Start** September **Days** Fits in with school hours if possible **Cost** Contact University **Entry Reqs** Subject to interview **Award** BSc(Hons)/Diploma/Certificate **Creche** Yes limited places
- **CONTACT** Course Enquiries Office 0171 753 5066/7

London

- **SUBJECT** Science 946
- **TITLE** Biochemical Engineering and Bioprocessing
- **PLACE** University College, London

Length 1 year **Start** October **Cost** Biotechnology & Biological Sciences Research Council award available **Entry Reqs** Graduates with first or upper second class honours degree in an appropriate subject **Award** MSc
- **CONTACT** Dr V Essex, BBSRC, 01793 413200

- **SUBJECT** Science 947
- **TITLE** Certificate in Science
- **PLACE** Birkbeck College, Central London

Length 1 year **Start** September **Days** 2 eves/week 6.00-9.00 for 28 weeks **Cost** Contact College **Entry Reqs** None but numeracy skills required **Award** University of London Extra-Mural Certificate gives university entrance **Creche** Yes evening creche available
- **CONTACT** Jane de Rennes 0171 631 6668

- **SUBJECT** Science 948
- **TITLE** Computer Vision, Image Processing, Graphics & Simulation: Research Masters Pilot Course
- **PLACE** University College, London

Length 2 years **Start** October **Cost** Engineering and Physical Sciences Research Council award available **Entry Reqs** Graduates with first or upper second class honours degree in an appropriate subject **Award** Master of Research Degree
- **CONTACT** Professor B Buxton 0171 380 7294

- **SUBJECT** Science 949
- **TITLE** HITECC Science and Engineering Foundation Year
- **PLACE** University of North London, Faculty of Science, Computing & Engineering

Length 1 year, modular **Start** September **Cost** Contact University. Mandatory grant for full-time/sandwich BSc course possible. **Entry Reqs** Interview, contact university **Award** Progress to full time/sandwich BSc (Hons) Science degree course
- **CONTACT** Dr Trushar Adatia 0171 753 7024

- **SUBJECT** Science 950
- **TITLE** Instrumentation Systems: Research Masters Pilot Course
- **PLACE** University College, London

Length 2 years **Start** October **Cost** Engineering and Physical Sciences Research Council award available **Entry Reqs** Graduates with first or upper second class honours degree in an appropriate subject **Award** Master of Research Degree
- **CONTACT** Dr M Esten 0171 387 7050

- **SUBJECT** Science 951
- **TITLE** Science: BTEC Advanced GNVQ
- **PLACE** Merton College

Length 2 years **Start** September **Cost** Contact College **Entry Reqs** Contact College **Award** BTEC Advanced GNVQ
- **CONTACT** Guidance and Entry Unit 0181 640 8001

- **SUBJECT** Science 952
- **TITLE** Science: BTEC Intermediate GNVQ
- **PLACE** City and Islington College, Islington Campus

Length 1 year **Start** September **Days** 19 hours/week **Cost** Contact College **Entry Reqs** Interview and assessment **Award** BTEC GNVQ Intermediate **Creche** Yes
- **CONTACT** Course Information Unit 0171 607 1132

- **SUBJECT** Science   953
- **TITLE** Telecommunications: Research Masters Pilot Course
- **PLACE** University College, London
Length 2 years   **Start** October   **Cost** Engineering and Physical Sciences Research Council award available   **Entry Reqs** Graduates with first or upper second class honours degree in an appropriate subject   **Award** Master of Research Degree
- **CONTACT** Professor J O'Reilly 0171 380 7303

- **SUBJECT** Secretarial   954
- **TITLE** Personal Assistant Course
- **PLACE** Kensington and Chelsea College, Hortensia Road
Length 3 weeks intensive   **Start** July   **Days** Mon-Fri 4 hours/day   **Cost** £65, £15 concessions   **Entry Reqs** Good level of literacy   **Award** College Certificate   **Creche** No
- **CONTACT** Cordelia Gerard-Sharpe 0181 964 1311 x321

- **SUBJECT** Secretarial   955
- **TITLE** Secretarial Studies
- **PLACE** Lewisham College
Length 1 year   **Start** September   **Days** 16-20 hours   **Cost** £648   **Award** LCCI NVQ Levels 2 or 3
- **CONTACT** Linda Woods 0181 692 0353

- **SUBJECT** Social Science   956
- **TITLE** BSc(Hons) Applied Social Science Modular Scheme
- **PLACE** University of North London, Ladbroke House
Length 3 years full time, 4-6 years part time   **Start** September   **Days** Fits in with school hours if possible   **Cost** Contact University   **Entry Reqs** Subject to interview   **Award** BSc(Hons)/Diploma/Certificate   **Creche** Yes limited places
- **CONTACT** Course Enquiries Office 0171 753 5066/7

- **SUBJECT** Social Studies   957
- **TITLE** Certificate and Diploma in Social Studies
- **PLACE** Various London locations
Length 48-hour courses, each 16 weeks: 3 courses for Certificate   **Start** September   **Days** Various   **Cost** £85/course, £28 concessions   **Entry Reqs** None   **Award** Certificate CATS accredited
- **CONTACT** Birkbeck College Social Studies Desk 0171 631 6653

- **SUBJECT** Sports Studies   958
- **TITLE** BTEC Sports Coaching
- **PLACE** Lambeth College, Norwood Centre
Length 1 year   **Start** September   **Days** 4 days/week 9.15-4.15   **Cost** Contact College   **Award** BTEC Sports Coaching   **Creche** Yes
- **CONTACT** Admissions Unit 0171 501 5000

- **SUBJECT** Sports Studies   959
- **TITLE** Sport and Recreation
- **PLACE** Lewisham College
Length 1 year   **Start** September   **Days** 16 hours/week   **Cost** £648   **Award** NVQ Levels I & II
- **CONTACT** Isobel Craddock 0181 692 0353

- **SUBJECT** Teaching   960
- **TITLE** C&G Further Education Teaching Certificate
- **PLACE** City of Westminster College, Maida Vale Centre
Length 1 year   **Start** September   **Days** Daytime   **Cost** Contact College   **Entry Reqs** Contact College   **Award** City & Guilds 7307
- **CONTACT** Course Information 0171 723 8826

- **SUBJECT** Teaching   961
- **TITLE** C&G Further Education Teaching Certificate
- **PLACE** College of North West London

Length 1 year   **Start** September   **Days** Day or eve   **Cost** Contact College   **Entry Reqs** FE full & part time teachers, people wishing to work in post-16 community education   **Award** City & Guilds 7307   **Creche** Yes

- **CONTACT** Course Enquiries 0171 328 3471

- **SUBJECT** Technology   962
- **TITLE** BSc(Hons) Women and New Technology
- **PLACE** University of East London, Department of Innovation Studies

Length Degree 3 years   **Start** September   **Days** Full or part time   **Entry Req** Completion of Access Course or relevant experience   **Award** Degree, Diploma in higher education, credits **Creche** Yes

- **CONTACT** Flis Henwood/Linda Stepulevage/Jo Sherman 0181 590 7722 x4216/849 3675

- **SUBJECT** Technology   963
- **TITLE** Foundation in New Technology
- **PLACE** NEWTEC (Newham Women's Training & Education Centre)

Length 1 year   **Start** September   **Days** Full time 10.00-3.00   **Cost** Free if unemployed/ unwaged   **Entry Reqs** None, reasonable level of numeracy   **Award** C&G Certificates, progress to further courses   **Creche** Yes

- **CONTACT** 0181 519 5843

- **SUBJECT** Technology   964
- **TITLE** Year Zero to New Technology Degrees
- **PLACE** NEWTEC/University of East London

Length 4 year extended degree programme   **Start** September   **Days** Full time 10.00-4.30   **Cost** Contact NEWTEC   **Entry Reqs** None, Maths & English assessment, 21+   **Award** Progression to years 1-3 of New Technology degree programmes at University of East London   **Creche** Yes

- **CONTACT** 0181 519 5843

- **SUBJECT** Tourism & Leisure   965
- **TITLE** GNVQ Leisure and Tourism 1. Intermediate 2. Advanced
- **PLACE** Lewisham College

Length 1.1 year 2.2 years   **Start** September   **Days** 16 hours/week   **Cost** £648   **Award** 1. GNVQ Intermediate 2. GNVQ Advanced

- **CONTACT** Isobel Craddock 0181 692 0353

- **SUBJECT** Tourism & Leisure   966
- **TITLE** GNVQ Leisure and Tourism 1. Foundation 2. Intermediate 3. Advanced
- **PLACE** City of Westminster College 1. Ladbroke Grove 2. &. 3 Paddington Centre

Length 1. &2. 1 year 3. 2 years   **Start** September   **Days** Daytime   **Cost** Contact College   **Entry Reqs** Contact College   **Award** GNVQ 1. Foundation 2. Intermediate 3. Advanced

- **CONTACT** Course Information 0171 723 8826

- **SUBJECT** Tourism & Leisure   967
- **TITLE** Travel Services
- **PLACE** Bromley College of Further & Higher Education

Length 1 year   **Start** September   **Days** 1 eve/week   **Cost** Contact College   **Entry Reqs** Suitable for people wishing to enter or re-enter the travel trade   **Award** NVQ Level II

- **CONTACT** Student Enquiries 0181 295 7001

- **SUBJECT**   Women's Studies   968
- **TITLE**   Certificate/Diploma in Women's Studies (23 courses)
- **PLACE**   Women's Centres and Colleges in London area

Length 48-hour modular courses of 24 weeks, 2 hours/week   **Start** September, January, April   **Days** Various, day/eve   **Cost** £1.77/hour. Concessionary 1/3 of full fees   **Entry Reqs** None   **Award** Certificate/Diploma of University of London, CATS Accredited   **Creche** At some centres

- **CONTACT**   Verity Barnett/Carol Walker 0171 631 6674

- **SUBJECT**   Women's Studies   969
- **TITLE**   Various Courses eg Women's Writing Workshop, Women Writers, Assertiveness
- **PLACE**   City University, Department of Continuing Education

Length Varies, 1-2 days/week and 10 weeks   **Start** Termly   **Days** Daytime and 1 eve/week 6.30-8.30   **Cost** £33-69   **Entry Reqs** None   **Award** None   **Creche** No

- **CONTACT**   Courses for Adults or Short Course Unit 0171 477 8000 x3268

- **SUBJECT**   Women's Studies   970
- **TITLE**   MA Women's Studies
- **PLACE**   University of Westminster, Regent Street, W1

Length 2 years part time   **Start** September   **Days** 1 eve/week 6.00-9.00+occasional Saturdays 10.00-5.00   **Cost** £600/year. Contact College   **Entry Reqs** First degree in any subject or appropriate experience   **Award** MA   **Creche** No

- **CONTACT**   Alex Warwick 0171 911 5000

- **SUBJECT**   Women's Studies   971
- **TITLE**   Women's Studies, Education and Media Studies
- **PLACE**   University of London, Institute of Education

Length 1 year full time, 2-4 years part time   **Start** October, January, April   **Days** Mon-Thurs eves 5.30-8.00+occasional Saturday. Part time 1 eve/week   **Cost** Full time £2430 Part time £1077   **Entry Reqs** Hons Degree and teaching (or equivalent experience). Also by work portfolio and essay   **Award** MA   **Creche** Nursery facilities available, £45/week

- **CONTACT**   Debbie Epstein 0171 612 6332/Diana Leonard 0171 612 6322

COUNTY CONTACTS

Information and advice:

Adult Guidance Service, Hounslow Careers Service, 4 School Road, Hounslow TW3 1QZ 0181 577 0555   *Contact:* Fiona Clark, Harbans Chana, Simon Crossley. Careers counselling, personal development.

Adult Guidance and Training Centre, Richmond upon Thames College, Egerton Road, Twickenham TW2 7SJ 0181 891 1899   *Contact:* Juliet Elliot

Brent Adult Guidance Service, Brent Adult & Community Education Service, 1 Library Parade, Craven Park Road, Harlesden NW10 8SG 0181 961 3703   *Contact:* Gloria Elliott. BACES provides information and guidance services as well as a wide range of courses

Career Dynamics, Kingston upon Thames 0181 541 9923. Adult careers guidance service provided by Surrey Careers Service

Croydon Adult Learning Advice Centre (CALAC), The Careers Centre, College Road, Croydon CR9 3SU 0181 401 0301

Educational & Occupational Advice Service/Services for the Unemployed, Education Shop, Chestnuts House, 398 Hoe Street, Walthamstow E17 9AA 0181 521 4311. Drop in Mon-Fri 9.30-12.30; 1.30-4.30. Closed Wed am and Fri pm

Hackney Education Advice for Adults, Careers, Employment and Advice Centre, 27B Dalston Lane, London E8 3DF 0171 275 0346   *Contact:* Lorna Ford-Panton, Rita Higginson, Naina Kent. Drop-in Mon-Fri 10.00-4.00 Appointments can be made

Hammersmith and Fulham Education and Training Advice for Adults, Community Education Centre, Macbeth Street, London W6 9JJ 0181 741 8441. Drop-in sessions Mon and Wed 1.00-4.00, Tues and Fri 10.00-1.00, Thurs 5.00-8.00

Haringey Careers Service, Education Offices, 48 Station Road, Wood Green, London N22 4TY 0181 862 3885

Havering Adult Educational Guidance Service, Holgate Court, Western Road, Romford RM1 3JS 01708 766896

Islington Adult Guidance Unit, Block G1, Barnsbury Complex, Barnsbury Park, London N1 1QF 0171 457 5785

LINK Educational Guidance, First Floor, Fountains Mill, 81 High Street, Uxbridge UB8 1JR 01895 234729   *Contact:* Stephanie Stuart, Ian Morton

Lewisham Careers Service, Lewisham Careers Centre, 68 Molesworth Street, London SE13 7EU 0181 318 9323

Merton Adult Guidance, Merton Adult College, Whatley Road, London SW20 9NS 0181 543 9292 x28

National Association for Educational Guidance for Adults, Regional representative, Anglia University Student Services, Victoria Road, Chelmsford CM1 1LL 01245 493131 x3298/9   *Contact:* Joan Boyton. Covers London region

Richmond Guidance Service, Richmond Adult and Community College, Clifden Road, Twickenham TW1 4LT 0181 891 5907

SETS (Southwark Education and Training Shop), Southwark Careers Centre, First Floor, Sumner Road, London SE15 5QS 0171 701 4001

Wandsworth Education Shop Guidance and Advice for Adults, 86 Battersea Rise, London SW11 1EJ 0171 350 1790   *Contact:* Any advice worker. Drop-in advice sessions, no appointment necessary

Westminster Careers Service for Adults, The Careers Centre, 3-4 Picton Place, London W1M 5DD 0171 487 4504. Offers education and training advice, vocational guidance, careers information library, psychometric testing, computerised guidance package, enquiry desk, group seminars. Services available to Westminster residents only.

Open University:

The Open University, London Region, 527 Finchley Road, London NW3 7BG 0171 433 6161

Other agencies:

Brunel University, Continuing Education Department, Uxbridge UB8 3PH 01895 274000   *Contact:* Anne Sheddick. Setting up a Lifetime Learning Centre, available to women returners. Range of management qualifications available through short courses, distance learning or workshops.

Camden ITEC, 7 Leighton Place, London NW5 2QL 0171 485 3324   *Contact:* Heather Menczer, Sadegh Jodieri. Runs Return to Work courses with work placements

Lambeth Women's Workshop, Unit 22, Parkhill Trading Estate, Martell Road, London SE21 8EA 0181 670 0339. Women's training centre

Lewisham Women's Workspace, Unit B 201, Faircharm Trading Estate, 8-10 Creekside, London SE8 3DX 0181 469 2281. Women's training centre

London Enterprise Agency, 4 Snow Hill, London EC1A 2BS 0171 236 3000

London Women and Manual Trades, 52-54 Featherstone Street, London EC1Y 8RT 0171 251 9192. Women's training in manual trades

Myrrh Education Centre, 1 Flint Street, Walworth, London SE17 1QD 0171 252 7015   *Contact:* Sarah

Myrrh Education Centre, 298-300 Brixton Hill, London SW2 1HT 0181 671 6327. Further education centre, training in NVQs Levels I-II: various practical skills

Myrrh Education Ltd, 42-44 Hassop Road, London NW2 0181 450 6993

NEWTEC, 22 Deanery Road, Stratford, London E15 4LP 0181 519 5843   *Contact:* Christine Leigh. Range of skills-based and other courses for women, also vocational guidance

Skillnet Surrey Quays Ltd, 10-11 The Dock Offices, Surrey Quays Road, London SE16 2XL 0171 252 1331   *Contact:* Liz Obire. NVQs, Access, Assessment and Job Preparation courses available

Southwark Women's Training Workshop, Community Education Annexe, Peckham Rye School, Whorlton Road, Peckham, London SE15 3PD 0171 732 4311

Women's Education in Building, 12-14 Malton Road, London W10 5UP 0181 968 9139. Construction skills training centre for women

Training and Enterprise Councils:

AZTEC, Manorgate House, 2 Manorgate Road, Kingston upon Thames KT2 7AL 0181 547 3934. Women into Management course

CENTEC (Central London), 12 Grosvenor Crescent, London SW1X 7EE 0171 411 3500

CILNTEC (City and Inner London North), 80 Great Eastern Street, London EC2A 3DP 0171 324 2424

London East TEC, Cityside House, 40 Adler Street, London E1 1EE 0171 377 1866

North London TEC, Dumayne House, 1 Fox Lane, Palmers Green, London N13 4AB 0181 447 9422. Women Returners course; Women in Business research programme; Women's Special Interest Group (part of the Enterprise Club); Information, advice and guidance (contact Colette Jones); ESF funded projects: Managment, Women and Refugees (focus on further education), Vocational guidance (placement generation programme for disadvantaged groups); Joint project with Kids Club Network on after school care; ESOL classes

North West London TEC, Kirkfield House, 118-120 Station Road, Harrow HA1 2RL 0181 424 8866

SOLOTEC (South London), Lancaster House, 7 Elmfield Road, Bromley BR1 1LT 0181 313 9232/ Freephone 0800 800222. Under Training for Work childcare support for lone parents may be available; Growing Places programme and Growth Loan available for business start-up

West London TEC, Sovereign Court, 15-21 Staines Road, Hounslow TW3 3HA 0181 577 1010

WEA office:

WEA London District, 44 Crowndale Road, London NW1 1TR 0171 388 7261   *Contact:* Ann Deutch

Publications:

Floodlight. Comprehensive guides to (a) part time day and evening classes (b) full time courses throughout the Greater London areas. Available in bookshops, public libraries, etc

LASER Advisory Council, Chenies House, 21 Bedford Square, London WC1B 3HH 0171 637 3073. LASER's Index of Courses covers adult and further education opportunities in London and the South East.

COURSES

- **SUBJECT**   Access   972
- **TITLE**   Access to Higher Education
- **PLACE**   Knowsley Community College, Roby Centre

Length 1 or 2 years   **Start** September   **Days** approx 15 hours/week   **Cost** Free to unemployed, LEA grants available   **Entry Reqs** None   **Award** Merseyside Open College Federation Credits   **Creche** Playgroup £2.50/session
- **CONTACT**   Lyn Eaton 0151 443 2657

- **SUBJECT**   Access   973
- **TITLE**   Pre Access Programme: English, Maths, Study Skills, IT
- **PLACE**   Knowsley Community College, Kirkby and Roby Centres

Length 1 year   **Start** September; late arrivals accepted   **Days** 4 x 3 hours sessions/week   **Cost** Free   **Entry Reqs** None   **Award** Merseyside Open College Federation Accreditation   **Creche** Playgroup £2.50/session
- **CONTACT**   Lyn Eaton 0151 443 2657

- **SUBJECT**   Civil Engineering   974
- **TITLE**   Women into Civil Engineering
- **PLACE**   City of Liverpool Community College, Old Swan Centre

Days Contact College   **Cost** Contact College   **Entry Reqs** None   **Award** Merseyside Open College Accreditation Levels 2&3, progess to BTEC or other qualifications   **Creche** Yes
- **CONTACT**   Old Swan Centre 0151 252 3000

- **SUBJECT**   Design   975
- **TITLE**   Women's Craft, Design & Technology
- **PLACE**   City of Liverpool Community College, Old Swan Centre

Days Wed 9.30-12.30   **Cost** Contact College   **Entry Reqs** None   **Award** Merseyside Open College Accreditation Levels 2&3   **Creche** Yes
- **CONTACT**   Old Swan Centre 0151 252 3000

- **SUBJECT**   Electronics   976
- **TITLE**   Women's Electronics & Electrical Engineering
- **PLACE**   City of Liverpool Community College, Old Swan Centre

Length Modular   **Days** Various   **Cost** Contact College   **Entry Reqs** Contact College   **Award** Progress to C&G, BTEC Certificates & Diplomas or other courses   **Creche** Yes
- **CONTACT**   Old Swan Centre 0151 252 3000

- **SUBJECT**   Floristry   977
- **TITLE**   Floristry NVQ Level II
- **PLACE**   Knowsley Community College, Prescot Centre

Length 36 weeks   **Start** September   **Days** Mon-Fri 9.30-1.30 (20 hours/week)   **Cost** Grant may be available   **Entry Reqs** No formal qualifications required   **Award** NVQ Level II Floristry   **Creche** Playgroup £2.50/session
- **CONTACT**   Lyn Eaton 0151 443 2657

- **SUBJECT**   Information Technology   978
- **TITLE**   Women into Information Technology
- **PLACE**   Knowsley Community College, Roby Centre

Length 36 weeks   **Start** September   **Days** Mon-Fri 9.30-1.30 (20 hours/week)   **Cost** Grant may be available   **Entry Reqs** No formal qualifications required   **Award** RSA CLAIT/RSA Word Processing/MOCF Credits   **Creche** Playgroup £2.50/session
- **CONTACT**   Lyn Eaton 0151 443 2657

- **SUBJECT** Information Technology 979
- **TITLE** Women into Information Technology
- **PLACE** St Helens College, Town Centre Campus
Length 12 weeks **Days** 15 hours/week **Cost** Contact Student Services **Entry Reqs** None **Award** Various qualifications offered
- **CONTACT** Student Services/Jan Bibby 01744 733766 x382

- **SUBJECT** Information Technology 980
- **TITLE** Women's Information Technology
- **PLACE** City of Liverpool Community College, Old Swan Centre
Length Modular **Cost** Contact College **Entry Reqs** None **Award** C&G/RSA CLAIT/ NVQ Level II/Open College Accreditation/Diploma in Information Technology **Creche** Yes
- **CONTACT** Old Swan Centre 0151 252 3000

- **SUBJECT** Media Studies 981
- **TITLE** Women into Media
- **PLACE** St Helens College, Town Centre Campus
Length 1 year **Start** September **Days** 15-20 hours/week. 9.30-12.00 & 1.00-3.30 **Cost** Contact Student Services **Entry Reqs** No formal qualifications. Interview **Award** C&G 770 Media Techniques + other modules **Creche** Yes
- **CONTACT** Student Services/Carmel Wills 01744 733766 x221

- **SUBJECT** Multi-Subject 982
- **TITLE** Various Courses: Basic Education, Computing, Business Admin, Art, Community Care
- **PLACE** City of Liverpool Community College, Wellesbourne Centre
Length 32 weeks **Start** September **Days** 2-12 hours/week **Cost** Free **Entry Reqs** Usually none **Award** Varies: Merseyside Open College Credits, GCSEs, NVQs **Creche** Yes
- **CONTACT** Pauline Flaherty/Alice Critchley 0151 226 3184

- **SUBJECT** NOW 983
- **TITLE** Fresh Start
- **PLACE** City of Liverpool Community College, Bankfield Centre
Length 36 weeks **Start** September **Days** Thurs 10.00-12.00, 1.00-3.00 **Cost** Free **Entry Reqs** None **Award** Merseyside Open College Federation Accreditation **Creche** Yes Free
- **CONTACT** Dorothy Hopwood 0151 252 3853

- **SUBJECT** NOW 984
- **TITLE** Fresh Start
- **PLACE** City of Liverpool Community College, Muirhead Centre
Length 36 weeks **Start** September **Days** Tues 10.00-12.00, 1.00-3.00 **Cost** Free **Entry Reqs** None **Award** Merseyside Open College Federation Accreditation **Creche** Yes
- **CONTACT** Christine Williams 0151 252 3616

- **SUBJECT** NOW 985
- **TITLE** Wider Opportunities for Women
- **PLACE** City of Liverpool Community College, Riversdale Centre
Length 1 year and shorter units **Start** September or any time **Days** Varies, Mon-Fri between 9.30 and 3.30, or eves **Cost** Contact College. Concessions available **Entry Reqs** None **Award** Merseyside Open College Federation Accreditation **Creche** Playgroup Free
- **CONTACT** Riversdale Centre 0151 427 1227

- **SUBJECT** Practical 986
- **TITLE** Women's Carpentry and Joinery
- **PLACE** City of Liverpool Community College, Old Swan Centre
Length 1 year **Start** September **Days** Mon 1.00-4.00 **Cost** Contact College **Entry Reqs** None **Award** Merseyside Open College Accreditation Level 2 **Creche** Yes
- **CONTACT** Old Swan Centre 0151 252 3000

- **SUBJECT** Preparatory 987
- **TITLE** Fresh Start: Assertiveness for Women
- **PLACE** City of Liverpool Community College, Bankfield Centre

Length 10 weeks **Start** September, January, April **Days** Fri 10.00-12.00 **Cost** Free **Entry Reqs** None **Award** Merseyside Open College Federation Accreditation **Creche** Yes

- **CONTACT** Pat Hopley 0151 252 3832

- **SUBJECT** Preparatory 988
- **TITLE** Women's Development Programme
- **PLACE** City of Liverpool Community College, Mabel Fletcher & Old Swan Centres

Length Various **Start** Various **Cost** Contact College **Entry Reqs** None **Award** Various including RSA/NVQs/Merseyside Open College Accreditation/C&G **Creche** Yes

- **CONTACT** Mabel Fletcher Centre 0151 252 3339/Old Swan Centre 0151 252 3000

- **SUBJECT** Preparatory 989
- **TITLE** Women Returners Programme
- **PLACE** Knowsley Community College, Kirkby and Roby Centres

Length 18 weeks **Start** September, February **Days** 4 halfdays/week **Cost** None **Entry Reqs** None **Award** Merseyside Open College Federation Accreditation **Creche** Playgroup £2.50/session

- **CONTACT** Muriel O'Hanlon 0151 443 5404

- **SUBJECT** Professional Updating 990
- **TITLE** Maternity Returners
- **PLACE** University of Liverpool, Centre for Continuing Education

Length 1 week **Start** July **Cost** £120 **Entry Reqs** Women Returners **Creche** Contact University

- **CONTACT** Pam Matfin 0151 794 2552

- **SUBJECT** Professional Updating 991
- **TITLE** Professional Women Returners Course
- **PLACE** University of Liverpool, Centre for Continuing Education

Length 4 weeks **Start** Various **Days** 4 days/week 10.00-12.30, 1.30-3.00 **Cost** Contact University **Entry Reqs** Women Returners **Award** Record of Achievement and Certificate **Creche** Contact University

- **CONTACT** Pam Matfin 0151 794 2552

- **SUBJECT** Professional Updating 992
- **TITLE** Three Steps to Success
- **PLACE** University of Liverpool, Centre for Continuing Education

Length Distance Learning + 2 workshops (each 1-day) **Start** Contact University **Cost** Contact University **Entry Reqs** Women Returners **Creche** Contact University

- **CONTACT** Pam Matfin 0151 794 2552

- **SUBJECT**   Science/Engineering   993
- **TITLE**   Surface and Interface Science and Engineering
- **PLACE**   University of Liverpool

Length 2 years   **Start** October   **Cost** Engineering & Physical Sciences Research Council award available   **Entry Reqs** Graduates with first or upper second class honours degree in an appropriate subject   **Award** Master of Research Degree
- **CONTACT**   Professor P Weightman 0151 794 3871

- **SUBJECT**   Women's Studies   994
- **TITLE**   Women's History
- **PLACE**   City of Liverpool Community College, Old Swan Centre

Length 1 year   **Start** September   **Days** Tues 12.30-3.00   **Cost** Contact College   **Entry Reqs** None   **Award** Merseyside Open College Accreditation Levels 2&3   **Creche** Yes
- **CONTACT**   Old Swan Centre 0151 252 3000

- **SUBJECT**   Women's Studies   995
- **TITLE**   Women's Studies
- **PLACE**   City of Liverpool Community College, Old Swan Centre

Days Thurs 1.00-3.00   **Cost** Contact College   **Entry Reqs** None   **Award** Merseyside Open College Accreditation Levels 2&3   **Creche** Yes
- **CONTACT**   Old Swan Centre 0151 252 3000

COUNTY CONTACTS

Information and advice:

Guidance Officers, Student Services, St Helens College, Town Centre Campus, Brook Street, St Helens WA10 1PZ 01744 733766 x382   *Contact:* Maureen, Dawn, Liz. Advice on college courses
Wirral Careers Service, Bebington Careers Office, 41-43 Bebington Road, New Ferry, Wirral L62 5BE 0151 645 5586   *Contact:* Monica May
Birkenhead Careers Office, Ground Floor, Conway Buildings, Conway Street, Birkenhead L41 6JD 0151 666 2121   *Contact:* Carolyn Scott
Deeside Careers Office, 1st Floor, West Kirby Concourse, Grange Road, West Kirby L48 4HX 0151 625 2716   *Contact:* Rose Weir
Wallasey Careers Office, Liscard Muncipal Buildings, 52 Seaview Road, Wallasey L45 4FY 0151 638 5625   *Contact:* Allan Mowl

Open University:

The Open University, North West Region, Chorlton House, 70 Manchester Road, Chorlton cum Hardy, Manchester M21 9UN 0151 862 6824

Other agencies:

Beechcroft Training, Price Street Business Centre, Price Street, Birkenhead L41 4LQ 0151 670 1122. Range of training courses including Women Returning to Work courses
Liverpool Women's Technology Scheme, Blackburne House, Hope Street, Liverpool L1 9JB 0151 709 4356. Women's training centre

Training and Enterprise Councils:

CEWTEC (Chester, Ellesmere Port, Wirral), Egerton House, 2 Tower Road, Birkenhead L41 1FN 0151 650 0555
Merseyside TEC, Tithebarn House, Tithebarn Street, Liverpool L2 2NZ 0151 236 0026. Professional Management foundation course; Telematics and Telecommunications project

for women, ESF funded; Business Enterprise Programme; Homebased IT training for lone parents and disabled people

WEA office:

WEA Cheshire, Merseyside & West Lancashire District, 7/8 Bluecoat Chambers, School Lane, Liverpool L1 3BX 0151 709 8023   *Contact:* Linda Pepper

NORFOLK

COURSES

- **SUBJECT**   Access/Arts/Social Science/Humanities   996
- **TITLE**   Modular Access Programme in Arts, Humanities and Social Sciences
- **PLACE**   City College Norwich

Length 36 weeks   **Start** September   **Days** Mon-Fri 9.00-4.00 full/part time   **Cost** Contact College   **Entry Reqs** 21+, interview   **Award** College Certificate, entry to higher education   **Creche** Yes £15.50/day

- **CONTACT**   Mark Wilson 01603 773162

- **SUBJECT**   Access/Computing   997
- **TITLE**   College Certificate in Computing: Access Mode
- **PLACE**   City College Norwich

Length 18 weeks   **Start** September, January   **Days** Tues, Wed, Thurs 9.00-3.00   **Cost** Contact College   **Entry Reqs** Aptitude test   **Award** College Certificate + course leads to Higher National Diploma in Computing or Business IT   **Creche** Yes £15.50/day

- **CONTACT**   David Payne 01603 773202

- **SUBJECT**   Access/Natural Sciences   998
- **TITLE**   Access to Natural Sciences
- **PLACE**   City College Norwich

Length 36 weeks   **Start** September   **Days** Mon-Fri 10.00-3.00   **Cost** Contact College   **Entry Reqs** 18+, interview   **Award** College Certificate, entry to higher education   **Creche** Yes £15.50/day

- **CONTACT**   Sue Sabac 01603 773167

- **SUBJECT**   Accounting   999
- **TITLE**   Accounting NVQ Level II
- **PLACE**   City College Norwich

Length 1 year   **Start** September   **Days** 1 day/week   **Cost** Contact College   **Entry Reqs** None   **Award** NVQ Level II Accounting   **Creche** Yes £15.50/day

- **CONTACT**   Mike Maggs 01603 773209

- **SUBJECT**   Art & Design   1000
- **TITLE**   Return to Art and Design
- **PLACE**   City College Norwich

Length 31 weeks   **Start** September   **Days** 6 hours/week   **Cost** Contact College   **Entry Reqs** Some previous knowledge or experience   **Creche** Yes £15.50/day

- **CONTACT**   Brenda Unwin 01603 773159

- **SUBJECT**   Business   1001
- **TITLE**   Women and Employment
- **PLACE**   City College Norwich

Length 10 weeks   **Start** September, January, April   **Days** 1 day/week 9.30-12.00, 1.00-3.00   **Cost** Contact College   **Entry Reqs** None. Women only   **Creche** Yes £15.50/day
- **CONTACT**   Suzanne Halliwell 01603 773257

- **SUBJECT**   Catering   1002
- **TITLE**   Cooks Certificate
- **PLACE**   City College Norwich

Length 1 year   **Start** September   **Days** 1 day/week 9.30-3.30 or 1 eve/week 6.00-9.00 + some open learning   **Cost** Contact College   **Entry Reqs** None   **Award** C&G 332/1, entry to Professional Cooks Certificate   **Creche** Yes £15.50/day
- **CONTACT**   Barbara Abrahams 01603 773415

- **SUBJECT**   Computing   1003
- **TITLE**   Computing Opportunities
- **PLACE**   City College Norwich

Length 10 weeks   **Start** September, January, April   **Days** 1 day/week 9.30-1.00   **Cost** Contact College   **Entry Reqs** None   **Award** Facilitates entry to other computing courses   **Creche** Yes £15.50/day
- **CONTACT**   David Payne 01603 773202

- **SUBJECT**   Fashion   1004
- **TITLE**   City and Guilds Fashion Part I+II (C&G 780)
- **PLACE**   City College Norwich

Length 2-3 years   **Start** September   **Days** 1 day/week   **Cost** Contact College   **Entry Reqs** Enthusiasm   **Award** C&G Fashion 780 Part I & II   **Creche** Yes £15.50/day
- **CONTACT**   Ruth Hughes 01603 773398

- **SUBJECT**   Information Technology   1005
- **TITLE**   Women into Information Technology
- **PLACE**   City College Norwich

Length 10 weeks   **Days** 1 day/week 10.00-1.00   **Cost** Contact College   **Entry Reqs** None   **Creche** Yes £15.50/day
- **CONTACT**   Tricial Harwood 01603 773272

- **SUBJECT**   Law   1006
- **TITLE**   Institute of Legal Executives
- **PLACE**   City College Norwich

Length 2 years   **Start** September   **Days** 1 afternoon+evening/week   **Cost** Contact College   **Entry Reqs** 4 GCSE/O Levels Grade C or above   **Award** Membership of Institute of Legal Executives   **Creche** Yes £15.50/day
- **CONTACT**   Anna Bannister 01603 773209

- **SUBJECT**   Management   1007
- **TITLE**   Women into Management
- **PLACE**   City College Norwich

Length 10 weeks   **Start** September, January, April   **Days** Wed 6.00-8.00   **Cost** £98   **Entry Reqs** None   **Creche** Yes
- **CONTACT**   Diane DeBell 01603 660011

- **SUBJECT**   NOW   1008
- **TITLE**   New Opportunities for Women
- **PLACE**   City College Norwich

Length 10 weeks   **Start** September, January, April   **Days** 1 day/week 9.30-12.00, 1.00-2.30   **Cost** £58   **Entry Reqs** None. Women only   **Creche** Contact College
- **CONTACT**   Suzanne Halliwell 01603 773257

- **SUBJECT** Office Skills   **1009**
- **TITLE** Updating and Retraining in Modern Office Skills
- **PLACE** City College Norwich

Length 12 weeks (modular)   **Start** September, January, April   **Days** Flexible, part time between 9.00-4.00   **Cost** Contact College   **Entry Reqs** Prior experience for some modules   **Award** RSA, Pitman, Teeline, NVQ qualifications possible   **Creche** Contact College

- **CONTACT** Margaret Garwood 01603 773210

- **SUBJECT** Personnel Management   **1010**
- **TITLE** Certificate in Personnel Practice
- **PLACE** City College Norwich

Length 1 year   **Start** September   **Days** 1 afternoon+evening/week   **Cost** Contact College   **Entry Reqs** None   **Award** IPD Certificate in Personnel Practice   **Creche** Contact College

- **CONTACT** Trudi Klaiber 01603 773372

- **SUBJECT** Practical   **1011**
- **TITLE** Basic Woodwork Skills (C&G)
- **PLACE** City College Norwich

Length 1 year   **Start** September   **Days** Tuesday 6.00-8.00   **Cost** £111   **Entry Reqs** None   **Award** Entry to furniture/carpentry courses   **Creche** No

- **CONTACT** Brian Moore 01603 660011

- **SUBJECT** Preparatory   **1012**
- **TITLE** Choosing the Way
- **PLACE** Women's Employment, Enterprise & Training Unit, Norwich

Length 12 weeks   **Start** Varies   **Cost** Free   **Entry Reqs** Women only   **Award** None   **Creche** Sometimes available

- **CONTACT** Erika Watson 01603 767367

- **SUBJECT** Preparatory   **1013**
- **TITLE** Return to Study
- **PLACE** Norfolk College of Arts & Technology

Length 8 weeks   **Start** Termly   **Days** Tues 10.00-12.00 or Wed 7.00-9.00   **Cost** £14   **Entry Reqs** None   **Award** None   **Creche** No

- **CONTACT** Rachel Phipps 01553 761144 x357

- **SUBJECT** Preparatory   **1014**
- **TITLE** Return to Study Options
- **PLACE** City College Norwich

Length Varies but 9 weeks maximum   **Start** January, April   **Days** Varies, 2-5 hours/week   **Cost** Contact College   **Entry Reqs** None   **Creche** Yes £15.50/day

- **CONTACT** Garth Clucas 01603 773162

COUNTY CONTACTS

Information and advice:

Career Development Centre, Great Yarmouth, 4 Church Plain, Great Yarmouth NR30 1PL 01493 332531

Career Development Centre, King's Lynn, 23 New Conduit Street, King's Lynn PE30 1DE 01553 771850

Career Development Centre, Norwich, 83-87 Pottergate, Norwich NR2 1DZ 01603 762079

Career Development Centre, Thetford, 2 Well Street, Thetford IP24 2BL 01842 762126

City College, Student Services Centre, Ipswich Road, Norwich

01603 660011   *Contact:* Carole Williams. Information Centre: Pam Breckenbridge

Norfolk Careers Service, County Hall, Martineau Lane, Norwich NR1 2DL 01603 222328. Information on the network of careers offices

Norfolk College of Arts & Technology, Tennyson Avenue, King's Lynn 01553 761144 x287 *Contact:* Caroline Coase, Rachel Phipps

WEETU (Women's Employment Enterprise Training Unit), The Music House, Wensum Lodge, King Street, Norwich NR1 1QW 01603 767367. Advice and guidance for individuals and groups, various courses

Open University:

The Open University, East Anglia Region, 12 Hills Road, Cambridge CB2 1PF 01223 61650

Training and Enterprise Council:

Norfolk and Waveney TEC, Partnership House, Whiting Road, Norwich NR4 6DJ 01603 763812. Women's Business Enterprise initiative; Audit of existing provision and identification of gaps; Development of out of school care facilities; Career Development Centres in Norwich, King's Lynn, Thetford, Great Yarmouth and Lowestoft

WEA office:

WEA Eastern District, Boltolph House, 17 Boltolph Lane, Cambridge CB2 3RE 01223 350978 *Contact:* Sue Young

NORTH YORKSHIRE

COURSES

- **SUBJECT**   Access   1015
- **TITLE**   Access Course in 1. Art, Design & Technology 2. Health Care
- **PLACE**   York College of Further & Higher Education

Length 1 year   **Start** September   **Days** Mon-Fri 9.30-3.00   **Cost** Contact College   **Entry Reqs** Age 21+, potential to benefit from course & committed to studying   **Award** College Certificate, entry to higher education   **Creche** Nursery

- **CONTACT**   Course Enquiries 01904 704141

- **SUBJECT** Access   **1016**
- **TITLE** Access Course in 1. Science, Technology & Engineering 2. Humanities & Social Science
- **PLACE** York College of Further & Higher Education

Length 1 year   **Start** September   **Days** Mon-Fri 9.30-3.00   **Cost** Contact College   **Entry Reqs** Age 21+, potential to benefit from course & committed to studying   **Award** College Certificate, entry to higher education   **Creche** Nursery

- **CONTACT** Course Enquiries 01904 704141

- **SUBJECT** Access   **1017**
- **TITLE** Access to Craft, Design & Technology
- **PLACE** University College of Ripon & York St John/York College of F&HE

Length 1 year   **Start** Autumn   **Days** 21 hours/week   **Cost** Contact College   **Entry Reqs** Interview   **Award** College Certificate, entry to higher education   **Creche** Yes

- **CONTACT** University College of Ripon &YSJ 01904 656771/York College F&HE 01904 704141

- **SUBJECT** Access/Art & Design   **1018**
- **TITLE** Access to Higher Education: Pathway in Art & Design
- **PLACE** Harrogate College

Length 36 weeks   **Start** September   **Days** Varied   **Cost** £496 full time, £294 part time   **Entry Reqs** By interview   **Award** Eligibility for entry to degree courses   **Creche** No

- **CONTACT** Chris Parker/Information Office 01423 879466

- **SUBJECT** Access/Business/Law   **1019**
- **TITLE** Access to Higher Education: Pathway in Business & Law
- **PLACE** Harrogate College

Length 36 weeks   **Start** September   **Days** Varied   **Cost** £496 full time, £294 part time   **Entry Reqs** By interview   **Award** Eligibility for entry to degree courses   **Creche** No

- **CONTACT** Chris Parker/Information Office 01423 879466

- **SUBJECT** Access/Health Studies   **1020**
- **TITLE** Access to Higher Education: Pathways in Health Professions and Health Science
- **PLACE** Harrogate College

Length 36 weeks   **Start** September   **Days** Varied   **Cost** £496 full time, £294 part time   **Entry Reqs** By interview   **Award** Eligibility for entry to degree courses   **Creche** No

- **CONTACT** Chris Parker/Information Office 01423 879466

- **SUBJECT** Access/Humanities/Social Science   **1021**
- **TITLE** Access to Higher Education: Pathway in Humanities and Social Science
- **PLACE** Harrogate College

Length 36 weeks   **Start** September   **Days** Varied   **Cost** £496 full time, £294 part time   **Entry Reqs** By interview   **Award** Eligibility for entry to degree courses   **Creche** No

- **CONTACT** Chris Parker/Information Office 01423 879466

- **SUBJECT** Access/Humanities/Social Science   **1022**
- **TITLE** Access to Humanities and Social Science
- **PLACE** University College of Ripon & York St John/York College of F&HE

Length 1 year   **Start** Autumn   **Days** 21 hours/week   **Cost** Contact College   **Entry Reqs** Interview   **Award** College Certificate, entry to higher education   **Creche** Yes

- **CONTACT** University College of Ripon &YSJ 01904 656771/York College F&HE 01904 704141

- **SUBJECT** Access/Science 1023
- **TITLE** Access to Higher Education: Pathway in Science
- **PLACE** Harrogate College

Length 36 weeks **Start** September **Days** Varied **Cost** £496 full time, £294 part time **Entry Reqs** By interview **Award** Eligibility for entry to degree courses **Creche** No

- **CONTACT** Chris Parker/Information Office 01423 879466

- **SUBJECT** Access/Science/Engineering/Mathematics 1024
- **TITLE** Access to Science, Engineering, Mathematics
- **PLACE** University College of Ripon & York St John/York College of F&HE

Length 1 year **Start** Autumn **Days** 21 hours/week **Cost** Contact College **Entry Reqs** Interview **Award** College Certificate, entry to higher education **Creche** Yes

- **CONTACT** University College of Ripon &YSJ 01904 656771/York College F&HE 01904 704141

- **SUBJECT** Business Administration 1025
- **TITLE** Business Administration NVQ Levels 1, 2, 3
- **PLACE** York College of Further & Higher Education

Length 1 or 2 years depending on level studied **Start** September **Days** Full time **Cost** Contact College **Entry Reqs** Contact College **Award** NVQ Levels 1, 2, 3 **Creche** Yes

- **CONTACT** Course Enquiries 01904 704141

- **SUBJECT** Environmental Sciences 1026
- **TITLE** Ecology and Environmental Management: Research Masters Training Programme
- **PLACE** University of York

Length 1 year **Start** October **Cost** Natural Environment Research Council award available **Entry Reqs** Graduates with first or upper second class honours degree in an appropriate subject **Award** MSc

- **CONTACT** Professor Alastair Fitter 01904 432814

- **SUBJECT** Management 1027
- **TITLE** Women into Management
- **PLACE** Harrogate College

Length 10 weeks **Start** March, October **Days** 1 day/week 9.00-4.30 **Cost** Contact College **Entry Reqs** Women seeking management positions **Award** College Certificate **Creche** No

- **CONTACT** Information Office 01423 878211

- **SUBJECT** Preparatory 1028
- **TITLE** Assertiveness and Communication Skills
- **PLACE** Harrogate College

Length 6 weeks **Start** September, October, January, April **Days** 1 eve/week 7.00-9.00 **Cost** £52+VAT **Entry Reqs** None **Award** College Certificate **Creche** No

- **CONTACT** Margaret Moffatt/Information Office 01423 879466

- **SUBJECT** Preparatory 1029
- **TITLE** Wider Opportunities for Women
- **PLACE** Harrogate College

Length 10 weeks **Start** September, January **Days** 2 days in College 9.15-3.00+ 1 day work placement **Cost** None **Entry Reqs** Ineligibility for employment training **Award** CLAIT **Creche** No

- **CONTACT** Information Office 01423 878211

North Yorkshire

- **SUBJECT** Science 1030
- **TITLE** Macromolecules and their Interactions: Masters Degree by Research
- **PLACE** University of York

Length 1 year **Start** October **Cost** Biotechnology & Biological Sciences Research Council award available **Entry Reqs** Graduates with first or upper second class honours degree in an appropriate subject **Award** MSc

- **CONTACT** Dr V Essex, BBSRC, 10793 413200

- **SUBJECT** Women's Studies 1031
- **TITLE** Women's Studies Degree Courses: MA, MPhil & DPhil
- **PLACE** University of York, Centre for Women's Studies

Length MA 12/24 months; MPhil 24/36 months; DPhil 36/48 months **Start** October **Days** Full time or part time **Cost** Contact University **Entry Reqs** Normally a degree but other qualifications considered **Award** MA degree, MPhil degree, DPhil degree **Creche** Contact Students' Union

- **CONTACT** Centre for Women's Studies 01904 433671

COUNTY CONTACTS

Information and advice:

Network North Yorkshire, c/o North Yorkshire Careers Guidance Services Ltd, Guidance House, York Road, Thirsk YO7 3BT 01845 526699. Educational and vocational guidance for adults. A range of leaflets and information available for adults from local careers centres
Harrogate Careers Centre, Jesmond House, Victoria Avenue, Harrogate HG1 5QP 01423 564331/2
Northallerton Careers Centre, Grammar School Lane, Northallerton DL6 1DW 01609 773593
Scarborough Careers Centre, 3rd Floor, Pavilion House, Westborough, Scarborough YO11 1UY 01723 373009
Selby Careers Centre, 2 Abbey Yard, Selby YO8 0PS 01757 703538
Skipton Careers Centre, Water Street, Skipton BD23 1PD 01756 792948
York Careers Centre, Merchant House, 11a Piccadilly, York YO1 1PB 01904 656655

Open University:

The Open University 2 Trevelyan Square, Boar Lane, Leeds LS1 6ED 0113 245 1466

Other agencies:

York Area Women Returners Network 01904 432027 *Contact:* June Hammond. Runs regular advice/information sessions and workshops, promotes opportunities for women

Training and Enterprise Council:

North Yorkshire TEC, TEC House, 7 Pioneer Business Park, Amy Johnson Way, Clifton Moorgate, York YO3 4TN 01904 691939. Out of school feasibility study; guidance for women returners; Returning to Teaching course; Returners courses in IT and Administration; Management and Training schemes, jointly funded; Widening Horizons; Women into Enterprise; out of school childcare

WEA office:

WEA Yorkshire North District, 6 Woodhouse Square, Leeds LS3 1AD 0113 245 3304 *Contact:* Wendy Formby

COURSES

- **SUBJECT**   Access   1032
- **TITLE**   Access to Higher Education
- **PLACE**   Northampton College, Military Road

Length 1 or 2 years   **Start** September   **Days** 10.00-3.00 in school terms   **Cost** Contact College   **Entry Reqs** None   **Award** Access to higher education   **Creche** Nursery

- **CONTACT**   Central Admissions Unit 01604 734228

- **SUBJECT**   Access   1033
- **TITLE**   Access to Higher Education in Sociology, Literature, History, Maths, Study Skills
- **PLACE**   Tresham Institute of Further & Higher Education, Corby

Length 2 years part time   **Start** September   **Days** 2 eves/week 7.00-9.00   **Cost** Contact College   **Entry Reqs** None   **Award** Access Certificate   **Creche** No

- **CONTACT**   J Morrison 01536 410252

- **SUBJECT**   Access/Business Studies/Engineering/Health Studies/Science   1034
- **TITLE**   Access to Business Studies, Engineering, Health Professions, Science
- **PLACE**   Northampton College, Booth Lane

Length 1 or 2 years   **Start** September   **Days** 10.00-3.00 in school terms   **Cost** Contact College   **Entry Reqs** None   **Award** Access to higher education   **Creche** Nursery

- **CONTACT**   Central Admissions Unit 01604 734228

- **SUBJECT**   Access/Business Studies/Information Technology   1035
- **TITLE**   Access to Business Studies & IT Applications
- **PLACE**   Tresham Institute of Further & Higher Education, Kettering

Length 1 year full time, 2 years part time   **Start** September   **Days** Mon-Fri 10.00-3.00   **Cost** None   **Entry Reqs** None   **Award** Access Certificate   **Creche** Yes £1.30/session

- **CONTACT**   A Reed 01536 402252 x3384

- **SUBJECT**   Access/Humanities/Social Science   1036
- **TITLE**   Access to Humanities and Social Sciences
- **PLACE**   Northampton College, Booth Lane

Length 1 or 2 years   **Start** September   **Days** 10.00-3.00 in school terms   **Cost** Contact College   **Entry Reqs** None   **Award** Access to higher education   **Creche** Nursery

- **CONTACT**   Central Admissions Unit 01604 734228

- **SUBJECT**   Access/Humanities/Social Science   1037
- **TITLE**   Access to Higher Education in Humanities, Social Science
- **PLACE**   Tresham Institute of Further & Higher Education, Kettering

Length 1 year full time, 2 years part time   **Start** September   **Days** Mon-Fri 10.00-3.00   **Cost** None   **Entry Reqs** None   **Award** Access Certificate   **Creche** Yes £1.30/session

- **CONTACT**   A Reed 01536 402252 x3384

- **SUBJECT**   Access/Teaching/Social Work   1038
- **TITLE**   Access to Teaching, Social Work
- **PLACE**   Northampton College, Military Road

Length 1 or 2 years   **Start** September   **Days** 10.00-3.00 in school terms   **Cost** Contact College   **Entry Reqs** None   **Award** Access to higher education   **Creche** Nursery

- **CONTACT**   Central Admissions Unit 01604 734228

- **SUBJECT** Administration 1039
- **TITLE** Administration: 1. NVQ II 2. NVQ III
- **PLACE** Northampton College

Length **Start** September **Days** Part time **Cost** Contact College **Entry Reqs** 1. None 2. Contact College **Award** 1. NVQ II 2. NVQ III **Creche** Nursery

- **CONTACT** Central Admissions Unit 01604 734228

- **SUBJECT** Business 1040
- **TITLE** Business & Finance Enhancement
- **PLACE** Northampton College

Length Modular **Start** September **Cost** Contact College **Entry Reqs** Contact College **Award** BTEC National Certificate **Creche** Nursery

- **CONTACT** Central Admissions Unit 01604 734228

- **SUBJECT** Care Studies 1041
- **TITLE** BTEC National Certificate in Caring Services (Social Care)
- **PLACE** Northampton College

Length 2 years **Start** September **Days** 1 day/week + work experience **Cost** Contact College **Entry Reqs** Mature students working or interested in working in caring services **Award** BTEC National Certificate **Creche** Nursery

- **CONTACT** Central Admissions Unit 01604 734228

- **SUBJECT** Care Studies 1042
- **TITLE** Certificate in Caring for People: The Elderly
- **PLACE** Northampton College

Length 1 year **Start** September **Days** 1 day/week **Cost** Contact College **Entry Reqs** Mature students working or interested in working with elderly people **Award** EMFEC Certificate in Caring for People **Creche** Nursery

- **CONTACT** Central Admissions Unit 01604 734228

- **SUBJECT** Catering 1043
- **TITLE** NVQ II 1. Food Preparation & Cooking 2. Food & Beverage Service
- **PLACE** Tresham Institute of Further & Higher Education

Length Varies according to units taken **Start** September onwards **Days** Flexible, by negotiation **Cost** Varies according to units taken and length **Entry Reqs** None. College interview **Award** Modules leading to NVQ Levels II&III **Creche** No

- **CONTACT** Chris Hole 01536 402252

- **SUBJECT** Catering 1044
- **TITLE** Sugar Craft, Cookery Certificate, Baking, Business Studies
- **PLACE** Moulton College

Length 36 weeks full time or part time **Start** September **Days** Various **Cost** Contact College **Entry Reqs** None **Award** C&Gs **Creche** Day Nursery £40-£66/week according to age

- **CONTACT** Roger Humphrey 01604 491131

- **SUBJECT** Catering/Hospitality Management 1045
- **TITLE** Diploma in Hospitality & Catering
- **PLACE** Northampton College

Length 2 years **Start** September **Days** Full time **Cost** Contact College **Entry Reqs** Contact College **Award** 1. BTEC GNVQ Intermediate 2. BTEC GNVQ Advanced **Creche** Nursery

- **CONTACT** Central Admissions Unit 01604 734228

- **SUBJECT** Childcare 1046
- **TITLE** BTEC National Certificate in 1. Nursery Nursing 2. Social Care
- **PLACE** Tresham Institute of F & HE, Kettering & Wellingborough

Length 2 years **Start** September **Days** 1 day + 1 eve/week **Cost** £185/year + £60 registration fee **Entry Reqs** College Interview **Award** BTEC National Certificate in Caring Services 1. Nursery Nursing 2. Social Care **Creche** No
- **CONTACT** 1. Bernie Sanders 01536 413224 2. Pam Stares 01536 413223

- **SUBJECT** Childcare 1047
- **TITLE** Conversion Course for NNEB to BTEC National Certificate in Nursery Nursing
- **PLACE** Tresham Institute of Further & Higher Education, Kettering

Length 9 months **Start** September **Days** Tues+Thurs eves **Cost** Approx £200 **Entry Reqs** NNEB Diploma **Award** BTEC National Certificate in Caring Services (Nursery Nursing) **Creche** No
- **CONTACT** Clive Delmonte 01536 410252 x236

- **SUBJECT** Childcare 1048
- **TITLE** NNEB Diploma in Nursery Nursing
- **PLACE** Tresham Institute of Further & Higher Education, Kettering

Length 2 years part time **Start** September **Days** Part time evenings **Cost** Contact College **Entry Reqs** Mature experienced students **Award** NNEB Diploma in Nursery Nursing **Creche** No
- **CONTACT** Clive Delmonte 01536 410252 x236

- **SUBJECT** Craft 1049
- **TITLE** 1. Creative Embroidery 2. Patchwork & Quilting
- **PLACE** Tresham Institute of Further & Higher Education, Kettering

Length 3 years **Start** September **Days** Mon 9.30-4.00 **Cost** £97.50 **Entry Reqs** None **Award** C&G Certificates **Creche** Contact College
- **CONTACT** Pam Keeling 01536 410252

- **SUBJECT** Craft 1050
- **TITLE** Upholstery, Soft Furnishing, Furniture Restoration, Business Studies
- **PLACE** Moulton College

Length 36 weeks full time or part time **Start** September **Days** Various **Cost** Contact College **Entry Reqs** None **Award** College Certificate and C&Gs **Creche** Day Nursery £40-£66/week according to age
- **CONTACT** Gerald Davies 01604 491131

- **SUBJECT** Engineering 1051
- **TITLE** Women into Engineering
- **PLACE** Northampton College

Length 1 year **Start** September **Cost** Contact College **Entry Reqs** No formal requirements. Women 25+, unemployed for 1 year or returning to work **Award** NVQ Level II, progress to BTEC or C&G courses **Creche** Nursery
- **CONTACT** Central Admissions Unit 01604 734228

- **SUBJECT** Fashion 1052
- **TITLE** Fashion, Machine Knitting, Business Studies
- **PLACE** Moulton College

Length 36 weeks full time or part time **Start** September **Days** Various **Cost** Contact College **Entry Reqs** None **Award** C&G **Creche** Day Nursery £40-£66/week according to age
- **CONTACT** Gerald Davies 01604 491131

- **SUBJECT** Floristry   **1053**
- **TITLE** Floristry NVQ Levels I, II, III
- **PLACE** Moulton College

Length 35 weeks day release or 1 year full time   **Start** September   **Days** Part I Tues, II Wed, III Thurs 9.30-4.30. Day release or eve or full time   **Cost** Contact College   **Entry Reqs** None   **Award** NVQ Levels I, II, III   **Creche** Day Nursery £40-£66/week according to age

- **CONTACT** Annette Claybrook 01604 491131

- **SUBJECT** Hairdressing   **1054**
- **TITLE** Foundation Certificate in Hairdressing for Mature Students
- **PLACE** Northampton College

Length 1 year   **Start** September   **Days** 4 hours/day, 4 days/week   **Cost** Contact College **Entry Reqs** None. 19+   **Award** NVQ Level II   **Creche** Nursery

- **CONTACT** Central Admissions Unit 01604 734228

- **SUBJECT** Hairdressing/Beauty/Sports Therapy   **1055**
- **TITLE** Units of NVQ Certificates in Hairdressing, Beauty Therapy, Sports Therapy
- **PLACE** Tresham Institute of Further & Higher Education, Corby

Length Varies according to units taken   **Start** Sept (other dates by negotiation)   **Days** Flexible by negotiation   **Cost** Varies according to units taken   **Entry Reqs** None. College interview   **Award** NVQs in Hair, Beauty Therapy, Sports Therapy   **Creche** No

- **CONTACT** Shirley Munden 01536 402252/413378

- **SUBJECT** Horticulture   **1056**
- **TITLE** Landscape, Garden Construction and Conservation; Organic Gardening
- **PLACE** Moulton College

Length 36 weeks full time, part time possible   **Start** September   **Days** Various   **Cost** Contact College   **Entry Reqs** None   **Award** National Certificate in Horticulture   **Creche** Day Nursery £40-£66/week according to age

- **CONTACT** Nick Brown 01604 491131

- **SUBJECT** Horticulture   **1057**
- **TITLE** Plant Production and Marketing
- **PLACE** Moulton College

Length 36 weeks full time, part time possible   **Start** September   **Days** Various   **Cost** Various   **Entry Reqs** None   **Award** National Certificate in Horticulture   **Creche** Day Nursery £40-£66/week according to age

- **CONTACT** Nick Brown 01604 491131

- **SUBJECT** Information Technology   **1058**
- **TITLE** Computer Literacy and Information Technology
- **PLACE** Northampton College

Length Contact College   **Start** September   **Days** Part time   **Cost** Contact College   **Entry Reqs** None   **Award** RSA CLAIT Stage 1   **Creche** Nursery

- **CONTACT** Central Admissions Unit 01604 734228

- **SUBJECT** Management   **1059**
- **TITLE** Management Studies
- **PLACE** Northampton College

Start September   **Days** Full or part time   **Cost** Contact College   **Entry Reqs** Contact College   **Award** BTEC GNVQ Advanced Management Studies   **Creche** Nursery

- **CONTACT** Central Admissions Unit 01604 734228

- **SUBJECT**   Office Skills   1060
- **TITLE**   Office Skills Workshop
- **PLACE**   Northampton College

Length Varies according to exams taken   **Start** Termly   **Days** Part time   **Cost** Contact College   **Entry Reqs** None   **Award** Various including RSA   **Creche** Nursery

- **CONTACT**   Central Admissions Unit 01604 734228

- **SUBJECT**   Preparatory   1061
- **TITLE**   Breakthrough
- **PLACE**   Northampton College, Booth Lane & Military Road Centres

Length 1 year part time   **Start** September   **Cost** Contact College   **Entry Reqs** None   **Award** RSA qualifications   **Creche** Nursery

- **CONTACT**   Central Admissions Unit 01604 734228

- **SUBJECT**   Preparatory   1062
- **TITLE**   Make Your Experience Count
- **PLACE**   Northampton College, Military Road Centre

Start Contact College   **Days** Part time   **Cost** Contact College   **Entry Reqs** None   **Creche** Nursery

- **CONTACT**   Central Admissions Unit 01604 734228

- **SUBJECT**   Preparatory   1063
- **TITLE**   New Opportunities (Pre Access)
- **PLACE**   Northampton College, Military Road Centre

Start September   **Days** Part time   **Cost** Contact College   **Entry Reqs** None   **Award** Open College Network Accreditation   **Creche** Nursery

- **CONTACT**   Central Admissions Unit 01604 734228

- **SUBJECT**   Preparatory   1064
- **TITLE**   Open University Preparation Course: An Approach to the Arts and Social Sciences
- **PLACE**   Tresham Institute of Further & Higher Education, Kettering

Length 10 weeks   **Start** September   **Days** Tues 7.00-9.00   **Cost** Approx £25   **Entry Reqs** None   **Award** None   **Creche** No

- **CONTACT**   Paul Taylor 01536 410252

- **SUBJECT**   Tourism & Leisure   1065
- **TITLE**   Leisure & Tourism 1. BTEC GNVQ Intermediate 2. BTEC GNVQ Advanced
- **PLACE**   Northampton College

Length 1.1 year 2.2 years   **Start** September   **Days** Full time   **Cost** Contact College   **Entry Reqs** Contact College   **Award** 1. BTEC GNVQ Intermediate 2. BTEC GNVQ Advanced   **Creche** Nursery

- **CONTACT**   Central Admissions Unit 01604 734228

COUNTY CONTACTS

Information and advice:

Northamptonshire Women's Network, Arch Villa, 23 High Street, Bozeat NN29 7NF 01933 665032   *Contact:* Rachel Mallows. Provides support and information for women seeking to return to work

The Training Shop, Royal Pavilion, Summerhouse Pavilion, Summerhouse Road, Moulton Park, Northampton NN3 1WD 01604 790908   *Contact:* Ann Masser, Val Foreman. Training information and Adult Vocational Guidance Service

Open University:

The Open University, East Midlands Region, The Octagon, 143 Derby Road, Nottingham NG7 1PH 0115 924 0121

Training and Enterprise Council:

Northamptonshire TEC, Royal Pavilion, Summerhouse Pavilion, Summerhouse Road, Moulton Park, Northampton NN3 1WD 01604 671200

WEA office:

WEA Eastern District, Boltolph House, 17 Boltolph Lane, Cambridge CB2 3RE 01223 350978 *Contact:* Sue Young

---

NORTHUMBERLAND

COURSES

- **SUBJECT**   Access   1066
- **TITLE**   Higher Education Foundation Course (Modular)
- **PLACE**   Northumberland College

Length 1 year   **Start** September   **Days** Various, modular   **Cost** Contact College   **Entry**
Reqs None   **Award** Certificate + entry to higher education   **Creche** Yes

- **CONTACT**   Advice Centre 01670 841202

- **SUBJECT**   Construction   1067
- **TITLE**   Women's Course in Construction Skills
- **PLACE**   Northumberland College

Length 35 weeks   **Start** September   **Days** 2 days/week   **Cost** Contact College   **Entry**
Reqs None   **Award** NVQ II, possibility of other awards   **Creche** Yes

- **CONTACT**   Advice Centre 01670 841202

- **SUBJECT**   Preparatory   1068
- **TITLE**   Adult Foundation Course
- **PLACE**   Northumberland College

Length 10 weeks   **Start** September, January, April   **Days** 3 hours/week   **Cost** Contact College   **Entry Reqs** None   **Creche** Yes
- **CONTACT**   Course Enquiries 01670 813248

- **SUBJECT**   Preparatory   1069
- **TITLE**   First Steps Forward
- **PLACE**   Hexham, Cramlington, Morpeth and centres throughout Northumberland

Length 12 days   **Start** Ongoing   **Days** 2 days/week 9.45-2.45   **Cost** Free   **Entry Reqs** None   **Award** Tyneside Open College Certificate Federation   **Creche** Help for childcare/travel costs if on benefit
- **CONTACT**   Beverley Hill, Newcastle Women's Training Centre, 0191 232 6159

- **SUBJECT**   Preparatory   1070
- **TITLE**   Preparing for Higher Education Foundation Course: Study Skills
- **PLACE**   Northumberland College

Length 1 year   **Start** September   **Days** Various, modular   **Cost** Contact College   **Entry Reqs** None   **Award** None   **Creche** Yes
- **CONTACT**   Advice Centre 01670 841202

- **SUBJECT**   Teaching   1071
- **TITLE**   Further and Adult Education Teaching Certificate (Part Time)
- **PLACE**   Northumberland College

Length 1 year   **Start** September   **Cost** Contact College   **Award** C&G 7307   **Creche** Yes
- **CONTACT**   Advice Centre 01670 841202

COUNTY CONTACTS

Information and advice:

Advice Centre, Northumberland College, College Road, Ashington NE63 9RG 01607 813248
Contact: Kathy McMonies, Avril Gibson
Northumberland Guidance Corporation, 7 Sextons House, Freehold Street, Blyth NE24 2BA 01670 361361

Open University:

The Open University, North Region, Eldon House, Regent Centre, Gosforth, Newcastle upon Tyne NE3 3PW 0191 284 1611

Training and Enterprise Council:

Northumberland TEC, Craster Court, Manor Walks, Cramlington NE23 6UT 01670 713303 Women Returners Centre; Foundation programmes for women returners; Gateways; First Steps to Management; Access courses; Turning Point; Women into Management; Women into Enterprise; Return to Work; Childcare initiative.

WEA office:

WEA Northern District, 51 Grainger Street, Newcastle upon Tyne NE1 5JE 0191 232 3957
Contact: Clare Brown, Ann Staines

COURSES

- **SUBJECT**   Access   1072
- **TITLE**   Modular Access to Higher Education
- **PLACE**   Clarendon College

Length Modular   **Start** September, January   **Days** Flexible   **Cost** Contact College   **Entry Reqs** Interview and written assessment   **Award** Access Certificate and Open College Network credits   **Creche** Yes 30 months+, £1.50/session

- **CONTACT**   Hazel Washington 0115 960 7201

- **SUBJECT**   Access/Arts/Design/Humanities/Science/Social Science/Technology   1073
- **TITLE**   Access to Higher Education
- **PLACE**   Clarendon College

Length 1 or 2 years   **Start** Continuous enrolment   **Days** Varies 6-17 hours/week   **Cost** Contact College. £10 enrolment fee for Nottinghamshire residents   **Entry Reqs** Mature students 20+   **Award** Open College Network Credits   **Creche** Yes 30 months+, £1.50/session

- **CONTACT**   Hazel Washington 0115 960 7201

- **SUBJECT**   Access/English/European Studies/Media Studies/Social Science/   1074
Science/Engineering/Computing/Psychology/Health Studies
- **TITLE**   Access to Higher Education
- **PLACE**   South Nottingham College

Length 1 year   **Start** September   **Days** Full time 9.15-3.00   **Entry Reqs** Contact College   **Award** Access to higher education   **Creche** Yes

- **CONTACT**   Course Information Service 0115 981 2161

- **SUBJECT**   Access/Science   1075
- **TITLE**   Fast Track Access Course in Science
- **PLACE**   Arnold & Carlton College

Length 9 months   **Start** September   **Days** 4 days/week, 'school-friendly' hours   **Cost** Full time, no fees   **Entry Reqs** Interest in science   **Award** NEMAP approved; students may choose to study GCSEs in English and Maths   **Creche** Yes

- **CONTACT**   Admissions 0115 953 1222

- **SUBJECT**   Access/Social Science   1076
- **TITLE**   Access to Social Science
- **PLACE**   Arnold & Carlton College

Length 1 year   **Start** September   **Days** 3 days/week 9.15-3.00 Tues, Wed, Thurs plus private study and workshops   **Cost** Free   **Entry Reqs** None   **Award** Provides introduction to subjects plus study skills. NEMAP approved.   **Creche** Yes

- **CONTACT**   Admissions 0115 953 1216

- **SUBJECT** Access/Social Work 1077
- **TITLE** Social Work Access Course
- **PLACE** Arnold & Carlton College, Bath Street Centre

Length 1 year **Start** September **Days** 2 days/week in college 9.15-4.00 and 2-3 days work experience **Entry Reqs** Contact College **Award** Certificate validated by NEMAP **Creche** Playgroup

- **CONTACT** Admissions 0115 953 1222

- **SUBJECT** Administration 1078
- **TITLE** Women Returners' RSA NVQ Level 2 Administration
- **PLACE** Arnold & Carlton College

Length 1 year **Start** September **Days** 4 days/week 10.00-4.00 or 5 days/week if studying shorthand **Cost** Full time, no fees **Entry Reqs** No formal entry requirements **Award** Internal assessments verified by RSA & exams offered in range of office skills **Creche** Playgroup

- **CONTACT** Admissions 0115 953 1222

- **SUBJECT** Administration/Management 1079
- **TITLE** Diploma in Administrative Management for Women
- **PLACE** Arnold & Carlton College & Nottingham Women's Centre, Chaucer Street

Length 1 or 2 years (includes work placement) **Start** April, September **Days** 4 days/week 9.30-3.00 **Cost** No fees, help with travel costs **Entry Reqs** Women with sound basic education and some experience of work **Award** Diploma in Administrative Management/ RSA CLAIT (Computer Literacy & Information Technology) **Creche** Playgroup (help with childcare costs)

- **CONTACT** Admissions 0115 953 1216

- **SUBJECT** Art & Design 1080
- **TITLE** Art & Design Foundation Studies validated by The Nottingham Trent University
- **PLACE** Arnold & Carlton College, Bath Street Centre

Length 1 year **Start** September **Days** 5 days/week **Cost** Free **Entry Reqs** Age 23+: interview+portfolio; age 17-22:5 GCSEs with Art, English/or experience+portfolio **Award** Leads to entry to The Nottingham Trent University or other higher education establishments **Creche** Playgroup

- **CONTACT** Admissions 0115 953 1222

- **SUBJECT** Beauty 1081
- **TITLE** Black Skin and Beauty Care
- **PLACE** Clarendon College

Length 9 weeks **Start** October **Days** Wed 9.30-1.00 **Cost** Free if unwaged or dependant **Entry Reqs** None **Award** College Certificate leading to C&G NVQ Level II **Creche** Yes

- **CONTACT** Lesley Johns 1005 960 7201

- **SUBJECT** Business/Finance 1082
- **TITLE** Business & Finance for Mature Students 1. BTEC Intermediate GNVQ 2. BTEC Advanced GNVQ
- **PLACE** Arnold & Carlton College, Digby Avenue Centre

Length 1.1 year 2.2 years **Start** September **Days** Up to 21 hours/week 9.30-3.00 **Cost** Free **Entry Reqs** Informal interview, no formal qualifications required **Award** 1. BTEC Intermediate GNVQ 2. BTEC Advanced GNVQ **Creche** Playgroup

- **CONTACT** Admissions 0115 953 1222

- **SUBJECT**   Business Administration   1083
- **TITLE**   Business Adminstration
- **PLACE**   South Nottingham College

Start September   **Days** Tues 1.00-3.00 or Thurs 6.00-7.50   **Entry Req**   **Award** NVQ Level I/II   **Creche** Yes

- **CONTACT** Course Information Service 0115 981 2161

- **SUBJECT**   Business Administration   1084
- **TITLE**   Business Adminstration
- **PLACE**   Basford Hall College of FE

Length 1-2 years   **Start** September   **Days** Mon-Fri 10.00-1.15   **Cost** Free for students in appropriate categories   **Entry Reqs** None   **Award** NVQ Business Administration   **Creche** Playgroup Approx 90p/session

- **CONTACT** Eileen Collings 0115 970 4541 x315

- **SUBJECT**   Care Studies   1085
- **TITLE**   Introductory Course in Caring
- **PLACE**   South Nottingham College

Start Contact College   **Days** Mon day/eve   **Entry Reqs** Contact College   **Creche** Yes

- **CONTACT** Course Information Service 0115 981 2161

- **SUBJECT**   Childcare   1086
- **TITLE**   BTEC Diploma in Nursery Nursing (Part time Modular)
- **PLACE**   South Nottingham College

Start September   **Days** Tues or Wed 6 hours/day, eve   **Cost** £167.30   **Award** BTEC National Diploma   **Creche** Yes

- **CONTACT** Course Information Service 0115 981 2161

- **SUBJECT**   Civil Engineering   1087
- **TITLE**   Civil Engineering: Research Masters Pilot Course
- **PLACE**   University of Nottingham

Length 2 years   **Start** October   **Cost** Engineering & Physical Sciences Research Council award available   **Entry Reqs** Graduates with first or upper second class honours degree in an appropriate subject   **Award** Master of Research Degree

- **CONTACT** Dr J Baker 0115 951 3895

- **SUBJECT**   Computing   1088
- **TITLE**   BTEC National Diploma in Computer Studies
- **PLACE**   Arnold & Carlton College

Length 2 years   **Start** September   **Days** Up to 21 hours/week   **Cost** Free   **Entry Reqs** For mature students entry by informal interview   **Award** BTEC National Diploma in Computer Studies   **Creche** Playgroup

- **CONTACT** Admissions 0115 953 1222

- **SUBJECT**   Computing   1089
- **TITLE**   Hello Computers
- **PLACE**   Muslim Women's Organisation, Nottingham

Length 20 weeks beginners, 15 weeks advanced   **Start** September   **Days** Beginners Mon 9.30-3.00; Advanced Tues 1.00-3.00   **Cost** Free   **Entry Reqs** For Asian women   **Award** RSA Text Processing 1 (beginners) 2 (Advanced)   **Creche** Playgroup

- **CONTACT** Rajinder Sandhu 0115 960 7201

- **SUBJECT** Computing   1090
- **TITLE** Word Processing for Asian Women
- **PLACE** Clarendon Women's Education/Resources Centre

Length 12 weeks   **Start** September   **Days** Tues 6.00-9.00   **Cost** Free if unwaged or dependant   **Entry Reqs** None   **Award** RSA Text Processing 1 & 2   **Creche** Yes

- **CONTACT** Rajinder Sandhu 0115 960 7201

- **SUBJECT** Computing/Multi-Subject   1091
- **TITLE** Job Link 2000
- **PLACE** Centre 2000, Nottingham

Length 15 weeks   **Start** September   **Days** Tues-Thurs 10.00-3.00   **Cost** Free if unwaged or dependant   **Entry Reqs** None   **Award** RSA Text Processing 1   **Creche** Playgroup

- **CONTACT** Joanne Fletcher 0115 960 7201

- **SUBJECT** Construction   1092
- **TITLE** GNVQ Intermediate Construction and the Built Environment
- **PLACE** Nottinghamshire Women's Training Centre, Nottingham

Length 1 year   **Start** September   **Days** 3 days/week   **Cost** Free   **Entry Reqs** Women. Priority if 25+, unemployed for 1 year or more, less than 5 GCSEs or equivalent   **Award** GNVQ Intermediate   **Creche** Nursery, free

- **CONTACT** 0115 958 6236

- **SUBJECT** Information Technology   1093
- **TITLE** GNVQ Intermediate IT for Women
- **PLACE** South Nottingham College

Start September   **Award** GNVQ Intermediate   **Creche** Yes

- **CONTACT** Course Information Service 0115 981 2161

- **SUBJECT** Management   1094
- **TITLE** Management Skills for African-Caribbean Women
- **PLACE** African Caribbean National Association, Nottingham

Length 20 weeks   **Start** September   **Days** 6.00-9.00   **Cost** Free if unwaged or dependant **Entry Reqs** None   **Award** OCN Level 3   **Creche** Playgroup

- **CONTACT** Eunice Campbell 0115 985 7566

- **SUBJECT** Multi-Subject   1095
- **TITLE** Women Stepping Out
- **PLACE** Greenfields Training Centre, Nottingham

Length 36 weeks   **Start** September, January   **Days** Mon-Thurs 10.00-3.00   **Cost** Free if unwaged or dependant   **Entry Reqs** None   **Award** RSA Text Processing/OCN Level 2 Wordpower+Numberpower   **Creche** Playgroup

- **CONTACT** Salma Mir 0115 970 0404

- **SUBJECT** Office Skills   1096
- **TITLE** First Steps (Office Skills)
- **PLACE** Nottingham Women's Centre, Chaucer Street, Nottingham

Length 18 weeks   **Start** Various   **Cost** Free plus possible help with childcare and travel costs   **Entry Reqs** No formal entry requirements   **Award** Various including RSA CLAIT (Computer Literacy & Information Technology)   **Creche** Playgroup

- **CONTACT** Admissions 0115 953 1222

- **SUBJECT** Office Skills   **1097**
- **TITLE** Mature Women's Secretarial Course
- **PLACE** Basford Hall College of FE

Length 1 year **Start** September **Days** Mon-Fri 10.00-1.15 **Cost** Free for students in appropriate categories **Entry Reqs** None **Award** Examinations in typewriting/audio/wordprocessing/NVQ Adminstration **Creche** Playgroup Approx 90p/session

- **CONTACT** Eileen Collings 0115 970 4541 x315

- **SUBJECT** Office Skills/Information Technology   **1098**
- **TITLE** Mature Students Typewriting/Information Technology
- **PLACE** South Nottingham College

Length 1.36 weeks 2.18 weeks **Start** 1. September 2. September, January **Entry Req** Contact College **Creche** Yes

- **CONTACT** Course Information Service 0115 981 2161

- **SUBJECT** Practical   **1099**
- **TITLE** Basics
- **PLACE** Nottinghamshire Women's Training Centre, Nottingham

Length 6 weeks **Start** November **Days** 1 day/week **Entry Req** Women, unemployed, 18+ with few or no qualifications **Creche** Nursery, free

- **CONTACT** 0115 958 6236

- **SUBJECT** Practical   **1100**
- **TITLE** Building and Engineering Trades, PSV/HGV Driving
- **PLACE** Nottinghamshire Women's Training Centre, Nottingham

Length 5 week taster courses, 6 months Foundation course **Start** Sept/Nov (taster), Jan (Foundation) **Days** Fits in with school hours & terms **Cost** Free. Travel and childcare allowances **Entry Reqs** Women, unemployed, 18+ with few or no qualifications **Award** Open College Network Credits (Level I & II), PSV or HGV licence **Creche** Nursery, free

- **CONTACT** 0115 958 6236

- **SUBJECT** Practical   **1101**
- **TITLE** Practical Courses in Non-Traditional Skills
- **PLACE** Nottinghamshire Women's Training Scheme, Worksop

Length Varies **Cost** Free **Entry Reqs** None, must be over 21, living in Bassetlaw, not working **Award** Accredited courses, can lead to NVQs **Creche** Yes free

- **CONTACT** Sally Laver/Rita Stringfellow 01909 474029

- **SUBJECT** Preparatory   **1102**
- **TITLE** Back to Work with New Skills and Confidence
- **PLACE** Clarendon College

Length Varies **Days** 2½ days/week **Entry Reqs** Contact College **Award** RSA/NVQ Level 2 Administration

- **CONTACT** Wendy Whitfield 0115 960 7201

- **SUBJECT** Preparatory   **1103**
- **TITLE** Women and Men in Transition
- **PLACE** Clarendon Women's Education/Resources Centre

Length 10 weeks **Start** September, January **Cost** Free if unwaged or dependant **Entry Reqs** None **Award** RSA Text Processing/OCN Level 2 **Creche** Yes

- **CONTACT** Annie Strong 0115 955 3119

- **SUBJECT** Preparatory
- **TITLE** Fresh Start
- **PLACE** Newark and Sherwood College

1104

Length 1 term   **Start** 3 times a year   **Days** 3 hours/week (morning)   **Cost** Free   **Entry Reqs** None   **Award** NEMAP Level 2   **Creche** Yes £5

- **CONTACT** S Bird 01636 680680

- **SUBJECT** Professional Updating/Medicine
- **TITLE** Re-entry to General Practice
- **PLACE** University of Nottingham, Faculty of Medicine & Health Sciences

1105

Length Contact University   **Days** Contact University   **Cost** Contact University   **Entry Reqs** Contact University

- **CONTACT** Jacky Williams 0115 970 9387

- **SUBJECT** Science
- **TITLE** GNVQ Intermediate Science for Women
- **PLACE** South Nottingham College

1106

Start September   **Award** GNVQ Intermediate   **Creche** Yes

- **CONTACT** Course Information Service 0115 981 2161

- **SUBJECT** Secretarial
- **TITLE** Secretarial and Office Skills for Adults
- **PLACE** Newark and Sherwood College

1107

Length 36 weeks   **Start** September, but join anytime   **Days** 14 hours/week 9.00-3.00   **Entry Reqs** None   **Award** LCC1/NVQ/RSA simple subjects/NEBSM Certificate Skills as a Supervisor   **Creche** Yes nominal charge

- **CONTACT** S Bird 01636 680680

- **SUBJECT** Textiles
- **TITLE** Tex-Train
- **PLACE** Clarendon Women's Education/Resources Centre

1108

Length 15 weeks   **Start** September, February   **Days** Tues, Wed, Thurs 10.00-3.00   **Cost** Free to unwaged or their dependants   **Entry Reqs** None   **Award** C&G Dressmaking/EMFEC Certificate in Multi-Cultural Fashion   **Creche** Yes

- **CONTACT** Joanne Fletcher 0115 970 0404

- **SUBJECT** Teaching
- **TITLE** City & Guilds Teacher Training for Women Stage 1 & 2
- **PLACE** Clarendon Women's Education/Resources Centre

1109

Length 1.7 weeks 2.27 weeks   **Start** 1. September 2. November   **Days** Fri 10.00-3.00   **Cost** Free if unwaged or dependant   **Entry Reqs** Must be some teaching/training eg part time or voluntary work   **Award** 1. C&G Stage 1 2. C&G Stage 2   **Creche** Playgroup

- **CONTACT** Margaret Healey/Tahira Khan 0115 960 7201/970 0404

Nottinghamshire

- **SUBJECT**   Training   **1110**
- **TITLE**   Training the Trainers for Women
- **PLACE**   African Caribbean National Association, Nottingham

Length 35 weeks   **Start** October   **Days** 1 day/week 10.00-3.00   **Cost** Free if unwaged or dependant   **Entry Reqs** None   **Award** OCN Level 3   **Creche** Playgroup

- **CONTACT**   Joanne Fletcher 0115 970 0404

COUNTY CONTACTS

Information and advice:

BEGIN (Basic Educational Guidance Service in Nottingham), Berridge Centre, Stanley Road, Forest Fields, Nottingham NG7 6HW 0115 978 0942   *Contact:* Fiona Vale. Central contact point and support for anyone needing help with basic maths, English and English for speakers of other languages
Nottingham Trent University, Centre for Access & Continuing Education, Burton Street, Nottingham NG1 4BU 0115 941 8418   *Contact:* Christine Davies x4247/2340

Open University:

The Open University, East Midlands Region, The Octagon, 143 Derby Road, Nottingham NG7 1PH 0115 924 0121

Other agencies:

Nottinghamshire Women's Training Scheme, Albion Close, Worksop S80 1RA 01909 474029. Women's training centre
Nottinghamshire Women's Training Scheme, Victoria Workshops, 1 Cairns Street, off Huntingdon Street, Nottingham NG1 3NN 01602 586236. Provides basic training for women in the construction trades and electronics. Trains LGV & PCV drivers

Training and Enterprise Councils:

Greater Nottingham TEC, Marina Road, Castle Marina Park, Nottingham NG7 1TN 0115 941 3313
North Nottinghamshire TEC, 1st Floor, Block C, Edwinstowe House, High Street, Edwinstowe, Mansfield NG21 9PR 01623 824624

WEA offices:

WEA East Midland District, Alfreton Hall, Church Street, Alfreton DE55 7AH 01773 832185 *Contact:* Chris Scarlett. Covers south Nottinghamshire
WEA Nottingham, Adult Education Centre, 16 Shakespeare Street, Nottingham NG1 4GF 0115 947 5162   *Contact:* Dr Cheryl Turner, Tutor Organiser
WEA Yorkshire South District, Chantry Buildings, Corporation Street, Rotherham S60 1NG 01709 837001   *Contact:* Trish Lands. Covers north Nottinghamshire

COURSES

- **SUBJECT** Access   1111
- **TITLE** Access to Higher Education
- **PLACE** Abingdon College

Length 1 year full time or 2 years part time   **Start** September   **Days** 5 days/week 9.30-3.00 (12-18 hours/week) or part time   **Cost** Free   **Entry Reqs** None   **Award** Access to HE Certificate, entry to Oxford Brookes University or other HE institution   **Creche** Yes Contact College

- **CONTACT** Diana Batchelor 01235 555585 x230

- **SUBJECT** Access   1112
- **TITLE** Access to Higher Education
- **PLACE** West Oxfordshire College

Length 36 weeks   **Start** September   **Days** Mon-Fri 9.20-2.45   **Cost** Free   **Entry Reqs** Open entry   **Award** Kitemarked by Oxford Brookes University   **Creche** No

- **CONTACT** D Mills 01993 703464

- **SUBJECT** Administration   1113
- **TITLE** Advanced Diploma in Administration
- **PLACE** Abingdon College

Length 1 year   **Start** September   **Days** Mon-Fri 9.00-5.00   **Cost** Contact College   **Entry Reqs** Mature students at discretion of interviewer   **Award** RSA Diploma in Administration NVQ Level III   **Creche** Yes

- **CONTACT** Karen Yorke 01235 555585 x241

- **SUBJECT** Administration/Secretarial   1114
- **TITLE** Higher Diploma in Administrative and Secretarial Procedures
- **PLACE** Abingdon College

Length 1 year   **Start** September   **Days** Mon-Fri 9.00-3.00   **Cost** Approx £750. Grants may be at discretion of LEA   **Entry Reqs** Degree, A Level. Mature students at discretion of interviewer   **Award** RSA Higher Diploma in Administrative & Secretarial Procedures **Creche** Yes Contact College

- **CONTACT** Jenny Stacey 01235 555585 x241

- **SUBJECT** Career Development   1115
- **TITLE** Career Development Programme for Lone Parents
- **PLACE** Oxford and other Training Centres

Length 18 weeks   **Start** March, September   **Days** 18 x 1 day workshops (generally Weds) **Cost** Free   **Entry Reqs** None, good command of English necessary   **Award** Westminster Certificate in Career Development   **Creche** Financial help available for childcare

- **CONTACT** Isabel Morris 01865 247644 x3293

- **SUBJECT** Computing   1116
- **TITLE** Computing Training Course with BTEC Modules or RSA Certificates
- **PLACE** Oxford Women's Training Scheme

Length 1 year   **Start** September   **Days** Mon-Fri 9.30-2.30   **Cost** Free   **Entry Reqs** Basic numeracy, literacy, interest in getting a job with computers   **Award** BTEC Module Certificates or RSA Certificates   **Creche** No. Childcare allowance

- **CONTACT** Jane Butcher 01865 741317

Oxfordshire

- **SUBJECT**   Computing   **1117**
- **TITLE**   Introduction to Computing with Asian Language Support
- **PLACE**   Oxford Women's Training Scheme

Length Termly but open-ended   **Start** September, January, April   **Days** 2 hours/week
Cost Free   **Entry Reqs** None   **Award** Basic computing familiarity, introduction to WP, RSA,
CLAIT option, access to other courses   **Creche** Yes free

- **CONTACT**   Jane Butcher 01865 741317

- **SUBJECT**   Information Technology   **1118**
- **TITLE**   Computer Literacy/Information Technology
- **PLACE**   Rycotewood College

Length 20 weeks   **Start** September   **Days** 2 hours/week   **Cost** Varies   **Entry Reqs** No
restriction   **Award** RSA CLAIT Stage 1/RSA Information Technology Stage 2   **Creche** No

- **CONTACT**   Pam Kermode 01844 212501

- **SUBJECT**   Information Technology   **1119**
- **TITLE**   Information Technology (City & Guilds)
- **PLACE**   Abingdon College

Length 1 year   **Start** September   **Days** Mon-Fri 9.30-3.00   **Cost** Contact College   **Entry
Reqs** None   **Award** City & Guilds Certificate   **Creche** Yes Contact College

- **CONTACT**   Jill James 01235 555585

- **SUBJECT**   Languages   **1120**
- **TITLE**   English as a Second Language
- **PLACE**   Oxford Women's Training Scheme

Length Termly but open-ended   **Start** September, January, April, but flexible   **Days** 2
hours/week   **Cost** Free   **Entry Reqs** None   **Award** Increased confidence in speaking/
writing English   **Creche** Yes free

- **CONTACT**   Jane Butcher 01865 741317

- **SUBJECT**   Languages   **1121**
- **TITLE**   Language Workshop
- **PLACE**   Abingdon College

Length 8-week blocks, part time   **Start** Roll-on, roll-off   **Days** Mon 1.30-4.30, 6.30-9.00/Tues
1.30-4.30/Wed 9.15-12.15, 1.30-4.30   **Cost** Contact College   **Entry Reqs** None   **Award** RSA.
GCSE, A Level (or none) by agreement   **Creche** Yes Contact College

- **CONTACT**   Mike Bloom 01235 555585 x229

- **SUBJECT**   NOW   **1122**
- **TITLE**   New Opportunities for Women
- **PLACE**   WEA Various locations in Oxfordshire

Length 10 weeks   **Start** Oct, Nov, Jan, Feb, March   **Days** Tues, Wed or Thurs 9.30-2.30
Cost Free   **Entry Reqs** None   **Award** 2 credits Levels 1/2 Oxon Open College Network
Creche Yes free

- **CONTACT**   Annie Winner 01865 361544

- **SUBJECT**   Office Skills   **1123**
- **TITLE**   Office Skills Workshop
- **PLACE**   Abingdon College

Length 1 term   **Start** Termly   **Days** Tues, Thurs 9.30-11.30/Tues 6.30-8.30   **Cost** Contact
College   **Entry Reqs** None   **Creche** Yes Contact College

- **CONTACT**   Janet Bracher 01235 555585 x261

- **SUBJECT** Practical 1124
- **TITLE** Home Maintenance
- **PLACE** Oxford Women's Training Scheme

Length Termly (12 weeks) **Start** September, January, April **Days** 5 hours/week **Cost** Free **Entry Reqs** None **Award** Confidence in tackling practical jobs at home **Creche** Yes free

- **CONTACT** Jane Butcher 01865 741317

- **SUBJECT** Practical 1125
- **TITLE** Painting & Decorating
- **PLACE** Oxford Women's Training Scheme

Length 4 terms **Start** September, January, April **Days** Term 1:Mon+Tues 9.30-2.30/Terms 2, 3, 4:Wed-Fri 9.30-2.30 **Cost** Free **Entry Reqs** Interest in entering painting and decorating trade **Award** C&G 6000 series **Creche** Free childcare. Contact Training Scheme

- **CONTACT** Jude Housago 01865 741317

- **SUBJECT** Practical 1126
- **TITLE** Woodworking Skills
- **PLACE** Oxford Women's Training Scheme

Length 12 weeks+12 weeks+3 terms **Start** September, January, April **Days** 2 days/week **Cost** Free **Entry Reqs** Interest in woodworking **Award** Open College Network accreditation throughout **Creche** Childcare allowance

- **CONTACT** Jane Butcher 01865 741317

- **SUBJECT** Preparatory 1127
- **TITLE** Basic Mathematics
- **PLACE** Oxford Women's Training Scheme

Length Termly but open-ended **Start** September, January, April **Days** Thurs (3 hours/week) **Cost** Free **Entry Reqs** None **Award** Individual objectives negotiated with tutor, optional Numberpower **Creche** No, subject to demand

- **CONTACT** Jane Butcher 01865 741317

- **SUBJECT** Preparatory 1128
- **TITLE** Next Step: Pre Access/Study Skills
- **PLACE** Abingdon College

Length 8 weeks **Start** Termly **Days** Variable **Cost** Free **Entry Reqs** None **Award** Pre Access Certificate **Creche** Yes Contact College

- **CONTACT** Student Services 01235 555585

- **SUBJECT** Preparatory 1129
- **TITLE** Return to Learn
- **PLACE** WEA Various locations in Oxfordshire

Length 10 weeks **Start** September, January, April **Days** Various days/eves 9.30-11.30, 7.00-9.00 **Cost** Free **Entry Reqs** None **Award** 1 credit Level 1/2 Oxon Open College Network **Creche** Yes free

- **CONTACT** 01865 361544

- **SUBJECT**   Professional Updating/Career Development   **1130**
- **TITLE**   Career Development Programme for Women
- **PLACE**   Westminster College and other Training Centres

Length 18 weeks   **Start** March, September   **Days** 18 x 1 day workshops   **Cost** Free for people not in paid employment   **Entry Reqs** None, good command of English necessary **Award** College Certificate, CATS Accreditation   **Creche** No
- **CONTACT**   Isabel Morris 01865 247644 x3293

- **SUBJECT**   Science   **1131**
- **TITLE**   Integrative Bioscience: Masters Degree by Research
- **PLACE**   University of Oxford

Length 1 year   **Start** October   **Cost** Biotechnology & Biological Sciences Research Council award available   **Entry Reqs** Graduates with first or upper second class honours degree in an appropriate subject   **Award** MSc
- **CONTACT**   Dr V Essex, BBSRC, 01793 413200

- **SUBJECT**   Science   **1132**
- **TITLE**   Neurosciences: Research Masters Pilot Course
- **PLACE**   University of Oxford

Length 1 year   **Start** October   **Cost** Medical Research Council award available   **Entry Reqs** Graduates with first or upper second class honours degree in an appropriate subject   **Award** MSc
- **CONTACT**   Mrs K Hartwell 01865 272497

- **SUBJECT**   Teaching   **1133**
- **TITLE**   Advice & Guidance for Mature Students Considering Teaching/Returning to Teaching
- **PLACE**   Department of Continuing Education, Westminster College

Length Ongoing   **Days** Counsellors generally available for regular briefing & information packs   **Entry Reqs** GCSE Maths & English   **Creche** Yes halfterm only £1/half day
- **CONTACT**   Alison Heynes 01865 247644 x3295

- **SUBJECT**   Teaching   **1134**
- **TITLE**   Specialist Teacher Assistant Certificate
- **PLACE**   Westminster College

Length 1 year   **Start** October   **Days** 15 days in College (fortnightly) 2 days/week school placement   **Cost** DFEE funded   **Entry Reqs** GCSE or equivalent English & Maths   **Award** Westminster Specialist Teacher Assistant Certificate   **Creche** No
- **CONTACT**   Carolyn Brooks 01865 247644 x3291

COUNTY CONTACTS

Open University:

The Open University, South Region, Foxcombe Hall, Boars Hill, Oxford OX1 5HR 01865 328038

Other agencies:

Oxford Women's Training Centre, Northway Centre, Maltfield Road, Oxford OX3 9RF 01865 741317. Women's training centre

Training and Enterprise Council:

Heart of England TEC, 26-27 The Quadrant, Abingdon Science Park, Off Barton Lane, Abingdon OX14 3YS 01235 553249

WEA office:

WEA Thames and Solent District, 6 Brewer Street, Oxford OX1 1QN 01865 246270   *Contact* Annie Winner

---

SHROPSHIRE

COURSES

- **SUBJECT**   Access/Health Studies/Science   **1135**
- **TITLE**   Access to Higher Education: Health Care and Science
- **PLACE**   Shrewsbury College of Arts & Technology, London Road & Radbrook
Length 1 year   **Start** September   **Days** Mon-Fri 9.30-3.00 (21 hours/week)   **Cost** Free   **Entry Reqs** None   **Award** Access qualification   **Creche** Yes free
- **CONTACT**   Dave Owen 01743 231544 x254

- **SUBJECT**   Access/Humanities/Social Science   **1136**
- **TITLE**   Access to Higher Education: Humanities and Social Science
- **PLACE**   Shrewsbury College of Arts & Technology, London Road & Radbrook
Length 1 year   **Start** September   **Days** Mon-Fri 9.30-3.00 (21 hours/week)   **Cost** Free   **Entry Reqs** None, 21+   **Award** Access qualification   **Creche** Yes free
- **CONTACT**   Linda Ackroyd 01743 231544

- **SUBJECT**   Access/Art/Design/Humanities/Nursing/Technology   **1137**
- **TITLE**   Access to Higher Education: 1. Humanities 2. Nursing 3. Art, Design & Technology
- **PLACE**   Telford College of Arts & Technology
Length 10 months   **Start** September   **Days** 9.30-2.45   **Cost** £5   **Entry Reqs** None   **Award** Black Country Access Federation Diploma which gives access to HE   **Creche** Yes £1/hour
- **CONTACT**   Student Services 01952 642237

- **SUBJECT**   Office Skills/Secretarial   **1138**
- **TITLE**   Office and Secretarial Studies
- **PLACE**   Telford College of Arts & Technology
Length Flexible   **Start** September, flexible   **Days** Flexible modules of 20 hours/term   **Cost** £65 for 20 hours   **Entry Reqs** Depends on module chosen   **Award** Exams taken as appropriate   **Creche** Yes £1/hour
- **CONTACT**   J Ellis 01952 642237

COUNTY CONTACTS

Information and advice:

North Shropshire College, College Road, Oswestry SY11 2SA 01691 653017
Shrewsbury College of Arts & Technology, London Road, Shrewsbury SY2 6PR 01743 231544
Telford College of Arts & Technology, Haybridge Road, Wellington, Telford 01952 642237

Open University:

The Open University. West Midlands Region, 66-68 High Street, Harborne, Birmingham B17 9NB 0121 428 1550

Training and Enterprise Council:

Shropshire TEC, Trevithick House, Stafford Park 4, Telford TF3 3BA 01952 208200   *Contact:* Simon Kite
Series of workshops and courses specifically for women wishing to start a business. Courses cover business idea generation and production of a business plan. One to one counselling support

WEA office:

WEA West Mercia District, 78/80 Sherlock Street, Birmingham B5 6LT 0121 666 6101   *Contact:* Jill Bedford

---

SOMERSET

COURSES

- **SUBJECT**   Access   **1139**
- **TITLE**   Access to Higher Education
- **PLACE**   Somerset College of Arts & Technology

Length 1 year   **Start** September   **Days** 4 days/week 9.30-3.00   **Cost** Contact College. Fees waived if in receipt of certain benefits   **Entry Reqs** None   **Award** Kitemarked Access Certificate   **Creche** Yes fees vary

- **CONTACT** Course Enquiry Service 01823 238403

- **SUBJECT**   Access   **1140**
- **TITLE**   Access to Higher Education
- **PLACE**   Strode College

Length 3 terms   **Start** October   **Days** 3-4 days/week   **Cost** £370   **Entry Reqs** By interview   **Award** Access Certificate, entry to higher education   **Creche** Yes Free

- **CONTACT** Judith Crawford 01458 844400

- **SUBJECT**   Access   **1141**
- **TITLE**   Access to Higher Education
- **PLACE**   Yeovil College

Length 1 year   **Start** September   **Days** Full time, daytime   **Cost** Contact College. LEA grants available   **Entry Reqs** None   **Award** Entry to higher education   **Creche** Yes

- **CONTACT** Course Information 01935 23921

- **SUBJECT**   Access/Mathematics/Physics   **1142**
- **TITLE**   Access to Mathematics & Physics
- **PLACE**   Somerset College of Arts & Technology

Length 1 term   **Start** April   **Days** 4 days/week 9.30-3.30   **Cost** Contact College. Fees waived if in receipt of certain benefits   **Entry Reqs** None   **Award** Open College Credits   **Creche** Yes fees vary

- **CONTACT** Course Enquiry Service 01823 238403

- **SUBJECT**   Multi-Subject   1143
- **TITLE**   Modular Degree, HND, Dip HE, Certificate, Postgraduate Courses
- **PLACE**   University of Plymouth, at centres in Somerset

Length Flexible   **Start** Flexible   **Cost** Contact University   **Entry Reqs** Mature students positively encouraged to apply with appropriate life/work experience   **Award** Degree, HND, Dip HE, University Certificate, Postgraduate qualifications
- **CONTACT**   Mature Student Enquiry Service 01752 232382

- **SUBJECT**   NOW   1144
- **TITLE**   Opportunities for Women
- **PLACE**   Strode College

Length Varies   **Start** Various   **Cost** Various   **Entry Reqs** Contact College   **Award** Various

Creche Yes Free
- **CONTACT**   Paul Facey-Hunter 01458 844400

- **SUBJECT**   Preparatory   1145
- **TITLE**   Make Your Experience Count/Return to Learn
- **PLACE**   Various locations throughout Somerset

Length Flexible   **Start** Flexible   **Days** 2 hours/week days or eves   **Cost** £1/week Concessions available   **Entry Reqs** None   **Award** South West Access Federation Open College Credit Level I   **Creche** Yes free
- **CONTACT**   Mary Smith 01278 444883

- **SUBJECT**   Preparatory   1146
- **TITLE**   New Start
- **PLACE**   Strode College

Length Varies   **Start** Various   **Cost** Free   **Entry Reqs** Contact College   **Award** Various

Creche Yes Free
- **CONTACT**   Gwen Scriven 01458 844400

- **SUBJECT**   Preparatory   1147
- **TITLE**   Work Experience for Adults
- **PLACE**   Various locations throughout Somerset

Length 6 weeks including 1 week work experience   **Start** Flexible   **Days** 5 hours/week (except work experience)   **Cost** £1/week   **Entry Reqs** None   **Award** South West Access Federation 3 Credits Levels 1/2   **Creche** Help with childcare may be available
- **CONTACT**   Mary Smith 01278 444883

COUNTY CONTACTS

Information and advice

Bridgwater College, Bath Road, Bridgwater TA6 4PZ 01278 441243   *Contact:* Annette Rigler
Education Counselling Service (Adults), Student and Customer Services, Somerset College of Arts & Technology, Wellington Road, Taunton TA1 5AX 01823 366352   *Contact:* Shirley Stollery
Educational Guidance Service for Adults, Strode College, Church Road, Street BA16 0AB 01458 844418   *Contact:* Paul Facey-Hunter
Learning Advice Centre, 72 South Street, Yeovil BA20 1QF 01935 75283   *Contact:* Jean Hoskins
National Association for Educational Guidance for Adults, Regional representative, Street Careers Office, 6 Leigh Road, Street BA16 0HA 01458 443051   *Contact:* Janet Palmer. Covers western region

Somerset Careers, 2 Crescent House, The Mount, Taunton TA1 3TT 01823 289214   *Contact:* Phil Spooner. Careers information and guidance interviews (charges for some services; enquire at local offices)
4-6 East Quay, Bridgwater TA6 5AZ 01278 423788   *Contact:* Anne Clarke
40-42 Hendford, Yeovil BA20 1UW 01935 27511   *Contact:* John Volrath
6 Leigh Road, Street BA16 0HA 01458 43051   *Contact:* Janet Palmer
Northover House, North Parade, Frome BA11 1AU 01373 456302   *Contact:* Tina Trevett
Somerset Learning Advice Service, Adult Learning, Parkway, Bridgwater TA6 4RL 01278 444883 *Contact:* Val Saunders, Community Education Co-ordinator. Provides adult guidance, work experience, courses for adults, Make Your Experience Count courses.
The Opportunity Shop, 3 Mendip House, High Street, Taunton TA1 3SY 01823 321165. Run by Somerset TEC, provides careers information and guidance. Open Mon-Fri 9.30-5pm (8pm Thurs)

Open University

The Open University, South West Region, 4 Portwall Lane, Bristol BS1 6ND 0117 925 6523

Training and Enterprise Council

Somerset TEC, Crescent House, 5-7 The Mount, Taunton TA1 3TT 01823 321188

WEA office

WEA Western District, 40 Morse Road, Redfield, Bristol BS5 9LB 1007 935 1764   *Contact:* Mavis Zutchi, Kath Ryder

---

SOUTH YORKSHIRE

COURSES

- **SUBJECT**   Access   **1148**
- **TITLE**   Access to Higher Education
- **PLACE**   Rotherham College of Arts & Technology

Length 1 year full time or 2 years part time   **Start** September   **Days** Various   **Cost** Grant available   **Entry Reqs** 21+   **Award** SYOC Accreditation, access to higher education **Creche** Playgroup

- **CONTACT**   Access Course Administrator 01709 362111

- **SUBJECT**   Access   **1149**
- **TITLE**   Headway: Access to Higher Education
- **PLACE**   Doncaster College, High Melton Site

Length 3 terms (30 weeks)   **Start** September   **Days** Mon-Thurs 9.30-3.00   **Cost** Free **Entry Reqs** Age 21+, no formal qualifications   **Award** SYOC Accreditation, access to higher education   **Creche** Help with childcare is available

- **CONTACT**   H Gordon 01302 533612

- **SUBJECT**   Access   **1150**
- **TITLE**   Mature Access Programme
- **PLACE**   University of Sheffield

Length 2 years (5 terms)   **Start** October   **Days** 2 sessions/week   **Cost** Contact University **Entry Reqs** None   **Award** Preparation for higher education   **Creche** No

- **CONTACT**   Division of Continuing Education 0114 276 8555

- **SUBJECT**   Access/Management/Technology/Science/Mathematics   **1151**
- **TITLE**   Women into Management and Technology
- **PLACE**   Sheffield College, Parson Cross Centre, Colley Site

Length 36 weeks   **Start** September   **Days** Mon-Fri 9.15-2.45 term time only   **Cost** Remission for women on an income of less than £60/week or on benefit   **Entry Reqs** Determination to succeed and an ability to benefit   **Award** Validated DEC/Access Course with SYOCF credits at level 4   **Creche** Yes Small charge for refreshments

- **CONTACT**   Rita Murray or Student Services 0114 260 2502

- **SUBJECT**   Access/Multi-Subject   **1152**
- **TITLE**   Step Forward (Modular)
- **PLACE**   Sheffield College, Norton Centre

Length Modular, normally 1 year   **Start** September/flexible   **Days** Modules operate over 5 days   **Cost** Varies, fee remission for those on benefit   **Entry Reqs** None. Counselling and guidance provided. Minimum age 20   **Award** Open College accredited   **Creche** Yes 0-5 years. Nominal charge

- **CONTACT**   Dorothy Donnison 0114 260 2342

- **SUBJECT**   Access/Science/Social Science   **1153**
- **TITLE**   A Level Alternative Access for Adults
- **PLACE**   Sheffield College, Parkwood Centre

Length 1 year   **Start** September   **Days** Mon-Thurs, up to 20 hours/week   **Cost** Contact College   **Entry Reqs** Interview   **Award** Nationally recognised kitemarked course   **Creche** Yes Free (places limited)

- **CONTACT**   David Pickersgill 0114 260 2400

- **SUBJECT**   Administration/Secretarial   **1154**
- **TITLE**   Office Administration & New Technology
- **PLACE**   Doncaster College

Length 15 weeks   **Start** February, September   **Days** 4 days/week Mon-Thurs 9.30-3.30   **Cost** Free (ESF funding)   **Entry Reqs** None   **Award** Various including NEBSM, C&G, RSA   **Creche** Yes Contact College

- **CONTACT**   Christine Herzberg/Sue Hussain 01302 533667

- **SUBJECT**   Business Administration   **1155**
- **TITLE**   Higher Diploma in Administrative Procedures
- **PLACE**   Sheffield College, Parson Cross Centre

Length 1 year full time, longer part time   **Start** September   **Days** 25 hours/week including workshop full time or 15 hours/week part time   **Cost** £683 Remission for women on benefit or earning under £60/week   **Entry Reqs** Usually 2 A Levels or equiv, women returning/changing direction, suitable for graduates   **Award** RSA Higher Diploma in Administrative Procedures   **Creche** Yes Small charge for refreshments

- **CONTACT**   Mary Prentice 0114 260 2502

- **SUBJECT**   Combined Studies   **1156**
- **TITLE**   1. BA Combined Studies 2. DipHE in Playwork
- **PLACE**   Sheffield College, Norton Centre

Length 1 year at Norton Centre then progress to HE for 2 years   **Start** September   **Days** Mon-Fri   **Cost** Mandatory award available   **Entry Reqs** Access Certificate, BTEC National, relevant work experience   **Award** 1. BA Combined Studies 2. DipHE in Playwork   **Creche** Yes

- **CONTACT**   1. Dorothy Donnison 2. Jackie Kivington 0114 260 2300

- **SUBJECT** Engineering   **1157**
- **TITLE** Foundation Year in Engineering
- **PLACE** Sheffield Hallam University

Length 1 year   **Start** September   **Days** Full time   **Cost** Mandatory grant available   **Entry Reqs** By interview   **Award** Engineering Diploma & Foundation Year, entry to degree/diploma courses   **Creche** Yes Limited availability

- **CONTACT** Access and Guidance Services 0114 253 3089

- **SUBJECT** Office Skills   **1158**
- **TITLE** Women's Office Skills and Technology
- **PLACE** Sheffield College, Parson Cross Centre

Length 18 weeks   **Start** September, February   **Days** Mon-Fri 9.15-2.45 term time only   **Cost** £246 Remission of fees for women on benefit or earning under £60/week.   **Entry Reqs** Determination, keyboard skills, previous office/commercial experience   **Award** RSA Certificates, NVQ Levels I, II & III   **Creche** Yes Small charge for refreshments

- **CONTACT** Shirley Mercer or Student Services 0114 260 2502

- **SUBJECT** Practical   **1159**
- **TITLE** Painting and Decorating, Signwork
- **PLACE** Doncaster College, Bessacarr Site

Length 26-52 weeks   **Start** Anytime   **Days** Mon-Fri 35 hours/week   **Cost** Funding through local TEC   **Entry Reqs** None   **Award** NVQ I/II/III   **Creche** Yes in main college

- **CONTACT** Frank Gorbutt 01302 553839

- **SUBJECT** Preparatory   **1160**
- **TITLE** Making Choices: Return to Work or Training, Confidence Raising
- **PLACE** Loxley College, various sites

Length 10 weeks   **Start** Termly   **Days** 2 hours/week, day & time varies termly   **Cost** None   **Entry Reqs** Basic literacy   **Award** 1 or 2 SYOCF Level 1 or 2 credits (if required)   **Creche** Yes Charge for refreshments only

- **CONTACT** Liz Cousins 0114 260 2200

- **SUBJECT** Science   **1161**
- **TITLE** Foundation Year in Science
- **PLACE** Sheffield College, Parkwood Centre

Length 1 year   **Start** September   **Days** Mon-Fri (20 hours/week)   **Cost** Mandatory grant available   **Entry Reqs** Interview   **Award** Foundation Year in Science Diploma; entry to School of Science at Sheffield Hallam University   **Creche** Yes Free

- **CONTACT** Kevin Richardson 0114 260 2400

- **SUBJECT** Science   **1162**
- **TITLE** Foundation Year in Science
- **PLACE** Sheffield Hallam University

Length 1 year   **Start** September   **Days** Full time   **Cost** Mandatory grant available   **Entry Reqs** By interview   **Award** Engineering Diploma & Foundation Year, entry to degree/diploma courses   **Creche** Yes Limited availability

- **CONTACT** Access and Guidance Services 0114 253 3089

- **SUBJECT** Science   **1163**
- **TITLE** Materials. Structures and Systems Engineering: Research Masters Pilot Course
- **PLACE** University of Sheffield

Length 2 years   **Start** October   **Cost** Engineering & Physical Sciences Research Council award available   **Entry Reqs** Graduates with first or upper second class honours degree in an appropriate subject   **Award** Master of Research Degree

- **CONTACT** Dr A Patterson 0114 282 5417

- **SUBJECT** Social Studies **1164**
- **TITLE** BA (Hons) Applied Social Studies
- **PLACE** Sheffield Hallam University, Collegiate Crescent Campus

Length 3 years full time, 2-6 years part time **Start** September **Days** Full time 5 days/week, part time variable. Evening only available **Cost** Part time £130 per 20 credit unit **Entry Reqs** Contact Admissions Office **Award** BA (Hons)/Diploma/Certificate **Creche** Yes, contact Nursery on 0114 253 2513 for fees
- **CONTACT** Admissions Office 0114 253 2169

- **SUBJECT** Women's Studies **1165**
- **TITLE** BA (Hons) Women's Studies
- **PLACE** Sheffield Hallam University, Collegiate Crescent Campus

Length 3 years full time, 5 years part time **Start** September **Days** 5 days/week **Cost** Contact University **Entry Reqs** Contact University **Award** BA (Hons) Women's Studies **Creche** Yes, contact Nursery on 0114 253 2513 for fees
- **CONTACT** Jill Le Bihan 0114 253 2223

COUNTY CONTACTS

Information and advice

Adult Guidance Service, Careers Advice and Guidance, Priory Campus, Pontefract Road, Lundwood, Barnsley S71 5PN 01226 770622   *Contact:* Amanda Green, Sue Sheridan
Doncaster Careers Service, Careers Centre, 24 Thorne Road, Doncaster DN1 2DH 01302 734243   *Contact:* Linda Orridge
REGA (Rotherham Educational Guidance for Adults), Starting Point, Eastwood Lane, Rotherham S65 1EG 01709 722820   *Contact:* Any Adult Adviser
Sheffield Careers Service for Adults, 42 Union Street, Sheffield S1 2JP 0114 273 5482

Open University

The Open University. Yorkshire Region, 2 Trevelyan Square, Boar Lane, Leeds LS1 6ED 0113 245 1466

Other agencies

Chamber of Commerce Training, Industry House, Summer Lane, Barnsley 01226 733838   *Contact:* Alice Clifford

Training and Enterprise Councils

Barnsley and Doncaster TEC, The Conference Centre, Eldon Street, Barnsley S70 2JL 01226 248088. Opportunity to access NVQ Business Adminstration Level II/III with local training provider
Rotherham TEC, Moorgate House, Moorgate Road, Rotherham S60 2EN 01709 830511
Sheffield TEC, St Mary's Court, 55 St Mary's Road, Sheffield S2 4AQ 0114 270 1911

WEA office

WEA Yorkshire South District, Chantry Buildings, 6-20 Corporation Street, Rotherham S60 1NG 01709 837001   *Contact:* Trish Lands

Publications

Women's Courses in Sheffield, Produced by Sheffield Careers Service, free of charge. Please send a large SAE for a copy.

COURSES

- **SUBJECT** Access   **1166**
- **TITLE** Access to Higher Education
- **PLACE** Newcastle under Lyme College

Length 1-2 years   **Start** September   **Days** Full time or part time   **Cost** Full time free if Staffs resident, part time £150/year payable termly (£50/term)   **Entry Reqs** None   **Award** Access Certificate, valid entry qualification for higher education   **Creche** Yes £6/3 hours, £2/3 hours if on benefit

- **CONTACT** Marion Bowler 01782 715111

- **SUBJECT** Access   **1167**
- **TITLE** Access to Higher Education
- **PLACE** Tamworth College, Tamworth & Lichfield Centres

Length 1 year   **Start** September   **Cost** Contact College   **Entry Reqs** 21+   **Award** Access to higher education   **Creche** Yes

- **CONTACT** Information Centre 01827 310202

- **SUBJECT** Access/English/History/Science/Psychology/Social Science   **1168**
- **TITLE** Access to Higher Education (Part Time Programme)
- **PLACE** Burton Technical College, Burton, Ashby, Etwall Centres

Length 1 year   **Start** September, February   **Days** Mon-Thurs 6.00-9.00   **Cost** Approx £160 May be free, contact College   **Entry Reqs** None, but must be able to cope with academic work   **Award** NEMAP Certificate of entry to Higher Education   **Creche** No

- **CONTACT** Linda Wyatt 01283 545401 x245

- **SUBJECT** Access/History/Science/Social Science/Psychology/English   **1169**
- **TITLE** Access to Anatomy & Physiology, History, Sociology, Psychology, Literature
- **PLACE** Stoke on Trent College

Length 1 year   **Start** September   **Days** Part time day or evening   **Cost** Contact College   **Entry Reqs** No formal qualifications   **Award** Access to higher education   **Creche** Yes

- **CONTACT** Central Enquiries 01782 208208

- **SUBJECT** Access/Humanities/Science/Social Science/Business/Computing   **1170**
- **TITLE** Modular Access Programme
- **PLACE** Burton Technical College, Burton & Rolleston

Length 1 year full time   **Start** September, February   **Days** Mon-Fri 10.00-3.00   **Cost** Free   **Entry Reqs** Age 21+, no formal qualifications but must be able to cope with academic work   **Award** NEMAP Certificate of entry to Higher Education   **Creche** Yes

- **CONTACT** Linda Wyatt 01283 545401 x245

- **SUBJECT** Accounting   **1171**
- **TITLE** Association of Accounting Technicians
- **PLACE** Tamworth College

Length 1, 2, or 3 years, depending on level   **Start** September   **Days** Mon-Fri 10.15-3.15   **Cost** Contact College   **Entry Reqs** Basic numeracy and communication skills   **Award** Membership of AAT and NVQ II, III, IV   **Creche** Yes

- **CONTACT** Information Centre 01827 310202

- **SUBJECT** Administration   **1172**
- **TITLE** Administration
- **PLACE** Stoke on Trent College

Length 1-2 years   **Start** September   **Days** Full time   **Cost** Contact College   **Entry Reqs** Contact College. No formal qualifications   **Award** NVQ Level II   **Creche** Yes

- **CONTACT** Central Enquiries 01782 208208

- **SUBJECT** Administration/Information Technology   **1173**
- **TITLE** Return to Work: Administration and Information Technology
- **PLACE** Stoke on Trent College

Length 36 weeks   **Start** September   **Days** 16 hours/week   **Cost** Contact College   **Entry Reqs** Interview. No formal qualifications   **Award** Range of qualifications available   **Creche** Yes

- **CONTACT** Central Enquiries 01782 208208

- **SUBJECT** Agriculture/Horticulture   **1174**
- **TITLE** Various Land-Based Courses to suit client needs & circumstances
- **PLACE** Rodbaston College, Penkridge

Length Flexible   **Start** Flexible   **Days** According to student needs   **Cost** Negotiable. Funding sources identified if possible   **Creche** Yes and playgroup, locally

- **CONTACT** Christine Duffield 01785 712209

- **SUBJECT** Beauty Therapy   **1175**
- **TITLE** Beauty Therapy for Mature Students
- **PLACE** Stoke on Trent College

Length 1 year   **Start** September   **Cost** Contact College   **Entry Reqs** No formal qualifications   **Award** C&G NVQ Level II   **Creche** Yes

- **CONTACT** Central Enquiries 01782 208208

- **SUBJECT** Business   **1176**
- **TITLE** BTEC National Certificate Business and Finance
- **PLACE** Stoke on Trent College

Length 1 year   **Start** September   **Days** Mon or Tues   **Cost** £82   **Entry Reqs** Contact College   **Award** BTEC National Certificate   **Creche** Yes

- **CONTACT** Central Enquiries 01782 208208

- **SUBJECT** Business   **1177**
- **TITLE** Customer Service
- **PLACE** Stoke on Trent College

Length 1 year   **Start** September   **Days** 1 day or 1 eve/week (4 hours/week)   **Cost** £110   **Entry Reqs** Contact College   **Award** NVQ Level III   **Creche** Yes

- **CONTACT** Central Enquiries 01782 208208

- **SUBJECT** Business   **1178**
- **TITLE** 1. GNVQ Intermediate Business 2. BTEC HND Business 3. BTEC HND Business and Finance
- **PLACE** Stoke on Trent College

Length 1.1 year 2. &3.2 years   **Start** September   **Days** Full time   **Cost** Contact College   **Entry Reqs** Contact College. Mature students welcome   **Award** 1. GNVQ Intermediate 2. BTEC HND Business 3. BTEC HND Business and Finance   **Creche** Yes

- **CONTACT** Central Enquiries 01782 208208

Staffordshire

- **SUBJECT** Business Administration   **1179**
- **TITLE** 1. Higher Diploma (NVQ 4) Administrative Procedures 2. NVQ 2/3 Business Administration
- **PLACE** Tamworth College 1. Tamworth 2. Lichfield

Start September   **Cost** Contact College   **Entry Reqs** Contact College. Mature students welcome   **Award** 1. NVQ 4/Higher Diploma 2. NVQ 2/3   **Creche** Yes

- **CONTACT** Information Centre 01827 310202

- **SUBJECT** Business Studies   **1180**
- **TITLE** BA Business Studies
- **PLACE** Tamworth College in conjunction with Staffordshire University

Length Year 1 at Tamworth College   **Start** September   **Cost** Contact College   **Entry Reqs** Contact College. Mature students welcome   **Award** Progress to years 2&3 at Staffordshire University leading to BA Business Studies   **Creche** Yes

- **CONTACT** Information Centre 01827 310202

- **SUBJECT** Business Studies   **1181**
- **TITLE** Training for Small Business and Self-Employment
- **PLACE** Tamworth College

Length Modular   **Start** Varies   **Cost** Contact College   **Entry Reqs** Contact College   **Creche** Yes

- **CONTACT** Information Centre 01827 310202

- **SUBJECT** Childcare   **1182**
- **TITLE** Certificate in Childcare and Education
- **PLACE** Tamworth College, Lichfield Centre

Length 1 year   **Start** September   **Cost** Contact College   **Entry Reqs** Contact College. Mature students welcome   **Award** NVQ II

- **CONTACT** Information Centre 01827 310202

- **SUBJECT** Childcare   **1183**
- **TITLE** Extended Diploma in Nursery Nursing
- **PLACE** Stoke on Trent College

Length 2 years+1 term   **Start** September   **Cost** Contact College   **Entry Reqs** Interview, GCSEs. Suitable for people with family commitments   **Award** NNEB Diploma   **Creche** Yes

- **CONTACT** Central Enquiries 01782 208208

- **SUBJECT** Computing   **1184**
- **TITLE** BTEC HNC Computer Studies
- **PLACE** Tamworth College

Length Contact College   **Start** September   **Cost** £401.90   **Entry Reqs** Contact College   **Award** BTEC HNC   **Creche** Yes

- **CONTACT** Information Centre 01827 310202

- **SUBJECT** Hairdressing   **1185**
- **TITLE** Hairdressing for Mature Students
- **PLACE** Stoke on Trent College

Length 2 years   **Start** September   **Cost** Contact College   **Entry Reqs** No formal qualifications   **Award** C&G NVQ Level II   **Creche** Yes

- **CONTACT** Central Enquiries 01782 208208

- **SUBJECT** Information Technology   **1186**
- **TITLE** Business Information Technology
- **PLACE** Tamworth College

Length 2 years   **Start** September   **Cost** Contact College   **Entry Reqs** Contact College. Mature students welcome   **Award** Coventry University/BTEC HND   **Creche** Yes

- **CONTACT** Information Centre 01827 310202

- **SUBJECT** Information Technology   1187
- **TITLE** Graduates Programme in Information Technology
- **PLACE** Stoke on Trent College

Length 1 year **Start** September **Days** Full time **Cost** Contact College **Entry Reqs** HNC/HND/first degree in other subjects **Award** C&G Advanced Diploma in Computer Applications **Creche** Yes
- **CONTACT** Central Enquiries 01782 208208

- **SUBJECT** Information Technology   1188
- **TITLE** Information Technology (Open Learning)
- **PLACE** Stoke on Trent College

Length Flexible **Start** Varies **Days** Flexible **Cost** Contact College **Entry Reqs** No formal qualifications **Creche** Yes
- **CONTACT** Central Enquiries 01782 208208

- **SUBJECT** Information Technology   1189
- **TITLE** Introductory Computing
- **PLACE** Tamworth College 1. Tamworth 2. Lichfield

Length 24 weeks **Days** 1. Thurs 11.15-1.15 2. Tues 10.00-12 **Cost** £54.56 **Entry Reqs** Contact College **Award** RSA CLAIT **Creche** Yes
- **CONTACT** Information Centre 01827 310202

- **SUBJECT** Information Technology   1190
- **TITLE** Return to Work in Information Technology
- **PLACE** Stoke on Trent College

Length 1 year **Start** September **Days** 16 hours/week **Cost** Contact College **Entry Reqs** Interview. No formal qualifications **Award** C&G Diploma in Computer Application **Creche** Yes
- **CONTACT** Central Enquiries 01782 208208

- **SUBJECT** Management   1191
- **TITLE** 1. BTEC GNVQ Management 2. BTEC HNC Management
- **PLACE** Tamworth College

Length 2 years **Start** September **Cost** Contact College **Entry Reqs** Contact College **Award** 1. BTEC GNVQ 2. BTEC HNC **Creche** Yes
- **CONTACT** Information Centre 01827 310202

- **SUBJECT** Management   1192
- **TITLE** 1. NEBSM Introductory Award 2. Certificate in Supervisory Management
- **PLACE** Stoke on Trent College

Length 1.13 weeks 2.34 weeks **Days** 1. Thurs 6.00-9.00 2.7 hours/week day or eve **Cost** 1. Free 2. £102 **Entry Reqs** No formal qualifications. Age 21+ **Award** 1. NEBSM Introductory Award 2. NEBSM Certificate in Supervisory Management **Creche** Yes
- **CONTACT** Central Enquiries 01782 208208

- **SUBJECT** Manufacturing   1193
- **TITLE** Return to Work: Manufacturing
- **PLACE** Stoke on Trent College

Length 1 year **Start** September **Cost** Contact College **Entry Reqs** Interview. No formal qualifications **Creche** Yes
- **CONTACT** Central Enquiries 01782 208208

- **SUBJECT** Office Skills   1194
- **TITLE** Beginners Shorthand, Typewriting & Word Processing for the Mature Student
- **PLACE** Tamworth College

Days Mon & Wed 10.15-3.15 **Cost** £269/20 **Entry Reqs** Contact College **Creche** Yes
- **CONTACT** Information Centre 01827 310202

- **SUBJECT** Office Skills   1195
- **TITLE** Return to Work: Medical Reception
- **PLACE** Stoke on Trent College

Length 1 year   **Start** September   **Days** 16 hours/week   **Cost** Contact College   **Entry Reqs** Contact College. Mature students welcome   **Creche** Yes
- **CONTACT** Central Enquiries 01782 208208

- **SUBJECT** Office Skills   1196
- **TITLE** Intensive Programme for Graduates
- **PLACE** Stoke on Trent College

Length 1 year   **Start** September   **Days** Full time   **Cost** Contact College   **Entry Reqs** First degree, Certificate in Education, BTEC Higher National   **Award** RSA Single Subject exams **Creche** Yes
- **CONTACT** Central Enquiries 01782 208208

- **SUBJECT** Preparatory   1197
- **TITLE** Access to Further Education
- **PLACE** Tamworth College

Length 10 weeks   **Start** September, January, April   **Cost** Contact College   **Entry Reqs** Contact College   **Award** Access to further education courses   **Creche** Yes
- **CONTACT** Information Centre 01827 310202

- **SUBJECT** Preparatory   1198
- **TITLE** Forward to New Skills
- **PLACE** Tamworth College

Start Contact College   **Cost** Contact College   **Entry Reqs** Contact College. Mature students welcome   **Creche** Yes
- **CONTACT** Information Centre 01827 310202

- **SUBJECT** Preparatory   1199
- **TITLE** Way Ahead
- **PLACE** Newcastle under Lyme College

Length 4 weeks   **Days** 3 days/week 10.00-3.00   **Cost** £3 registration   **Entry Reqs** None
- **CONTACT** Marion Bowler 01782 715111

- **SUBJECT** Science   1200
- **TITLE** Foundation Year to Degree in Science, Engineering and Applied Science
- **PLACE** Tamworth College in conjunction with Coventry University

Length Year 1 at Tamworth College   **Start** September   **Cost** Contact College   **Entry Reqs** Contact College. Mature students welcome   **Award** Progress to further study for degrees at Coventry University   **Creche** Yes
- **CONTACT** Information Centre 01827 310202

- **SUBJECT** Secretarial   1201
- **TITLE** 1. General Secretarial 2. Medical Secretarial
- **PLACE** Tamworth College

Start September   **Cost** Contact College   **Entry Reqs** Contact College. Mature students welcome   **Award** 1. NVQ 2   **Creche** Yes
- **CONTACT** Information Centre 01827 310202

- **SUBJECT** Technology   1202
- **TITLE** Women into Technology
- **PLACE** Stoke on Trent College

Length 1 year   **Start** September   **Days** Full time   **Cost** Contact College   **Entry Reqs** Contact College. Mature students welcome   **Award** BTEC National Certificate   **Creche** Yes
- **CONTACT** Central Enquiries 01782 208208

- **SUBJECT** Tourism & Leisure   **1203**
- **TITLE** Association of British Travel Agents (ABTAC) Primary
- **PLACE** Stoke on Trent College

Length 30 weeks   **Start** September   **Days** Tues (4 hours/week)   **Cost** £90   **Entry Reqs** No formal qualifications. Suitable for work returners or those seeking a career change **Award** ABTAC Primary Award   **Creche** Yes

- **CONTACT** Central Enquiries 01782 208208

COUNTY CONTACTS

Information and advice

Staffordshire Careers Service Adult Guidance, Careers Headquarters, Old Education Offices, Earl Street, Stafford ST16 2DJ 01785 223121 x8734   *Contact:* Eileen Manley

Open University

The Open University, East Midlands Region, The Octagon, 143 Derby Road, Nottingham NG7 1PH 0115 924 0121. Covers Burton on Trent area
West Midlands Region, 66-68 High Street, Harborne, Birmingham B17 9NB 0121 428 1550. Covers most of Staffordshire

Training and Enterprise Council

Staffordshire TEC, Festival Way, Festival Park, Stoke on Trent ST1 5TQ 01782 202733

WEA office

WEA West Mercia District, 78/80 Sherlock Street, Birmingham B5 6LT 0121 666 6101   *Contact:* Jill Bedford

SUFFOLK

COURSES

- **SUBJECT** Access   **1204**
- **TITLE** Access to Higher Education
- **PLACE** Suffolk College

Length 1 year   **Start** September   **Days** Full time   **Cost** Contact College   **Entry Reqs** No formal requirements. Age 21+   **Award** Access Certificate

- **CONTACT** Marketing Unit 01473 255885

- **SUBJECT** Access/Humanities/Social Science/Health Studies/Business Studies/   **1205**
            Management
- **TITLE** Access to 1. Higher Education 2. Health Professions
- **PLACE** West Suffolk College

Length 1 year   **Start** September   **Cost** Contact College   **Entry Reqs** No formal requirements. Interview. Age 21+   **Award** Access to 1. degree level study in Humanities/ Social Science/Business 2. Health Care professions   **Creche** Yes

- **CONTACT** Infoline 01284 716344

- **SUBJECT** Access/Humanities/Social Studies/Science/Technology **1206**
- **TITLE** Access to Humanities and Social Studies, Life Science, Technology
- **PLACE** Lowestoft College

Length 1 year **Start** September **Cost** Contact College **Entry Reqs** No formal requirements. Age 21+ **Award** Access to higher education **Creche** Yes
- **CONTACT** Information Centre 01502 583521

- **SUBJECT** Access/Social Science **1207**
- **TITLE** Access to Social Science: Part Time
- **PLACE** Lowestoft College

Start September **Days** Part time **Cost** Contact College **Entry Reqs** No formal requirements. Age 21+ **Award** Access to Social Science degree courses **Creche** Yes
- **CONTACT** Information Centre 01502 583521

- **SUBJECT** Administration **1208**
- **TITLE** Administrative Procedures
- **PLACE** West Suffolk College

Length Modules of 12 weeks x 3 hours **Start** Flexible **Days** Mondays **Cost** £90/module **Entry Reqs** Experience of working and supervising in admin environment **Award** RSA Higher Diploma in Administrative Procedures **Creche** Yes
- **CONTACT** Elizabeth Smith 01284 701301 x252

- **SUBJECT** Administration **1209**
- **TITLE** Administrative Studies
- **PLACE** Suffolk College

Length 1 year **Start** September **Days** Full time **Cost** Contact College **Entry Reqs** Contact College **Award** RSA Higher National Diploma
- **CONTACT** Marketing Unit 01473 255885

- **SUBJECT** Administration **1210**
- **TITLE** Evening Courses in WP, Computing, Typing/Audiotyping, Shorthand, Keyboarding
- **PLACE** West Suffolk College

Length 1 year **Start** September **Days** Weekdays 7.00-9.00 **Cost** According to subject and duration **Entry Reqs** None: can enrol for one or several courses **Award** RSA & Pitman single subjects **Creche** Yes and playgroup
- **CONTACT** Pauline Tapp 01284 701301 x252

- **SUBJECT** Administration/Secretarial **1211**
- **TITLE** RSA Higher Diploma in Administrative and Secretarial Procedures
- **PLACE** West Suffolk College

Length 1 year full time **Start** September **Days** 4 days/week 9.00-5.00 **Cost** £650 **Entry Reqs** Mature students with past experience, degree or A Levels accepted **Award** RSA Higher Diploma in Administrative & Secretarial Procedures (with WP, Computing & Shorthand) **Creche** Yes
- **CONTACT** Elizabeth Smith 01284 701301 x252

- **SUBJECT** Art & Design **1212**
- **TITLE** BA(Hons) Art and Design
- **PLACE** Suffolk College

Length 3 years **Start** September **Days** Full time **Cost** Contact College **Entry Reqs** Contact College **Award** BA (Hons) Art and Design
- **CONTACT** Marketing Unit 01473 255885

- **SUBJECT** Beauty Therapy   1213
- **TITLE** Beauty Therapy
- **PLACE** West Suffolk College

Length 2 years full time   **Start** September   **Cost** Contact College   **Entry Reqs** 2 GCSEs or equivalent + science subject. Exceptional entry for mature students   **Award** C&G Certificate   **Creche** Yes
- **CONTACT** Infoline 01284 716347

- **SUBJECT** Business   1214
- **TITLE** BA (Hons) Business Studies
- **PLACE** Suffolk College

Length Normally 3 years   **Start** September   **Days** Full time   **Cost** Contact College   **Entry Reqs** Contact College   **Award** BA (Hons)
- **CONTACT** Marketing Unit 01473 255885

- **SUBJECT** Business   1215
- **TITLE** BTEC Higher National Diploma in Business and Finance
- **PLACE** Suffolk College

Length 2 years full time, 3 years sandwich   **Start** September   **Cost** Contact College   **Entry Reqs** Contact College   **Award** BTEC HND
- **CONTACT** Marketing Unit 01473 255885

- **SUBJECT** Business   1216
- **TITLE** BTEC GNVQ Intermediate Business
- **PLACE** Lowestoft College

Start September   **Cost** Contact College   **Entry Reqs** Contact College   **Award** BTEC GNVQ Intermediate   **Creche** Yes
- **CONTACT** Information Centre 01502 583521

- **SUBJECT** Business   1217
- **TITLE** Higher National Diploma in Business and Finance
- **PLACE** West Suffolk College

Length 2 years full time   **Start** September   **Cost** Contact College   **Entry Reqs** Mature student entry based on interview   **Award** HND (Anglia Polytechnic University) Business and Finance   **Creche** Yes
- **CONTACT** Infoline 01284 716342

- **SUBJECT** Business Studies   1218
- **TITLE** Gateway to Work in Business
- **PLACE** Lowestoft College

Length Varies   **Cost** Contact College   **Entry Reqs** Programmes tailored to individual needs   **Award** Various qualifications available   **Creche** Yes
- **CONTACT** Information Centre 01502 583521

- **SUBJECT** Childcare   1219
- **TITLE** Childcare and Education
- **PLACE** Lowestoft College

Length 1 year full time   **Start** September   **Cost** Contact College   **Entry Reqs** Mature students welcome   **Award** Childcare and Education Certificate   **Creche** Yes
- **CONTACT** Information Centre 01502 583521

- **SUBJECT** Electrical Engineering/Electronic Engineering   1220
- **TITLE** BTEC HND in Engineering (Electrical and Electronic)
- **PLACE** Suffolk College

Length 2 years   **Start** September   **Days** Full time   **Cost** Contact College   **Entry Reqs** Contact College   **Award** BTEC HND
- **CONTACT** Marketing Unit 01473 255885

- **SUBJECT** Electronic Engineering   1221
- **TITLE** Electronic Engineering: City & Guilds and BTEC Modular Programmes
- **PLACE** West Suffolk College

Length Flexible   **Start** Varies   **Cost** Contact College   **Entry Reqs** Contact College
Award C&G/BTEC awards   **Creche** Yes
- **CONTACT** Brian Crossland 01284 701301

- **SUBJECT** Engineering   1222
- **TITLE** BTEC HND in Engineering (Mechatronics)
- **PLACE** Suffolk College

Length 2 years   **Start** September   **Days** Full time   **Cost** Contact College   **Entry Reqs**
Mature students, especially female applicants, welcome   **Award** BTEC HND
- **CONTACT** Marketing Unit 01473 255885

- **SUBJECT** Engineering   1223
- **TITLE** BTEC HND in Engineering (Motor Vehicle Studies)
- **PLACE** Suffolk College

Length 2 years   **Start** September   **Days** Full time   **Cost** Contact College   **Entry Reqs**
Mature students, especially female applicants, welcome   **Award** BTEC HND
- **CONTACT** Marketing Unit 01473 255885

- **SUBJECT** Food Studies   1224
- **TITLE** BTEC National Diploma in Food and Consumer Studies
- **PLACE** Suffolk College

Length 2 years   **Start** September   **Days** Full time   **Cost** Contact College   **Entry Reqs**
Mature students welcome   **Award** BTEC National Diploma
- **CONTACT** Marketing Unit 01473 255885

- **SUBJECT** Hairdressing   1225
- **TITLE** Hairdressing
- **PLACE** Lowestoft College

Length 2 years part time modular   **Days** 2 eves/week and 1 Saturday/month   **Cost** Contact
College   **Entry Reqs** Mature students welcome   **Award** NVQ Level II
- **CONTACT** Information Centre 01502 583521

- **SUBJECT** Hairdressing   1226
- **TITLE** Hairdressing
- **PLACE** West Suffolk College

Length 2 years full time   **Start** September   **Cost** Contact College   **Entry Reqs** 2 GCSEs or
equivalent. Exceptional entry possible for mature students   **Award** NVQ Level II   **Creche**
Yes
- **CONTACT** Infoline 01284 716344

- **SUBJECT** Hairdressing   1227
- **TITLE** Hairdressing (Mature Learners)
- **PLACE** Suffolk College

Length 1 year   **Start** September   **Days** Full time   **Cost** Contact College   **Entry Reqs** No
formal requirements   **Award** NVQ Level II
- **CONTACT** Marketing Unit 01473 255885

- **SUBJECT** Humanities/Social Science   1228
- **TITLE** BA (Hons) in Humanities and Social Science (Anglia Polytechnic University)
- **PLACE** West Suffolk College

Length 3 years (modular)   **Days** Each module comprises 30 hours/week over a 10 week
period   **Cost** Contact College   **Entry Reqs** Contact College   **Award** BA (Hons) Humanities
and Social Science   **Creche** Yes
- **CONTACT** Infoline 01284 716344

- **SUBJECT** Information Technology 1229
- **TITLE** Using Information Technology
- **PLACE** Lowestoft College

Length Modular **Cost** Contact College **Entry Reqs** None **Creche** Yes

- **CONTACT** Information Centre 01502 583521

- **SUBJECT** Information Technology 1230
- **TITLE** Women's Technology
- **PLACE** West Suffolk College

Length 1 year **Start** September **Days** Mon 7.00-9.00 **Cost** £80 **Entry Reqs** None **Award** RSA CLAIT 1 & 2 **Creche** Yes

- **CONTACT** Pauline Tapp 01284 701301 x252

- **SUBJECT** Law/Secretarial 1231
- **TITLE** ILEX Legal Secretaries Certificate Level II
- **PLACE** West Suffolk College

Length 1 year **Start** September **Days** Tues 7.00-9.00 **Cost** £80 **Entry Reqs** Experience of working in a legal environment **Award** ILEX Certificate Level II **Creche** Yes

- **CONTACT** Pauline Tapp 01284 701301 x252

- **SUBJECT** Manufacturing 1232
- **TITLE** BTEC HND in Product Design and Manufacture
- **PLACE** Suffolk College

Length 2 years **Start** September **Days** Full time **Cost** Contact College **Entry Reqs** Mature students, especially female applicants, welcome **Award** BTEC HND

- **CONTACT** Marketing Unit 01473 255885

- **SUBJECT** Media Studies 1233
- **TITLE** BTEC National Diploma in Media
- **PLACE** Suffolk College

Length 2 years **Start** September **Days** Full time **Cost** Contact College **Entry Reqs** Mature students welcome **Award** BTEC National Diploma

- **CONTACT** Marketing Unit 01473 255885

- **SUBJECT** Multi-Subject 1234
- **TITLE** BA(Hons)/BSc(Hons) Individually Negotiated Route
- **PLACE** Suffolk College

Length Normally 3 years, individual programme of study **Start** September **Cost** Contact College **Entry Reqs** Mature students welcome **Award** BA(Hons)/BSc(Hons)

- **CONTACT** Marketing Unit 01473 255885

- **SUBJECT** Multi-Subject 1235
- **TITLE** Suffolk Modular Degree Programme
- **PLACE** Suffolk College, in partnership with the University of East Anglia

Length Flexible **Start** September **Days** Flexible **Cost** Contact College **Entry Reqs** Contact College **Award** BA(Hons)/BSc(Hons)

- **CONTACT** Programmes Unit 01473 255885 x6472

- **SUBJECT**   Office Skills   1236
- **TITLE**   Keyboarding and Word Processing
- **PLACE**   West Suffolk College

Length 1 year   **Start** September   **Days** Thurs 7.00-9.00   **Cost** £80   **Entry Reqs** None
Award RSA   **Creche** Yes
- **CONTACT**   Pauline Tapp 01284 701301 x252

- **SUBJECT**   Office Skills   1237
- **TITLE**   Open Learning Shorthand, Beginners & Speed Development
- **PLACE**   West Suffolk College

Length Flexible   **Start** Flexible   **Days** Open Learning with tutorials at agreed times   **Cost**
£90   **Entry Reqs** Reasonable ability in English   **Award** RSA   **Creche** Yes
- **CONTACT**   Margaret Place 01284 701301 x252

- **SUBJECT**   Office Skills   1238
- **TITLE**   Short Courses in Typing, Basic Computing, Word Processing, DTP, Office
  Technology, Women's Technology, Word for Windows & Wordperfect
- **PLACE**   West Suffolk College

Length 10 weeks   **Start** January, April, September   **Days** 2 hour daytime classes at various
times   **Cost** £60   **Entry Reqs** None: can enrol for one or several courses   **Award** RSA &
Pitman single subjects   **Creche** Yes
- **CONTACT**   Pauline Tapp 01284 701301 x252

- **SUBJECT**   Office Skills/Business Administration   1239
- **TITLE**   Office Skills and Business Administration NVQ Levels I-III
- **PLACE**   Lowestoft College

Length 6 week modules   **Start** Flexible   **Days** Negotiable   **Cost** £33/6-week module at 3
hours attendance   **Entry Reqs** None   **Award** NVQ Levels I, II, & III   **Creche** Yes
- **CONTACT**   Information Centre 01502 583521

- **SUBJECT**   Practical   1240
- **TITLE**   1. Furniture Crafts 2. Advanced Craft Furniture Making
- **PLACE**   Suffolk College

Length 1.1 year 2.2 years   **Start** September   **Days** Full time   **Cost** Contact College   **Entry
Reqs** Mature students welcome   **Award** 1. C&G 2. C&G/Suffolk College Diploma/NVQ
- **CONTACT**   Marketing Unit 01473 255885

- **SUBJECT**   Preparatory   1241
- **TITLE**   Get Ready Course for Women
- **PLACE**   Community Education Centre, Ipswich

Length 1 term   **Start** September   **Days** Thurs+Fri 9.45-11.45   **Cost** £1.50/week   **Entry
Reqs** None   **Creche** Yes free
- **CONTACT**   Community Education Centre 01473 212165

- **SUBJECT**   Preparatory   1242
- **TITLE**   New Start
- **PLACE**   West Suffolk College

Length 20 weeks   **Start** September, January   **Days** Thurs 9.30-12.30   **Cost** Free   **Entry
Reqs** None   **Award** Possible entry to other courses   **Creche** Yes Contact College
- **CONTACT**   Peter Dudley 01284 716348

- **SUBJECT**   Preparatory   1243
- **TITLE**   Starting Again
- **PLACE**   West Suffolk College, sites at Thurston, Stowmarket, Ixworth, etc

Length 6 weeks   **Start** September, January, April   **Days** Contact College   **Cost** Contact
College   **Entry Reqs** None   **Award** Possible entry to other courses   **Creche** No
- **CONTACT**   Peter Dudley 01284 716348

- **SUBJECT** Science   1244
- **TITLE** BSc (Hons) Interdisciplinary Science
- **PLACE** Lowestoft College with University of East Anglia

Length 4 years (1st year at Lowestoft College)   **Start** September   **Cost** Contact College **Entry Reqs** Mature students without usual entrance qualifications welcome **Award** BSc (Hons) Interdisciplinary Science   **Creche** Yes

- **CONTACT** Information Centre 01502 583521

- **SUBJECT** Science   1245
- **TITLE** Foundation Science Programme
- **PLACE** Suffolk College

Length 1 year   **Start** September   **Days** Full time   **Cost** Contact College   **Entry Reqs** Contact College   **Award** Progression to science degrees in the Suffolk Modular Degree Programme

- **CONTACT** Marketing Unit 01473 255885

- **SUBJECT** Secretarial   1246
- **TITLE** Advanced Secretarial/Administrative Diploma 1. Daytime 2. Evening
- **PLACE** West Suffolk College

Length 1-2 years   **Start** September   **Days** 1. Thurs 9.00-5.00 2. Wed 5.30-7.30 or Thurs 5.30-7.30   **Cost** 1. £263 2. £115   **Entry Reqs** Relevant experience or NVQ II   **Award** 1. RSA Business Admin (Secretarial), NVQ III & RSA single subjects 2. RSA Bus Admin NVQ III **Creche** Yes

- **CONTACT** Pat Pemberton 01284 701301 x252

- **SUBJECT** Secretarial   1247
- **TITLE** Intensive Secretarial Course
- **PLACE** West Suffolk College

Length 11 weeks   **Start** January, April, September   **Days** Mon-Fri 10.00-3.00   **Cost** £700 **Entry Reqs** None   **Award** RSA & Pitman   **Creche** Yes

- **CONTACT** Marian Clayton 01284 701301 x252

- **SUBJECT** Secretarial   1248
- **TITLE** RSA Secretarial/Administrative Diploma 1. Daytime 2. Evening
- **PLACE** West Suffolk College

Length 1-2 years   **Start** September   **Days** 1. Wed 9.00-5.00 2. Wed 5.30-7.30   **Cost** 1. £218 2. £108   **Entry Reqs** None   **Award** 1. RSA Bus Admin, NVQ I/II & RSA single subjects 2. Bus Admin NVQ II   **Creche** Yes

- **CONTACT** Dorothy Patterson 01284 701301 x252

- **SUBJECT** Secretarial   1249
- **TITLE** RSA Secretarial Diploma
- **PLACE** West Suffolk College

Length 1 year full time   **Start** September   **Days** 4 days/week 9.00-5.00   **Cost** £650   **Entry Reqs** None   **Award** RSA Administration NVQ Level II   **Creche** Yes

- **CONTACT** Dorothy Patterson 01284 701301 x252

- **SUBJECT** Secretarial   1250
- **TITLE** Secretarial Diploma
- **PLACE** Lowestoft College

Length Modular   **Cost** Contact College   **Entry Reqs** None. Mature students welcome **Creche** Yes

- **CONTACT** Information Centre 01502 583521

- **SUBJECT** Secretarial · **1251**
- **TITLE** Secretarial Training Centre
- **PLACE** West Suffolk College

Length Flexible · **Start** Flexible · **Days** Flexible, 1 hour workshop facilities · **Cost** £3/hour
Entry Reqs None · **Award** RSA & Pitman single subject exams · **Creche** Yes

- **CONTACT** Dorothy Patterson 01284 701301 x252

COUNTY CONTACTS

Information and advice

BEGIN (Bury Educational Guidance and Information Network), Bury Central Library, Sergeants Walk, Bury St Edmunds IP33 1TZ 01284 706524. Service operates Monday and Wednesday 10.00-12.30 and by appointment
Career Development Centre, Lowestoft, 124 London Road North, Lowestoft NR32 1HB 01502 531474
Northern Area Community Education Office, Adrian House, Alexandra Road, Lowestoft NR32 1PC 01502 562262
Southern Area Community Education Office, Murryside Centre, Nacton Road, Ipswich IP3 9JL 01473 712645. Educational guidance; also informal groups/courses for women
Western Area Community Education Office, Shire Hall, Bury St Edmunds IP33 1RX 01284 722137. Adult career guidance, also range of groups/courses

Open University

The Open University, East Anglia Region, 12 Hills Road, Cambridge CB2 1PF 01223 61650

Training and Enterprise Council

Suffolk TEC, 2nd Floor, Crown House, Crown Street, Ipswich IP1 3HS 01473 218951. Restricted pre-returner courses; Training for Work; details of local training providers

WEA office

WEA Eastern District, Botolph House, 17 Botolph Lane, Cambridge CB2 3RE 01223 350978
Contact: Sue Young

SURREY

COURSES

- **SUBJECT** Access/Art & Design/Humanities/Mathematics/Science/Business Studies · **1252**
  Social Science/Engineering/Teaching
- **TITLE** Access to Higher Education
- **PLACE** North East Surrey College of Technology

Length 1 year · **Start** September · **Days** Full time 10.00-3.00 · **Cost** Contact College · **Entry Reqs** Contact College · **Award** Access to university entrance

- **CONTACT** Course Enquiries 0181 394 3038

- **SUBJECT** Access/Engineering/Mathematics/Science   1253
- **TITLE** Access to Engineering, Maths, Physics, Chemistry, Biology
- **PLACE** Guildford College of Further & Higher Education

Length 1 year   **Start** September   **Days** 3.5 days/week   **Cost** Varies. Contact College **Entry Reqs** 20+, interview   **Award** Entry to degree courses at wide range of universities and other HE establishments   **Creche** Yes
- **CONTACT** Mrs A Welton 01483 448500

- **SUBJECT** Accounting   1254
- **TITLE** AAT: Accounting Technician Professional Qualification
- **PLACE** North East Surrey College of Technology

Length 1 year   **Start** September   **Cost** Contact College   **Award** AAT awards
- **CONTACT** Course Enquiries 0181 394 3038

- **SUBJECT** Administration   1255
- **TITLE** Administration and Information Processing for Postgraduates
- **PLACE** North East Surrey College of Technology

Length 2 terms   **Days** Full time   **Cost** Contact College   **Entry Reqs** Degree, HND, HNC or professional qualification   **Award** RSA/LCCI awards
- **CONTACT** Course Enquiries 0181 394 3038

- **SUBJECT** Administration   1256
- **TITLE** Diploma in Administrative Procedures
- **PLACE** Brooklands College, Faculty of Professional Studies

Length 9 months   **Start** September   **Days** Mon-Fri   **Cost** Approx £650   **Entry Reqs** Degree/A Levels/experience   **Award** RSA Higher Diploma in Administrative Procedures **Creche** No
- **CONTACT** Course Enquiries 01932 853300 x432

- **SUBJECT** Biological Sciences   1257
- **TITLE** Biological Sciences Modular Degree Programme
- **PLACE** North East Surrey College of Technology

Length 3 years or less   **Start** September   **Days** Full time or part time   **Cost** Contact College   **Entry Reqs** Contact College   **Award** Open University BSc Hons
- **CONTACT** Course Enquiries 0181 394 3038

- **SUBJECT** Biological Sciences   1258
- **TITLE** HNC 1. Applied Biology 2. Biotechnology
- **PLACE** North East Surrey College of Technology

Length 1 year   **Start** September   **Cost** Contact College   **Award** 1. HNC Applied Biology 2. HNC Biotechnology
- **CONTACT** Course Enquiries 0181 394 3038

- **SUBJECT** Business Administration   1259
- **TITLE** Business Administration
- **PLACE** Guildford College of Further & Higher Education

Length Average 23 weeks   **Start** Flexible   **Days** 30 hours/week   **Cost** None Skills Plus £10/week Training Allowance   **Entry Reqs** Initial interview & 6 months registered unemployed   **Award** NVQ Level II, C&G/RSA   **Creche** Yes. Lone parent grant
- **CONTACT** Pam Eaton 01483 448640

- **SUBJECT** Business Administration   1260
- **TITLE** HNC Business and Finance
- **PLACE** North East Surrey College of Technology

Length 1 year   **Start** September   **Cost** Contact College   **Award** HNC Business and Finance
- **CONTACT** Course Enquiries 0181 394 3038

- **SUBJECT**   Business Information Technology   **1261**
- **TITLE**   Business Information Technology 1. BTEC HNC 2. BTEC HND
- **PLACE**   North East Surrey College of Technology

Length 1.2 years 2.3 years **Start** September **Days** 1 day/week or 2 eves/week **Cost** Contact College **Entry Reqs** Contact College **Award** 1. BTEC HNC 2. BTEC HND
- **CONTACT** Course Enquiries 0181 394 3038

- **SUBJECT**   Childcare   **1262**
- **TITLE**   1. Childcare and Education 2. Nursery Nursing
- **PLACE**   North East Surrey College of Technology

Length 1.1 year or modular 2.2 years **Start** September **Cost** Contact College **Entry Reqs** Mature students welcome **Award** 1. CACHE Certificate in Childcare and Education 2. CACHE (NNEB) Diploma in Nursery Nursing
- **CONTACT** Course Enquiries 0181 394 3038

- **SUBJECT**   Civil Engineering/Construction   **1263**
- **TITLE**   HNC 1. Civil Engineering 2. Computing in Construction Management
- **PLACE**   North East Surrey College of Technology

Length 1 year **Start** September **Cost** Contact College **Award** 1. HNC Civil Engineering 2. HNC Computing in Construction Management
- **CONTACT** Course Enquiries 0181 394 3038

- **SUBJECT**   Computing   **1264**
- **TITLE**   Computer Automation and Networking
- **PLACE**   North East Surrey College of Technology

Length 2 years **Start** September **Days** Full time **Cost** Contact College **Entry Reqs** Adult returners, particularly women, welcomed **Award** BTEC HND
- **CONTACT** Course Enquiries 0181 394 3038

- **SUBJECT**   Computing   **1265**
- **TITLE**   Computing, with a European Option
- **PLACE**   North East Surrey College of Technology

Length 2 years or 3 years with work placement **Start** September **Days** Full time **Cost** Contact College **Entry Reqs** Mature students admitted with BTEC approval **Award** BTEC HND
- **CONTACT** Course Enquiries 0181 394 3038

- **SUBJECT**   Counselling   **1266**
- **TITLE**   Counselling Skills: Introductory Course
- **PLACE**   North East Surrey College of Technology

Length 10 weeks **Days** 2 hours/week **Cost** Contact College **Entry Reqs** No formal entry requirements **Award** Certificate in Counselling Skills
- **CONTACT** Course Enquiries 0181 394 3038

- **SUBJECT**   Environmental Studies   **1267**
- **TITLE**   HNC Pollution Management
- **PLACE**   North East Surrey College of Technology

Length 1 year **Start** September **Cost** Contact College **Award** HNC Pollution Management
- **CONTACT** Course Enquiries 0181 394 3038

- **SUBJECT**   Information Technology   **1268**
- **TITLE**   BTEC National Diploma Information Technology
- **PLACE**   North East Surrey College of Technology

Length 2 years **Start** September **Days** Full time **Cost** Contact College **Entry Reqs** Mature students admitted with BTEC approval **Award** BTEC National Diploma (GNVQ Advanced Information Technology)
- **CONTACT** Course Enquiries 0181 394 3038

- **SUBJECT** Management   1269
- **TITLE** Management
- **PLACE** North East Surrey College of Technology

Length 1 year **Start** September **Days** Part time day and evening/evening only **Cost** Contact College **Entry Reqs** Special provision for women returners and unemployed candidates **Award** BTEC Certificate/NVQ Level 4
- **CONTACT** Course Enquiries 0181 394 3038

- **SUBJECT** Mathematics/Preparatory   1270
- **TITLE** Beginner and Refresher Courses in Numeracy & Maths
- **PLACE** Guildford College of Further & Higher Education

Length Various plus drop-in workshop facilities **Start** Flexible **Days** Flexible **Cost** Varies. Contact College **Entry Reqs** No formal entry requirements unless studying for A Level **Award** Depends on individual eg Basic Numeracy, GCSE Maths, A Level Maths **Creche** Yes
- **CONTACT** Mrs L Brunton-Smith 01483 448500 x8388

- **SUBJECT** Office Skills   1271
- **TITLE** Beginner & Refresher Courses in Office Skills
- **PLACE** Guildford College of Further & Higher Education

Length Various plus drop-in workshop facilities **Start** Flexible **Days** Flexible, evenings possible **Cost** Varies. Contact College **Entry Reqs** Subject to discussion **Award** Secretarial Exams/Bus Admin/NVQ I-III/WP/Shorthand **Creche** Yes Concessions possible
- **CONTACT** Customer Services 01483 448500

- **SUBJECT** Office Skills   1272
- **TITLE** Business Skills Workshop
- **PLACE** Brooklands College

Length Varies according to need **Start** Flexible **Days** Flexible. Workstations bookable as required **Cost** £5-£8/hour **Entry Reqs** None **Award** Varies **Creche** No
- **CONTACT** Course Enquiries 01932 853300 x432

- **SUBJECT** Office Skills   1273
- **TITLE** Business Skills for Returning to Work
- **PLACE** Brooklands College, Faculty of Professional Studies

Length 10 weeks **Start** September, January, April **Days** Tues, Wed, Thurs 9.30-2.30 **Cost** Approx £150 (free if on benefits) **Entry Reqs** Some previous office experience **Award** None **Creche** No
- **CONTACT** Course Enquiries 01932 853300 x432

- **SUBJECT** Office Skills   1274
- **TITLE** 1. Keyboarding/Typing 2. Office Technology
- **PLACE** North East Surrey College of Technology

Length 1.1 term 2.10 weeks **Days** 1.1 afternoon or evening/week 2.3 days/week **Cost** Contact College **Entry Reqs** None **Award** RSA awards
- **CONTACT** Course Enquiries 01932 853300 x432

- **SUBJECT** Medicine/Physics/Paramedical Studies   1275
- **TITLE** Medical Physics and Physiological Measurement
- **PLACE** North East Surrey College of Technology

Length 2 years **Start** September **Days** 8 or 9 1-week blocks throughout the academic year **Cost** Contact College **Entry Reqs** Special consideration given to mature students **Award** BTEC HNC
- **CONTACT** Course Enquiries 0181 394 3038

- **SUBJECT** Preparatory   1276
- **TITLE** Study Workshop
- **PLACE** Guildford College of Further & Higher Education

Length 8 or 13 weeks   **Start** September   **Days** Thurs 7.00-9.00   **Cost** 8 weeks £35, 13 weeks £55   **Entry Reqs** None

- **CONTACT** Keith Please 01483 448500 x8380/1

- **SUBJECT** Preparatory   1277
- **TITLE** Women Returners' Course
- **PLACE** North East Surrey College of Technology

Length 3 weeks   **Start** Contact College   **Cost** Free   **Entry Reqs** None   **Creche** Yes Playscheme

- **CONTACT** Course Enquiries 0181 394 3038

- **SUBJECT** Science/Computing   1278
- **TITLE** Science and Computer Technology
- **PLACE** North East Surrey College of Technology

Length 2 years   **Start** September   **Days** Full time   **Cost** Contact College   **Entry Reqs** Adult returners, particularly women, welcomed   **Award** BTEC HND

- **CONTACT** Course Enquiries 0181 394 3038

- **SUBJECT** Secretarial   1279
- **TITLE** 1. Intensive Secretarial Course 2. Legal Secretaries' Course 3. Medical Secretaries' Course
- **PLACE** North East Surrey College of Technology

Length 1.1 year 2. &3.2 years   **Start** September   **Days** Full time   **Cost** Contact College **Entry Reqs** Contact College. Mature students without specificed qualifications considered **Award** 1. &2. RSA Diploma Administration 3. RSA/AMSPAR Diploma

- **CONTACT** Course Enquiries 0181 394 3038

- **SUBJECT** Secretarial   1280
- **TITLE** Secretarial/Administration Skills Workshop
- **PLACE** North East Surrey College of Technology

Length 1 term to 1 year   **Days** 1 afternoon or 1 evening/week   **Cost** Contact College **Entry Reqs** None   **Award** RSA Certificates/NVQ Levels 2-4

- **CONTACT** Course Enquiries 0181 394 3038

- **SUBJECT** Tourism & Leisure   1281
- **TITLE** HNC 1. Facilities Management 2. Leisure Management
- **PLACE** North East Surrey College of Technology

Length 1 year   **Start** September   **Cost** Contact College   **Award** HNC 1. Facilities Management 2. Leisure Management

- **CONTACT** Course Enquiries 0181 394 3038

COUNTY CONTACTS

Information and advice

Surrey Careers Services Ltd, Head Office, Farncombe Place, 10 Farncombe Street, Farncombe, Godalming GU7 3HE 01483 860668
Camberley Careers Centre, Portesbury Road, Camberley GU15 3SZ 01276 27172
Epsom Careers Centre, 83 East Street, Epsom KT17 1DN 01372 722291
Guildford Careers Centre, Finance House, Park Street, Guildford GU1 4XB 01483 576121
Redhill Careers Centre, 3 London Road, Redhill RH1 1LY 01737 773801
Staines Careers Centre, Fairacre House, Fairfield Avenue, Staines TW18 4AB 01784 455081
Woking Careers Centre, Lismore, 9c Heathside Road, Woking GU22 7EU 01483 760041

Open University

The Open University, South East Region, St James's House, 150 London Road, East Grinstead RH19 1ES 01342 410545

Training and Enterprise Council

Surrey TEC, Technology House, 48-54 Goldsworth Road, Woking GU21 1LE 01483 728190

WEA office

WEA London District, 44 Crowndale Road, London NW1 1TR 0171 388 7261   *Contact:* Ann Deutch

---

TYNE AND WEAR

COURSES

- **SUBJECT**   Access   1282
- **TITLE**   Access to Higher Education
- **PLACE**   Monkwearmouth College, various centres

Length Modular   **Start** September, January, April   **Days** 8-12 hours/week   **Cost** £200
Entry Reqs Interview   **Award** Open College Certificate   **Creche** Yes
- **CONTACT**   Bill Trenbitt, Access Co-ordinator, 0191 516 2000

- **SUBJECT**   Access   1283
- **TITLE**   Access to Higher Education
- **PLACE**   Wearside College, Bede and Tunstall Centres

Length Varies   **Start** Contact College   **Award** Access to higher education
- **CONTACT**   Course Information 0191 511 0515/567 0794

- **SUBJECT**   Access   1284
- **TITLE**   Higher Education Foundation Course
- **PLACE**   Gateshead College

Length 1, 2 or 3 years   **Start** Autumn   **Days** Various (modular)   **Cost** Contact College
Entry Reqs None, age 21+   **Award** University of Northumbria at Newcastle HE Foundation Course Certificate (CNAA validated)   **Creche** Yes limited places
- **CONTACT**   Information Centre 0191 450 2246/7

- **SUBJECT**   Access/Information Technology   **1285**
- **TITLE**   Access to Information Technology
- **PLACE**   North Tyneside College

Length 10 weeks   **Start** September   **Days** Tues 6.30-9.00, Thurs 6.30-9.00, Sat 9.30-12.00
Cost College fees   **Entry Reqs** None   **Creche** No
- **CONTACT**   R Archer/H Page 0191 229 5000

- **SUBJECT**   Access/Nursing   **1286**
- **TITLE**   Towards a Career in Nursing
- **PLACE**   North Tyneside College

Length 18 weeks   **Start** September   **Days** Part time day or eve   **Cost** Contact College
Entry Reqs None   **Award** DC Test   **Creche** No
- **CONTACT**   Margaret Gow 0191 229 5000

- **SUBJECT**   Accounting   **1287**
- **TITLE**   Association of Accounting Technicians: Preliminary Stage
- **PLACE**   Gateshead College

Length 1 year   **Start** September   **Days** Part time day or evening   **Cost** Contact College
Entry Reqs Various and interview   **Award** AAT Preliminary, Intermediate and Technician
Stages   **Creche** Yes
- **CONTACT**   Information Centre 0191 450 2246/7

- **SUBJECT**   Business Administration/Management Studies   **1288**
- **TITLE**   BTEC CE in Business Administration, Certificate in Management Studies
- **PLACE**   North Tyneside College, Open Learning Unit

Length Flexible   **Start** Anytime   **Days** Open learning   **Cost** Contact College   **Entry Reqs**
None   **Award** BTEC Continuing Education Cert in Business Administration, Cert in
Management Studies   **Creche** Yes Free
- **CONTACT**   M A Rule 0191 229 5000

- **SUBJECT**   Care Studies   **1289**
- **TITLE**   1. Family & Community Care 2. Community Care Practice
- **PLACE**   North Tyneside College

Length 3 terms   **Start** 1. September 2. Sept, January, April   **Days** 1. Mon-Fri 9.00-4.00 2. Wed
9.00-4.00   **Cost** Contact College   **Entry Reqs** 1. Interview, references 2.18+   **Award** 1. CGLI
331 Family & Community Care Certificate 2. CGLI 325/1 Community Care Practice   **Creche**
Yes Contact College
- **CONTACT**   1. Anne Dodd/2. Linda Jordan 0191 229 5000

- **SUBJECT**   Childcare   **1290**
- **TITLE**   1. Nursery Nursing 2. Caring for Children 0-7 years
- **PLACE**   North Tyneside College

Length 1.2 years 2.1year   **Start** September   **Days** Tues+Thurs 6.00-9.00 + 2 halfdays in
placement   **Cost** £130/year+registration fees   **Entry Reqs** Satisfactory academic
background   **Award** 1. BTEC National Certificate in Nursery Nursing 2. C&G 324   **Creche**
No
- **CONTACT**   Linda Jordan 0191 229 5000

- **SUBJECT**   Childcare   **1291**
- **TITLE**   NNEB Diploma
- **PLACE**   North Tyneside College, Riverside Centre

Length 9 terms   **Start** September   **Days** Placement Mon 9.00-4.15+College Wed-Fri
10.00-2.15   **Cost** Contact College   **Entry Reqs** Interview, references, evidence of work with
children   **Award** NNEB Diploma   **Creche** Yes Limited places Contact College
- **CONTACT**   Veronica Dawson 0191 229 5000

- **SUBJECT** Combined Studies   **1292**
- **TITLE** BA Combined Honours (part time)
- **PLACE** University of Northumbria at Newcastle

Length Varies   **Start** September   **Days** Various   **Cost** £250 per part route   **Entry Reqs** A Levels. HEFC/GCSE/maths for psychology **Award** BA (Hons) Combined Honours **Creche** Yes

- **CONTACT** Alan Saunders/Janice Woods 0191 227 4067

- **SUBJECT** Computing   **1293**
- **TITLE** 1. Computing for Beginners 2. Introduction to Computing 3. Computing & Information Technology
- **PLACE** Wearside College, Tunstall Centre

Length 1.10 weeks 2&3.1 year   **Start** Contact College   **Award** 1. Open College accredited 2&3 City & Guilds

- **CONTACT** Course Information 0191 567 0794

- **SUBJECT** Engineering   **1294**
- **TITLE** Engineering in Marine Technology: Research Masters Pilot Course
- **PLACE** University of Newcastle upon Tyne

Length 2 years   **Start** October   **Cost** Engineering & Physical Sciences Research Council award available   **Entry Reqs** Graduates with first or upper second class honours degree in an appropriate subject   **Award** Master of Research Degree

- **CONTACT** Professor G Hearn 0191 222 6749

- **SUBJECT** Information Technology   **1295**
- **TITLE** C&G Introduction to Information Technology
- **PLACE** Gateshead College

Length 1 year   **Start** September   **Days** Part time day   **Cost** Contact College   **Entry Reqs** No formal entry qualifications   **Award** C&G 726 Introduction to Information Technology **Creche** Yes

- **CONTACT** Information Centre 0191 450 2246/7

- **SUBJECT** Information Technology   **1296**
- **TITLE** Information Technology Applications 1. BTEC First Cert 2. BTEC National Certificate
- **PLACE** North Tyneside College

Length 35 weeks   **Start** September   **Cost** Contact College   **Entry Reqs** 1. None 2.4 GCSEs or equivalent   **Award** 1. BTEC First Cert 2. BTEC Nat Cert in Information Technology Applications

- **CONTACT** H Wright 0191 229 5000

- **SUBJECT** Information Technology   **1297**
- **TITLE** Information Technology in the Office
- **PLACE** North Tyneside College, Open Learning Unit

Length Flexible   **Start** Anytime   **Days** Open learning   **Cost** £45x2 (materials only)   **Entry Reqs** None   **Award** BTEC Continuing Education Half Credit   **Creche** Yes free

- **CONTACT** M A Rule 0191 229 5000

- **SUBJECT** Information Technology   **1298**
- **TITLE** Introduction to Word Processing
- **PLACE** Working for Women, Gateshead

Length 8 weeks   **Start** Termly   **Days** 1 session/week   **Cost** Free   **Entry Reqs** None **Award** Open College Federation Level 1   **Creche** Yes & playgroup. Free

- **CONTACT** Anne Britton 0191 477 1011 x2055

- **SUBJECT**   Multi-Subject   **1299**
- **TITLE**   CATS: Awards by Credit Accumulation & Transfer
- **PLACE**   University of Northumbria at Newcastle

Length Varies   **Start** Usually September. Apply early   **Days** 2-3 hrs/week/unit. Part time or full time study may be possible   **Cost** Part time approx £6.75/credit point. Standard unit=10 points=80 hours   **Entry Reqs** Various. All applicants must be ready to study at HE level   **Award** HE & postgraduate diplomas, first degrees, Masters degree   **Creche** Yes/34 places. Sliding scale of charges

- **CONTACT**   CATS Administrator/CATS Adviser 0191 227 4067

- **SUBJECT**   NOW   **1300**
- **TITLE**   New Opportunities for Women
- **PLACE**   Durham University Adult Education at Sunderland Women's Support Centre

Length 10 weeks   **Start** September   **Days** Wed 10.00-3.00   **Cost** Free   **Entry Reqs** None   **Award** Certificate of Attendance   **Creche** Yes Free

- **CONTACT**   Anne Staines 0191 514 4652

- **SUBJECT**   Office Skills   **1301**
- **TITLE**   Refreshers in Shorthand/Typing/Audio/Wordprocessing
- **PLACE**   North Tyneside College, Wallsend and Whitley Bay

Length 1 or 2 years   **Start** September and various   **Days** 2, 3 or 6 hours/week part time, 5 days/week full time   **Cost** College fees   **Award** Various including NVQ Levels I, II, III   **Creche** Yes

- **CONTACT**   Maureen Douglas 0191 229 5000

- **SUBJECT**   Office Skills   **1302**
- **TITLE**   Secretarial Modules (Shorthand, Typewriting, WP, Office Practice, Book-keeping)
- **PLACE**   Gateshead College, Broadway Annexe

Length 1 year (flexible)   **Start** September (flexible)   **Days** Part time day, 3-hour sessions   **Award** Various (RSA NCFE etc)   **Creche** Yes

- **CONTACT**   Information Centre 0191 450 2246/7

- **SUBJECT**   Practical   **1303**
- **TITLE**   Bricklaying for Women
- **PLACE**   Wearside College, Tunstall Centre

Length 1 term   **Start** Contact College   **Days** Tues 9.30-11.30   **Award** Open College accredited

- **CONTACT**   Course Information 0191 567 0794

- **SUBJECT**   Practical   **1304**
- **TITLE**   Painting and Decorating for Women
- **PLACE**   Wearside College, Bede Centre

Length 1 term   **Start** Contact College   **Days** Mon-9.30-11.30   **Award** Open College accredited

- **CONTACT**   Course Information 0191 511 0515

- **SUBJECT**   Practical   **1305**
- **TITLE**   Woodwork for Women
- **PLACE**   Wearside College, Tunstall Centre

Length 1 term   **Start** Contact College   **Days** Fri 9.30-11.30   **Award** Open College accredited

- **CONTACT**   Course Information 0191 567 0794

- **SUBJECT** Preparatory   1306
- **TITLE** Gateway to Learning: Return to Study Courses
- **PLACE** Gateshead College

Length 10 weeks **Start** September, January, April **Days** Various 2-hour modules **Cost** £17/module **Entry Reqs** None **Award** Tyneside Open College Federation Certificate **Creche** Yes Contact College

- **CONTACT** Information Centre 0191 450 2246/7

- **SUBJECT** Preparatory   1307
- **TITLE** 1. Return to Work 2. Assertiveness 3. Confidence Building
- **PLACE** Working for Women, Gateshead

Days 2-3 hours/week **Cost** Free **Entry Reqs** Women only **Creche** Yes & playgroup. Free

- **CONTACT** Anne Britton 0191 477 1011 x2055

- **SUBJECT** Preparatory   1308
- **TITLE** Return to Learn 1. English 2. Maths
- **PLACE** Wearside College, Bede Centre

Length 1 year **Days** Mon 6.30-8.30, Tues 9.15-11.15 or Wed 1.15-3.15 **Entry Reqs** None **Award** Could lead to City & Guilds Certificate **Creche** Yes 65p/session

- **CONTACT** Andrew Wrightson 0191 511 0515

- **SUBJECT** Preparatory   1309
- **TITLE** Stepping Out
- **PLACE** Working for Women, Gateshead

Length 10 weeks **Start** Termly **Days** Tues 9.30-12.30 **Cost** Free **Entry Reqs** Initial guidance session needed **Award** Open College Federation Level 1/2 **Creche** Yes & playgroup. Free

- **CONTACT** Anne Britton 0191 477 1011 x2055

- **SUBJECT** Preparatory   1310
- **TITLE** Stepping Stones
- **PLACE** Newcastle Women's Training Centre

Length 16 days **Start** Ongoing **Days** 2 days/week 9.45-2.45 **Cost** Free **Entry Reqs** None **Award** Tyneside Open College Federation Certificate **Creche** Help for child/ dependant care & travel costs

- **CONTACT** Beverley Hill/Elizabeth Best 0191 232 6159

- **SUBJECT** Preparatory   1311
- **TITLE** Taster Courses
- **PLACE** Women into Work, Howard House, Howard St, North Shields & in community

Length 6-8 days **Start** Throughout the year **Days** Various **Cost** Free **Entry Reqs** Free to women returners from Wallsend, Howdon, North Shields in North Tyneside **Award** Tyneside Open College Federation qualification **Creche** Yes Free

- **CONTACT** Women into Work 0191 296 1111

- **SUBJECT** Preparatory   1312
- **TITLE** Various Courses (WEA)
- **PLACE** Durham University Adult Education at Wheel Centre, Albany, Washington

Length 10-20 weeks **Start** September **Days** Various days 10.00-12.00, 1.00-3.00 **Cost** Free **Entry Reqs** None **Award** None **Creche** Yes 25p

- **CONTACT** Anne Staines 0191 514 4652

Tyne and Wear

- **SUBJECT** Preparatory   1313
- **TITLE** What the Hell Can I Do?: Taster Courses
- **PLACE** Monkwearmouth College, Swan Street

Length 8 weeks   **Start** Various, according to demand   **Days** 2 hours/week, day & time negotiable   **Cost** Free   **Entry Reqs** None   **Award** Open College Network Certificate in progress   **Creche** Yes Free
- **CONTACT** Maggie Smith 0191 516 2004/Mary Blake 0191 516 2018

- **SUBJECT** Secretarial   1314
- **TITLE** School Secretaries Course
- **PLACE** South Tyneside College

Length 1 year   **Start** September   **Days** Various, 2½-3 days/week   **Cost** £7 registration only if unemployed   **Entry Reqs** Typing and/or WP qualification or clerical experience   **Award** RSA Single Subject qualifications and First Aid   **Creche** Yes if places available
- **CONTACT** Joan Dawson 0191 427 3530

- **SUBJECT** Secretarial   1315
- **TITLE** Secretarial Skills for Unemployed Adults
- **PLACE** South Tyneside College

Length 1 year   **Start** September onwards   **Days** Various 2½ days/week 9.00-3.00 or flexible   **Cost** £7 registration only if unemployed   **Entry Reqs** None   **Award** RSA Single Subject qualifications   **Creche** Yes if places available
- **CONTACT** Joan Dawson 0191 427 3530

- **SUBJECT** Secretarial   1316
- **TITLE** Secretarial Skills for Unemployed/Mature Students
- **PLACE** South Tyneside College, Mill Lane, Hebburn

Length 1 year   **Start** September onwards   **Days** 2½ days/week   **Cost** £7 registration only if unemployed   **Entry Reqs** None   **Award** NVQ II and RSA Single Subjects
- **CONTACT** Joan Dawson 0191 427 3530

- **SUBJECT** Secretarial/Law   1317
- **TITLE** Legal Secretarial Course
- **PLACE** South Tyneside College

Length 1 year   **Start** September onwards   **Days** 2½ days/week + 1 day/week work experience   **Cost** £7 registration only if unemployed   **Award** NVQ II and RSA Single Subjects + ParaLegal exams
- **CONTACT** Joan Dawson 0191 427 3530

- **SUBJECT** Secretarial/Medicine   1318
- **TITLE** Medical Receptionist/Secretarial Course
- **PLACE** South Tyneside College, Mill Lane, Hebburn

Length 1 year   **Start** September onwards   **Days** 2½ days/week + 1 day/week work experience   **Cost** £7 registration only if unemployed   **Award** NVQ II and RSA Single Subjects + Medical Secretarial exams
- **CONTACT** Joan Dawson 0191 427 3530

COUNTY CONTACTS

Information and advice:

Adult Guidance Unit, Gateshead, Interchange Centre, West Street, Gateshead NE8 1BH 0191 490 1717
Adult Guidance Unit, Jarrow, Town Hall, Grange Road, Jarrow NE32 3LE 0191 489 1141
Adult Guidance Unit, South Shields, Stanhope Complex, Gresford Street, South Shields NE33 4SD 0191 456 3932/455 2632

Education Advice and Guidance for Adults, Linskill Centre, Linskill Terrace, North Shields NE30 2AY 0791 259 1166

Educational Guidance Unit, Careers Centre, College Street, Newcastle upon Tyne NE1 8DX 0191 232 9471   *Contact:* Margaret McPhail

Educational Guidance Unit, Central Library, Princess Square, Newcastle upon Tyne NE99 1DX 0191 261 0691 x247   *Contact:* Jane Glass

Tyneside Careers, Careers Centre, Adult Guidance Unit, College Street, Newcastle upon Tyne NE1 8DX 0191 232 9471   *Contact:* Margaret Grale

Open University:

The Open University, Northern Region, Eldon House, Regent Centre, Gosforth, Newcastle upon Tyne NE3 3PW 0191 284 1611

Other agencies:

Angelou Centre, 2 Brighton Grove, Fenham, Newcastle upon Tyne NE4 5NR 0191 226 0395. Women's training centre

Local Initiatives Team, Gateshead Council, Civic Centre, Regent Street, Gateshead NE8 1HH 0191 477 1011 x2055   *Contact:* Women's Employment Issues Officer

Women into Work, Howard House Commercial Centre, Howard Street. North Shields NE30 1AR 0191 296 1111   *Contact:* Liz Armstrong

Women's Training Centre, 1st Floor, Union Chambers, 41 Grainger Street, Newcastle upon Tyne NE1 5JE 0191 232 6159   *Contact:* Jan Anthony

Training and Enterprise Councils:

Sunderland TEC, Business and Innovation Centre, Sunderland Enterprise Park, Riverside, Sunderland SR5 2TA 0191 516 0222

Tyneside TEC, Moongate House, 5th Avenue Business Park, Team Valley, Gateshead NE11 0HF 0191 491 6000. Women's Advisory Group; Fresh Start within Training for Work; Ethnic Women's Initiatives; Research into flexible provision - training and employment; Childcare survey and Childcare Conference for Employers; After school and holiday care project; Free Tyneside Childcare Directory; Experience Enterprise; Small Business Management and Management Development course; Women into Self-Employment; Enterprise Allowance changes; Wider Horizon Days; First Step Back courses, ESF joint funded; Tyneside Women's Training Centre, ESF joint funded Return to Study courses; Opportunity 2000 Award Scheme; Employers' Equal Opportunities Network.

WEA office:

WEA Northern District, 51 Grainger Street, Newcastle upon Tyne NE1 5JE 0191 232 3957 *Contact:* Clare Brown, Ann Staines

WARWICKSHIRE

COURSES

- **SUBJECT**   Access   1319
- **TITLE**   Access to Higher Education
- **PLACE**   North Warwickshire College

Length 30 weeks   **Start** September   **Days** Tues & Thurs 6.30-9.30   **Cost** £160   **Entry Reqs**
Contact College   **Award** Access to higher education   **Creche** Yes
- **CONTACT**   Information Unit 01203 349321 x2132

- **SUBJECT** Access   1320
- **TITLE** Access to Higher Education
- **PLACE** Rugby College of Further Education

Length 36 weeks   **Start** September   **Days** Mon-Thurs 9.30-3.15, Fri 9.30-2.15   **Cost** Free   **Award** College Certificate   **Creche** Yes. £1.50-£1.75/hour (free if on certain benefits)

- **CONTACT** Kate Rix 01926 413505

- **SUBJECT** Access/Engineering/Science   1321
- **TITLE** Foundation Year for Engineering and Science (HITECC)
- **PLACE** Rugby College of Further Education

Length 36 weeks   **Start** September   **Days** Mon-Thurs 9.30-3.15, Fri 9.30-2.15   **Cost** Grant available   **Entry Reqs** GCSE Maths grade C or above   **Creche** Yes. £1.50-£1.75/hour (free if on certain benefits)

- **CONTACT** Peter Lock 01926 413426

- **SUBJECT** Access/Multi-Subject/Information Technology/Mathematics/Science   1322
- **TITLE** Open Access Programme
- **PLACE** Stratford upon Avon College

Length Modular   **Start** September, December, March   **Award** Central Access Network credits and Certificate

- **CONTACT** Access Team 01789 266245

- **SUBJECT** Administration   1323
- **TITLE** People into Administrative Management
- **PLACE** Rugby College of Further Education

Length 1 year   **Start** September   **Days** Mon-Thurs 9.30-3.15   **Cost** Free   **Entry Reqs** No formal requirements   **Award** RSA awards in Word processing, Book-keeping, Computer Literacy, Administrative Management Certificate   **Creche** Yes. £1.50-£1.75/hour (free if on certain benefits)

- **CONTACT** Jill Titley 01926 413476

- **SUBJECT** Art   1324
- **TITLE** Foundation Course (Flexible)
- **PLACE** Rugby College of Further Education

Length 1 year   **Start** September   **Days** Flexible   **Cost** Free   **Entry Reqs** No formal qualifications, but examples of previous art work required   **Award** BTEC Diploma in Foundation Studies   **Creche** Yes. £1.50-£1.75/hour (free if on certain benefits)

- **CONTACT** Sally Kenyon 01926 413461

- **SUBJECT** Business   1325
- **TITLE** BTEC: 1. HND Business and Finance 2. HNC Business
- **PLACE** Mid-Warwickshire College

Length 2 years   **Start** September   **Days** 1. Full time 2.1 afternoon+1 eve or 2 eves/week   **Cost** Contact College   **Entry Reqs** Contact College. Mature students 21+ with relevant experience   **Award** 1. BTEC HND in Business and Finance 2. BTEC HNC Business   **Creche** Day Nursery

- **CONTACT** L Haynes 01926 311711 x273

- **SUBJECT** Business   1326
- **TITLE** BTEC HND Business and Finance
- **PLACE** Stratford upon Avon College

Length 2 years   **Start** September   **Days** Full time   **Entry Reqs** Contact College   **Award** BTEC HND in Business and Finance

- **CONTACT** Admissions Officer 01789 266245

- **SUBJECT**   Business   1327
- **TITLE**   Business Studies 1. GNVQ Intermediate 2. GNVQ Advanced
- **PLACE**   North Warwickshire College

Start September   **Days** Full time   **Cost** Contact College   **Entry Reqs** Contact College
Award 1. GNVQ Intermediate 2. GNVQ Advanced   **Creche** Yes

- **CONTACT**   Information Unit 01203 349321 x2132

- **SUBJECT**   Business Administration   1328
- **TITLE**   Administrative Procedures
- **PLACE**   Stratford upon Avon College

Length 1 year full time, 2 years part time   **Start** September   **Entry Reqs** Contact College
Award RSA Higher Diploma

- **CONTACT**   Admissions Officer 01789 266245

- **SUBJECT**   Business Administration   1329
- **TITLE**   Business Administration
- **PLACE**   North Warwickshire College

Length 30 weeks   **Start** September   **Days** Part time, various days   **Cost** £55   **Entry Reqs**
Contact College   **Award** NVQ Level II   **Creche** Yes

- **CONTACT**   Information Unit 01203 349321 x2132

- **SUBJECT**   Business/Information Technology   1330
- **TITLE**   Back to Business Technology
- **PLACE**   Stratford upon Avon College

Length 20 weeks   **Cost** Contact College   **Award** NEBSM Certificate/C&G Information
Technology

- **CONTACT**   Ann Carter 01789 266245 x3196

- **SUBJECT**   Care Studies   1331
- **TITLE**   BTEC HND Caring Services
- **PLACE**   Mid-Warwickshire College

Length 2 years   **Start** September   **Days** Up to 5 days/week   **Cost** Contact College   **Entry
Reqs** Contact College. Interview for mature students with suitable academic/practical
experience   **Award** BTEC HND Caring Services   **Creche** Day Nursery

- **CONTACT**   C Morris 01920 311711 x265

- **SUBJECT**   Care Studies   1332
- **TITLE**   Welfare Studies 1. Certificate 2. Diploma
- **PLACE**   North Warwickshire College

Length 30 weeks   **Start** September   **Days** 1. Wed 10.00-4.00 2. Tues or Fri 10.00-4.00   **Cost**
1. £154 + registration 2. £215 + registration   **Entry Reqs** Contact College   **Award** 1. BTEC
Certificate 2. BTEC Diploma   **Creche** Yes

- **CONTACT**   Information Unit 01203 349321 x2132

- **SUBJECT**   Childcare   1333
- **TITLE**   1. Childcare and Education 2. Nursery Nursing
- **PLACE**   North Warwickshire College

Start September   **Days** Full time   **Cost** Contact College   **Entry Reqs** Contact College
Award 1. BTEC Certificate 2. NNEB Diploma   **Creche** Yes

- **CONTACT**   Information Unit 01203 349321 x2132

- **SUBJECT** Design 1334
- **TITLE** Design Communications: Information Graphics
- **PLACE** Mid-Warwickshire College

Length 2 years **Start** September **Days** 3 days/week **Cost** Contact College **Entry Reqs** Contact College. Mature students need to demonstrate appropriate skills levels and commitment **Award** BTEC Higher National Certificate in Information Graphics **Creche** Day Nursery
- **CONTACT** Secretary 01926 311711 x259

- **SUBJECT** Design 1335
- **TITLE** Design Communications: Media
- **PLACE** Mid-Warwickshire College

Length 2 years **Start** September **Days** 1 day+1 evening/week **Cost** Contact College **Entry Reqs** Contact College. Mature students need to demonstrate appropriate skills levels and commitment **Award** BTEC Higher National Certificate in Communication Media **Creche** Day Nursery
- **CONTACT** Secretary 01926 311711 x259

- **SUBJECT** Environmental Studies 1336
- **TITLE** BA/BSc Environmental Studies
- **PLACE** Mid-Warwickshire College in conjunction with the University of Warwick

Length 4 years (Years 1&2 at Mid Warwickshire College) **Start** September **Days** 5 days/week **Cost** Contact College. Grant may be available **Entry Reqs** Normally 21+. No formal qualifications **Award** BA/BSc in Environmental Studies **Creche** Day Nursery
- **CONTACT** C Morris 01920 311711 x265

- **SUBJECT** Information Technology 1337
- **TITLE** Information Technology
- **PLACE** North Warwickshire College

Length 30 weeks **Start** September **Days** Part time, various days and evenings **Cost** £54 **Entry Reqs** Contact College **Award** Various depending on course: NVQ, BTEC National Diploma, etc **Creche** Yes
- **CONTACT** Information Unit 01203 349321 x2132

- **SUBJECT** Music/Performing Arts 1338
- **TITLE** Flexible Foundation in Music/Dance
- **PLACE** Rugby College of Further Education

Length 1 year **Start** September **Days** Flexible **Cost** Free **Entry Reqs** No formal requirements **Award** Graded Music and Dance exams **Creche** Yes. £1.50-£1.75/hour (free if on certain benefits)
- **CONTACT** Val Brodie 01926 413316

- **SUBJECT** Office Skills 1339
- **TITLE** Office Skills/Keyboard
- **PLACE** North Warwickshire College

Length 30 weeks **Start** September **Days** Thurs 1.00-3.00 **Cost** None **Entry Reqs** None **Creche** Yes
- **CONTACT** Information Unit 01203 349321 x2132

- **SUBJECT** Office Skills 1340
- **TITLE** Typewriting, Wordprocessing
- **PLACE** North Warwickshire College

Length 30 weeks **Start** September **Days** Various, day and evening **Cost** Contact College **Entry Reqs** None **Award** RSA exams **Creche** Yes
- **CONTACT** Information Unit 01203 349321 x2132

- **SUBJECT** Preparatory   1341
- **TITLE** Adult Returners' Course
- **PLACE** Stratford upon Avon College

Start Contact College   **Days** Flexible   **Entry Regs** None   **Award** Progression to further courses

- **CONTACT** Admissions Officer 01789 266245

- **SUBJECT** Preparatory   1342
- **TITLE** Pathway: Return to Learn
- **PLACE** Mid-Warwickshire College

Length Modular   **Start** Open Learning   **Days** Varies   **Cost** Free   **Entry Reqs** None **Award** Open College Network Accreditation

- **CONTACT** Moira Riggs 01926 883413

- **SUBJECT** Preparatory   1343
- **TITLE** Women Back to Business
- **PLACE** Rugby College of Further Education

Length 3 terms   **Start** September   **Days** Mon-Fri 9.15-3.15 (16 hours/week)   **Cost** Free **Entry Reqs** None   **Award** NVQ in Office Skills, Wordprocessing; Typing exams can be taken **Creche** Yes. £1.50-£1.75/hour (free if on certain benefits)

- **CONTACT** Jean Vivian 01926 413470

- **SUBJECT** Science/Engineering   1344
- **TITLE** Coventry University Foundation Course in Applied Science and Engineering
- **PLACE** Mid-Warwickshire College

Length 1 yr at Mid-Warwickshire, then 3 yrs elsewhere   **Start** September   **Days** Full time (1 day/week spent at Coventry University)   **Cost** Contact College. Grant may be available   **Entry Reqs** 21+. GCSE Maths Grade C+ or diagnostic test.   **Award** Progress to BSc/HND courses at Coventry University or other univ or College of Higher Education **Creche** Day Nursery

- **CONTACT** C Morris 01920 311711 x265

- **SUBJECT** Social Studies   1345
- **TITLE** BA Social Studies
- **PLACE** Mid-Warwickshire College in conjunction with the University of Warwick

Length 4 years (Years 1&2 at Mid Warwickshire College)   **Start** September   **YDays** 5 days/ week   **Cost** Contact College. Grant may be available   **Entry Reqs** No formal requirements. Evidence of commitment to serious study and/or relevant work experience   **Award** BA Social Studies   **Creche** Day Nursery

- **CONTACT** C Morris 01920 311711 x265

- **SUBJECT** Social Studies   1346
- **TITLE** BA (Hons) Social Studies
- **PLACE** Rugby College of Further Education

Length 4 years   **Start** September   **Days** Mon-Fri 9.00-5.00   **Cost** Mandatory grant   **Entry Reqs** No formal requirements   **Award** BA (Hons)   **Creche** Yes. £1.50-£1.75/hour (free if on certain benefits)

- **CONTACT** Sue Minton 01926 413505

Warwickshire

- **SUBJECT** Technology   **1347**
- **TITLE** Women into Technology
- **PLACE** Rugby College of Further Education

Length Varies   **Start** Varies   **Days** 3½ days/week to fit in with school hours   **Cost** £180
Entry Reqs None   **Award** City & Guilds 726 Basic Technology or 224 Electronic Servicing
Creche Yes. £1.50-£1.75/hour (free if on certain benefits)

- **CONTACT** Peter Lock 01926 413426

COUNTY CONTACTS

Information and advice:

Adult Guidance Service, Atherstone and Coleshill Careers Office, Long Street, Atherstone CV9 1AX 01827 712482
Leamington Spa Careers Office, 2 Euston Square, Leamington Spa CV32 4ND 01926 334241
Nuneaton and Bedworth Careers Office, King Edward Road, Nuneaton CV11 4BB 01203 347677
Rugby Careers Office, Newton Hall, Lower Hillmorton Road, Rugby CV21 3TU 01788 541333
Stratford upon Avon Careers Office, The Willows, Alcester Road, Stratford upon Avon CV37 9QP 01789 266841
Stratford upon Avon College, The Willows North, Stratford upon Avon CV37 9QR 01789 266245. Adult guidance sessions

Open University:

The Open University, West Midlands Region, 66-68 High Street, Harborne, Birmingham B17 9NB 0121 428 1550

Training and Enterprise Council:

Coventry and Warwickshire TEC, see West Midlands County Contacts

WEA office:

WEA West Mercia District, 78-80 Sherlock Street, Birmingham B5 6LT 0121 666 6101   *Contact:* Jill Bedford

---

WEST MIDLANDS

COURSES

- **SUBJECT** Access   **1348**
- **TITLE** Access to Higher Education
- **PLACE** Dudley College of Technology

Length 1 or 2 years   **Start** September   **Days** Full or part time between 9.45-3.00 (21 hour rule)   **Cost** None   **Entry Reqs** Reasonably literate and numerate   **Award** Entry to various degree courses   **Creche** Yes

- **CONTACT** Ursula Demwell/Lesley Marshall 01384 455433 x4205

- **SUBJECT**   Access/Art & Design   1349
- **TITLE**   Access to Art & Design (Central Access Network)
- **PLACE**   Coventry Technical College

Length 36 weeks   **Start** September   **Days** Part time 3 days/week, Tues, Wed, Thurs 9.00-4.30 **Cost** Contact College. Concessions available   **Entry Reqs** Commitment to art and design   **Award** Central Access Certificate (kitemarked) for progression to higher education   **Creche** No

- **CONTACT**   Maureen Dix 01203 526700 x6890

- **SUBJECT**   Access/Art & Design/Business/Humanities/Social Studies/Science/   1350
  Health Studies
- **TITLE**   Access to Art & Design, Humanities and Business, Social and Community
  Work, Science and Health Studies
- **PLACE**   Coventry Technical College

Length 1-2 years   **Start** September   **Days** Open/flexible arrangements   **Cost** Contact College. Free depending on individual circumstances   **Entry Reqs** Commitment. Interview   **Award** Entry to higher education or specialised training   **Creche** Yes, nearby and childcare funding possible

- **CONTACT**   Julia Horsman 01203 526700 x6844

- **SUBJECT**   Access/Art & Design/Media Studies   1351
- **TITLE**   Access to 1. Art & Design 2. Media Studies 3. Electronic Media 4. CDT
- **PLACE**   Dudley College of Technology

Length 32 weeks/3 terms   **Start** September   **Days** 4 days/week (16 hours/week)   **Cost** None   **Entry Reqs** Enthusiasm for subject 2. Age 19+   **Award** HE Access Certificate, entry to degree course or HND in Design, Communication   **Creche** Yes

- **CONTACT**   1. Sue Denson/2, 3&4 Tim Joplin/Anthony Wright 01384 455433x201

- **SUBJECT**   Access/Business Studies   1352
- **TITLE**   Access to Higher Education in Business Studies
- **PLACE**   Dudley College of Technology

Length 1 year (32 weeks)   **Start** September   **Days** 5 days/week (16 hours/week)   **Cost** Free   **Entry Reqs** No formal qualifications   **Award** Access Certificate   **Creche** Yes

- **CONTACT**   David Payne 01384 455433

- **SUBJECT**   Access/Business Studies/Computing/Economics/Law/Politics   1353
- **TITLE**   Access to Business Studies, Computing, Economics, Law, Politics
- **PLACE**   Tile Hill College, Coventry

Length 1 year   **Start** September   **Cost** Free   **Entry Reqs** Contact College   **Award** Entry to higher education   **Creche** Yes

- **CONTACT**   Course Information 01203 694200

- **SUBJECT**   Access/Computing   1354
- **TITLE**   Access to Computing and Higher Education
- **PLACE**   Dudley College of Technology

Length 1 year   **Start** September   **Days** 16 hours/week to take account of family commitments   **Cost** None   **Entry Reqs** Competence in oral and written language skills **Award** Entry to HNC/HND or Degree course   **Creche** Yes 80p/hour

- **CONTACT**   Brenda Cook 01384 455433 x4217

- **SUBJECT**   Access/Design/Performing Arts   1355
- **TITLE**   Access to Costume Design & Propmaking for Display & Theatre
- **PLACE**   Coventry Technical College

Length 1 year   **Start** September   **Days** 3 days/week   **Cost** None   **Entry Reqs** Interview. Enthusiasm and commitment   **Award** Kitemarked Access Certificate Central Access Network Credit. Entry to higher education   **Creche** No

- **CONTACT**   Maureen Dix/Ann Bast 01203 526700 x6890

- **SUBJECT** Access/Education/Social Work/Sociology/Women's Studies **1356**
- **TITLE** Access to Higher Education
- **PLACE** South Birmingham College, Digbeth Centre

Length Flexible **Start** September **Days** Flexible, up to 16 hours/week **Cost** Concessionary fee £10 **Entry Reqs** Desire to enter higher education **Award** Access Certificate in HE **Creche** Yes £3/day

- **CONTACT** Sue Lassman/Lynne Sheridan 0121 694 5122

- **SUBJECT** Access/Health Studies/Nursing **1357**
- **TITLE** Access to Health Studies and Nursing
- **PLACE** Dudley College of Technology

Length 1 or 2 years **Start** September **Days** Full or part time between 9.45-3.00 (16 hours/week) **Cost** None **Entry Reqs** Reasonably literate and numerate **Award** Entry to degree and diploma courses **Creche** Yes 80p/hour

- **CONTACT** Grace Walsh 01384 455433 x4239

- **SUBJECT** Access/Health Studies/Nursing/Sports Studies **1358**
- **TITLE** Access to Health, P. E. , Nursing
- **PLACE** Tile Hill College, Coventry

Length 1 year **Start** September **Days** Mon, Tues, Thurs, Fri (16 hours/week) **Cost** Free **Entry Reqs** Contact College **Award** Entry to higher education **Creche** Yes

- **CONTACT** Course Information 01203 694200

- **SUBJECT** Access/History **1359**
- **TITLE** Access to History and Theory of Visual Culture
- **PLACE** Coventry Technical College

Length 1-2 years **Start** September **Days** Open/flexible arrangements **Cost** Contact College. Free depending on individual circumstances **Entry Reqs** Commitment. Interview **Award** Entry to higher education **Creche** Yes, nearby and childcare funding possible

- **CONTACT** Julia Horsman 01203 526700 x6844

- **SUBJECT** Access/Humanities/Social Science **1360**
- **TITLE** Access to Higher Education (Part Time)
- **PLACE** Tile Hill College, Coventry

Length 2 years **Start** September **Days** 4-7 hours/week **Cost** Contact College **Entry Reqs** Contact College **Award** Entry to higher education **Creche** Yes

- **CONTACT** Course Information 01203 694200

- **SUBJECT** Access/Humanities/Social Science/Teaching **1361**
- **TITLE** Access to Higher Education: Social Sciences, Humanities, Teacher Training
- **PLACE** Tile Hill College, Coventry

Length 1 year **Start** September **Days** 16 hours/week **Cost** Free **Entry Reqs** Contact College **Award** Entry to higher education **Creche** Yes

- **CONTACT** Course Information 01203 694200

- **SUBJECT** Access/Media Studies **1362**
- **TITLE** Access to Media and Communications
- **PLACE** Tile Hill College, Coventry

Length 1 year **Start** September **Days** 16 hours/week **Cost** Free **Entry Reqs** Contact College **Award** Entry to higher education **Creche** Yes

- **CONTACT** Course Information 01203 694200

- **SUBJECT**   Access/Social Science/Social Work   1363
- **TITLE**   Access to Social Work/Social Policy: Preparation for Professional Training
- **PLACE**   Dudley College of Technology

Length 1 academic year   **Start** September   **Days** 4 days/week (16 hours/week)   **Cost** Free if unemployed   **Entry Reqs** Good oral/written language skills, minimum 1 year relevant experience (can be voluntary)   **Award** Entry to Diploma/BA in Social Work/Social Science degrees   **Creche** Yes 80p/hour
- **CONTACT**   Val Vinall 01384 455433 x4270

- **SUBJECT**   Access/Social Science/Teaching   1364
- **TITLE**   Access to Social Science, Teaching
- **PLACE**   Matthew Boulton College

Length 1 year   **Start** Autumn   **Days** 3 days/week, part time evening   **Cost** Contact College. Concessions available   **Entry Reqs** None   **Award** Access Certificate, entry to higher education   **Creche** Yes
- **CONTACT**   Course Enquiries 0121 446 4545

- **SUBJECT**   Access/Social Work   1365
- **TITLE**   Access to Higher Education: Social Work
- **PLACE**   Tile Hill College, Coventry

Length 1 year   **Start** September   **Days** 4 days/week (16 hours/week)   **Cost** Free   **Entry Reqs** Contact College   **Award** Entry to higher education   **Creche** Yes
- **CONTACT**   Course Information 01203 694200

- **SUBJECT**   Access/Teaching   1366
- **TITLE**   Access to Teacher Training (BEd)
- **PLACE**   Dudley College of Technology

Length 1 year full time or 2 years part time   **Start** September   **Days** Full or part time between 9.45-3.00, part time hours negotiable   **Cost** None   **Entry Reqs** Reasonably literate and numerate   **Award** Access to Higher Education Certificate   **Creche** Yes 80p/hour
- **CONTACT**   Joyce Asbury 01384 455433 x4205

- **SUBJECT**   Art & Design   1367
- **TITLE**   Art & Design 1. GNVQ Intermediate 2. GNVQ Advanced
- **PLACE**   Tile Hill College, Coventry

Length 1.1 year 2.2 years   **Start** September   **Days** Various (18hours/week)   **Cost** Free   **Entry Reqs** Contact College   **Award** 1. GNVQ Intermediate 2. GNVQ Advanced   **Creche** Yes
- **CONTACT**   Course Information 01203 694200

- **SUBJECT**   Biological Sciences   1368
- **TITLE**   Biology: Masters Degree by Research
- **PLACE**   University of Warwick

Length 1 year   **Start** October   **Cost** Biotechnology & Biological Sciences Research Council award available   **Entry Reqs** Graduates with first or upper second class honours degree in an appropriate subject   **Award** MSc
- **CONTACT**   Dr V Essex, BBSRC, 01793 413200

- **SUBJECT**   Biological Sciences   1369
- **TITLE**   Molecular and Cellular Biology and its Applications: Masters Degree by Research
- **PLACE**   University of Birmingham

Length 1 year   **Start** October   **Cost** Biotechnology & Biological Sciences Research Council award available   **Entry Reqs** Graduates with first or upper second class honours degree in an appropriate subject
- **CONTACT**   Dr V Essex, BBSRC, 01793 413200

- **SUBJECT** Business   **1370**
- **TITLE** 1. Business Skills Workshop 2. Advanced Business Skills Workshop
- **PLACE** Tile Hill College, Coventry

Length 1.1 term 2.18 weeks   **Start** 1. Sept, Jan, April 2. Sept, February   **Cost** Free   **Entry Reqs** Contact College   **Creche** Yes

- **CONTACT** Course Information 01203 694200

- **SUBJECT** Business   **1371**
- **TITLE** Women into Business
- **PLACE** Bond House, Wolverhampton

Length 20 weeks   **Start** 2 courses/year   **Days** 4 days/week   **Cost** Free   **Entry Reqs** Basic knowledge of English   **Award** NVQ   **Creche** Yes, free

- **CONTACT** Hardeep Nijjar 0121 609 7100

- **SUBJECT** Business Administration   **1372**
- **TITLE** BTEC Certificate in Business Administration
- **PLACE** Tile Hill College, Coventry

Length 1 year   **Start** September   **Cost** Free   **Entry Reqs** Contact College   **Award** BTEC Certificate in Business Administration   **Creche** Yes

- **CONTACT** Course Information 01203 694200

- **SUBJECT** Business Administration   **1373**
- **TITLE** Business Administration
- **PLACE** Matthew Boulton College

Length 1 year   **Start** September   **Days** 1 day or 1 eve/week   **Cost** Contact College   **Entry Reqs** Interview   **Award** RSA NVQ awards   **Creche** Yes

- **CONTACT** Course Enquiries 0121 446 4545

- **SUBJECT** Business Administration   **1374**
- **TITLE** Business Administration/Personal Assistant for Graduates (with Language Options)
- **PLACE** Coventry Technical College

Length 1 year   **Start** September   **Days** 20.5 hours/week Mon-Fri 9.00-4.30   **Cost** Contact College. Concessions available   **Entry Reqs** Mature students with work experience, degree or good O/A Levels   **Award** LCCI Private & Executive Secretary's Diploma, RSA Single Subjects   **Creche** No

- **CONTACT** Trudi Wattison-Ridge 01203 526700 x6896

- **SUBJECT** Business Administration   **1375**
- **TITLE** NVQ Adminstration
- **PLACE** Women's Job Change, Birmingham Settlement

Length 23 weeks   **Start** Autumn, Spring   **Days** 4 days/week   **Entry Req** Some office experience, basic keyboard skills   **Award** RSA/NVQ2/RSA CLAIT

- **CONTACT** Diane Thomas 0121 359 3562

- **SUBJECT** Care Studies   **1376**
- **TITLE** Foundation Course in Social Care
- **PLACE** Tile Hill College, Coventry

Length 1 year   **Start** September   **Days** 3 days/week (16 hours/week)   **Cost** Free   **Entry Reqs** Contact College   **Award** Foundation Certificate   **Creche** Yes

- **CONTACT** Course Information 01203 694200

- **SUBJECT** Childcare   1377
- **TITLE** 1. Certificate in Childcare and Education 2. CACHE Diploma in Nursery Nursing 3. BTEC National Diploma
- **PLACE** Tile Hill College, Coventry

Length 1.1 year 2. &3.2 years   **Start** September   **Days** Various   **Cost** Free   **Entry Reqs** Contact College   **Award** 1. CACHE Certificate in Childcare & Education 2. CACHE Diploma in Nursery Nursing 3. BTEC Nat Diploma   **Creche** Yes

- **CONTACT** Course Information 01203 694200

- **SUBJECT** Childcare   1378
- **TITLE** Introduction to Childcare
- **PLACE** Women's Job Change, Birmingham Settlement

Length 8 weeks   **Start** Varies   **Days** 9.30-3.00 1 day/week   **Cost** Free   **Entry Reqs** None, except interest in childcare   **Creche** Yes nominal charge

- **CONTACT** Kate Ward 0121 359 3562

- **SUBJECT** Computing   1379
- **TITLE** Managing with Computers
- **PLACE** Coventry University, Women and Work Programme

Length 12 weeks   **Start** September, January, April   **Days** Mon-Wed/Wed-Fri 10.00-3.00   **Cost** Free to Coventry residents   **Entry Reqs** Unwaged women living in Coventry   **Award** University Certificate/RSA/C&G   **Creche** No but childcare costs refunded

- **CONTACT** Women and Work Programme 01203 838903

- **SUBJECT** Computing   1380
- **TITLE** Women into Computing
- **PLACE** Dudley College of Technology

Length 1 year   **Start** September   **Days** Mon-Fri 9.30-2.30   **Cost** None   **Entry Reqs** None **Award** C&G 7621   **Creche** Yes 80p/hour

- **CONTACT** Janet Connigale 01384 455433 x4217

- **SUBJECT** Computing   1381
- **TITLE** Women into Computing
- **PLACE** University of Wolverhampton, School of Computing & IT

Length 6 weeks   **Start** Summer term   **Days** Modular   **Cost** Contact University (ESF funded)   **Entry Reqs** None   **Award** Possible to apply for place on HND in Computing or MSc in Computing   **Creche** Yes

- **CONTACT** School of Computing & IT 01902 321000

- **SUBJECT** Computing/Business Administration   1382
- **TITLE** 1. Information Technology 2. Business Administration
- **PLACE** Women's Job Change, Birmingham Settlement

Length 12 weeks   **Start** Autumn, Spring   **Days** 1 day/week   **Cost** Free   **Entry Reqs** Basic keyboard skills   **Award** 1. RSA CLAIT Level 1/RSA NVQ Level 2

- **CONTACT** Diane Thomas 0121 359 3562

- **SUBJECT** Computing/Desk Top Publishing   1383
- **TITLE** 1. Apple Mac Computer Training 2. Desk Top Publishing
- **PLACE** Women's Job Change, Birmingham Settlement

Length 8 weeks   **Start** Varies, please phone   **Days** 2 hours, 1 day/week   **Cost** Free **Entry Reqs** Unemployed or in part time work; preferred if able to use/for 1. keyboard/for 2. computer   **Creche** Yes nominal charge

- **CONTACT** Diane Thomas 0121 359 3562

- **SUBJECT** Construction   **1384**
- **TITLE** Construction for Women
- **PLACE** South Birmingham College

Length 18 weeks **Start** September, February **Days** 4 days/week (16 hours) **Cost** None
Entry Reqs None **Award** Open College Certificate **Creche** Yes free

- **CONTACT** Mark Scott/Sally Nightingale 0121 694 5089

- **SUBJECT** Engineering   **1385**
- **TITLE** Engineering: Research Masters Pilot Course
- **PLACE** University of Warwick

Length 2 years **Start** October **Cost** Engineering & Physical Sciences Research Council
award available **Entry Reqs** Graduates with first or upper second class honours degree in an
appropriate subject **Award** Master of Research Degree

- **CONTACT** Professor P Carpenter 01203 523152

- **SUBJECT** Engineering   **1386**
- **TITLE** Women's Technology Training Programme
- **PLACE** Matthew Boulton College

Length 1 year **Start** September **Days** 20 hours/week **Cost** Free **Entry Reqs** None
Award C&G, BTEC **Creche** Yes

- **CONTACT** Course Enquiries 0121 446 4545

- **SUBJECT** Humanities/Social Studies   **1387**
- **TITLE** Part Time Degree Scheme (7 Programmes)
- **PLACE** University of Warwick

Length 4-10 years (depending on number of course modules yearly **Start** October **Days**
Various days and evenings **Cost** £216/course module (12 in total). Bursaries available
Entry Reqs No specific requirements for mature students **Award** BA **Creche** Yes limited
places

- **CONTACT** Sally Blakeman 01203 523683/Peter Byrd 01203 523533

- **SUBJECT** Information Technology   **1388**
- **TITLE** C&G Information Technology Applications
- **PLACE** Tile Hill College, Coventry

Length 1 term **Start** September, January, April **Cost** Free **Entry Reqs** Contact College
Award C&G 726 IT Applications **Creche** Yes

- **CONTACT** Course Information 01203 694200

- **SUBJECT** Information Technology   **1389**
- **TITLE** Wordprocessing, Spreadsheets, Database, DTP
- **PLACE** Flexible Learning Centres in Willenhall, Stoke Heath & Stoke Aldermoor

Length Negotiable **Start** Flexible **Days** Varies **Cost** Free to people on benefit/dependent
Entry Reqs None **Award** Open College Credits, RSA **Creche** Yes Free

- **CONTACT** Sue Wyatt/Richard Heath 01203 511228

- **SUBJECT** Information Technology   **1390**
- **TITLE** Women's Technology
- **PLACE** South Birmingham College

Length 18 weeks **Start** September, February **Days** 3 days/week 9.30-3.00 **Cost** Contact
College **Entry Reqs** Women intending to return to work **Award** C&G 726/IT **Creche**
Yes

- **CONTACT** Sheena Elder 0121 694 5000

- **SUBJECT** Laboratory Skills 1391
- **TITLE** Laboratory Technicians' Course for Women
- **PLACE** South Birmingham College, Hall Green Centre

Length 1 year **Start** September **Days** 16 hours/week in school hours **Cost** £10 **Entry Reqs** Interest in working in field **Award** Institute of Science Technology Certificate **Creche** Yes £3/day
- **CONTACT** Chris Thompson/Keith Tromans 0121 694 5119

- **SUBJECT** Management 1392
- **TITLE** Certificate in Management (BTEC)
- **PLACE** South Birmingham College

Length 24 weeks **Start** September **Days** 4 days/week 9.30-3.30 **Cost** None **Entry Reqs** Women capable of work at management or supervisory levels **Award** Certificate in Management **Creche** Yes free
- **CONTACT** Jenny Rankin 0121 694 5077

- **SUBJECT** Management 1393
- **TITLE** 1. Insight into Management for Women 2. Women into Management
- **PLACE** Bilston Community College, Open Management Centre

Length Flexible **Start** Flexible **Days** Distance learning **Cost** £200+VAT **Entry Reqs** Women only **Award** College Certificate, progression route to NVQ, MCI Management training
- **CONTACT** Jane Seabourne 01902 408791

- **SUBJECT** Medicine 1394
- **TITLE** Molecular and Cellular Immunology and Oncology: Research Masters Pilot Course
- **PLACE** University of Birmingham

Length 1 year **Start** October **Cost** Medical Research Council award available **Entry Reqs** Graduates with first or upper second class honours degree in an appropriate subject **Award** MSc
- **CONTACT** Professor J Gordon 0121 414 4034

- **SUBJECT** Multi-Subject 1395
- **TITLE** Women Returner Programmes: Associate of Accounting Technicians, Return to Office, Certificate in Personnel Practice, Computing
- **PLACE** Bournville College

Length 30 weeks **Start** September **Days** 4-5 days/week 9.30-2.30 **Cost** None **Entry Reqs** None **Award** Academic or professional qualifications **Creche** Yes £3.40/day
- **CONTACT** Maggie Dilloway 0121 411 1414

- **SUBJECT** NOW 1396
- **TITLE** New Opportunities for Women
- **PLACE** Bournville College and other community venues

Length 10 weeks **Start** October, January **Days** Tues (College), Thurs (Northfield) 10.00-12.00
Cost None **Entry Reqs** None **Award** West Midlands Access Federation Accreditation **Creche** Yes
- **CONTACT** Maggie Dilloway 0121 411 1414

- **SUBJECT** NOW 1397
- **TITLE** New Opportunities for Women: Confidence Building and Personal Development
- **PLACE** Selly Oak Adult Education Centre, Bristol Road

Length 10 weeks, including taster sessions at Bournville College **Start** September, January **Days** Fri 10.00-12.00 **Cost** Free to Passport to Leisure holders **Entry Reqs** None **Creche** Yes 2 years+, £1/session
- **CONTACT** Kathy Kirk 0121 459 9919/Mary Ellson 0121 472 5933

- **SUBJECT** NOW   **1398**
- **TITLE** Women into Work
- **PLACE** Coventry University, Women and Work Programme

Length 12 weeks **Start** September, January, April **Days** Mon-Wed/Wed-Fri 10.00-3.00 **Cost** Free to Coventry residents **Entry Reqs** Unwaged women living in Coventry **Award** University Certificate/RSA/C&G **Creche** No but childcare costs refunded

- **CONTACT** Women and Work Programme 01203 838903

- **SUBJECT** Office Skills   **1399**
- **TITLE** Office Procedures, Office Skills
- **PLACE** Matthew Boulton College

Length 1 year **Start** September **Cost** Contact College. Concessions possible **Entry Reqs** None **Award** RSA CLAIT, NVQ Level II **Creche** Yes

- **CONTACT** Course Enquiries 0121 446 4545

- **SUBJECT** Office Skills   **1400**
- **TITLE** Office Skills, Office Technology
- **PLACE** Henley College

Length 12 weeks **Start** Flexible **Days** 3 days/week (16 hours/week) **Cost** Free if in receipt of benefit **Entry Reqs** None **Creche** Yes

- **CONTACT** Joy Webb 01203 611021

- **SUBJECT** Office Skills   **1401**
- **TITLE** Modular Office Skills: Wordprocessing, SAGE Financial Accounting, Business Admin, IT, Programming
- **PLACE** Tile Hill College, Coventry

Length 1 term/module **Start** September, January, April **Days** Various **Cost** Contact College **Entry Reqs** Contact College **Award** NVQ Levels I, II&III/RSA CLAIT **Creche** Yes

- **CONTACT** Course Information 01203 694200

- **SUBJECT** Office Skills   **1402**
- **TITLE** 1. Return to the Office 2. New to the Office
- **PLACE** South Birmingham College

Length 1.18 weeks 2.1 year **Start** 1. Twice a year 2. September **Days** 1.4 days/week 9.30-3.15 2.5 mornings/week **Cost** Contact College **Entry Reqs** 1. Previous office experience 2. None **Award** Various certificates possible **Creche** Yes

- **CONTACT** Angela Donohoe 0121 694 5000

- **SUBJECT** Practical   **1403**
- **TITLE** Basic Woodwork
- **PLACE** Coventry Job Change Ltd

Length 6 weeks **Start** Ongoing **Days** 3 days/week 10.00-3.00 **Cost** Free but pay for wood used on own project **Entry Reqs** Unemployed/unwaged over 35 years **Award** Open College Network Levels I & II and entry level **Creche** Yes Free

- **CONTACT** Vera Davies/Robert Oakey 01203 673310

- **SUBJECT** Preparatory   **1404**
- **TITLE** Access Foundation Course
- **PLACE** Tile Hill College, Coventry

Length 1 term or 1 year **Start** September **Days** Various (15 hours/week) **Cost** Free **Entry Reqs** Contact College **Award** Progress to Access courses **Creche** Yes

- **CONTACT** Course Information 01203 694200

- **SUBJECT** Preparatory   1405
- **TITLE** Asian Women's Access Course
- **PLACE** Community centres & other venues in Sandwell

Length 16 weeks   **Start** 2 courses/year   **Days** 3 days/week 10.00-2.30   **Cost** Free   **Entry Reqs** Basic knowledge of English   **Award** Certificate   **Creche** Yes
- **CONTACT** Hardeep Nijjar 0121 609 7100

- **SUBJECT** Preparatory   1406
- **TITLE** Building on Your Experience
- **PLACE** Coventry Job Change Ltd

Length 10 weeks   **Start** Ongoing   **Days** 2 days/week between 10.00-1.00   **Cost** Free   **Entry Reqs** Unemployed/unwaged over 35 years   **Award** Open College Network Levels I, II, III Accredited   **Creche** Yes Free
- **CONTACT** Vera Davies/Nimi Kaur 01203 673310

- **SUBJECT** Preparatory   1407
- **TITLE** Have a Go for Women
- **PLACE** Bournville College

Length 16 weeks   **Start** September, February   **Days** Fri 9.30-1.00   **Cost** £20 enrolment fee   **Entry Reqs** None   **Award** West Midlands Access Federation Accreditation   **Creche** Yes £1.70
- **CONTACT** Maggie Dilloway 0121 411 1414

- **SUBJECT** Preparatory   1408
- **TITLE** New Woman: Confidence Building
- **PLACE** Dudley College of Technology

Length 1 term   **Start** September, January, April   **Days** 1 day/week 10.00-2.30   **Cost** Free   **Entry Reqs** All welcome   **Award** Black Country Access Federation Credits   **Creche** Yes 80p/hour
- **CONTACT** Julie Frew/Annie Killin 01384 455433 x2100/454291

- **SUBJECT** Preparatory   1409
- **TITLE** Outreach Programme
- **PLACE** Henley College, at Primary Schools & Community Centres across Coventry

Length 1 term to 1 year   **Start** Autumn, January, April   **Days** Various 9.30-11.30, 1.15-3.15, 6.30-8.30   **Cost** Free or £5   **Entry Reqs** None   **Award** Some lead to GCSE/AS/A levels/ RSA NVQ Bus Admin/CLAIT/Typing & Bookkeeping/Assertiveness   **Creche** At some centres. Approx £1/session
- **CONTACT** Henley College 01203 611021

- **SUBJECT** Preparatory   1410
- **TITLE** Pre Access: Breakthrough
- **PLACE** Dudley College of Technology

Length 1 term   **Start** September, January, April   **Days** 1 day/week 10.00-2.30   **Cost** Free   **Entry Reqs** Anyone of Asian or African-Caribbean origin   **Award** Credits towards Access Courses   **Creche** Yes 80p/hour
- **CONTACT** Christine Braddock/Julie Frew 01384 455433 x304

- **SUBJECT** Preparatory   1411
- **TITLE** Various courses: Women's Section
- **PLACE** Women's Job Change, Birmingham Settlement

Length Various   **Start** Various   **Cost** Free   **Entry Reqs** Unemployed women   **Creche** Yes
- **CONTACT** Chris Higgins 0121 359 3562

- **SUBJECT** Preparatory   **1412**
- **TITLE** Woman's Career Change
- **PLACE** Dudley College of Technology

Length 1 term   **Start** September, January, April   **Days** 1 eve/week 7.00-9.00   **Cost** None   **Entry Reqs** All welcome   **Award** Black Country Access Federation Credits   **Creche** Yes 80p/hour

- **CONTACT** Annie Killin/Julie Frew 01384 455433 x2100/454291

- **SUBJECT** Preparatory   **1413**
- **TITLE** Women: What's New
- **PLACE** Coventry Unemployed Workers Project

Length 10 weeks   **Start** Contact Project   **Days** 3 days/week   **Cost** Free   **Entry Reqs** None   **Award** NVQ Level I, CLAIT   **Creche** Yes

- **CONTACT** G Tsakirakis 01203 714082

- **SUBJECT** Preparatory   **1414**
- **TITLE** 1. Women's Rethink 2. Women Moving On
- **PLACE** Halesowen College

Length 15 weeks   **Start** September, February   **Days** Tues 10.30-3.00   **Cost** £5   **Entry Reqs** None   **Award** WMAF Credits   **Creche** Nursery Free

- **CONTACT** Sue Mickiewicz/Heather Knight 0121 550 1451

- **SUBJECT** Professional Updating/Management   **1415**
- **TITLE** Women into Professions/Management
- **PLACE** Coventry University, Women and Work Programme

Length 12 weeks   **Start** September, January, April   **Days** Mon-Wed/Wed-Fri 10.00-3.00   **Cost** Free to Coventry residents   **Entry Reqs** Women returners and those who want to enter a profession   **Award** University Certificate   **Creche** No but childcare costs refunded

- **CONTACT** Women and Work Programme 01203 838903

- **SUBJECT** Retail   **1416**
- **TITLE** C&G Retail Certificate NVQ Levels I&II
- **PLACE** Tile Hill College, Coventry

Length 12 weeks   **Start** September, December, March   **Cost** Free   **Entry Reqs** Contact College   **Award** C&G Retail Certificate NVQ Levels I/II   **Creche** Yes

- **CONTACT** Course Information 01203 694200

- **SUBJECT** Science   **1417**
- **TITLE** Materials Science and Engineering: Research Masters Pilot Course
- **PLACE** University of Birmingham

Length 2 years   **Start** October   **Cost** Engineering & Physical Sciences Research Council award available   **Entry Reqs** Graduates with first or upper second class honours degree in an appropriate subject   **Award** Master of Research Degree

- **CONTACT** Professor Colin Gough 0121 414 4669

- **SUBJECT** Science   **1418**
- **TITLE** Science 1. GNVQ Intermediate 2, GNVQ Advanced
- **PLACE** Tile Hill College, Coventry

Length 1 year   **Start** September   **Days** Various (18 hours/week)   **Cost** Free   **Entry Reqs** Contact College   **Award** 1. GNVQ Intermediate 2. GNVQ Advanced   **Creche** Yes

- **CONTACT** Course Information 01203 694200

- **SUBJECT**　Sports Studies　　　　　　　　　　　　　　　　　　　**1419**
- **TITLE**　　BSc in Sport Science with Leisure Studies and Health Studies
- **PLACE**　　Tile Hill College, Coventry

Start October　**Days** 16 hours/week　**Cost** Free　**Entry Reqs** Contact College　**Award** BSc in Sports Science with Leisure Studies and Health Studies　**Creche** Yes
- **CONTACT**　Course Information 01203 694200

- **SUBJECT**　Sports Studies　　　　　　　　　　　　　　　　　　　**1420**
- **TITLE**　　BTEC National Diploma in Sports Studies
- **PLACE**　　Tile Hill College, Coventry

Length 2 years　**Start** September　**Days** Various (18.5 hours/week)　**Cost** Free　**Entry Reqs** Contact College　**Award** BTEC National Diploma　**Creche** Yes
- **CONTACT**　Course Information 01203 694200

- **SUBJECT**　Teaching　　　　　　　　　　　　　　　　　　　　　**1421**
- **TITLE**　　C-Tel: Certificate in Teaching a European Language
- **PLACE**　　Coventry Technical College

Length 1. Full time, 4 weeks/140 hours 2. Part time, 3 terms eves　**Start** Various　**Days** 1. Mon-Fri+1 or 2 eves 2. Mon eve + teaching practice　**Cost** Contact College (concessions available)　**Entry Reqs** Proficient native speaker or graduate in European language　**Award** Trinity College London Certificate in Teaching a European Language. Entry to teaching **Creche** Yes
- **CONTACT**　Genevieve Hartop 01203 526743

- **SUBJECT**　Teaching　　　　　　　　　　　　　　　　　　　　　**1422**
- **TITLE**　　Certificate in ESOL (Teaching English to Speakers of Other Languages)
- **PLACE**　　Coventry Technical College

Length 1. Full time, 4 weeks/140 hours 2. Part time, 3 terms/140 hrs　**Start** 1. Various 2. September　**Days** 1. Mon-Fri 2. Mon 6.00-8.30　**Cost** Contact College (concessions available)　**Entry Reqs** Degree or similar qualification or high level of proficiency in English Language　**Award** Trinity College London Certificate in TESOL. Entry to teaching EFL/ESL **Creche** No
- **CONTACT**　Christopher Fry 01203 526742/3

- **SUBJECT**　Teaching　　　　　　　　　　　　　　　　　　　　　**1423**
- **TITLE**　　Learning to Teach a Language
- **PLACE**　　Coventry Technical College

Length 15 weeks　**Start** Various　**Days** Mon 6.00-8.00　**Cost** Contact College (concessions available)　**Creche** No
- **CONTACT**　Nicola Mooney/Christopher Fry 01203 257221 x327

- **SUBJECT**　Teaching　　　　　　　　　　　　　　　　　　　　　**1424**
- **TITLE**　　Teachers' Certificate in Further and Adult Education 1. Stage 1 2. Stage 2
- **PLACE**　　Tile Hill College, Coventry

Length 1.20 weeks 2.26 weeks　**Start** 1. September, February 2. January　**Days** Evenings　**Cost** 1. £45 2. £113.40+£40 moderation fee　**Entry Reqs** Contact College　**Award** 1. C&G 730 Stage 1 2. C&G 730 Stage 2　**Creche** Yes
- **CONTACT**　Gill Manthorpe 01203 694200 x304

- **SUBJECT**　Teaching　　　　　　　　　　　　　　　　　　　　　**1425**
- **TITLE**　　Teachers' Certificate in Further and Adult Education Combined C&G 1&2
- **PLACE**　　Tile Hill College, Coventry

Length 35 weeks　**Start** September　**Days** 10.00-3.30　**Cost** £195.20+£40 moderation fee **Entry Reqs** Contact College　**Award** C&G 730 Combined (Stages 1&2)　**Creche** Yes
- **CONTACT**　Glynis Cousins 01203 694200 x304

- **SUBJECT** Women's Studies 1426
- **TITLE** Assertiveness Training
- **PLACE** Women's Job Change, Birmingham Settlement

Length 8x2 hour sessions **Start** Various **Cost** Free to non-waged women **Creche** Yes

- **CONTACT** Chris Higgins 0121 359 3562

- **SUBJECT** Women's Studies 1427
- **TITLE** BA Modules or Combined Degree with Social Science/Social Policy/Politics
- **PLACE** Coventry University

Length 3 years full time, 5 years part time or single modules **Start** October **Days** Contact University **Cost** Approx £70/module, 75% reductions if on benefit **Entry Reqs** Usual degree entry or able to benefit if single modules studied **Award** BA **Creche** Yes but limited places

- **CONTACT** Tina Barnes Powell 01203 631313

- **SUBJECT** Women's Studies 1428
- **TITLE** 1. MA/Diploma (Interdisciplinary) Women's Studies 2. MA/Diploma Gender & International Development 3. MA Gender, Literature & Modernity
- **PLACE** University of Warwick

Length 1. &2.1 year full time, 2 years part time 3.1 year full time **Start** October **Cost** £2430 full time, £730 part time **Entry Reqs** Arts or Social Science degree **Award** MA or Diploma where indicated **Creche** Yes limited places

- **CONTACT** Terry Lovell 01203 523600

- **SUBJECT** Women's Studies 1429
- **TITLE** Open Studies Certificate
- **PLACE** University of Warwick

Length 2 years (6x10 week modules) **Start** October **Days** Wed 7.30-9.30 **Cost** Each 10 week module £38 (or £28 or £11 concessionary) **Entry Reqs** None **Award** Certificate and exemption from 1 unit of part time degree programme **Creche** No

- **CONTACT** Open Studies Office 01203 523831

- **SUBJECT** Women's Studies 1430
- **TITLE** Women's Studies 1. BA 2. MA/Diploma
- **PLACE** University of Wolverhampton, Centre for Women's Studies, Dudley

Length 1.3 years 2.2 years or longer **Start** September, modular scheme **Days** Varies **Cost** Contact Dudley Campus **Entry Reqs** 1. No specific requirements 2. First degree and/or professional qualification/experience **Award** 1. BA or BA(Hons) Degree 2. MA or Postgraduate Diploma in Women's Studies **Creche** Yes 2-5 year olds daytime

- **CONTACT** Jenny Williams 01902 321000 x3416/x3413

COUNTY CONTACTS

Information and advice:

Adult Education Advice Service, Ashleigh House, 2 Edman Road, Dudley DY1 1HL 01384 453150

Adult Guidance Service, Tile Hill College, Tile Hill Lane, Tile Hill, Coventry CV4 9SU 01203 694200

Careers Guidance Service, Coventry University, Alma Building, Alma Street, Coventry 01203 536323

Educational Advice Centre, Solihull College, Blossomfield Campus, Blossomfield Road, Solihull B91 1SB 0121 711 6025/6 *Contact:* Joyce Bennett

Educational Advice and Admissions, Solihull College, Chelmsley Campus, Partridge Close, Chelmsley Wood B37 6UG 1021 770 5651 *Contact:* Linda Britcliffe

GATE: Guidance For Adults on Training and Education, 11 Clarence Street, Wolverhampton WV1 4JL 01902 311878 *Contact:* Sue Kidson. Open weekdays 9.30-12.30 and 1.30-4.30. Offers a free service to all

Information Centre, Handsworth College, The Council House, Soho Road, Birmingham B21 9DP 0121 515 1500

Quality Careers Services Ltd, Casselden House, Greyfriars Lane, Coventry CV1 2GZ 01203 831776. Adult guidance and information on careers, education and training.

Women's Studies Resource Centre. University of Wolverhampton, Dudley Campus, Castleview, Dudley DY1 3HR 01902 321000 *Contact:* Pat Green, Jenny Williams

Open University:

The Open University, West Midlands Region, 66-68 High Street, Harborne, Birmingham B17 9NB 0121 428 1550

Other agencies:

Birmingham Women's Workshop, Unit 9, Whitworth Industrial Park, Tilton Road, Small Heath, Birmingham B9 4PE 0121 773 5511. Women's training centre

Childcare Information Bureau, Centre for the Child, Central Library, Chamberlain Square, Birmingham B3 3HQ 0121 235 4386 *Contact:* Bel Saini. Drop-in centre providing information about all aspects of childcare for parents and carers

Coventry Unemployed Workers' Project, Unit 15, The Arches Industrial Estate, Spon End, Coventry CV1 3JQ 01203 714082 *Contact:* G Tsakirakis

Foleshill Women's Training Ltd, 70-72 Elmsdale Avenue, Coventry CV6 6ES 01203 637693

Women & Work Programme, Coventry University, Priory Street, Coventry CV1 1QN 01203 631313 *Contact:* Helen Gurden

Women's Business Development Agency Ltd, Enterprise House, Sheriff's Orchard, Coventry CV1 1QN 01203 633737

Women's Centre, Solihull College, Chelmsley Campus, Partridge Close, Chelmsley Wood B37 6UG 0121 770 5651 *Contact:* Janet Clark

Women's Development Network (Birmingham), c/o Birmingham TEC, Chaplin Court, 80 Hurst Street, Birmingham B5 4TG 0121 622 4419 *Contact:* Lesley Pinder. Aims to open up fair opportunities in employment, training, education and enterprise to enable all women and girls to participate to their full potential in a high skill economy in Birmingham. Produces a directory of local programmes and services targetted at women returning to work, changing jobs or in employment.

Women's Development Network (Coventry), c/o City Development Directorate, Coventry City Council, Tower Block, Much Park Street, Coventry CV1 2PY 01203 831288 *Contact:* Hilda Francis. Comprises representatives of various statutory and voluntary organisations concerned with disadvantaged women in Coventry. Can advise and provide information on education, training, employment and enterprise initiatives

Training and Enterprise Councils:

Birmingham TEC, Chaplin Court, 80 Hurst Street, Birmingham B5 4TG 0121 622 4419

Coventry and Warwickshire TEC, Brandon Court, Progress Way, Coventry CV3 2TE 01203 635666. Out-of-School Childcare initiative provides support to people wishing to set up childcare facilities for school aged children. Holds information on childcare facilities for school aged children in Coventry and Warwickshire accessible for people returning to work and other working parents with childcare difficulties. Advice on training provision is available through the Helpline 0800 252198

Dudley TEC, Dudley South Court, Waterfront East, Level Street Brierley Hill DY5 1XN 01384 485000

Sandwell TEC, 1st Floor, Kingston House, 438/450 High Street West Bromwich B70 9LD 0121 525 4242. Business Administration for Women Returners with twinning for counselling, mentoring and work shadowing with women managers; Training co-ordinator funded at Women's Enterprise Development Agency in Sandwell to promote women's training and opportunities in business; Childcare survey.

Walsall TEC, 5th Floor, Townend House, Townend Square, Walsall WS1 1NS 01922 32332

Wolverhampton TEC, Pendeford Business Park, Wobaston Road, Wolverhampton WV9 5HA 01902 397787

WEA office:

WEA West Mercia District, 78-80 Sherlock Street, Birmingham B5 6LT 0121 666 6101   *Contact:* Jill Bedford

Publication:

Birmingham Women's Development Directory, produced by Birmingham Women's Development Network. Contact Lesley Pinder at Birmingham TEC 0121 622 4419

WEST SUSSEX

COURSES

- **SUBJECT**   Computing   **1431**
- **TITLE**   BTEC National Certificate in Computer Studies
- **PLACE**   Chichester College of Arts, Science and Technology

Length 36 weeks   **Start** September   **Days** 4 days/week (approx 15 hours/week between 9.00-3.00)   **Cost** Contact College   **Entry Reqs** Aptitude test   **Award** BTEC National Certificate   **Creche** Yes Nursery £10/session

- **CONTACT** Mary Ann Bart 01248 812218

- **SUBJECT**   NOW   **1432**
- **TITLE**   1. New Opportunities for Women 2. Further Opportunities for Women
- **PLACE**   Chichester College of Arts, Science and Technology

Length 1.1 year or termly 2.1 year   **Start** September or termly   **Days** Full time (5 days/week) or part time (choice of days)   **Cost** Contact College   **Entry Reqs** Interview   **Award** GCSEs, RSA qualifications, employment   **Creche** Yes Nursery £10/session

- **CONTACT** Sue Chequer/Patricia Hall 01243 786321 x2268

- **SUBJECT**   Office Skills   **1433**
- **TITLE**   Office Update
- **PLACE**   Chichester College of Arts, Science and Technology

Length 1 year   **Start** September, October, January   **Days** 3 days/week or 4 mornings/week   **Cost** Contact College   **Entry Reqs** None   **Award** RSA, NVQ Level II   **Creche** Yes Nursery £10/session

- **CONTACT** J Holmes/M Quiney 01243 812216

- **SUBJECT**   Professional Updating/Teaching   **1434**
- **TITLE**   Keeping in Touch with Teaching
- **PLACE**   West Sussex Teacher Recruitment Base, at various centres

Length Flexible, as long as support is required   **Start** Flexible   **Days** 1 meeting/month 9.45-11.30   **Cost** £25/year subscription   **Entry Reqs** Qualified teachers   **Creche** Yes free

- **CONTACT**   Aileen Skenlake 01243 777269

COUNTY CONTACTS

Information and advice:

Chichester College of Arts, Science and Technology, Westgate Fields, Chichester PO19 1SB 01243 786321   *Contact:* Mary Anne Bart

Open University:

The Open University, South East Region, St James's House, 150 London Road, East Grinstead RH19 1ES 01342 410545

Training and Enterprise Council:

Sussex TEC, 2nd Floor, Electrowatt House, North Street, Horsham RH12 1RS 01403 271471

WEA office:

WEA South Eastern District, 4 Castle Hill, Rochester ME1 1QQ 01634 842140   *Contact:* Wilma Fraser, Joy Pascoe

WEST YORKSHIRE

COURSES

- **SUBJECT**   Access   **1435**
- **TITLE**   Access to Higher Education
- **PLACE**   Thomas Danby College, Leeds

Length 1 year full time   **Start** Autumn   **Days** Daily   **Cost** Discretionary grant available   **Entry Reqs** None. Black adults interested in higher education   **Award** Access Certificate, GCSE Maths and English   **Creche** Yes Contact College

- **CONTACT**   Guidance & Information Centre 0113 259 4912

- **SUBJECT**   Access/Art & Design   **1436**
- **TITLE**   Access to Art & Design: Certificate for Mature Students
- **PLACE**   Bradford & Ilkley Community College

Length 2 years   **Start** Various   **Days** 2½ days/week   **Entry Req** No formal qualifications **Award** Access to higher education   **Creche** Yes

- **CONTACT**   Sue Davis 01274 753168/7533240

- **SUBJECT**   Access/Black Studies/Humanities/Social Science/Health/   **1437**
  Business Studies/Science/Engineering
- **TITLE**   Certificate for Mature Students (Modular)
- **PLACE**   Bradford & Ilkley Community College

Length 1 or 2 years depending on course   **Days** Varies   **Cost** Contact College Concessions available   **Entry Reqs** Interview   **Award** Certificate for Mature Students, access to higher education   **Creche** Limited places, contact Playcare 01274 547047

- **CONTACT**   Access Courses Secretary 01274 753180

- **SUBJECT**   Access/Childcare   **1438**
- **TITLE**   Access Opportunities in Child Care (BEd)
- **PLACE**   Thomas Danby College, Leeds

Length 1 year   **Start** September   **Days** Full time   **Cost** Discretionary grant available   **Entry Reqs** 20+, good basic level in English & Maths   **Award** Access Certificate, GCSE Maths and English   **Creche** Contact Kay Martin 0113 262 3955

- **CONTACT**   Guidance & Information Centre 0113 259 4912

- **SUBJECT**   Access/Computing/Media Studies/Humanities/Social Science/   **1439**
  Health Studies/Environmental Sciences/European Studies
- **TITLE**   Mature Access General
- **PLACE**   Park Lane College

Length 1 or 2 years Foundation course available   **Start** September   **Days** Modular course 1 or 2 days/week 9.30-3.00   **Cost** Concessions for most students   **Entry Reqs** Suitable level of literacy   **Award** Access Certificate awarded by WNYAN for Open College   **Creche** Yes

- **CONTACT**   Heather Fry 0113 235 5492

- **SUBJECT**   Access/Humanities/Social Science   **1440**
- **TITLE**   Humanities and Social Sciences: Women's Route
- **PLACE**   Bradford & Ilkley Community College

Length 1/2 years   **Days** 3/4 days 9.30-3.00   **Cost** Contact College Concessions available **Entry Reqs** Interview   **Award** Certificate for Mature Students, access to higher education **Creche** Nursery, small charge

- **CONTACT**   Access Courses Secretary 01274 753180

- **SUBJECT**   Access/Humanities/Social Studies   **1441**
- **TITLE**   Access to Higher Education in Humanities and Social Studies
- **PLACE**   University of Leeds

Length 32 weeks   **Start** September   **Days** 1 day/week or 2 eves/week   **Cost** £187 Concessions available   **Entry Reqs** By interview   **Award** Access Certificate (Open College West & North Yorkshire Access Network)   **Creche** Yes subject to demand. Small charge

- **CONTACT**   Jill Liddington 0113 233 3185/Jane Fisher 0113 233 3200

- **SUBJECT**   Access/Information Technology/Computing   **1442**
- **TITLE**   Access to Higher Education: A Programme for Women in Computing and IT
- **PLACE**   Thomas Danby College, Leeds

Length 1 year   **Start** September   **Days** Times arranged to suit childcare demands   **Cost** Discretionary awards should be available   **Entry Reqs** Mature, motivated and ability to study   **Award** Access Certificate, GCSE Maths and English if appropriate   **Creche** Contact Kay Martin 0113 262 3955

- **CONTACT**   Guidance & Information Centre 0113 259 4912

- **SUBJECT** Access/Mathematics/Science
- **TITLE** Mature Access: Mathematics/Science
- **PLACE** Park Lane College

1443

Length 1 year **Start** September **Days** 10.00-3.00 (Minimum 3 days/week) **Cost** Full time fees Concessions available **Entry Reqs** Basic mathematical skills **Award** CNAA validated Certificate awarded by WNYAN for Open College **Creche** Yes and nursery
- **CONTACT** Shelagh Ross 0113 235 5562/0113 244 3011

- **SUBJECT** Access/New Technology
- **TITLE** Access to New Technology Programme
- **PLACE** Park Lane College, Community Centres, Home, Workplace

1444

Length Flexible **Start** Flexible **Cost** Full time fees Concessions available **Entry Reqs** None required except literate **Award** NVQ Levels I, II/Certificate of completion/Open College validation **Creche** Yes and nursery
- **CONTACT** Margaret Simmonds 0113 235 5462/0113 244 3011

- **SUBJECT** Accounting
- **TITLE** Bookkeeping (Women Only)
- **PLACE** Bradford & Ilkley Community College, Asian Women & Girls' Centre

1445

Length 30 weeks **Start** September **Days** Thurs 1.00-3.00 **Cost** £48 Concessions available **Award** RSA Level II
- **CONTACT** Bolton Royd Centre 01274 546812

- **SUBJECT** Art/Design/Textiles
- **TITLE** 1. British Display Society (BDS) Technician Certificate 2. CATS
- **PLACE** Bradford & Ilkley Community College

1446

Length Contact College **Days** Wed 9.30-5.00 1 day/week **Cost** Concessions may apply **Entry Reqs** 1. No formal qualifications 2. Depends on course **Award** 1. BDS Technician Certificate Levels 1, 2, 3 3. Entry to part time degree courses **Creche** Yes
- **CONTACT** 1. Sue Daniels 01274 753250 2. Lester Hall 01274 753448

- **SUBJECT** Business
- **TITLE** New Working Women Business Course
- **PLACE** New Working Women, Leeds and locations in North of England

1447

Length 12 weeks **Start** January/September **Days** 2 days/week 9.30-3.30 **Cost** Free (Leeds City Council & ESF funded) **Entry Reqs** None **Creche** No but childcare costs paid
- **CONTACT** Sally Gilding 0113 243 2474

- **SUBJECT** Business Administration/Secretarial
- **TITLE** Business Administration with Secretarial Skills
- **PLACE** Park Lane College

1448

Length Each course 1 year (less if student finds employment) **Start** September **Days** Under 21 hours/week **Cost** £618 **Entry Reqs** 19+ and good English and/or prior experience **Award** RSA NVQ Business Administration Level 1, 2, 3 **Creche** Playgroup
- **CONTACT** Elaine Ozyer 0113 235 5456

- **SUBJECT** Business Studies/Secretarial/Office Skills/Information Technology
- **TITLE** Business Skills Workshop: Part Time Secretarial, Word Processing & Information Technology Skills
- **PLACE** Bradford & Ilkley Community College

1449

Length Flexible **Days** Open access between 9.00-8.00 Mon-Thurs, Fri 9.00-4.00 **Cost** Contact College **Award** RSA/RSA CLAIT Stages I/II/III **Creche** Yes
- **CONTACT** 01274 753119/753164/753388

- **SUBJECT**   Care Studies   1450
- **TITLE**   BTEC National Certificate in Caring Services (Social Care)
- **PLACE**   Thomas Danby College, Leeds

Length 2 years part time   **Start** September   **Days** Varies   **Cost** Approx £480. Discretionary rates available   **Entry Reqs** 4 Grade C GCSEs or equivalent or evidence of ability to study at that level   **Award** BTEC National Certificate   **Creche** Yes
- **CONTACT**   Guidance & Information Centre 0113 259 4912

- **SUBJECT**   Care Studies   1451
- **TITLE**   Community Care Practice (C&G 325-1)
- **PLACE**   Thomas Danby College, Leeds

Length 1 year flexible modular system   **Start** September, January, April   **Days** 1 day/week 9.15-4.30 or 1 evening/week   **Cost** £390 Discretionary rates available   **Entry Reqs** Appropriate qualities and interest in caring for others   **Award** C&G 325-1   **Creche** Yes Contact College
- **CONTACT**   Guidance & Information Centre 0113 259 4912

- **SUBJECT**   Childcare   1452
- **TITLE**   1. Introduction to Working with Children 2. Working with Children: the Next Step to Good Practice
- **PLACE**   Bradford & Ilkley Community College, Newby Centre

Length 12 weeks   **Start** 1. September 2. January   **Days** Wed 9.30-11.30   **Cost** 1. & 2. £19 each Concessions available   **Award** Open College Network Certificate Level I/II   **Creche** Yes
- **CONTACT**   Newby Road Centre 01274 753570

- **SUBJECT**   Civil Engineering   1453
- **TITLE**   Built Environment: Research Masters Pilot Course
- **PLACE**   University of Leeds

Length 2 years   **Start** October   **Cost** Engineering & Physical Sciences Research Council award available   **Entry Reqs** Graduates with first or upper second class honours degree in an appropriate subject   **Award** Master of Research Degree
- **CONTACT**   Professor A May 0113 233 2268

- **SUBJECT**   Community Studies   1454
- **TITLE**   BA(Hons) Community Studies: Social & Public Policy
- **PLACE**   Bradford & Ilkley Community College

Length 3 years full time, 5 years+ part time   **Start** September   **Days** 1 or 2 sessions/week, negotiable   **Cost** Mandatory grants available   **Entry Reqs** Unqualified mature students encouraged to apply   **Award** BA(Hons) degree   **Creche** Yes
- **CONTACT**   Course Enquiries 01274 753450

- **SUBJECT**   Computing   1455
- **TITLE**   Computing Applications (various courses)
- **PLACE**   Wakefield College, Wakefield, Thornes Park & Whitwood Centres

Start Contact College   **Days** 3-4 days/week 10.00-2.30   **Cost** Free   **Entry Reqs** Women only   **Creche** Yes Contact College
- **CONTACT**   01924 810514

- **SUBJECT**   Computing/Information Technology   1456
- **TITLE**   Computer Literacy and Information Technology for Women: RSA
- **PLACE**   Bradford & Ilkley Community College, Millan Centre

Length 30 weeks   **Start** September   **Days** Thurs 9.30-11.30   **Cost** £48 Concessions available   **Entry Reqs** None   **Award** RSA CLAIT Level I   **Creche** Yes
- **CONTACT**   Bolton Royd Centre 01274 546812

- **SUBJECT** Design   1457
- **TITLE** Design: BTEC
- **PLACE** Bradford & Ilkley Community College

Length 2 years part time   **Start** September   **Cost** Contact College   **Entry Reqs** Interview and portfolio   **Award** BTEC National Certificate

- **CONTACT** Martin Dutton 01274 753239/753241

- **SUBJECT** Electronics   1458
- **TITLE** Electronic Servicing
- **PLACE** Wakefield College, Five Towns Centre

Start Contact College   **Days** 2.5 days/week 9.30-2.30   **Cost** Free   **Entry Reqs** Women only   **Creche** Yes Contact College

- **CONTACT** 01924 810514

- **SUBJECT** Fashion   1459
- **TITLE** Fashion Design and Clothing Technology
- **PLACE** Bradford & Ilkley Community College

Length 2 years part time   **Start** September   **Days** Flexible   **Cost** Contact College   **Entry Reqs** Contact College   **Award** Diploma of Higher Education

- **CONTACT** Alan Smith 01274 753238/Martin Dutton 01274 753240

- **SUBJECT** Fashion   1460
- **TITLE** Introduction to Fashion Design for Women
- **PLACE** Bradford & Ilkley Community College, Karmand Centre

Length 1 year   **Start** September   **Days** Thurs 1.00-3.00   **Cost** £48 Concessions available   **Award** Access to further courses   **Creche** Yes

- **CONTACT** South East Area Team 01274 753570

- **SUBJECT** Floristry/Horticulture   1461
- **TITLE** Horticulture and Floristry
- **PLACE** Wakefield College, Hemsworth Centre

Start Contact College   **Days** 2 days/week 10.00-2.30   **Cost** Free   **Entry Reqs** Women only   **Creche** Yes Contact College

- **CONTACT** 01924 810514

- **SUBJECT** Hairdressing   1462
- **TITLE** Flexible Adult Training: Hairdressing Training Board & City & Guilds
- **PLACE** Bradford & Ilkley Community College

Length Flexible   **Cost** Contact College   **Entry Reqs** Contact College   **Award** HTB/C&G Level II Foundation Certificate in Hairdressing   **Creche** Yes

- **CONTACT** Jackie Hewitt/Terri Sykes 01274 753414/753405

- **SUBJECT** Health Studies   1463
- **TITLE** BTEC National Certificate in Science (Health Studies)
- **PLACE** Thomas Danby College, Leeds

Length Full time 1 year or day release for 2 years   **Start** Full time: January, part time: Sept   **Cost** Discretionary grant available   **Entry Reqs** 21+, with commitment to care   **Award** Entry to nursing, radiography and related careers   **Creche** Contact Kay Martin 0113 262 3955

- **CONTACT** Guidance & Information Centre 0113 259 4912

- **SUBJECT** Health Studies 1464
- **TITLE** Health and Social Care NVQ Level II/III
- **PLACE** Park Lane College, Burton Road Centre

Length 30 weeks **Start** Flexible **Days** Flexible + Thurs 9.30-12.00 **Cost** £73+accreditation (approx £50) Fee waivers and reductions available **Entry Reqs** None, some voluntary or paid experience preferable **Award** C&G/CCETSW Award in Health & Social Care II/III **Creche** Yes 35p/session

- **CONTACT** Jill Kibble 0113 2778228

- **SUBJECT** Information Technology 1465
- **TITLE** Certificate in Business Information Technology
- **PLACE** Leeds Metropolitan University

Length 1 year part time **Start** October **Days** Mon-Fri 10.00-3.00 **Cost** Registration fee £72, Tuition fees £516 **Entry Reqs** Applications treated on individual merit, previous computer experience not necessary **Award** University Certificate in Business Information Technology **Creche** No

- **CONTACT** Doug Kemp, Linda Broughton 0113 283 7421

- **SUBJECT** Information Technology 1466
- **TITLE** IT for Women
- **PLACE** Bradford & Ilkley Community College, Bolton Royd Centre

Length 10 weeks **Days** Mon 11.15-12.45 **Cost** £24 Concessions available **Entry Reqs** None

- **CONTACT** Bolton Royd Centre 01274 546812

- **SUBJECT** Interior Design 1467
- **TITLE** Introduction to Interior Design for Women
- **PLACE** Bradford & Ilkley Community College, Karmand Centre

Length 1 year **Start** September **Days** Tues 1.00-3.00 **Cost** £48 Concessions available **Award** Access to further courses **Creche** Yes

- **CONTACT** South East Area Team 01274 753570

- **SUBJECT** Manufacturing 1468
- **TITLE** MSc in Manufacturing Management
- **PLACE** University of Bradford, Dept of Industrial Technology

Length 1 year (6 months at University+6 months in placement) **Start** October **Days** Full time 9.00-5.00 5 days/week **Cost** For West Yorkshire applicants, scholarships are available **Entry Reqs** First degree or equivalent in Engineering, Science, or related subjects **Award** MSc in Manufacturing Management **Creche** Yes & playgroup. Approx £40/week

- **CONTACT** Professor I J McColm 01274 384249

- **SUBJECT** Multi-Subject 1469
- **TITLE** BA/MA/Diploma (Various Subjects)
- **PLACE** Bradford & Ilkley Community College

Length Various **Cost** Contact College **Entry Reqs** Contact College **Award** BA(Hons)/ MA/Diploma **Creche** Yes

- **CONTACT** School of Teaching & Community Studies 01274 751600

- **SUBJECT** Multi-Subject 1470
- **TITLE** Certificate in Personal & Professional Skills (Study, Career, Meetings, WP, etc)
- **PLACE** Leeds Metropolitan University

Length 15x3-hour sessions **Start** September, February **Days** Variable **Cost** £50/ module+£5 registration for the award **Entry Reqs** Ability to benefit from the course **Award** University Certificate **Creche** No

- **CONTACT** Viv Anderson/Adele Parks 0113 283 2600

- **SUBJECT** Multi-Subject   1471
- **TITLE** Courses for Women: Various Subjects
- **PLACE** Bradford & Ilkley Community College

Length Various   **Days** Variable   **Cost** Contact College   **Creche** Yes
- **CONTACT** Sharon Brooke 01274 546812

- **SUBJECT** Multi-Subject   1472
- **TITLE** Women Returners' Non-Traditional Courses eg Motor Vehicle, IT, Garden Design, Horticulture, Painting & Decorating, Computer Aided Design
- **PLACE** Wakefield College

Length 1 year   **Start** September   **Days** 2-3 days/week 10.00-2.30   **Cost** Free   **Entry Reqs** None   **Award** C&G/NVQ   **Creche** Yes free, places limited
- **CONTACT** Lizzie Daley 01924 810514

- **SUBJECT** NOW   1473
- **TITLE** New Opportunities for Women
- **PLACE** Dewsbury College

Length 28 weeks   **Start** September   **Days** Tues 9.30-3.00   **Cost** Assistance possible. Contact College   **Entry Reqs** None   **Award** Open College Accreditation applied for   **Creche** Yes
- **CONTACT** Jenny Humphreys 01924 465916 x400

- **SUBJECT** NOW   1474
- **TITLE** New Opportunities for Women
- **PLACE** Wakefield College, various centres

Length 2 terms   **Start** September   **Days** 1 day/week (school hours)   **Cost** Free   **Entry Reqs** None   **Award** Open College Accreditation applied for   **Creche** Yes
- **CONTACT** 01924 810385

- **SUBJECT** Office Skills   1475
- **TITLE** Basic Office Skills, Typing, Word Processing
- **PLACE** Keighley Access to Training

Length Variable up to 22 weeks   **Start** April, September, January   **Days** Daytime only   **Cost** Free   **Entry Reqs** Available to unemployed and certain part time workers   **Award** Most lead to RSA or NVQ qualifications   **Creche** Limited free places on some courses
- **CONTACT** Derek Hird/Andrew Hall 01535 618256

- **SUBJECT** Office Skills   1476
- **TITLE** Medical Reception/Office Skills
- **PLACE** Park Lane College

Length 16 weeks   **Start** September, February   **Days** 2.5 days/week 10.00-1.00   **Cost** £318   **Entry Reqs** None   **Award** RSA, NVQ certificates   **Creche** Yes
- **CONTACT** Elaine Ozyer 0113 235 5456

- **SUBJECT** Photography   1477
- **TITLE** Certificate in Photography: C&G
- **PLACE** Bradford & Ilkley Community College

Length 12 weeks   **Days** 2 hours/module/week   **Cost** Contact College   **Entry Reqs** None   **Award** C&G 9231, Licentiate Membership of Royal Photographic Society
- **CONTACT** John Dickson 01274 753386

- **SUBJECT** Practical   1478
- **TITLE** Home Design and Decorating
- **PLACE** Wakefield College, Thorns Park Centre

Start Contact College   **Days** 2 days/week 9.30-3.00   **Cost** Free   **Entry Reqs** Women only   **Creche** Yes Contact College
- **CONTACT** 01924 810514

- **SUBJECT**   Practical   1479
- **TITLE**   Motor Mechanics
- **PLACE**   Wakefield College, Whitwood Centre

Start Contact College   **Days** 2 halfdays/week   **Cost** Free   **Entry Reqs** Women only
Creche Yes Contact College

- **CONTACT**   01924 810514

- **SUBJECT**   Practical   1480
- **TITLE**   Painting and Decorating (Women Only)
- **PLACE**   Bradford & Ilkley Community College

Length 36 weeks   **Start** September   **Days** 4 days/week 9.30-2.30   **Cost** Contact College
Award NVQ Levels I/II   **Creche** Assistance with childcare

- **CONTACT**   Kevin Young 01274 753013

- **SUBJECT**   Practical   1481
- **TITLE**   Repair and Service of Road Vehicles (Women Only)
- **PLACE**   Bradford & Ilkley Community College

Length 36 weeks   **Start** September   **Days** 4 days/week 9.15-3.15   **Entry Req** Contact
College   **Award** C&G Repair & Service of Road Vehicles Level I/II   **Creche** Assistance with
childminding

- **CONTACT**   Karen Griffiths/Annette Williams 01274 753346

- **SUBJECT**   Practical   1482
- **TITLE**   Woodwork for Women
- **PLACE**   Bradford & Ilkley Community College, Bolton Royd Centre

Length 30 weeks   **Start** September   **Days** Thurs 1.00-3.00   **Cost** £48 Concessions available
Entry Reqs None

- **CONTACT**   Bolton Royd Centre 01274 546812

- **SUBJECT**   Preparatory   1483
- **TITLE**   Into Learning: Foundation Course for Returning to Learning/Work
- **PLACE**   Park Lane College, Adult Learning Centre

Length 18 weeks   **Start** January   **Days** Up to 21 hours/week (school hours)   **Cost** None
Entry Reqs Commitment and enthusiasm   **Award** Open College Credits   **Creche** Yes 35p/
session

- **CONTACT**   Jill Kibble 0113 2778228

- **SUBJECT**   Preparatory   1484
- **TITLE**   Make Your Experience Count: Portfolio Preparation
- **PLACE**   Thomas Danby College, Leeds

Length 6 weeks   **Start** Rolling programme   **Days** Variable 3 hours/week   **Cost** Contact
College   **Entry Reqs** None   **Creche** Yes Contact College

- **CONTACT**   Alec Main/Cathy Bragg 0113 249 4912

- **SUBJECT**   Preparatory   1485
- **TITLE**   Open Learning Workshops: English, Maths, Study Skills, Basic IT Skills)
- **PLACE**   Bradford and Ilkley Community College

Length Varies from drop-in to full courses   **Start** Continuous enrolment   **Days** Between 9am
and 9pm, not Fri eve   **Cost** Varies   **Entry Reqs** None   **Award** Basic to A Levels   **Creche**
Yes

- **CONTACT**   Ruth Wright 01274 753317

- **SUBJECT** Preparatory   **1486**
- **TITLE** Various: Maths, English, Computing, Study Skills, English as Second Language
- **PLACE** Park Lane College, Adult Learning Centre

Length Flexible   **Start** Flexible   **Days** Open 42 weeks/year, 32 hours/week + Sat mornings   **Cost** None   **Entry Reqs** None   **Award** Various accreditations. RSA, C&G, Open College Credits & course support for training   **Creche** Yes 35p/session

- **CONTACT** Jill Kibble 0113 2778228

- **SUBJECT** Preparatory   **1487**
- **TITLE** Women into Work
- **PLACE** Various venues in South and East Leeds

Length 11 weeks   **Start** September, January, April   **Days** 15 hours/week (school hours and terms)   **Cost** Free £5/week training allowance   **Entry Reqs** None - recruit mainly from women without qualifications. Admission by interview   **Award** NEBSM Introductory Supervisory Award, HSE First Aid at Work + opportunity to enter other courses   **Creche** Yes 35p/session

- **CONTACT** Jill Kibble 0113 2778228

- **SUBJECT** Secretarial/Administration   **1488**
- **TITLE** Administrative and Secretarial Procedures
- **PLACE** Park Lane College

Length 1 year   **Start** September   **Days** Mon-Fri 9.00-4.30   **Cost** Contact College   **Entry Reqs** 19+, post A level, postgraduate   **Award** NVQ Level IV Higher Diploma   **Creche** Playgroup

- **CONTACT** Marilyn Handley 0113 235 5563

- **SUBJECT** Teaching   **1489**
- **TITLE** Returning to Teaching
- **PLACE** Bradford & Ilkley Community College

Length Contact College   **Cost** Contact College   **Creche** Yes

- **CONTACT** Frances Murdoch 01274 75610

- **SUBJECT** Women's Studies   **1490**
- **TITLE** Women's Studies:1. BA 2. MA 3. Diploma
- **PLACE** University of Bradford

Length 1.3 years 2. &3.1 year full time, 2 years part time   **Start** October   **Days** 1.5 days/week 2. &3. 1 or 2 days/week   **Cost** Contact University   **Entry Reqs** 1. Contact University 2. &3. Degree in related subject but other qualifications accepted   **Award** 1. BA 2. MA 3. Diploma   **Creche** Nursery

- **CONTACT** Course Information 01274 733466

COUNTY CONTACTS

Information and advice:

Access and Guidance Centre, Bradford and Ilkley Community College, Grove Building, Bradford BD7 1AY 01274 753052/3   *Contact:* Mavis Hill, Janet Juryta
CEASA (Careers and Educational Advice Service for Adults), Careers Office, Upperhead Row, Huddersfield HD1 2JS 01484 443523/4
Careers Bradford, Third Floor, Midland House, 14 Cheapside, Bradford BD1 4JA 01274 829400
EASA (Educational Advice Service for Adults), 7th Floor, Central Library, Princes Way, Bradford BD1 1NN 01274 753658

West Yorkshire

National Association for Educational Guidance for Adults, Regional representative, Calderdale & Kirklees Careers Service, Northgate House, Northgate, Halifax HX1 1UN 01422 392579 *Contact:* Helen Oldham. Covers Yorkshire and Humberside region

Prospect Corner, 25 Northgate, Wakefield, Freephone 0800 834170. Free information and advice service offering careers guidance and counselling, CV writing, information on female friendly employers, local childcare facilities, working from home, advice on training, placements and grants. Mobile Prospect Corner visits Hemsworth, Airedale, Normanton, Featherstone and Upton weekly. Service run by Wakefield TEC

Prospect Corner, 9 Market Place, Pontefract,Freephone 0800 834170

Open University:

The Open University, Yorkshire Region, 2 Trevelyan Square, Boar Lane, Leeds LS1 6ED 0113 245 1466

Other agencies:

ASHA Neighbourhood Project, 43 Stratford Street, Leeds LS9 8AJ 0113 270 4600. Women's training centre

Access and Guidance Centre, Bradford & Ilkley Community College, Grove Building, Great Horton Road, Bradford BD7 1AY 01274 7503052/3   *Contact:* Mavis Hill, Janet Jumita. Information on Access and other courses

Airedale & Wharfedale College, Calverley Lane, Horsforth, Leeds LS18 4RQ 0113 239 5800 *Contact:* Gill Barber

Bradford and Ilkley Community College, Access and Guidance Centre, Great Horton Road, Bradford BD7 1AY 01274 753053   *Contact:* Mavis Hill, Janet Juryta

East Leeds Women's Workshop, Newtonhill House, Newtonhill Road, Leeds LS7 4JE 0113 237 4718. Women's training centre

Hooner Kelah Training Project, Roseville Centre, Gledhow Road, Leeds LS8 5ES 0113 235 0484. Women's training centre

New Working Women, 3 St Peter's Building, York Street, Leeds LS9 8AJ 0113 243 2474. Women's training centre

Student Access Office, University of Leeds, Leeds LS2 9JT 0113 243 1751

Wakefield College, Margaret Street, Wakefield WF1 2DH 01924 370501   *Contact:* Sally Raby, Careers Adviser/Lizzie Daley, Women Returners Courses

Training and Enterprise Councils:

Bradford and District TEC, Mercury House, 4 Manchester Road, Bradford BD5 0QL 01274 723711. Training for Work; For women who are interested in self-employment, women only provision in Ideas Generation Workshops, Confidence Building Workshops, Open Days for Awareness Raising and Business Planning Courses; Pre-vocational and basic skills courses with ESOL support; Training, guidance and counselling for women with disabilities

Calderdale and Kirklees TEC, Park View House, Woodvale Office Park, Woodvale Road, Brighouse HD6 4AB 01484 400770

Leeds TEC, Belgrave Hall, Belgrave Street, Leeds LS2 8DO 0113 234 7666

Wakefield TEC, Grove Hall, 60 College Grove Road, Wakefield WF1 3RN 01924 299907. Range of training courses; 'Women in Business' register; Prospect Corner information and advice centre

WEA office:

WEA Yorkshire North District, 6 Woodhouse Square, Leeds LS3 1AD 0113 245 3304   *Contact:* Wendy Formby

COURSES

- **SUBJECT**   Access   1491
- **TITLE**   Access to Higher Education
- **PLACE**   Trowbridge College

Length 1 year full time, 2 years part time   **Start** September   **Days** Mon-Fri 9.15-4.15   **Cost** Contact College   **Award** Access to higher education
- **CONTACT**   Sue Brister 01225 766241

- **SUBJECT**   Access/Health Studies   1492
- **TITLE**   Access to Higher Education (Nursing Studies)
- **PLACE**   Chippenham College

Length 1 year   **Start** September   **Cost** Contact College   **Entry Reqs** By interview   **Award** Access to higher education and nurse training   **Creche** Yes
- **CONTACT**   J West 01249 444501

- **SUBJECT**   Access/Social Studies   1493
- **TITLE**   Access to Social Studies
- **PLACE**   Chippenham College

Length 36 weeks   **Start** September   **Days** Wed 9.00-4.30   **Cost** £186   **Entry Reqs** By interview   **Award** 1 A level, university entry   **Creche** Yes £2/3 hours am £1.50/2 hours pm
- **CONTACT**   David Cornwell/Patrick Harmon 01249 444501

- **SUBJECT**   Accounting   1494
- **TITLE**   Bookkeeping and Accounts
- **PLACE**   Trowbridge College

Length 1 year   **Start** September   **Days** Thurs 2.00-4.00   **Cost** £70   **Award** RSA Bookkeeping and Accounts
- **CONTACT**   01225 766241

- **SUBJECT**   Archaeology   1495
- **TITLE**   Archaeology Foundation Course
- **PLACE**   Chippenham College

Length 1 or 2 years   **Start** September   **Cost** Contact College   **Entry Reqs** 3 GCSEs including Maths & English. Mature students may not need these requirements   **Award** GCE A Level, College Certificate, progress to degree courses   **Creche** Yes
- **CONTACT**   Information Officer 01249 444501

- **SUBJECT**   Art & Design   1496
- **TITLE**   Art & Design (Multidisciplinary)
- **PLACE**   Chippenham College

Length 2 years   **Start** September   **Cost** Contact College   **Entry Reqs** College interview for mature students   **Award** BTEC Advanced GNVQ   **Creche** Yes
- **CONTACT**   Information Officer 01249 444501

- **SUBJECT**   Childcare   1497
- **TITLE**   1. NNEB Certificate in Childcare & Education 2. NNEB Diploma in Nursery Nursing
- **PLACE**   Chippenham College

Length 1.1 year 2.2 years   **Start** September   **Cost** Contact College   **Entry Reqs** Interview. Mature students welcome   **Award** 1. NNEB Certificate in Childcare & Education 2. NNEB Diploma in Nursery Nursing   **Creche** Yes
- **CONTACT**   Information Officer 01249 444501

Wiltshire

- **SUBJECT**   Hairdressing   **1498**
- **TITLE**   Hairdressing for Adults
- **PLACE**   Trowbridge College

Length 1 year   **Start** September   **Days** Mon & Thurs 9.00-2.45   **Cost** £425.40   **Award** NVQ Level II
- **CONTACT**   01225 766241

- **SUBJECT**   Information Technology   **1499**
- **TITLE**   IT in Business
- **PLACE**   Trowbridge College

Length Flexible   **Start** September, January, April   **Days** Mon-Thur 9.00-3.00   **Cost** £190
- **CONTACT**   01225 766241

- **SUBJECT**   Office Skills   **1500**
- **TITLE**   Office Skills Drop-in Centres
- **PLACE**   Trowbridge College, Trowbridge, Devizes and Warminster Centres

Length Flexible   **Days** Varies   **Cost** £3/hour   **Entry Reqs** None
- **CONTACT**   Trowbridge 01225 766241 x216/Devizes 01380 723989/Warminster 01985 213316

- **SUBJECT**   Office Skills   **1501**
- **TITLE**   Office Skills Training Programme: NVQ
- **PLACE**   Trowbridge College

Length 12 weeks   **Start** September, January, April   **Days** Mon-Thur 9.00-3.00   **Cost** £190
Award NVQ Levels I/II/III
- **CONTACT**   01225 766241

- **SUBJECT**   Practical   **1502**
- **TITLE**   Painting and Decorating
- **PLACE**   Trowbridge College

Length 1 year   **Start** September   **Days** Part time 9.00-5.15   **Cost** Contact College   **Award** NVQ Levels I/I/III
- **CONTACT**   01225 766241

- **SUBJECT**   Preparatory   **1503**
- **TITLE**   Opportunities
- **PLACE**   Trowbridge College

Length 10 weeks   **Start** September, January, April   **Days** Tues-Fri 9.30-3.30   **Cost** £25
Entry Reqs None
- **CONTACT**   Pippa Hawkins 01225 767788

- **SUBJECT**   Social Science   **1504**
- **TITLE**   Social Science First Year BA (Hons) University of West of England
- **PLACE**   Chippenham College

Length 30 weeks   **Start** September/October   **Days** Wed, Thurs, Fri to suit domestic arrangements   **Cost** Mandatory grant available   **Entry Reqs** A levels, HND, HNC, Access course   **Award** Entry to 2nd year BA (Hons) at University of the West of England, Bristol **Creche** Yes £2/3 hours am £1.50/2 hours pm
- **CONTACT**   David Cornwell/Patrick Harmon/Ron Wilcox 01249 444501

COUNTY CONTACTS

Information and advice:

Adult Careers Guidance Service, 4 Temple Chambers, Temple Street, Swindon SN1 1SQ 01793 549200

65 Milford Street, Salisbury 01722 413178
66 St Mary's Street, Chippenham 01249 447446
Careers Service Annexe, By the Sea Road, Trowbridge 01225 776881
Guidance Team, Chippenham College, Cocklebury Road, Chippenham SN15 3QD 01249 444501
West Wiltshire Educational Advice for Adults, Devizes College, Southbroom, Devizes SN10 5AB 01380 723989   *Contact:* Marcus Toyne. Education and training advice for adults
Trowbridge College, College Road, Trowbridge BA14 0ES 01225 766241 x264   *Contact:* Claire Wilson, Hester Messom
Warminster College, 5 The Avenue, Warminster BA12 9AA 01985 213316   *Contact:* Judy Tongue

Open University:

The Open University, South West Region, 4 Portwall Lane, Bristol BS1 6ND 0117 925 6523

Training and Enterprise Council:

Wiltshire TEC, The Bora Building. Westlea Campus, Westlea Down, Swindon SN5 7EZ 01793 513644

WEA office:

WEA Western District, 40 Morse Road, Redfield, Bristol BS5 9LB 0117 935 1764   *Contact:* Mavis Zutchi, Kath Ryder

---

NORTHERN IRELAND: Belfast

COURSES

- **SUBJECT**   Access/Science/Technology   **1505**
- **TITLE**   Certificate in Foundation Studies for Mature Students: University of Ulster Course
- **PLACE**   Belfast Institute of Further & Higher Education

Length 2 years part time   **Start** September   **Cost** Contact Institute   **Entry Reqs** Age 21+, some previous experience in/knowledge of science & technology   **Award** University Certificate in Foundation Studies, entry to higher education   **Creche** Contact Institute

- **CONTACT**   General Inquiries 01232 327244

- **SUBJECT**   Access/Social Science/Humanities   **1506**
- **TITLE**   Certificate in Foundation Studies for Mature Students: University of Ulster Course
- **PLACE**   Belfast Institute of Further & Higher Education

Length 2 years part time   **Start** September   **Cost** Contact Institute   **Entry Reqs** Age 23+, no formal requirements   **Award** University Certificate in Foundation Studies, entry to higher education   **Creche** Contact Institute

- **CONTACT**   General Inquiries 01232 327244

- **SUBJECT**   Preparatory   **1507**
- **TITLE**   Going Places: Return to Learn for Adults
- **PLACE**   Castlereagh College

Length 10 weeks   **Start** Flexible, 3 times/year   **Days** 2 mornings/week   **Cost** £35 (£5 if in receipt of benefit)   **Entry Reqs** Open access   **Award** College Certificate   **Creche** Contact College

- **CONTACT**   Sharon Rivers/Mary Gallagher 01232 797144

Northern Ireland: Belfast

- **SUBJECT**   Preparatory   **1508**
- **TITLE**   Time for Me (Personal Development/Choice of Options)
- **PLACE**   University of Ulster at Jordanstown, at centres in Belfast

Length 10 weeks (1 term)   **Start** October, January, April   **Days** 1 day/week
10.00-12.00+1.00-3.00   **Cost** £28, concessionary fee £14   **Entry Reqs** Women   **Award**
Certificate of Attendance, University of Ulster   **Creche** Yes free in some centres

- **CONTACT**   Pauline Murphy 01232 366679

- **SUBJECT**   Preparatory   **1509**
- **TITLE**   Women Moving On
- **PLACE**   Belfast Women's Training Services at women's centres across Belfast

Length 9 weeks   **Start** Throughout the year   **Days** 2 mornings/week   **Cost** None. £80 Bonus
to trainees on completion   **Entry Reqs** None   **Award** Open College 2 Credits Level I   **Creche**
Yes Free

- **CONTACT**   Claire Keating 01232 323904

COUNTY CONTACTS

Information and advice:

Educational Guidance Service for Adults, 2nd Floor, Glendinning House, 4 Murray Street, Belfast BT1 6DN 01232 244274   *Contact:* Eileen Kelly, Eleanor Speers. Educational guidance and information for adults interested in returning to or continuing in learning at any level.

Open University:

The Open University, Northern Ireland, 40 University Road, Belfast BT7 1SU 01232 245025

Other agencies:

Belfast Women's Training Services, 30 Donegall Street, Belfast BT1 2GQ 01232 323904 *Contact:* Claire Keatinge. Provides courses suitable for women returners.
Falls Women's Centre, 170a Falls Road, Belfast 01232 327672   *Contact:* Oonagh Mallon
Greenway Women's Centre, 19 Greenway, Belfast BT6 0DT 01232 799912   *Contact:* Kathy Small, Patricia Turner. Advice and information on all issues relevant to women; organises a community education programme which responds to identified needs.
Institute of Continuing Education, Queen's University of Belfast, University Road, Belfast BT7 1NN 01232 245133   *Contact:* Heather O'Callaghan
Lenadoon Women's Group, 41a Suffolk Road, Lenadoon, Belfast BT11 01232 600380   *Contact:* Greta Doherty
Shankill Women's Centre, 151-157 Shankill Road, Belfast BT13 1FD 01232 240642   *Contact:* Anne McVicker, Karen Snoddy
Women Too, Windsor Women's Centre, 130-144 Broadway, Belfast BT12 6HY 01232 235451. Range of courses available
Women's Resource and Development Agency, 6 Mount Charles, Belfast BT7 1NZ 01232 230212 *Contact:* Judy Seymour. Resource and development agency for women, networking with local groups and providing an education and training programme

WEA office:

WEA Northern Ireland, 1 Fitzwilliam Street, Belfast BT9 6AW 01232 329718

COURSES

- **SUBJECT**   Access   1510
- **TITLE**   Certificate in Foundation Studies for Mature Students: University of Ulster Course
- **PLACE**   Lisburn College of Further Education

Length 2 years part time   **Days** Contact College   **Cost** Contact College   **Entry Reqs** Age 23+, no formal requirements   **Award** University Certificate in Foundation Studies, entry to higher education   **Creche** Contact College

- **CONTACT**   General Inquiries 01846 677225

- **SUBJECT**   Access   1511
- **TITLE**   Certificate in Foundation Studies for Mature Students: University of Ulster Course
- **PLACE**   Newtownabbey College of Further Education

Length 2 years part time   **Days** Contact College   **Cost** Contact College   **Entry Reqs** Age 23+, no formal requirements   **Award** University Certificate in Foundation Studies, entry to higher education   **Creche** Contact College

- **CONTACT**   General Inquiries 01232 864331

- **SUBJECT**   Information Technology   1512
- **TITLE**   Certificate in Information Technology (Specialism in Telematics)
- **PLACE**   University of Ulster at Jordanstown, Dalriada House

Length Minimum of 42 weeks   **Start** January-December   **Days** Mon-Fri 9.30-3.30   **Cost** Free (EC funded NOW initiative) Student's allowance £100/week   **Entry Reqs** GCSE standard or equivalent   **Award** University of Ulster Certificate: Information Technology Studies (Specialism in Telematics)   **Creche** Yes

- **CONTACT**   Pauline Murphy 01232 366679

- **SUBJECT**   Information Technology/Management   1513
- **TITLE**   Certificate in Information Technology Studies: IT, Management, Enterprise Skills
- **PLACE**   University of Ulster at Jordanstown, Dalriada House

Length 42 weeks   **Start** September-June   **Days** Mon-Thurs 9.30-12.001. 00-3.00, Fri study optional   **Cost** Free (EC funded) Student's allowance £100/week   **Entry Reqs** Women, unemployed, 21+, no stipulated formal qualifications. Computer aptitude test given   **Award** Certificate in Information Technology Studies, University of Ulster

- **CONTACT**   Pauline Murphy 01232 366679

- **SUBJECT**   Preparatory   1514
- **TITLE**   Wider Opportunities for Women
- **PLACE**   Lisburn College of Further Education, Downtown Centre

Length 12 weeks   **Start** September, January   **Days** Wed or Thurs 9.30-12.00   **Cost** £24.60 or £6 if receiving benefit   **Entry Reqs** None   **Creche** Yes Free

- **CONTACT**   Marcella Adair 01846 677225

- **SUBJECT**   Preparatory   1515
- **TITLE**   Time for Me (Personal Development/Choice of Options)
- **PLACE**   University of Ulster at Jordanstown

Length 10 weeks (1 term)   **Start** October, January, April   **Days** 1 day/week 10.00-12.00+1.00-3.00   **Cost** £28, concessionary fee £14   **Entry Reqs** Women   **Award** Certificate of Attendance, University of Ulster   **Creche** Yes

- **CONTACT**   Pauline Murphy 01232 366679

Northern Ireland: North Eastern/South Eastern

- **SUBJECT** Preparatory   1516
- **TITLE** Time for Me Pre Vocational Training Course: IT/Personal Development
- **PLACE** Workspace, 80-82 Rainey Street, Magherafelt

Length 10 weeks   **Start** October   **Days** 1 day/week 10.00-12.00+1.00-3.00   **Cost** Free (EC funded NOW initiative)   **Entry Reqs** Women. No stipulated entry qualifications   **Award** Course leads to CLAIT exams & University of Ulster Certificate of Attendance   **Creche** Yes free to students (EC funded)

- **CONTACT** Pauline Murphy 01232 366679

- **SUBJECT** Women's Studies   1517
- **TITLE** 1. Postgraduate Diploma 2. MSc in Women's Studies
- **PLACE** University of Ulster at Jordanstown

Length 1. Diploma 2 years part time 2. MSc 1 year   **Start** Contact University   **Days** 1.2 eves/week 2. No classes:tutorials+dissertation   **Cost** Contact University   **Entry Reqs** Interview 1. Hons degree(2nd)PG diploma/professional qualification/or equivalent 2. Completion of 1. **Award** 1. Postgraduate Diploma, possible entry to MSc 2. MSc in Women's Studies   **Creche** Daytime 6wks-5 yrs Tel 01232 365433 x2539

- **CONTACT** General Inquiries 01232 365131 x2920

COUNTY CONTACTS

Open University:

The Open University, Northern Ireland, 40 University Road, Belfast BT7 1SU 01232 245025

Other agencies:

Newtownabbey Women's Centre, 20a The Diamond, Rathcoole, Newtownabbey, Antrim BT37 9BJ 01232 854041   *Contact:* Wilma Lennox, Rosaleen McAlister
Northern Ireland Small Business Institute, Ulster Business School, BP Enterprise Centre, Shore Road, Newtownabbey, Antrim BT37 0QB 01232 332720

WEA office:

WEA Northern Ireland, 1 Fitzwilliam Street, Belfast BT9 6AW 01232 329718

NORTHERN IRELAND: South Eastern

COURSES

- **SUBJECT** Access/Social Science   1518
- **TITLE** Certificate in Foundation Studies/Social Sciences
- **PLACE** East Down Institute of Further & Higher Education

Length 2 years part time   **Start** September   **Days** Tues & Fri 9.30-12.30   **Cost** £130 + £25 university registration fee   **Entry Reqs** Personal interview   **Award** No

- **CONTACT** Anne Anderson 01396 615815 x230

- **SUBJECT** Business Administration/Information Technology 1519
- **TITLE** Business Update Skills: Business Administration, Word Processing, CLAIT
- **PLACE** North Down & Ards College of FE, Newtownards

Length 30 weeks **Start** September **Days** Mon 9.00-12.45, Tues 9.00-2.30 **Cost** £114 (Concessionary fees available) **Award** RSA Levels 1-3, NVQ Level 2 **Creche** No

- **CONTACT** Edith Martin 01247 812116 x204

- **SUBJECT** Counselling 1520
- **TITLE** Certificate(s) in Counselling
- **PLACE** East Down Institute of Further & Higher Education

Length 1 year part time **Start** October **Days** Mon or Thurs 1.00-3.00 **Cost** £285 **Entry Reqs** Open entry/mature students **Award** Certificate in counselling **Creche** No

- **CONTACT** Anne Anderson 01396 615815 x230

- **SUBJECT** English/Mathematics/Social Science/Psychology/History/ 1521 European Studies
- **TITLE** Adult Studies: GCSEs
- **PLACE** North Down & Ards College of FE, Newtownards

Length 30 weeks **Start** September **Days** 2 hours/subject/week (mornings) **Cost** £64/1st subject, £32/subsequent subjects. Concessions available **Entry Reqs** None **Award** GCSE **Creche** No

- **CONTACT** Jayne Walkingshaw 01247 271254

- **SUBJECT** English/Social Science/Psychology 1522
- **TITLE** Adult Studies: A Levels
- **PLACE** North Down & Ards College of FE, Newtownards & Bangor

Length 30 weeks **Start** September **Days** 2x3 hours/subject/week (mornings) **Cost** £96 Concessions available **Entry Reqs** None but GCSEs preferred **Award** A Level **Creche** No

- **CONTACT** Jayne Walkingshaw 01247 271254

- **SUBJECT** Information Technology 1523
- **TITLE** Adult Part Time Courses: CLAIT, Information Technology, Word Processing
- **PLACE** East Down Institute of Further & Higher Education

Length Contact College **Days** Mornings **Cost** CLAIT £64 (£21 concessions) **Award** RSA CLAIT **Creche** No

- **CONTACT** Edith Martin 01247 812116 x204

- **SUBJECT** Preparatory 1524
- **TITLE** Return to Study
- **PLACE** North Down & Ards College of FE, Newtownards, Bangor & Holywood

Length 30 weeks **Start** Anytime **Days** 1½ hours/subject/week (daytime or evening study) **Cost** £9 daytime, £12 evenings **Entry Reqs** None **Award** C&G Numeracy Stages 1-4, AEB Communication Skills, RSA Practical Skills Profile **Creche** No

- **CONTACT** Jayne Walkingshaw 01247 271254

- **SUBJECT**   Women's Studies   1525
- **TITLE**   Women to Women Discussion Group
- **PLACE**   North Down & Ards College of FE, Bangor

Length 30 weeks   **Start** Anytime   **Days** Thurs morning (1½ hours/week)   **Cost** £9   **Entry Reqs** None   **Award** None   **Creche** No

- **CONTACT**   Jayne Walkingshaw 01247 271254

COUNTY CONTACTS

Open University:

The Open University, Northern Ireland, 40 University Road, Belfast BT7 1SU 01232 245025

Other agencies:

Ballybeen Women's Centre, 34 Ballybeen Square, Dundonald BT7 1SU 01232 481632   *Contact:* Anne Graham. Educational guidance and practical support for women returners
Northern Ireland Childminding Association, 17a Court Street, Newtownards BT23 5NX 01247 811015   *Contact:* Bridget Nodder, Director

WEA office:

WEA Northern Ireland, 1 Fitzwilliam Street, Belfast BT9 6AW 01232 329718

NORTHERN IRELAND: Southern

COURSES

- **SUBJECT**   Access/Humanities/Social Studies   1526
- **TITLE**   Certificate in Foundation Studies for Mature Students: University of
  Ulster Course
- **PLACE**   Banbridge College of Further Education

Length 2 years part time   **Days** Contact College   **Entry Req** Age 23+, no formal requirements   **Award** University Certificate in Foundation Studies, entry to higher education **Creche** Contact College

- **CONTACT**   General Inquiries 018206 62289

- **SUBJECT**   Access/Humanities/Social Studies   1527
- **TITLE**   Certificate in Foundation Studies for Mature Students: University of
  Ulster Course
- **PLACE**   Newry College of Further Education

Length 2 years part time   **Days** Day and evening provision   **Entry Req** Age 23+, no formal requirements   **Award** University Certificate in Foundation Studies, entry to higher education **Creche** Yes Contact College

- **CONTACT**   Tom Torley 01693 69359/61071

- **SUBJECT**   Access/Science/Technology   1528
- **TITLE**   Certificate in Foundation Studies for Mature Students: University of Ulster Course
- **PLACE**   Portadown College of Further Education

Length 2 years part time   **Days** Contact College   **Entry Req** Age 21+, some previous experience in/knowledge of science & technology   **Award** University Certificate in Foundation Studies, entry to higher education   **Creche** Contact College

- **CONTACT**   General Inquiries 01762 337111

- **SUBJECT**   Catering/Craft   1529
- **TITLE**   1. Catering NVQ I&II 2. Creative Studies c&G 790: Patchwork & Quilting/ Floristry
- **PLACE**   Armagh College of Further Education

Start 1. Continuous enrolment 2. September   **Cost** Contact College   **Award** 1. NVQ Levels I&II Catering 2. C&G 790 Creative Studies

- **CONTACT**   1. Mr O Grimes/2. Adult Education Centre 01861 522205

- **SUBJECT**   Food Studies   1530
- **TITLE**   HNC/HND Food Supply Technology
- **PLACE**   Loughry College: The Food Centre

Length Depends on subjects studied   **Start** September, January   **Cost** £250/module. No charge for candidates who register for full award   **Entry Reqs** 1 A Level   **Award** HNC/ HND   **Creche** No

- **CONTACT**   Catherine Devlin 016487 62491

- **SUBJECT**   Food Studies   1531
- **TITLE**   Science (Food Technology) Modular Courses: First/National/ Higher Nat Cert/Diploma
- **PLACE**   Loughry College: The Food Centre

Length 10 days/module   **Start** Usually September and January   **Days** Depends on subjects studied. Open Learning available   **Cost** Approx £230/module   **Entry Reqs** First Level: English/Maths; Nat Level: 4 GCSEs (1 Science); Higher Nat: 1 A Level Science   **Award** Individual modules NC/HNC/HND/Intermediate GNVQ Manufacturing (Food)   **Creche** No

- **CONTACT**   Catherine Devlin 016487 62491

- **SUBJECT**   Preparatory   1532
- **TITLE**   Return to Learn
- **PLACE**   Newry College of FE, Adult Education Centre

Length 10 weeks   **Start** Termly   **Days** Thurs 9.30-12.30   **Cost** £21.60, £6 if in receipt of benefit   **Entry Reqs** None   **Creche** Yes £5/session

- **CONTACT**   Marietta Farrell 01693 69359/61071

- **SUBJECT**   Preparatory   1533
- **TITLE**   Time for Women: Assertiveness, Confidence Building, Women's Issues
- **PLACE**   Newry College of FE at Newry and Kilkeel College

Length 10 weeks   **Start** Termly   **Days** Mon 10.00-12.30   **Cost** £21.60, £6 if in receipt of benefit   **Entry Reqs** None   **Creche** Yes £5/session

- **CONTACT**   Marietta Farrell 01693 69359/61071

COUNTY CONTACTS

Open University:

The Open University, Northern Ireland, 40 University Road, Belfast BT7 1SU 01232 245025

WEA office:

WEA Northern Ireland, 1 Fitzwilliam Street, Belfast BT9 6AW 01232 329718

NORTHERN IRELAND: Western

COURSES

- **SUBJECT** Access   1534
- **TITLE** Certificate in Foundation Studies for Mature Students: University of Ulster Course
- **PLACE** Fermanagh College of Further Education

Length 2 years part time **Days** Contact College **Cost** Contact College **Entry Reqs** Age 21+, no formal requirements **Award** University Certificate in Foundation Studies, entry to higher education **Creche** Contact College

- **CONTACT** General Inquiries 01365 322431

- **SUBJECT** Access/Science   1535
- **TITLE** Certificate in Foundation Studies in Science
- **PLACE** N W Institute of Further & Higher Education, Londonderry

Length 2 years part time **Days** Contact Institute **Entry Req** Age 21+, some previous experience in/knowledge of science **Award** University Certificate in Foundation Studies in Science, entry to higher education **Creche** No

- **CONTACT** General Inquiries 01504 266711

- **SUBJECT** Access/Social Science/Humanities   1536
- **TITLE** Certificate in Foundation Studies for Mature Students: University of Ulster Course
- **PLACE** University of Ulster, Magee College

Length 2 years part time **Days** Contact College **Entry Req** Age 23+, no formal requirements **Award** University Certificate in Foundation Studies, entry to higher education **Creche** Yes

- **CONTACT** General Inquiries 01504 265621

- **SUBJECT** Preparatory   1537
- **TITLE** 1. Time for Me 2. Learning Links for Women
- **PLACE** University of Ulster at Jordanstown, Bellaghy & Coalisland venues

Length 10 weeks (1 term) **Start** October, January, April **Days** 1 day/week 10.00-12.00+1.00-3.00 **Cost** £28, concessionary fee £14 **Entry Reqs** Women **Award** Certificate of Attendance, University of Ulster **Creche** At some centres

- **CONTACT** Pauline Murphy 01232 366679

- **SUBJECT** Women's Studies   1538
- **TITLE** Certificate in Women's Studies
- **PLACE** University of Ulster, Magee College

Length 1 year   **Start** Contact College   **Days** 1 day/week   **Cost** Contact College   **Entry Reqs** 21+; English Grade C GCSE/GCE or equiv or entrance test. Under 21; 5 GCSE/GCE Grade C or equiv   **Award** University Certificate in Women's Studies   **Creche** Yes
- **CONTACT** General Inquiries 01504 265621

COUNTY CONTACTS

Open University:

The Open University, Northern Ireland, 40 University Road, Belfast BT7 1SU 01232 245025

Other agencies:

Women's Centre, 3-3a Abbey Street, Coleraine BT52 1AD 01265 56573   *Contact:* Avril A Watson. Range of courses available

WEA office:

WEA Northern Ireland, 1 Fitzwilliam Street, Belfast BT9 6AW 01232 329718

SCOTLAND: Borders

COURSES

- **SUBJECT** Art & Design   1539
- **TITLE** Access to Art and Design
- **PLACE** Borders College

Length 1 year   **Start** Usually August   **Days** Full or part time depending on subject   **Cost** Student may be eligible for LEA bursary   **Entry Reqs** Age 21+, no formal entry requirements   **Award** SCOTVEC Certificate, entry to higher education   **Creche** Yes
- **CONTACT** Scottish Wider Access Programme/SWAP 0131 458 5469

- **SUBJECT** Arts/Divinity/Social Science   1540
- **TITLE** Access to Arts, Divinity, Social Science
- **PLACE** Borders College

Length 1 year   **Start** Usually August   **Days** Full or part time depending on subject   **Cost** Student may be eligible for LEA bursary   **Entry Reqs** Age 21+, no formal entry requirements   **Award** SCOTVEC Certificate, entry to higher education   **Creche** Yes
- **CONTACT** Scottish Wider Access Programme/SWAP 0131 458 5469

- **SUBJECT** Business/Management   1541
- **TITLE** Access to Business Studies, Management
- **PLACE** Borders College

Length 1 year   **Start** Usually August   **Days** Full or part time depending on subject   **Cost** Student may be eligible for LEA bursary   **Entry Reqs** Age 21+, no formal entry requirements   **Award** SCOTVEC Certificate, entry to higher education   **Creche** Yes
- **CONTACT** Scottish Wider Access Programme/SWAP 0131 458 5469

- **SUBJECT**   Health Studies   **1542**
- **TITLE**   Access to Health Studies
- **PLACE**   Borders College

Length 1 year   **Start** Usually August   **Days** Full or part time depending on subject   **Cost** Student may be eligible for LEA bursary   **Entry Reqs** Age 21+, no formal entry requirements **Award** SCOTVEC Certificate, entry to higher education   **Creche** Yes

- **CONTACT**   Scottish Wider Access Programme/SWAP 0131 458 5469

- **SUBJECT**   Science/Engineering/Technology   **1543**
- **TITLE**   Access to Science, Engineering, Technology
- **PLACE**   Borders College

Length 1 year   **Start** Usually August   **Days** Full or part time depending on subject   **Cost** Student may be eligible for LEA bursary   **Entry Reqs** Age 21+, no formal entry requirements **Award** SCOTVEC Certificate, entry to higher education   **Creche** Yes

- **CONTACT**   Scottish Wider Access Programme/SWAP 0131 458 5469

COUNTY CONTACTS

Information and advice:

Borders Regional Council Education Department, Newtown St Boswells, Melrose TD6 0SA 01835 823301
Pathways. 01896 755110. Free adult educational guidance service in the Scottish Borders. Free courses for adult returners arranged locally. Individual interviews arranged.

Local Enterprise Council:

Scottish Borders Enterprise, Bridge Street, Galashiels TD1 1SW 01896 758991

Open University:

The Open University, Scotland, 10 Drumsheugh Gardens, Edinburgh EH3 7QJ 0131 225 2889

WEA office:

Scottish WEA, Riddles Court, 322 Lawnmarket, Edinburgh EH1 3PG 0131 226 3456   *Contact:* Hilary Lawson

SCOTLAND: Central

COURSES

- **SUBJECT**   Access/Business/Hospitality Management   **1544**
- **TITLE**   Access to Business, Hospitality Operations
- **PLACE**   Clackmannan College of Further Education

Length 38 weeks   **Start** Contact College   **Days** Full or part time depending on subject   **Cost** Student may be eligible for LEA bursary   **Entry Reqs** Age 21+, no formal entry requirements **Award** SCOTVEC Certificate, entry to higher education   **Creche** Yes

- **CONTACT**   Access Co-ordinator 01259 215121

- **SUBJECT** Access/Teaching 1545
- **TITLE** Access to Primary Bachelor of Education
- **PLACE** Clackmannan College of Further Education

Length 38 weeks **Start** Contact College **Cost** Student may be eligible for LEA bursary **Entry Reqs** Age 21+, no formal entry requirements **Award** SCOTVEC Certificate, entry to BEd degree courses **Creche** Yes
- **CONTACT** Access Co-ordinator 01259 215121

- **SUBJECT** Access/Teaching/Science & Technology/Mathematics/Computing 1546
- **TITLE** Access to Secondary Teaching, Science & Technology, Maths & Computing
- **PLACE** Clackmannan College of Further Education

Length 38 weeks **Start** Contact College **Days** Full or part time depending on subject **Cost** Student may be eligible for LEA bursary **Entry Reqs** Age 21+, no formal entry requirements **Award** SCOTVEC Certificate, entry to higher education **Creche** Yes
- **CONTACT** Access Co-ordinator 01259 215121

- **SUBJECT** Business Administration 1547
- **TITLE** Women in Business
- **PLACE** 1. Clackmannan College of FE 2. Falkirk College of Technology

Length 1 year **Start** August **Days** Full time 9.00-4.00 **Cost** Free **Entry Reqs** Applicants must have been unemployed for 6 months **Award** Higher National Certificate **Creche** Yes at Clackmannan College
- **CONTACT** Pat Clark, Central Regional Council Skill Training Unit 01786 814193

- **SUBJECT** Business Studies 1548
- **TITLE** Enterprise Training for Women: Starting Your Own Business
- **PLACE** University of Stirling

Length 13 weeks **Start** February, September **Days** 3 days/week 9.30-2.00 **Cost** Free **Entry Reqs** None **Award** Completion of Course Diploma **Creche** Yes
- **CONTACT** Christina Hartshorn 01786 467352

- **SUBJECT** Community Studies 1549
- **TITLE** Introduction to Working With People in the Community
- **PLACE** Falkirk College of Technology

Length 36 weeks **Start** August **Days** 3 days/week part time **Cost** £40/unit. Local Authority bursary may be available **Entry Reqs** Usually 21+, experience of voluntary work **Award** SCOTVEC National Certificate **Creche** Yes £25/week
- **CONTACT** Frank Monaghan 01324 624981

- **SUBJECT** Computing 1550
- **TITLE** Computing Skills Course
- **PLACE** Alloa Women's Technology Centre

Length 1 year **Start** April **Days** Mon-Fri 9.30-4.30 **Cost** Free **Entry Reqs** Currently unemployed, 18+, no formal qualifications required **Award** SCOTVEC Modules **Creche** Contribution towards childcare costs
- **CONTACT** Pam Courtney 01259 211180

- **SUBJECT** Management 1551
- **TITLE** Management Training for Women: Certificate in Small & Medium Enterprise Management
- **PLACE** University of Stirling

Length 26 weeks **Start** October **Days** Mon-Thurs 9.30-4.00 **Cost** Free **Entry Reqs** Age 25+, good general education, some previous supervisory/management experience, not employed **Award** University of Stirling Certificate **Creche** From 6 months, £40-£44/week
- **CONTACT** Christina Hartshorn 01786 467352

- **SUBJECT** Multi-Subject
- **TITLE** BA/BSc
- **PLACE** University of Stirling

1552

Length Approx 4 years (flexible system for individual progress)   **Start** September, February
Days Approx 2 eves/week   **Cost** £175/unit (16 units needed to complete degree)   **Entry Reqs**
Age 21+, no formal entry requirements   **Award** BA/BSc   **Creche** Yes

- **CONTACT** Dorothy Kelso/Susan McGiffin 01786 467955/467947

- **SUBJECT** Preparatory
- **TITLE** Women into Work
- **PLACE** Alloa Women's Technology Centre

1553

Length 5 weeks   **Start** Throughout the year   **Days** 3 days/week 10.15-3.15   **Cost** Free
Entry Reqs Unemployed for at least 12 months   **Award** Course Completion Certificate
Creche Contribution towards childcare costs

- **CONTACT** Pam Courtney 01259 211180

- **SUBJECT** Technology
- **TITLE** Women into Technology
- **PLACE** Clackmannan College of Further Education

1554

Length 38 weeks   **Start** Contact College   **Cost** Contact College   **Entry Reqs** Age 21+, no
formal entry requirements   **Award** SCOTVEC Certificate, entry to higher education   **Creche**
Yes

- **CONTACT** Access Co-ordinator 01259 215121

- **SUBJECT** Technology/Education
- **TITLE** Access to Bachelor of Technological Education
- **PLACE** Clackmannan College of Further Education

1555

Length 38 weeks   **Start** Contact College   **Cost** Student may be eligible for LEA bursary
Entry Reqs Age 21+, no formal entry requirements   **Award** SCOTVEC Certificate, entry to
Bachelor of Technological Education   **Creche** Yes

- **CONTACT** Access Co-ordinator 01259 215121

COUNTY CONTACTS

Information and advice:

Careers Central Ltd, Head Office, Cape Unicentre, Kerse Road, Stirling FK7 7RW 01786 446150
Contact: Margaret Graham. Adult guidance service to individuals and groups in the Forth Valley
area.
Central Adult Guidance Network, West Block, Park Street, Falkirk FK1 1RE 0800 585892.
Individual guidance, access to information, freephone help and advice on work, training or
study.
Centre for Open Learning and Flexible Training, West Block, Park Street, Falkirk FK1 1RE 01324
613334/613331. Advice, guidance and information on all aspects of open learning locally or
nationally. Does not deliver any open learning courses.
Alloa Careers Office, 6 Marshill, Alloa 01259 215214   *Contact:* Heather McDonald/Rona
Neilson. Alloa, Bo'ness and Grangemouth areas
Falkirk Careers Office, 9-11 Vicar Street, Falkirk 01324 620311   *Contact:* Lawrence Durden.
Falkirk, Denny and Bonnybridge areas
Stirling Careers Office, 2 Viewfield Place, Stirling 01786 462036   *Contact:* John Gilligan Stirling
area

Local Enterprise Council:

Forth Valley Enterprise, Laurel House, Laurelhill Business Park, Stirling FK7 9JQ 017864 51919

Open University:

The Open University, Scotland, 10 Drumsheugh Gardens, Edinburgh EH3 7QJ 0131 225 2889

Other agencies:

Alloa Women's Technology Centre, 14 Bank Street, Alloa FK10 1HP 01259 211180. Offers full time computing skills course and women into work short courses specifically for women returners.
Clackmannan College, Branshill Road, Alloa FK10 3BT 01259 215121
Community Education Service, Grendon, 9 Snowdon Place, Stirling FK8 2NH 01786 442247
Falkirk College, Grangemouth Road, Falkirk FK2 9AD 01324 624981
Falkirk Women's Technology Centre, Unit H, Newhouse Business Park, Newhouse Road, Falkirk FK3 8LL 01324 471000. Offers full-time computing skills course.
Skill Training Unit, Hut E4, Bannockburn High School, Broomridge, Bannockburn FK7 0HJ 01786 814193. Training including Women onto Business courses for women returners.
Stirling Women's Technology Centre, The Arcade, King Street, Stirling FK8 1DN 01786 450980. Offers full-time computing skills course and an access course.
University of Stirling, Stirling FK9 4LA 01786 467945. Range of provision including access course, part time degree course and continuing education.

WEA offices:

Grendon, 9 Snowdon Place, Stirling FK8 2NH 01786 447567
Scottish WEA, Riddles Court, 322 Lawnmarket, Edinburgh EH1 3PG 0131 226 3456   *Contact:* Hilary Lawson

---

SCOTLAND: Dumfries & Galloway

COURSES

- **SUBJECT**   Computing   1556
- **TITLE**   Various Computer Courses
- **PLACE**   Dumfries and Galloway College, Open Learning Unit

Length Contact College   **Start** Various   **Days** Variable. Home study and drop-in computer centre   **Cost** Contact College   **Entry Reqs** Contact College

- **CONTACT** Irene Lennox 01387 261261

- **SUBJECT**   Multi-Subject   1557
- **TITLE**   1. SCOTVEC National Certificate Modules 2. SCOTVEC Higher National Certificate Units
- **PLACE**   Dumfries and Galloway College, Open Learning Unit

Length 1.40 hours 2.40 hours or various   **Start** Various   **Days** Variable. Home study and drop-in centre   **Cost** £40/credit   **Entry Reqs** 1. None 2. H Grade or National Certificate recommended   **Award** 1. SCOTVEC National Certificates 2. SCOTVEC Higher National Certificates

- **CONTACT** Irene Lennox 01387 261261

- **SUBJECT**   Office Skills   1558
- **TITLE**   Wordprocessing, Accounting, Record-Keeping
- **PLACE**   Dumfries and Galloway College, Open Learning Unit

Length Contact College   **Start** Various   **Days** Variable. Home study and drop-in computer centre   **Cost** Contact College   **Entry Reqs** Contact College   **Award** Contact College

- **CONTACT**   Irene Lennox 01387 261261

- **SUBJECT**   Preparatory   1559
- **TITLE**   Springboard
- **PLACE**   Dumfries and Galloway College, Open Learning Unit

Length Variable, usually 6 weeks   **Start** Various   **Days** Variable. Home study + workshops **Cost** Contact College   **Entry Reqs** None   **Award** College Certificate

- **CONTACT**   Irene Lennox 01387 261261

COUNTY CONTACTS

Information and advice:

Dumfries and Galloway Careers Service, Adult Guidance Unit, Dumfries Careers Office, Newall Terrace, Dumfries DG1 1LW 01387 260066   *Contact:* Sally Burn
Annan Careers Office, Ednam Street, Annan DG12 6EF 01461 204916. For Annan and Gretna
Castle Douglas Careers Office, Market Street, Castle Douglas DG7 1BE 01556 502351. For Castle Douglas and Dalbeattie
Dumfries Careers Office, Newall Terrace, Dumfries DG1 1LW 01387 260068. For Dumfries town area, Thornhill, Sanquhar and Moffat.
Lockerbie Careers Office, Council Offices, Dryfe Road, Lockerbie DG11 2AP 01576 202287. For Lockerbie, Langholm and Canonbie.
Newton Stewart Careers Office, Peninghame Centre, Auchendoon Road, Newton Stewart DG8 6HD 01671 402692. For Newton Stewart and the Machars.
Stranraer Careers Office, 76 Ashwood Drive, Stranraer DG9 7PD 01776 702151. For Stranraer and the Rhins.

Local Enterprise Council:

Dumfries and Galloway Enterprise Company, Cairnsmore House, Bankend Road, Dumfries DG1 4TA 01387 54444

Open University:

The Open University, Scotland, 10 Drumsheugh Gardens, Edinburgh EH3 7QJ 0131 225 2889

Other agencies:

Women's Forum, Community Education, Library Building, North Strand Street, Stranraer DG9 7LQ 01776 706753   *Contact:* Donna Mounce, Secretary. Provides a co-ordinated voice for women in the area and produces a newsletter 'Women's Voices'

WEA office:

Scottish WEA, Riddles Court, 322 Lawnmarket, Edinburgh EH1 3PG 0131 226 3456   *Contact:* Hilary Lawson

COURSES

- **SUBJECT** Access/Arts/Social Science   **1560**
- **TITLE** Access to Arts and Social Science
- **PLACE** Lauder College

Length 36 weeks   **Start** August   **Days** Full time   **Cost** Fees may be paid if eligible for a bursary award   **Entry Reqs** 21+   **Award** SCOTVEC National Certificate, access to higher education   **Creche** Yes Free

- **CONTACT** Joham Parry 01383 726201 x249

- **SUBJECT** Access/Teaching   **1561**
- **TITLE** Access to Teaching
- **PLACE** Lauder College

Length 36 weeks   **Start** August   **Days** Full time   **Cost** Contact College   **Entry Reqs** 21+ **Award** SCOTVEC modules, access to higher education   **Creche** Yes Free

- **CONTACT** Joham Parry 01383 726201 x249

- **SUBJECT** Business Administration   **1562**
- **TITLE** Business Administration
- **PLACE** Kirkland High School & Community College, Methil

Length 1 year   **Days** Full time   **Cost** Bursary support   **Entry Reqs** None   **Award** SCOTVEC National Certificate   **Creche** Yes Free

- **CONTACT** Evelyn Davie 01333 592403

- **SUBJECT** Business Administration   **1563**
- **TITLE** Small Business Workshop
- **PLACE** Kirkland High School & Community College, Methil

Length 8 weeks   **Start** Various   **Days** 1 day/week   **Cost** Contact College   **Entry Reqs** Contact College   **Creche** Yes

- **CONTACT** Evelyn Davie 01333 592403

- **SUBJECT** Electronics/Electrical Engineering   **1564**
- **TITLE** Electronics and Electrical Engineering
- **PLACE** Dunfermline Women's Technology Centre

Length 52 weeks   **Start** October   **Days** Mon-Fri 9.30-4.30   **Cost** Free   **Entry Reqs** Unemployed, no qualifications, residing in Dunfermline district   **Award** National Certificate in Electronic & Electrical Engineering   **Creche** Childcare costs paid

- **CONTACT** Lorraine Clark 01383 621038

- **SUBJECT** Engineering   **1565**
- **TITLE** Engineering Practice
- **PLACE** Kirkland High School & Community College, Methil

Length 1 year   **Days** Full time   **Cost** Bursary support   **Entry Reqs** None   **Award** SCOTVEC National Certificate Group Award in Engineering Practice   **Creche** Yes Free

- **CONTACT** Evelyn Davie 01333 592403

- **SUBJECT** Finance   **1566**
- **TITLE** Financial Administration
- **PLACE** Kirkland High School & Community College, Methil

Length 1 year   **Days** Full time   **Cost** Bursary support   **Entry Reqs** None   **Award** SCOTVEC National Certificate   **Creche** Yes Free

- **CONTACT** Evelyn Davie 01333 592403

- **SUBJECT** Information Technology   **1567**
- **TITLE** Information Technology
- **PLACE** Kirkland High School & Community College, Methil

Length 1 year   **Days** Full time   **Cost** Bursary support   **Entry Reqs** None   **Award** SCOTVEC GSVQ Information Technology Level 3   **Creche** Yes Free

- **CONTACT** Evelyn Davie 01333 592403

- **SUBJECT** Office Skills   **1568**
- **TITLE** Office Administration, Business Administration, Computing and Accounts
- **PLACE** Kirkland High School & Community College, Methil

Length 12 weeks - 1 year   **Start** August, November, March   **Days** Varies   **Cost** Bursary support   **Entry Reqs** None   **Award** SVQ, GSVQ   **Creche** Yes Free

- **CONTACT** Mrs Veronica Kirk 01333 592343

- **SUBJECT** Preparatory   **1569**
- **TITLE** Options and Choices: Preparation for a Return to Training/Employment/ Education
- **PLACE** Glenrothes College

Length 12 weeks   **Start** October, April   **Days** Mon-Fri 9.00-2.45   **Cost** Fife Regional Bursary available   **Entry Reqs** None   **Award** SCOTVEC National Certificate modules   **Creche** No

- **CONTACT** Shirley Scott 01592 772233

- **SUBJECT** Preparatory   **1570**
- **TITLE** Women's Studies: Blueprint Return to Education and Training
- **PLACE** Lauder College

Length 13 weeks   **Start** August   **Days** Full time   **Cost** Contact College   **Award** SCOTVEC National Certificiates   **Creche** Yes Free

- **CONTACT** Mireille Pouget 01383 726201 x245

- **SUBJECT** Preparatory   **1571**
- **TITLE** Working for Women
- **PLACE** Glenrothes College

Length 10 months   **Start** September   **Days** Mon-Fri 9.00-2.30   **Cost** Fife Regional Bursary available   **Entry Reqs** No formal entry qualifications   **Award** Range of Higher National Certificates available   **Creche** No

- **CONTACT** June Smith 01592 772233

COUNTY CONTACTS

Information and advice:

Fife Adult Guidance & Education Services, Auchterderran Centre, Woodend Road, Cardenden KY5 0NE 01592 414738. Free impartial advice to adults in Fife on education, jobs and training. Individual appointments arranged in Careers Offices, Local Services Offices and other community venues across Fife. A range of workshops is also offered.
Anstruther Careers Service, East Newk Centre, Lady Walk, Anstruther 01333 310728

National Association for Educational Guidance for Adults, Regional representative, Fife Adult Guidance Service, ASDARC, Woodend Road, Cardenden KY5 0NE 01592 414738   *Contact:* Ian Ledward. Covers Scotland

Local Enterprise Council:

Fife Enterprise Ltd, Huntsman's House, 33 Cadham Centre, Glenrothes KY7 6RU 01592 621000

Open University:

The Open University, Scotland, 10 Drumsheugh Gardens, Edinburgh EH3 7QJ 0131 225 2889

Other agencies:

Dunfermline Women's Technology Centre, Unit 10, Elgin Industrial Park, Dickson Street, Dunfermline KY12 7SL 01383 621038   *Contact:* Lorraine Clark. Women's training centre

WEA office:

Scottish WEA, Riddles Court, 322 Lawnmarket, Edinburgh EH1 3PG 0131 226 3456 Hil0131 226 3456   *Contact:* Hilary Lawson

SCOTLAND: Grampian

COURSES

● **SUBJECT**	Access/Arts/Social Science	1572
● **TITLE**	Access to Arts and Social Science	
● **PLACE**	Scottish Wider Access Programme, Elgin, Aberdeen	

Length 1 year full time or negotiable part time   **Start** August   **Days** Varied   **Cost** Full time £750, part time £30 for 40 hours (subject to review)   **Entry Reqs** None   **Award** Arts & Social Science Certificate, access to courses at Aberdeen University   **Creche** Yes at Aberdeen

● **CONTACT** Stephen Masser 01224 313142

● **SUBJECT**	Access/Building/Surveying	1573
● **TITLE**	Access to Building, Surveying and Architectural Technology	
● **PLACE**	Scottish Wider Access Programme, Aberdeen, Fraserburgh, Elgin	

Length 1 year full time or negotiable part time   **Start** August   **Days** Varied   **Cost** Full time £750, part time £30 for 40 hours (subject to review)   **Entry Reqs** None   **Award** SCOTVEC National Certificate, access to higher education   **Creche** Yes at Aberdeen

● **CONTACT** Stephen Masser 01224 313142

● **SUBJECT**	Access/Engineering/Science	1574
● **TITLE**	Access to Engineering. Science	
● **PLACE**	Scottish Wider Access Programme, Aberdeen, Fraserburgh, Elgin	

Length 1 year full time or negotiable part time   **Start** August   **Days** Varied   **Cost** Full time £750, part time £30 for 40 hours (subject to review)   **Entry Reqs** None   **Award** SCOTVEC National Certificate, access to higher education   **Creche** Yes at Aberdeen

● **CONTACT** Stephen Masser 01224 313142

- **SUBJECT**   Access/Languages   1575
- **TITLE**   Access to Languages
- **PLACE**   Scottish Wider Access Programme, Aberdeen, Elgin

Length 1 year   **Start** August   **Days** Full time or part time   **Cost** Full time £750, part time £30 (subject to review)   **Entry Reqs** 1 modern language at SCE Higher Grade pass   **Award** SCOTVEC modules, access to degree at Aberdeen University   **Creche** Yes at Aberdeen

- **CONTACT**   Stephen Masser 01224 313142

- **SUBJECT**   Access/Nursing   1576
- **TITLE**   Access to Nursing
- **PLACE**   Scottish Wider Access Programme. Elgin, Aberdeen, Fraserburgh

Length 1 year full time   **Start** August   **Days** Full time   **Cost** £750 (subject to review)   **Entry Reqs** None   **Award** Entry to Pre-registration First Level Nursing course at college in Aberdeen, Inverness   **Creche** Yes at Aberdeen

- **CONTACT**   Stephen Masser 01224 313142

- **SUBJECT**   Access/Teaching   1577
- **TITLE**   Access to Primary Teaching
- **PLACE**   Aberdeen, Elgin

Length 1 year full time or 2 years part time   **Start** August   **Days** Full time or part time   **Cost** Full time £750, part time £30 (subject to review)   **Entry Reqs** Interview   **Award** SCOTVEC National Certificate, access to teacher training   **Creche** Yes at Aberdeen

- **CONTACT**   Stephen Masser 01224 313142

- **SUBJECT**   Horticulture   1578
- **TITLE**   Horticulture
- **PLACE**   Aberdeen College, Sector of Rural & Recreational Studies

Length Full time 36 weeks or part time   **Start** September or flexible   **Days** Mon-Fri 9.00-4.30 or modular open access   **Cost** Full time approx £740, part time approx £44/module (=40 hours)   **Entry Reqs** None but must be physically fit   **Award** SCOTVEC National Certificate SVQ Levels 1 and 2   **Creche** No

- **CONTACT**   B Gilliland 01224 640366

- **SUBJECT**   Preparatory   1579
- **TITLE**   Action for Employment
- **PLACE**   Various locations in Grampian Region

Length 12 weeks   **Days** Mon-Fri 9.30-12.30   **Entry Req** None   **Award** SCOTVEC modules

- **CONTACT**   Linda McFarlane, Grampian Training 01224 707071

- **SUBJECT**   Science   1580
- **TITLE**   Postgraduate Diploma/MSc in Instrumental Analytical Sciences
- **PLACE**   The Robert Gordon University, School of Applied Sciences

Length 30 weeks/48 weeks   **Start** September   **Days** 5 days/week (Mon+Fri afternoons generally free). Part time 1 day/week   **Cost** SAAS (Scotland) & ESF funded places available, pays fees + living expenses   **Entry Reqs** Science degree or appropriate experience   **Award** Postgraduate Diploma/MSc   **Creche** Nursery, contact Customer Services

- **CONTACT**   M A Sweet 01224 262815

COUNTY CONTACTS

Information and advice:

Careers Office, 11 North Guildry Street, Elgin IV30 1JR 01343 548884
Careers Office, Old Aberdeen House, Dunbar Street, Aberdeen AB2 1UE 01224 483314
Careers Office, Unit 6, Garioch Centre, Constitution Street, Inverurie AB51 4SQ 01467 623623
Grampian Enterprise Guidance Service, STEPahead, 381 Union Street, Aberdeen 01224 210300
Contact: Dorothy Elder. Careers information and guidance
STEPahead, Neighbourhood Learning Centre, 9 Marischal Street, Peterhead AB42 6BS 01779 481054
Training Access Point, Unit 3, Elgin Business Centre, Maisondieu Road, Elgin IV30 1RH 01343 551858   *Contact:* Roddy Innes. Access to a database of training information

Local Enterprise Councils:

Grampian Enterprise, 27 Albyn Place, Aberdeen AB1 1YL 01224 211500
Moray, Badenoch and Strathspey Enterprise Ltd, Elgin Business Centre, Maisondieu Road, Elgin IV30 1RH 01343 550567. Runs TAP information service, training courses

Open University:

The Open University, Scotland, 10 Drumsheugh Gardens, Edinburgh EH3 7QJ 0131 225 2889

Other agencies:

Grampian Training, Kessock Industrial Estate, Kessock Road, Fraserburgh AB43 5UE 01346 519172
Grampian Training, Raeden Park Road, Aberdeen AB2 4PE 01224 312550
KADET, Unit 1, Aboyne Business Centre, Huntly Road, Aboyne AB34 5AG 01339 887222

WEA office:

Scottish WEA, Riddles Court, 322 Lawnmarket, Edinburgh EH1 3PG 0131 225 3456   *Contact:* Hilary Lawson

SCOTLAND: Highland

COURSES

- **SUBJECT**   Access/Arts/Social Science   1581
- **TITLE**   Access to Arts & Social Science
- **PLACE**   Scottish Wider Access Programme, Inverness, Thurso

Length 1 year full time or negotiable part time   **Start** August   **Days** Varied   **Cost** Full time £750, part time £30 for 40 hours (subject to review)   **Entry Reqs** None   **Award** Arts & Social Science Certificate, access to courses at Aberdeen University   **Creche** Yes at Inverness

- **CONTACT**   Stephen Masser 01224 313142

- **SUBJECT** Access/Building/Surveying · 1582
- **TITLE** Access to Building, Surveying and Architectural Technology
- **PLACE** Scottish Wider Access Programme, Inverness, Thurso

Length 1 year full time or negotiable part time **Start** August **Days** Varied **Cost** Full time £750, part time £30 for 40 hours (subject to review) **Entry Reqs** None **Award** SCOTVEC National Certificate, access to higher education **Creche** Yes at Inverness

- **CONTACT** Stephen Masser 01224 313142

- **SUBJECT** Access/Engineering/Science · 1583
- **TITLE** Access to Engineering, Science
- **PLACE** Scottish Wider Access Programme, Inverness, Thurso

Length 1 year full time or negotiable part time **Start** August **Days** Varied **Cost** Full time £750, part time £30 for 40 hours (subject to review) **Entry Reqs** None **Award** SCOTVEC National Certificate, access to higher education **Creche** Yes at Inverness

- **CONTACT** Stephen Masser 01224 313142

- **SUBJECT** Access/Languages · 1584
- **TITLE** Access to Languages
- **PLACE** Scottish Wider Access Programme. Inverness, Thurso

Length 1 year full time or negotiable part time **Start** August **Days** Varied **Cost** £750 full time (subject to review) **Entry Reqs** 1 modern language at SCE Higher Grade pass **Award** SCOTVEC modules, access to degree at Aberdeen University **Creche** Yes at Inverness

- **CONTACT** Stephen Masser 01224 313142

- **SUBJECT** Access/Nursing · 1585
- **TITLE** Access to Nursing
- **PLACE** Scottish Wider Access Programme, Inverness, Thurso

Length 1 year full time **Start** August **Days** Full time **Cost** £750 (subject to review) **Entry Reqs** None **Award** Entry to Pre-registration First Level Nursing Course at colleges in Inverness, Aberdeen **Creche** Yes at Inverness

- **CONTACT** Stephen Masser 01224 313142

- **SUBJECT** Accounting · 1586
- **TITLE** Accounting and Finance
- **PLACE** Inverness College

Length Flexible **Days** Open learning **Cost** Contact College **Entry Reqs** Contact College **Award** Progress towards HNC/D Business Administration or Chartered Assoc of Certified Accountants awards

- **CONTACT** Open Learning Unit 01463 236681

- **SUBJECT** Business Administration · 1587
- **TITLE** Business Administration 1. HNC 2. HND
- **PLACE** Inverness College

Length 1.2-3 years 2.5 years **Start** Flexible **Days** Open learning **Cost** Contact College **Entry Reqs** Contact College **Award** 1. HNC 2. HND Business Administration

- **CONTACT** Open Learning Unit 01463 236681

- **SUBJECT** Communication Studies/English Literature · 1588
- **TITLE** Communication and Literature
- **PLACE** Inverness College

Length Flexible **Days** Open learning **Cost** Contact College **Entry Reqs** Contact College **Award** SCOTVEC modules

- **CONTACT** Open Learning Unit 01463 236681

- **SUBJECT** Electronics   1589
- **TITLE** 1. Electrical Engineering 2. Electronic Engineering 3. Instrumentation
  4. Electronics
- **PLACE** Inverness College

Length Flexible   **Days** Open learning   **Cost** Contact College   **Entry Reqs** Contact College
Award 1, 2 & 3. HNC 4. National Certificate in Electronics

- **CONTACT** Open Learning Unit 01463 236681

- **SUBJECT** Engineering   1590
- **TITLE** 1. Preparatory Modules for HNC Engineering 2. HNC Multi Disciplinary
  Engineering 3. HNC Mechanical Engineering
- **PLACE** Inverness College

Length Flexible   **Days** Open learning   **Cost** Contact College   **Entry Reqs** Contact College
Award 1. Access to HNC courses in Engineering subjects 2. &3. HNC

- **CONTACT** Open Learning Unit 01463 236681

- **SUBJECT** Information Technology   1591
- **TITLE** Women Returners' Information Technology Course
- **PLACE** Highland ITEC, Inverness

Length 16 weeks   **Days** Part time, morning or afternoon   **Entry Req** Contact College. Must
not be in employment. Keyboarding an advantage   **Award** RSA CLAIT

- **CONTACT** Highland ITEC 01463 226505

- **SUBJECT** Mathematics   1592
- **TITLE** Mathematics
- **PLACE** Inverness College

Length Flexible   **Days** Open learning   **Cost** Contact College   **Entry Reqs** Contact College
Award SCOTVEC Modules

- **CONTACT** Open Learning Unit 01463 236681

- **SUBJECT** Multi-Subject   1593
- **TITLE** SCOTVEC Modules (Various Subjects)
- **PLACE** Inverness College

Length Flexible   **Days** Open learning   **Cost** Contact College   **Entry Reqs** None   **Award**
SCOTVEC Modules

- **CONTACT** Open Learning Unit 01463 236681

- **SUBJECT** Preparatory   1594
- **TITLE** Women Returner Course
- **PLACE** Highland JET, Alness

Length 12 weeks   **Start** May, September   **Days** 3 hours/day   **Entry Reqs** Contact College
Award RSA CLAIT

- **CONTACT** Margaret MacDonald 01349 882545

- **SUBJECT** Travel & Tourism   1595
- **TITLE** Tourism
- **PLACE** Inverness College

Length Flexible   **Days** Open learning   **Cost** Contact College   **Entry Reqs** Contact College
Award SCOTVEC Modules

- **CONTACT** Open Learning Unit 01463 236681

COUNTY CONTACTS

Information and advice:

Highland Careers Services Ltd, Area Careers Office, 2b Fodderty Way, Dingwall Business Park, Dingwall IV15 9XB 01349 864914
Area Careers Office, 46 Church Street, Inverness IV1 1EH 01463 236114
Area Careers Office, 92-94 High Street, Fort William PH33 6AD 01397 704369
Area Careers Office, Traill House, 7a Olrig Street, Thurso KW14 7BJ 01847 895310
Careers Office, Elgin Hostel, Dunvegan Road, Portree IV51 9EE 01478 612328
Careers Office, Town House, Bridge Street, Wick KW1 4AJ 01955 602325
Part time Careers Office, Nairn Community Centre, King Street, Nairn 01667 454633

Local Enterprise Councils:

Caithness and Sutherland Enterprise, Scapa House, Castlegreen Road, Thurso KW14 7LS 01847 66115
Inverness and Nairn Enterprise, Castle Wynd, Inverness IV3 3DW 01463 713504
Lochaber Ltd, St Mary's House, Gordon Square, Fort William PH33 6DY 01397 702160/704326
Ross and Cromarty Enterprise, 62 High Street, Invergordon IV18 0DH 01349 853666
Skye and Lochalsh LEC, King's House, The Green, Portree, Isle of Skye IV51 9BS 01478 612841
Contact: Claire Scaife. Enterprising Women courses

Open University:

The Open University, Scotland, 10 Drumsheugh Gardens, Edinburgh EH3 7QJ 0131 225 2889

WEA office:

Scottish WEA, Riddles Court, 322 Lawnmarket, Edinburgh EH1 3PG 0131 226 3456   *Contact:* Hilary Lawson

SCOTLAND: Lothian

COURSES

- **SUBJECT**   Access   1596
- **TITLE**   1. Options and Choices 2. Access for Women
- **PLACE**   Edinburgh Telford's College

Length Flexible   **Start** Ongoing   **Days** Ongoing   **Cost** Varies £1.25/65p/Student hour, eves £45.50 course   **Entry Reqs** None   **Award** SCOTVEC modules or College Certificates   **Creche** Yes 55p/day

- **CONTACT**   1. Roz Chetwynd/2. Liz Leith 0131 332 2491

- **SUBJECT**   Access/Arts/Social Science/Divinity/Law   1597
- **TITLE**   Access to Undergraduate Entry in Arts, Social Sciences, Divinity and Law
- **PLACE**   University of Edinburgh, Centre for Continuing Education

Length 1 or 2 years   **Start** September   **Days** 2 halfdays/week, or eves   **Cost** Approx £175 (evening costs slightly less)   **Entry Reqs** 23+   **Award** Access Certificate endorsed by the University of Edinburgh and Stevenson College   **Creche** No

- **CONTACT**   Access Secretary 0131 650 4400

- **SUBJECT** Access/Arts/Social Science/Media Studies 1598
- **TITLE** Access to Arts, Social Science, Media Studies
- **PLACE** Edinburgh Telford's College

Length **Start** August **Days** Full time 9.00-4.00 **Entry Req** 21+ **Award** SED Higher, access to higher education **Creche** Yes

- **CONTACT** John McCusker 0131 332 2491 x2233

- **SUBJECT** Access/Nursing 1599
- **TITLE** Access to Nursing Programme
- **PLACE** Jewel and Esk Valley College, Eskbank Centre

Length 1 year **Start** August **Days** Full time **Entry Req** 21+, in good health **Award** SCOTVEC modules leading to direct entry to Diploma in Nursing **Creche** Yes

- **CONTACT** Norma Young 0131 654 5258 (direct dial)

- **SUBJECT** Access/Nursing/Health Studies 1600
- **TITLE** Access to 1. Nursing 2. Health Related Studies
- **PLACE** Edinburgh Telford's College

Length **Start** August **Days** Full time 9.00-4.00 **Entry Req** 21+ **Award** SCOTVEC modules, access to higher education **Creche** Yes

- **CONTACT** 1. Jane Jowitt/2. Anne Elder 0131 332 2491

- **SUBJECT** Access/Science/Engineering 1601
- **TITLE** Science and Engineering Degree Access Course (GSVQ Science Level 3)
- **PLACE** Stevenson College

Length 39 weeks **Start** August **Days** Full time, shortened timetable 9.15/9.30-3.00 **Cost** Bursary available and concessions **Entry Reqs** 21+, GCSE Maths or equivalent **Award** SCOTVEC National Certificate. Success on course provides access to HE **Creche** Yes 80p/day

- **CONTACT** Barclay MacIntosh 0131 453 6161

- **SUBJECT** Access/Science/Engineering/Technology 1602
- **TITLE** Access to Science, Engineering and Technology
- **PLACE** Edinburgh Telford's College

Length 1 year **Start** August, December **Days** Full time, evening or distance learning **Entry Reqs** 21+ **Award** SCOTVEC modules, access to higher education **Creche** Yes

- **CONTACT** David Heathcote 0131 332 2491

- **SUBJECT** Access/Teaching/Technology 1603
- **TITLE** Access to 1. BEd (Primary) 2. BEd (Technology)
- **PLACE** Various Further Education Colleges in Lothian & Fife

Length 1 year **Start** August/September **Days** Full time **Cost** LEA bursaries available **Entry Reqs** Must be over 21 **Award** Place on 1. BEd (Primary) course 2. BEd (Technology) course **Creche** No

- **CONTACT** David Thomson 0131 558 6195

- **SUBJECT** Art & Design/Architecture 1604
- **TITLE** Access to Art & Design, Access to Architecture & Landscape Architecture
- **PLACE** Edinburgh Telford's College, Stevenson College

Length 1 year **Start** Usually August **Days** Full time **Cost** Student may be eligible for LEA bursary **Entry Reqs** Age 21+, no formal qualifications required **Award** Guaranteed offer of place on diploma or degree course **Creche** Yes

- **CONTACT** Scottish Wider Access Programme/SWAP East 0131 650 6861

- **SUBJECT** Arts/Divinity/Social Science/Languages   **1605**
- **TITLE** Access to Arts, Divinity and Social Sciences
- **PLACE** Jewel & Esk College, Stevenson College, University of Edinburgh

Length 1 year **Start** August/September **Days** Full time or part time (day or evening) **Cost** Student may be eligible for LEA bursary (full time); approx £200 part time **Entry Reqs** Age 21+, no formal qualifications required **Award** Guaranteed offer of place on degree course **Creche** Yes in some locations

- **CONTACT** Scottish Wider Access Programme/SWAP East 0131 650 6861

- **SUBJECT** Business/Management/Hospitality Management/Tourism & Leisure **1606**
- **TITLE** Access to Business & Management Studies, Management Studies in Hospitality Tourism & Leisure
- **PLACE** Edinburgh Telford's College, Stevenson College

Length 1 year **Start** August **Days** Full time or part time depending on subject **Cost** Student may be eligible for LEA bursary **Entry Reqs** Age 21+, no formal qualifications required **Award** Guaranteed offer of place on diploma or degree course **Creche** Yes

- **CONTACT** Scottish Wider Access Programme/SWAP East 0131 650 6861

- **SUBJECT** Business Studies **1607**
- **TITLE** Women in Business: Business Training for Women, Women's Entrepreneurship
- **PLACE** Queen Margaret College, Business Development Centre

Length 16 weeks **Start** September, March **Days** Flexible **Cost** Free (ESF funded) **Entry Reqs** Aged over 25 and not in paid employment **Award** Certificate of Course Completion **Creche** No (childcare allowance paid)

- **CONTACT** J Anderson 0131 539 7095

- **SUBJECT** Computing **1608**
- **TITLE** Computer Drop-in Centre: Applications, Software, Programming
- **PLACE** Edinburgh Telford's College

Length Varies **Start** Flexible **Days** Wed 9.00-4.15, Tues, Thurs, Fri 9.00-12.15 **Cost** Contact College **Award** SCOTVEC National Certificate modules **Creche** Yes

- **CONTACT** Liz Guthrie 0131 332 2491 x2308

- **SUBJECT** Computing/Electronics **1609**
- **TITLE** Computing and Electronics Training for Women (including Personal Development)
- **PLACE** Edinburgh Women's Training Centre

Length 16 months including 4-months work placement **Start** January **Days** Full time 9.00-4.00, 5 days/week **Cost** Training allowance+childcare costs paid to trainees **Entry Reqs** Women 25+, living in Edinburgh, unemployed, with few qualifications **Award** SCOTVEC Accreditation **Creche** Childcare costs paid

- **CONTACT** Sheila Thynne 0131 557 1139

- **SUBJECT** Counselling **1610**
- **TITLE** Foundation Course in Advice, Guidance, Counselling
- **PLACE** Edinburgh Telford's College

Length 1 year **Start** September **Days** Various **Cost** £750, bursaries available **Entry Reqs** None **Award** SCOTVEC modules, HNC Counselling **Creche** Yes 50p/session

- **CONTACT** Roz Chetwynd 0131 332 2491 x2352

- **SUBJECT**   Electronics   1611
- **TITLE**   Electronics for Women
- **PLACE**   Jewel and Esk Valley College, Milton Road Centres

Length 10 months (short period of work experience included)   **Start** August   **Days** Full time, shortened-day timetable (8.45-2.15)   **Cost** Approx £740. LEA bursary possible. No fee if unemployed   **Entry Reqs** Potential ability in Maths & Technology   **Award** National Certificate (SCOTVEC) in Electronic Engineering. Entry to HNC & HND Courses   **Creche** Yes

- **CONTACT**   Derek Landells 0131 657 7288 (direct dial)

- **SUBJECT**   Engineering   1612
- **TITLE**   1. Women into Engineering 2. Women into Mechatronics
- **PLACE**   Edinburgh Telford's College

Length 1 year   **Start** August   **Days** Full time 9.00-4.30   **Entry Reqs** Contact College   **Award** Access to higher education   **Creche** Yes

- **CONTACT**   Bruce Heil 0131 332 2491 x2268

- **SUBJECT**   Environmental Sciences   1613
- **TITLE**   Research in the Natural Environment: Research Masters Training Programme
- **PLACE**   University of Edinburgh

Length 1 year   **Start** October   **Cost** Natural Environment Research Council award available   **Entry Reqs** Graduates with first or upper second class honours degree in an appropriate subject   **Award** MSc

- **CONTACT**   Dr John Underhill 0131 650 8518

- **SUBJECT**   Information Technology/Management   1614
- **TITLE**   Graduate Women into Management with Information Technology Skills
                Update
- **PLACE**   University of Edinburgh

Length 24 weeks   **Start** August   **Days** Mon-Fri 9.30-2.30   **Cost** Free through Training for Work   **Entry Reqs** Graduate   **Creche** No

- **CONTACT**   Shona Nichols 0131 650 3475

- **SUBJECT**   Library & Information Management   1615
- **TITLE**   European Information Services: HNC
- **PLACE**   Edinburgh Telford's College

Length 1 year full time, 1-2 years part time, open learning   **Start** August, December   **Days** 3 days full time, 1-2 days part time   **Cost** £750 full time, £45/unit part time or open learning   **Entry Reqs** 2 SCE Highers or equivalent   **Award** SCOTVEC Higher National Certificate   **Creche** Yes

- **CONTACT**   Donald Steele 0131 332 2491 x2310

- **SUBJECT**   Library & Information Management   1616
- **TITLE**   Library and Information Science: 1. HNC 2. National Certificate
- **PLACE**   Edinburgh Telford's College

Length 1.1 year full time, 1-2 years part time 2. Open learning   **Start** August, December   **Days** 1.2. 5 days/week 9.00-4.30 2.5-6 hours/week   **Cost** 1. £750 full time, £45/unit part time 2. £47 module   **Entry Reqs** 1.2 SCE Highers or equivalent 2. O Grade or Standard Grade 3 English or equivalent   **Award** 1. SCOTVEC Higher National Certificate 2. SCOTVEC National Certificate   **Creche** Yes

- **CONTACT**   1. Bert Robertson 2. Maggie Young 0131 332 2491 x2275

- **SUBJECT**   Multi-Subject   **1617**
- **TITLE**   Headway: Core (Communication, Maths, IT and Student Support)
               and Options
- **PLACE**   Stevenson College

Length 13, 26 or 39 weeks   **Start** August, December, March   **Days** Full time or part time
Cost Bursary available and concessions   **Entry Reqs** None   **Award** SCOTVEC modules
Creche Yes £2/half day

- **CONTACT**   Andree Carruthers 0131 535464

- **SUBJECT**   Preparatory   **1618**
- **TITLE**   1. Choices: Options in Study, Career & Leisure 2. Assertiveness Pts 1 & 2
- **PLACE**   Stevenson College

Length 10 weeks   **Start** September, January, April   **Days** Half day/week 9.30-11.30 or
6.45-8.45   **Cost** 1. £20 2. £20 Concessions if in receipt of benefit   **Entry Reqs** None   **Award**
None   **Creche** Yes £2/half day

- **CONTACT**   James Stirton 0131 535 4668

- **SUBJECT**   Preparatory   **1619**
- **TITLE**   Arts & Social Science: Pre Access Taster Course
- **PLACE**   Stevenson College

Length 8 weeks   **Start** May   **Days** 2 half days/week   **Entry Reqs** None   **Award** Useful for
adults wishing to do Access to Arts & Social Science course   **Creche** Yes £2/half day

- **CONTACT**   Liz Highet 0131 453 4600 x1524

- **SUBJECT**   Preparatory   **1620**
- **TITLE**   New Horizons: First Step Back to Learning
- **PLACE**   University of Edinburgh, Centre for Continuing Education

Length Flexible (2 terms-2 years)   **Start** October   **Days** 1 day/week Tues, Wed or Thurs or 1
eve/week   **Cost** Contact Centre   **Entry Reqs** None   **Award** None   **Creche** No

- **CONTACT**   Margaret Gordon 0131 650 4400

- **SUBJECT**   Preparatory   **1621**
- **TITLE**   Returning to Education: Guidance to Scottish Wider Access Programme
- **PLACE**   Stevenson College

Length 6 weeks   **Start** January, April   **Days** Half day/week 1.30-3.30 or 6.45-8.45   **Cost**
Approx £10 Concessions if in receipt of benefit   **Entry Reqs** For adults seeking guidance and
information about Scottish Wider Access Programme   **Award** None   **Creche** Yes £2/half day

- **CONTACT**   Liz Highet 0131 453 4600 x1524

- **SUBJECT**   Preparatory   **1622**
- **TITLE**   Returning to Work or Study: Issues, Options, Strategies
- **PLACE**   University of Edinburgh, Centre for Continuing Education

Length 2 terms   **Start** January   **Days** Fri mornings+4 days job sampling   **Cost** Approx £70
Entry Reqs For adults absent from study or labour market due to domestic responsibilities
Award None   **Creche** No

- **CONTACT**   Joanna Highton 0131 650 4400

- **SUBJECT**   Preparatory   **1623**
- **TITLE**   Stepping Stones
- **PLACE**   University of Edinburgh, Centre for Continuing Education

Length 6 sessions   **Start** October, January, May   **Days** Thurs 1.30-3.30   **Cost** Approx £40
Entry Reqs None   **Award** None   **Creche** No

- **CONTACT**   Margaret Gordon 0131 650 4400

- **SUBJECT**   Preparatory   1624
- **TITLE**   Training for Work
- **PLACE**   Various locations throughout Edinburgh and Lothian

Length Varies depending on course. 9-26 weeks   **Start** Throughout the year   **Days** Usually full time 9.00-5.00 but some courses use flexible learning methods   **Cost** None. Small allowance   **Entry Reqs** 18+ Must be registered unemployed or away from workplace for 2 years or more   **Award** NVQs Level II-V   **Creche** No but childcare costs for lone parents

- **CONTACT** Jacqui Nagib (Lothian & Edinburgh Enterprise Ltd) 0131 313 6111

- **SUBJECT**   Professional Updating   1625
- **TITLE**   Women into Technology
- **PLACE**   University of Edinburgh

Length 24 weeks   **Start** August   **Days** Mon-Fri 9.30-2.30   **Cost** Contact University   **Entry Reqs** Graduate, unemployed women returners   **Award** Certificate   **Creche** Yes

- **CONTACT** Jane Ansell 0131 650 4651

- **SUBJECT**   Professional Updating/Teaching   1626
- **TITLE**   Refresher Courses for Returners to Teaching
- **PLACE**   Moray House Institute of Education

Length Contact College   **Days** Contact Institute   **Cost** Contact Institute   **Entry Reqs** Qualified teachers   **Creche** No

- **CONTACT** David Turner 0131 558 6103

- **SUBJECT**   Rural Studies   1627
- **TITLE**   Access to Rural Studies
- **PLACE**   Edinburgh's Telford College

Length 1 year   **Start** August   **Days** Full time   **Cost** Student may be eligible for LEA bursary   **Entry Reqs** Age 21+, no formal qualifications required   **Award** Guaranteed offer of place on diploma or degree course   **Creche** Yes

- **CONTACT** Scottish Wider Access Programme/SWAP East 0131 650 6861

- **SUBJECT**   Science/Engineering/Technology/Information Technology   1628
- **TITLE**   Access to Science, Engineering & Technology, Information Technology
- **PLACE**   Edinburgh's Telford College, Jewel & Esk Valley College, Stevenson Clge

Length 1 year   **Start** Usually August   **Days** Full time or part time depending on subject   **Cost** Student may be eligible for LEA bursary   **Entry Reqs** Age 21+, no formal qualifications required   **Award** Guaranteed offer of place on diploma or degree course   **Creche** Yes at some locations

- **CONTACT** Scottish Wider Access Programme/SWAP East 0131 650 6861

- **SUBJECT**   Teaching   1629
- **TITLE**   Access to Primary Teaching
- **PLACE**   Jewel & Esk Valley College

Length 1 year   **Start** Usually August   **Days** Full time or part time depending on subject   **Cost** Student may be eligible for LEA bursary   **Entry Reqs** Age 21+, no formal qualifications required   **Award** Guaranteed offer of place on diploma or degree course   **Creche** Yes

- **CONTACT** Scottish Wider Access Programme/SWAP East 0131 650 6861

COUNTY CONTACTS

Information and advice:

Career Development Edinburgh and Lothians, Adult Guidance Service, Atholl House, Edinburgh EH3 8EG 0131 228 7528   *Contact:* Ann Southwood. Information on careers and training opportunities at locations throughout Edinburgh and Lothian
Lothian TAP Agency, 8 St Mary Street, Edinburgh EH1 1SU 0131 557 5822   *Contact:* Denny Colley

Local Enterprise Council:

Lothian and Edinburgh Enterprise Ltd, Apex House, 99 Haymarket Terrace, Edinburgh EH12 5HD 0131 313 4000   *Contact:* Jacqui Nagib. Range of training opportunities

Open University:

The Open University, Scotland, 10 Drumsheugh Gardens, Edinburgh EH3 7QJ 0131 225 2889

Other agencies:

Edinburgh Training Centre, 5 Hillside Crescent, Edinburgh EH7 0131 557 1139. Women's training centre
Women on to Work, 137 Buccleuch Street, Edinburgh EH8 9ME 0131 662 4514. Women's training schemes

WEA office:

Scottish WEA, Riddle's Court, 322 Lawnmarket, Edinburgh EH1 3PG 0131 226 3456   *Contact:* Hilary Lawson

SCOTLAND: Orkney

COURSES

- **SUBJECT**   Access/Arts/Social Science   1630
- **TITLE**   Access to Arts and Social Science
- **PLACE**   Scottish Wider Access Programme, Kirkwall

Length 1 year full time or negotiable part time   **Start** August   **Days** Varied   **Cost** Full time £750, part time £30 for 40 hours (subject to review)   **Entry Reqs** None   **Award** Arts & Social Science Certificate, access to courses at Aberdeen University   **Creche** No

- **CONTACT** Stephen Masser 01224 313142

- **SUBJECT**   Access/Engineering/Science   1631
- **TITLE**   Access to Engineering, Science
- **PLACE**   Scottish Wider Access Programme, Kirkwall

Length 1 year full time or negotiable part time   **Start** August   **Days** Varied   **Cost** Full time £750, part time £30 for 40 hours (subject to review)   **Entry Reqs** None   **Award** SCOTVEC National Certificate, access to higher education   **Creche** No

- **CONTACT** Stephen Masser 01224 313142

COUNTY CONTACTS

Information and advice:

Orkney Opportunities Centre, The Brig, 2 Albert Street, Kirkwall KW15 1HP 01836 873535 x2425. Careers information

Local Enterprise Council:

Orkney Enterprise, 14 Queen Street, Kirkwall KW15 1JE 01856 874638

Open University:

The Open University, Scotland, 10 Drumsheugh Gardens, Edinburgh EH3 7QJ 0131 225 2889

WEA office:

Scottish WEA, Riddles Court, 322 Lawnmarket, Edinburgh EH1 3PG 0131 226 3456   *Contact:* Hilary Lawson

SCOTLAND: Shetland Islands

COURSES

- **SUBJECT**   Access/Arts/Social Science   1632
- **TITLE**   Access to Arts and Social Science
- **PLACE**   Scottish Wider Access Programme, Lerwick

Length 1 year full time or negotiable part time   **Start** August   **Days** Varied   **Cost** Full time £750, part time £30 for 40 hours (subject to review)   **Entry Reqs** None   **Award** Arts & Social Science Certificate, access to courses at Aberdeen University   **Creche** No

- **CONTACT**   Stephen Masser 01224 313142

- **SUBJECT**   Access/Engineering/Science   1633
- **TITLE**   Access to Engineering, Science
- **PLACE**   Scottish Wider Access Programme, Lerwick

Length 1 year full time or negotiable part time   **Start** August   **Days** Varied   **Cost** Full time £750, part time £30 for 40 hours (subject to review)   **Entry Reqs** None   **Award** SCOTVEC National Certificate, access to higher education   **Creche** No

- **CONTACT**   Stephen Masser 01224 313142

COUNTY CONTACTS

Information and advice:

Lerwick Careers Office, Toll Clock Shopping Centre, 26 North Road, Lerwick ZE1 0PE 01595 5791

Local Enterprise Council:

Shetland Enterprise, Toll Clock Shopping Centre, 26 North Road, Lerwick ZE1 0PE 01595 3177

Open University:

The Open University, Scotland, 10 Drumsheugh Gardens, Edinburgh EH3 7QJ 0131 225 2889

WEA office:

Scottish WEA, Riddles Court, 322 Lawnmarket, Edinburgh EH1 3PG 0131 266 3456   *Contact:* Hilary Lawson

---

SCOTLAND: Strathclyde

COURSES

- **SUBJECT**   Access/Arts/Marketing/Media Studies/Social Science   1634
- **TITLE**   Access to 1. Arts and Social Science 2. Marketing and Media
- **PLACE**   Cardonald College

Length 38 weeks   **Start** August   **Days** Full time   **Cost** Student may be eligible for LEA bursary   **Entry Reqs** Age 21+, no formal entry requirements   **Award** SCOTVEC Certificate, access to higher education   **Creche** Yes

- **CONTACT**   0141 883 6151 x242

- **SUBJECT**   Access/Business Administration/Social Science/Science/Technology   1635
- **TITLE**   Access to Business Administration, Office Technology & Administration, Social Science, Science & Technology
- **PLACE**   Coatbridge College

Length 40 weeks   **Start** Contact College   **Days** Full time or part time depending on subject   **Cost** Student may be eligible for LEA bursary   **Entry Reqs** Age 21+, no formal entry requirements   **Award** SCOTVEC Certificate, access to higher education   **Creche** Yes

- **CONTACT**   Access Co-ordinator 01236 436000

- **SUBJECT**   Access/Business/Biology/Teaching/Social Science/Science &   1636
Technology
- **TITLE**   Access to Business, Biology, Primary Education, Social Sciences, Science & Technology
- **PLACE**   Kilmarnock College

Length 38 weeks   **Start** Contact College   **Days** Full time or part time depending on subject   **Cost** Student may be eligible for LEA bursary   **Entry Reqs** Age 21+, no formal entry requirements   **Award** SCOTVEC Certificate, access to higher education   **Creche** No

- **CONTACT**   Moira Finlayson 01563 523501

- **SUBJECT**   Access/Business/Engineering/Information Technology   1637
- **TITLE**   Access to Business, Engineering, Computing, IT, Office Administration
- **PLACE**   Glasgow College of Nautical Studies

Length 40 weeks   **Start** Contact College   **Days** Full time or part time depending on subject   **Cost** Student may be eligible for LEA bursary   **Entry Reqs** Age 21+, no formal entry requirements   **Award** SCOTVEC Certificate, access to higher education   **Creche** Yes

- **CONTACT**   Access Co-ordinator 0141 429 3201

- **SUBJECT**   Access/Design/Built Environment   1638
- **TITLE**   Access to Design, Built Environment
- **PLACE**   Glasgow College of Building and Printing

Length 40 weeks   **Start** Contact College   **Days** Full time or part time depending on subject
Cost Student may be eligible for LEA bursary   **Entry Reqs** Student may be eligible for LEA
bursary   **Award** SCOTVEC Certificate, access to higher education   **Creche** Contact College
- **CONTACT**   Access Co-ordinator 0141 332 9969

- **SUBJECT**   Access/Health Studies   1639
- **TITLE**   Access to Health
- **PLACE**   Cardonald College

Length 38 weeks   **Start** August   **Cost** Bursaries available   **Entry Reqs** 21+   **Award**
SCOTVEC Certificate, access to higher education   **Creche** Yes £3.50/day
- **CONTACT**   0141 883 6151 x304

- **SUBJECT**   Access/Hospitality Management/Business   1640
- **TITLE**   Access to Business, Hospitality Operations
- **PLACE**   Motherwell College

Length 38 weeks   **Start** Contact College   **Days** Full time or part time depending on subject
Cost Student may be eligible for LEA bursary   **Entry Reqs** Age 21+, no formal entry
requirements   **Award** SCOTVEC Certificate, entry to HE   **Creche** Yes £1.30/halfday
- **CONTACT**   Access Co-ordinator 01698 232323

- **SUBJECT**   Access/Hospitality Management/Information Technology   1641
- **TITLE**   Access to Hospitality Operations, Office Administration, IT
- **PLACE**   Reid Kerr College

Length 38 weeks   **Start** Contact College   **Days** Full time (7x½ days)   **Cost** Student may be
eligible for LEA bursary   **Entry Reqs** Age 21+, no formal entry requirements   **Award**
SCOTVEC Certificate, access to higher education   **Creche** Yes
- **CONTACT**   Student Services Unit 0141 889 4225

- **SUBJECT**   Access/Information Technology/Science & Technology/Teaching   1642
- **TITLE**   Access to IT, Science & Technology, Secondary Teaching
- **PLACE**   Motherwell College

Length 38 weeks   **Start** Contact College   **Days** Full time or part time depending on subject
Cost Student may be eligible for LEA bursary   **Entry Reqs** Age 21+, no formal entry
requirements   **Award** SCOTVEC Certificate, entry to HE   **Creche** Yes £1.30/halfday
- **CONTACT**   Access Co-ordinator 01698 232323

- **SUBJECT**   Access/Nursing/Paramedical Studies   1643
- **TITLE**   Access to 1. Nursing 2. Pre-Nursing and Paramedical Course
- **PLACE**   Motherwell College

Length 1.32 weeks 2.39 weeks   **Start** August   **Days** 24 hours/week (4 days)   **Cost** Contact
College   **Entry Reqs** 1. None 2. Standard Grade in English or equivalent   **Award** Entry to nurse
education   **Creche** Yes £1.30/halfday
- **CONTACT**   Helen Singleton 01698 232323

- **SUBJECT**   Access/Science/Technology/Hospitality Management/Business/   1644
                 Social Science
- **TITLE**   Access to Science, Technology, Catering & Hotel Management,
                 Business Admin, Social Science
- **PLACE**   Motherwell College

Length 1 year full time   **Start** August   **Days** 24 hours/week   **Cost** Contact College   **Entry
Reqs** None   **Award** Entry to HNC/HND or degree   **Creche** Yes £1.30/halfday
- **CONTACT**   John Govan 01698 232323

- **SUBJECT** Access/Science & Technology/Mathematics/Computing **1645**
- **TITLE** Access to Science & Technology, Maths & Computing
- **PLACE** Reid Kerr College

Length 38 weeks **Start** Contact College **Days** Full time (7x½ days) **Cost** Student may be eligible for LEA bursary **Entry Reqs** Age 21+, no formal entry requirements **Award** SCOTVEC Certificate, entry to HE **Creche** Yes

- **CONTACT** Student Services Unit 0141 889 4225

- **SUBJECT** Art & Design **1646**
- **TITLE** Art & Design
- **PLACE** North Glasgow College, Barmulloch Campus

Length 40 weeks **Start** August **Days** Mon-Fri 24 hours/week **Cost** Bursaries available **Entry Reqs** By interview **Award** SCOTVEC National Certificate **Creche** Yes

- **CONTACT** Information Centre 0141 558 9001

- **SUBJECT** Art & Design **1647**
- **TITLE** 1. 3D Design (Industrial, Pottery, Jewellery) 2. Drawing & Painting
  3. Graphic Design
- **PLACE** Cardonald College

Length 38 weeks **Start** August **Days** 8 halfdays/week between 9.00-4.30 **Cost** Bursaries may be available **Entry Reqs** By interview for mature students **Award** NC leads to HNC/HND **Creche** Yes £3.50/day

- **CONTACT** 1. &2. David Sloan 3. David Heggie 0141 883 6151

- **SUBJECT** Business Studies **1648**
- **TITLE** Access to Business Studies
- **PLACE** North Glasgow College, Springburn Campus

Length 40 weeks **Start** August **Days** 24 hours/week **Cost** Bursaries available **Entry Reqs** None **Award** Entry to higher education **Creche** Yes

- **CONTACT** Information Centre 0141 558 9001

- **SUBJECT** Care Studies/Health Studies **1649**
- **TITLE** Pre-Nursing, Pre-Social Care & Other Courses
- **PLACE** Cardonald College

Length 1 academic year including 6 weeks work placement **Start** August **Days** Full time 8 halfdays/week+work placements, or part time **Cost** Bursaries available **Entry Reqs** By interview **Award** SCOTVEC NC modules **Creche** Yes limited places £3.50/day

- **CONTACT** Sue Bates 0141 883 6151 x264

- **SUBJECT** Clothing Studies **1650**
- **TITLE** 1. C&G Embroidery 2. Central NC Knitwear
- **PLACE** Cardonald College

Length Various 1-3 years **Start** August **Days** Various **Cost** Contact College **Entry Reqs** By interview **Award** 1. C&G 2. Central NC **Creche** Yes £3.50/day

- **CONTACT** 1. Mattie Davidson/2. Isobel Bann 0141 883 6151 x282

- **SUBJECT** Clothing Studies/Fashion **1651**
- **TITLE** NC Clothing Studies
- **PLACE** Cardonald College

Length 38 weeks **Start** August **Days** 8 halfdays/week between 9.00-4.30 **Cost** Bursaries may be available **Entry Reqs** By interview **Award** NC leads to HNC/HND **Creche** Yes £3.50/day

- **CONTACT** Joyce Draffan/Bill Granger 0141 883 6151

- **SUBJECT** Communications/Media Studies 1652
- **TITLE** 1. Communication Studies 2. Media Studies
- **PLACE** Cardonald College

Length 38 weeks **Start** August **Days** 8 halfdays/week between 9.00-4.30 **Cost** Bursaries may be available **Entry Reqs** None for mature students **Award** SCOTVEC, NC **Creche** Yes £3.50/day

- **CONTACT** Mrs Smith 0141 883 6151 x242

- **SUBJECT** Computing/Electronics 1653
- **TITLE** National Certificate in Computer Installation Support Engineering
- **PLACE** Cardonald College

Length 1 year **Start** August **Entry Reqs** By interview for mature students **Award** NC, HNC Computer Installation Support Engineering **Creche** By interview for mature students

- **CONTACT** A Ure 0141 883 6151

- **SUBJECT** Fashion 1654
- **TITLE** Fashion Studies
- **PLACE** North Glasgow College, Barmulloch Campus

Length 40 weeks **Start** August **Days** Mon-Fri, 24 hours/week **Cost** Bursaries available **Entry Reqs** None, entry by interview **Award** SCOTVEC National Certificate **Creche** Yes

- **CONTACT** Information Centre 0141 558 9001

- **SUBJECT** Food Studies 1655
- **TITLE** Food and Nutrition
- **PLACE** Cardonald College

Length 38 weeks **Start** August **Days** 4 days/week full time **Cost** Bursaries may be available **Entry Reqs** By interview **Award** NC **Creche** Yes £3.50/day

- **CONTACT** Isabell Ross 0141 883 6151 x268

- **SUBJECT** Health Studies 1656
- **TITLE** Access to Nursing
- **PLACE** North Glasgow College, Barmulloch Campus

Length 1 year full time **Start** August **Days** Mon-Fri 9.30-4.00 **Cost** Contact College. Bursaries available **Entry Reqs** By interview **Award** Entry to higher education **Creche** Yes

- **CONTACT** Information Centre 0141 558 9001

- **SUBJECT** Information Technology 1657
- **TITLE** Business Information Technology
- **PLACE** University of Paisley

Length 1 year **Start** October **Days** Mon-Fri daytime attendance **Cost** SOED funded **Entry Reqs** Good Honours degree or degree & 3/4 years work **Award** MSc or Postgraduate Diploma **Creche** Nursery 3-5 years £20-£25/week

- **CONTACT** Mr J G Howell 0141 848 3313

- **SUBJECT** Information Technology/Electronic Engineering 1658
- **TITLE** 1. Access to Information Technology 2. Electronic Engineering
- **PLACE** Cardonald College

Length 1 year **Start** 1 year **Days** 8 halfdays/week **Cost** Bursaries may be available **Entry Reqs** None **Award** NC, HNC, HND **Creche** Yes £3.50/day

- **CONTACT** 1. D Nutley/2. A Ure 0141 883 6151

Strathclyde

- **SUBJECT** Languages   **1659**
- **TITLE** Conversational French/German/Spanish/Business Languages
- **PLACE** Kilmarnock College

Length 12 weeks   **Start** Any time subject to demand   **Days** Half day/week   **Cost** £36   **Entry Reqs** None   **Award** SCOTVEC Certificate Language 1/2   **Creche** No

- **CONTACT** Nancy McPherson 01563 523501 x247

- **SUBJECT** Mathematics/Computing   **1660**
- **TITLE** Access to Maths and Computing
- **PLACE** North Glasgow College, Springburn Campus

Length 40 weeks   **Start** August   **Days** Mon-Fri, 24 hours/week   **Cost** Bursaries available **Entry Reqs** None   **Award** SCOTVEC modules, entry to higher education   **Creche** Yes

- **CONTACT** Information Centre 0141 558 9001

- **SUBJECT** Multi-Subject   **1661**
- **TITLE** Open Learning
- **PLACE** Motherwell College

Length Flexible, open learning   **Start** Flexible   **Days** Flexible   **Cost** Contact College   **Entry Reqs** Contact College   **Award** Various   **Creche** Yes £1.30/halfday

- **CONTACT** Mary McCall 01698 232323

- **SUBJECT** NOW   **1662**
- **TITLE** New Horizons for Women
- **PLACE** University of Strathclyde, Continuing Education Centre

Length 10 weeks   **Start** Twice yearly   **Days** 1 day/week 10.00-3.00   **Cost** £115   **Entry Reqs** None   **Creche** No

- **CONTACT** Libby Lamb 0141 552 4400 x4314

- **SUBJECT** Office Skills   **1663**
- **TITLE** Office Skills
- **PLACE** North Glasgow College, Springburn Campus

Length 40 weeks   **Start** August   **Days** 24 hours/week   **Cost** Bursaries available   **Entry Reqs** None, entry by interview   **Award** SCOTVEC National Certificate   **Creche** Yes

- **CONTACT** Information Centre 0141 558 9001

- **SUBJECT** Office Skills   **1664**
- **TITLE** Secretarial & Clerical Skills for Women Returners
- **PLACE** Glasgow College of Nautical Studies

Length 20 weeks   **Start** Contact College   **Days** 3 days/week 9.30-2.00   **Cost** Student may be eligible for fee waivers   **Entry Reqs** By interview   **Award** SCOTVEC Certificate   **Creche** No

- **CONTACT** Mrs M Paton/Mrs B Fisher 0141 429 3201

- **SUBJECT** Preparatory   **1665**
- **TITLE** Return to Study
- **PLACE** Cardonald College

Length 38 weeks   **Start** August   **Days** Part time or full time   **Cost** Bursaries may be available   **Entry Reqs** By interview   **Award** NC   **Creche** Yes £3.50/day

- **CONTACT** Isabell Ross 0141 883 6151 x268

- **SUBJECT** Preparatory 1666
- **TITLE** Return to Study: Using Information Retrieval Skills
- **PLACE** Kilmarnock College, General Education Division

Length 4 weeks **Start** May, June **Days** Varies, usually mornings. Contact College **Cost** £18 **Entry Reqs** None **Award** SCOTVEC Certificate, learning and study skills **Creche** No

- **CONTACT** Linda Muir 01563 523501 x250

- **SUBJECT** Preparatory 1667
- **TITLE** Skills Plus: Core Skills, Communication, Numeracy, Confidence Building
- **PLACE** Cardonald College, outreach at Priesthill

Length Determined by need of student, usually 6 months minimum **Start** Anytime **Days** Negotiable, hours and days to suit circumstances **Cost** Free **Entry Reqs** Must not be in full time employment **Award** SCOTVEC NC modules where appropriate, entry to work, further study **Creche** Yes

- **CONTACT** 0141 883 6151 x335

- **SUBJECT** Science 1668
- **TITLE** Biomedical and Life Sciences: Research Masters Pilot Course
- **PLACE** University of Glasgow

Length 1 year **Start** October **Cost** Medical Research Council award available **Entry Reqs** Graduates with first or upper second class honours degree in an appropriate subject **Award** MSc

- **CONTACT** Professor G Milligan 0141 330 5557

- **SUBJECT** Science/Technology 1669
- **TITLE** Access to Science and Technology
- **PLACE** North Glasgow College, Barmulloch Campus

Length Normally 1 year full time **Start** August **Days** Mon-Fri 9.30-4.00 **Cost** Contact College. Bursaries available **Entry Reqs** By interview **Award** Entry to higher education **Creche** Yes

- **CONTACT** Information Centre 0141 558 9001

- **SUBJECT** Social Science 1670
- **TITLE** NC Social Science
- **PLACE** Cardonald College

Length 38 weeks **Start** August **Days** Full time **Cost** Bursaries may be available **Entry Reqs** None for mature students **Award** NC **Creche** Yes £3.50/day

- **CONTACT** Lesley Smith 0141 883 6151 x242

- **SUBJECT** Social Studies 1671
- **TITLE** Social Care
- **PLACE** North Glasgow College, Barmulloch Campus

Length 40 weeks **Start** August **Days** 24 hours/week **Cost** Bursaries available **Entry Reqs** By interview **Award** GSVQ Level II/III **Creche** Yes

- **CONTACT** Information Centre 0141 558 9001

- **SUBJECT** Teaching 1672
- **TITLE** Access to Primary Education
- **PLACE** North Glasgow College, Barmulloch Campus

Length 2 years part time **Start** August **Days** Part time **Cost** Bursaries available **Entry Reqs** None, entry by interview **Award** Entry to higher education **Creche** Yes Contact College

- **CONTACT** Information Centre 0141 558 9001

Strathclyde

- **SUBJECT** Teaching   **1673**
- **TITLE** Preparation for Primary School Teaching
- **PLACE** Reid Kerr College

Length 38 weeks   **Start** August, contact College   **Days** Full time (7x½ days)   **Cost** Student may be eligible for LEA bursary   **Entry Reqs** Age 21+, no formal entry requirements   **Award** SCOTVEC Certificate, entry to HE   **Creche** Yes, free

- **CONTACT** Student Services/Access Co-ordinator 0141 889 4225

- **SUBJECT** Travel & Tourism/Secretarial/Business Studies   **1674**
- **TITLE** Travel & Tourism, Secretarial Studies, Business Studies
- **PLACE** Cardonald College

Length 38 weeks   **Start** August   **Days** 8 halfdays/week between 9.00-4.30   **Cost** Bursaries and grants available   **Entry Reqs** None for mature students   **Award** SCOTVEC, NC, HNC **Creche** Yes £3.50/day

- **CONTACT** Mrs Kirkwood/Mr Campbell 0141 883 6151 x243

COUNTY CONTACTS

Information and advice:

Continuing Education Gateway, 199 Nithsdale Road, Glasgow G41 5EX 0141 422 1070   *Contact:* Freephone 0800 838122 Joan Rees, Catherine Garvie. Telephone helpline and over 300 advice points in careers offices, colleges and community education centres for adults seeking educational guidance.
Regional HQ: Principal Careers Officer, Strathclyde Region, Department of Education, Strathclyde House, 20 India Street, Glasgow G2 4PF 0141 249 4167

Local Enterprise Councils:

Argyll and the Islands Enterprise, The Enterprise Centre, Kilmory, Lochgilphead PA31 8SH 01546 602281/602563
Dunbartonshire Enterprise, Spectrum House, Clydebank Business Park, Clydebank G81 2DR 0141 951 2121   *Contact:* Linda Murray/John Gilles. Wide range of opportunities through the Training for Work Programme at all levels. Two specific Women Returner courses in the Dumbarton and Kirkintillock areas. Out of School Childcare Project
Enterprise Ayrshire Ltd, 17-19 Hill Street, Kilmarnock KA3 1HA 01563 26623
Glasgow Development Agency, Atrium Court, 50 Waterloo Street, Glasgow G2 6HQ 0141 204 1111
Lanarkshire Development Agency, New Lanarkshire House, Willow Drive, Strathclyde Business Park, Bellshill ML4 3AD 01698 745454
Renfrewshire Enterprise, 27 Causeyside Street, Paisley PA1 1UL 0141 848 0101   *Contact:* Fiona Kennedy. Redirect Adult Guidance Service; Training and Employment grants scheme; Options for Women - ESF funded part time course run by ITT Ltd.

Open University:

The Open University, Scotland, 10 Drumsheugh Gardens, Edinburgh. EH3 7QJ 0131 225 2889

Other agencies:

ITT Ltd, 19 Bogle Street, Greenock PA15 1ER 01475 892197   *Contact:* Veronica de Blieck, Chief Executive. Run a range of training courses

WEA office:

Scottish WEA, Riddles Court, 322 Lawnmarket, Edinburgh EH1 3PG 0131 266 3456   *Contact:* Hilary Lawson

COURSES

- **SUBJECT** Access/Arts/Social Science/Divinity/Languages   **1675**
- **TITLE** Access to Higher Education
- **PLACE** Dundee College, Melrose Terrace Centre

Length 1 year   **Start** August   **Days** Mon-Fri 9.00-12.15, 1.15-4.30 (21 hours/week)   **Cost** None+course carries a bursary   **Entry Reqs** None. Entry by application and interview   **Award** SCOTVEC National Certificate, SCE Highers Optional   **Creche** No
- **CONTACT** Anne Wake 01382 834882

- **SUBJECT** Access/Education   **1676**
- **TITLE** Access to Community Education
- **PLACE** Dundee College, Melrose Terrace Centre

Length 1 year   **Start** August   **Days** Mon-Fri 9.00-12.15, 1.15-4.30 (21 hours/week)   **Cost** None+course carries a bursary   **Entry Reqs** None. Voluntary work experience & acceptance by Northern College, Dundee must be demonstrated   **Award** SCOTVEC NC   **Creche** No
- **CONTACT** Bernadette Barry, Northern College 01382 464000/Anne Wake, Dundee College
             01382 834834

- **SUBJECT** Access/Science   **1677**
- **TITLE** Access to Science
- **PLACE** Dundee College, Old Glamis Road

Length 1 year   **Start** August   **Days** Full time   **Entry Reqs** None. Interview   **Award** SCOTVEC, access to higher education   **Creche** No
- **CONTACT** Harry Racionzer 01382 834834

- **SUBJECT** Access/Science   **1678**
- **TITLE** Access to Science
- **PLACE** Perth College

Length 1 year   **Start** August   **Days** Full time   **Cost** Student may be eligible for LEA bursary **Entry Reqs** By personal interview   **Award** SCOTVEC National Certificate and access to higher education at university   **Creche** Yes
- **CONTACT** L Foster 01738 621171

- **SUBJECT** Access/Science/Engineering   **1679**
- **TITLE** Access to Science and Engineering
- **PLACE** University of Dundee, Faculty of Science and Engineering

Length 1 year (3 terms)   **Start** October   **Days** 1 day/week Wed 9.30-3.15   **Cost** £510 Grants available   **Entry Reqs** None   **Award** Normally university entry   **Creche** Yes £20-£30/week
- **CONTACT** Anna Spackman 01382 344896

- **SUBJECT** Access/Teaching   **1680**
- **TITLE** Access to Teaching (BEd Primary)
- **PLACE** Dundee College

Length 1 year   **Start** August   **Days** Full time   **Entry Req** None   **Award** SCOTVEC, access to higher education   **Creche** No
- **CONTACT** Anne Wake 01382 834882

- **SUBJECT** Access/Town Planning/Environmental Studies   **1681**
- **TITLE** Access to Town & Regional Planning, Environmental Management
- **PLACE** Dundee College, Melrose Terrace Centre

Length 1 year   **Start** August   **Days** Mon-Fri 9.00-12.15, 1.15-4.30 (21 hours/week)   **Cost** None+course carries a bursary   **Entry Reqs** None. Entry by application   **Award** SCOTVEC National Certificate, SCE Highers Optional   **Creche** No
- **CONTACT** Anne Wake 01382 834882

- **SUBJECT**   Art & Design   1682
- **TITLE**   HND Graphics/HND Advertising
- **PLACE**   Perth College, Goodlyburn Building

Length 2 years full time or equivalent part time   **Start** September   **Days** Varies   **Cost** SOED Grant-aided   **Entry Reqs** Entry by interview, evidence of prior interest/achievement   **Award** HND Graphics or Advertising   **Creche** Yes

- **CONTACT**   Pieter Deuling 01738 621171

- **SUBJECT**   Arts/Divinity/Social Science/Languages   1683
- **TITLE**   Access to Arts, Divinity, Social Science, Languages
- **PLACE**   Dundee College

Length 1 year   **Start** Usually August   **Days** Full time or part time depending on subject   **Cost** Student may be eligible for LEA bursary   **Entry Reqs** Age 21+, no formal qualifications required   **Award** Guaranteed offer of place on diploma or degree course   **Creche** Yes

- **CONTACT**   Scottish Wider Access Programme/SWAP East 0131 650 6861

- **SUBJECT**   Business/Management Studies   1684
- **TITLE**   Access to Business & Management Studies
- **PLACE**   Dundee College

Length 1 year   **Start** Usually August   **Days** Full time   **Cost** Student may be eligible for LEA bursary   **Entry Reqs** Age 21+, no formal qualifications required   **Award** Guaranteed offer of place on diploma or degree course   **Creche** Yes

- **CONTACT**   Scottish Wider Access Programme/SWAP East 0131 650 6861

- **SUBJECT**   Construction   1685
- **TITLE**   HND in Built Environment
- **PLACE**   Perth College, Braman Estate

Length 2 years   **Start** September   **Days** Full time   **Cost** Student may be eligible for LEA bursary   **Entry Reqs** By personal interview   **Award** SCOTVEC HND   **Creche** Yes

- **CONTACT**   J Martin 01738 6211171

- **SUBJECT**   Electronics   1686
- **TITLE**   Electronics 1. National Certificate 2. HNC
- **PLACE**   Perth College

Length 1 year   **Start** 1. August 2. September   **Days** Full time   **Cost** Student may be eligible for LEA bursary   **Entry Reqs** By personal interview   **Award** 1. National Certificate 2. HNC Electronic Engineering   **Creche** Yes

- **CONTACT**   Paul Balfour 01738 621171

- **SUBJECT**   Engineering   1687
- **TITLE**   Computer-Aided Engineering
- **PLACE**   Perth College

Length 1 year   **Start** August   **Days** Full time   **Cost** Student may be eligible for LEA bursary   **Entry Reqs** By personal interview   **Award** SCOTVEC National Certificate in Engineering   **Creche** Yes

- **CONTACT**   Paul Balfour 01738 621171

- **SUBJECT** Food Studies/Social Studies   **1688**
- **TITLE** Access to Food & Welfare Studies
- **PLACE** Dundee College

Length 1 year   **Start** Usually August   **Days** Full time   **Cost** Student may be eligible for LEA bursary   **Entry Reqs** Age 21+, no formal qualifications required   **Award** Guaranteed offer of place on diploma or degree course   **Creche** Yes

- **CONTACT** Scottish Wider Access Programme/SWAP East 0131 650 6861

- **SUBJECT** Food Studies/Social Studies   **1689**
- **TITLE** MA in Food & Welfare Studies
- **PLACE** Duncan of Jordanstone College, University of Dundee

Length 3 years (MA), 4 years (MA Hons)   **Start** October   **Days** Mon-Fri 9.00-5.00   **Cost** £1855 (sponsored), £696 (self-funded)   **Entry Reqs** For mature students via Access Course at Dundee College   **Award** MA/MA Hons   **Creche** No

- **CONTACT** Anne Colquhoun 01382 223261

- **SUBJECT** Information Technology   **1690**
- **TITLE** Computer Courses for Women
- **PLACE** The MicroCentre, University of Dundee

Length Varies   **Cost** Contact University

- **CONTACT** Professor Alan Newell 01382 344145

- **SUBJECT** Office Skills   **1691**
- **TITLE** Workshops: WP/Text Processing (Typing)/Shorthand/Desk top Publishing/IT/Audio
- **PLACE** Perth College

Length 12 weeks (3 hours/week/subject)   **Start** August, November, March   **Days** 3 hours/week, various days 9.00-12.15, 1.00-4.15   **Cost** £40-£50   **Entry Reqs** Elementary level, none. Intermediate/Advanced level, contact college   **Award** Can lead to SCOTVEC/College Certificate   **Creche** Playgroup 3-5 years

- **CONTACT** Wendy Thomson 01738 621171 x214

- **SUBJECT** Office Skills   **1692**
- **TITLE** National Certificate in Office Skills & Technology
- **PLACE** Perth College

Length 39 weeks   **Start** August   **Days** 3.5 days/week minimum 9.00-4.15   **Cost** Regional Council grants available or £42.40 modular fee/subject   **Entry Reqs** None   **Award** SCOTVEC National Certificate, SVQ Level II Administration or Secretarial   **Creche** Playgroup 3-5 years

- **CONTACT** Linda M McKernan 01738 621171 x214

- **SUBJECT** Science/Engineering/Technology   **1693**
- **TITLE** Access to Science, Engineering & Technology
- **PLACE** Dundee College

Length 1 year   **Start** Usually August   **Days** Full time   **Cost** Student may be eligible for LEA bursary   **Entry Reqs** Age 21+, no formal qualifications required   **Award** Guaranteed offer of place on diploma or degree course   **Creche** Yes

- **CONTACT** Scottish Wider Access Programme/SWAP East 0131 650 6861

Tayside

- **SUBJECT** Teaching   **1694**
- **TITLE** Access to Primary Teaching, Access to Secondary Teaching
- **PLACE** Dundee College

Length 1 year   **Start** Usually August   **Days** Full time   **Cost** Student may be eligible for LEA bursary   **Entry Reqs** Age 21+, no formal qualifications required   **Award** Guaranteed offer of place on degree course   **Creche** Yes

- **CONTACT** Scottish Wider Access Programme/SWAP East 0131 650 6861

COUNTY CONTACTS

Information and advice:

Tayside Careers Service, Information Services Unit, Floor 3, 5 Whitehall Crescent, Dundee DD1 4AR 01382 303521. Tayside Careers Service also has a network of Sub-Offices in several of the smaller population centres. Sub-Office appointments can be arranged by phoning the nearest Area Careers Office
Aberfeldy Careers Office, Breadalbane Academy, Aberfeldy PH15 2DU 01887 820428. First Tues/ month 2.00-4.00
Angus Careers Office, Bellevue House, Springfield Terrace, Arbroath DD11 1EL 01241 870441
Blairgowrie Careers Office, The Community Education Office, Rowanbank Community Centre, Newton Terrace, Blairgowrie PH10 6HD. Mon & Wed 9.30-11.30
Crieff Careers Office, King Street, Crieff PH7 3AX 01764 652351. Tues twice monthly 10.00-12 noon
Dundee Careers Office, Argyll House, Marketgait, Dundee DD1 1QP 01382 304100
Perth Careers Office, 6-8 South Methven Street, Perth PH1 5PF 01738 638101

Local Enterprise Council:

Scottish Enterprise Tayside, Enterprise House, 45 North Lindsay Street, Dundee DD1 1HT 01382 23100

Open University:

The Open University, Scotland, 10 Drumsheugh Gardens, Edinburgh EH3 7QJ 0131 225 2889

WEA office:

Scottish WEA, Riddles Court, 322 Lawnmarket, Edinburgh.EH1 3PG 0131 226 3456   *Contact:* Hilary Lawson

COURSES

- **SUBJECT** Access/Arts/Social Science 1695
- **TITLE** Access to Arts and Social Science
- **PLACE** Scottish Wider Access Programme, Stornoway

Length 1 year full time or negotiable part time **Start** August **Days** Varied **Cost** Full time £750, part time £30 for 40 hours (subject to review) **Entry Reqs** None **Award** Arts & Social Science Certificate, access to courses at Aberdeen University **Creche** No

- **CONTACT** Stephen Masser 01224 313142

- **SUBJECT** Access/Engineering/Science/Teaching 1696
- **TITLE** Access to 1. Engineering, Science 2. Primary Teaching
- **PLACE** Scottish Wider Access Programme, Stornoway

Length 1 year full time or negotiable part time **Start** August **Days** Varied **Cost** Full time £750, part time £30 for 40 hours (subject to review) **Entry Reqs** None **Award** 1. SCOTVEC National Certificate, access to HE 2. Entry to Northern College teacher training **Creche** No

- **CONTACT** Stephen Masser 01224 313142

- **SUBJECT** Care Studies 1697
- **TITLE** Caring GSVQ 1. Care 2. Health 3. Social Care
- **PLACE** Lews Castle College, Stornoway

Length 1.30 weeks 2. & 3. 40 weeks **Start** August **Days** Full time Mon-Fri 9.00-4.00 **Cost** Contact College **Entry Reqs** 2. & 3. Some experience in a Caring job or completion of GSVQ Level 2 **Award** 1. GSVQ Level 2 Care 2. GSVQ Level 3 Health 3. GSVQ Level 3 Social Care **Creche** No

- **CONTACT** David Matheson/Ina MacIver 01851 703311

- **SUBJECT** Office Skills 1698
- **TITLE** Office Technology Refresher Course
- **PLACE** Lews Castle College, Stornoway

Length 15 weeks **Start** September, January **Days** Mon-Fri 10.00-3.00 **Cost** Contact College **Entry Reqs** Previous office experience useful but not essential **Award** SCOTVEC NC Modules **Creche** No

- **CONTACT** Margaret MacLeod 01851 703311

COUNTY CONTACTS

Information and advice:

Western Isles Careers Service, Council Offices, Sandwick Road, Stornoway HS1 2BW 01851 703773 x445

Local Enterprise Council:

Western Isles Enterprise, Cromwell Street Quay, Stornoway PA87 2DF 01851 703625/703905

Open University:

The Open University, Scotland, 10 Drumsheugh Gardens, Edinburgh EH3 7QJ 0131 225 2889

WEA office:

Scottish WEA, Riddles Court, 322 Lawnmarket, Edinburgh EH1 3PG 0131 226 3456

COURSES

- **SUBJECT** Access/Arts/Design/Business/Engineering/Humanities/Science/ **1699**
  Social Science
- **TITLE** Access to Higher Education
- **PLACE** Yale College

Length 1 year   **Start** Contact College   **Days** Full time 9.30-3.00   **Cost** Free   **Entry Reqs** None   **Award** Access to higher education   **Creche** Yes

- **CONTACT** Central Admissions 01978 311794

- **SUBJECT** NOW **1700**
- **TITLE** New Opportunities for Women
- **PLACE** Yale College

Start Contact College   **Cost** Free   **Entry Reqs** None   **Creche** Yes

- **CONTACT** Central Admissions 01978 311794

- **SUBJECT** Secretarial **1701**
- **TITLE** Refreshers' Course in Secretarial Studies
- **PLACE** Yale College

Start Contact College   **Cost** Free   **Creche** Yes

- **CONTACT** Central Admissions 01978 311794

- **SUBJECT** Women's Studies **1702**
- **TITLE** Women's Studies (various courses)
- **PLACE** University of Wales Bangor, Dept of Extramural Studies, Wrexham Office

Length 10 weeks   **Cost** £18.50 Concessions available   **Entry Reqs** None   **Award** Certificate in Women's Studies

- **CONTACT** Wrexham Office 01978 364277

COUNTY CONTACTS

Open University:

The Open University, Wales, 24 Cathedral Road, Cardiff CF1 9SA 01222 665636

Other agencies:

University of Wales Bangor, University Adult Education Office, 51 Regent Street, Wrexham LL11 1PF 01978 364277
Yale College, Grove Park Road, Wrexham LL12 7AA 01978 311794. The School of Continuing Education provides a range of useful courses for women wishing to return to work.

Training and Enterprise Council:

North East Wales TEC, Wynnstay Block, Hightown Barracks, Kingsmill Road, Wrexham LL13 8BH 01978 290049

WEA offices:

WEA North East Wales 01978 720145   *Contact:* Nick Taylor, WEA Tutor Organiser
WEA North Wales, 33 College Road, Bangor 01248 353254   *Contact:* Rufus Adams

COURSES

- **SUBJECT** Access/Art & Design/Business/Law/Humanities/Social Science/ **1703**
  Health Studies/Computing
- **TITLE** Access to: Visual Awareness, Business & Law, Humanities & Social Science,
  Nursing & Health Professions, Business & Computing
- **PLACE** Coleg Ceredigion, various sites

Start September **Cost** Contact College **Entry Reqs** Contact College **Award** Access to higher education
- **CONTACT** 01970 624511

- **SUBJECT** Administration **1704**
- **TITLE** Administration
- **PLACE** Coleg Ceredigion, Cardigan & Llanbadarn Fawr campuses

Start September **Cost** Contact College **Entry Reqs** Contact College **Award** NVQ II
- **CONTACT** Cardigan 01239 621059/Llanbadarn Fawr 01970 624511

- **SUBJECT** Biological Sciences **1705**
- **TITLE** Integrated Studies on Plant Development, Adaptation and Productivity:
  Masters Degree by Research
- **PLACE** University of Wales, Aberystwyth

Length 1 year **Start** October **Cost** Biotechnology & Biological Sciences Research Council Award available **Entry Reqs** Graduates with first or upper second class degree in an appropriate subject **Award** MSc
- **CONTACT** Dr V Essex, BBSRC, 01793 413200

- **SUBJECT** Business Studies/Teleworking **1706**
- **TITLE** Teleworking Course
- **PLACE** Narberth, Fishguard

Start September, November
- **CONTACT** Janet Davies 01834 861712

- **SUBJECT** Catering/Hospitality Management **1707**
- **TITLE** Professional Hospitality and Catering
- **PLACE** Coleg Ceredigion, Cardigan & Plas Tanybwlch campuses

Start September **Days** Contact College **Cost** Contact College **Entry Reqs** Contact College **Award** NVQ Level I/II/III
- **CONTACT** Cardigan 01239 621059/Plas Tanybwlch 01970 627787

- **SUBJECT** Childcare **1708**
- **TITLE** NNEB Diploma in Nursery Nursing
- **PLACE** Coleg Ceredigion, Llanbadarn Fawr campus

Start September **Cost** Contact College **Entry Reqs** Contact College **Award** NNEB Diploma
- **CONTACT** 01970 624511

- **SUBJECT** Computing **1709**
- **TITLE** Community Outreach: Computer Training in Your Village
- **PLACE** Various locations in Dyfed

Length Various **Days** Flexible **Cost** £1.30/hour Concessions available **Award** RSA CLAIT/RSA WP
- **CONTACT** Jan Waite/Ian Goddard 01834 861642/861712

- **SUBJECT**   Computing/Business Studies   **1710**
- **TITLE**   Various Computing/Business Technology Courses
- **PLACE**   Crymych, Fishguard, Narberth, Llandeilo, Saundersfoot, St David's

Length Various   **Days** Various
- **CONTACT**   Janet Davies 01834 861712

- **SUBJECT**   Desk Top Publishing   **1711**
- **TITLE**   Desk Top Publishing
- **PLACE**   Coleg Ceredigion, Cardigan & Llanbadarn Fawr campuses

Length Contact College   **Start** September   **Cost** Contact College   **Entry Reqs** Contact College
- **CONTACT**   Cardigan 01239 621059/Llanbadarn Fawr 01970 624511

- **SUBJECT**   Information Technology   **1712**
- **TITLE**   Developing Skills in New Technology
- **PLACE**   Coleg Ceredigion, Cardigan & Llanbadarn Fawr campuses

Length Contact College   **Start** September   **Cost** Contact College   **Entry Reqs** Contact College
- **CONTACT**   Cardigan 01239 621059/Llanbadarn Fawr 01970 624511

- **SUBJECT**   Information Technology   **1713**
- **TITLE**   Information Technology for PC Users
- **PLACE**   Coleg Ceredigion, Cardigan & Llanbadarn Fawr campuses

Length Contact College   **Start** September   **Cost** Contact College   **Entry Reqs** Contact College   **Award** RSA NVQ I/II/III
- **CONTACT**   Cardigan 01239 621059/Llanbadarn Fawr 01970 624511

- **SUBJECT**   Information Technology   **1714**
- **TITLE**   Women in Technology: IT & Job Seeking Skills for Women Returners
- **PLACE**   Carmarthenshire College, Llanelli and Carmarthen

Length 12 weeks   **Start** September, January, April/May   **Days** 3/4 days/week 9.30-3.30   **Cost** Free   **Entry Reqs** Basic literacy and numeracy   **Award** City & Guilds Information Technology modules & Open College Network Credits   **Creche** Yes, free in Llanelli
- **CONTACT**   Lesley Darwin/Sonya Passey 01554 759165

- **SUBJECT**   Management   **1715**
- **TITLE**   NEBSN Introductory Award in Supervisory Management
- **PLACE**   Coleg Ceredigion, Cardigan & Llanbadarn Fawr campuses

Length Contact College   **Start** September   **Cost** Contact College   **Entry Reqs** Contact College   **Award** NEBSM Introductory Award in Supervisory Management
- **CONTACT**   Cardigan 01239 621059/Llanbadarn Fawr 01970 624511

- **SUBJECT**   Office Skills   **1716**
- **TITLE**   Office Technology and Administration
- **PLACE**   Coleg Ceredigion, Cardigan & Llanbadarn Fawr campuses

Length 18 weeks   **Start** September   **Cost** Contact College   **Entry Reqs** Contact College
- **CONTACT**   Cardigan 01239 621059/Llanbadarn Fawr 01970 624511

- **SUBJECT**   Office Skills   **1717**
- **TITLE**   Typewriting/Welsh Typewriting
- **PLACE**   Coleg Ceredigion, Cardigan, Felinfach & Llanbadarn Fawr campuses

Length Contact College   **Start** September   **Cost** Contact College   **Entry Reqs** Contact College   **Award** RSA Typewriting/Welsh Typewriting Stages 1, 2 & 3
- **CONTACT**   Cardigan 01239 621059/Felinfach 01570 470209/Llanbadarn Fawr 01970 624511

- **SUBJECT** Office Skills   **1718**
- **TITLE** Word Processing
- **PLACE** Coleg Ceredigion, Cardigan, Felinfach & Llanbadarn Fawr campuses

Length Contact College   **Start** September   **Cost** Contact College   **Entry Reqs** Contact College   **Award** RSA Word Processing Stages 1, 2, & 3

- **CONTACT** Cardigan 01239 621059/Felinfach 01570 470209/Llanbadarn Fawr 01970 624511

- **SUBJECT** Office Skills   **1719**
- **TITLE** 1. Word Processing Familiarisation 2. Advanced Databases and Spreadsheets, Introduction to Windows
- **PLACE** Coleg Ceredigion, various sites

Length Contact College   **Start** September   **Cost** Contact College   **Entry Reqs** Contact College

- **CONTACT** 01970 624511

- **SUBJECT** Physics   **1720**
- **TITLE** BSc Access Degree in Physics
- **PLACE** University of Wales, Aberystwyth

Length 4 years   **Start** September   **Cost** LEA awards available   **Entry Reqs** Open access, but aptitude in Maths necessary   **Award** BSc   **Creche** Yes and playgroup £4.50/halfday

- **CONTACT** Dr K Birkinshaw 01970 622806

COUNTY CONTACTS

Open University:

The Open University, Wales, 24 Cathedral Road, Cardiff CF1 9SA 01222 665636

Other agencies:

Glanaman Community Education Centre, High Street, Glanaman, Ammanford SA18 1DX 01269 823162   *Contact:* Harold Jones
Simtra Project, c/o Bloomfield Centre, Redstone Road, Narbeth SA67 7EP 01834 861712   *Contact:* Annette Quelch. An information technology training project operating throughout Dyfed offering general and specific training in computer applications.

WALES: Gwent

COURSES

- **SUBJECT** Access/Health Studies/Social Science/Women's Studies   **1721**
- **TITLE** Access to Health and Social Science (with Women's Studies Components)
- **PLACE** Gwent Tertiary College, Ebbw Vale Campus

Length 36 weeks   **Start** September   **Days** Mon-Fri 10.30-3.15   **Cost** Free if unemployed. Grants available   **Entry Reqs** None   **Award** Access Diploma   **Creche** Yes

- **CONTACT** Jan Hiscox 01495 302083

- **SUBJECT**   Access/Humanities/Science/Catering/Art & Design   1722
- **TITLE**   Access Combined Studies
- **PLACE**   Gwent Tertiary College, Pontypool

Length 1 year   **Start** September   **Days** 5 day/week 10.00-12.00, 1.00-3.00   **Cost** Contact College. Concessions available   **Entry Reqs** None   **Award** Access kitemarked diploma via South East Wales Access Consortium   **Creche** No

- **CONTACT** Colin Clarke 01495 755141

- **SUBJECT**   Access/Science/Technology/Information Technology/Environmental   1723
                 Studies/Humanities/Social Studies/Labour Studies/Business
- **TITLE**   Access and Foundation Programme
- **PLACE**   Gwent College of Higher Education

Length 1 year   **Start** September   **Days** Full time 10.00-3.00   **Cost** Contact College   **Entry Reqs** None   **Award** Access to higher education

- **CONTACT** 01633 430088

- **SUBJECT**   Combined Studies   1724
- **TITLE**   BA (Hons) Combined Studies
- **PLACE**   Gwent College of Higher Education

Length 3 years full time, 6 years part time   **Start** September   **Cost** Mandatory grant available   **Entry Reqs** Contact College   **Award** BA (Hons) Combined Studies

- **CONTACT** Admissions Office 01633 432432/430088

- **SUBJECT**   Electronic Engineering/Electrical Engineering   1725
- **TITLE**   BEng (Hons) 1. Electronics & Instrumentation Systems 2. Electrical &
                 Instrumentation Systems
- **PLACE**   Gwent College of Higher Education

Length 3 years full time, 4 years part time   **Start** September   **Cost** Mandatory grant available   **Entry Reqs** Contact College   **Award** BA (Hons) 1. Electronics & Instrumentation Systems 2. Electrical & Instrumentation Systems

- **CONTACT** Admissions Office 01633 432432/430088

- **SUBJECT**   NOW/Business   1726
- **TITLE**   Small Business Skills for Women: Rural Diversification/Tourism,
                 Business Start-up
- **PLACE**   Various: Training Van to any location with electricity supply

Length Flexible, modular courses   **Start** Varies. Contact College   **Days** Negotiable   **Cost** Free   **Entry Reqs** Women living in Gwent   **Award** Various   **Creche** Free on-site or costs elsewhere paid

- **CONTACT** Judy Chaloner 01291 672311

- **SUBJECT**   Office Skills   1727
- **TITLE**   Adult Returners Course
- **PLACE**   Gwent Tertiary College, Ebbw Vale Campus

Length 1 year   **Start** September   **Days** Modular 10.00-3.00   **Cost** Free if unemployed   **Entry Reqs** None   **Award** RSA & NVQ awards leading to employment or higher education   **Creche** Yes £1.50/session

- **CONTACT** Linda Swanson/Pat Harvey 01495 333000

COUNTY CONTACTS

Information and advice:

Adult Prospects, Pontypool Careers Centre, Town Bridge, Park Road, Pontypool NP4 6JE 01495 750015   *Contact:* Judy Evans. Free adult guidance service
Gwent College of HE, College Crescent, Caerleon, Newport NP6 1XJ 01633 432062   *Contact:* Willie Stewart. Access courses, undergraduate and postgraduate courses

Open University:

The Open University, Wales, 24 Cathedral Road, Cardiff CF1 9SA 01222 665636

Training and Enterprise Council:

Gwent TEC, Glyndwr House, Cleppa Park, Newport NP1 9BA 01633 817777. Women into Management course

WALES: Gwynedd

COURSES

● **SUBJECT**	Access		1728
● **TITLE**	Access to Higher Education		
● **PLACE**	Coleg Menai, Bangor, Llangefri, Holyhead & Caernarfon		

Length 36 weeks   **Start** September   **Days** 4 days/week 10.15-3.15   **Cost** None   **Entry Reqs** Age 21+   **Award** North Wales Access Consortium Certificate, entry to higher education **Creche** No

● **CONTACT** Student Services 01248 370125

● **SUBJECT**	Computing		1729
● **TITLE**	Computing Courses (Various)		
● **PLACE**	University of Wales Bangor, Dept of Extramural Studies		

Length Various   **Days** Various   **Cost** Contact College

● **CONTACT** Dept of Extramural Studies 01248 382256/383896

● **SUBJECT**	General Studies		1730
● **TITLE**	University of Wales Diploma in General Studies		
● **PLACE**	Coleg Harlech		

Length Variable, part time   **Cost** Free   **Entry Reqs** None   **Award** University of Wales Diploma in General Studies

● **CONTACT** Nia Griffiths, Short Course Unit 01766 780363

● **SUBJECT**	Multi-Subject		1731
● **TITLE**	Various Short Courses		
● **PLACE**	Coleg Harlech		

Length Various   **Start** September   **Days** Various   **Cost** Free   **Entry Reqs** Contact College

● **CONTACT** Nia Griffiths, Short Course Unit 01766 780363

- **SUBJECT**   Preparatory   1732
- **TITLE**   Return to Learning
- **PLACE**   Coleg Menai, Bangor, Llangefri, Holyhead & Caernarfon

Length 10 weeks   **Start** Sept/Oct, January, April/May   **Days** 2½-3 days/week (rotating) **Cost** Free   **Entry Reqs** None   **Award** OCN Credits Level I & II   **Creche** No. Vouchers could be available subject to status

- **CONTACT**   Gill Williams 01248 370125

- **SUBJECT**   Women's Studies   1733
- **TITLE**   Women's Studies (various courses)
- **PLACE**   University of Wales Bangor, Dept of Extramural Studies

Length 10 weeks   **Cost** £18.50 Concessions available   **Entry Reqs** None   **Award** Certificate in Women's Studies

- **CONTACT**   Dept of Extramural Studies 01248 382256/383896

COUNTY CONTACTS

Other agencies:

University of Wales, Bangor, Department of Extramural Studies, 45 Fford y Coleg, Bangor LL57 2DG 01248 383356

Training and Enterprise Council:

North West Wales TEC, Llys Britannia, Parc Menai, Bangor LL57 4BN 01248 671444

WEA offices:

WEA Anglesey 01248 371693   *Contact:* Trefor Owen, WEA Tutor Organiser
WEA North Wales, 33 College Road, Bangor 01248 353254   *Contact:* Rufus Adams

---

WALES: Mid-Glamorgan

COURSES

- **SUBJECT**   Access   1734
- **TITLE**   Access to Higher Education (Modular)
- **PLACE**   Pontypridd College

Length 1 year full time, 2 years part time   **Start** September   **Days** 15-18 hours/week   **Cost** None   **Entry Reqs** None   **Award** Access to higher education   **Creche** No

- **CONTACT**   Dave Isaacs 01443 486121

- **SUBJECT**   Access/Business/Humanities/Law/Science/Tourism & Leisure   1735
- **TITLE**   Access to Higher Education (Modular)
- **PLACE**   Pontypridd College

Length 9 months   **Start** September   **Days** Mon-Fri 10.00-3.00   **Cost** None   **Entry Reqs** None   **Award** Access Course Certificate, entry to higher education   **Creche** No

- **CONTACT**   Dave Isaacs/Jocelyn Andrews 01443 486121

- **SUBJECT** Business Studies/Office Skills   **1736**
- **TITLE** Modern Office Techniques for Adults
- **PLACE** Pontypridd College

Length 9 months   **Start** Flexible   **Days** Mon-Fri 10.00-3.00   **Cost** None   **Entry Reqs** None
Award RSA single subjects, Secretarial Skills, NVQ Level 2 Business   **Creche** No
- **CONTACT** Adela Smith/Sue Gale 01443 486121

- **SUBJECT** Preparatory   **1737**
- **TITLE** Women into Vocational Training
- **PLACE** Merthyr Tydfil College

Length 8 weeks   **Start** Throughout the year   **Days** Mon-Fri 10.00-3.00   **Cost** None   **Entry Reqs** Women 18-60 years   **Award** Higher education or employment   **Creche** Yes Free
- **CONTACT** Sue Lewis 01685 723663 x225

COUNTY CONTACTS

Information and advice:

Pontypridd College Basic Skills Unit, Ynys Terrace, Rhydyfelin, Pontypridd 01443 407863
Contact: Marilyn Morgan

Open University:

The Open University, Wales, 24 Cathedral Road, Cardiff CF1 9SA 01222 665636

Training and Enterprise Council:

Mid-Glamorgan TEC, Unit 17-20, Centre Court, Main Avenue, Treforest Industrial Estate, Pontypridd CF37 5YL 01656 841594. Opportunity Centres provide information, advice and guidance for women; Option Centres provide guidance and occupational 'Tasters' for women; Participation in events organised by Chwarae Teg, Valley Women's Roadshow and Women in Business; Women in Management courses; Access courses; Establishment of women returner groups in the community; Women in Management workshops; Careers Fairs for girls; Exhibitions, seminars and conferences

WALES: Powys

COURSES

- **SUBJECT** Preparatory   **1738**
- **TITLE** People into Work
- **PLACE** Coleg Powys, Brecon, Llandrindod, Newtown

Length 12 weeks   **Start** September, January, April   **Days** 3 days/week 9.00-4.00 approx
Cost Free   **Entry Reqs** None   **Award** RSA CLAIT   **Creche** No
- **CONTACT** Mrs C Burnside 01597 822616

- **SUBJECT** Preparatory   **1739**
- **TITLE** Return to Learn
- **PLACE** Coleg Powys, Brecon, Llandrindod, Newtown & other venues across Powys

Length 10 weeks   **Start** Sept, Jan, April subject to demand   **Days** 1 day/week 10.00-3.00
Cost £18 but bursary may be available   **Entry Reqs** None   **Award** UWACC Credits   **Creche** No
- **CONTACT** Jackie Protheroe 01874 623009

COUNTY CONTACTS

Open University:

The Open University, Wales, 24 Cathedral Road, Cardiff CF1 9SA 01222 665636

Training and Enterprise Council:

Powys TEC, First Floor, St David's House, Newtown SY16 1RB 01686 622494. Out of school childcare; Community Enterprise Workers.

WEA offices:

WEA Mid Wales 01686 650337   *Contact:* Cyril Jones, WEA Tutor Organiser
WEA Powys, 26 Garth Road, Builth Wells LD2 3AR   *Contact:* Robin Cain

WALES: South Glamorgan

COURSES

- **SUBJECT**   Access/Art & Design   1740
- **TITLE**   Access to Art & Design
- **PLACE**   Coleg Glan Hafren, Trowbridge Road Centre

Length 1 year   **Start** January   **Days** Mon-Fri 10.00-3.00   **Cost** Contact College   **Entry Reqs** None   **Award** Progression to higher education   **Creche** Yes

- **CONTACT**   Beverley Beauchamp 01222 794226 x241

- **SUBJECT**   Access/Business/Computing   1741
- **TITLE**   Access to Higher Education
- **PLACE**   Barry College

Length 1 year full time   **Start** September   **Days** Mon-Fri 10.00-3.00   **Cost** Contact College   **Entry Reqs** 21+   **Award** Access Diploma   **Creche** Playgroup

- **CONTACT**   Mike Carter 01446 743519

- **SUBJECT**   Access/Business Studies   1742
- **TITLE**   Access to Business Studies
- **PLACE**   Coleg Glan Hafren, Trowbridge Road Centre

Length 1 year   **Start** September   **Days** Mon-Fri 10.00-3.00   **Cost** Contact College   **Entry Reqs** None   **Award** Progression to higher education   **Creche** Yes

- **CONTACT**   Judith Larsen 01222 794226

- **SUBJECT**   Access/Health Studies   1743
- **TITLE**   Access to Health Studies
- **PLACE**   Barry College

Length 1 year full time   **Start** September   **Days** Mon-Fri 10.00-3.00   **Cost** Contact College   **Entry Reqs** 21+   **Award** Access Diploma   **Creche** Playgroup

- **CONTACT**   Mike Carter 01446 743519

- **SUBJECT** Access/Humanities 1744
- **TITLE** Access to Humanities
- **PLACE** Coleg Glan Hafren, Trowbridge Road Centre

Length 1 year   **Start** September   **Days** Mon-Fri 10.00-3.00   **Cost** Contact College   **Entry Reqs** None   **Award** Progression to higher education   **Creche** Yes

- **CONTACT** Judith Larsen 01222 794226

- **SUBJECT** Access/Science 1745
- **TITLE** Access to Life Sciences
- **PLACE** Coleg Glan Hafren, Trowbridge Road Centre

Length 1 year   **Start** September   **Days** Mon-Fri 10.00-3.00   **Cost** Contact College   **Entry Reqs** None   **Award** Progression to higher education   **Creche** Yes

- **CONTACT** Judith Larsen 01222 794226

- **SUBJECT** Access/Social Science/Humanities 1746
- **TITLE** Access to Higher Education
- **PLACE** Barry College

Length 1 year full time   **Start** September   **Days** Mon-Fri 10.00-3.00   **Cost** Contact College   **Entry Reqs** 21+, interview   **Award** Access Diploma   **Creche** Playgroup

- **CONTACT** Mike Carter 01446 743519

- **SUBJECT** Business Studies 1747
- **TITLE** BTEC National Diploma in Business and Finance
- **PLACE** Coleg Glan Hafren, Parade Centre

Length 2 years   **Start** September   **Days** Mon-Fri 10.00-3.00   **Cost** Contact College   **Entry Reqs** By informal interview   **Award** BTEC National Diploma   **Creche** No

- **CONTACT** Course Enquiries 01222 794226

- **SUBJECT** Childcare 1748
- **TITLE** Nursery Nursing
- **PLACE** Coleg Glan Hafren, Parade Centre

Length 2 years   **Start** September   **Days** Full time   **Cost** Contact College   **Entry Reqs** Contact College   **Award** NNEB Diploma   **Creche** No

- **CONTACT** Course Enquiries 01222 794226

- **SUBJECT** Computing 1749
- **TITLE** Various Short Courses in Business Computing and Related Courses
- **PLACE** South Glamorgan Women's Workshop

Length 10 weeks   **Start** Variable   **Days** Weekday evenings/Saturday mornings   **Cost** Reasonable   **Creche** Contact Workshop

- **CONTACT** Chris O'Connell 01222 493351

- **SUBJECT** Computing 1750
- **TITLE** Women in Computing
- **PLACE** South Glamorgan Women's Workshop

Length 1 year   **Start** September   **Days** 2½ days/week 10.00-4.00 to fit in with school terms   **Cost** Free   **Entry Reqs** Women aged 25 years+, unemployed, South Glamorgan residents   **Award** NVQ Level II and Open College Network Accreditation units   **Creche** Yes Free

- **CONTACT** Chris O'Connell 01222 493351

- **SUBJECT** Preparatory   1751
- **TITLE** Introductory Course for Minority Ethnic Women: Technical English, Maths, Computing
- **PLACE** South Glamorgan Women's Workshop

Length 6-8 weeks   **Start** May   **Days** 2 days/week, 4 hours/day 10.00-3.00   **Cost** Free **Entry Reqs** Women from ethnic minority communities, over 25, living in South Glamorgan, with good English   **Award** Entry for successful trainees to Workshop's 1 year part time or full time courses   **Creche** On site nursery free

- **CONTACT** Rakhshanda Shahzad 01222 493351

COUNTY CONTACTS

Information and advice:

Radyr Adult Education Centre, Radyr Comprehensive School, Heol Isaf, Radyr, Cardiff CF4 8XG 01222 842056   *Contact:* Tim Ward, Megan Langmay. Wide range of wide range of non-vocational and vocational part-time classes

Open University:

The Open University, Wales, 24 Cathedral Road, Cardiff CF1 9SA 01222 665636

Other agencies:

South Glamorgan Women's Workshop, Edena House, East Canal Wharf, Cardiff CF1 5AQ 01222 493351. Women's training centre

Training and Enterprise Council:

South Glamorgan TEC, 3-7 Drakes Walk, Waterfront 2000, Atlantic Wharf, Cardiff CF1 5AN 01222 451000

WEA office:

WEA South Wales, Tawney House, 11 Station Terrace, Cowbridge Road West, Ely, Cardiff CF5 4AA 01222 552277

WALES: West Glamorgan

COURSES

- **SUBJECT** Access   1752
- **TITLE** Access to Social Sciences, Arts, Modern Languages
- **PLACE** University College Swansea, various centres

Length 2 years part time   **Start** September   **Days** Variable   **Cost** Contact College. Concessions available   **Entry Reqs** None   **Award** SWWOCAC Access Certificate   **Creche** Yes Free

- **CONTACT** Sheila Inglis 01792 295691

- **SUBJECT** Access/Accounting
- **TITLE** Access to Accountancy
- **PLACE** Swansea College

1753

Length 36 weeks   **Start** September   **Days** Mon-Thurs 10.00-3.00   **Cost** Free if in receipt of benefit   **Entry Reqs** No formal entry requirements   **Award** Access to higher education courses   **Creche** Yes
- **CONTACT** Hywel Vaughan 01792 284078

- **SUBJECT** Access/Art & Design
- **TITLE** Access to Art and Design
- **PLACE** Swansea College

1754

Length 36 weeks   **Start** September   **Days** Mon-Thurs 10.00-3.00   **Cost** Free if in receipt of benefit   **Entry Reqs** No formal entry requirements   **Award** Access to higher education courses   **Creche** Yes
- **CONTACT** Hywel Vaughan 01792 284078

- **SUBJECT** Access/Art & Design/Craft
- **TITLE** Access to Art, Design and Craft
- **PLACE** Afan College

1755

Length Modular, 1 year full time 2 years part time   **Start** September   **Days** 15 hours/week full time, 8 hours/week part time   **Cost** £35+£10 registration fee full time, £5 registration fee part time   **Entry Reqs** None   **Award** SWWOCAC Certificate (HEQC/Higher Education Quality Council validated)   **Creche** Yes £11/day
- **CONTACT** Sue Beresford 01639 882107

- **SUBJECT** Access/Business Studies
- **TITLE** Access to Business Studies
- **PLACE** Swansea College

1756

Length 36 weeks   **Start** September   **Days** Mon-Thurs 10.00-3.00   **Cost** Free if in receipt of benefit   **Entry Reqs** No formal entry requirements   **Award** Access to higher education courses   **Creche** Yes
- **CONTACT** Hywel Vaughan 01792 284078

- **SUBJECT** Access/Health Studies/Social Studies
- **TITLE** Access to Health and Social Studies
- **PLACE** Afan College

1757

Length Modular, usually 1 year   **Start** September   **Days** Approx 8 hours/week. Daytime/evening programme   **Cost** £35/year+£5 registration fee   **Entry Reqs** None   **Award** SWWOCAC Certificate (HEQC validated)   **Creche** Yes £11/day
- **CONTACT** Dr Huw Davies 01639 882107

- **SUBJECT** Access/Humanities
- **TITLE** Access to Higher Education: Humanities
- **PLACE** Afan College

1758

Length Modular, usually 1 year   **Start** September   **Cost** £35/year+£5 registration fee   **Entry Reqs** None   **Award** SWWOCAC Certificate (HEQC validated)   **Creche** Yes £11/day
- **CONTACT** Pam Luke 01639 882107

- **SUBJECT** Access/Humanities/Law/Business Studies
- **TITLE** Ways of Seeing 1. Humanities 2. Law 3. Business Studies
- **PLACE** Swansea College

1759

Length 36 weeks full time   **Start** September   **Days** Mon-Thurs 10.00-3.00   **Cost** Free if in receipt of benefit, otherwise £35   **Entry Reqs** Very open   **Award** Access Certificate   **Creche** Daytime. Assistance with cost possible
- **CONTACT** Lyn Jones 01792 206871

- **SUBJECT**   Access/Social Studies   **1760**
- **TITLE**   Access to Social Welfare Studies
- **PLACE**   Swansea College

Length 36 weeks   **Start** September   **Days** Mon-Thurs 10.00-3.00   **Cost** Free if in receipt of benefit   **Entry Reqs** No formal entry requirements   **Award** Access to higher education courses   **Creche** Yes
- **CONTACT**   Hywel Vaughan 01792 284078

- **SUBJECT**   Access/Sports Studies   **1761**
- **TITLE**   Access in Sports and Leisure
- **PLACE**   Swansea College

Length 36 weeks   **Start** September   **Days** Mon-Thurs 10.00-3.00   **Cost** Free if in receipt of benefit   **Entry Reqs** No formal entry requirements   **Award** Access to higher education courses   **Creche** Yes
- **CONTACT**   Hywel Vaughan 01792 284078

- **SUBJECT**   Access/Tourism & Leisure   **1762**
- **TITLE**   Access in Tourism
- **PLACE**   Swansea College

Length 36 weeks   **Start** September   **Days** Mon-Thurs 10.00-3.00   **Cost** Free if in receipt of benefit   **Entry Reqs** No formal entry requirements   **Award** Access to higher education courses   **Creche** Yes
- **CONTACT**   Hywel Vaughan 01792 284078

- **SUBJECT**   Engineering   **1763**
- **TITLE**   Materials Engineering: Research Masters Pilot Course
- **PLACE**   University of Wales Swansea

Length 2 years   **Start** October   **Cost** Engineering & Physical Sciences Research Council award available   **Entry Reqs** Graduates with first or upper second class honours degree in an appropriate subject   **Award** Master of Research Degree
- **CONTACT**   Dr V Randle 01792 295841

- **SUBJECT**   Hairdressing   **1764**
- **TITLE**   Hairdressing for Beginners
- **PLACE**   Afan College

Length 2 years   **Start** September   **Days** Mon+Wed 10.00-3.00   **Cost** £250 + purchase of materials & £5 registration fee   **Award** C&G Level II Preferred Scheme for Hairdressing (NVQ II)   **Creche** Yes £11/day
- **CONTACT**   Georgina Missen 01639 882107

- **SUBJECT**   Information Technology   **1765**
- **TITLE**   People in Technology
- **PLACE**   University of Wales Swansea, at Banwen, Tairgwaith, Glynneath & Porth

Length 20 weeks   **Start** Various   **Days** 2/3 days/week 9.15-3.15   **Cost** Free (ESF Funded)   **Entry Reqs** Age 18+, unemployed for 6 mnths, literacy, numeracy   **Award** 10 Open College Credits   **Creche** Yes
- **CONTACT**   Charlotte Rees 01792 295464

- **SUBJECT**   Management   **1766**
- **TITLE**   Women into Management Modules 1, 2 & 3
- **PLACE**   University of Wales Swansea

Length 10 weeks   **Start** September, January, April   **Days** 1 eve/week 7.00-9.00   **Cost** £60 Concessionary £10 per module   **Entry Reqs** None   **Award** University of Wales Swansea 10 credits on level I per module   **Creche** No
- **CONTACT**   Charlotte Rees 01792 295464

- **SUBJECT**   Preparatory/Humanities/Social Science/Languages   1767
- **TITLE**   Foundation Studies: Humanities, Social Science, Modern Languages
- **PLACE**   University of Wales Swansea, Dept of Adult Continuing Education

Length 2 years part time   **Start** October   **Days** Varies   **Cost** £125 full wage, £65 low wage, £15 unwaged   **Entry Reqs** None   **Award** UWS Foundation Studies Certificate   **Creche** Yes

- **CONTACT**   Dr K Fitzpatrick 01792 295691

- **SUBJECT**   Secretarial   1768
- **TITLE**   Secretarial Workshop
- **PLACE**   Afan College

Length Determined by completion of Action Plan   **Start** Flexible   **Days** 10.00-3.00 4 days/week, 6.00-9.00 3 eves/week   **Cost** £35 for up to 8 1½ hour modules/year + £5 registration fee   **Entry Reqs** None   **Award** C&G NVQ II/III, RSA, Pitman qualifications   **Creche** Yes £11/day

- **CONTACT**   Stella Noyes 01639 882107

- **SUBJECT**   Women's Studies   1769
- **TITLE**   Certificate in Women's Studies
- **PLACE**   University of Wales Swansea, Dept of Adult Continuing Education

Length Flexible, but 2 years minimum part time (120 credits)   **Start** Flexible   **Days** Varies according to module   **Cost** £30 per 10 credits. Concessionary rates available   **Entry Reqs** None   **Award** University of Wales Swansea Certificate   **Creche** Possibly. Contact College

- **CONTACT**   Jane Elliott 01792 295499

- **SUBJECT**   Women's Studies   1770
- **TITLE**   Women's Studies MSc (Econ)
- **PLACE**   University of Wales Swansea, Dept of Adult Continuing Education

Length 3 years part time   **Start** October   **Days** 1 eve/week+day schools   **Cost** Years 1 & 2 approx £600 per year. Year 3: dissertation (ESF subsidy)   **Entry Reqs** Initial degree or university approved nongraduate qualification or relevant experience   **Award** MSc (Econ) **Creche** Possibly. Contact College

- **CONTACT**   Jane Elliott 01792 295499

COUNTY CONTACTS

Information and advice:

West Glamorgan Careers & Education Business Co. Ltd, West Wing, County Hall, Swansea SA1 3SN 01792 471229   *Contact:* John Talbot
Neath Careers Centre, Ty Dwr-y-Felin, Dwr-y-Felin Road, Neath SA10 7ST 01639 636391
Port Talbot Careers Centre, Theodore Road, Port Talbot SA13 1SP 01639 882081   *Contact:* Pamela Berry

Open University:

The Open University, Wales, 24 Cathedral Road, Cardiff CF1 9SA 01222 665636

Training and Enterprise Council:

West Wales TEC, Orchard House, Orchard Street, Swansea SA1 5DJ 01792 460355

COURSE SUBJECT INDEX

The entries are indexed to entry numbers and not page numbers

Administration
Bedfordshire, 61
Berkshire, 75, 76
Durham, 291
East Sussex, 309
Essex, 327, 328, 329
Hampshire, 438, 439, 440
Hertfordshire, 513, 515
Isle of Wight, 557
Northamptonshire, 1039
Nottinghamshire, 1078, 1079
Oxfordshire, 1113, 1114
South Yorkshire, 1154
Staffordshire, 1172, 1173
Suffolk, 1208, 1209, 1210, 1211
Surrey, 1255, 1256
Warwickshire, 1323
West Yorkshire, 1488
Wales: Dyfed, 1704

Agriculture
Staffordshire, 1174

Animal Care
Isle of Wight, 558

Antiques
Hampshire, 441

Archaeology
Wiltshire, 1495

Art
Isle of Wight, 559
Kent, 571, 601
London, 713
Shropshire, 1137
Warwickshire, 1324
West Yorkshire, 1446

Art & Design
Avon, 1, 22
Bedfordshire, 59
Derbyshire, 211
East Sussex, 310
Hampshire, 442
Kent, 572, 575
Leicestershire, 654
Lincolnshire, 677
London, 703, 704, 759, 760, 761,
    762, 763, 764
Norfolk, 1000
North Yorkshire, 1018
Nottinghamshire, 1080
Suffolk, 1212
Surrey, 1252
West Midlands, 1349, 1350, 1351,
    1367

West Yorkshire, 1436
Wiltshire, 1496
Scotland: Borders, 1539
Scotland: Lothian, 1604
Scotland: Strathclyde, 1646, 1647
Scotland: Tayside, 1682
Wales: Dyfed, 1703
Wales: Gwent, 1722
Wales: South Glamorgan, 1740
Wales: West Glamorgan, 1754,
    1755

Arts
Devon, 231
Essex, 325
Gloucestershire, 362, 363
Greater Manchester, 380
London, 702, 705, 706, 765
Norfolk, 996
Nottinghamshire, 1073
Scotland: Borders, 1540
Scotland: Fife, 1560
Scotland: Grampian, 1572
Scotland: Highland, 1581
Scotland: Lothian, 1597, 1598,
    1605
Scotland: Orkney, 1630
Scotland: Shetland Islands, 1632
Scotland: Strathclyde, 1634
Scotland: Tayside, 1675, 1683
Scotland: Western Isles, 1695
Wales: Clywd, 1699

Beauty
Bedfordshire, 62
Cornwall, 166
Devon, 236
Kent, 602
Lincolnshire, 682
London, 766
Northamptonshire, 1055
Nottinghamshire, 1081

Beauty Therapy
Dorset, 271
Essex, 330
Staffordshire, 1175
Suffolk, 1213

Biological Sciences
Greater Manchester, 386, 387
Leicestershire, 659
Surrey, 1257, 1258
West Midlands, 1368, 1369
Wales: Dyfed, 1705

Biology
Scotland: Strathclyde, 1636

Black Studies
London, 707, 708, 767, 807
West Yorkshire, 1437

Building
Scotland: Grampian, 1573
Scotland: Highland, 1582

Built Environment
Avon, 2
Scotland: Strathclyde, 1638

Business
Avon, 3, 23, 24
Berkshire, 77
Cheshire, 112
Cumbria, 188
Dorset, 272
Essex, 331, 332, 333
Gloucestershire, 363
Greater Manchester, 388
Hampshire, 443
Hereford and Worcester, 481
Hertfordshire, 508
Humberside, 551
Isle of Wight, 560
Kent, 603
Leicestershire, 663
London, 702, 704, 705, 706, 709,
    710, 711, 712, 713, 768, 769,
    770, 771, 772, 773, 774,
    775, 776
Norfolk, 1001
North Yorkshire, 1019
Northamptonshire, 1040
Nottinghamshire, 1082
Staffordshire, 1170, 1176, 1177,
    1178
Suffolk, 1214, 1215, 1216, 1217
Warwickshire, 1325, 1326, 1327,
    1330
West Midlands, 1350, 1370, 1371
West Yorkshire, 1447
Scotland: Borders, 1541
Scotland: Central, 1544
Scotland: Lothian, 1606
Scotland: Strathclyde, 1636, 1637,
    1640, 1644
Scotland: Tayside, 1684
Wales: Clywd, 1699
Wales: Dyfed, 1703
Wales: Gwent, 1723, 1726
Wales: Mid-Glamorgan, 1735
Wales: South Glamorgan, 1741

Business Administration
Avon, 25
Cheshire, 113

Cleveland, 141
Cornwall, 184
Cumbria, 189
Essex, 334
Greater Manchester, 389
Hertfordshire, 516
Kent, 604
Leicestershire, 660, 661
London, 777, 778, 779, 780, 781, 782, 783, 784, 785
North Yorkshire, 1025
Nottinghamshire, 1083, 1084
South Yorkshire, 1155
Staffordshire, 1179
Suffolk, 1239
Surrey, 1259, 1260
Tyne and Wear, 1288
Warwickshire, 1328, 1329
West Midlands, 1372, 1373, 1374, 1375
West Yorkshire, 1448
Northern Ireland: South Eastern, 1519
Scotland: Central, 1547
Scotland: Fife, 1562, 1563
Scotland: Highland, 1587
Scotland: Strathclyde, 1635

Business Information Technology
Devon, 237
Essex, 335
Surrey, 1261

Business Studies
Avon, 4, 5, 6
Bedfordshire, 59
Berkshire, 78
Cheshire, 114
Cleveland, 131
Cornwall, 163
Devon, 232, 238
Dorset, 266, 273
Durham, 287
East Sussex, 308
Essex, 325, 336
Hampshire, 434
Hereford and Worcester, 484
Hertfordshire, 509
Kent, 573, 574, 575, 578
Leicestershire, 652, 653
London, 714, 715, 716, 717, 786, 787
Northamptonshire, 1034, 1035
Staffordshire, 1180, 1181
Suffolk, 1205, 1218
Surrey, 1252
West Midlands, 1352, 1353

West Yorkshire, 1437, 1449
Scotland: Central, 1548
Scotland: Lothian, 1607
Scotland: Strathclyde, 1648, 1674
Wales: Dyfed, 1706, 1710
Wales: Mid-Glamorgan, 1736
Wales: South Glamorgan, 1742, 1747
Wales: West Glamorgan, 1756, 1759

Care Studies
Bedfordshire, 63, 64
Cleveland, 132
Cornwall, 186
Devon, 239
Durham, 292
Essex, 337, 338, 339
Gloucestershire, 364
Hereford and Worcester, 487
Hertfordshire, 517
Isle of Wight, 561, 562
Kent, 605
London, 788, 789
Northamptonshire, 1041, 1042
Nottinghamshire, 1085
Tyne and Wear, 1289
Warwickshire, 1331, 1332
West Midlands, 1376
West Yorkshire, 1450, 1451
Scotland: Strathclyde, 1649
Scotland: Western Isles, 1697

Career Development
Oxfordshire, 1115, 1130

Careers Guidance
Kent, 606

Catering
Avon, 43
Bedfordshire, 62, 65
Berkshire, 79
Cheshire, 115
Cleveland, 138
Cornwall, 167, 168
Cumbria, 191
Hertfordshire, 518
Lincolnshire, 679, 680
London, 790, 791, 792, 793
Norfolk, 1002
Northamptonshire, 1043, 1044, 1045
Northern Ireland: Southern, 1529
Wales: Dyfed, 1707
Wales: Gwent, 1722

Chemistry
Hampshire, 444
Leicestershire, 653
London, 794

Childcare
Avon, 26, 27, 28
Cheshire, 116
Cleveland, 139
Cornwall, 169, 170
Cumbria, 192
Durham, 293, 294, 295, 296
Essex, 340
Hampshire, 445
Hereford and Worcester, 485, 486, 487
Hertfordshire, 519, 520, 521, 522, 523, 524, 525
Leicestershire, 662
Lincolnshire, 681
London, 789, 795, 796, 797, 798, 799, 800, 801, 802, 803, 804
Northamptonshire, 1046, 1047, 1048
Nottinghamshire, 1086
Staffordshire, 1182, 1183
Suffolk, 1219
Surrey, 1262
Tyne and Wear, 1290, 1291
Warwickshire, 1333
West Midlands, 1377, 1378
West Yorkshire, 1438, 1452
Wiltshire, 1497
Wales: Dyfed, 1708
Wales: South Glamorgan, 1748

Civil Engineering
Merseyside, 974
Nottinghamshire, 1087
Surrey, 1263
West Yorkshire, 1453

Clothing Studies
Scotland: Strathclyde, 1650, 1651

Combined Studies
Cumbria, 190
South Yorkshire, 1156
Tyne and Wear, 1292
Wales: Gwent, 1724

Communication Studies
Scotland: Highland, 1588

Communications
Leicestershire, 663
Scotland: Strathclyde, 1652

Community Studies
Avon, 17, 29, 43
Cumbria, 193
Durham, 292
Greater Manchester, 380
Kent, 576, 607
London, 718, 805, 806, 807
West Yorkshire, 1454
Scotland: Central, 1549

Computing
Avon, 7, 40, 43
Bedfordshire, 66
Cheshire, 117, 118
Cleveland, 140, 141
Cornwall, 176
Cumbria, 194, 195
Devon, 240
Dorset, 266, 283
Essex, 341, 342
Greater Manchester, 390
Hertfordshire, 508, 526
Humberside, 552
Isle of Wight, 563
Kent, 575, 577, 578, 592, 627
Lancashire, 637
Leicestershire, 674
London, 702, 704, 705, 706, 714,
    717, 719, 720, 808, 809,
    810, 811, 812, 813, 814, 815,
    816, 817, 818, 819
Norfolk, 997, 1003
Nottinghamshire, 1074, 1088,
    1089, 1090, 1091
Oxfordshire, 1116, 1117
Staffordshire, 1170, 1184
Surrey, 1264, 1265, 1278
Tyne and Wear, 1293
West Midlands, 1353, 1354, 1379,
    1380, 1381, 1382, 1383
West Sussex, 1431
West Yorkshire, 1439, 1442, 1455,
    1456
Scotland: Central, 1546, 1550
Scotland: Dumfries and
    Galloway, 1556
Scotland: Lothian, 1608, 1609
Scotland: Strathclyde, 1645, 1653,
    1660
Wales: Dyfed, 1703, 1709, 1710
Wales: Gwynedd, 1729
Wales: South Glamorgan, 1741,
    1749, 1750

Construction
Avon, 30, 43
Devon, 232
Hampshire, 446

London, 820, 821
Northumberland, 1067
Nottinghamshire, 1092
Surrey, 1263
West Midlands, 1384
Scotland: Tayside, 1685

Contemporary Studies
London, 822

Counselling
Cleveland, 142
Durham, 297
Hampshire, 447
Kent, 608
London, 823, 824, 825, 826, 827,
    828
Surrey, 1266
Northern Ireland: South Eastern,
    1520
Scotland: Lothian, 1610

Craft
Cornwall, 171
Hereford and Worcester, 488, 495
London, 887
Northamptonshire, 1049, 1050
Northern Ireland: Southern, 1529
Scotland: West Glamorgan, 1755

Cultural Studies
Greater Manchester, 381
London, 704, 721, 722, 728

Dentistry
London, 829

Design
Greater Manchester, 391
Hampshire, 448
Hertfordshire, 527, 528
Kent, 609
London, 713, 717, 830, 894
Merseyside, 975
Nottinghamshire, 1073
Shropshire, 1137
Warwickshire, 1334, 1335
West Midlands, 1355
West Yorkshire, 1446, 1457
Scotland: Strathclyde, 1638
Wales: Clwyd, 1699

Desk Top Publishing
Cheshire, 119
Hampshire, 449
London, 830, 831, 832, 833
West Midlands, 1383
Wales: Dyfed, 1711

Divinity
Scotland: Borders, 1540
Scotland: Lothian, 1597, 1605
Scotland: Tayside, 1675, 1683

Economics
Greater Manchester, 392
Kent, 592
West Midlands, 1353

Education
Greater Manchester, 393
London, 834
West Midlands, 1356
Scotland: Central, 1555
Scotland: Tayside, 1676

Electrical Engineering
Hertfordshire, 529
London, 835
Suffolk, 1220
Scotland: Fife, 1564
Wales: Gwent, 1725

Electronic Engineering
Suffolk, 1220, 1221
Scotland: Strathclyde, 1658
Wales: Gwent, 1725

Electronics
Devon, 232
Dorset, 274
Isle of Wight, 564
Lancashire, 638
London, 704, 819, 836
Merseyside, 976
West Yorkshire, 1458
Scotland: Fife, 1564
Scotland: Highland, 1589
Scotland: Lothian, 1609, 1611
Scotland: Strathclyde, 1653
Scotland: Tayside, 1686

Engineering
Avon, 14, 18
Bedfordshire, 67
Cleveland, 143
Cumbria, 196, 197
Dorset, 267, 275
Essex, 343
Greater Manchester, 381, 394,
    395
Hereford and Worcester, 502
Hertfordshire, 529
Kent, 579
Lancashire, 639, 640
Leicestershire, 658
London, 714, 723, 837, 838, 839,
    840, 841

Scotland: Grampian, 1578

Hospitality Management
Cheshire, 115
Cleveland, 144
Cornwall, 173, 174
London, 702
Northamptonshire, 1045
Scotland: Central, 1544
Scotland: Lothian, 1606
Scotland: Strathclyde, 1640, 1641, 1644
Wales: Dyfed, 1707

Housing
Avon, 33

Humanities
Avon, 6, 11
Berkshire, 74
Buckinghamshire, 88
Cambridgeshire, 94
Devon, 232, 235
Dorset, 268
Durham, 288
East Sussex, 306, 307, 308
Gloucestershire, 362
Greater Manchester, 380, 383
Hampshire, 435, 436, 437
Hereford and Worcester, 478
Hertfordshire, 511, 533
Kent, 575, 584, 585, 586, 587, 597, 598
Leicestershire, 654, 655
Lincolnshire, 678
London, 725, 726, 727, 728, 729, 730, 731, 757, 855
Norfolk, 996
North Yorkshire, 1021, 1022
Northamptonshire, 1036, 1037
Nottinghamshire, 1073
Shropshire, 1136, 1137
Staffordshire, 1170
Suffolk, 1205, 1206, 1228
Surrey, 1252
West Midlands, 1350, 1360, 1361, 1387
West Yorkshire, 1437, 1439, 1440, 1441
Northern Ireland: Belfast, 1506
Northern Ireland: Southern, 1526, 1527
Northern Ireland: Western, 1536
Wales: Clywd, 1699
Wales: Dyfed, 1703
Wales: Gwent, 1722, 1723
Wales: Mid-Glamorgan, 1735
Wales: South Glamorgan, 1744, 1746

Wales: West Glamorgan, 1758, 1759, 1767

Information Technology
Avon, 7, 34, 35
Cleveland, 143, 145, 146, 147, 148, 149
Cornwall, 175, 176
Cumbria, 200
Derbyshire, 218, 219, 220
Devon, 241, 242, 247
Dorset, 273, 278
East Sussex, 313
Essex, 347, 348, 349, 350
Gloucestershire, 365
Greater Manchester, 381, 399
Hampshire, 439, 452, 453, 454
Hereford and Worcester, 489, 490
Hertfordshire, 509, 516
Isle of Wight, 566
Kent, 593, 597, 613, 620
Leicestershire, 665, 666
Lincolnshire, 683
London, 721, 732, 733, 841, 856, 857, 858, 859, 860, 861, 862, 863, 864, 865, 866, 867, 868, 869, 870, 871, 872, 873, 874, 875, 876, 944
Merseyside, 978, 979, 980
Norfolk, 1005
Northamptonshire, 1035, 1058
Nottinghamshire, 1093, 1098
Oxfordshire, 1118, 1119
Staffordshire, 1173, 1186, 1187, 1188, 1189, 1190
Suffolk, 1229, 1230
Surrey, 1268
Tyne and Wear, 1285, 1295, 1296, 1297, 1298
Warwickshire, 1322, 1337
West Midlands, 1388, 1389, 1390
West Yorkshire, 1442, 1449, 1456, 1465, 1466
Wiltshire, 1499
Northern Ireland: North Eastern, 1512, 1513
Northern Ireland: South Eastern, 1519, 1523
Scotland: Fife, 1567
Scotland: Highland, 1591
Scotland: Lothian, 1614, 1628
Scotland: Strathclyde, 1637, 1641, 1642, 1657, 1658
Scotland: Tayside, 1690
Wales: Dyfed, 1712, 1713, 1714
Wales: Gwent, 1723
Wales: West Glamorgan, 1765

Interior Design
Hampshire, 455
West Yorkshire, 1467

Laboratory Skills
West Midlands, 1391

Labour Studies
Wales: Gwent, 1723

Landscape Design
London, 854

Languages
Avon, 12, 36
Dorset, 272
Kent, 588
London, 702, 705, 734
Oxfordshire, 1120, 1121
Scotland: Grampian, 1575
Scotland: Highland, 1584
Scotland: Lothian, 1605
Scotland: Strathclyde, 1659
Scotland: Tayside, 1675, 1683
Wales: West Glamorgan, 1767

Law
Avon, 13, 20
Bedfordshire, 59
Cambridgeshire, 96
Greater Manchester, 400
Kent, 575, 589, 590
Leicestershire, 663
London, 704, 713, 735, 757, 877
Norfolk, 1006
North Yorkshire, 1019
Suffolk, 1231
Tyne and Wear, 1317
West Midlands, 1353
Scotland: Lothian, 1597
Wales: Dyfed, 1703
Wales: Mid-Glamorgan, 1735
Wales: West Glamorgan, 1759

Leisure Studies
London, 736

Library & Information Management
Greater Manchester, 401, 402
Scotland: Lothian, 1615, 1616

Life Sciences
Hertfordshire, 509

Management
Avon, 37
Berkshire, 81

Cheshire, 120
Cleveland, 150
Cumbria, 201
Derbyshire, 221
Essex, 351, 352
Gloucestershire, 362, 366, 367
Greater Manchester, 403
Hampshire, 456
Hereford and Worcester, 491
Hertfordshire, 534
Isle of Wight, 567
Kent, 614
Lincolnshire, 685, 686
London, 702, 715, 874, 878, 879,
    880, 881, 882, 883, 884,
    885, 886, 887
Norfolk, 1007
North Yorkshire, 1027
Northamptonshire, 1059
Nottinghamshire, 1079, 1094
South Yorkshire, 1151
Staffordshire, 1191, 1192
Suffolk, 1205
Surrey, 1269
West Midlands, 1392, 1393, 1415
Northern Ireland: North Eastern,
    1513
Scotland: Borders, 1541
Scotland: Central, 1551
Scotland: Lothian, 1606, 1614
Wales: Dyfed, 1715
Wales: West Glamorgan, 1766

Management Development
Avon, 38

Management Studies
Cambridgeshire, 97, 98, 99
Tyne and Wear, 1288
Scotland: Tayside, 1684

Manufacturing
Avon, 39
Bedfordshire, 67, 69
Staffordshire, 1193
Suffolk, 1232
West Yorkshire, 1468

Marketing
Gloucestershire, 368
Greater Manchester, 381
Kent, 615
Leicestershire, 663
Scotland: Strathclyde, 1634

Mathematics
Avon, 40, 53
Cambridgeshire, 95

Derbyshire, 214
Devon, 233
Durham, 289
East Sussex, 308
Kent, 591, 592, 593
Lancashire, 638
North Yorkshire, 1024
Somerset, 1142
South Yorkshire, 1151
Surrey, 1252, 1253, 1270
Warwickshire, 1322
West Yorkshire, 1443
Northern Ireland: South Eastern,
    1521
Scotland: Central, 1546
Scotland: Highland, 1592
Scotland: Strathclyde, 1645, 1660

Media Studies
Cleveland, 151
Essex, 353
Kent, 575
London, 713, 717, 722, 737, 887,
    888
Merseyside, 981
Nottinghamshire, 1074
Suffolk, 1233
West Midlands, 1351, 1362
West Yorkshire, 1439
Scotland: Lothian, 1598
Scotland: Strathclyde, 1634, 1652

Medicine
Greater Manchester, 387
Leicestershire, 659
Nottinghamshire, 1105
Surrey, 1275
Tyne and Wear, 1318
West Midlands, 1394

Multi-Subject
Bedfordshire, 70
Buckinghamshire, 89
Cambridgeshire, 100
Cleveland, 152
Cornwall, 177
Devon, 243, 244
Dorset, 279, 280
Essex, 350, 354
Gloucestershire, 369
Greater Manchester, 404, 405,
    406, 407, 408
Hertfordshire, 535
Kent, 616, 617
Lancashire, 642
Leicestershire, 656, 667, 668, 669
Lincolnshire, 677
London, 889, 890, 891

Merseyside, 982
Nottinghamshire, 1091, 1095
Somerset, 1143
South Yorkshire, 1152
Suffolk, 1234, 1235
Tyne and Wear, 1299
West Midlands, 1395
West Yorkshire, 1469, 1470, 1471,
    1472
Scotland: Central, 1552
Scotland: Dumfries and
    Galloway, 1557
Scotland: Highland, 1593
Scotland: Lothian, 1617
Scotland: Strathclyde, 1661
Wales: Gwynedd, 1731

Music
Devon, 231
London, 702, 892
Warwickshire, 1338

Natural Sciences
Norfolk, 998

New Technology
Lincolnshire, 687
West Yorkshire, 1444

**NOW (New Opportunities for
    Women)**
Cheshire, 121
Cleveland, 153, 154, 155
Devon, 245
Gloucestershire, 370
Hampshire, 457
Hertfordshire, 536
Kent, 618
Lancashire, 643, 644
London, 893, 894
Merseyside, 983, 984, 985
Norfolk, 1008
Oxfordshire, 1122
Somerset, 1144
Tyne and Wear, 1300
West Midlands, 1396, 1397, 1398
West Sussex, 1432
West Yorkshire, 1473, 1474
Scotland: Strathclyde, 1662
Wales: Clywd, 1700
Wales: Gwent, 1726

Nursing
Cambridgeshire, 93
Cleveland, 133
Hereford and Worcester, 479, 501
Leicestershire, 657
London, 706, 713, 738, 739, 740,
    741, 742, 743

COLLEGE INDEX

The entries are indexed to entry numbers and not page numbers

Bromley College of Further and Higher Education, Rookery Lane, Bromley, Kent BR2 8HE   743, 755, 768, 782, 835, 879, 967

Brooklands College, Heath Road, Weybridge, Surrey KT13 8TT   1256, 1272, 1273

Brunel College of Arts and Technology, Ashley Down, Bristol BS7 9BU   6, 14, 41, 50

Burnley College, Ormorod Road, Burnley, Lancashire BB11 2RX   639, 640, 645, 649

Burton Technical College, Lichfield Street, Burton upon Trent, Staffordshire DE11 8BN   1168, 1170

C

Canterbury College, New Dover Road, Canterbury CT1 3AJ   577, 597, 584, 594

Capel Manor Horticultural and Environmental Centre, Bullsmoor Lane, Enfield, Middlesex EN1 4RQ   854

Cardonald College, 690 Mosspark Drive, Glasgow G52 3AY   1634, 1639, 1647, 1649, 1650, 1651, 1652, 1653, 1655, 1658, 1665, 1667, 1670, 1674

Carlisle College, Victoria Place, Carlisle, Cumbria CA1 1HS   187, 188, 189, 191, 192, 193, 194, 195, 196, 197, 198, 201, 202, 203, 204, 205, 206, 207

Carmarthenshire College of Technology & Art, Llanelli Campus, Alban Road, Llanelli, Dyfed SA15 1NG   1714

Carshalton College, Nightingale Road, Carshalton, Surrey SM5 2EJ   695, 696, 725, 783, 792, 809, 864, 874, 876, 899, 908, 918

Castlereagh College, Montgomery Road, Belfast, Co. Antrim BT6 9JD   1507

Charles Keene College, Painter Street, Leicester LE1 3WA   652, 655, 658, 660, 665, 669

Chelmsford College, Moulsham Street, Chelmsford, Essex CM2 0JQ   322, 326, 327, 331, 341

Cheltenham and Gloucester College of Higher Education, The Park Campus, The Park, Cheltenham, Gloucestershire GL50 2QF   364, 366, 368, 369, 372, 376

Chesterfield College, Infirmary Road, Chesterfield, Derbyshire S41 7NG   211, 212, 213, 214, 215, 216, 218, 219, 221, 222, 223

Chichester College of Arts, Science and Technology, Westgate Fields, Chichester, West Sussex PO19 1SB   1431, 1432, 1433

Chippenham College, Cocklebury Road, Chippenham, Wiltshire SN15 3QD   1492, 1493, 1495, 1496, 1497, 1504

Cirencester College, Stroud Road, Cirencester, Gloucestershire GL7 1XA   363, 370

City College, Arden Centre, Sale Road, Northenden, Manchester M23 0DD   379, 383, 418

City College Norwich, Ipswich Road, Norwich NR2 2LJ   996, 997, 998, 999, 1000, 1001, 1002, 1003, 1004, 1005, 1006, 1007, 1008, 1009, 1010, 1011, 1014

City University, Department of Continuing Education, Northampton Square, London EC1V 0HB   727, 868, 883, 885, 923, 944, 969

City and Islington College, 444 Camden Road, London N7 0SP   717, 741, 749, 758, 769, 777, 788, 804, 817, 839, 848, 898, 906, 919, 940, 952
      Bunhill Row, London EC1Y 8LQ   698, 737, 863, 909
      Willen House, 8-26 Bath Street, London EC1V 9PL   778, 869, 896

City of Liverpool Community College, Division Adult & Continuing Education, Bankfield Centre, Bankfield Road, Liverpool L13 0BQ   983, 984, 985, 987
      Myrtle Street Centre, Liverpool L7 7DN   974, 975, 976, 980, 986, 988, 994, 995
      Westbourne Adult Centre, Westbourne School, Abbotsford Road, Liverpool L11   982

City of Westminster College, Department of Continuing Education, Elgin Avenue, London W9 2NR   714, 726, 730, 760, 771, 850, 907, 960, 966

Clackmannan College of Further Education, Branshill Road, Alloa, Clackmannanshire FK10 3BT   1544, 1545, 1546, 1554, 1555

Clarendon College Nottingham, Pelham Avenue, Mansfield Road, Nottingham NG5 1AL   1072, 1073, 1081, 1089, 1090, 1091, 1094, 1095, 1102, 1103, 1108, 1109, 1110

Coalville Technical College, Bridge Road, Coalville, Leicestershire LE6 2QR   654, 661, 662, 664

Coatbridge College, Kildonan Street, Coatbridge, Lanarkshire ML3 3LS   1635

Colchester Institute, Sheepen Road, Colchester, Essex CO3 3LL   324, 356

Coleg Ceredigion, Llanbadarn Fawr, Aberystwyth, Dyfed SY23 4PZ   1703, 1704, 1707, 1708, 1711, 1712, 1713, 1715, 1716, 1718, 1719

Coleg Glan Hafran, Trowbridge Road, Rumney, Cardiff, South Glamorgan CF3 8XZ   1740, 1742, 1744, 1745, 1747, 1748

Coleg Harlech, Harlech, Gwynedd LL46 2PU   1730, 1731

Coleg Menai, Fford Ffriddoedd, Bangor, Gwynedd LL57 2TP   1728, 1732

Coleg Powys, Peulan, Brecon, Powys LO3 9SR   1738, 1739

College of Care and Early Education, Broadlands Drive, Lawrence Weston, Bristol BS11 0NT   26, 27, 44

College of North East London, Tottenham Centre, High Road, London N15 4RU   712, 732, 750, 756, 784, 926, 931

Kensington and Chelsea College, Hortensia Road, London SW10 0QS   786, 795, 801, 849, 860, 954

    Wornington Road, London W10 5QQ   707, 715, 731, 759, 762, 763, 787, 846, 917, 930

Kent Adult Education, St Faith's Street Centre, St Faith's Street, Maidstone ME14 1LH   608, 612, 620, 623

Kent Institute of Art & Design, Oakwood Park, Maidstone ME16 8AG   571, 601, 609

Kilmarnock College, Holehouse Road, Kilmarnock KA3 7AT   1636, 1659, 1666

Kingsway College, Clerkenwell Centre, Sans Walk, London EC1R 0AS   894

Kirkland High School and Community College, Methil Brae, Methil, Fife KY8 3LT   1562, 1563, 1565, 1566, 1567, 1568

Knowsley Community College, Cherryfield Drive, Kirkby, Liverpool L32 8SF   972, 973

    Rupert Road, Roby, Merseyside L36 9TD   977, 978, 989

L

Lambeth College, Clapham Centre, 45 Clapham Common South Side, London SW4 9BL   739, 746, 748, 752, 764, 748, 752, 764, 785, 797, 800, 802, 818, 819, 826, 828, 829, 830, 851, 853, 856, 872, 873, 875, 928, 929, 932, 937, 942, 958

    Norwood Centre, Knights Hill, West Norwood, London SE27 0TX   862

Lancaster and Morecambe College, Morecambe Road, Lancaster LA1 2TY   634, 635, 636

Lauder College, North Fod, Halbeath Road, Dunfermline KY11 5DY   1560, 1561, 1570

Leeds Metropolitan University, Calverley Street, Leeds LS1 3HE   1465, 1470

Leicester Adult Education College, Wellington Street, Leicester LE1 6HL   670

Lewes Tertiary College, Mountfield Road, Lewes, East Sussex BN7 2XH   305

Lewisham College, Lewisham Way, London SE4 1UT   709, 718, 719, 723, 738, 744, 754, 761, 766, 772, 776, 780, 790, 791, 793, 796, 803, 810, 812, 816, 824, 825, 827, 831, 832, 836, 838, 840, 841, 844, 852, 857, 858, 859, 865, 866, 867, 871, 888, 892, 900, 902, 903, 904, 911, 955, 959, 965

Lews Castle College, Stornoway, Isle of Lewis PA86 0XR   1697, 1698

Lincolnshire College of Art and Design, Lindum Road, Lincoln LN2 1NP   677, 682

Lisburn College of Further Education, Castle Street, Lisburn, Co. Antrim BT27 4SU   1510, 1514

London College of Fashion, 20 John Prince's Street, London W1M 0BJ   887

Lothian and Edinburgh Enterprise Ltd, Apex House, 99 Haymarket Terrace, Edinburgh EH12 5HD   1624

Loughry College, The Food Centre, Cookstown Co. Tyrone BT80 9AA   1530, 1531

Lowestoft College, St Peters Street, Lowestoft, Suffolk NR32 2NB   1206, 1207, 1216, 1218, 1219, 1225, 1229, 1239, 1244, 1250

Loxley College, Myers Grove Lane, Sheffield S11 9FP   1160

Lucy Cavendish College, Lady Margaret Road, Cambridge CB3 0BU   97, 101

M

Macclesfield College, Park Lane, Macclesfield, Cheshire SK11 8LF   107, 111, 112, 113, 115, 116, 117, 118, 119, 120, 121, 125

Mackworth College, Prince Charles Avenue, Mackworth, Derbyshire DE22 4LR   209, 217, 224, 226, 228

Manchester Adult Education Service, Birtles Centre, Town Centre, Wythenshawe, Manchester M22 5RF   413, 416, 427

Manchester College of Arts and Technology, City Centre Campus, Lower Hardman Street, Manchester M3 3ER   378, 397, 412, 417, 426

Manchester Metropolitan University, All Saints, Manchester M15 6BH   114, 128, 392, 396, 398, 400, 401, 402, 404, 405, 406, 407, 421, 424, 428

    Department of Business Studies, Aytoun Building, Aytoun Street, Manchester M1 3GH   420

Matthew Boulton College, Sherlock Street, Birmingham B5 7DB   1364, 1373, 1386, 1399

Merthyr Tydfil College, Ynysfach, Merthyr Tydfil, Mid-Glamorgan CE48 1AR   1737

Merton College of Further Education, Morden Park, London Road, Morden, Surrey SM4 5QX   702, 781, 799, 811, 897, 935, 951

Mid-Cheshire College, Chester Road, Hartford, Northwich, Cheshire CW8 1LJ   108, 124

Mid-Kent College of Higher & Further Education, City Way Centre, City Way, Rochester, Kent ME1 2AD   602, 610, 611

    Horsted Centre, Maidstone Road, Chatham, Kent ME5 9UQ   578, 580, 582, 585, 588, 589, 595, 603, 619, 627, 629

Mid-Warwickshire College, Warwick New Road, Leamington Spa, Warwickshire CV32 5JE   1325, 1331, 1334, 1335, 1336, 1342, 1344, 1345

Middlesbrough College, Roman Road, Middlesbrough, Cleveland TS5 5PJ   138, 139, 141, 144, 148, 149

Milton Keynes College, Chaffron Way Centre, Loughton Campus West, Leadenhall, Milton Keynes, Buckinghamshire MK6 5LP   88, 89, 90, 91

South Devon College, Newton Road, Torquay,
Devon TQ2 5BY   232, 242, 245, 247, 249,
251, 252, 253, 254, 255, 256

South Downs College, College Road, Purbrook Way,
Havant, Hampshire PO7 8AA   433, 471

South East Community Education, Stretton Avenue,
Willenhall, West Midlands CV3 3HY   1389

South East Essex College, Carnarvon Road,
Southend SS2 6LS   323, 332, 333, 340,
342, 343, 345, 346, 347, 353

South Glamorgan Women's Workshop, Clarence
House, Clarence Road, Cardiff CF1
6JB   1749, 1750, 1751

South Kent College, Jemmett Road, Ashford, Kent
TN23 2RJ   573, 581, 582, 590, 592, 598
Maison Dieu Road, Dover CT16 1DH   599,
600

South Nottingham College, Greythorn Drive, West
Bridgford, Nottingham NG2 7GA   1074,
1083, 1085, 1086, 1093, 1098, 1106

South Tyneside College, St George's Avenue, South
Shields, Tyne and Wear NE34 6ET   1314,
1315, 1316, 1317, 1318

Southampton City College, St Mary Street,
Southampton SO14 1AR   446, 454, 455,
460, 464, 465, 472, 774

St Helens College, Town Centre Campus, Brook
Street, St Helens WA10 1PZ   979, 981

Staffordshire College of Agriculture, Rodbaston,
Penkridge, Stafford ST19 5PG   1174

Stamford College, Drift Road, Stamford,
Lincolnshire PE9 1XA   678, 688

Stevenson College, Bankhead Avenue, Sighthill,
Edinburgh EH12 4DE   1601, 1617, 1618,
1619, 1621

Stockport College of Further and Higher Education,
Wellington Road South, Stockport SK1
3UQ   385, 389, 393, 399, 408, 409, 410

Stockton & Billingham College of Further
Education, Dept of Arts & Science, The
Causeway, Billingham, Cleveland TS23
2DB   130, 133, 135, 158, 159

Stoke on Trent Collegem Stoke Road, Shelton, Stoke
on Trent, Staffordshire ST4 2BR   1169.
1172, 1173, 1175, 1176, 1177, 1178, 1183, 1185,
1187, 1188, 1190, 1192, 1193, 1195, 1196, 1202,
1203

Stratford upon Avon College, The Willows North,
Stratford upon Avon, Warwickshire CV37
9QR   1322, 1326, 1328, 1330, 1341

Strode College, Church Road, Street, Somerset
BA16 0AB   1140, 1144, 1146

Stratford Road, Stroud, Gloucestershire GL5
4AH   362, 371, 373, 374, 375

Suffolk College Rope Walk, Ipswich IP4 1LT
1204, 1209, 1212, 1214, 1215, 1220, 1222,
1223, 1224, 1227, 1232, 1233, 1234, 1235, 1240,
1245

Suffolk Community Education Service, Southern
Area, Murrayside Community Centre, Nacton
Road, Ipswich IP1 2AQ   1241

Swansea College, Tycoch, Swansea SA2 9EB
1753, 1754, 1756, 1759, 1760, 1761, 1762

T

Tameside College of Technology, Beaufort Road,
Ashton-under-Lyne OL6 6BR   377, 382,
388, 390, 391, 411, 414, 415, 419, 425

Tamworth College, Tamworth, Staffordshire B79
7BR   1167, 1171, 1179, 1180, 1181, 1182,
1184, 1186, 1189, 1191, 1194, 1197, 1198, 1200,
1201

Teeside Tertiary College, Marton Campus, Marton
Road, Middlesbrough, Cleveland TS4
3RZ   132, 136, 142, 146, 147, 151, 152, 157

Telford College of Arts & Technology, Haybridge
Road, Wellington, Telford, Shropshire TF1
2NP   1137, 1138

Thanet College, Ramsgate Road, Broadstairs, Kent
CT10 1PN   572, 574, 576, 586, 591, 593,
596

The Adult College Lancaster, PO Box 603, White
Cross Education Centre, Quarry Road,
Lancaster LA1 3SE   647, 648

The Business Team/Black Country Co-operative
Development Agency, West Midlands House,
Gypsy Lane, Willenhall, West Midlands WV13
2HA   1371, 1405

The City Lit Centre, Stukely Street, Drury Lane,
London WC2B 5LJ   701, 913, 914, 916

The College of Guidance Studies, College Road,
Hextable, Swanley, Kent BR8 7RN   606

The College of Osteopaths Educational Trust, 13
Furzehill Road, Borehamwood, Hertfordshire
WD6 2DG   531

The Robert Gordon University, School of Applied
Sciences, St Andrew Street, Aberdeen AB1
1HG   1580

Thomas Danby College, Roundhay Road, Sheepscar,
Leeds LS7 3BG   1435, 1438, 1442, 1450,
1451, 1463, 1484

Thurrock College, Love Lane, Aveley, South
Ockenden, Essex RM15 4HT   361
Woodview, Grays, Essex RM16 4YR   329,
330, 334, 337, 338, 339, 344, 348, 349. 350

Tile Hill College, Tile Hill Lane, Coventry CV4
9SU   1353, 1358, 1360, 1361, 1362, 1365,
1367, 1370, 1372, 1376, 1377, 1388, 1401, 1404,
1416, 1418, 1419, 1420, 1424, 1425

Tower Hamlets College, Jubilee Street, London E1
3HA   905

Tresham Institute of Further and Higher Education,
George Street, Corby, Northamptonshire N17
1QA   1033, 1043, 1055
St Mary's Road, Kettering, Northamptonshire
NN15 7BS   1035, 1037, 1046, 1047, 1048,
1049, 1064

Trowbridge College, College Road, Trowbridge, Wiltshire BA14 0ES   1491, 1491, 1498, 1499, 1500, 1501, 1502, 1503

U

University College of Ripon and York St John, Lord Mayor's Walk, York YO3 7EX   1017, 1022, 1024

University College, London, Gower Street, London WC1E 6BT   843, 946, 948, 950, 953

University of Birmingham, Edgbaston, Birmingham B15 2TT   1369, 1394, 1417

University of Bradford, Bradford BD7 1DP   1468, 1490

University of Bristol, Department for Continuing Education, 8-10 Berkeley Square, Clifton, Bristol BS8 1HH   56, 57
    School for Policy Studies, Rodney Lodge, Grange Road, Bristol BS8 4EA   32, 33, 38, 46

University of Central Lancashire, Corporation Street, Preston PR1 2TQ   638

University of Dundee, Nethergate, Dundee DD1 4HN   1679, 1690

University of East London, Livingstone House, Livingstone Road, London E15 2LL   924, 962

University of Edinburgh, Centre for Continuing Education, 11 Buccleuch Place, Edinburgh EH8 9LW   1597, 1620, 1622, 1623, 1625
    Industrial Liaison, Abden House, 1 Marchall Crescent, Edinburgh EH16 5HP   1614
    Old College, South Bridge, Edinburgh EH8 9YL   1613

University of Exeter, Northcote House, The Queen's Drive, Exeter EX4 4QJ   259

University of Glasgow, Glasgow G12 8QQ   1668

University of Greenwich, Avery Hill Campus, Southwood Site, Avery Hill Road, Eltham, London SE9 2HB   794
    Riverside House, Beresford Street, Woolwich, London SE18 6BU   614, 615, 775, 880, 882, 884
    Wellington Street, Woolwich, London SE18 6PF   845

University of Hertfordshire, Hatfield Campus, College Lane, Hatfield, Hertfordshire AL10 9AB   533, 534, 535, 536, 544, 545

University of Hull, Centre for Continuing Education Development & Training, 49 Salmon Grove, Hull HU6 7SZ   555

University of Kent at Canterbury, Canterbury, Kent CT2 7NX   628
    School of Continuing Education, University Centre at Tonbridge, Avebury Avenue, Tonbridge, Kent TN9 1TG   587, 616, 617, 624, 626

University of Lancaster, University House, Lancaster LA1 4YW   641

University of Leeds, Leeds LS2 9JT   1453
    Dept of Adult Continuing Education, Leeds LS2 9JT   1441

University of Leicester, University Road, Leicester LE1 7RH   659

University of Liverpool, Centre for Continuing Education, PO Box 147, 19 Abercromby Square, Liverpool L69 3BX   990, 991, 992
    PO Box 147, Liverpool L69 3BX   993

University of London, Institute of Education, 55 Gordon Square, London WC1H 0NT   971

University of Luton, Park Square, Luton LU1 3JU   70, 71

University of Manchester, Oxford Road, Manchester M13 9PL   386, 387, 395, 422, 423

University of Manchester Institute of Science and Technology, Sackville Street, Manchester M60 1QD   394

University of Newcastle upon Tyne, 6 Kensington Terrace, Newcastle upon Tyne NE1 7RU   1294

University of North London, Holloway Road, London N7 8DB   855, 945, 949, 956

University of Northumbria at Newcastle, Unilink, Sutherland Building, Northumberland Road, Newcastle upon Tyne NE1 8ST   190, 1292, 1299

University of Nottingham, Faculty of Medicine and Health Sciences, The Medical School, Queen's Medical Centre, Nottingham NG7 2UH   1105

University Park, Nottingham NG7 2RD   1087

University of Oxford, University Offices, Wellington Square, Oxford OX1 2JD   1131, 1132

University of Paisley, High Street, Paisley PA1 2BE   1657

University of Plymouth, Drake Circus, Plymouth PL4 8AA   177, 230, 233, 241, 243, 244, 260, 261, 1143

University of Reading, Whiteknights, Reading RG6 2AH   80

University of Sheffield, Sheffield S10 2TN   1163
    Division of Adult Continuing Education, 196-198 West Street, Sheffield S1 4ET   1150

University of Southampton, Dept of Adult Continuing Education, Highfield, Southampton SO9 5NH   467
    Highfield, Southampton SO17 1BJ   444

University of Stirling, Airthrey Castle, Stirling, Stirlingshire FK9 4LA   1548, 1551, 1552

University of Strathclyde, Continuing Education Centre, McCance Building, Glasgow G1 1XQ   1662

University of Ulster at Jordanstown, Shore Road, Newtownabbey, Co. Antrim BT37 0QB   1508, 1512, 1513, 1515, 1516, 1517, 1537

University of Ulster, Magee College, Northland Road, Londonderry, Co. Derry BT48 7JL   1536, 1538

INDEX TO NATIONAL SCHEMES AND ORGANISATIONS